SPAIN

CATAL
& BARCELONA

INCLUDING PYRÉNÉES-ORIENTALES

DANA FACAROS & MICHAEL PAULS
WITH MARY-ANN GALLAGHER

www.bradtguides.com

Bradt Guides Ltd, UK
The Globe Pequot Press Inc, USA

Bradt GUIDES

TRAVEL TAKEN SERIOUSLY

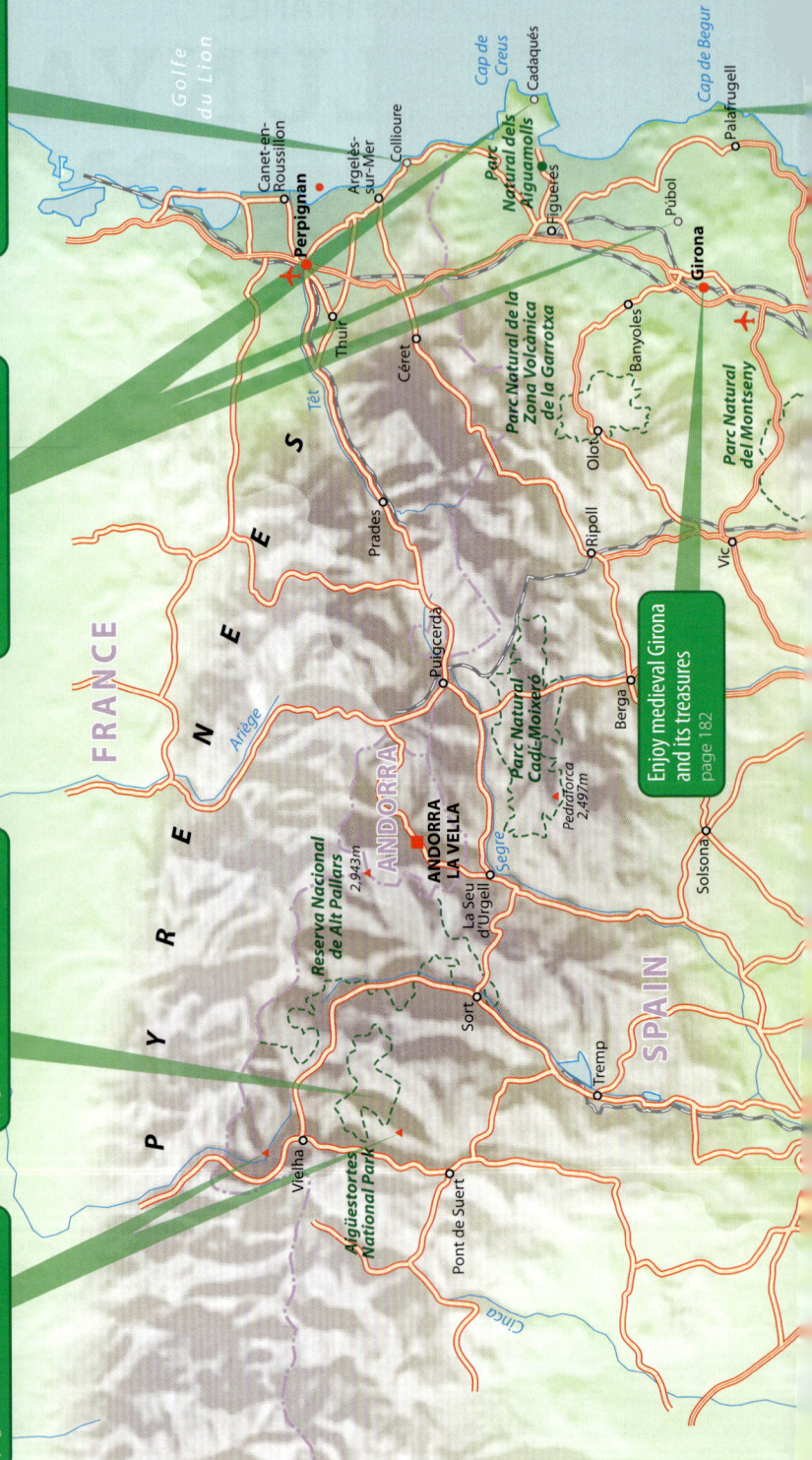

Seek out unique Romanesque churches in the remote Vall de Boí and Vall d'Aran pages 304 & 308

Explore Parc Nacional de Aigüestortes i Estany de Sant Maurici — grandeur in the Pyrenees page 308

Explore the Dalí Triangle — his homes in Púbol and Cadaqués, and the Teatre-Museu Dalí in Figueres pages 168, 177 & 195

Don't miss Collioure and the Côte Vermeille, which have inspired artists from Matisse to Picasso page 326

Enjoy medieval Girona and its treasures page 182

FRANCE

SPAIN

ANDORRA

P Y R E N E E S

Golfe du Lion

Cap de Creus

Cap de Begur

Canet-en-Roussillon
Argelès-sur-Mer
Collioure
Perpignan
Thuir
Céret
Prades
Puigcerdà
Figueres
Cadaqués
Púbol
Palafrugell
Girona
Banyoles
Olot
Ripoll
Vic
Solsona
Berga
La Seu d'Urgell
ANDORRA LA VELLA
Sort
Tremp
Pont de Suert
Vielha

Tét
Ariège
Segre
Cinca

Parc Natural dels Aiguamolls
Parc Natural de la Zona Volcànica de la Garrotxa
Parc Natural del Montseny
Parc Natural Cadí-Moixeró
Pedraforca 2,497m
Reserva Nacional de Alt Pallars
2,943m
Aigüestortes National Park

KEY

● Main town or city	
○ Town	
○ Village	
✈ Airport	
Main road	
Other road	
Railway	
Regional boundary	
Park/reserve	

Relax on the beaches along the Cap de Begur, on the Costa Brava page 167

Soak up culture in Barcelona, one of Europe's liveliest cities page 58

Climb the extraordinary holy mountain of Montserrat page 140

Head to Catalunya's wine country: the Penedès and the Priorat pages 145 & 252

Visit Roman and medieval sites in Tarragona page 226

Costa Brava

Blanes

Mataró

Barcelona

Granollers

Terrassa

Llobregat

Parc Natural De Garraf

Manresa

Montserrat

Igualada

Montblanc

Vals

Cervera

Reus

Tarragona

Miami Platja

Balaguer

Falset

Costa Dorada

MEDITERRANEAN SEA

Gandesa

Ebro

Parc del Delta d'Ebre

Lleida

Segre

Deltebre

Bradt

N

0   10 miles

0   20km

CATALUNYA & BARCELONA
DON'T MISS...

FESTIVALS
Castellers, or human towers, are a feature of many traditional Catalan festivals, often achieving eight or more tiers PAGE 46
(CSP/D)

BARCELONA
The Rambla is Barcelona's showcase promenade, full of flower stalls, street theatre, Modernista dragons and an iconic market PAGE 82
(NW/S)

BEACHES

Catalunya has beaches in every shape and size, from miniature coves to golden swathes like this one in Tossa de Mar PAGE 161
(PS/D)

ANCIENT SITES

Tarragona's seaside Roman amphitheatre is a vivid reminder of the ancient importance of Tarraco PAGE 236
(CE/S)

FOOD AND DRINK

Catalunya's natural abundance translates into one of the world's most celebrated cuisines, where fresh local produce shines PAGE 43
(N/S)

CATALUNYA & BARCELONA
IN COLOUR

above left
& right
(SS & SS)

The singular imagination of Antoni Gaudí finds its fullest expression in his greatest passion project, the Sagrada Família PAGE 112

below
(EF/S)

The arcaded Plaça Reial hums day and night, with cafés, bars and restaurants tucked beneath the colonnades PAGE 83

With almost 5km of sandy beaches, Barcelona regularly ranks as one of the best beach cities in the world PAGE 105

above
(S3/S)

Time seems to stand still in the Barri Gòtic, a medieval maze of narrow lanes and dreamy squares PAGE 84

right
(E/S)

Trencadís – colourful mosaics made from broken china – are found everwhere in Gaudí's Park Güell, including this snaking ceramic bench PAGE 124

below
(VE/S)

AUTHOR

Dana Facaros wrote her first travel guide to the Greek Islands in 1977, then married her college sweetheart, **Michael Pauls**, and dragged him into the fray. They have been at it ever since, writing guides and apps and contributing to a number of UK publications, including the *Sunday Times, Daily Telegraph*, the *i*, *Wanderlust, National Geographic Traveller* and *Which*? Over the past decades they have lived in Greece, Spain, Italy, Ireland and southwest France.

UPDATER

Originally from the UK, **Mary-Ann Gallagher** is a writer, translator and editor who has lived in Barcelona for the past 20 years and has contributed to more than two dozen guidebooks on Catalunya and Spain. She's explored every nook and cranny of the region over the years, gaining a deep understanding of its unique culture, traditions and landscape. It's hard to resist a place which builds human castles that are ten storeys high, unleashes fire-spitting dragons at every festival, and where food – from humble *pa amb tomàquet* to the fanciest foams – is always front and centre of every gathering. A long-time friend and collaborator of the extraordinary Dana Facaros and Michael Pauls writing duo, she is thrilled to be a part of this book's journey.

First edition published January 2026
Bradt Travel Guides Ltd
31a High Street, Chesham, Buckinghamshire, HP5 1BW, England
www.bradtguides.com
Print edition published in the USA by The Globe Pequot Press Inc,
PO Box 480, Guilford, Connecticut 06437-0480

Photographs copyright © Individual photographers, 2026 (see below)
Project Manager: Susannah Lord
Copy Editor: Gina Rathbone
Cover research: Pepi Bluck, Perfect Picture

Thank you for buying an authorised edition of this book published by Bradt Travel Guides. For over 50 years, Bradt Travel Guides has encouraged adventurous, immersive and responsible travel, and this is only possible because of the support of our readers. By purchasing our books, you are enabling us to continue to commission expert authors who genuinely know and love the places they write about, and who write their books after thorough, on-the-ground research.

ISBN: 9781804693087

British Library Cataloguing in Publication Data
A catalogue record for this book is available from the British Library

Importer to the EU: Freytag-Berndt u. Artaria KG, Ölzeltgasse 3/10, 1030 Wien, Österreich

Photographs AWL Images: Karol Kozlowski (KK/AWL); Dreamstime.com: Andrey Ivanov (AI/D), Andrey Omelyanchuk (AO/D), Carlos Sanchez Pereyra (CSP/D), Gurb101088 (G/D), H368k742 (H36/D), Johnypan (J/D), Juan Bautista Cofreces (JBC/D), Llopartic (L/D), Manuel Milan Checa (MMC/D), Maria Luisa Lopez Estivill (ML/D), Oksana Byelikova (OB/D), Pere Sanz (PS/D), Sirboumanphoto (S/D), Vicnt (V/D), VladyslaV Travel photo (VT/D); Shutterstock.com: AlbertoGonzales (AG/S), Chizhevskaya Ekaterina (CE/S), Efired (EF/S), elxeneize (E/S), foto_and_video (FV/S), gg-foto (GG/S), Ivo Antonie de Rooij (IAR/S), Lady Kirschen (LK/S), M. Vinuesa (MV/S), Mazur Travel (MT/S), Michaelpuche (MP/S), Nandi Estevez (NE/S), nito (N/S), Noppasin Wongchum (NW/S), Olha Solodenko (OS/S), Roman Belogorodov (RB/S), saiko3p (S3/S), tartaphotography (TP/S), trabantos (T/S), V_E (VE/S), Vladimir Koshkarov (VK/S); SuperStock (SS)
Front cover Temple Expiatori del Sagrat Cor at sunset, Barcelona (KK/AWL)
Back cover, clockwise from top left Port de Vendres, Cote Vermeille (J/D); Sant Joan de les Abadesses (MMC/D); castellers at Santa Ursula's Festival, Colla Vella de Valls (LK/S); detail of carving on the Romanesque cathedral of Santa Maria in La Seu d'Urgell (NE/S)
Title page, clockwise from left Old houses, Tossa De Mar (AI/D); Blanes (AO/D); a sculpture in Park Güell, Barcelona (VT/D)

Maps David McCutcheon FBCart.S. FRGS, assisted by Simonetta Giori

Typeset by Ian Spick, Bradt Guides
Production managed by Page Bros; printed in the UK
Digital conversion by www.dataworks.co.in

Paper used for this product comes from sustainably managed forests, and recycled and controlled sources.

In 1980 Franco was only five years in the grave when we first washed up in Catalunya with a baby in tow. What is now Barcelona's Port Vell was the smelly ferry port, bobbing with bags of garbage. The Sagrada Família was little more than Gaudí's original façade and its four towers. Flats in the seedy Raval were selling for peanuts. You could just wander into the Park Güell. The star tourist attraction, judging by the postcards anyway, was the albino gorilla Snowflake in the zoo. The food ranged from bland to bad. But there was such a buzz and fizz, such energy in the air, such a longing to make up for lost time. One unforgettable evening we hung out on the Ramblas with the veterans of the International Brigade, who were in Barcelona for a reunion. To say they were full of beans is an understatement!

How it has changed – our baby is a dad, and Barcelona and Catalunya, still buzzing, still fizzing, are almost unrecognisable. And if the veterans could look down from heaven, we're sure they'd be pleased that it all turned out so well.

HOW TO USE THIS GUIDE

AUTHORS' FAVOURITES Finding genuinely characterful accommodation or that unmissable off-the-beaten-track café can be difficult, so the authors have chosen a few of their favourite places throughout the country to point you in the right direction. These 'authors' favourites' are marked with a ✳.

PRICE CODES Throughout this guide we have used price codes to indicate the cost of those places to stay and eat listed in the guide.

Accommodation Prices below are for a double room; expect to pay about three-quarters for single occupancy.

Luxury	€€€€€	€280+
Upmarket	€€€€	€200–280
Mid-range	€€€	€150–200
Budget	€€	€100–150
Shoestring	€	less than €100

Eating out Prices are based on the average price of a main course.

Expensive	€€€€€	€25+
Above average	€€€€	€20–25
Moderate	€€€	€15–20
Cheap and cheerful	€€	€10–15
Rock bottom	€	less than €10

MAPS

Keys and symbols Maps include alphabetical keys covering the locations of those places to stay, eat or drink that are featured in the book. Note that regional maps may not show all hotels and restaurants in the area: other establishments may be located in towns shown on the map.

Grids and grid references Several maps use gridlines to allow easy location of sites. Map grid references are listed in square brackets after the name of the place or site of interest in the text, with page number followed by grid number, eg: [85 C3].

Acknowledgements

We would like to thank Mary-Ann, updater extraordinaire and dear friend for taking on the guide.

Dana Facaros and Michael Pauls

Moltíssimes gràcies to Dana and Michael, the best writers in the business, for the chance to see Catalunya through their eyes. Huge thanks to Carmen and Sally and to my inspirational travel pals, Graham, Dani, Lucy, Anke, Cécile, Max, Casper, Lenny and Johnny.

Mary-Ann Gallagher

Contents

Introduction

> Do you believe that, since the earth is round, you will find landscapes everywhere? Does a round face have several noses? There are very few landscapes. They all converge here. Catalunya is the nose of the earth!
>
> Salvador Dalí

That explains everything, right? But Mr Dalí, as ever, was simply stating the obvious. Catalunya even looks like an upside-down nose, a triangle culturally wedged between France and the Mediterranean, sniffing bemusedly at the rest of Spain. Dalí was right about the landscapes, too. He painted endless versions of the extraordinary ones near his home in Cadaqués, the strangely eroded rocks bathed in a light that has had all its humidity whipped away by the wind. The rest of the landscapes come in a dozen flavours: Catalunya's 12,414 square miles squeeze in the golden beaches of the Costa Daurada, the mighty, pyramidal Pyrenees, the bijou coves of the Costa Brava, the Tuscan charms of Empordà's olive groves and cypresses, the wetlands of the Ebro Delta.

People have lived here for at least a million years. The Iberians, Greeks, Romans, Visigoths, Moors and Franks all passed through, but beginning in the 9th century, a precocious, mercurial people who came to be known as the Catalans have ruled the roost. Before the rest of Europe realised they were there, the Catalans built a Mediterranean empire for themselves, and then, just as quickly, in an orgy of folly they threw it away. While it lasted, it was a golden age for Catalunya; Romanesque and Gothic villages, monasteries, churches and castles litter the great nasal landscape; remarkable works of medieval art fill its museums.

After the golden age came centuries of oppression, under the thumb of rotten kings in far-off Madrid who tried to make the Catalans forget even their own language and culture. In spite of everything, they made their comeback. Led by industrial Barcelona the Catalans grew rich again, and rebuilt their cities in a fantastical new architecture that was part medieval and part Martian. Then came Franco's dictatorship, and this boisterous nation found itself muffled once more. But only 17 years after Franco died, the Catalans were hosting the Olympics, and Barcelona was the toast of the world. Not many peoples get such a historical rollercoaster to ride, something to consider when you start to think, as many visitors do, that the Catalans are just a little bit eccentric. These are people who bottle their own bubbly – cava from the Penedès – and like to have a glass with tapas in the early afternoon. Some drink it for breakfast.

Like a lot of eccentric people, the Catalans believe they are paragons of hard-headed common sense. They have a word for it, *seny*, and the people who brought the Industrial Revolution to the Med think of it as a national virtue. That's only one of the contradictions that keep Catalunya's creative tension in balance. The Catalan is at once a Spaniard and the anti-Spaniard. The average fellow works in an auto plant or a bank, but he's part of a nation that's passionate about art and serves up one of Europe's most creative cuisines. A big part of the Catalan contradiction is the contrast between cosmopolitan, effervescent Barcelona and the conservative, earthy, well-rooted interior (and it's no small part of this book's purpose to show you that the little-known hinterlands are well worth a visit too).

Their absurd and dangerous history has taught the Catalans that life is no dress rehearsal. They started partying the night Franco died in 1975, and they've been doing their best to keep it going ever since. While you're there you may notice that one of their greatest charms is making us feel a little more alive too.

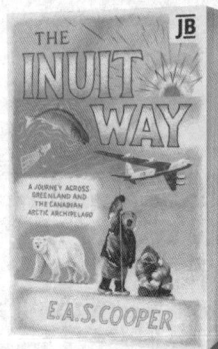

Part One

GENERAL INFORMATION

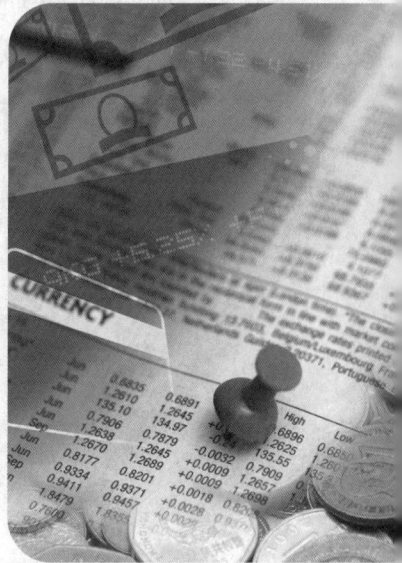

CATALUNYA AT A GLANCE

Location Northeastern Spain and southwest France
Size Northeastern Spain: 32,108km^2; southwest France: 4,116km^2
GDP per capita Northeastern Spain: Approx. €32,000; southwest France: €26,232
Population Northeastern Spain: 7.8 million; southwest France: 480,000
Life expectancy Northeastern Spain: 83 years; southwest France: 82.9 years
Climate Mediterranean
Regional capitals Northeastern Spain: Barcelona, Girona, Tarragona, Lleida; southwest France: Perpignan
Other main towns Northeastern Spain: Reus, Sabadell, Terrassa, Badalona; southwest France: Canet-en-Roussillon, Saint-Estève, Saint-Cyprien, Cabestany, Argelès-sur-Mer, Saint-Laurent-de-la-Salanque
Main airports Northeastern Spain: Barcelona El-Prat, Girona-Costa Brava, Reus; southwest France: Perpignan
Language Northeastern Spain: Spanish and Catalan; southwest France: French and Catalan
Religion Roman Catholic
Currency Euro (€)
Exchange rate £1=€1.13; US$1=€0.87 (November 2025)
International telephone code +34
Time GMT +1
Electrical voltage 220V/50H, two-pin or three-pin round plugs
Public holidays Northeastern Spain: 1 January, 6 January, Easter Monday, 1 May, 15 August, 11 September, 1 November, 25 December, 26 December; southwest France: 1 January, Easter Monday, 1 May, 8 May , 29 May, 9 June, 24 June, 14 July, 15 August, 1 & 11 November, 25 December

1

Background Information

GEOGRAPHY

Catalunya is what happens when nature refuses to pick a lane. Within one compact patch of Europe, you get sun-drenched beaches, the jagged peaks of a mountain wilderness, volcanic craters wrapped in beech forest, and a rice-growing delta with clouds of pink flamingos.

To the east, there are 500km of glorious Mediterranean coastline. The southern stretch, Costa Daurada, is all soft sand and wide skies, while the Costa Brava to the north is all about tumbling cliffs and sapphire coves.

Move inland and the land rises into low plains and gently rolling hills etched with vineyards, olive groves and cereal fields.

To the west, the terrain is more arid but equally dramatic, with gorges carving through the Montsec mountain range. Sparsely populated and serene, it's one of the best places in Europe for stargazing, an officially certified international Starlight Reserve. Meanwhile, down in the south, the Ebro Delta fans out into a flat, otherworldly expanse, with rice paddies and lagoons that attract an extraordinary wealth of birdlife.

To the north, the Pyrenees form a rugged natural border with France, with peaks of more than 3,000m and a string of ski resorts. On the French side is Canigó (2,784m), the Catalan 'holy mountain'. The wooded foothills of the French Pyrenees give way to valleys filled with vines and orchards, before reaching the dramatic reddish cliffs of the Costa Vermella (Côte Rouge in French, meaning 'Red Coast'). Heading north, the beaches grow longer, flatter and sandier as they meet the Roussillon plain, a fertile low-lying region with *étangs* (coastal lagoons) that attract flamingos and other birdlife. Heading inland, the dreamy, timeless Fenouillèdes region is scattered with quiet villages, dramatic ridges and deep gorges.

CLIMATE

The climate is Mediterranean, fairly temperate but often quite humid: July and August are the hottest months, but the sea breeze often comes to the rescue to keep it from being stiflingly so. Northern parts of the region, influenced by the wild tramuntana wind off the Pyrenees, are most variable. No matter where you go in winter, you'll want a nice warm coat. You may need an umbrella any time up to June; spring in particular tends to be changeable. January can be surprisingly sunny; February is great for walking.

NATURAL HISTORY AND CONSERVATION

Catalunya's natural history is exceptionally rich, shaped by its varied geography and climate. From alpine peaks to Mediterranean woodlands and coastal wetlands, the region supports a wide range of habitats and a remarkable diversity of wildlife.

There are over 300 protected areas, including national parks, natural reserves and special conservation zones, covering around 30% of the region. Among the most notable are Aigüestortes i Estany de Sant Maurici National Park, with its glacial lakes and pine forests; the Cadí-Moixeró Natural Park, known for limestone cliffs and alpine meadows; and the Zona Volcànica de la Garrotxa, home to extinct volcanoes and ancient beech forests. North of the Pyrenees, in North Catalunya, the Parc naturel régional des Pyrénées catalanes protects a vast area of high mountain landscapes, forests and traditional pastures, offering continuity to the ecological corridors shared with southern Catalunya. Wetland areas near the Étang de Canet-Saint-Nazaire and the lagoons of the Roussillon plain also provide critical stopover points for migratory birds. Offshore, the Cap de Creus marine reserve and the protected coastal waters near Banyuls-sur-Mer help preserve seagrass meadows, coral habitats and marine species, highlighting the region's remarkable underwater biodiversity.

These areas support species such as the bearded vulture, golden eagle, Pyrenean chamois (isard), and wild boar, as well as rarer animals like the European wildcat and the recently reintroduced brown bear, which occasionally crosses from neighbouring valleys in the French Pyrenees. Amphibians, reptiles and butterflies thrive in the wetter, lower-lying habitats, while the Mediterranean woodlands are home to genets, hoopoes, and Hermann's tortoises. Birdlife is especially rich, with Catalunya lying on a major migratory route. Wetlands like the Aiguamolls de l'Empordà and the Ebro Delta offer vital stopovers for flamingos, herons, glossy ibises, and many species of ducks and waders.

Traditional land-use practices, such as transhumant grazing, dry-stone terracing and low-intensity olive and vine cultivation, continue to shape many rural landscapes, supporting biodiversity and maintaining fragile ecosystems, particularly in upland areas of both Spanish and French Catalunya. There is also increasing cross-border co-operation between conservation bodies on either side of the Pyrenees, recognising the shared ecology of the region and promoting joint strategies for species protection, rewilding and ecological connectivity.

Yet these ecosystems face growing threats. One of the most urgent is the prolonged drought that has affected the region in recent years. Although reservoirs have been replenished recently, the drought has placed severe stress on freshwater habitats, as well as agriculture and human supply. Forests are also more vulnerable to fire, pests and disease – 2019 saw the worst wildfires across the region in more than two decades.

The Ebro Delta, one of Spain's most important wetlands, is under particular strain. Rising sea levels, coastal erosion and reduced sediment from upstream dams are all contributing to the gradual shrinking of the delta. Saltwater intrusion is damaging rice fields and freshwater habitats, threatening both biodiversity and the traditional farming economy. Conservationists have called for urgent action to restore sediment flow, improve water management, and plan for a changing climate.

Other pressures include the spread of invasive species such as the Coypu (*Myocastor coypus*), American mink (*Neovison vison*) and red swamp crayfish (*Procambarus clarkii*), as well as habitat fragmentation caused by roads and infrastructure. In some areas, increasing visitor numbers, second-home development and over-tourism are placing further strain on fragile coastal and mountain ecosystems, prompting calls for more sustainable land use and nature-friendly tourism.

Despite these challenges, there are ongoing efforts to protect and restore Catalunya's natural environment. Local and national organisations are working on reintroduction projects, wildlife corridors and environmental education, while increasing numbers of visitors are exploring these areas through low-impact, nature-focused tourism.

There is growing public awareness of the need for conservation, and regional authorities have adopted ambitious biodiversity and climate strategies. The balance between protecting ecosystems and supporting local communities remains delicate, but Catalunya continues to be a leader in environmental stewardship.

HISTORY

1,000,000BC–AD711: CATALUNYA BEFORE THERE WERE ANY CATALANS As nations go, Catalunya is practically a newborn, a precocious little love child hatched in the confusions of the Dark Ages. Salvador Dalí probably would have said that through the ages the world was just waiting for it. In any case, the first million years on the southern slopes of the Pyrenees were pretty much a non-event. That is the approximate age of the earliest human remains found here, in the Vallparadís park in the industrial city of Terrassa.

It's all a blank from there to roughly 6000BC, when Palaeolithic people were painting game animals and ladies in flouncy skirts in caves around the Ebro valley. Where they went, nobody knows, and no-one else comes to occupy the stage until the Neolithic era. Catalunya lay far on the rustic fringes of the first great European civilisation, the one that built Stonehenge, Newgrange and Carnac, leaving only a crop of dolmens (c2500–1700BC), mostly in the Empordà, to testify to their presence.

By 800BC, the Mediterranean shores of Spain were occupied by the tribes that would come to be known as the Iberians. They were warriors and farmers, economically primitive compared to peoples further east, and they were about to get a rude shock. The big dogs of the day were moving in, bringing new ideas, new technologies and plenty of a recent invention called money.

First came the Carthaginians, who colonised parts of Andalusia and Ibiza. The Greek settlers came later, establishing themselves at Emporion and Rode (now Roses) c575BC. Between them, the fiercely antagonistic Greeks and Carthaginians had opened up Spain to the emerging Classical world. The bewildered Iberians had to adjust: they got assimilated into a money economy, and learned to turn ore into iron. In the 3rd century BC, Rome replaced the Greeks as the Carthaginians' nemesis. Carthage now assumed direct control where it could, making eastern Spain the heart of its empire, and in the Second Punic War Hannibal marched his elephants through Catalunya on their way to Italy. But, while Hannibal was fighting inconclusive battles on that peninsula, the Romans opened a second front. They landed at Emporion in 218BC, and in 15 years won control of Catalunya and all Spain.

The Iberians weren't overjoyed to see them. But a massive revolt in 197BC was brutally put down, and the Romans got down to Romanising their new conquest. An Iberian village became the new metropolis: Tarraco, now Tarragona, has more Roman ruins today than any town west of Italy itself. The Romans built roads and aqueducts, founded new cities, such as Colonia Faventia Julia Augusta Paterna Barcino – Barcelona – and integrated Hispania into the Mediterranean world.

As the western Roman Empire fell apart in the Germanic invasions of the 5th century AD, Catalunya became one of the barbarians' first prizes. The Visigoths (the lusty crew that sacked Rome in 410), soon learned that pickings in impoverished Italy were slim, and they headed their wagons back over the Alps into Gaul and

1

Hispania. Here they founded an out-of-the-way, low-rent kingdom that – at least south of the Pyrenees – would survive until the coming of the Moors.

AD711–985: WITH A LITTLE HELP FROM WILFRED THE HAIRY, A NATION IS BORN
That Visigothic Kingdom of Spain, after a promising start, went to pieces amid the ambitions of its barons, religious bloody-mindedness and economic disarray. The Franks might well have eventually gobbled it up, had not a fiercer foe come out of nowhere to beat them to the job.

This foe was the Arab-led army of Islam, which had rolled over all the Middle East and North Africa in less than a century after the death of Mohammed. Their invasion of Spain began in AD711; two years later the Moors destroyed Tarraco. Barcelona took note and surrendered without a fight. The Arabs pushed halfway up through Gaul before they were stopped by Charles Martel at Poitiers in 732. Martel's son and grandson, Pepin the Short and Charlemagne, would revive the Frankish Kingdom under their new Carolingian dynasty, while the Arabs consolidated their gains in the new Emirate of al-Andalus (a Caliphate after 756), occupying most of the Iberian peninsula. For some of the lands in between, however, the new dispensation meant confusion.

That, as history likes to remind us, can be a blessing. In this case, it allowed the Christian Visigothic nobles in the remote northern mountains to organise new power centres, the seeds of what would one day become Castile, Navarre, Aragon and Catalunya. Catalunya? No-one is recorded using that name before the 12th century, the same time that Catalan first appears as a written language. Its origins are shadowy: some say it was originally 'Gothalanda', while another guess has it 'Castle-onia', like Castile.

All through the later Dark Ages, in the safety of the Pyrenees, a population that included many refugees from the Moorish conquest was developing a distinct language and cultural identity. They were becoming a new nation, the Catalans. In 801, the Franks conquered northern 'Gothalanda', but after Charlemagne's death their empire rapidly fell into decay, and the Catalans were increasingly left to their own devices.

Local lords took the title of count from the Franks, and organised the Catalan lands into a number of counties, of which the County of Barcelona soon became the most powerful. In 870, the Franks installed an energetic count of Barcelona named Guifré el Pilós, or 'Wilfred the Hairy'.

HAIRY WILFRED AND THE FOUR BARS

It may sound like a yarn from Daniel Boone, but it's Catalunya's foundation myth. The Count of Barcelona, Guifré el Pilós (Wilfred the Hairy), is heroically defending Barcelona from the Moors led by Lobo ibn Mohammed, in around AD898. He is mortally wounded, and, when the Frankish king Charles the Bald comes to his hirsute hero's tent, Guifré confesses that his one regret is that he is dying without having earned a coat of arms for his golden shield. The king responds by dipping his fingers in Guifré's blood and running them down the shield. Hence the *quatre barres* (those four blood-red stripes you see on the Catalan flag) are born. It's a good story, even if the most ardent nationalists have to admit that Charles the Bald died 20 years before Guifré. Even so, Catalunya's flag is one of the oldest national flags in the world, first documented on the royal seal of Alfons II of Aragon in 1159.

According to the chroniclers this Wilfred was hairy indeed, down to the very soles of his feet. Legends about him are numerous, for later Catalans made him into a nearly mythological founding hero. Guifré took control of three other counties, while he resettled abandoned lands and endowed Barcelona and the region with churches and monasteries. After Guifré's death, his sons took over the counties – not as Frankish fiefs, but in their own right.

Barcelona's counts grew ever more confident, and in AD985, when their city was sacked by the great caliph al-Mansur of Córdoba and the Franks failed to respond to requests for aid, Count Borrell II declared his county's sovereign independence. The Franks could do nothing about it.

AD985–1213: AWASH IN WOOL AND IRON, THE CATALANS MAKE A PRECOCIOUS AND SLIGHTLY ECCENTRIC START

When things finally settled down, the Moorish-Christian boundary ran through the massif of Montsec in the west, and then down the valley of the Llobregat. Tortosa, Lleida and Balaguer grew into prosperous Muslim cities, sharing in the golden age of the Caliphate of al-Andalus. When the Caliphate broke up in 1010, Lleida and Balaguer briefly became the capitals of kingdoms (taifas) of their own.

On the Christian side, some remarkable things were happening. People were spilling down from the overpopulated Pyrenees onto the foothills' border zone, living like frontiersmen and building odd round towers for protection; many of these would grow up into castles.

Catalunya was growing wealthy too, far in advance of most of its neighbours. It was blessed with three of the most useful gifts a medieval economy could ask for: iron, wool and a free port. Barcelona was probably the key. Recovering nicely from the assault of al-Mansur, the city managed to develop one of the first real urban economies in Christian Europe. The town became a centre of cloth manufacture, while in the Pyrenees the Catalans found a little iron ore and invented an advanced technique for smelting it.

By the 1030s Barcelona had the first stable gold currency in western Europe. The business interests of the city and the ambitions of the counts found a happy symbiosis and, as both grew in power, trade and the flag went hand in hand. At the same time, the balance of power between Christians and Moors was shifting decisively. Under Ramon Berenguer I (1035–76), Barcelona extended its control as far as Carcassonne and Montpellier in Languedoc, while at the same time the counties of Barcelona and Urgell expanded westwards at the expense of the Moorish taifas.

After Ramon Berenguer I, with typical Catalan peculiarity, rule was shared by twin brothers named Ramon Berenguer II (1076–82) and Berenguer Ramon II (1076–97); the first was called 'the Towhead' and the second was nicknamed the 'Fratricide', for which crime he was eventually forced into exile. The twins and their successors continued to direct their efforts at expansion towards the north. To the west and south lay Zaragoza and Valencia, defended by El Cid, and they couldn't beat him; the Cid in fact captured Berenguer Ramon twice.

Berenguer Ramon was succeeded by his twin's son Ramon Berenguer III (1097–1131), who added new lands over the Pyrenees in what is now French Catalunya, or Roussillon. He and his son Ramon Berenguer IV (1131–1162) presided over the conquest of 'New Catalunya', over a few decades nearly doubling the nation's size ('Old Catalunya' was mainly the counties of Barcelona and Urgell). Tarragona fell in 1118. Tortosa's turn came in 1148, with the biggest prize, Lleida, following a year later. The last Moorish redoubts in what is now Catalunya succumbed in 1153.

ST JORDI AND THE DRAGON

The bull – that passionate, earthy archetype of fertility and death – may be the totem beast of Iberia, but he has little place in Catalunya. No, the creature the Catalans hold to their hearts is more fiery, more dangerous and quirkier. Ever since 1229, when Count-King Jaume I had a vision of Sant Jordi (St George) lending a hand at the siege of Mallorca, this most chivalrous of saints has been the patron of Catalunya.

The legend of Jordi and his dragon was seamlessly grafted on to Catalunya's favourite 9th-century dragon saga. It seems that the Moors, realising they couldn't defeat the Counts of Barcelona, decided to play dirty and brought a baby dragon over from North Africa, setting it loose at Montblanc near Tarragona. When it began to grow fat on the surrounding peasants and the boldest knights, the father of Wilfred the Hairy had the Christian derring-do to slay it at last. It was skinned and displayed on feast days, the grandad of the dragons who come out to play during Catalan *festes*, spewing fireworks in the pandemonium of the *correfoc*, or fire-running.

In 1456, the Generalitat made St George's Day (23 April) the Festival of the Rose, when men give their love a rose, just as George gave his princess the rose that sprang from the dragon's blood. Since 1926 women have given their men a book, in honour of Cervantes and Shakespeare, who both died on 23 April 1616. These days, it's less prescribed: women give roses, men give books, and many give both.

As the Catalan Reconquista neared completion, the new nation transformed itself from a collection of counties into a kingdom. The marriage in 1137 between Ramon Berenguer IV, Count of Barcelona, and the heiress of Aragon, Petronila, brought the city the crown of Aragon and all the prestige and patronage of royalty. Now the counts were 'count-kings', and rulers of the second most powerful kingdom on the peninsula.

The unusual title is a hint of just how important Barcelona continued to be in the new state; it also reflects the Catalans' ancient tradition of rights and privileges, codified as the Usatges in the time of Ramon Berenguer I. Their count-king ruled not by divine right, but on a down-to-earth contractual basis, evident in the people's oath of allegiance: 'We who are as good as you, swear to you, who are no better than we, to accept you as our king and sovereign lord, provided you observe all our liberties and laws; but if not, not.'

That famous oath, in fact, tells only part of the story. The 'we' who are swearing it were an increasingly grasping nobility. The Catalunya of Wilfred the Hairy's time, if not really egalitarian, had at least been a place where the average person could get ahead. Now, with their increasing wealth and power, the bosses were putting on the screws. In the 12th century, wealthy merchants in Barcelona coalesced as a political force and immediately started claiming privileges that shut out the smaller operators. Even before Catalunya reached its medieval heyday, we can see signs of the social strife that would eventually bring its downfall.

Meanwhile, though, the new state continued to rack up successes. Alfons I (Alfonso II of Aragon, 1162–96) absorbed the rest of Roussillon. Pere I (Pedro II of Aragon, 1196–1213) took part in the greatest victory of the Reconquista, the 1212 Battle of Las Navas de Tolosa that resulted in the fall of all of al-Andalus, save only the kingdom of Granada, to Castile.

1213–1355: CATALUNYA RULES THE WAVES Jaume I the Conqueror (1213–76) led Catalunya into its Golden Age, beginning its new maritime empire with the acquisition of Valencia and the Balearics. Jaume's descendants, by way of conquest, treaties and marriage, expanded this empire across the Mediterranean.

In some ways, it was a remarkably advanced and progressive state. Barcelona's trade was regulated by a maritime code, the *Llibre del Consolat de Mar*, written under Jaume I in 1259. The same king gave Catalunya a parliament, the Corts, in 1249 (only 34 years after England's Magna Carta) and a permanent governing body, the Generalitat. Jaume I's will divided his kingdom into two parts: Pere II (Pedro III of Aragon, 1276–85) got Aragon, including Catalunya and Valencia, while his younger brother Jaume ruled the trans-Pyrenean possessions and Mallorca as his vassal. As long as these two were alive the arrangement worked out well.

Later Mallorcan and Aragonese rulers, though cousins, often had a hard time getting along. Occasional tiffs did little harm – they were out building an empire in the Mediterranean. Under Alfons II (Alfonso III of Aragon, 1285–91), Jaume II the Just (1291–1327), Alfons III (IV of Aragon, 1327–36) and Pere III the Ceremonious (Pedro IV of Aragon, 1336–87), Catalan culture was at its height. It was the time of such notable figures as the philosopher and mystic Ramon Llull (d1311) and Abraham Cresques (d1387), the first scientific map-maker. Catalan painters and architects created works the equal of any in Europe, as Barcelona embellished itself with splendid Gothic monuments. For what had been a nation of farmers and shepherds only a few centuries before, the Catalans had come a long way.

1355–1479: IN WHICH GREAT AMBITIONS LEAD TO A GREAT FALL For all Catalunya's wealth and exploits overseas, things were not always going well at home. Barcelona in the midst of its opulence became a discontented and dangerous place, plagued by unemployment, poverty and crime. Big merchants fought against workers, while churchmen stirred up violence against the city's Jews. Despite royal protection, the first wave of pogroms occurred in 1391.

Overextension, and competition in trade from Genoa, brought hard times, and thanks to a string of bad harvests the city's poor even knew recurrent famines. Epidemics were also common. The Black Death arrived in 1348, killing off a third of the population. As oppression at home made peasant life unattractive, the new empire gave young men who could get out plenty of opportunities overseas.

In 1410, when Martí I died without an heir, the Compromise of Caspe gave the throne to a member of the ruling house of Castile, the Trastámara. The first of the Trastámara kings, Ferran I (1412–16) and Alfons IV (Alfonso V of Aragon, 1416–58), showed a greater interest in Castilian affairs than in Aragon's. This broke the final tie of mutual interest that had held Catalunya-Aragon's delicately balanced system together. Popular revolts in Barcelona in 1436 and 1437 were only the prelude to worse struggles to come; the real troubles began in 1462 with the Remença Revolt (named for a new tax). This was the curtain-raiser for the ten-year Catalan Civil War, which ended with the surrender of a city under siege by its own king, the notoriously brutal Joan II (1397–1479). Barcelona was ruined.

For the last act of the tragedy, the villain would be the son of Joan II. He was Ferran II to the Catalans, but he would have preferred to call himself by his Castilian name, Fernando El Católico. He had been married to Isabel of Castile in the middle of the wars and, when his father died and he assumed the throne in 1479, Castile and Aragon were effectively united. Spain was one, and Catalunya was suddenly a small corner of a very large kingdom; its capital was an exhausted, bankrupt metropolis that had no prospects and no friends.

1479–1830: LIFE IN SPAIN'S 'GOLDEN AGE' – IMPOVERISHMENT, OPPRESSION AND DESPAIR Historians tend to give Fernando and Isabel much better reviews than they deserve. This grasping, brutal and bigoted couple were interested only in squeezing all they could out of Catalunya to finance their own ambitions; their only gift to the region was the Inquisition, which arrived in 1487. The new rulers even took steps to ensure Catalunya would have no share in new opportunities: a codicil in Isabel's will specifically prohibited Catalan merchants from trading with the New World.

For Spain in its 'Golden Age', power and decadence went hand in hand, as the Habsburg successors to Fernando and Isabel strove to extend their power over three continents while condemning the nation to exhaustion and poverty at home. They drove the Castilian heartland bust, too, but Catalunya, its old ways of making a living torn away, was reduced to despair.

The region had the added burden of being on the front lines of the long wars between Spain and France. The government quartered troops on the populace, and the soldiers distinguished themselves more in pillage and robbery than fighting the French. That, along with Madrid's continued assaults on Catalan liberties and institutions, sparked off a revolt in 1640 that Catalans call the Reapers' War, the Guerra dels Segadors, as it began with a riot by a mob of labourers who were gathered in Barcelona looking for employment on the harvest. The Generalitat, under Pau Claris, raised an army, which with French help defeated the Castilians in a battle underneath Montjuïc, but the affair was hardly settled. The Catalan leaders managed it badly, and their region lapsed into anarchy through 12 years of inconclusive struggles before the French finally betrayed them. Barcelona, left on its own, was besieged and starved into submission in 1652. Under the Treaty of the Pyrenees in 1659, France annexed the northern counties of Catalunya, including Roussillon and parts of the Cerdanya, a loss that continues to shape Catalan identity to this day.

In the decades that followed, Spain pursued a more conciliatory policy towards Catalunya. Nevertheless, the Catalans chose to revolt again the next chance they had, in the pan-European commotion called the War of the Spanish Succession (1701–14). When they backed the Austrian archduke Charles's claim to the throne against the French Bourbon Philip V, it was a costly bet on the wrong horse. In the end, the Catalans were alone again and Barcelona came under siege once more. After 15 months of desperate resistance the city fell in November 1714, and down with it, this time, went Catalunya's Usatges, its institutions and the last vestiges of its autonomy. From now on, Madrid treated Catalunya as just another colony, and ruled it through a viceroy. In an effort to kill off whatever remained of Catalan spirit, the publication of books in Catalan was forbidden, and the universities were closed.

But once the Catalans had been suitably punished, the Bourbon dynasty tried to earn Catalan loyalty by giving them a chance to make a living again, and through the 1700s business started to pick up. The results were dramatic. The old instincts had never died, and, like some capitalist Sleeping Beauty, the mercantile elite magically popped up from its 200-year slumber, ready to make some deals.

The Catalans found two very profitable new businesses. Depressed farmers replaced subsistence crops with vines, and Barcelona distilled their grapes into cheap brandy (*aiguardent*) and shipped it off to thirsty Latin America. After about 1730, Barcelona specialised in the manufacture of printed cotton cloth; the empty spaces outside the city walls became the *prats d'indianes*, 'fields of calico', where the cloth was hung out to dry. In 1778, Madrid finally removed the last restrictions on trading with the colonies, and the build-up turned into a boom.

By 1780, when the population stood at 110,000 (it had more than doubled since 1714), the first industrial cotton mill was founded. Factory production soon replaced the medieval guilds, as Barcelona began its career as the 'Mediterranean Manchester'. The Napoleonic Wars were a rude interruption. Britain's blockade stopped the American trade cold. Catalunya went into a deep depression while Napoleon's men raided and looted its churches and monasteries. Meanwhile, across the Pyrenees, northern Catalans under French rule faced growing centralisation from Paris, and the gradual erosion of their language and institutions. As much as they hated Madrid, the Catalans learned from experience that the French were even worse.

1830–88: AS BOMBS AND BULLETS FLY, CATALUNYA MAKES ITS UNEXPECTED COMEBACK

After the big Napoleonic shake-up, the powers of Europe thanked Spain for its heroic resistance by throwing away its new constitution and propping the reactionary king Fernando VII (1814–33) back on his throne. When a coup in 1820 installed a liberal regime, they sent in 100,000 French troops to crush it. Spain was hopping mad, and no corner of it more so than Catalunya, which by now had once again become the most modern and forward-looking part of the country.

When Fernando finally died in 1833, and the infant Isabel II became queen, Catalans hoped for better things. Instead, what they got was a wild rollercoaster ride of conflict, progress and setbacks that made Spain seem the very image of the banana republics that were just winning their independence from her in Latin America. Barcelona was enlivened by regular riots, rebellions, strikes, factory burnings and assassinations over the next two decades.

Out in the countryside, the trouble was coming from the opposite end of the political spectrum. Supporters of the pretender Don Carlos, Fernando VII's brother, launched three major rebellions, the three Carlist Wars (1833–36, 1846–49 and 1872–76), and Catalunya was at the centre of all of them. All Carlists wanted was to turn the clock back a few centuries, and that included restoring the Catalan Usatges, as these mostly increased the power of the landowning nobility and the Church. Rural Catalunya, still deeply traditional and pious, found Carlism entirely to its liking, and local peasants supplied many of the recruits in the Carlist armies. Across the Pyrenees, the same rural conservatism lingered on, but without the same political outlet; Catalan identity there was increasingly filtered through religion, language and resistance to French centralisation.

Quite amazingly, for all the troubles, Catalunya was making tremendous progress, pushed through and paid for by industry. Barcelona's businessmen dragged Spain kicking and screaming into the Industrial Revolution. The nation's first steam engine appeared in 1833, the first Catalan-built steamship only three years later; the first railroad (from Barcelona to Mataró) opened in 1848. Barcelona filled up with factories, or *vapors* ('steamers'), and spawned a whole constellation of burgeoning industrial towns: Reus, Mataró, Badalona, Terrassa, Sabadell, Manresa. In textiles and iron, Catalunya became one of the first places in Europe to steal markets from industrial Britain.

For the second time in its history, Catalunya astounded the world, and its metropolis Barcelona enjoyed a second blossoming. The modern city, with its enormous expansion and glittering cosmopolitanism, evoked comparisons with the medieval golden age, and fostered a new pride in things Catalan. The *Renaixença*, or Renaissance, began with a movement to redeem and re-establish the Catalan language, long submerged by the forced Castilianisation of Madrid. The medieval poetry competitions, the *Jocs Florals*, were revived in 1859, and the literary

RAUXA VS SENY: WITHIN EVERY CATALAN THERE IS AN ANARCHIST
Joan Maragall

Catalans consider *seny*, 'common sense' or 'practical wisdom', as their principal virtue. It makes them rich and sets them apart from the rest of Spain, or at least from old romantic Spain and its haughty nobility that regarded work and commerce with disdain. *Seny*, however, has a Catalan counterpart: *rauxa*, or 'uncontrolled passion'. While the bosses sought Utopia in Modernista culture, their workers looked for theirs in Anarchism. The bourgeoisie sublimated their *rauxa* in Wagner, architectural excess and exotic sex (at least judging by the bills of fare at Barcelona's bordellos), while the Anarchists expressed it by erecting barricades.

But there was *seny* on the Anarchist side as well. The one thing that the Anarchists and bourgeoisie shared was a resentment of central authority. For the bourgeoisie, this meant Madrid, especially after the government lost Cuba and the Philippines, both Catalan cash cows, in 1898. For the Anarchists, of course, 'authority' was anyone who lorded it over the brotherhood of man, be it Church, government or capital, all of whom made man evil by assuming he was so.

The history of the class struggle in Spain began in Barcelona's Bonoplata factory, one of the country's first steam-powered plants; in 1835, during the first spate of church burnings, Luddite saboteurs set it on fire, too. Things became serious in 1855, when the government banned trade unions and Barcelona responded with Spain's first general strike. This happened at a time when a family of four living in the city needed a minimum of 4,000 *reales* a year to live; an unskilled labourer made less than 2,500. And no matter who was in charge – 19th-century Spain was a banana republic without the bananas – nothing changed. Like Pirandello's characters in search of a play, Barcelona's frustrated workers were in search of a belief.

It arrived by train in October 1868 in the person of Giuseppe Fanelli, an apostle of Bakunin, the famous Russian theorist of Anarchism. Fanelli spoke only

crusade was carried on by Catalunya's finest 19th-century poets, Jacint Verdaguer (1843–1902) and Joan Maragall (1860–1911), who led the way in bridging the historic Catalan spoken by the troubadours with the everyday language still spoken by the people. From there, the Renaixença grew into a fervent nationalist cultural movement in all the arts, from music to architecture. In this heady climate, Barcelona put on its first World's Fair, the Universal Exhibition in 1888; it showed the world, in the mayor's words, that the Catalans were the 'Yankees of Europe'.

1888–1939: A MOST DANGEROUS, MOST BRILLIANT HALF-CENTURY ENDS IN DISASTER By the end of the 19th century, Barcelona had one of the most developed economies of Europe, based on iron, textiles and trade – just as it had been in the Middle Ages. But, just as in those times, the new generation of the business elite proved just a little too piggish to share any of the prosperity. For a while, boom times papered over the growing discontent, but in the 1870s the city was ready to explode once more – this time, with the heat of a new ideology, known as Anarchism. The movement grew rapidly in Barcelona and took a violent turn after it was driven underground in 1874. While violence increased, Barcelona was paradoxically enjoying a most creative era. In the 1890s, Catalan culture flowered impressively, with the painters Ramon Casas and Santiago Rusinyol and their circle. The city's converging artistic style soon acquired a name, Modernisme. Its painting

Italian and French, but he had some newspaper clippings of Bakunin's speeches and pamphlets, and they were enough. In that same year, the Anarchist paper *Solidaritat Obrera* was founded, and gave meaning to the sporadic uprisings of Catalan farm labourers and workers. The Anarchists staged strikes and inevitably lost; which only made them more radical. Die-hards drifted into political terrorism. After the troubles reached a crescendo in the Setmana Tràgica of 1909, Anarchists dubbed Barcelona *La Rosa de Foc*, the Rose of Fire.

Two years later, the Anarchist trade union CNT was founded, and 80% of Barcelona's workers joined. Between 1910 and 1923, 800 strikes rocked Barcelona. The Civil War would be their finest hour, and their last. Anarchist military units worked effectively under elected officers, without hierarchies or salutes. In the areas they controlled, including much of Barcelona and its industrial belt, their collectivised economy ran efficiently and did more than its bit for the Republican war effort. Though Anarchists had their doubts about collaboration with any government, one of their leaders, Federica Montseny, became the Republic's minister of health – the first woman cabinet minister in Europe – and radically advanced women's rights while creating a first-rate public health system.

The end came in the middle of that war, not at the hands of Franco but of the Anarchists' allies in the Republic. Communist propagandists such as La Pasionaria called them traitors in the pay of Franco, and, when the two factions came to blows (absurdly enough in a fight over the Barcelona telephone company building), the Republican army intervened on the side of the Communists. After the war, Anarchist leaders who didn't escape to Mexico or France mostly died in Franco's gulags, and, when democracy returned, the Catalan workers would be listening to calmer voices who never mentioned utopias at all.

and poetry would not make much of an impression outside Catalunya, but in architecture the Modernistas were about to astound the world. Antoni Gaudí, the greatest among them, began work on the Sagrada Família in 1883. The Spanish–American War of 1898 was an earthquake for all of Spain. The loss of Spain's last important colonies closed off trade opportunities, and, in the decade that followed, hard times increased popular discontent. Anarchist violence culminated in 1909 with the Setmana Tràgica, the 'Tragic Week' of riots in Barcelona, when 116 died and Anarchist leaders were executed by the army. Spain's neutrality in World War I brought more boom times, as exports to the belligerents soared. The end of the war brought a wave of strikes and agitation, and in 1921 the captain general of Barcelona, Miguel Primo de Rivera, declared a military dictatorship with the approval of King Alfons XIII.

The dictatorship of Primo de Rivera was proof, if the Catalans needed any, that nothing had really changed since the time of Fernando and Isabel. But after he retired, Spain voted a left-wing landslide in the 1931 municipal elections, a dramatic renunciation of the old order that led to the abdication of Alfonso XIII and the birth of the Second Republic. In Catalunya, the big winner was the popular old ex-colonel Francesc Macià, head of the left-wing Republicans (Esquerra Republicana), who declared the 'Republic of Catalunya', although three days later he agreed for the sake of the young Spanish Republic to limit this to autonomy under the rule of a revived Generalitat. The patricians and their Lliga de Catalunya did not lose gracefully. Barcelona had always been theirs, and, when the elections of 1934 brought in a right-wing national government, they incited an insurrection that resulted in the jailing of both leftist and Catalan nationalist leaders, including Lluís Companys, the liberal trade union lawyer who succeeded Macià as head of the Esquerra Republicana, and ran the Generalitat until 1939.

The 1936 national elections brought the leftists back to power, but extremists on both sides seemed determined to settle the quarrel in the streets. A few months of shocking violence set the stage for Francisco Franco's coup and the outbreak of the Spanish Civil War. The ascendant left easily won control of Catalunya and used the opportunity to start a revolution. For ten months, Barcelona made history as the only city ever to have been governed by millennial Anarchists; shops and cafés became collectives, while wearing a tie on the streets was considered a provocation. As Franco's army made major gains across Spain in 1937, Barcelona became the theatre of a left-wing war-within-a-war, which was emphatically won by the Republican Army and the Communists.

By 1938 the Republican zone was largely limited to Catalunya, Madrid and Valencia. As refugees flooded into Barcelona and other cities, Franco and his German and Italian allies bombed them to terrorise the populations. When the Nationalists reached the sea and cut the Republican zone in two, the Republicans staked the outcome on one big offensive. The Battle of the Ebro (page 260), the bloodiest fight of the Civil War, ran for three months, and, when the Nationalists began their counter-offensive in October, the contest was effectively over. Half a million Republicans fled towards France in January 1939 as Barcelona surrendered. Tens of thousands crossed the snowbound Pyrenees into French Catalunya, a mass exodus known as the 'Retirada'. Refugees were herded into hastily erected internment camps along the coast, such as Argelès-sur-Mer and Saint-Cyprien, where they endured freezing conditions, hunger and disease. While the French government was hostile, for many locals the influx of Catalan-speaking exiles helped intensify a shared sense of identity that had long been marginalised by the state, although some resented the burden of housing and feeding the desperate newcomers.

Franco took particular delight in humiliating the Catalans. Lluís Companys, caught by the Nazis in France, was sent back to Franco and executed. The new regime returned Catalunya to direct rule from Madrid and banned all things Catalan; through the 1940s, even speaking Catalan in the street was risking jail.

1939–75: FOUR STULTIFYING DECADES WITH FRANCISCO FRANCO AND, THIS TIME, A HAPPY ENDING
The next two sad and impoverished decades saw food, electricity and everything else in short supply; in 1947 Catalan cities came very close to famine. Other parts of Spain were suffering too, and Franco did everything to encourage the unemployed to move to Catalunya, hoping a tidal wave of poor Andalucians would dilute Catalanism into a harmless eccentricity. The Catalans called Franco Paco Rana, 'Frank the Frog'. It was clear that he was never going to win their hearts and minds, and he never tried. By the 1950s, however, the dictator had given up on overt repression as part of a new image he was trying to project for his new friends in Washington. In 1952, the Catalan language was tentatively decriminalised.

By 1960, Franco had given up his attempt at economic self-sufficiency too, and a new generation of economists and technocrats was tooling up the country for its impressive industrial take-off of the next two decades, while the invention of the Costa Brava launched Spain's profitable new-found vocation for mass tourism.

The 1960s were a strange decade; many Catalans look back on it with a shudder: the philistine tastelessness of a new bourgeoisie interested only in 'peseta pragmatism', caught between *seny*, the famous Catalan common sense, and the urge to protest, between forgetting and remembering. Still, shoots of new life were poking up through the cracks of the Castilian concrete. In 1960, future Catalan president Jordi Pujol was arrested and imprisoned for two years after devising a protest at the Palau de la Música – singing the *Song of the Catalan Flag* at a concert while a delegation of Franco's ministers was in the audience. Cultural resistance, too, was slowly being reborn. In the last decade of Francoism, while both the regime and the dictator were losing their faculties, a half-hearted machine of repression was increasingly unable to contain the critical culture that was emerging in the streets.

When Franco finally died, on 20 November 1975, every single bottle of cava in Barcelona was emptied. The morning after, like the rest of Spain, the Catalans started wondering what would happen next. As it became clear that their new king, Juan Carlos, was moving them towards democracy with a steady hand, the Catalans kept their cool and did nothing to make it more difficult for him.

When the king's appointed prime minister, Adolfo Suárez, won the first elections in 1977, he invited Josep Tarradellas, Catalunya's long-time president-in-exile, to return and restore the Generalitat. The gesture was an example, one among many, of just how mature and progressive Spaniards had become while waiting for Paco Rana to croak. The ideal of a monolithic Spain died with the same tick of the clock that took Franco; even in Madrid, they saw that the new Spain was going to be liberal and federal, and they welcomed it. Across the border in France, nothing much changed: Catalan culture and language continued to be marginalised by the centralising French state, with little official recognition. Still, the establishment of the Bressola network of Catalan-language schools in 1976 marked a turning point. Community radio, local publications, and festivals also supported cultural renewal, and finally, in 2007, Catalan was symbolically recognised as a regional language.

The spectacular 1992 Barcelona Olympics was a coming-out party for the city and for the new Catalunya, a place to show off their accomplishments to the world. By any measure, those accomplishments have been remarkable. The creative channelling of decades of pent-up energy and Catalan quirkiness have made Barcelona the most dynamic city on the Mediterranean. It likes to see itself as the southernmost city of northern Europe and the northernmost city of the south, with a hard Protestant nose for making money, sweetened by Mediterranean colour and spontaneity.

Not the least of the Catalans' achievements has been defusing the little time bomb Paco Rana left for them: the hundreds of thousands of poor immigrants from southern Spain. This they managed with an effort towards good faith and fairness, and by compromising their nationalism enough to define a Catalan as anyone who wanted to be one (and who learned the language). Their non-racial inclusiveness could be a blueprint for other nationalities struggling to keep heart and soul intact in a multi-cultural world.

Today, with the population nudging 8 million, the question of identity remains potent. In the 2010s, the quest for independence moved from the fringes to the mainstream, culminating in an explosive referendum (deemed illegal by the Spanish government) in 2017. The Catalan government claimed victory, Madrid invoked direct rule and President of the Generalitat, Carles Puigdemont, fled into exile. The political crisis that followed was the most serious Spain had faced since its return to democracy. In Perpignan, the capital of Northern Catalunya, solidarity demonstrations were held, drawing thousands of participants. In early 2020,

Perpignan hosted a massive rally organised by Puigdemont, underlining a sense of cross-border Catalan identity.

Although few Catalans in France call for outright independence, they have demanded cultural recognition, particularly after the administrative regions of Languedoc-Roussillon and Midi-Pyrénées were merged into a super-region named Occitanie in 2016. This, they believed, erased their Catalan identity, and local leaders and small parties such as Unitat Catalana and Oui au Pays Catalan, have campaigned to rename the region 'Occitanie–Pays Catalan'.

Back in Spain, with the election of a more conciliatory socialist Spanish government, the global pandemic and a cost-of-living crisis, the independence issue has lost much of its fire, although it simmers in the background. Meanwhile, Catalunya is positioning itself as a forward-looking, green, tech-savvy region, with a focus on sustainability and digital innovation. Still, although busy with other ambitions – smarter cities, greener energy – it hasn't forgotten the eternal dream of running things its own way.

GOVERNMENT AND POLITICS

Catalunya is an autonomous community of Spain, and its government, the Generalitat, controls its own education, police (the Mossos d'Esquadra), healthcare, transport, agriculture, environment policy, and municipal governments and gets to keep most of their tax money. But ever since the death of Franco, there is a powerful yearning to become truly independent, as it was before Ferdinand married Isabella.

In 2010, Spain's Constitutional Court struck down key parts of Catalunya's newly revised Statute of Autonomy, including a symbolic reference to Catalunya as a 'nation'. Suddenly, Catalan independence was back in the spotlight. More than a million people came out to protest under the slogan, '*Som una nació. Nosaltres decidim*' (We are a nation. We decide). More massive, peaceful pro-independence demonstrations filled the streets every 11 September (the Diada, Catalunya's national day) and the Catalan government committed itself to a democratic vote on self-determination. But Madrid's response remained firm: such a vote was unconstitutional, insisting that the whole country – not just Catalunya – would have to vote on it.

A symbolic, non-binding vote was held by the Generalitat under President Artur Mas in 2014, and the result was overwhelmingly in favour of independence. Madrid declared it illegal, but over 2.3 million people took part, and Mas was later barred from holding office for two years for defying the courts. In 2015, pro-independence parties won a slim majority in the Catalan parliament and pledged to hold a binding referendum. In 2017, the Catalan government's Centre for Opinion Studies found 48.7% of Catalans supported independence, while 43.6% did not.

Despite repeated warnings from Madrid and the Constitutional Court, a unilateral referendum was held in October 2017 under President Carles Puigdemont, a former journalist leading the centre-right Junts per Catalunya (Together for Catalunya) party, in coalition with the more moderate Esquerra Republicana de Catalunya (ERC, Republican Left of Catalunya) led by Oriol Junqueras. The Spanish state declared it illegal and sent in riot police to seize ballot boxes. The images of violence shocked the world, and Spain was plunged into a political crisis.

Puigdemont declared independence but then immediately suspended it. Within days, Madrid invoked Article 155 of the constitution, dissolved the Catalan parliament, and imposed direct rule. Puigdemont fled to Waterloo in Belgium, where he has remained ever since as an MEP and the leader of what he calls a

Catalan 'government in exile', wanted by Spanish courts on charges of sedition and misuse of public funds. Junqueras and other leaders were arrested and sentenced to long prison terms.

When Pedro Sánchez of the left-of-centre Partido Socialista Obrero Español (PSOE) became prime minister in 2018, the approach from Madrid changed. He sought to 'turn the page' by restarting dialogue and mending the rift between Madrid and Barcelona. His controversial 2021 decision to pardon Junqueras and eight other jailed separatists, in the interests of 'coexistence and harmony', helped lower the political temperature.

The Catalan branch of the PSOE finished first in the Catalan regional election held in February 2021, even though Junts and the ERC went on to form a fragile coalition government. But it was only after finishing second in July's inconclusive general election – and sitting down to do the electoral maths – that Sánchez showed precisely how placatory he was prepared to be in return for winning the support he needed from the Catalan parties. Sánchez agreed not just to continued dialogue, but to a highly contentious amnesty deal for those involved in the 2017 referendum – including, potentially, Puigdemont himself. The move triggered furious backlash across Spain but kept Sánchez in office.

THE CATALAN CRAPPER

While attending Mass one day in Barcelona in 1959, Luís de Galinsoga, the pro-Franco director of the newspaper *La Vanguardia* couldn't stand it any longer. He stood up in church and shouted: ¡*Todos los catalanes son una mierda!* (All Catalans are shit!). Enough protests were raised for Franco to sack the newspaperman personally. Catalans didn't have much to laugh about that year, but Galinsoga's fate must have evoked at least a few smiles. They probably weren't even that miffed. Medieval Barcelona grew up between two torrents, the Cagallel and the Merdança: 'turd-taker' and 'shit-stream'. Both were buried centuries ago, under what are now the Rambla and the Rec Comtal, only to become chthonic scatological streams of consciousness.

The *caganer*, or Christmas crapper, a figurine with bare buttocks suspended over a lovingly carved pyramid of poo, has been an essential figure in Catalunya's Christmas cribs since the 1500s, placed just downwind from the main event in the manger. Not even Christmas-crib-mad Italy has anything like a caganer: plates of spaghetti, elephants, camels and Turks, yes; crappers, no. Catalunya squats alone. Ethno-psychoanalysts wonder: is the caganer the fertility symbol of an obsessive anal-retentive race? An expression of down-to-earth reality – the Messiah may have come, but the duodenum pushes on? The embodiment of Catalan opposition to central authority, even divine authority?

Traditional caganers wear traditional Catalan costume (red Phrygian cap, white shirt and breeches), but there are variations for collectors – yes, you can buy a King Charles III caganer (it's a compliment). All wear beatific smiles. The value of a good crap is brought home in another tradition, the *tió*, or Christmas log, which the children beat with sticks, shouting, '*Caga, Tió, caga!*' (Shit, Log, shit!) until *Tió* excretes sweets. After all, as cookbook writer Josep Canill de Bosch wrote in *La Cuyna Catalana* (1907): 'Regular body functions make nations strong. Strong nations lead the pack, and eventually become masters of the world.'

1

Another survey, conducted in July 2023, found that 52% of Catalans were opposed to independence and 42% in favour. Today, one of the biggest issues in Spanish politics isn't whether Catalunya will leave, but how far Madrid is willing to go to keep it on board, and at what cost. The proposed amnesty for Puigdemont and other exiled leaders remains a national flashpoint. Yet for many Catalans, other concerns – such as housing, inflation, climate and jobs – are now more urgent. Independence is still a political hot potato, but it's no longer the only story.

ECONOMY

Even in an economy modernising as formidably as Spain's has been, Catalunya has managed to stay in the lead. The region has 16% of Spain's population but produces 20% of national GDP and 25% of exports, thanks to its sophisticated industrial base. Catalunya's €200-billion economy is now bigger than Finland's. As soon as you leave Barcelona and take a look at the suburbs, you'll see just how important industry remains.

Traditionally, Catalunya has been a land of textile mills and machinery, but today the economy rests on three pillars: advanced manufacturing, export-oriented industry and a diversified services sector led by tourism, tech, logistics and culture.

The automotive sector remains a major employer, with SEAT and other international suppliers based in and around Martorell. Pharma and life sciences are booming, anchored by multinationals like Grifols and a web of research centres tied to Catalan universities. Then there's food and drink: Catalan wine, cava, olive oil, and cured meats are exported far and wide.

Barcelona, of course, powers the services sector, with a thriving ecosystem of start-ups, creative industries and logistics. The port of Barcelona is one of the busiest in the Mediterranean, handling everything from container traffic to cruise ships. Tourism is a major contributor, but so is finance, fashion and digital tech. The city styles itself as southern Europe's tech capital, and it's not just hype: Mobile World Congress, one of the world's biggest tech expos, is held here each year.

Catalunya is also a leader in green innovation. The regional government has prioritised sustainability and digital transformation, investing in renewables, smart transport and circular economy schemes.

That said, the cost of living, especially housing, has surged, particularly in Barcelona, and younger Catalans worry about stagnant wages. But, for all the tension, Catalunya remains one of Spain's most dynamic, inventive and productive economic engines.

The story across the border in France is less rosy: the Pyrénées-Orientales region faces challenges including limited industry, the exodus of young people in search of work, and a dependency on tourism. But efforts to boost economic growth are underway, including the establishment of campuses like 42 Perpignan which provides innovative education in high-demand coding and digital skills. And the Pyrenees–Mediterranean Euroregion (EPM), which encompasses both north and south Catalunya, as well as the Balearic Islands, promotes cross-border economic activities to strengthen regional economies and make the region more resilient to environmental challenges, as well as improved mobility to enhance youth movement and economic exchange.

PEOPLE

Catalunya's population has been shaped by centuries of movement, settlement and cultural blending. The earliest peoples were the Iberians, who established fortified settlements along the coast and interior, engaging in trade with Phoenicians and Greeks. Under Roman rule, the region became an important Mediterranean trading hub, a role it expanded during the medieval period when the Catalan counties joined the Crown of Aragon and their merchants reached across the sea to Italy and North Africa. The biggest demographic shift happened in the 20th century, when hundreds of thousands of people moved to Catalunya from other parts of Spain, particularly Andalucía and Extremadura, drawn by industrial jobs in Barcelona and surrounding areas. This internal migration fundamentally changed the region's makeup, with entire neighbourhoods developing distinct cultural identities.

Northern Catalunya presents a different picture. Rural and less populated, it maintains strong Catalan cultural ties despite being administratively French. The region's Catalan identity persists in language, traditions and local politics, even as French systems govern daily life.

Since the 1990s, immigration has become more international. North African communities, particularly from Morocco, form significant populations in Barcelona and other cities. Latin Americans, Eastern Europeans and Chinese immigrants have also established themselves, often concentrating in specific neighbourhoods and economic sectors. Each group has brought its own businesses, cultural associations and festivals.

Today, Catalunya reflects both continuity and change, with traditional identities coexisting alongside increasingly multi-cultural communities. FC Barcelona's teenage prodigy Lamine Yamal, embodies this new Catalunya, celebrating his multi-cultural background – Moroccan, Equatoguinean and Catalan – both on and off the pitch.

LANGUAGE

Catalan is a Romance language spoken by over 9 million people, mainly in Catalunya, Valencia, and the Balearic Islands, as well as in parts of southern France, Andorra (where it's the official language), and even in a corner of Sardinia. It developed from the Latin spoken in the northeastern Iberian peninsula during the early Middle Ages, gradually taking shape as a distinct language by the 9th or 10th century.

By the 12th century, Catalan had already emerged as a language of both daily use and literary expression. Its first known texts, like the *Homilies d'Organyà*, show a language fully distinct from Latin and clearly on its own path. As the Crown of Aragon expanded its influence across the Mediterranean, so too did the language. For several centuries, Catalan thrived as a language of literature, law and commerce.

In 1714, when Catalunya backed the losing side in the War of the Spanish Succession, the new Bourbon monarchy in Madrid wasted no time in stamping out regional autonomy. The Catalan language was banned from government, courts and education under the Nueva Planta decrees. From then on, Castilian (Spanish) was the language of power. Catalan retreated into the home, the church and folk traditions. Meanwhile in France, French authorities were systematically promoting French as the sole national language. Catalan was banned from schools and public administration, seen as a threat to national unity. This suppression intensified during the French Revolution and again under the Third Republic (late 19th–early 20th century), when monolingual French education became mandatory.

In the 19th century in Spain, industrialisation in Catalunya helped spark a cultural reawakening. The Renaixença ('rebirth') revived interest in Catalan literature and identity. Catalans worked to restore the language's public role, a movement that continued into the early 20th century and saw Catalan reintroduced in schools and public life under the short-lived Second Republic.

Franco's victory in 1939 undid those gains almost overnight. Catalan was banned from classrooms, censored from newspapers, and pushed out of public life. Speaking it in public could get you arrested. Still, the language never disappeared. It was spoken at home, in churches, and among those determined to keep it alive. By the 1960s, even as the regime loosened slightly and Spain opened up economically, Catalan culture began to cautiously re-emerge. Similarly in France, after a period of decline there was a revival of interest in Catalan language and traditions from the 1970s, boosted by the La Bressola school immersion program.

The end of the dictatorship in Spain in 1975 marked a turning point. Democracy brought the return of Catalan institutions, and the language was made co-official with Spanish. Since then, it's become the main language of education, widely used in the media, and a key part of public life. It's a requirement for all public sector jobs, whether teachers, doctors or town hall clerks, and all street signs are in Catalan. In France, Catalan was finally recognised as a regional language by the French state in 2007, although its use has diminished considerably and fewer than a third of the population speak it fluently. Nonetheless, it is used in cultural events and signage and students can now take their baccalaureate exam in Catalan.

RELIGION AND BELIEFS

Christianity became dominant under Roman and Visigothic rule and remains the majority religion today, though observance varies widely. The region is dotted with Romanesque and Gothic churches as well as important monasteries, such as Montserrat, a major European pilgrimage site. Nearly every town and village celebrates its patron saint with a *festa major* blending religious ritual, music, and all the popular Catalan traditions, from *capgrosses* (fatheads) to *correfocs* (fire-running).

In recent decades, immigration has diversified religious life. Islam is now the second-largest religion, with a growing number of mosques across Catalunya, particularly in urban areas. Smaller communities of Evangelical Christians, Jehovah's Witnesses, Buddhists, Hindus and Jews also practise freely, reflecting the region's legal commitment to religious freedom.

Although Catalunya is increasingly secular, especially among younger generations, religious architecture and customs continue to shape its collective identity and festivals.

EDUCATION

Education in Catalunya follows the broader Spanish system, but with regional distinctions. Schooling is compulsory from ages 6–16, beginning with primary education (ages 6–12), followed by secondary education (ESO, ages 12–16). Students may then continue to *batxillerat* (pre-university) or vocational training. Public education is free and secular, and Catalunya manages its own education system, meaning Catalan is the primary language of instruction in schools.

There is a wide network of public, semi-private (*concertat*) and private schools. Religious schools, especially Catholic ones, remain influential. University education is well developed, with major institutions such as the University of Barcelona and Pompeu Fabra University consistently ranking among Spain's best.

In French Catalunya, the education system follows the centralised French model, with instruction primarily in French, though Catalan is offered in some bilingual programmes and extracurricular activities.

ART AND ARCHITECTURE

The earliest art The first art in Catalunya goes back to c6000BC, in the caves in Ulldecona and Cogul, and the first monumental buildings are the walled Iberian oppida – the biggest of which is just off the Costa Brava in Ullastret. Not by accident, Ullastret is only a few miles from the first of Catalunya's ancient Greek colonies, Emporion (Empúries) and Rode (Roses). The Romans left substantially more – the spectacular ruins in and around Tarragona, but also walls and towers, the Temple of Augustus and the streets under the Museu d'Història de Barcelona.

The Middle Ages In one sense, Catalunya's great achievement in medieval art is unique. The buildings remain, but for most of the painting and sculpture that once embellished them you'll have to visit the great Museu Nacional d'Art de Catalunya in Barcelona and some of the smaller local museums, especially those of Girona, Vic, La Seu d'Urgell and Solsona. In North Catalunya, important Romanesque works survive in places like Elne, with its remarkable cloister, and in the sculptures attributed to the mysterious Master of Cabestany, whose distinctive, expressive style appears in churches throughout Roussillon and beyond.

The 11th and 12th centuries are marked by sturdy Romanesque churches in 'Old Catalunya' around the Pyrenees. Many of these were built or influenced by the Lombard masons of northern Italy, as shown in their tall bell towers and trademark blind arcading. Some were decorated with lively sculpture and painting, influenced by the artists of Occitan France. The painters' eccentric style and use of bold, flat colours later exerted a powerful influence on Joan Miró.

Among the most notable Romanesque churches are the great cathedral of La Seu d'Urgell, Ripoll's magnificent portal and cloister, the atmospheric Sant Joan de les Abadesses, Sant Cugat del Vallès, little Santa Maria at Porqueres, Sant Pere de Rodes high over the Costa Brava, Santa Maria de l'Estany's cloister, and Sant Vicenç at Cardona. Scores of charming Romanesque churches survive in the remote valleys of the Pyrenees. Those of the Vall de Boí are internationally famous for their highly stylised paintings, but there are many others, particularly in the Vall d'Aran. In North Catalunya, the Romanesque tradition is most powerfully embodied in the abbeys of Sant Miquel de Cuixà and Sant Martí del Canigó, two masterpieces of early medieval architecture.

The arrival of Gothic architecture in the late 12th century coincided with the conquest of New Catalunya and the tremendous upsurge of Catalan culture and political power. Catalan Gothic developed into a true national style in the late 13th century. Instead of the dizzying heights, pointed arches and flying buttresses that characterised the original Gothic of the Île-de-France, Catalan Gothic is restrained, practical and solid. What fascinated the Catalans was width and mass, and in their conquest of horizontal space they were as daring as the masters of Chartres. Among the earliest works are the three great Cistercian monasteries around Montblanc, at Poblet, Vallbona and Santes Creus. Nowhere is the style more striking than in Girona cathedral, with the widest Gothic nave in Christendom, or more beautiful than in Barcelona's Santa Maria del Mar.

Barcelona's medieval core is full of secular wonders as well: the merchants' palaces, the Drassanes (now the Museu Marítim), the Antic Hospital de la Santa Creu, the Llotja, and, perhaps most remarkable of all, the Saló de Tinell, with the widest masonry arches ever built in Europe. Later cathedrals of New Catalunya deserve a mention too, impressive works at Tarragona and Lleida that were begun after reconquest from the Moors.

While following international trends, Catalan painters too developed a national style, with a naturalism of expression and gesture. Ferrer Bassa's frescoes (1346) at Pedralbes are among the finest works of the century. Brothers Jaume and Pere Serra (active 1357–1405; Manresa cathedral, Sant Cugat) created the first large-scale altarpieces, or retables, of lavish colour and detail. They fell out of favour when International Gothic became the vogue; Lluís Borrassà (d1424), known for his elegant gestures, was the Catalan pioneer in the new style, followed by the very courtly Bernat Martorell (active 1427–52). His student Jaume Huguet (1412–92) was the leading Catalan artist of the 15th century.

Gothic Catalunya also produced some excellent sculptors, notably Jaume Cascalls (d1378), who is considered the greatest of the 'School of Lleida' sculptors (works also at Tarragona, Poblet, Ripoll). In the north, Gothic elements appear in the cathedrals of Elne and Perpignan, where the architectural vocabulary of southern France – pointed arches, ribbed vaults, and a more vertical emphasis – blended with the Catalan preference for wide, unbroken interior spaces and austere structural clarity. Just above Perpignan, the Palace of the Kings of Majorca stands as a striking example of secular Catalan Gothic architecture, built in the late 13th century when Perpignan served as the capital of the short-lived Kingdom of Majorca.

As Catalunya decayed in the 16th and 17th centuries, so did its art, both in quantity and quality. There is very little of art or architecture from the Renaissance, Baroque and Neoclassical eras, and even less that is distinctly Catalan.

Modernisme (1880–1910) Things changed when Barcelona burst outside its walls into the Eixample in 1860. Now that they had money and room to build, how should they build? In the spirit of the Renaixença, Catalan architects studied Viollet-le-Duc; they agreed with Ruskin that 'ornament [was] the origin of architecture', and adored a book called *Der Stil* (1861–63) by German architect Gottfried Semper, one of the first to describe how a building should express its function. To mimic historical styles was repulsive. It was essential to be modern, and Modernisme, as the new style came to be known, would be based on Semper's dictum that 'originality is a return to origins'.

Catalunya's Modernista architects responded to Semper in surprisingly diverse ways. What they had in common, however, was their nationalism, a trait they shared with Catalunya's newly assertive bourgeoisie. Although part of the late-19th-century Arts and Crafts movement, Modernista architecture has no fin-de-siècle tristesse; it is vigorous, bold, colourful and playful.

The first great Modernista, Lluís Domènech i Montaner (1849–1923), took Semper's 'return to origins' as a return to traditional Catalan brick and iron. His use of the latest technologies saved the bacon of Barcelona's 1888 Universal Exhibition, when he orchestrated the building of a massive hotel in only 59 days. His masterpieces, the Palau de la Música Catalana, the Casa Lleó Morera and the Hospital de Sant Pau, are remarkable for their complete integration of decoration. Josep Puig i Cadafalch (1857–1956) was more historically minded; for him, Semper meant an imaginative reinterpretation of Catalan Gothic. He left Barcelona some highly individualistic works: Casa Amatller, Els Quatre Gats, Casa de les Punxes, and the Fábrica Casaramona (now the CaixaForum exhibition space). He later adapted his style to fit Noucentista currents (see opposite); his last buildings, for the 1929 Exhibition, are almost Baroque.

By far the greatest genius of the whole international Art Nouveau movement, Antoni Gaudí i Cornet (1852–1926) went deep into uncharted territory; his 'return to origins' was a return to the forms and structure of nature herself. The son of a coppersmith in Reus, he had grown up watching his father make cauldrons from flat sheets of metal, a hands-on creating of volumes. Gaudí would approach architecture in the same way. He was more a sculptor and poet than an architect, and improvised as he went along. 'He didn't make plans,' said Miró. 'He made gestures.'

Gaudí's life and career (page 24) are a remarkable study in paradox and contrariness. He hated being called a Modernista, because as a good Catholic he didn't believe in modernity. He was a reactionary, yet he went far beyond any architect of his time into the realms of pure imagination; while others drew on Gothic, his goal was to take it to a higher stage of evolution. Convinced that 'the straight line is man's creation; the curved line, God's', he studied Moorish and Hindu designs that he would later combine with Gothic, natural forms and his own imagination, and changed the face of Barcelona.

Beyond these Modernista big three are some delightful talents. Gaudí's sometime collaborator Josep Maria Jujols i Gibert (1879–1949) was 'one of the most subtle, original, unprejudiced and provocative personalities of contemporary art', as Carlos Flores called him. He created the serpentine bench at the Park Güell, the balconies of La Pedrera, the roof of the Casa Batlló – but he also left some of his most imaginative works in villages around Tarragona. Joan Rubió i Bellvé (1871–1952), from Reus, created some of Barcelona's imaginative brickwork. In Perpignan, the Palais des Congrès (originally the Hôtel Pams), with its ornate ironwork and decorative interiors, reflects a local interpretation of Art Nouveau aesthetics.

Modernista painters never rose to the level of the architects, but at the start of the 20th century they nurtured a young Andalucian genius named Picasso. Ramon Casas (1866–1932), the 'Catalan Toulouse-Lautrec' painted a handful of bold, almost photographic, political paintings, but later turned to churning out society portraits and advertisements. Santiago Rusinyol (1861–1931) painted landscapes, gardens and genre scenes; his legendary Modernista festivals at Sitges flirted with Symbolism. Isidre Nonell (1873–1911) painted poor gypsy women, inspiring Picasso's Blue Period. Rodin was the strongest influence on Modernista sculptors such as Miquel Blay and the delightful Eusebi Arnau. The most Rodin-like was Josep Llimona (1864–1934), whose masterpiece is Barcelona's *Monument to Dr Robert*.

In North Catalunya, artists from Picasso and Braque to Miró and Tàpies were drawn to Céret, attracted by the light and the landscape, and the Musée d'Art Moderne de Céret still houses one of the finest modern art collections in the south of France. Matisse and Derain painted in the nearby coastal town of Collioure in 1905, launching the Fauvist movement, which vividly echoed the bold colours and expressive lines in Catalan Romanesque frescoes.

Post-Modernisme (1910–present) A reaction to the eccentricities of Modernisme expressed itself in Noucentisme, 'nineteen-hundredism', which sought balance and order in a return to Mediterranean roots. In art, the Noucentista reaction is represented by a Cézanne-inspired search for structure, in the paintings by Joaquim Sunyer of Sitges (1874–1956) and sculpture of Josep Clarà. Two of the more original figures of the time were Juli González (1876–1942) and the muralist Josep Maria Sert (1874–1945).

Even while Noucentisme held forth in the 1920s, change was in the air. Picasso and the Cubists were first exhibited at Barcelona's Dalmau Galleries in 1912.

During World War I the city became a refuge for artists: André Breton's Surrealist manifestos were signed by the two great Catalan painters of the 20th century, Joan Miró (1893–1983; page 122) and Salvador Dalí (1904–89; page 196). Under Franco, architectural creativity ground to a halt, but Antoni Tàpies (1923–2012), who used found objects as a means of expression, emerged in the 1950s doldrums as one of the leading artists in Spain. One bright spot was Barcelona's luminous-white Fundació Joan Miró by Josep Lluís Sert (nephew of Josep Maria Sert), who went into exile after the Civil War and returned to design his best building in 1972.

Barcelona's post-Franco rulers have been Socialists, but they were also solid bourgeois and wanted to make their mark on the city. Being awarded the 1992 Olympics fitted right in with their plans for revitalising old neighbourhoods on a dazzling scale. They haven't stopped yet, although the 'vicious circle of design' – the parade of trendy architects constantly upstaging each other to be the boldest, the newest – has been at best a mixed blessing, resulting more often than not in a force-fed architecture that looks the way hothouse tomatoes taste; the 2004 Fòrum is a glowing example. Rare exceptions include the Torre de Telefònica (1992) on Montjuïc, by engineer-architect Santiago Calatrava of Valencia, and striking works by outsiders: Arata Isozaki's Palau Sant Jordi (1990), Norman Foster's Torre de Collserola (1992) and the Museu d'Art Contemporani (1995) by Richard Meier.

GENIUS AND CRANK

Antoni Gaudí i Cornet (1852–1926) was one of the most innovative architects of any era. Although Gaudí was regarded as an eccentric or even a hippy architect in the architectural Ice Age of the 1960s, you don't have to be in Barcelona long to realise that his reputation has since been polished and used to fuel an industry of its own. You can take an all-Gaudí tour or purchase models of his benches in Park Güell; the opera *Gaudí*, by Joan Guinjoan and Gaudí scholar Josep M Carandell, premiered at the Liceu in 2000.

Although classed as a Modernista, Gaudí's creation of new forms and textures, and his vision of decoration as being as integral to the structure as its walls or roof, went far beyond anything built by his colleagues. No architect ever studied nature more intently; in his buildings, stone became organic, sensuous, dripping; iron was wrought into whiplash ribbons, trailing leaves and spiders' webs; the old Muslim art of covering surfaces with broken tiles (*trencadís* in Catalan) was given a new vibrant, abstract meaning, reaching an epiphany in the Park Güell. Gaudí ingeniously reinvented the parabolic arch, last seen with the ancient Hittites. Much of the mathematical work he and his colleagues had to do in those pre-computer days is astonishing.

Gaudí, however, might not have become world famous had he not caught the eye of Eusebi Güell. Güell's father Joan was an Americano who made a fortune in Cuba, and Eusebi had a privileged son's knack for spending, and fancied himself the Lorenzo de' Medici of Barcelona. Perhaps he and Gaudí were destined to meet, but the actual conjunction occurred at the Paris Exhibition of 1878, when the 31-year-old Güell saw an extraordinary 10ft-tall glass, iron and mahogany display case for a glove company.

It was love at first sight. Güell tracked down its 26-year-old designer. Gaudí at the time was something of a dandy and man about town, ripe to be patronised, and Güell's first commission was for the gate, lodge and stables for the Finca Güell in 1884. Güell was so pleased that two years later he asked Gaudí to build

Barcelona has entered another phase of quiet transformation, with recent changes focused less on spectacle and more on livability, sustainability and reclaiming urban space. Jean Nouvel's **Torre Glòries** (2004), the **Disseny Hub** (Design Museum, 2014) and a fancy new mirrored home for the historic **Encants** flea market (2013) have transformed the Plaça de les Glòries, once a traffic-choked junction. New gardens and outdoor cafés have made it one of the most inviting corners of the city to relax. Similarly, for the 2024 America's Cup, the city avoided grand new builds, instead revitalising the **Port Vell** area and restoring historic buildings like the Llotja de Pescadors.

Inland, the *superilla* **(superblock) programme**, launched in 2016, continues to remake neighbourhood life. In the Eixample, plans are underway to convert one in every three streets into green, pedestrian-first areas by 2030. The Sant Antoni *superilla*, the first to be introduced and now nearing completion, will reclaim over 22,000m^2 from traffic, replacing asphalt with trees, benches and shaded social spaces.

Meanwhile, the 22@ district in Poblenou, once industrial, is now a hub for innovation and contemporary design. Notable new buildings include the **LCI Barcelona campus** and the **Can Framis Museum**, a modern art space housed in a former textile factory.

him a mansion, with money no object. The result, the Palau Güell, was fit for a Renaissance prince. So it tends to come as a surprise to learn that Gaudí, whose very name in Catalan means 'delight', was the last man you'd want to invite over for dinner (to begin with, he was probably the only Catalan vegan ever). Gaudí was always proud to be the son of a craftsman, but in the circle of Güell he became increasingly anti-democratic and authoritarian, and the worst sort of neo-medieval religious crank. Obsessive, morbidly pious, he told friends that he saw himself as God's humble servant in a world made of punishment and pain.

Yet the crankier he got, the more wonderfully he built. For his next project, the church for the Colònia Güell in Santa Coloma del Cervelló, he cut loose completely from historical eclecticism and soared into the realms of pure imagination. Only the crypt was ever finished, but it stands as a revolutionary architectural sculpture, a cave held together by mathematics and Catalan craftsmanship. Güell and Gaudí's last collaboration was the Park Güell, ostensibly a residential colony for the rich but incidentally a secret garden of their beliefs on Catholicism and Masonry.

Crankier and crankier, Gaudí reached his pinnacle of fame in 1910, with La Pedrera (Casa Milà) – which he designed as a pedestal for a 12m-high statue of the Virgin Mary and a pair of angels, an idea his client prudently vetoed after the 1909 Setmana Tràgica, when Barcelona was still smoking from another of bout of church-burning. It never seemed to occur to the pious Gaudí that the industrialists who hired him made their bundles by keeping Barcelona's workers so downtrodden that Anarchism seemed to be their only hope.

Gaudí just didn't get it. After La Pedrera, he became increasingly reclusive, devoting the rest of his life trying to expiate the church-torching sins of his fellow citizens by building the Sagrada Família. The Association for the Beatification of Antoni Gaudí was founded in 1992, and in 2000 the Vatican announced that it would open the case. His followers are now busy trying to prove that he performed non-architectural miracles, too.

CINEMA Catalan cinema is known for its artistic innovation and strong regional character, with directors such as Isaki Lacuesta, Albert Serra and Carla Simón drawing international acclaim. Simón's *Alcarràs*, which won the Golden Bear at the Berlinale in 2022, captured the struggles of a farming family in Catalunya with authenticity and warmth, while Isabel Coixet, one of the country's most prolific filmmakers, has achieved global success with English-language films like *The Bookshop* and *The Secret Life of Words*.

The history of filmmaking in Catalunya stretches back to the early 20th century, when Barcelona was one of Spain's most dynamic production centres. Silent films, comedies and experimental works flourished, often influenced by European avantgarde movements. The Spanish Civil War and Franco's dictatorship brought this momentum to an abrupt halt, as the Catalan language was banned in public life, and cinema in Catalan was almost impossible to make.

Despite censorship, Catalan filmmakers kept experimenting. In the 1960s, the School of Barcelona emerged, a loose group of directors which included Pere Portabella, Jacinto Esteva and Joaquim Jordà, who embraced modernist aesthetics inspired by the French New Wave. Their films were cerebral, critical and defiantly out of step with the official culture promoted by Madrid.

After Franco's death in 1975 and Spain's transition to democracy, Catalunya regained autonomy, and with it came renewed support for film production. The Catalan Institute for Cultural Companies (ICEC), established in 1981, began offering grants and backing local productions, laying the groundwork for a new generation. Since then, Catalan cinema has steadily grown in confidence and visibility. Alongside public grants and tax incentives, festivals and institutions such as the Filmoteca de Catalunya have helped professionalise and internationalise local production.

For many filmmakers, choosing to work in Catalan is not just an artistic decision but a cultural and political one: it is a way of affirming identity and giving the language a place on screen. Albert Serra has become a Cannes regular with his austere, often provocative films, while Isaki Lacuesta continues to blur the boundaries between documentary and fiction. Coixet proves that Catalan filmmakers can succeed abroad in other languages, while Carla Simón embodies the power of cinema to bring Catalan voices to the world stage.

MUSIC In the early 20th century, Catalan composers Isaac Albéniz (1860–1909) and Enrique Granados (1867–1916) were among the most renowned in all Spain, famous for combining classical music with folkloric lyricism. Granados, born in Lleida, was also a pioneering teacher and founded the conservatory that would later train many of Catalunya's greats. Albéniz created the *Iberia Suite*, considered one of the finest pieces for piano of all time. Perhaps the most famous Catalan musician of the 20th century was Pau Casals (1876–1973), or Pablo Casals, as the world knew him, a cello virtuoso and conductor from El Vendrell (page 240). A fierce advocate for peace and democracy, he went into exile after the Civil War and refused to perform in countries that recognised Franco's regime.

Catalunya has a deep-rooted choral tradition, with *corals* (choirs) in every town and village. The most famous of them all, the Orfeó Català, founded in 1891, still sings to packed houses at the Palau de la Música Catalana (page 102). This region has also produced some of the world's most renowned opera singers, including Montserrat Caballé, born in Barcelona and famous for her vocal power, her flamboyant stage presence and her unforgettable duet with Freddie Mercury.

There's plenty of traditional music to be heard throughout Catalunya. At every *festa major*, you're bound to hear the *cobla*, the traditional ensemble that

THE SARDANA

As with so much that the Catalans do, they go about their national dance, the *sardana*, with a workaday seriousness. Coats and bags are placed in a pile in the centre, hands are joined to form a ring, and everyone steps intricately to the right, then to the left – slowly or vigorously, depending on the music. The feeling that this is a communal rite is always there, an affirmation of Catalan identity and unity, of Catalan feet gently awakening Catalan earth – it's as far from the wild, pounding, passionate *duende* or goblin of flamenco as you can get.

The dance is harder than it looks but, if you want to give it a go, don't goof about: 'To dance the sardana imperfectly is to commit a sin against art; it is to insult Catalunya,' according to Aureli Capmany. Franco, needless to say, banned it. The Catalans learned the *ballo sardo* during their unwelcome occupation of Sardinia and, as the Sards claim their circle dances are Neolithic in origin, the *sardana's* roots are very deep indeed. So what comes as a surprise, seeing the serious faces, is the music, which is nothing like any folk tune you've ever heard, but rather in the vein of boulevard tunes; nearly all *sardanes* were composed in the mid 19th century by one Pep Ventura. There's an occasional melancholy strain, but it never lasts long; sometimes the tempo picks up, and the younger dancers in the inner circles even work up a bit of a sweat.

accompanies the *sardana* (see above), a mix of woodwinds, brass and the strange, nasal tenora. And, along the coast, the *indianos* who set sail for the Americas to find their fortunes brought back different melodies and rhythms, including the *havaneres* (sea shanties), which are still sung today in fishing towns like Calella de Palafrugell (page 167).

Under Franco, music became a means of political expression. The Nova Cançó movement of the 1960s and 70s, led by artists like Lluís Llach, Maria del Mar Bonet and Raimon, gave voice to Catalan identity and turned protest into poetry. Today, it's Rosalía, a flamenco-trained prodigy turned international pop icon, who has captivated the world with a sound that's all her own.

LITERATURE A *mestre en gay saber*, or 'master of joyous knowledge', was a troubadour, and, if it seems peculiar that they were still running around Catalunya in the mid 19th century, it's because of the overwhelmingly nostalgic nature of the Catalan cultural reawakening, the Renaixença. The first Jocs Florals, or Floral Games, a poetry competition between troubadours, took place in Toulouse in May 1324. In 1388, Queen Violante de Bar brought the games to Barcelona, where the third prize was a silver violet, the second a golden rose and the first prize a real rose, because, like the greatest poetry, a rose can never be imitated.

Medieval Catalan verse is powerful, pithy stuff. In 1490 the genre kicked off with a bang with Joanot Martorell's *Tirant lo Blanc*, Europe's first prose novel, a mix of chivalry and satire. The heroics may well have been based on the 'White Knight', the Romanian-Hungarian Turk-crushing hero John Hunyadi, but the bawdy, ribald bits are pure Catalan. It was one of Cervantes' favourite books.

After dying out in the 15th century, the Jocs Florals were revived by Barcelona's Ajuntament in May 1859 as a way to promote Catalan verse, which had all but died out. 'Fatherland, Faith and Love' were the mottoes. A jury selected the winner, and the first prize once again was a real rose. A poet who earned three roses was deemed a modern *mestre en gay saber*. The Jocs even produced some good verse: Joan Maragall and Jacint Verdaguer, other *mestres*, are still read today. In the other arts, the Jocs Florals and their twee quaintness were perhaps most important for the reaction they provoked in the 1890s: Modernisme.

SPORT Football is big all over Spain, but in Catalunya it is truly a religion. FC Barcelona isn't just a club – *més que un club*, as their slogan declares. Founded in 1899 by a Swiss expat and quickly embraced by the locals, Barça has long symbolised Catalan identity, particularly during the Franco era when flying the *senyera* or speaking Catalan could land you in trouble. Today, the Camp Nou remains one of Europe's great sporting cathedrals, even as it undergoes major renovations to modernise its facilities. Barcelona's second team, RCD Espanyol, also has a loyal following and a striking stadium of its own in Cornellà, but it's Barça that dominates hearts and headlines.

In North Catalunya, rugby reigns supreme, with Perpignan team the Catalan Dragons embodying Catalan identity and regional pride and competing in the English Super League.

Cycling is hugely popular throughout Catalunya, both professionally and recreationally, with routes winding through the Pyrenees, Montseny and the Priorat vineyards. Girona, in particular, has become a magnet for international cyclists, but there are also lots of beautiful routes, including the Vies Verdes – former train lines, now converted into easy bike paths through the countryside – which bikers of any level can enjoy.

In winter, the Catalan Pyrenees offer skiing and snowboarding at resorts like La Molina, Masella, Font Romeu and Baqueira-Beret (the latter a favourite with the Spanish royals). In summer, the mountains become playgrounds for hiking, paragliding, canyoning and climbing. Catalunya is a renowned climbing destination, with legendary crags like Siurana and Montserrat drawing elite climbers from around the world.

The coastline, meanwhile, delivers its own brand of adrenaline. The Costa Brava and Costa Daurada, as well as the beaches around Argelès-sur-Mer and Canet in France, are hotspots for sailing, windsurfing and kayaking, while Barcelona's beaches attract locals year-round for volleyball and paddleboarding. Many of the Olympic venues from 1992, such as the Palau Sant Jordi and the Olympic swimming pools on Montjuïc, are still in use today.

2

Practical Information

For general touring Catalunya is a year-round destination. January can be surprisingly sunny; February is great for walking. In August many shops and restaurants close altogether – except along the coast. If you can pick and choose and want to do more than sit on a beach, February to May or September and October are usually the most delicious months, and September has the added attraction of great festivals, while early October is the peak time for wild mushrooms. In winter, of course, the mountain resorts have all the winter sports activities imaginable. Do check the calendar of events – Catalans put on a good show.

HIGHLIGHTS

Since it made its splash into the world's consciousness with the summer Olympics in 1992, Catalunya's dazzling capital **Barcelona** needs no introduction. You could easily spend a week there, exploring its Gothic core, the unique Modernista architectural legacy left by Gaudí and his colleagues, its superb museums, fabulous restaurants, wild array of shops and hyperactive nightlife. An excellent train network waits to whisk you out to marvels on the outskirts. This includes a sprinkling of Modernista architecture, beaches and superb restaurants on the **Costa Maresme**, and fascinating churches in the old centres of **Sant Cugat del Vallès**, **Manresa** and **Terrassa**. There's startling **Montserrat**, the Catalan holy mountain, and Gaudí's equally startling crypt at the **Colonia Güell**. South of Barcelona lies the **Alt Penedès**, source of Catalunya's delightful, bubbly cava. Popularised by artists a century ago, **Sitges** is a lively bohemian resort.

The **Costa Brava** concentrates some of Spain's most beautiful beaches and coastal scenery, especially along Cap de Begur. In delightful **Cadaqués** you can visit Dalí's house; nearby **Figueres** has his playful museum. **Girona** is one of Spain's great medieval towns, with more than its share of secrets. The lush volcanic landscapes and lovely medieval villages of the **Natural Park of the Garrotxa** lie just to the west. Towards the Pyrenees you have the historic towns of **Vic**, **Ripoll**, and **Berga**, the latter on the route to the towering **Serra de Cadí**.

Tarragona is a fascinating city with tremendous Roman ruins, a sublime cathedral and miles of beaches. Its province includes the **Costa Daurada**, Catalunya's 'Golden Coast' for a beach break. Three great **Cistercian monasteries**, Poblet, Vallbona and Santes Creus, are the medieval showcases of the region, and the beautiful countryside of **the Priorat** yields superb red wines. Catalunya's southern frontier is marked by the **Ebro Delta**, full of rice paddies and flamingos.

Lleida has a great landmark in its Seu Vella (the old cathedral) and plenty of provincial charm takes in western or 'New Catalunya', the last wedge to be reconquered from the Moors. **Solsona** and **Cervera** are two of the most beautiful medieval towns

2

in Catalunya; the surrounding countryside is dotted with medieval relics. Up in the High Pyrenees you'll find **La Seu d'Urgell**, with another great cathedral, just down the road from the duty-free, sweaty-palmed ski paradise of **Andorra** and some of the most beautiful and secluded valleys in the Pyrenees: the **Vall d'Àneu**, **Vall d'Aran** and the **Vall de Boí**, filled with Romanesque marvels, and the majestic **Aigüestortes National Park**.

Across the border in North Catalunya, you can explore **Perpignan** with its palm-lined squares and the Palace of the Kings of Majorca and the reddish, vine-clad cliffs of the **Côte Vermeille**, which is dotted with colourful fishing villages like **Collioure**. Heading into the Pyrenees are striking Vauban fortresses like **Mont-Louis** and **Villefranche-de-Conflent**, linked by the panoramic **Little Yellow Train**, and the sacred Catalan mountain of **Canigó**. On its slopes is the stunning, Romanesque abbey of **Saint-Michel-De-Cuxa**, with more fine Romanesque architecture to explore elsewhere in Roussillon, from the cloister at **Elne** to the early medieval churches of the **Fenouillèdes**.

SUGGESTED ITINERARIES

A WEEK IN AND AROUND BARCELONA Perfecting dynamic, dazzling, dizzying Barcelona is an ongoing Catalan project, and one suspects that once the Sagrada Família is finished, they'll start something else even grander.

Day 1 Take the obligatory stroll along the Rambla and visit Barcelona's medieval heart: the cathedral, the Museu d'Història de la Ciutat, Santa Maria del Mar and the Gothic mansions of La Ribera.
Day 2 Change pace and spend a day with the Modernistas – walk up the Passeig de Gràcia to see the 'Block of Discord' by Gaudí, Domènech i Montaner and Puig i Cadifalch, and Gaudí's extraordinary La Pedrera; in the afternoon take the metro over to the Sagrada Família and Domènech i Muntaner's magical Hospital de Santa Creu i Sant Pau. In the evening attend a concert at the Palau de la Música Catalana.
Day 3 For a day trip, take the train and cableway up to Montserrat for a visit to the monastery and a walk among the peaks.
Day 4 For an intermission, take the train down to Sitges to laze on the beach and take in its two excellent museums, Maricel and Can Ferrat.
Day 5 A day on Montjuïc, starting with the marvels of the Museu Nacional d'Art de Catalunya; after lunch wander through the gardens and visit the Fundació Miró, then take the aerial cableway over to Barceloneta for a seafood dinner.
Day 6 Go out to Santa Coloma de Cervelló to see Gaudí's sublime Colonia Güell crypt, and drink cocktails overlooking Barcelona from the top of Tibidabo.
Day 7 Get up early to visit the Picasso Museum and spend a last lazy afternoon with Gaudí in the wonderland of the Park Güell.

BEYOND BARCELONA: THE BEST OF CATALUNYA IN TWO WEEKS

Days 1–2 Head down to Tarragona and visit the great cathedral, its Roman buildings and museum, the beautiful Pont del Diable aqueduct and Villa de Centcelles; there's time for a swim on one of the Costa Daurada's big beaches, and if you've brought the kids, you may have to slot in a day for Port Aventura.
Day 3 Spend a morning exploring the lovely vineyards of El Priorat, then over to Montblanc to see the Cistercian sisters: Santes Creus, Poblet and Vallbona, then spend the night in Cervera.
Day 4 Visit the lovely town of Cervera, then westwards to Lleida to see La Seu Vella and the museum.

Day 5 Time to head into the Pyrenees: take the scenic route up to Tremp and then follow the Vall de Noguera Ribagorçana up to remote Vall de Boí to spend a day with its lovely Romanesque churches; spend the night in Vielha.

Day 6 Take the gorgeous ride in the mountains through the Vall d'Aran and Vall d'Aneu to Sort and La Seu d'Urgell.

Day 7 Visit La Seu d'Urgell's cathedral and Museu Diocesà then head south to visit the beautiful small cities of Solsona and salty Cardona; stay in the parador if you can.

Day 8 Make your way east to Vic to see Josep Maria Sert's astonishing murals and the Museu d'Art Medieval, then head north to Ripoll to see the famous portal and cloister; spend the night in Ribes de Freser.

Day 9 Take the ride up the *cremallera* (rack-and-pinion railway) to Núria, and in the afternoon head to Olot.

Day 10 Spend a day in the pretty Garrotxa; visit Besalú in the afternoon, then head to Figueres.

Day 11 Visit the Dalí Museum in the morning, then head to the coast; visit spectacularly set Sant Pere de Rodes, Cadaqués and Dalí's house in Port Lligat (be sure to book in advance). Overnight in Cadaqués.

Day 12 Have a look at Castelló d'Empúries and the ancient Greek and Roman site of Empúries; eat anchovies for lunch in L'Escala and drive over to Girona to visit the cathedral, its treasure, and all the rest.

Day 13 See the rest of Girona and one or two of the pretty medieval towns nearby (Pals, Peratallada, Torroella de Montgrí), then go for a swim at one of the beautiful beaches around Cap de Begur or Palafrugell, where you can spend the night.

Day 14 Visit Palamós and Sant Feliu de Guíxols, then take the beautiful corniche road to Tossa de Mar. Explore the old town and carry on to Lloret de Mar to visit the Jardí Santa Clotilde, then back to Barcelona.

TOURIST INFORMATION

The **tourist information** services across Catalunya are exceptionally good – helpful, efficient and adept at providing a wide range of information. You'll find them in every city, town and resort, with extra booths and info points during the peak summer season. Even in the tiniest towns and villages, there will usually be someone at the town hall who can provide local info (as well as the keys to churches and other rarely visited sights). The Catalan government runs a comprehensive tourism website for the whole region (w catalunya.com), which is a very useful overall resource. Every region, city and town also has its own website too, most of which are excellent. On the French side of the border, the regional tourism website is w tourism-mediterraneanpyrenees.com.

In many places you'll see **Centres d'Interpretació** – part museum, part tourist office, with exhibitions on what there is to see in an area.

TOUR OPERATORS

UK AND IRELAND

Activities Abroad w activitiesabroad.com. Family adventures in the Catalan Pyrenees.

Audley Travel w audleytravel.com. Custom-designed itineraries focusing on Catalunya's heritage & nature.

Exodus Travel w exodus.co.uk. Self-guided walking trips & cycling on the coast.

Explore Worldwide w explore.co.uk. Family adventure in the Pyrenees, cycling from Marseille to Barcelona.

HF Holidays w hfholidays.co.uk. Guided walking holidays through the Catalan countryside & coastal paths.

Inntravel w inntravel.co.uk. Self-guided cycling & walking throughout Catalunya.

Mac's Adventure w macsadventure.com. Walking holidays on the Costa Brava & Pyrenees.

Pura Aventura w pura-aventura.com. Barcelona & Catalan wine route.

Ramble Worldwide w rambleworldwide.co.uk. Walks in the Collsacabra & the Garrotxa Natural Park, Vall de Boí, Catalan coast culture tour.

Trailfinders w trailfinders.com. Tailor-made travel experiences across Catalunya, including cultural & culinary tours.

TravelLocal w travellocal.com. A UK-based website where you can book direct with selected local travel companies, allowing you to communicate with a ground operator without having to go through a 3rd-party travel operator or agent. Your booking with the local company has full financial protection, but note that travel to the destination is not included. Member of ABTA, ASTA.

Unicorn Trails w unicorntrails.com. Riding holidays, including a Catalan extreme trail.

USA

Backroads w backroads.com. Active travel company offering biking & hiking tours in the Catalan countryside.

Classic Journeys w classicjourneys.com. Cultural walking tours through Catalunya's historic towns & villages.

Exodus Travels w exodustravels.com. Guided & self-guided cycling & walking tours, also in the Pyrenees.

Experience Plus w experienceplus.com. Cycling the Costa Brava.

VBT Bicycling Vacations w vbt.com. Bicycle tours along Catalunya's scenic routes, including the Costa Brava.

Wilderness Travel w wildernesstravel.com. Hiking across the Pyrenees.

FRANCE AND SPAIN

Catalan Adventures w catalanadventures.com. A small, family-run specialist operator based near Girona & Barcelona, offering walking, cycling & multi-activity holidays.

Catalan Wine Escape w catalan-wine-escape. com. Based in Perpignan, this offers small group guided tours & tastings in the vineyards of North (French) Catalunya.

Cycle Tours Catalonia w cycletourscatalonia. com. Cycling & hiking tours (both guided & self-guided) in the Girona region, including the Costa Brava.

Explore Catalunya w explorecatalunya. com. Based in Barcelona, this company leads small-group day tours around Catalunya, including Montserrat, the Costa Brava, winery visits & more.

Feeling Pyrénées w feeling-pyrenees.com. A wide range of outdoor mountain activities in the Pyrenees, including mountain-biking, skiing, hot-air ballooning, thermal spas, etc.

Njoy Catalonia w njoycatalonia.com. All kinds of tours, including lots of gastronomic tours (wine, olive oil, food experiences), as well as more unusual experiences, such as spring blossom-viewing tours in the Ebro Valley.

RED TAPE

VISAS Holders of EU, UK, US, Canadian, Australian and New Zealand passports do not need a visa to enter Spain for stays of up to three months; most other nationals do.

Note that, from the last quarter of 2026, citizens of visa-exempt countries, including the UK, USA, Canada and Australia, will be required to pay a fee and obtain an ETIAS travel authorisation (w travel-europe.europa.eu/etias_en) in order to enter France and Spain. A new Entry-Exit System (EES; w travel-europe. europa.eu/ees_en) is also set to be introduced on 12 October 2025, to replace the requirement for stamping passports. This will be rolled out gradually at border crossings over the following six months, with full implementation across the EU by 10 April 2026. Check before you travel.

If you aren't an EU citizen and intend staying longer in Spain, you should report to the Foreign Nationals Office (*oficina de extranjeros*). Non-EU citizens should apply for a TIE card (*Tarjeta de Identidad de Extranjero*). EU citizens will be issued with a printed Residence Certificate stating name, address, nationality, NIE number

(*Número de Identificación Extranjeros*) and date of registration. Non-EU citizens had best apply for an extended visa at home, a complicated procedure requiring proof of income, etc. You can't get a TIE without this visa.

In France, you must apply for a long-stay visa (*visa de long séjour*) before arrival if you want to stay more than 90 days: there are different types of visa available, depending on your circumstances and how long you want to stay (see w service-public.fr/particuliers/vosdroits/F16162 for detailed information).

EMBASSIES All embassies are in Madrid or Paris, but there are consulates in Barcelona. For a constantly updated list, visit w embassypages.com/spain.

GETTING THERE AND AWAY

BY AIR Catalunya has international airports in Barcelona, Girona and Reus (near Tarragona), and an astounding variety of flight options, especially from the UK and EU. Sometimes national airlines British Airways and Iberia offer special deals equal to those offered by the low-cost carriers. Numerous airlines from the USA, Canada or Australia fly direct to Barcelona. There are smaller domestic airports, used especially during ski season including Andorra-La Seu Urgell (flights from Madrid and Palma de Mallorca) and Lleida (with flights from Palma de Mallorca and Ibiza). Perpignan airport in France has regular flights to the UK and most of Europe, but travellers from the USA, Canada and Australia will need to change in Paris, London or another large European hub.

BY RAIL From the UK, travelling from London St Pancras to Barcelona on the Eurostar and fast trains takes 12 to 14 hours, changing stations in Paris, but you can do it in 9 hours 45 minutes if you're lucky. From London to Perpignan is about 9 hours 30 minutes, but you can shave an hour off that if you don't mind extremely tight connections in Paris. If you purchase a ticket well in advance you can save money, although it's rare to find a train cheaper than a flight.

BY CAR It's 1,492km from London to Barcelona; the journey takes around 17 hours and costs around €92 in tolls and €260 in petrol. The distance from London to Perpignan is about 1,250km, with a driving time of around 13 hours and costs €75 in tolls and about €220 in petrol. A car entering France and Spain must have its registration and insurance papers. If you're coming from the UK or Ireland, the dip of the headlights must be adjusted to the right. Carrying a yellow vest and warning triangle is mandatory; the triangle should be placed 50m behind the car if you have a breakdown. Drivers with a valid licence from an EU country, the UK, Canada, the USA or Australia don't need an international licence. If you plan to hire a car, look into air and holiday package deals to save money.

The Eurotunnel (w eurotunnel.com) from Dover to Calais runs 24 hours a day, all year round, with a service at least once an hour through the night.

HEALTH *with Dr Daniel Campion*

On the whole, health risks are no different from those in other European countries. It is wise to be up to date with routine vaccinations in the UK such as measles, mumps and rubella, and diphtheria, tetanus and polio.

Check any current insurance policies you hold to see if they cover all the activities you plan to do and under what circumstances, and consider whether you need a special travel insurance policy for the journey. EU citizens with an European Health Insurance Card (EHIC) are entitled to the same health services as Spanish and French citizens, as are Britons with a UK Global Health Insurance Card (UK GHIC), available for free from the NHS. Note that neither EHIC nor GHIC cards are an alternative to travel insurance, and do not cover such health-related costs as medical repatriation or any private treatment, so it is still important to take out comprehensive travel insurance. Other visitors should also be insured: this should include 24/7 medical assistance, medical expenses and emergency evacuation or repatriation, accidental death and permanent disability, baggage loss or delay, money and passport, trip cost cancellation and personal liability. Accidents resulting from sports may not be covered by ordinary travel insurance. At the coast, stick to beaches with lifeguards.

The tap water in Catalunya is safe to drink, though has quite a strong chlorine taste in Barcelona. Those who find this unpleasant may wish to purchase bottled water.

MEDICAL PROBLEMS
Insect- and tick-borne diseases In summer, aside from the danger posed by over-exposure to the sun, there's the nuisance of mosquitoes and blackflies, which can leave painful bites. Hydrocortisone or antihistamine cream from a pharmacy can help relieve the discomfort. There's also the possibility of being bitten by an Asian tiger mosquito (*Aedes albopictus*) during daylight hours, so bring a good repellent containing DEET or icaridin. Occasionally, imported cases of dengue fever have led to small local outbreaks – transmitted by these mosquitoes – in Catalunya and Pyrénées-Orientales.

Ticks can carry Lyme disease and dangerous rarities such as Crimean–Congo haemorrhagic fever. Make sure that you are wearing long trousers with socks and boots and long-sleeved top when hiking in the spring and summer. Check yourself for ticks at the end of the day.

Altitude Before walking or cycling in the mountains, check the weather report (storms can come on suddenly) and make sure your mobile phone is fully charged. The Pyrenees have some peaks higher than 2,500m (eg: Vignemale), so altitude sickness is possible: a gradual ascent and good hydration can help prevent this. If you are at high altitude and develop headache, nausea or dizziness, you should stop and rest. If this doesn't work, return to a lower altitude.

TICK REMOVAL
Ticks should ideally be removed intact, and as soon as possible, to reduce the chance of infection. You can use special tick tweezers, which can be bought in good travel shops; or failing this, with your fingernails, grasp the tick as close to your body as possible, and pull it away steadily and firmly at right angles to your skin without jerking or twisting. Applying irritants (eg: Olbas oil) or lit cigarettes is to be discouraged as a means of removal since they can cause the ticks to regurgitate and therefore increase the risk of disease. Once the tick is removed, if possible douse the wound with alcohol (any spirit will do), soap and water, or iodine. If you are travelling with small children, remember to check their heads, and particularly behind the ears, for ticks. Spreading redness around the bite and/or fever and/or aching joints after a tick bite imply that you have an infection that requires antibiotic treatment. In this case seek medical advice.

Rabies Although rabies in terrestrial mammals has been eliminated from the Spanish mainland, bats may carry rabies-like viruses. Avoid any physical contact with bats – bites may go unrecognised. If you are exposed, wash any wound with soap and water and seek urgent medical advice. Rabies vaccination before travel may be recommended for some travellers involved in activities that could bring them into contact with bats, such as caving.

HEALTH CARE In the event of a **medical emergency**, call ✆112 an ambulance, or go directly to *urgencies* (A&E) at a hospital. Tourist offices can supply lists of English-speaking doctors, but if it's not an emergency, go to a pharmacy. Pharmacists are highly skilled both in France and Spain, and in Spain many drugs that require a prescription elsewhere are available freely. Look in local papers or in pharmacy windows for the rota of pharmacies that stay open at night and on holidays.

TRAVEL CLINICS AND HEALTH INFORMATION A list of current travel clinic websites worldwide is available on w istm.org. For other journey preparation information, consult w travelhealthpro.org.uk (UK) or w wwwnc.cdc.gov/travel (USA). Information about various medications may be found on w netdoctor.co.uk/travel. All advice found online should be used in conjunction with expert advice received prior to or during travel.

SAFETY

Barcelona with all its visitors has more than its share of street crime, so be aware. Pickpocketing, bag snatching and robbing parked cars are the specialities; except for some quarters of the largest cities, walking around at night is no problem. Note that in Spain less than 8g of marijuana is legal; anything else may easily earn you the traditional 'six years and a day'.

The Catalan police, the Mossos d'Esquadra or just *mossos*, are under the authority of the Generalitat and are the main force in Catalunya, although you may also see the Policia Nacional and Guardia Civil, particularly on the borders. Report thefts (called making a *denuncia*) to the nearest police station: the reward is the bit of paper you need for an insurance claim. If your passport is stolen, contact the police and your nearest consulate for emergency travel documents. The mossos also patrol the highways. On-the-spot fines of between €100 and €600 can be imposed for traffic violations; if you don't have the money they may impound your car until you do.

WOMEN TRAVELLERS

Women travelling alone should not encounter any problems. If possible, try to avoid arriving or leaving big city stations late at night. There have been a few complaints of harassment in Barcelona, though no more or less than in any other European city. If you are hesitant about travelling alone, download apps such as Find My Phone, Noonlight, bSafe and Life360 that can be used to check in with family or alert the police to your location.

TRAVELLING WITH A DISABILITY

Eurotunnel is a good way to travel to Catalunya by car from the UK, since passengers are allowed to stay in their vehicles. By train, Eurostar gives wheelchair passengers first-class travel for second-class fares. Most ferry companies will offer special facilities if contacted beforehand. Airports all offer free assistance although it's important to let them know at least 48 hours in advance of your needs.

The UK's **gov.uk** website (w gov.uk/government/publications/disabled-travellers/disability-and-travel-abroad) has a downloadable guide giving general advice and practical information for travellers with a disability (and their companions) preparing for overseas travel. The US-based Travel for All (w travel-for-all.com) and the Society for Accessible Travel and Hospitality (w sath.org) also provide some general information. The website Wheelmap (w wheelmap.org) has an interactive global map showing accessible and partially accessible properties, including museums, hotels and restaurants.

In Catalunya, hotels, B&Bs, holiday homes, bars and restaurants, and the most important museums and churches **are nearly all accessible** to wheelchair users, but steep hill villages less so, although there are often specially designated parking spots near the top, and at tourist attractions, supermarkets and elsewhere. Barcelona is especially accessible, with dedicated website w barcelona-enabled.com packed full of useful information. All city buses take wheelchairs, and most metro lines (except lines L1, L4 and L5) now have lifts in all stations. The rail operator RENFE usually provides wheelchairs at main city stations, and many trains are slowly being upgraded to provide services (lift access to platforms, etc). All Barcelona's beaches are wheelchair-accessible and some (in particular, the Bogatell and Nova Icària beaches) have assisted bathing facilities, including accessible changing rooms and ramps into the water. For accessible beaches elsewhere in Catalunya, see w tourismforall.catalunya.com/en. To hire an electric scooter or power chair, see w cosmoscooter.com.

In North Catalunya, accessibility is also improving. Perpignan train station is equipped with lifts and wheelchair ramps, and offers a free passenger assistance service called Assist'enGare at all main stations (w sncf-voyageurs.com/en/travel-with-us/prepare-your-trip/accessibility/assistance-services-and-assistengare). Some of the TER regional trains have been upgraded and offer significantly improved accessibility, but the older trains are often not suitable for wheelchair users. All liO regional buses comply with France's accessibility standards, however. Perpignan Airport offers assistance services for travellers with reduced mobility. Several tourist offices in the region have received the 'Tourisme & Handicap' certification, covering auditory, mental, motor and visual disabilities.

Specialist holiday companies that can provide assistance' and/or other specific services are Accessible Spain Travel (w accessiblespaintravel.com) and Enable Holidays (w enableholidays.com/spain). Disabled Accessible Travel (w disabledaccessibletravel.com) provides holidays across Europe, including French Catalunya, as does Disabled Holidays (w disabledholidays.com).

LGBTQIA+ TRAVELLERS

Catalunya is a very tolerant, gay-friendly destination; Sitges has long been a leading gay resort. In country towns and villages, a certain amount of discretion may be called for as you may encounter confusion, especially among the elderly. In North Catalunya, Perpignan has a small but active LGBTQIA+ community, and hosts Pride events and queer-friendly venues, though rural areas remain a little more conservative.

TRAVELLING WITH KIDS

Catalans love kids, and there's plenty for them to do. Family life is central to Catalan culture, and children are warmly welcomed in restaurants, museums and public spaces.

In Barcelona, there's a wealth of child-friendly attractions: sandy city beaches for paddling and castle-building; the colourful mosaics and fairytale architecture of Park Güell; the dizzying spires of the Sagrada Família; and a Chocolate Museum that combines history with plenty of tasting. Kids also love the Barcelona Zoo, the L'Aquàrium at Port Vell with its walk-through shark tunnel, and the interactive Olympic and Sports Museum on Montjuïc.

PortAventura World near Tarragona is one of Europe's biggest theme parks, with white-knuckle rides for teens and tamer zones for younger children, plus the water-focused Caribe Aquatic Park with wave pools and giant slides, and Ferrari Land, with more adrenaline-pumping rollercoasters, next door. There are lots of family-friendly resorts with long, sandy beaches on the Costa Daurada, while the Costa Brava offers boat trips, calm coves for snorkelling, and kid-friendly medieval villages like Pals and Besalú.

For active kids, the Catalan Pyrenees offer plenty of adventures, from skiing and sledging in winter to pony trekking and climbing in summer.

In North Catalunya, the coast offers miles of beaches, waterparks like Aqualand in Saint-Cyprien, and easy boat excursions. The Yellow Train (Le Train Jaune), which winds through dramatic mountain scenery from Villefranche-de-Conflent to Latour de Carol – Enveitg on the Spanish border, is a big hit with children and parents alike. For a taste of history, there are hilltop forts and castles to explore, like Fort Liberia, often reached via scenic trails or mountain lifts.

Wherever you go, family-friendly accommodation is easy to find, and many museums and attractions offer discounted or free entry for children.

WHAT TO TAKE

Pack any medications you need to take regularly. Layers of warm clothing are a good idea for winter and at least a light jacket for summer evenings or trips into the mountains. You'll be doing a lot of walking: comfortable, broken-in shoes are essential. Sun protection is a must (although easily available in Catalunya), including sunscreen (SPF 50+), ideally eco-friendly if you're heading to the beaches, as well a wide-brimmed hat and lightweight clothing.

As in the rest of mainland Europe, Spain and France use **electricity** at a current of 220V at 50 cycles per second (50H). If you don't have the necessary plug adaptors and power converters, they are easy to find at international airports before you leave, and in all the major towns and cities.

MONEY AND BUDGETING

MONEY The currency in France and Spain is the euro (€). Credit cards are accepted at most major points of sale, though not always at the smallest B&Bs, *gîtes* or small family-run restaurants. **ATMs** are widely available and will spout cash with your bank card and PIN number for the price of a significant commission; check with your bank if it has an agreement with any banks in France or Spain which will allow you to withdraw cash without paying international ATM access fees. Americans using credit cards without the right chip may find that ticket machines and self-serve petrol pumps won't work, so, again, check with your bank before leaving. You might check out prepaid bank cards such as Visa's Netspend (w netspend.com) or use WISE (w wise.com) to transfer currencies and top up as you go along.

BUDGETING Catalunya can suit a range of budgets. Travelling on a shoestring – staying in hostel dorms, picnicking from markets or bakeries, exploring free sights and using public transport – you can get by on around €50–65 per day. Mid-range travellers, especially couples sharing hotel rooms, dining at casual restaurants and occasionally renting a car or joining tours, should expect to spend closer to €130–160 daily. Costs rise notably in summer (in the resorts in particular) and during festivals. Across the border in France, accommodation and dining are typically pricier, though rural gîtes and set-menu lunches can offer good value.

1-litre bottle water	€0.70 (France/Spain)
½ litre beer	€2.50–3 (Spain)/€3.50–4 (France)
loaf of bread	€2–2.50 (Spain)/ €1.50–2 (France)
street snack	€5 (France/Spain)
T-shirt	€8–10
litre of petrol	€1.77 (France)/€1.51 (Spain)

GETTING AROUND

If you're using public transport, Catalunya's Mou-te website and app (w mou-te. gencat.cat/itinerary) will give you all the options of getting from A to B. In the greater Perpignan region of North Catalunya, you can use the Sankéo website and app (w sankeo.com) to find out how to get around.

BY RAIL Spain's national rail network RENFE (w renfe.com) operates high-speed AVE trains between Barcelona and Madrid with stops at Tarragona and Lleida, as well as from Barcelona to Perpignan. Other operators also run high-speed services including Ouigo (w ouigo.com), which is a low-cost service, Iryo (w iryo.eu) and TGV inoui (w oui.sncf/tgv-inoui). There is a regional service (R11, about 3.5hrs) from Barcelona to Cerbère, just across the border, where you can change for French regional trains.

There is a generally good network of regional lines as well as *rodalies* (commuter trains) emanating from Barcelona that will take you across much of Catalunya (w rodalies.gencat.cat), although the north and northwest of the region is less well served. Catalunya also operates its own rail line, the Ferrocarrils de la Generalitat de Catalunya (FGC; w fgc.cat), which runs commuter trains around Barcelona, as well as scenic routes such as the rack-and-pinion railways in Montserrat (page 140) and Vall de Núria (page 218), among others. In France, regional trains around the Pyrénées-Orientales are operated by TER Occitanie (w ter.sncf.com/occitanie). The panoramic Train Jaune (w letrainjaune.fr) runs through the Pyrenees from Villefranche-le-Conflent to Latour de Carol-Enveitg.

BY BUS Like the trains, buses in Catalunya are cheap by northern European standards. Small towns and villages can normally be reached by bus only through their provincial capitals. Different companies serve different regions, which can be confusing, but tourist information offices are usually extremely helpful about explaining which bus you need. Main companies in the region are listed below. Across the border in Pyrénées-Orientales (Northern Catalunya), regional bus services are primarily operated under the liO (Lignes Intermodales d'Occitanie) network (w lio-occitanie. fr), but note that services are considerably less frequent outside the Perpignan area.

Alsa w alsa.es. Long-distance & intercity routes across Spain, including Barcelona, Lleida, Girona & connections to Madrid & France.
AMPSA w ampsa.org. Local routes around Andorra & connections to La Seu d'Urgell.
Autocars Julià w autocaresjulia.com. Regional services around the Costa Brava, Girona & Barcelona.
BusPlana w busplana.com. Connects Barcelona, Tarragona, Reus Airport & coastal towns along the Costa Daurada.
Hispano Igualadina w catalunya.monbus.es. Connects Igualada, Manresa & Barcelona; part of the Igualadina-Monbus group.

Monbus w monbus.es. Regional & national routes, especially in Lleida, Tarragona & across northeast Spain.
Moventis Sarfa w moventis.es. Major operator along the Costa Brava, Girona, & Barcelona area.
Sagalés w sagales.com. Extensive network across Barcelona, Vallès Oriental, Osona & airport routes.
Teisa w teisa-bus.com. Serves Girona, Olot, Banyoles & inland towns in Northern Catalunya.
TGO DX w gruptg.com. Regional routes in Baix Llobregat, Bages, Anoia, & connections to FGC rail services.

BY CAR This is the easiest way of getting about, though the convenience is balanced by a considerable cost. In cities, parking is often difficult; another problem is that only a few hotels – usually the more expensive ones – have garages or any sort of parking. The highway network in both France and Spain is good, and most major cities are linked by motorways (called *autovies* or, if a toll is charged, *autopistes*, in Catalan) or dual carriageways.

Be warned that tolls are sheer highway robbery (although the toll was lifted on the main AP-7 motorway between La Jonquera and Tarragona in 2021, which will give you some respite). The speed limit in Spain is 120kph (75mph) on the *autopistes*, and 90kph (56mph) on all other national highways unless marked. In France, the speed limit is 130kph (81mph) on motorways and 80kph (50mph) on national/departmental roads outside built-up areas.

In 2023 Spain introduced Low Emission Zones (LEZs) in cities; they have already come into effect in Barcelona and Lleida, with Girona introducing them in late 2025, Tarragona between 2025 and 2027. In France, Perpignan will introduce its LEZ in 2026. See w urbanaccessregulations.eu for an up-to-date list of requirements and details for purchasing the windscreen stickers you need if you are driving a diesel or older car.

Car hire Hertz (w hertz.co.uk), Avis (w avis.co.uk) and Europcar (w europcar. co.uk), have branches at airports and some of the larger train stations; most domestic one-way rentals carry no surcharge. You must be at least 18 (age may vary by car category) and have held your licence for at least a year. Some companies will rent only to drivers aged 21 and over; drivers under 25 may incur a surcharge. Autoeurope (w autoeurope.com), which covers most firms, is a good place to start looking.

BY CITY BUS AND TAXI Every Catalan city has a perfectly adequate system of public transport. You won't need to make much use of it, though, for even in the bigger cities nearly all attractions are within walking distance. In most cities, the entire route will be displayed on the signs at each bus stop.

In a taxi there are surcharges (for luggage, night or holiday trips, to the train or airport, etc), and if you cross the city limits there will be a surcharge. It's rarely hard

2

to hail a cab from the street, and there will always be a few around the stations. If you call a radio taxi, be aware that the fare will start as the taxi-driver makes his way to you. Cabify (w cabify.com) is currently the most widely used app-based taxi service.

In France, you will usually need to call taxis in advance as it's unusual to hail them on the street, except in Perpignan. There are supplements for luggage, trips at night and at weekends and station/airport runs.

BY BICYCLE Getting around Catalunya by bicycle is a fun and increasingly accessible option, whether in cities or through the countryside. Cities like Barcelona, Girona and Tarragona have expanding networks of bike lanes, bike-sharing schemes, and rental shops offering everything from e-bikes to mountain bikes. Bike-touring through the countryside is also becoming more common, with converted railway paths (Vies Verdes) winding through gorgeous landscapes. North Catalunya is becoming more cycle-friendly, especially around Perpignan and the coast, where there are some quiet rural roads and sections of the EuroVelo 8 (the famous European bike route that encompasses much of the Mediterranean coastline). Regional trains generally allow bikes on board, although always check restrictions in advance.

Bike hire is available in pretty much every town and tourist resort on both sides of the border.

ACCOMMODATION

There's a wide range of options in Catalunya, from extremely luxurious contemporary hotels, paradors and apartments to simple *hostals* and campsites. Room prices must be posted in hotel lobbies and in rooms, and if there's a problem you can ask for the complaints book (Llibre de Reclamacions. Prices for single rooms will average about 80% of a double, while triples or an extra bed are around 35% more.

PARADORS The government, in its plan to develop tourism in 1928, started this nationwide chain of classy hotels to draw attention to little-visited areas. They restored old palaces, castles and monasteries for the purpose, furnished them with antiques and installed fine restaurants featuring local specialities. Not all are historic landmarks; in resort areas, they are as likely to be cleanly designed modern buildings. In most cases both the rooms and the restaurant will be the most expensive in town, though most offer substantial off-season discounts. Catalunya has eight paradores: at Vic, Tortosa, Cardona, Lleida, La Seu d'Urgell, Vielha, Arties and Aiguablava on the Costa Brava.

HOTELS (H) are rated from one to five stars according to the services they offer; the very best are designated Gran Luxe (Grand Luxury). Even a one-star hotel will be a comfortable, middle-range establishment. Many have some rooms available at prices lower than those listed; you'll have to ask. You can often get discounts in the off season but will be charged higher rates during big festivals and in high season; book for these as far in advance as possible.

HOSTALS (Hs) are more modest options, rated from one to three stars; a hostal-residence (HsR) means it has no restaurant, but probably still serves breakfast. *Pensions* (P) and *fondes* (now rare but similar to a pension) are often family-run places, sometimes a floor in an apartment block. Hostals and pensions often have cheaper rooms with shared bathrooms. At the bottom of the scale used to be the

ACCOMMODATION PRICE CODES

Prices for a double room; expect to pay about three-quarters for single occupancy.

Luxury	€€€€€	€280+
Upmarket	€€€€	€200–280
Mid-range	€€€	€150–200
Budget	€€	€100–150
Shoestring	€	less than €100

fonda (F), little different from a one-star *hostal*. Today though, some rather stylish new hotel-restaurants have taken to calling themselves *fondes*. Larger monasteries and convents often welcome guests. Accommodation and meals are simple and guests can usually take part in the religious ceremonies.

CAMPING Campsites are rated from one to five stars, depending on their facilities, in both Spain and France. Facilities in most first-class sites include shops, restaurants, bars, laundries, hot showers, first aid, swimming pools, phones and, occasionally, a tennis court. Caravans (trailers) converge on all the more developed sites, but, if you just want to pitch your little tent or sleep out in some quiet field, ask around in the bars or at likely farms. Wild camping is prohibited in many areas because of the danger of fire, as well as on the beaches: in French Catalunya, it is very strictly regulated. For more info, see w camping.info and **Campings de España** (w fedcamping.com), which also has an app, or w campingfrance.com.

SELF-CATERING *Cases rurals* – accommodation in farms or country houses – have become extremely popular and are a wonderful way to enjoy the spectacular countryside. Some are rented whole, while others offer B&B accommodation. Some even offer special activities such as cheese-making. Kitchen facilities may or may not be available, and prices generally fall in the range of €80–150 per day for a double room. The **Catalan tourist board** website has a section on rural accommodation (w turismeacatalunya.cat), or you could try **Som Rurals** (w somrurals.com), which specialises in Catalunya, **Casas Rurales** (w casasrurales.net) or **Escapada Rural** (w escapadarural.com). All the accommodation platforms, such as Airbnb and Booking.com, also have rural accommodation listings.

Spain
Charming Villas Catalunya w charmingvillas.net. Villas mainly along the Costa Brava.
Rustical Travel w rusticaltravel.com. Villas in the countryside.
Interhome Spain w interhome.com. Apartments & houses.

UK
Casamundo w casamundo.com. Apartments & holiday homes.
Catalonia Holiday Lettings w holidaylettings.co.uk. Properties through the region.

Oliver's Travels w oliverstravels.com. High-end holiday & villa rentals.
Vintage Travel w vintagetravel.co.uk. Range from mountain cottages to seaside.

USA and Canada
Holiday Homes w holidayhomes.com. Wide choice of houses by the sea or inland, many with a pool.
Owner Direct w ownerdirect.com. Condo, apartment & villa rentals.
Vrbo w vrbo.com. Vast range of properties, listed by owners.

EATING AND DRINKING

Catalans are the early diners of Spain but they still may eat later than you are used to. In the morning it's a coffee and a roll grabbed at the bar, followed by a huge meal at around 2pm, then some nibbles – perhaps olives or a small dish of cheese or charcuterie – after work at 8pm to hold them over until supper at 9 or 9.30pm. In touristy areas restaurants tend to open earlier to accommodate foreigners (some as early as 5pm).

RESTAURANTS You'll find some of the world's finest restaurants here but in non-touristy areas, restaurants are inconspicuous and few. Just ask someone, and you will find a nice *comedor* with home cooking tucked in a back room behind a bar. If you dine where the locals do, you'll be assured of a good deal if not necessarily a good meal. Many restaurants offer a set weekday lunch, the *menú del migdia*, featuring a starter, a main course, dessert, bread and drink at a set price. Cheaper places may offer *plats combinats*, an all-on-one-plate quick meal. Unless it's explicitly written on the bill (*el compte*), service is not included in the total, so tip accordingly. Otherwise, locals rarely tip, beyond rounding up a euro or two, although restaurant and bar staff may hope for a little something from foreigners.

Both Spain and France have strict national smoking bans in hospitality venues, and there are no indoor smoking areas. Terraces are another story, though, and smoking is fairly common.

Learning to eat the Catalan way In Catalunya, you may have to learn to eat all over again; dining is a much more complex affair here than in many countries. The essential fact to learn is that Catalans like to eat all day long – this scheme spreads the gratification evenly through the day, and it facilitates digestion. Give it some consideration.

Start out by heading to a bar to order a big coffee, a *café amb llet*, and perhaps a pastry. Mid-morning, it's time for a sandwich (*entrepà*), typically with *fuet* or perhaps a slice of *truita* (thick Spanish omelette) or some cheese. Then there's lunch, which is usually substantial; a Catalan would scoff at a sandwich crammed down next to a computer. In the afternoon, you can snack on something delicious from a *pastisseria* (cake shop) or a *forn* (bakery). There are ice-cream shops everywhere – you will never be more than a hundred feet from ice cream in a Catalan town.

The best restaurants are almost always those specialising in regional cuisine, although at the upmarket end of the scale you'll find plenty of new restaurants with innovative dishes with a lot of surprising combinations, peculiar sauces and an obsession with appearances. There are still many old-fashioned restaurants, but avoid the ones with little flags, photos of the dishes and ten-language menus (you'd usually do better to buy some bread, cheese and a bottle of Penedès and have a picnic).

The regions along the coast have a repertoire of traditional dishes as gratifying as any in the country, and seafood is undoubtedly the star of the show. In any coastal town or village, the best seafood restaurants will be around the harbour. The fancier ones will post set menus, while at the rest you'll find only a chalkboard with prices listed for a plate of grilled fish, or prawns or whatever else came in that day.

Tapas culture is not the same in Catalunya as in other parts of Spain. Typical Catalan snacks or drink accompaniments might include some *pa amb tomàquet* (bread rubbed with tomato) and a platter of local cheeses and cured meats with some olives. Locals might also throw in some *truita* (Spanish omelette) and *patates braves* if they're feeling hungry. You'll find places that serve a wider range of tapas,

RESTAURANT PRICE CODES

Prices are based on the average price of a main course.

Expensive	€€€€€	€25+
Above average	€€€€	€20–25
Moderate	€€€	€15–20
Cheap and cheerful	€€	€10–15
Rock bottom	€	less than €10

similar to the rest of Spain, but they're not seen as a local tradition. Lots of fancy new places have sprung up serving *platets* – small dishes of often creative dishes to share, which is a wonderful way to try lots of tasty specialities. But, in general, Catalans keep their eyes on the prize: a good, filling lunch (with a couple of courses as a minimum) and a lighter supper.

Vegetarians and vegans There has been an explosion in vegetarian and vegan restaurants in the last decade or so across Catalunya. You'll find several options in the bigger cities and most restaurants will have at least a couple of veggie or vegan dishes on the menu. It can be trickier out in the smaller towns and villages, but not impossible. You'll find some restaurants listed at w happycow.net/europe/spain.

The **Slow Food movement** (known in Catalunya as 'Kilometre 0' or 'Km0'), with its emphasis on locally sourced, seasonal produce (already a core principle of Mediterranean cuisine), and the growing awareness of sustainability issues, have helped galvanise interest in eating healthily and sustainably. Many restaurants advertise their 'Km0' menus, and these places are likely to offer a wider range of vegetarian and vegan dishes.

CATALAN CUISINE

Pecat de gola Déu el perdona (God forgives the sin of gluttony).

Old Catalan proverb

Catalunya's Renaixença saw a renewal of many arts, but the most ephemeral, the one in the pot, had to wait a century – until the late 1960s, to be precise, when Josep Mercader, chef-owner of Figueres' Hotel Empordà, the 'father of New Catalan Cuisine', started tweaking traditional recipes. What followed since is an explosion of creativity that's been heard around the world. In 1994, the path first trodden by Mercader received its international culinary kudos when the late Santi Santimaria of the Can Fabes (now closed) became the first Catalan chef to be awarded three Michelin stars and when Ferran Adrià the 'Dalí of the Kitchen' who invented molecular cuisine at El Bulli (now a museum), was chosen as the world's best chef for several years running.

Memorably at the Madrid Fusion conference in 2007, Santimaria was given a standing ovation when he stated, like a true Catalan: 'The only truth that matters is the product that comes out of the earth, passes through the ovens to the mouth of the eater, and is then defecated.' Catalunya vies with the Basque Lands, another world-famous culinary destination, for the highest number of Michelin stars and other gastronomy awards.

Catalan specialities The approaches may be new, but the roots are ancient: many features go back to the Romans, especially the Catalan propensity for mixing the savoury with the sweet (salt cod with honey is a classic). The materials at hand are astonishing, as any visitor to Barcelona's La Boqueria market on the Rambla knows – a larder of Mediterranean and mountain delights that led to iconic *mar i muntanya* ('sea and mountain') dishes that can combine lobster, chicken and bitter chocolate.

In his classic *Catalan Cuisine*, Colman Andrews describes how four concoctions underpin most dishes: *all-i-oli* (garlic pounded with olive oil); *sofregit* (usually onions, olive oil and tomatoes fried until they melt together); *picada* (almonds, hazelnuts, fried bread, garlic, parsley and sometimes saffron or chocolate, thrown into a dish at the last minute); and *samfaina* (like ratatouille, but cooked down to a thick paste). The province of Tarragona adds a fifth: *romesco*, a sauce of red peppers, tomatoes, garlic, almonds and hazelnuts.

The classic Catalan accompaniment or starter is *pa amb tomàquet* (thickly sliced country bread, rubbed with tomato and garlic and drizzled with olive oil). Its cousin is the *coca* (plural *coques*), a sort of Catalan pizza, with tomatoes and garlic on top, and maybe anchovies, or aubergines and courgettes, or sausage.

Catalans love their *amanides*, or salads. *Amanida Catalana* is a variant on chef's salad; *esqueixada* is made with salt cod, tomatoes, onions and olives. A variation on that is *xatò*, an obsession in lands between Sitges and Tarragona. Every town and village has its own recipe for it (usually, they'll include lettuce or endives, anchovies, tuna, olives and raw salt cod, with *romesco* sauce on top). *Escalivada* (roasted or grilled aubergines, peppers, onions, garlic and herbs) is another popular starter. The local *embutits* (charcuterie) is excellent. Try the ham from the Cerdanya and the bewilderingly large variety of sausages all called *botifarra*; cured sausages include *fuet*, spicy *llonganissa*, and *xoriç* (chorizo). In early spring, especially in Tarragona province, you might come upon another fond obsession: the *calçotada* is a meal which centres on barbecued spring onions called *calçots* (page 246).

Two things Catalans take very seriously are olives and anchovies. Olives appear everywhere; the variety called *arbequina* (originally from Arbeca, near Lleida) is particularly prized. Catalan anchovies (page 171) are arguably the best in the world, and they'll be a revelation if you've only tasted the ones in the little tins back home. Like everyone else in Spain, the Catalans are wild about seafood; the variety and quality of fish and shellfish on offer in the markets is astounding. In some fishing towns, such as Palamós (page 163), you can watch the fleet come in and then pick up ultra-fresh fish from the Llotja (fish market) in the harbour.

Seafood and rice in various forms is a favourite, with *arròs negre* ('black' rice tinted with cuttlefish ink) perhaps the favourite of favourites (bring a friend, since most restaurants will only make it for two). Everything you can do with rice can also be done with *fideus* (thin noodles). *Bacallà* (salt cod) is always a treat, and there are at least a dozen traditional ways of preparing it. You'll also see *sarsuela* (an elaborate seafood casserole), but more often *suquet de peix*, usually made from hake (*lluç*) and monkfish (*rap*) boiled in a thick broth with *sofregit*, garnished with mussels. Try *graellada de peix i marisc* (a platter of grilled fish and shellfish), or *cim i tomba* – a Costa Brava fisherman's fish and potato dish with all-i-oli.

Inland, the pig holds pride of place; if you find a restaurant in the Pyrenees that doesn't serve trotters, let us know. The list of local sausages includes 17 officially recognised types, but the most important is *botifarra*, similar to a mild Italian sausage, which is the star of the mainstay *botifarra amb mongetes* (with fat white beans). Other dishes include *escudella*, a pork, chicken and vegetable stew with a million recipes, including a celebratory version, *escudella i carn d'olla*, that includes (wait for it): veal, bacon, beef, chicken, pig's ear and trotters, pork, *botifarra*, chickpeas, beans, potatoes, cauliflower, egg, turnip, carrot, garlic, pepper, cinnamon and parsley. Autumn is the season for wild mushroom and truffles, and many people head for the forest to find their own (particularly around Berga and Olot). The closer you get to the mountains, the more game dishes appear on the menu.

Catalunya's cheeses are having a moment, with new producers creating artisan cheeses using traditional and time-honoured methods. There are now almost 200 cheeses made here – more than any other region of Spain – and you'll have the chance to buy and try them at markets and specialist shops. The most famous is *mató*, a ricotta-type white cheese (Montserrat's is famous), which is usually served as a dessert with honey. Serrat, a cured sheep's milk cheese which is similar to Manchego, has been made in Catalunya for more than a thousand years, and is definitely worth seeking out. Catalans generally don't devote a lot of thought to desserts; *crema catalana*, similar to *crème brûlée*, is the inevitable classic.

WHAT TO DRINK No matter how much other costs have risen in Spain and France, wine has remained refreshingly inexpensive by northern European or American standards. What's more, Catalunya produces some of Spain's best. A restaurant's *vi de la casa* is always your least expensive option while dining out; at the more old-fashioned places, it may come from a barrel or glass jug and may be a surprise either way. Anyone with more than a passing interest in wine will want to visit a bodega or two. Across the Pyrenees in North Catalunya, there are also plenty of enjoyable, drinkable wines to try, although none is particularly outstanding. The one exception is the famous dessert wine from Banyuls (page 332).

Many locals prefer beer, particularly on the hottest days. The most popular brands are Estrella or Moritz, but now there are also several places to try local craft beers. The classic aperitif is *vermut* – a delicious, fortified wine with a skoosh of soda water, lots of ice and usually a slice of orange and a couple of olives.

Coffee, tea, all the international soft-drink brands and the locally made Kas round off the average café fare. Spanish coffee in any bar is good and strong – French coffee, on the other hand, is usually weak and mediocre. But the worldwide boom in specialist coffee shops has also hit France and Spain, and they have mushroomed all over the region.

WINES, CAVA AND OTHER DRINKS The region of Catalunya is the second biggest wine producer in Spain, although ever since the ancient Greeks planted the first vines, Catalan wines have had an up-and-down history. In the Middle Ages, the peasants tended vineyards under an agreement known as *rabassa mort* – which meant they could keep them for as long as the vines were alive. They became very good at keeping them alive – and the monasteries became very good at helping them turn the grapes into wine. Everything changed in the late 18th century, when Madrid finally let Catalunya trade with the New World. The Americas, the Catalans quickly discovered, were thirsty. The wine was made into a brandy called *aiguardent*, which took up less room in the ships. Business boomed – until phylloxera killed off every last vine.

Today Catalunya has 12 DOs (Denominació d'Origen), nearly all to the west and south of Barcelona. The most famous of these is bubbly cava (page 146), produced since the 1860s around Sant Sadurní d'Anoia. Pre-phylloxera, most of Catalunya's grapes were red, but when the vineyards were replanted, the rising popularity of cava reversed the proportions: today 70% are white. The fruity, non-fizzy Penedès whites are a perfect match with the region's tasty seafood. Catalunya's red minority, however, is noteworthy, especially Priorat (page 254), the only one to achieve Denominació d'Origen Qualificada (DOQ, or DOC in Spanish) stature along with La Rioja. There are good rosés too, mostly from Empordà.

BARS AND CAFÉS These collect much of the Spaniards' leisure time. They are wonderful institutions, where you can eat breakfast, nibble tapas or linger over a glass of beer until four in the morning. Some have music; some have great snacks, some have games (one-armed bandits seem to be everywhere). Some bars put on Parisian airs; others are resolutely proletarian.

Many night-time bars and clubs are totally invisible in the day, exploding into blue-light noise palaces punctually at midnight until 6am. This is the twilight world of *la marcha*, the all-night pub crawl that finds a reflection in any Spanish city, especially on weekends if it has a university.

PUBLIC HOLIDAYS AND FESTIVALS

PUBLIC HOLIDAYS

	Catalunya	French Catalunya
1 January		
6 January		–
Easter Monday	Easter Monday	Easter Monday
1 May	Labour Day	Labour Day
8 May	–	Victory in Europe Day
29 May	–	Ascension
9 June	–	Whit Monday
24 June	St John's Day	–
14 July	–	Bastille Day
15 August	Asssumption	Assumption
11 September	National Day of Catalunya	–
1 November	All Saint's Day	All Saint's Day
11 November	–	Armistice Day
25 December	Christmas Day	Christmas Day
26 December	St Stephen's Day	–

FESTIVALS Catalans take festivals seriously; they love to swan around in medieval costumes or don their *barretines* (floppy red hats) and set off as many firecrackers as possible. Traditional events, especially the Festes Majors, are occasions for a very specialised battery of Catalan folklore and traditional music. You'll find processions of *gegants* (12ft figures of wood and papier-mâché, supported by someone in the skirts) and *capgrossos* (demonically grinning 'fat heads', made of the same materials), dragons and other creatures. There are the daring human towers, made of competing teams of *castellers* who climb on each other's shoulders to the eerie music of the *gralles* (wind instruments) and *timbals* (drums), attaining eight or even nine levels (w castellscat.cat/en/schedule). Common dances include the national circle dance, the *sardana* (page 27), the Ball de Gitanes (Gypsy Dance), and the Ball de Bastons (Stick Dance). At night,

NIGHT OF THE MUSEUMS

The Nit dels Museus or Night of the Museums is held each May – also across the border, where it's called the La Nuit Européenne des Musées – to coincide with International Museum Day, when hundreds of museums and cultural sites open their doors for free late into the night, often with concerts, guided tours and special events.

the big event is the *correfoc*, or 'fire-running', when terrifying dragons (made up of teams under canvas and wood) spit fireworks into the crowds, chased by devils brandishing fireworks; sometimes the devils have the show to themselves. Similar traditions thrive across the border in Northern Catalunya, especially in the summer, when towns like Céret and Prats-de-Mollo celebrate with correfocs, *sardanes* and *gegants*.

Note that dates for most festivals vary from year to year; they tend to be fluid, flowing towards the nearest weekend. If the actual date falls on a Thursday or a Tuesday, Catalans 'bridge' the date with the weekend to create a four-day whoopee. The following is only a taste: for a complete list, see w femturisme.cat, w catalunya. com and w tourisme-pyreneesorientales.com. For Barcelona, see page 77.

January

Everywhere	**New Year** The new year is brought in with big parties and the custom of gulping down a grape for each bell-chime at midnight, for luck.
	Festa dels Tres Tombs Parades of horses, carts and riders in traditional costume to honour Saint Anthony, patron of animals.
Lleida	**Festival Internacional Enric Granados** (w auditorienricgranados.cat) Classical music; third week of the month; 17 January.
Valls	**Grand Festa de la Calçotada** (w festacalcotadavalls.cat) A feast of spring onions; late January.

February

Arles-sur-Tech, Prats-de-Mollo and Saint-Laurent-de-Cerdans	**Festa de l'Os** (The Festival of the Bear) Costumed 'bears' chase the townsfolk.
Everywhere	**Carnestoltes** (carnival) Celebrated throughout Catalunya. Ten days of costumes, dancing and parades in Barcelona and many cities, including a battle of sweets ('Comparsa') in Vilanova i la Geltrú (w carnavaldevilanova.cat) and a week-long gay carnival in **Sitges** (w visitsitges.com). **Solsona** (w carnavalsolsona.com) has a carnival with the explosive 'marriage of the mad giant' and the ascent of a donkey (now an effigy) up the church tower.
L'Ametlla del Mar	**Candelera Festa Major** (w terresdelebre.travel/es) 1–5 February.
Olesa de Montserrat	**Passion Play** (w lapassio.cat) Also historic performances at **Cervera** (w turismecervera.cat); during Lent; mid-March to May; variable.

March

Terrassa	**Jazz Terrassa** (w jazzterrassa.org) Held at different venues all over the city throughout the month.
Verges	**Processó i Dansa de la Mort** (w laprocesso.cat) A re-enactment of the Passion, and costumed skeletons performing the medieval Dance of Death; Holy Thursday.

2

April

Everywhere	**Festes de Sant Jordi** Exchange of books and roses on the Catalan version of Valentine's Day; 24 April.
Montblanc	**Setmana Medieval** (w setmanamedieval.cat) Costumes, music, food; mid month.
Montserrat	**Festa de la Mare de Déu de Montserrat** *Sardanes* and *castellers*; 27 April.
Tarragona	**International Dixieland Festival** (w tarragonaturisme.cat) Late April.

May

Badalona	**Festes de Maig** On the eve and St Anastasi's Day, with the burning of the devil (*la cremada del demoni*); 10–11 May.
Berga	**La Patum** (page 218) One of Catalunya's oldest and most spectacular traditional festivals. On Corpus Christi; late May/early June.
Girona	**Temps de Flors** (w tempsdeflors.girona.cat) A glorious flower show, with intricate 'carpets' of flowers, flower sculptures and more; mid-May.
Lleida	**Festa Major** (w turismedelleida.cat) Lleida's patron saint, Sant Anastasi, is celebrated with parades featuring the oldest *gegants* in Catalunya, battle of flowers, etc; 10–11 May.
Lleida	**Aplec del Caragol** (w aplec.org) World's biggest snail festival, where 584 cooks serve snails to 300,000 people. Late May.
Montblanc	**Trobada Gegantera** (w viuelsgegants.com) Festival of *gegants*; mid-May.
Ripoll	**Festa de Llana I de Casament a Pagés** (w ripoll.cat) Wool and country wedding festival; variable weekend.
Sitges	**Corpus Christi** (w visitsitges.com) The streets are covered with flower carpets, and eggs dance on fountains ('l'ou com balla'); late May/early June.
Solsona	**Corpus Christi** (w turismesolsones.com) Giants and dragons parade, fireworks, etc; late May/early June.
Tarragona	**Fòrum Vinarium Primavera** (w tarragonaturisme.cat) Big wine festival, with tastings and food stalls; second weekend.

June

Isil	**Falles d'Isil** (w fallesisil.cat) Part of the midsummer celebrations in honour of Sant Joan (see below): huge bonfires are lit on the mountain top, and the burning logs carried down in a zigzag ('the snake of fire') to the village, where another huge bonfire is lit, around which the locals dance.
Everywhere	**Nit de Sant Joan** (St John's Eve) is the maddest night of the year in Catalunya, especially in the Pyrenees. The 'Flama de Canigó' – a flame from the sacred mountain of Canigó – is carried to towns, villages and cities all over Catalunya, where it is used to light the bonfires that kick

off the night's fiery madness. Celebrations, bonfires and fireworks, followed by dancing everywhere; 23 June.

L'Ametlla del Mar — **Festa de Sant Pere** (w visitametllademar.com) Traditional festival in honour of one of the patron saints of sailors; late June.

Reus — **Festa de Sant Pere** (w reus.cat) City festival, featuring *tronada* (explosions) and *castellers;* late June.

Terrassa — **Festa Major** (w festamajorterrassa.cat) Late June–early July.

July

Balaguer — **Festa del Transsegre** (w transsegre.org) A mock naval battle between the village neighbourhoods; mid month.

Cadaqués — **Music Festival** (w festivalcadaques.com) Mid month.

Calella de Palafrugell — **Cantada d'Havaneres** (w havanerescalella.cat) Sea shanty song festival; early July.

Cambrils — **Festa de la Mare del Déu del Carme** Boat parades, in honour of one of the patron saints of sailors; also in **Sant Carles de la Ràpita** and **L'Ampolla**; 16 July.

Guissona — **Mercat Romà de Iesso** (w mercatroma.cat) Roman festival and market (with gladiators); third Saturday.

Igualada — **European Balloon Festival** (w ebf.cat) Variable dates.

L'Espluga de Francolí — **Festa Major** (w esplugadefrancoli.cat) Last week.

Lloret de Mar — **Festa Major** Castellers and dances, etc; 24 July.

Olot — **Aplec de la Sardana** (w olotcultura.cat) Big Catalan dance and music festival; around 14 July.

Peralada — **Peralada Festival** (w festivalperalada.com) A prestigious performing arts festival with a spectacular castle setting; early/mid-July.

Pobla de Segur — **Els Raiers** (w elsraiers.cat) River raft races, music and food; variable dates.

Prades — **Fira del Vi I del Cava** Festival of wine and cava, with music; third weekend.

Puigcerdà — **Festa Major del Roser** (w puigcerda.cat) Four days of concerts, correfoc, theatre, traditional and popular culture; mid month.

SortNoguera Pallaresa Rally — (w riu.sort.cat) International whitewater competition; end June/early July.

Tarragona — **International Fireworks Festival** (w tarragonaturisme.cat) On the first weekend.

Torroella de Montgrí — **Festival de Torroella** (w festivaldetorroella.cat) Festival of performing arts; July and August.

Vilanova i la Geltrú — **International World Music Festival** July–August.

August

Castellar de N'Hug — **Concurs Internacional de Gossos d'Atura** (w castellardenhug.net) Catalan sheepdog trials; last Sunday.

Cervera — **Aquelarre** (w aquelarre.cat) Parades of witches, dragons and monsters; end August/early September.

Manresa — **Festa Major** (w web.lafestamajor.cat) Last weekend.

Roda de Bará	**Festa Major** Third week.
Salou	**El Castell de Foc** (**w** visitsalou.eu) Big fireworks; 15 August.
Sitges	**Festa Major de Sant Bartomeu** 23/24 August.
Tarragona	**Festa Major de Sant Magí** Third week.
Ulldecona	**Festa Major** (**w** ulldecona.cat) Late August/early September.
Valls	**Firagost** (**w** valls.cat) August farmer's market and fair; first week.
Vilabertran	**Schubertiada** (**w** schubertiada.cat) Chamber music festival; late August/early September.
Vilafranca del Penedès	**Festa Major** (**w** festamajor.vilafranca.cat) With fiery devils' dances; last weekend.
Vilanova I la Geltrú	**Festa Major** (**w** vilanovaturisme.cat) First week.

September

Barcelona	**La Mercé** (**w** barcelona.cat/lamerce/en) A huge five-day party in honour of the city's patron saint, with over 600 events; around 24 September.
Besalú	**Medieval Festival** (**w** visitpirineus.com/en/node/56) First weekend.
Calella	**Festa Major de la Minerva** (**w** calellabarcelona.com) Lots of *sardana* dancing; late September–early October.
Cardona	**Corre de Bou and Ball de Bastons** (**w** cardonaturisme. cat) Bull running and the 'dance of the sticks'; 9 September.
Castelló d'Empúries	**Terra del Trobadors** (**w** terradetrobadors.com) Medieval festival; mid month.
Cervera	**Festa Major del Sant Crist** Fourth Sunday.
Gandesa	**Festa Major** (**w** gandesa.cat) *Correfocs*, parades and more; 4 September.
L'Escala	**Festa de la Sal** (**w** lescala.cat) Anchovy-salting festival; 16 September.
Reus	**Festa de la Misericòrdia** (**w** reus.cat) The city's festa major; mid month.
Salou	**Festa de Rei Jaume I** (**w** visitsalou.eu) Celebrating the medieval king's departure to conquer Mallorca; first weekend.
Solsona	**Festa Major** (**w** solsonaturisme.com) With *gegants* and *correfocs*; early September.
Tarragona	**Festa Major de Santa Tecla** (**w** tarragonaturisme.cat) Huge 12-day festival; around 23 September.
Torredembarra	**Festa Major** In honour of Santa Rosalia; early September.
Tortosa	**Festa Major/Festes de la Cinta** (**w** tortosa.cat/festes) In honour of the city's patron saint, the Virgin of the Ribbons; first weekend.

October

Esterri d'Aneu	**Fira de Santa Teresa** (**w** esterrianeu.cat) Traditional livestock fair (since 1163) with food, crafts and festivities; third week.

Girona	**Fires de Sant Narcís** (**w** girona.cat) Concerts, fireworks, parades, giants, the works in honour of the city's patron saint; late October–early November.
Sitges	**Cinema Festival** (**w** sitgesfilmfestival.com) Second Sunday.
Valls	**Fira de Santa Úrsula** (**w** valls.cat) With major *casteller* action; 21 October.

November
Altafulla	**Festa Major de Sant Martí** (**w** visitaltafulla.cat) 11 November.
Balaguer	**Festes del Sant Crist** (**w** balaguer.cat) With plenty of concerts; 8–12 November.
Maçanet de Cabrenys	**Festa Major** (**w** maçanetdecabrenys.cat/fires-i-festes) Lots of *correfocs*; 11 November.

December
| Besalú | **Fira de la Ratafia** (**w** besalu.cat) Ratafia competition; mid month. |
| Vic | **Early Medieval Christmas market** (**w** victurisme.cat) First Sunday. |

SHOPPING

Popular souvenirs from Catalunya include hand-painted ceramics, the straw-soled canvas shoes *espardanyes* (espadrilles), and a fantastic range of food and drink. Every town has a local market, where you could pick up cured meats like *fuet* or some of the region's wonderful cheeses, and most market stalls will be able to vacuum pack for you (*envasat al buit*). Other good options are local olive oil, *turró* (nougat, mainly available around Christmas), and Catalan wines and cava, which all make excellent gifts.

Fashion shoppers will also find plenty of choice. Global Spanish brands like Zara and Mango are everywhere, usually at slightly lower prices than in other parts of the world. Catalunya also boasts a thriving community of home-grown designers, with Barcelona in particular known for independent fashion labels and concept stores.

Note that most shops don't open on Sundays, except in the run-up to Christmas and for a month during the summer sales, so time your shopping trips accordingly. In high season, shops will open every day in the resorts.

In French Catalunya, Roussillon ceramics, Collioure anchovies, and Banyuls sweet wine are classic local products.

ARTS AND ENTERTAINMENT

CINEMA Barcelona is the production hub and home to the Filmoteca de Catalunya, which offers a programme of classics, indie films and retrospectives (international films, as well as home-grown). The Institut Jean Vigo in Perpignan plays a similar archival and educational role as the Filmoteca.

Film culture is vibrant all over Catalunya, and summer brings wonderful outdoor screenings like Cinema Lliure a la Platja (free indie films on the beach) and the world-renowned Sitges Film Festival, specialising in horror, fantasy and sci-fi. Other festivals include DocsBarcelona (documentary), D'A Film Festival (emerging auteurs), and numerous local events in Girona, Lleida and Reus.

Most cinemas show films dubbed into Spanish, but screenings marked VO (*versió original*) retain the original language with subtitles, especially in arthouse and independent cinemas. On one day a week, usually a Wednesday, most cinemas offer discounted tickets for the '*dia de l'espectador*' (literally, 'the day of the spectator').

MUSEUMS AND HISTORICAL SITES Many museums and historical sites have explanations only in Catalan; if that's the case, ask if they have a leaflet, app or audio guide with English translations. In Barcelona, many city museums are free on Sunday afternoons or one day a month (page 87). Most museums give discounts if you have a student ID card or are an EU citizen under 18 or over 65 years old. Don't be surprised if cathedrals and famous churches charge for admission – just consider the cost of upkeep.

MUSIC Catalans love music, from the traditional *cobla* that accompanies the *sardana* (page 27) and the *havaneres* (sea shanties, page 167) of the Costa Brava, to the internationally renowned dance music festivals in Barcelona.

Sónar (w sonar.es), a globally renowned festival of electronic music and digital art, is Barcelona's biggest contemporary music event. Almost as big are Primavera Sound (w primaverasound.com), one of Europe's leading festivals for indie, rock and cutting-edge pop, and Cruïlla (w cruillabarcelona.com), which mixes genres from reggae to rock. All attract huge international audiences and top-tier line-ups.

There are scores of fabulous music festivals in beautiful settings throughout the summer. The Cap Roig Festival (w caproigfestival.com) offers pop and classical performances in a stunning botanical setting overlooking the sea. The Festival de Peralada w festivalperalada.com) and Barcelona's Grec Festival (w barcelona.cat/grec) include opera, classical concerts and ballet under the stars. Jazz lovers can explore events in Terrassa, Girona, and Barcelona (especially in October's Voll-Damm Barcelona Jazz Festival).

Early and classical music also flourish here, from the Schubertiada Festival (w schubertiada.cat) in Vilabertran to the Festival de Música Antiga dels Pirineus (FeMAP; w femap.cat), which brings medieval, Renaissance and Baroque works to Romanesque churches and rural spaces. Major classical institutions include the Liceu Opera House (w liceubarcelona.cat), the Auditori (w auditori.cat) and the Palau de la Música Catalana (w palaumusica.cat), all in Barcelona, offering full seasons of opera, orchestral, choral and contemporary works.

In Northern Catalunya, particularly in Roussillon, traditional music survives in folk dances and community festivals, often blending French chanson with Catalan instruments. The Festival Pablo Casals (w prades-festival-casals.com) in Prades, founded by the exiled cellist, remains a cornerstone of summer classical programming in the region.

SPORTS AND ACTIVITIES

Catalunya offers a dazzling array of sports, but one it doesn't have is bullfighting. It is so unpopular that in 1989 Tossa de Mar became the first place to declare itself 'an anti-bullfighting city'. Many municipalities followed suit, and it was banned across the region in 2010.

AIR SPORTS AND BALLOONING There are quite a few opportunities to look down on Catalunya. The updraughts at the Noguera make it perfect for paragliding, with several firms based at Àger. Empuriabrava has a popular sky-diving school (w skydiveempuriabrava.com). Several firms across the region offer hot-air balloon rides (some of the most popular are in La Garrotxa, so you can look down on the volcanoes). Igualada, 35km west of Barcelona, has a gliding club (w volavela.com).

CANOEING AND KAYAKING There are quite a few ways to get wet in Catalunya. The Noguera Pallaresa is the star river for whitewater adventure, with kayaking and rafting trips running from Sort (w riu.sort.cat). Nearby La Seu d'Urgell has a purpose-built Olympic whitewater park. On the coast, sea kayaking is a great way to explore the coves of the Costa Brava and there are several operators based around Tamariu, Llafranc and Cadaqués. Across the border in French Catalunya, the calmer stretches of the Tech and Tet rivers are popular for gentler canoeing, and guided trips are available from Céret and Argelès-sur-Mer.

CYCLING Catalunya takes cycling extremely seriously, both as a hobby and sport – especially in Girona province, where Lance Armstrong used to train. The region has four Vías Verdes – long-distance walking and bike routes along former rail lines (w viasverdes.com/en). Otherwise, many of the rural roads get very little traffic, but the hills aren't for sissies. Fifteen marked mountain bike (BTT in Catalan) areas have been laid out in the natural parks by the Generalitat covering 3,300km; the longest is the 800km GR11 Transpirenaica route from Catalunya to Cabo de Higuer in the Basque Lands. Information on the bike routes within each of the natural parks is found on their respective page (although in Catalan and Spanish only) at w parcsnaturals.gencat.cat. Given the popularity of cycling, you're never far from a bike hire shop and e-bikes are readily available all over the region.

FISHING Fishing is a long-standing Spanish obsession. Recreational permits (*licència de pesca*) are required for both sea and inland fishing, and separate permits are needed for underwater (spear) fishing. All are issued by the Generalitat de Catalunya, and you can apply online (in Spanish or Catalan) at w licenciascazapesca. com. Sea fishing along the Costa Brava is popular, but many fisherfolk prefer to try their luck on the rivers Ter, Onyar and Segre, and Lake Banyoles.

GOLF Catalunya's sunny, warm winters, combined with greens of international tournament standard, attract golfing enthusiasts from all over the world throughout the year. There are more than 50 golf courses in the region, including some of the best on the continent. Notably, Camiral Golf and Wellness (formerly PGA Catalunya) in Caldes de Malavella features two championship courses: the Stadium Course, consistently ranked among Europe's top courses, and the Tour Course. Other renowned courses in the Costa Brava region include Club de Golf Costa Brava in Santa Cristina d'Aro and Empordà Golf Club in Gualta. Many hotels cater specifically for golfers. The Federació Catalana de Golf (w catgolf.com) lists all the clubs by province

HIKING The Centre Excursionista de Catalunya (CEC) is in the very heart of the Barri Gòtic in Barcelona, symbolising hiking's importance in a country where walkabouts seem to be part of the DNA: all the great figures of the Renaixença from Gaudí to Verdaguer were constantly going off on expeditions to explore Catalunya's natural beauty. Today the coast and mountains are crisscrossed with beautiful paths: long distance (over 50km) Senders de Gran Recorregut (GR), waymarked in red and white; short distance (10–50km) Senders de Petit Recorregut (PR), waymarked in yellow and white; and Senders Locals (under 10km), waymarked

2

in green and white. The Federació d'Entitats Excursionistes de Catalunya (FEEC; w senders.feec.cat, Catalan and Spanish only) oversees the maintenance and promotion of these trails; the website lists all the routes. In summer it's advisable to book at guarded *refugis* (mountain huts) to make sure you have a bed. You can book at w refugisdecatalunya.com (Catalan and Spanish only).

HORSERIDING Catalunya has scores of riding stables, many connected with rural accommodation. They are located all over the region, particularly in the Pyrenees, the Empordà and the Garrotxa region, and most offer classes and rides for all levels and ages. There are some wonderful long-distance trails as well; try Catalonia Horse Trails (✆606 949 338; w catalonia-horse-trails.cat), which organises riding holidays in the Pyrenees and along the coast.

MOUNTAIN SPORTS Outside of the Alps, Catalunya's Pyrenees have some of the best venues in Europe for high-altitude sports: distinctive twin-peaked Pedraforca (page 221) is a favourite of both mountain and rock climbers. Siurana (page 255), with its limestone crags, attracts elite climbers from around the world, and Montserrat offers hundreds of traditional and sport climbing routes. There are also several via ferratas around the region, both in the mountains and on the craggier stretches of coast. Canyoning is also huge, particularly in the mountains along the border with Aragon, the Pallars Sobirà region and around Ripoll. Barcelona is the seat of the Spanish Mountain Sports Federation (Federación Espanola de Deportes de Montana y Escalada; w fedme.es, Spanish only).

TENNIS There is as much fervour in Spain for tennis as for golf, inspired by Rafael Nadal and Carlos Alcaraz. Every resort hotel has its own courts; municipal ones are everywhere.

WATERSPORTS L'Estartit on the Costa Brava is the diving capital of Catalunya, thanks to the proximity of the Medes islets, a protected nature and marine reserve (Parc Natural del Montgrí, les Illes Medes i el Baix Ter; w parcsnaturals.gencat.cat/ ca/xarxa-de-parcs/illes-medes) teeming with marine life, waiting to be explored. But there are diving centres in most resorts, and sea kayaks for exploring the secret coves of the coast.

WINTER SPORTS Catalunya has 17 ski stations, with 612km of slopes served by 130 ski lifts; when you add in the little Catalan duty-free mountain principality of Andorra you have the best skiing in Europe outside of the Alps – both downhill runs and cross-country (*esquí nordic*). Resorts such as Baqueira-Beret, La Molina and Masella offer excellent downhill skiing, while Nordic centres like Guils Fontanera, Aransa and Tuixent-La Vansa provide lovely cross-country trails through forests. Many have other features as well: snow parks for free-style snowboarding, toboggan runs, and more. Puigcerdà is the cradle of hockey in Spain, and has an ice palace that hosts figure skating as well.

OPENING TIMES

Most **banks** in Spain are open 09.00–14.00 Monday–Friday. A few open until 16.00 on Thursdays. All have ATMs (*caixer automàtic*). In France, banks usually open 08.30–17.30 Monday–Friday, but many close for lunch between noon and 14.00. Occasionally they also open on Saturday mornings. Officially, **main post office** opening hours are 08.30–20.30 Monday–Friday, 09.30–13.00 Saturday. This isn't necessarily the case outside the big cities, and small post offices may close early in summer.

Shops usually open at 10.00, boutiques an hour or so later. Except the bigger shops and chains in cities, most shops close for 2–3 hours in the afternoon and stay open until 20.00 or 21.00. Shops are closed on Sundays, except during the run-up to Christmas and for the summer sales (*rebaixes*). Most larger towns and cities have convenience stores that are open daily for essential groceries.

Museums and historical sites tend to follow shop hours, though they are shorter in winter. Nearly all close on Mondays. Note that many stop admitting visitors half an hour before the official closing time and most close on national holidays (page 46).

MEDIA AND COMMUNICATIONS

PRINT AND ONLINE MEDIA The two main newspapers are *La Vanguardia* and *El Periódico de Catalunya*, both published in Spanish and Catalan editions. *Ara* and *El Punt Avui* are Catalan-only dailies with a slightly more explicit nationalist emphasis. For English-speaking visitors, *Catalan News* (w catalannews.com) has good online coverage, and *Metropolitan* (w barcelona-metropolitan.com) provides cultural coverage, listings and expat-focused features. North of the border, *L'Indépendant* (published in Perpignan) is the main local paper, with occasional bilingual content.

TELEVISION AND RADIO Public broadcaster TV3 is the main Catalan-language TV channel, known for high-quality news and documentaries, while Betevé covers Barcelona-specific news. On radio, Catalunya Ràdio and RAC1 are the most popular Catalan stations.

POST Post offices will often be crowded, but unless you have packages to send you may never need visit one: most tobacconists sell stamps (*segells*) and they'll usually know the correct postage for whatever you're sending. Post boxes are bright yellow.

INTERNET Hotels, restaurants, bars, tourist offices and even taxis offer free Wi-Fi these days, so you can spend your whole holiday staring at your phone. Beware that hackers often use free hotspots, so don't log on to your bank etc unless you use a VPN.

TELEPHONES Spain's international dialling code is 34; to make an international call from Spain, dial 00, then the country code, followed by the area code (omitting any initial 0) and the number. International dialling codes include Australia 61, Canada 1, Republic of Ireland 353, UK 44 and USA 1. Visitors from the EU/EEA can usually use their mobile phones without incurring roaming charges under the 'Roam Like at Home' policy, but non-EU mobile users are subject to roaming charges. Consider using an eSIM or local SIM: there are plans offered by e-SIM provider Airalo (w airalo.com) or from big, international service providers like Movistar (w movistar.es), Vodafone (w vodafone.es) and Orange (w orange.es). Spain has strong mobile coverage, including 5G in most urban areas.

CULTURAL ETIQUETTE

Catalans are welcoming and warm, but also proud of their distinct culture, and there are a few things to keep in mind if you want to be respectful of local sensibilities.

- **Catalunya is not Spain** Top of the list: don't assume Catalunya is just a region of Spain or that Catalan is a dialect of Spanish. Catalans are proud of their culture and language and showing an interest in the language and culture goes a long way. A few words in Catalan (*bon dia, si us plau, gràcies*) will win you real points.
- **Politeness and personal space** Catalans tend to be more reserved than other Spaniards. Public behaviour is a little quieter, and people generally respect personal space. You're unlikely to see loud phone calls on the metro or overly animated debates in cafés.
- **Meeting and greeting** Handshakes are the usual way to greet someone new. Among friends, two cheek kisses are normal. Formal titles like *senyor* or *senyora* are still used in more traditional settings.
- **Punctuality and business** Catalans are pretty punctual, especially for work or formal meetings, so turning up late without a good reason won't go down well. Business culture is polite but to the point, pleasantries are brief and things tend to move quickly.
- **Dress** Catalans like to look good and you'll rarely see locals wandering around town in beachwear. Shirts off in the city? Absolutely not.
- **North (French) Catalunya** Over the border in North Catalunya, local culture blends French formality with a quieter kind of Catalan pride. French is the main language, and while Catalan is still spoken, especially by older generations, it's much less visible. Show a bit of interest in the region's Catalan heritage and you'll be warmly received.

TRAVELLING POSITIVELY

As with anywhere in the world, you should try to buy local and think global. Catalunya offers plenty of ways to travel sustainably, support the local economy and connect with its landscapes and communities.

Much of Catalunya's tourism revenue concentrates in Barcelona and the Costa Brava, leaving rural and inland communities behind. By staying in small family-run pensions, *cases rurals* or *agroturismes* (farm stays) and buying from local markets or co-operatives, you're helping to keep traditional crafts, foods and ways of life alive. When shopping in cities, head to the amazing local markets, and use the refill shops and plastic-free grocers that are becoming more and more.

Catalunya has faced severe droughts in recent years, so be mindful of water use wherever you are – take short showers, report leaks, and re-use towels. In natural parks and nature reserves, stick to marked trails and avoid disturbing flora and fauna.

If you want to get involved, there are several organisations that encourage volunteers. GEPEC (w gepac.cat) and Sèlvans (w selvans.ong) run tree-planting, beach clean-ups and other conservation volunteer days. Espigoladors (which means 'gleaners'; w espigoladors.cat), which tackle food waste, invite volunteers to help 'glean' fields of produce that is then distributed to those in need or used in their delicious food products (the 'im-perfecte' range, available in lots of shops in and around Barcelona).

Part Two

THE GUIDE

3

Barcelona

Barcelona, the treasure house of courtesy, the refuge of strangers...although the adventures that befell me there occasioned me no great pleasure, but rather much grief, I bore them the better for having seen that city.

Cervantes, *Don Quixote*, Part II

Barcelona, the capital of the Catalans, is a city that goes about its business and pleasure with such ballistic intensity that you can't tell whether it's insanely serious or seriously insane, or both. In 1975, 3 million Barcelonins danced in the streets like drunken banshees when they heard of Franco's death; the next day they rolled up their sleeves and channelled their energy into making up for 40 stale, flat years. They've done it: Barcelona fizzes and sizzles like a bottle of Catalan cava spiked with a red pepper.

With its superb legacy of Gothic and Modernista architecture, its business acumen and ambitious immigrants, its taste for the avant-garde and manic obsession with design, Barcelona is a little New York – and in many ways the only really successful modern city in old Europe. Nor is it shy about saying so. A compulsive exhibitionist, Barcelona held two great international fairs, in 1888 and 1929, and staged one hell of a show for the 1992 Olympics. We are all the better for having seen it.

HISTORY

In later years, when this prancing peacock of a city felt the lack of a foundation myth, Barcelona's literati would summon up no less a personage than Hercules to play the role of city father. Hercules would have passed this way on his Tenth Labour, while driving the cattle of Geryon back to Greece. He had already founded Cádiz and built the Pillars of Hercules, and the Barcelonins thought they could sneak their town on to the list, too. A different story, based on the similarity of the names, credited with the founding a leader of Carthage's most prominent family – Hamilcar Barca, Hannibal's father.

As far as anyone can tell, the first real Barcelonins were the Celto-Iberian Laietanos, who lived in scattered villages on the rich plain, with a citadel or religious centre on Montjuïc. In 15BC, in the reign of Augustus, the Romans founded Colonia Faventia Julia Augusta Paterna Barcino on a low hill between two small streams, just north of Montjuïc. Although surrounded by fertile land, Barcino lacked a good harbour, and it never became half as important as Roman Tarraco (Tarragona).

Roman Barcino, a typical walled, rectangular castrum of the sort found all over the empire, covered what is now the core of the Barri Gòtic; an impressive patch of Roman foundations, still intact under the medieval city, can be visited under the Museu d'Història de la Ciutat (page 191). In AD262, Barcino suffered a sacking at the hands of the Franks, in a raid that was a prelude to the Germanic invasions that would overwhelm the western empire a century and a half later. The Franks did far more damage to Tarraco, and, after the Roman legions regained control of the situation, Barcino seems to have gradually supplanted it as top town in the region.

The newly strengthened walls failed to keep out the Visigoths in AD415 but, rather than rape and pillage, they moved in and briefly made Barcelona the seat of their court. When a new foe, the Arab-led army of Islam, destroyed Tarraco in AD713, Barcelona took note and surrendered without a fight. The Barcelonins couldn't know it, but the Arabs had just made their fortune. From now on Barcelona, and not Tarragona, would be the leading city of northern Iberia. In the meantime, Barcelona would merely be an outpost of the new state of al-Andalus.

In AD801, Charlemagne's son Louis the Pious reconquered northern 'Gothalanda'. Barcelona was an important walled fortress, and in AD874 – a year of clashing coiffures – the Frankish king Charles the Bald made the local baron Guifré el Pilós, or 'Wilfred the Hairy', its first count. Guifré brought much of what is now Catalunya under his control, and he endowed Barcelona and the region with churches and monasteries. As Frankish power decayed after Charlemagne's death, Barcelona was increasingly on its own. In AD985, when it was attacked by the great al-Mansur of Córdoba, the Franks failed to respond to its requests for aid. Count Borrell II declared his county's sovereign independence, and the Franks could not stop him.

Barcelona faced the new millennium with a population of probably little more than 1,000. Over the next two centuries, however, this insignificant town would quite suddenly and startlingly grow fat and rich. It isn't entirely clear how they managed it. Its main economic assets were the two most useful gifts a medieval town could ask for: iron and wool. Yet more profit came from the produce of the surrounding farmland, and from the booty acquired by Barcelona's counts in the wars of the Reconquista against the Moors. The pennies were piling up and the city invested some of its surplus wisely, building ships and developing maritime links across the Mediterranean.

By the 1030s Barcelona had the first stable gold currency in western Europe. The business interests of the city and the ambitions of the counts found a happy symbiosis and, as both grew in power, trade and the flag went hand in hand. The marriage in 1137 between Barcelona's Count Ramon Berenguer IV and the heiress of Aragon, Queen Petronila, brought the city the Crown of Aragon and all the prestige of royalty. Now the counts were 'count-kings', the unusual name proof of the continuing importance of Barcelona.

As it acquired a new maritime empire, Barcelona's trade, and nearly everyone else's in medieval Europe, was regulated by a maritime code, the

BARCELONA Overview
For listings, see from page 72

⌂ Where to stay
1	Casa Bonay	F2
2	Central House Hostel	C2
3	Ciutat Vella	D4
4	Hotel 54	G5
5	Hotel Casa Fuster	C2
6	Hotel Arts	H4
7	Mesón Castilla	D4
8	Motel One Barcelona	F3
9	Pol & Grace	B1

✕ Where to eat and drink
10	Alkimia	D4
11	Bar Jai Ca	G5
12	Besta	C3
13	Biocenter	D4
14	Botafumeiro	C2
15	Ca l'Isidre	D5
16	Can Majó	G5
17	Can Solé	G5
18	Casa Alfonso	E3
19	Cinc Sentits	C5
20	Cova Fumada	G5
21	Disfrutar	C3
22	La Nena	C1
23	Quimet i Quimet	D6
24	Sésamo	D5
25	Terraza Martínez	E7
26	Vaso de Oro	G5
Off map		
	Aranda's Grill	B1
	Bar Tomás	A2

3

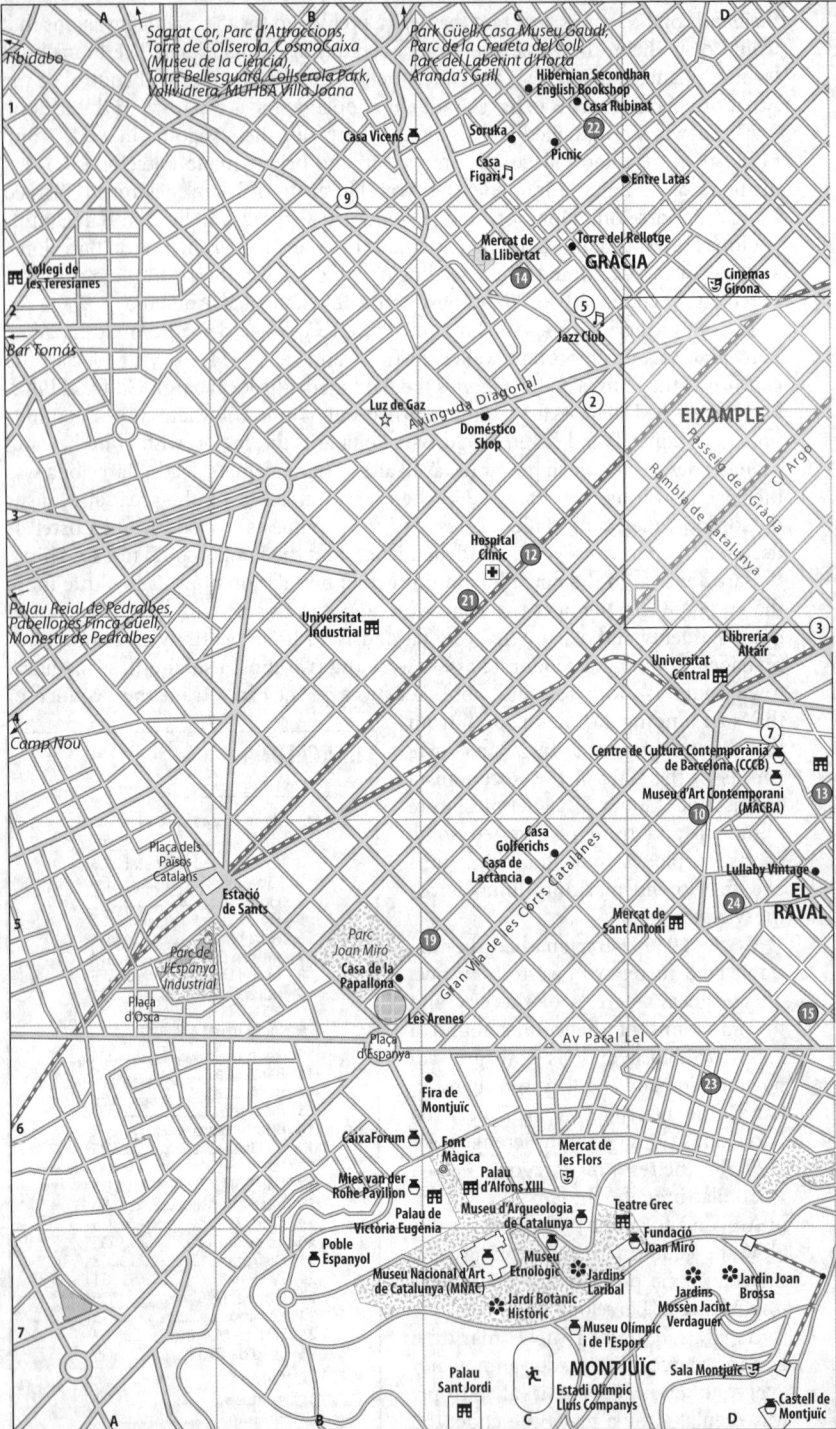

Sagrat Cor, Parc d'Attraccions,
Torre de Collserola, CosmoCaixa
(Museu de la Ciència),
Torre Bellesguard, Collserola Park,
Vallvidrera, MUHBA Villa Joana

Park Güell/Casa Museu Gaudí,
Parc de la Creueta del Coll,
Parc del Laberint d'Horta
Aranda's Grill

Tibidabo

Hibernian Secondhan
English Bookshop

Casa Rubinat

Casa Vicens

Soruka

Picnic

22

Casa
Figari

Entre Latas

9

Col·legi de
les Teresianes

Mercat de
la Llibertat

Torre del Rellotge

GRÀCIA

14

Cinemas
Girona

5

Bar Tomás

Jazz Club

EIXAMPLE

Luz de Gaz

Avinguda Diagonal

2

Doméstico
Shop

Passeig de Gràcia

C Arg

Rambla de Catalunya

Palau Reial de Pedralbes,
Pabellones Finca Güell,
Monestir de Pedralbes

Hospital
Clínic

12

21

Universitat
Industrial

Llibreria
Altaïr

3

Universitat
Central

Camp Nou

Centre de Cultura Contemporània
de Barcelona (CCCB)

7

13

Museu d'Art Contemporani
(MACBA)

10

Casa
Golferichs

Casa de
Lactància

Lullaby Vintage

EL
RAVAL

24

Plaça dels
Països
Catalans

Estació
de Sants

Parc
Joan Miró

19

Gran Via de les Corts Catalanes

Mercat de
Sant Antoni

Parc de
l'Espanya
Industrial

Casa de la
Papallona

Plaça
d'Osca

Les Arenes

15

Av Paral·lel

Plaça
d'Espanya

23

Fira de
Montjuïc

CaixaForum

Font
Màgica

Mercat de
les Flors

Mies van der
Rohe Pavilion

Palau
d'Alfons XIII

Teatre Grec

Palau de
Victoria Eugènia

Museu d'Arqueologia
de Catalunya

Fundació
Joan Miró

Poble
Espanyol

Museu
Etnològic

Museu Nacional d'Art
de Catalunya (MNAC)

Jardins
Laribal

Jardin Joan
Brossa

Jardí Botànic
Històric

Jardins
Mossèn Jacint
Verdaguer

Museu Olímpic
i de l'Esport

MONTJUÏC

Sala Montjuïc

Palau
Sant Jordi

Estadi Olímpic
Lluís Companys

Castell de
Montjuïc

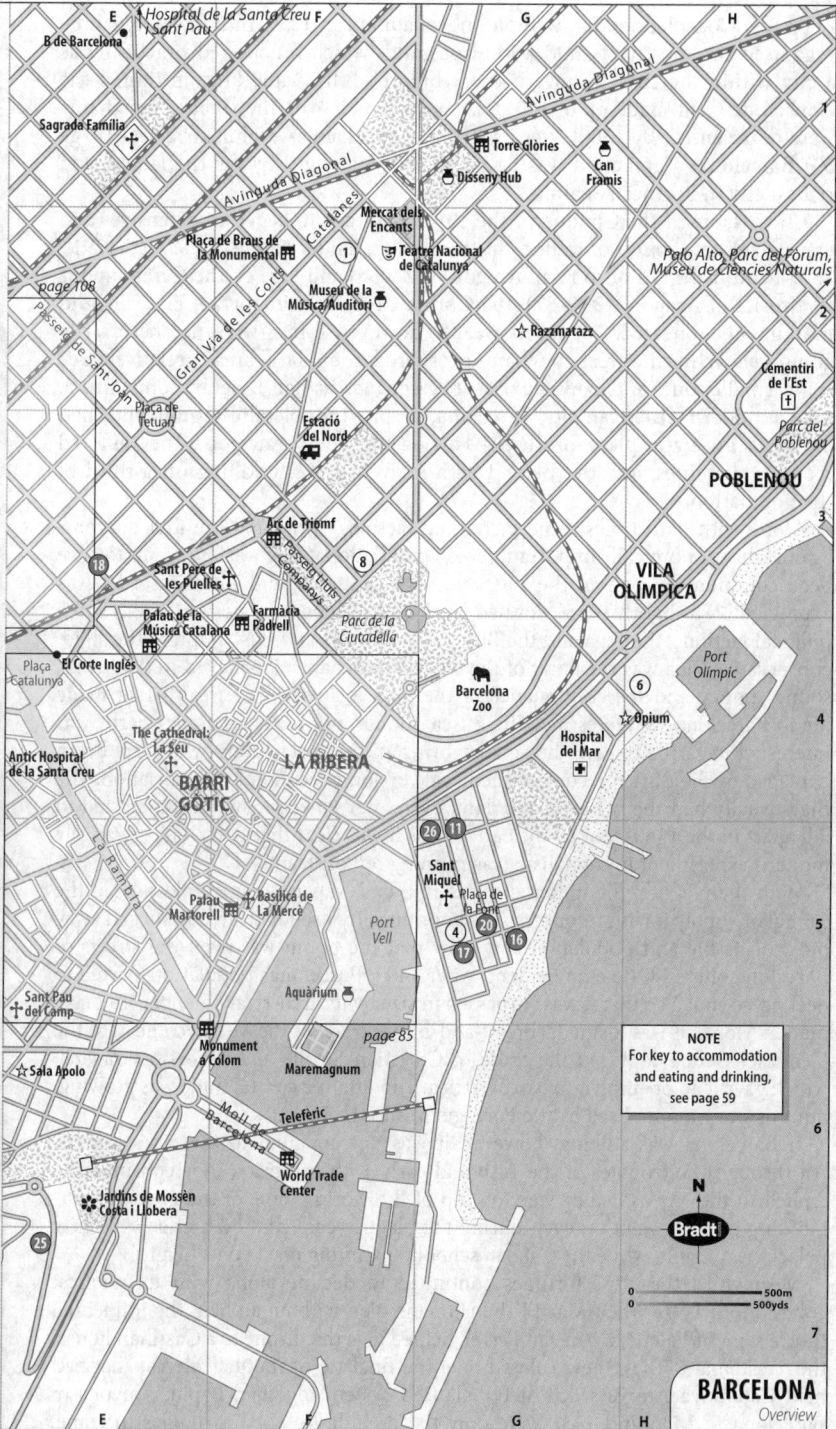

E
Hospital de la Santa Creu i Sant Pau
F
G
H

B de Barcelona

Avinguda Diagonal

1

Sagrada Família

Torre Glòries

Can Framis

Avinguda Diagonal

Disseny Hub

Plaça de Braus de la Monumental

Mercat dels Encants

Catalanes

1

Teatre Nacional de Catalunya

Palo Alto, Parc del Fòrum, Museu de Ciències Naturals

page 108

Gran Via de les Corts

Museu de la Música/Auditori

2

Passeig de Sant Joan

Razzmatazz

Cementiri de l'Est

Plaça de Tetuan

Estació del Nord

Parc del Poblenou

POBLENOU

3

Arc de Triomf

18

Sant Pere de les Puelles

8

Passeig Lluís Companys

VILA OLÍMPICA

Palau de la Música Catalana

Farmàcia Padrell

Parc de la Ciutadella

Port Olímpic

El Corte Inglés

Plaça Catalunya

The Cathedral: La Seu

LA RIBERA

Barcelona Zoo

6

Ópium

4

Antic Hospital de la Santa Creu

BARRI GÒTIC

Hospital del Mar

26

11

Sant Miquel

Plaça de la Font

5

Rambla

Palau Martorell

Basílica de La Mercè

Port Vell

20

4

17

16

Sant Pau del Camp

Aquàrium

page 85

NOTE
For key to accommodation
and eating and drinking,
see page 59

Sala Apolo

Monument a Colom

Maremàgnum

6

3

Moll de Barcelona

Telefèric

N

World Trade Center

Bradt

Jardins de Mossèn Costa i Llobera

25

0   500m
0   500yds

7

E

F

G

H

BARCELONA
Overview

61

Llibre del Consolat de Mar, written under Jaume I in 1259. In Barcelona, Jaume organised the merchants into a kind of guild, which functioned practically as a city within the city. To govern everything else, the same king instituted the Consell de Cent made up of 100 citizens, in which even the smaller merchants were represented. By 1300, after its string of spectacular exploits overseas (page 59) Barcelona's population was up to 50,000, making it by far the largest and richest city in northern Spain.

Under Jaume I the Conqueror the city was forced to begin an extensive (and expensive) new circuit of walls to fit them all in. Under Jaume II the Just (1291–1327), Alfons III (Alfonso IV of Aragon, 1327–36) and Pere IV the Ceremonious (Pedro III of Aragon, 1336–87), the Gothic city's most important and splendid monuments appeared. For all its wealth, however, things were not necessarily going well. While the great merchants prospered from a large area of relatively free trade, smaller ones and manufacturers became increasingly beset by competition. Like a modern American city, Barcelona, despite the splendid monuments, had become a miserable place for the city's increasingly desperate poor. They suffered recurrent famines, and the Black Death arrived in 1348, killing off a third of the population.

Along with hard times came increasing factional strife and the first pogroms against the economically important Jewish population. Gang warfare seems to have been common throughout the 14th and 15th centuries, and social disorder was expressed on a slightly more elevated level in the bitter struggles of the city's two political factions, the Biga and the Busca – the 'Beam' and the 'Splinter'. The solid, conservative Biga was the party of the biggest merchants; it believed in free trade, sound money and the continuance of the great disparities of wealth that made life in Barcelona so interesting. The Busca, though not really a popular party, was interested in tariffs to save the smaller firms and manufacturers who were being damaged by the Biga's precocious medieval version of economic globalisation. The Biga usually had the better of the fight, even after its economic vision started to fall apart in the 1380s, but by the early 1400s it was clear that Barcelona's strangely modern experiment in capitalism was running out of steam.

With the plagues, the hinterland was in a bad way, no longer able to feed the capital or supply it with resources. The booming city itself had already sucked away most of its life and population and, now that the boom was over, the streets of Barcelona offered little employment. After 1400, Barcelona's population started to decline, so much so that it was surpassed in size by its arch-rival Valencia. To make matters worse, it was losing its bread-and-butter trade in the Mediterranean to the Genoese; Genoa captured the trade of Christian Seville and Moorish Granada, which gave it an opening into North Africa. The Atlantic coastal trade was growing, but this was monopolised by the Portuguese and the Basques.

If Barcelona was sinking, however, it was not apparent to the city's leaders. All through the troubles of the 14th and early 15th centuries, they continued to embellish the city as if they were on top of the world. Some of the great church-building projects went on even during the plague years, and even after 1400 new palaces were built, while the Catalan school of painting reached its height.

Meanwhile, the city's fortunes continued to decline along with its political cohesion. In 1410, when Martí I the Humane died without an heir, the influential future saint of Valencia, Vincent Ferrer, helped give the throne to a Castilian house, the Trastámara. These new rulers broke the final tie of mutual interest that had held Catalunya-Aragon's delicately balanced system together. Popular revolts in Barcelona in 1436 and 1437 were only the prelude to worse struggles to come.

The great revolt that began in 1462 was essentially a struggle between Barcelona's ruling class and King Joan II. Ten years of civil war followed, finally ending with the surrender of a city under siege by its own king. Barcelona was ruined.

Joan's son was Ferran II to the Catalans, but he would have preferred to call himself by his Castilian name, Fernando. He had been married to Isabel of Castile in the middle of the wars and, when his father died and he assumed the throne in 1479, Castile and Aragon were effectively united. Barcelona was an exhausted, bankrupt metropolis that had no prospects and no friends.

1479–1830: A PROVINCIAL CITY IN SPAIN

At first, Barcelona entertained some wan hopes that Aragon's union with powerful Castile would supply a much-needed transfusion of money and vitality. What happened was quite different. Fernando and Isabel ensured it would have no share in the new opportunities; a codicil in Isabel's will specifically prohibited Catalan merchants from trading with the New World. A lesser city than Barcelona might have disintegrated altogether, but the city's merchants showed remarkable resilience. In spite of everything, they endured decreased trade and then a series of rebellion and wars with and against France. Finally, they chose the wrong side in the War of the Spanish Succession (1701–14). After 15 months of resistance the city fell to the Bourbon faction in November 1714, and down with it went Catalunya's Usatges, its institutions and the last vestiges of its autonomy. The city's leaders were drawn and quartered, and a large number of die-hard resisters were buried in a mass grave near Santa Maria del Mar.

The old capital of the count-kings became just another provincial city of Spain, and Felipe V punished it with the construction of the Ciutadella, a huge pentagonal fort intended to protect the city from its own people. The Barcelonins were forced to pay for it themselves, and its building meant the demolition of half of a neighbourhood, La Ribera, in a city that was already suffocatingly overcrowded. To make matters worse, Madrid decreed that no-one would be allowed to live outside the walls. The city began to consume itself, expanding at the expense of patios and gardens; the current maze of dark canyons in the old city is the result.

For the next century and a half, Barcelona acquired taller and taller buildings, and the conditions in which its people lived became increasingly unhealthy. The new quarter of Barceloneta, built on reclaimed land around the harbour, appeared in 1753. Originally planned to house the families displaced for the Ciutadella, it came – with typical Bourbon efficiency – some 40 years too late. At least Barcelonins were working again.

Once the Catalans had been punished, Bourbon policy was never quite as black-hearted as Fernando and Isabel's. The new dynasty hoped it could eventually earn the Catalans' loyalty by giving them a chance to make a living again. The results were dramatic. Like some capitalist Sleeping Beauty, the city's mercantile elite popped up from its 200-year slumber, full of entrepreneurial fizz. The city found two very profitable new businesses: the manufacture of cotton cloth, and cheap brandy which was shipped off to thirsty Latin America.

In 1778, Madrid finally removed the last restrictions on trading with the colonies, and the long build-up turned into a boom. By 1780, Barcelona's population had more than doubled since 1714, to 110,000. The first industrial cotton mill was founded the same year, and factory production soon replaced the old medieval guilds, as Barcelona began its career as the 'Manchester of the Mediterranean'. The merchants returned to their exchange, the Llotja, and new palaces rose along the new promenade, the Rambla. Barcelona was back in business. The Napoleonic

Wars were a rude interruption. Britain's blockade stopped the American trade cold, and the city went into a deep depression while Napoleon's men raided and looted its churches and monasteries. As much as they hated Madrid, the Catalans had learned from experience that the French were even worse. They remained steadfastly loyal to Spain this time, but, even after the French were chased out in 1814, recovery was slow. Epidemics of yellow fever and cholera hit the overcrowded city in 1821 – the worst of many. The wheels of Barcelona industry didn't get back to full speed until the 1830s.

1830–1923: VIOLENT BIRTH OF THE MODERN CITY One habit that the new Barcelona had in common with its medieval counterpart was treating its workers like dirt. Barcelona's industrialists, Spain's politicians and the Church connived to squeeze them to the limit; working conditions were appalling, especially for the women and children, who generally worked 15 hours a day. They lived in slums so unhealthy that epidemics raged and mortality rates were among the highest in Europe. Dissent or attempts at organisation were ruthlessly suppressed. Anger was not limited to the workers. Barcelona's progressive middle classes had complaints of their own about the reactionary regime that King Fernando VII (1814–33) brought in after Napoleon's defeat.

Between the two, the city became a hotbed of radical ideas, and it boiled over in increasingly violent revolts. The first outbreak, in July 1835, brought the burning of most of Barcelona's monasteries and convents. Regular riots and Luddite attacks on factory machinery enlivened the next two decades. The biggest riot, in 1842, was called the Jamància, in which the rebels took control of the city but were bombarded into submission by the cannons of Montjuïc Castle.

To the industrialists, these were relatively minor irritations. They kept making money. In 1848, they built Spain's first railway, from Barcelona to Mataró. Bursting at the seams, Barcelona finally got permission from Madrid in the late 1850s to demolish its walls and expand. The great grid of the Eixample, designed by Ildefons Cerdà, was one of the most ambitious planning schemes of 19th-century Europe, and nearly quintupled the size of the city. Later, two new wide streets, Passeig de Colom and Vía Laietana, were driven through the old town, following the example of Baron Haussmann's transformation of Paris.

The modern city, with its impressive expansion and cosmopolitanism, evoked comparisons to Barcelona's medieval golden age, and fostered a new pride in things Catalan, leading to a flowering in the arts that would be called the Catalan Renaixença. In this heady climate, under dynamic mayor Francesc de Paula Rius i Taulet, the city put on the Universal Exhibition in 1888; it showed the world, in the mayor's words, that the Catalans 'were the Yankees of Europe', and it saw the beginnings of Barcelona's distinctive Modernista architecture. By the end of the 19th century, Barcelona had one of the most developed economies of Europe.

Prosperity, however, brought little improvement in the conditions of working people, and the issues that caused all the trouble in the 1830s were still unsettled. For a while, boom times papered over the growing discontent, but in the 1870s the city was ready to explode once more – this time, with the heat of a new ideology, known as Anarchism. Even after it was driven underground in 1874, this movement gave an ideological home to those workers – increasingly, a majority of them – who were willing to meet the violence of the army and the employers' gangs of thugs with violence of their own.

The two sides battled through the streets intermittently for the next three decades, while Barcelona became the bomb capital of Europe: in 1893, Anarchist bombs killed 20; the next year, one exploded into the expensive seats at the Liceu; and, in 1896, they blew up the religious procession of Corpus Christi. While bombs and bullets flew, Barcelona was paradoxically enjoying its most creative era. In the 1890s, Catalan culture flowered, with the painters Ramon Casas and Santiago Rusinyol and their circle – which included the young Picasso – at the café Els Quatre Gats.

The city's converging artistic style soon acquired a name, Modernisme. Its painting and poetry would not make much of an impression outside Catalunya, but in architecture the Modernistas were about to astound the world. Antoni Gaudí, the greatest among them, began work on the Sagrada Família in 1883, and built La Pedrera on the Passeig de Gràcia in 1905.

The Modernistas' buildings set the tone for the rapidly developing Eixample, giving the city a new look, almost a new identity, while back in the old centre Barcelona's bohemians were perfecting the louche demi-monde life of the Barri Gòtic.

The Spanish-American War of 1898 was an earthquake for all of Spain. Many among Barcelona's elite had started by amassing fortunes in the colonies in tobacco, shipping or enslaved people; they were called *indianos* or *americanos*. The loss of Spain's last important colonies closed off considerable trade opportunities, and the end of the war filled the city with disgusted ex-soldiers with little chance of employment. By 1909 the city was a tense, dry tinderbox. The conscription of young Catalans for an unpopular imperialist war in Morocco led to a general strike on 26 July. The strike turned into a revolt, and a leaderless mob took over the city. Though discouraged by lack of support from the rest of Spain, Barcelona turned the revolt into a head-on collision with the army.

At the end of what was called the Setmana Tràgica, or Tragic Week, 116 people were dead and 80 buildings torched, 70 of them churches or monasteries. Barcelona, Anarchism's 'rose of fire' had confirmed its role as the most radical city in Europe, and its workers gained considerable sympathy afterwards, as the army's execution in the fortress of Montjuïc of even moderate leaders shocked Europe. Spain's neutrality in World War I brought more boom times, as exports to the belligerents soared and the city's industrialists diversified and modernised to meet demand.

Rural Catalans, impoverished by wartime inflation and seeking jobs, moved into the city; the population doubled between 1910 and 1930 as Barcelona became the largest city in Spain. In the same period the city was rocked with more than 800 strikes. Workers' conditions only grew worse; by 1919, the Anarchist workers' union of Catalunya (the CNT) had over 50,000 members in Barcelona alone, but remained unrecognised by the employers even after a devastating, two-month general strike. The violence escalated, as employers hired thugs to kill unionists and the workers lashed back in kind. The chaos and the rising body count gave Spain's rightists the excuse to close down parliamentary democracy. The captain general of Barcelona, Miguel Primo de Rivera, declared a military dictatorship and the 'abolition of the class struggle', with the approval of King Alfonso XIII.

1923–75: DICTATORSHIP, CIVIL WAR AND FRANCO

The dictatorship of Primo de Rivera was proof, if the Catalans needed any, that nothing had really changed since the time of Fernando and Isabel. Spain still looked on Barcelona with a mixture of contempt and fear, and was prepared to do anything to suppress it. The dictator banned the CNT and attempted to do the same to the Catalan language and its nationalist symbols, but he did promote Barcelona's International Exhibition of 1929 to show his version of Spain to the world.

This initiated another building boom, one that included the city's first metro line. It also gave it its first great wave of immigrants from other corners of Spain, especially from Andalucía, Murcia and Galicia. The old dictator retired the next year, and a left-wing landslide in the 1931 municipal elections provided a dramatic renunciation of the old order, leading to the abdication of Alfonso XIII and the birth of the Spanish Republic.

In Catalunya, the big winner was the popular old ex-colonel Francesc Macià, head of the left-wing Republicans (Esquerra Republicana), who declared the 'Republic of Catalunya', although three days later he agreed to limit this to Catalan autonomy under the rule of a revived Generalitat, and was later succeeded by liberal trade union lawyer Lluís Companys. The other patricians and their Lliga de Catalunya were not about to support Macià's mix of Republican leftists, CNT Anarchists, professors and trade unionists.

When the right won the 1934 national elections, many of the Catalan leftists got thrown in jail. When the left came back with the Popular Front in 1936, the stage was set for Francisco Franco's coup and the outbreak of the Civil War. In Barcelona, the success of the workers and loyal Republican troops in defeating the rightists revolutionised the city; churches were set alight and Falangist supporters rooted out and summarily shot, while the anguished Companys tried desperately to contain the mobs and control the situation to avoid state intervention.

The CNT remained in control for the remainder of 1936 and part of 1937, making Barcelona unique in Europe as the only city ever to have been governed by Anarchists. Shops and cafés became collectives; progressive schools were established; women's rights and healthcare were seriously addressed for the first time in Spain; servile and ceremonial forms of speech were abolished; buildings seized by workers were given rent-free to the poor. Many workers were as naive as they were idealistic, and they ignored the darker side of organised Anarchism, the *patrulles de control*, with its old scores to settle. Many who had volunteered to be *patrulles* left in disgust at the massacres of clergy, who were especially singled out for the Church's long-standing support of the propertied classes.

As Franco made gains across Spain in 1937, Barcelona became the theatre of a left-wing war-within-a-war. Typically, the CNT lost its hold in chaotic circumstances – George Orwell, who was there, was hardly the only one to be confused. On 3 May 1937, Companys, at the time president of Catalunya only in name, but supported by the Communists, ordered a takeover of the telephone company from the CNT.

The Anarchists rose one last time; supported reluctantly by the Trotskyist POUM, they built barricades and won the streets, but true to their name they didn't follow through and take political control. It was suicide, as the defeated Communists leaped forward to fill the void. In three days at least 1,500 people were killed in the fighting, until the Anarchists and POUM laid down their arms for the sake of the Republic; the next day, the Republican Army and the Communists started to round them up, saving Franco the trouble later. Anarchists and Trotskyites who weren't shot often found themselves imprisoned in the same cells as Falangists.

Near the end of the war more than 200,000 refugees filled the city, while hundreds of civilians died in the indiscriminate bombings ordered by Franco and his German friends; the historic centre and Barceloneta suffered the most. In January 1939, half a million Republicans fled towards France as Barcelona surrendered. In the confusion, the Generalitat left behind enough incriminating documents for Franco's reprisal squads to have little trouble finishing off the thousands of Republicans who stayed behind.

Franco took particular delight in humiliating the city. All things Catalan were banned; even speaking Catalan in the street was risking jail. The next two sad and impoverished decades saw food, electricity and everything else in short supply; in 1947 the city came very close to famine. Other parts of Spain were suffering too; immigrants flocked to the city, and Franco did everything to encourage them, hoping a tidal wave of poor Andalucians would dilute Catalanism into a harmless eccentricity.

Unlike earlier immigrants, the new arrivals didn't integrate but lived together in their shanty towns and ghettos; the banning of Catalan meant they never learned the language. But Franco could never hope to get Spain back on its feet without Barcelona's industry. By 1960, he had given up his attempt at national self-sufficiency, and a new generation of economists was tooling up the country for its impressive industrial take-off.

Barcelona's appointed mayor, Josep Maria de Porcioles, presided over a building boom of soulless, high-rise housing projects and factories on the outskirts, and disfigured old Barcelona with massive car parks and roads. Still, shoots of new life were poking up through the cracks of the Castilian concrete. In 1960, future Catalan president Jordi Pujol was arrested and imprisoned for two years after devising a protest at the Palau de la Música – singing the Song of the Catalan Flag at a concert while Franco's ministers were in the audience. Not long afterwards, Barcelonins formed their first neighbourhood groups. These were the seeds of a new participatory democracy, and they became very active by the mid-1970s, leading most of the protests of the period, demanding basic services and better public transport, and complaining against exploitation and the siting of factories.

1975 TO THE PRESENT: BECOMING THE CITY OF COOL When Franco died, on 20 November 1975, every single bottle of cava in Barcelona was emptied. The morning after, like the rest of Spain, they wondered what would happen next. When the first city elections were held in 1978, the Socialists under Narcís Serra won control of the city government, the Ajuntament, and they have kept it ever since.

From 1982 to 1997 the mayor was the popular Pasqual Maragall, grandson of the poet Joan Maragall, tireless improver and promoter of his city. By any measure, the accomplishments of Maragall, Pujol and company have been remarkable; their creative channelling of 40 years of pent-up energy and Catalan quirkiness have made Barcelona the most dynamic city on the Mediterranean (it likes to see itself as the southernmost city of northern Europe and the northernmost city of the south), with a hard nose for making money, sweetened by Mediterranean colour and spontaneity.

The continuation of Gaudí's Sagrada Família, a project so big and eccentric and so essentially Catalan, is the symbol of the city's cultural *continuitat*. All the designer tinsel of Barcelona's obsessive hipness is only the shop window dressing of a city that works hard for its living, and knows how to sell itself. The real Barcelona runs on metals and machine industries, textiles and chemicals and publishing (more in Spanish than Catalan). There is a busy stock exchange and countless trade fairs in complexes on Montjuïc and the Gran Via.

For all that, it has been the tinsel that gets the world's attention. Mayor Maragall, with a bit of help from Olympics czar Joan Antoni Samaranch, a Catalan, secured the 1992 Olympics and used it as a vehicle to push through a huge building programme, which radically transformed the city. It gave it a fresh orientation towards the sea, restored its monuments, cleaned up its seedier quarters and gentrified others, making it the model for any up-and-at-'em metropolis wanting to break into the ranks of the 'world cities'.

The Olympics are long over, but the city-perfecting momentum shows no sign of stopping. Barcelona's astonishing array of other projects, including the Diagonal Mar high-tech innovation district, District 22@, the extensive port expansion for the 2024 America's Cup, and the total revamp of the old Poblenou industrial quarter around the Plaça de les Glòries Catalanes have changed the face of the city. New Gaudí-inspired pavilions by Japanese architect Toyo Ito have made the trade fair on the Gran Via the largest in Europe, and the legendary Camp Nou is getting a €900 million makeover. In 2027, a new outpost of the Thyssen-Bornemisza museum will open in a grand old cinema on the Passeig de Gràcia, and several museums, including the Museu Nacional d'Art de Catalunya, are being expanded.

All this relentless reinvention and expansion has taken place against a backdrop of resurgent nationalism. The Catalans brilliantly defused the challenge of mass immigration from elsewhere in Spain (encouraged by Franco in an attempt to dilute their culture) by embracing an open, inclusive identity that welcomed anyone willing to become Catalan and learn the language. But after Spanish courts stripped the word 'nation' from Catalunya's Statute of Autonomy in 2010, calls for independence began to grow. This culminated in a dramatic 2017 referendum, a government crackdown, and a serious political crisis (page 16), eased only by the election of a new, more conciliatory Spanish government in 2023.

Meanwhile, Barcelona is cementing its place as a pioneer in smart, sustainable urban innovation. From the *superilles* ('superblocks'), which prioritise pedestrians and reduce emissions, to expanded green spaces, bike lanes and clever water-saving innovations, it's become a global leader for climate action. Restless, forward-thinking and always in search of the new, Barcelona's boundless energy continues to reinvent the city while remaining unmistakably, irresistibly itself.

GETTING THERE AND AWAY

BY AIR Spain's second busiest airport, **Josep Tarradellas Barcelona-El Prat Airport** is pretty efficient. Located 12km southwest of the centre in El Prat de Llobregat, it has two main terminals, T1 (designed by Ricardo Bofill) and T2. The two terminals are 4km apart and linked by a free 24-hour shuttle bus that runs every 5–10 minutes.

Getting to and from the airport
By train The commuter line R2 (w rodalies.gencat.cat) links the airport (T2) to Passeig de Gràcia and Sants railway station in the city centre (€4.90 single). Trains run every 30 minutes between approximately 05.30 and 23.30.

By metro There is a supplement for metro travel to and from the airport. City metro L9 (orange) serves both terminals. A single airport ticket costs €5.50, which includes ongoing travel on the metro.

By bus City **bus 46** from T1 and T2 goes to the Plaça d'Espanya every 10–15 minutes between 04.50 and 23.50 daily. **NitBus lines** (night buses) link Plaça de Catalunya from 21.50 to 04.50 to T1 (N7) or T2 (N18). Note that these are regular city buses, without extra space for luggage. Single tickets are €2.55 (travel passes such as the T-Casual, see page 69, are valid on local buses). **Aerobús** (w aerobusbarcelona.es; €6.75/11.65 single/return) operates two lines, A1 for T1 and A2 for T2, which have a lot of luggage space and link each terminal to Plaça de Catalunya, Plaça Espanya, Gran Via-Urgell and Plaça Universitat, all of which have metro stations. **Sagalés** (w sagalesairportline.com) provides direct buses from the airport to major Costa Brava resorts Girona and Figueres.

By taxi These take approximately 30 minutes from T1 and 25 minutes into the city centre from T2. Fares to the city centre are approximately €30–40.

Airport car hire There are several car hire companies at the airport, including Avis (w avis.es), Enterprise (w enterprise.es), Europcar (w europcar.es), Hertz (w hertz.es) and Sixt (w sixt.es).

BY SEA Barcelona has ferry links to the Balearic Islands, Rome, Savona, Porto Torres (Sardinia), Genoa, Tangier and Nador. The port is by the World Trade Center, a 10-minute walk from the Rambla. The main ferry companies are Baleària (w balearia.com), Trasmed (w trasmed.com), GNV (w gnv.it) and Grimaldi Lines (w grimaldi-lines.com).

BY TRAIN All trains, whether AVE high-speed trains, regional or suburban arrive at the **Estació de Sants** [60 A5] (w renfe.com; metro: Sants), south of the centre. It is large and can be confusing; if you can buy tickets online, do so. Many trains also stop at the more central Passeig de Gràcia station. Sants has a left-luggage service, tourist information and car hire (Avis ✆902 11 02 93; Enterprise ✆934 91 01 89; Europcar ✆911 50 50 00). The enormous new La Sagrera station, which will be the main hub for high-speed services, has been plagued by delays but is due to open in 2026.

DISCOUNT AND TRAVEL CARDS

Barcelona is an expensive city but you could save money if you're planning to pack in a lot of sights with the **Barcelona Card** (w barcelonacard. org), good for three, four or five consecutive days (not by hours, so best to activate it in the morning), offering free public transport on the TMB's metro, bus and trams, train to Barcelona's airport and RENFE trains Zone 1. It includes free or discounted entry and the chance to skip the queue at 70 museums, attractions, tours, gardens and restaurants. Prices start at €55 for three days for an adult, and €32 for ages 4–12. You can order it online and bring the voucher to the tourist offices at the airport or train station, or pick it up at the tourist offices in the airport, at Sants station or on the Plaça de Catalunya.

Another option is the **Hola Barcelona** transport card (w holabarcelona. com), good between two (€17.50) and five (€40.80) consecutive days of travel including to and from the airport (there's a 10% discount if you buy online). TMB, via **T-mobilitat** (w t-mobilitat.atm.cat) offers the **T-Casual** card for €12.15, good for ten journeys in Zone 1; and the **T-Usual** for €21.35, valid for a month's travel for single users. You will need to pay a small supplement (€0.50) for the ticket when first purchased, as it is rechargeable. Passes can be purchased at any ticket machine, at tobacco shops (*estancs*), newspaper kiosks, in a ticket office (you will need your passport or ID number for the T-Usual) or through the TMB app. Single tickets do not allow for transfers (*transbord*).

3

BY COACH Nearly all coaches from abroad or around Catalunya call at the Barcelona Nord Bus Station (C/ d'Alí Bei 80; 🚇 Arc de Triomf; w barcelonanord.barcelona/en).

BY CAR Like many European cities, nearly all of Barcelona is a restricted low emission zone (ZBE) between 07.00 and 20.00 Mon–Fri. To find out more, and to register your car, visit w zbe.barcelona; daily permits are available. If you do drive into the city, the best thing to do is find a safe place to leave your vehicle for the duration. On-street parking is practically non-existent: for visitors, the only on-street option is the 'blue zones' (*zona blava*), which have blue street markings (resident-only on-street marking is green) and are only available for 1- or 2-hour slots (€2.50–3.50/hr, free for electric vehicles). If your accommodation doesn't have parking (few do), book a spot in a garage; see w aparcamentsbsm.cat/en (for official municipally run car parks) or w car-parking.eu/spain/Barcelona.

GETTING AROUND

BY TRAIN RENFE's Rodalíes network (R lines; w renfe.com/es/en/suburban/rodalies-catalunya) meet up in Plaça de Catalunya and Sants and are useful for crossing the city, for example, from Sants to Estació de França in the Born neighbourhood. Destinations in Zone 1 are included in the Barcelona Card (page 69), along with buses and metro.

The FGC lines (w fgc.cat), which depart from the Plaça Espanya station, are useful for reaching the Parc de Collserola and destinations beyond the city, but otherwise not useful for travelling around the city.

BY METRO, TRAM AND BUS Barcelona's metro lines, trams and buses are part of an integrated system run by TMB (w tmb.cat), and tickets and passes are valid on all of them. The most useful and cost-effective pass for visitors is the **T-Casual** or, for longer stays, the **T-Usual** – for details, see page 69. Single tickets are €2.55: buy via the app, or at ticket machines for the metro or tram, or use a contactless debit card on buses (no cash accepted). On buses and trams, validate tickets or passes at the clearly marked machines. Note that you cannot transfer (*transbord*) between lines or transport types with a single ticket. There are ten metro lines, which are fast and efficient. The city also has an extensive bus network, with maps showing routes at most bus stops. There are 22 night bus (NitBus) routes, most of which depart from the Plaça Catalunya in the city centre. Trams primarily serve outer districts and suburbs.

BY BIKE OR SCOOTER The city's Bicing bike-sharing service (w bicing.barcelona) is also run by TMB, but it is aimed at city residents, with passes valid for a year. There are lots of private rental companies, with bikes available by the hour or day, including:

Bicycle hire
Barcelona Rent a Bike C/ Tallers 45; 📞 933 17 19 70; w barcelonarentabike.com
Bike Rental Barcelona C/ Montserrat 8; 📞 666 05 76 55; w bikerentalbarcelona.com
Orange Fox C/ Sant Pere Més Alt 57; 📞 605 201 773; w orangefox.tours

Scooter hire
Cooltra C/ Consell de Cent 181; 📞 664 41 53 44; w cooltra.com
Vesping Ptge Simó 24; 📞 936 67 78 77; w vesping.com

BY TAXI Official city taxis are black and yellow and can be flagged down or found at taxi stands. Radio taxis can be summoned at ☎933 03 30 33, 932 25 00 00 or 933 22 22 22. Fares are higher at night, at weekends and on public holidays. Uber and Cabify also function in Barcelona.

ORIENTATION

Barcelona is situated on a plain gently descending to the sea, wrapped in an amphitheatre of hills and mountains. At the south end of the harbour rises its oldest landmark, the smooth-humped mountain of **Montjuïc**, once key to the city's defence and now its pleasure dome and **Olympic 'ring'**; on the landward side, the highest peak in the Serra de Collserola is **Tibidabo**, with its amusements and priceless views. Old Catalans may have bewailed their eclipse during the days of Imperial Spain, but moderns may be thankful that the lack of prosperity has left intact the historic centre or **Barri Gòtic**, the greatest concentration of medieval architecture in Europe. This is bounded on the southwest by the **Rambla**, Barcelona's showcase promenade; south of the Rambla and north of Avingunda del Paral·lel, **El Raval** remains the most piquant, with a few last remnants of the once notorious red-light district, the Barri Xinès.

The part of the map that looks as if it were stamped by a giant waffle iron is the **Eixample**, the 19th-century extension that quadrupled the size of Barcelona, and coincided with the careers of the Modernista architects, whose colourful buildings brighten its monotonous chamfered blocks. West of the Eixample the city has digested once independent towns like **Gràcia** and **Sarrià** and spread as far up the hills as gravity permits. With the 1992 Olympics, Barcelona turned its attention to its long-neglected seafront: just south of **Barceloneta**, a planned popular neighbourhood from the 18th century, the **Port Vell** (old port), has been transformed into an urban playground, while to the north of Barceloneta the **Vila Olímpica**, founded to house Olympic athletes, has become a swanky address, while neighbouring **Poblenou** has become the heart of the city's design and innovation district.

TOURIST INFORMATION AND TOUR OPERATORS

Barcelona's hyperactive **tourist office** (☎ 932 85 38 34; w barcelonaturisme.com; ⏰ 08.30–20.30 daily) is located on Plaça Catalunya, in a large, underground office opposite the El Corte Inglés department store. It sells tickets, discount cards, tours, etc, as well as providing information on all the many sights and attractions. There are other offices in both airport terminals, Sants station, the coach station, at the Sagrada Família and other main sites. They also run a call centre (☎ 932 85 38 32; ⏰ 08.00–20.00 daily).

LOCAL TOUR OPERATORS

✳ **Barcelona Design Tours** ☎ 696 56 56 62; w barcelonadesigntours.com. Offers insider-led architecture, design & shopping tours, including custom itineraries & experiences like 'Consuming Architecture' that blend food & design.

Devour Food Tours ☎ 931 84 02 97; w devourtours.com. Food & history tours with a focus on local markets, family-run eateries & Catalan culinary traditions.

Spanish Civil War Tours ☎ 661 05 09 54; w thespanishcivilwar.com. Offers in-depth & award-winning walking tours exploring Barcelona's role in the Spanish Civil War, including a George Orwell-themed tour.

Green Barcelona w barcelonawildlife.com (online only). Offers nature-focused walking tours led by a biologist, exploring urban wildlife & green spaces in Barcelona.

3

WHERE TO STAY

There are good places to stay all over the city, but wherever you stay, it's essential to book in advance.

THE RAMBLA AND THE BARRI GÒTIC

1898 [85 A2] La Rambla 109; ☎935 52 95 52; w hotel1898.com. The former Philippines Tobacco Company is now a designer hotel with lovingly preserved details, a rooftop oasis & a plush spa, right in the middle of the Rambla. €€€€

Kimpton Vividora [85 A1] C/ del Duc 15; ☎936 42 54 00; w kimptonvividorahotel.com. A glamorous hotel with chic rooms in Mediterranean shades of sea blue & ochre, which does yoga classes on its roof terrace (with plunge pool). Super-central & handy for all the main sights in the old centre. €€€€

Neri [85 E2] C/ Sant Sever 5; ☎933 04 06 55; w hotelneri.com. One of the loveliest hotels in the Gothic quarter, with just 22 rooms in a beautifully restored 18th-century palace, & a terrace on the time-capsule square of Plaça Sant Felip Neri (page 90). It has stylish contemporary décor & an enchanting roof terrace. €€€€

Soho House [85 C4] Pl del Duc de Medinaceli 4; ☎932 20 46 00; w sohohouse.com/en-us/houses/soho-house-barcelona. Sumptuous celebrity retreat in a fashionably remodelled 18th-century mansion, with its own cinema, a Cowshed spa & chic rooftop bar & plunge pool with views over the port. €€€€

Lamaro [85 F1]Av de la Catedral 7; ☎933 01 14 04; w lamarohotel.com. A handsomely revamped hotel right in the heart of the Barri Gòtic, with elegant, classic rooms in a large historic building. The rooftop tapas bar has fine views of the cathedral opposite. €€€

Hostal Jardí [85 B2]Pl de Sant Josep Oriol 1; ☎933 01 59 00; w eljardi.com. Very popular budget hotel with clean, plain, AC rooms at a slightly inflated price on one of the loveliest squares in the Barri Gòtic. €€

EL RAVAL

Ciutat Vella [60 D4] C/ Tallers 66; ☎934 81 37 99; w hotelciutatvella.com. Just a 5-min stroll from the Rambla, this friendly little budget option offers simple, modern rooms – some with their own private terrace or balcony – & has a pocket-sized roof terrace with sun beds & a hot tub. €€

Gaudí [85 B3] C/ Nou de la Rambla 12; ☎933 17 90 32; w hotelgaudi.es. The renovated rooms are modern rather than Modernista, but there are views of the great roof of the Palau Güell & a plunge pool & sun deck on the roof. €€

Mesón Castilla [60 D4] C/ de Valldonzelia 5; ☎933 18 21 82; w mesoncastilla.atiramhotels.com. This is tucked down a quiet side street near the Museu d'Art Contemporani. It has a delightful interior garden, & spacious bedrooms furnished with antiques. €

LA RIBERA

Borneta [85 D1] Pg de Picasso 26–30; ☎935 47 86 00; w miirohotels.com/hotelborneta. The cool new kid on the block, this is a gorgeous mid-sized boutique hotel right opposite the Parc de la Ciutadella, with one of the city's hottest restaurants, Volta, on the ground floor. €€€€

H10 Cubik [85 B1] Via Laietana 69; ☎933 20 22 00; w h10hotels.com/en/barcelona-hotels/h10-cubik. This medium-sized, central hotel boasts a stylish, retro-inspired interior by Spanish design maven Lázaro Rosa-Violán & a rooftop plunge pool & bar – just a 2-min walk from the Plaça Catalunya. €€€

chic&basic Born Boutique [85 D1] C/ Princesa 50; ☎932 95 46 52; w chicandbasic.com/en/hotel-born-barcelona. Bright white ultra-modern hotel in a mansion with high ceilings in the ultra-hip Born neighbourhood. It's part of a smallish chain, with 5 hotels & 2 hostels across the city, all featuring their trademark contemporary style. €€€

✳ **chic&basic Habana Hoose** [85 C2] C/ de l'Argenteria 37; ☎935 95 65 05; w chicandbasic.com/en/hotel-habana-hoose-barcelona. Fun, quirky décor which combines Cuban tropicana with Scottish tartan, a gorgeous courtyard restaurant filled with greenery, & all the chic boutiques & bars of the Born on the doorstep. €€€

Ciutat de Barcelona [85 D1] C/ Princesa 33–35; ☎932 69 74 75; w ciutatbarcelona.com. A great-value, mid-sized option with immaculate rooms & a colourful rooftop tapas bar & plunge pool. It's right in the heart of the fashionable Born neighbourhood, a short stroll from the Parc de la Ciutadella. €€

Motel One Barcelona [61 F3] Ciutadella Pg de Pujades 11–13; ☎ 936 26 19 00; w motel-one. com/en/hotels/barcelona/hotel-barcelona-ciutadella. A large, modern hotel with simple, pristine rooms & a huge, sunny roof terrace offering views of the lovely Parc de la Ciutadella across the street. €€

SEASIDE BARCELONA

Hotel Arts [61 H4] C/ Marina 19–21; ☎ 932 21 10 00; w ritzcarlton.com. Occupies one of the 2 Olympic towers of the Port Olímpic & in a class of its own, with 44 floors of spectacular rooms, suites & penthouses offering stunning views of the sea & city & with a fantastic seaside pool. Superb dining & spa. €€€€€

Hotel 54 [61 G5] Pg Joan de Borbó 54; ☎ 932 25 00 54; w hotel54 barceloneta.es. One of few affordable places to stay by the sea, with sunny blue-&-white rooms & panoramic views from the roof terrace. €€€

THE EIXAMPLE

Hotel Palace [108 D3] Gran Via de les Corts Catalanes 668; ☎ 935 10 11 30; w hotelpalacebarcelona.com. Formerly known as the Ritz, this remains Barcelona's classic grand hotel, as it has been since 1919; outrageously opulent, from the liveried & top-hatted staff at the door to the Mayan-themed spa. Service is extraordinary – although you may not be able to get a horse sent up, as Dalí once did. €€€€€

Mandarin Oriental [108 C3] Pg de Gràcia 38–40; ☎ 931 51 88 88; w mandarinoriental.com/en/barcelona/passeig-de-gracia. Consistently topping rankings of the world's best hotels, the Mandarin Oriental exudes 5-star luxury from its golden catwalk entrance to its Michelin-starred restaurant, superlative spa & ultra-luxurious rooms & suites. €€€€€

Claris [108 B2] C/ Pau Claris 150; ☎ 934 87 62 62; w derbyhotels.com. Gives luxury a twist, blending refined modern design with a connoisseur's collection of Egyptian & Roman art. The superb spa is one of the city's best. €€€€

Sir Victor [108 A1] C/ Rosselló 265; ☎ 934 54 00 00; w sirhotels.com/es/victor. A sleek über-cool hotel in a striking contemporary building that has become a fave of the fashion pack. The

rooftop plunge pool & tapas bar offer views of La Pedrera's chimneys, & its steakhouse & cocktail bar, the Mr Porter, is one of the city's hottest addresses. €€€€

Casa Bonay [61 F2] Gran Via de les Corts Catalanes 700; ☎ 935 45 80 70; w casabonay. com. This hipster-favourite boutique hotel is a real charmer, with a laid-back vibe, a spacious, low-lit café/bar full of velvet sofas on the ground floor & a delightful rooftop oasis with floral sofas & armchairs where you can soak up the sun. €€€

Gran Via [108 D4] Gran Via de les Corts Catalanes 642; ☎ 933 18 19 00; w hotelgranvia. com. This handsomely converted *palau* preserves a touch of 19th-century grace, from the glorious courtyard garden to the sweeping original staircase. €€€

Jazz [108 D4] C/ Pelai 3; ☎ 935 52 96 96; w hoteljazz.com. Just off the Plaça de Catalunya, this mid-sized modern hotel offers everything you need – immaculate rooms, central location, friendly staff & a small rooftop pool – at a great price. €€€

✴ **Margot House** [108 B3] Pg de Gràcia 47; ☎ 932 72 00 76; w margothouse.es. Named for a character in a Wes Anderson film, this is a quirky little boutique hotel with just 9 rooms right opposite the Casa Batlló. Make yourself at home in the sitting room, with an honesty bar & complimentary tea & cakes. €€€

Paseo de Gràcia [108 A2] Pg de Gràcia 102; ☎ 932 15 06 03; w hotelpaseodegracia.es. Just 1 block from Gaudí's La Pedrera & tucked among the chi-chi designer boutiques on the swanky Passeig de Gràcia, this is a rare affordable option in this upmarket neighbourhood. It has simple, inviting rooms, some with private balconies. €€€

Hostal Oliva [108 C4] Pg de Gràcia 32; ☎ 934 88 01 62; w hostaloliva.com. A friendly, long-running guesthouse with 16 traditionally decorated, cosy rooms in a classic Eixample townhouse, just 1 block from the Casa Batlló. Great value & fantastically located for sightseeing & shopping. €€

Praktik Èssens [108 C4] Pg de Gràcia 24; ☎ 933 42 87 30; w hotelpraktikessens.com. There is a handful of Praktik hotels in central Barcelona, each with a different theme, from the Praktik Garden to the Praktik Bakery, all offering chic design at an affordable price. This alluring small hotel is their newest offering, dedicated to perfume. €€

3

OUTSIDE THE CENTRE

Hotel Casa Fuster [60 C2] Pg de Gràcia 132; 932 55 30 00; w hotelcasafuster.com. A grand, landmark Modernista building by Domènech i Montaner, meticulously restored to become one of the city's most opulent hotels, complete with a panoramic roof terrace with pool. It's just steps from the fancy shops of the Passeig de Gràcia. €€€€€

Pol & Grace [60 B1] C/ Guillem Tell 49; 934 15 40 00; w polgracehotel.es. Large, stylish & friendly option in the elegant Sarrià neighbourhood, just a short walk from the boutiques & bars of Gràcia & 10mins by public transport to the city centre. Spacious, great-value rooms. €€

Central House Hostel [60 C2] C/ Còrsega 32; 932 17 19 44; w thecentralhousehostels.com. This popular hostel offers a choice of AC dorms or private rooms, a lovely garden courtyard & relaxed café-bar in the lively & authentic Gràcia neighbourhood, only a 10min walk from La Pedrera. €

✖ WHERE TO EAT AND DRINK

From dazzling exponents of molecular gastronomy to hole-in-the-wall bars serving fried sardines, Barcelona is the perfect destination for gourmets and foodies of every stripe. Catalan food is renowned all over the world, and you'll find a wonderful range of eateries that showcase the delicious regional produce.

LA RAMBLA AND BARRI GÒTIC
Restaurants

Passadís d'en Pep [85 D2] Pla del Palau 2; 933 10 10 21; w passadis.com; ⏰ 20.00–23.30 Mon, 13.30–23.30 Tue–Sat. Gourmet heaven, tucked down a tiny passage & hard to spot. There are no menus, but the freshest seasonal specialities (mainly seafood), accompanied by fine wines, are served. Expect to pay around €100 per head. €€€€€

7 Portes [85 D2] Pg d'Isabel II 14; 933 19 30 33; w 7portes.com; ⏰ 13.00–midnight daily. One of the city's most famous restaurants, founded in 1836, & still popular, serving delicious rice & seafood. €€€€

Ca l'Agut [85 C3] C/ d'En Gignàs 16; 933 15 17 09; 📷 restaurantcalagut; ⏰ 13.00–15.45 & 20.00–22.30 Tue–Sat, 13.00–16.00 Sun. After a brief hiatus in which its future hung in the balance, this legendary Catalan restaurant with a century of history has reopened & is better than ever. Top-notch regional cuisine with a creative touch. €€€

Cuines de Santa Caterina [85 C1] Avda Francesc Cambó 29; 932 68 99 18; w grupotragaluz.com/restaurantes/cuines-santa-caterina; ⏰ 10.00–midnight daily. Bright, loft-style restaurant in the market offering a fresh & interesting mix of traditional Mediterranean & world cuisine. €€€

Els Quatre Gats [85 E2] C/ Montsió 3; 933 02 41 40; w 4gats.com; ⏰ 11.00–23.00 Tue–Sat, 11.00–16.00 Sun. Once a famous Modernista taverna, now a smart but touristy Catalan restaurant. Good-value lunch menu. €€€

Cafè de l'Acadèmia [85 G2] C/ Lledó 1; 933 19 82 53; w gruposantelmo.com/restaurant/el-cafe-de-lacademia; ⏰ noon–23.30 daily. Take in the enchanting Plaça Sant Just from the candlelit terrace. Tapas, dishes to share & Catalan classics. €€

Tapas bars and cafés

Cafè de l'Òpera [85 B3] La Rambla 74; 933 17 75 85; w cafeoperabcn.com; ⏰ 08.30–02.30 daily. An institution & the classiest place on the Rambla, this café was founded in 1929, opposite the Liceu. With a terrace, but pricey. €€€

La Pineda [85 B2] C/ del Pi 16; 933 02 43 93; w xarcuterialapineda.com; ⏰ 09.00–16.00 Mon, 09.00–21.00 Wed–Sat, 11.00–16.00 Sun. A delightful, old-fashioned delicatessen hung with hams, with just a couple of tables. €€

Bodega La Plata [85 D3] C/ Mercè 28; 611 647 688; w barlaplata.com; ⏰ 11.00–15.00 & 18.00–23.00 Mon–Sat. A tiny old-fashioned bar, serving just a few dishes, including their famed sardines, all washed down with wine from the barrel. €

LA RIBERA

Cal Pep [85 D2] Pl de les Olles; 933 10 79 61; w calpep.com; ⏰ 13.00–15.30 & 19.30–23.30

Tue–Sat. A much-loved local stalwart in La Ribera; excellent tapas, & a charismatic owner. €€€

✳ **The Green Spot** [85 D2] C/ de la Reina Cristina 12; ☎ 93 802 55 65; w encompaniadelobos.com/the-green-spot; ⏰ 13.00–17.00 & 19.30–01.00 daily. Widely regarded as one of the best veggie restaurants in town, with an airy, super-stylish dining room. €€€

EL RAVAL

Ca l'Isidre [60 D5] C/ Flors 12; ☎ 934 41 11 39; w calisidre.com; ⏰ 13.00–15.00 & 20.00–22.00 Tue–Sat. Long a favourite of artists & royals, this serves elaborate, top-notch Catalan cuisine in an elegant, classic dining room. €€€€

Sésamo [60 D5] C/ Sant Antoni Abat; ☎ 934 41 64 11; ◙ sesamobcn; ⏰ 19.00–midnight daily. A hip little spot that serves inspired veggie dishes prepared with fresh, locally grown produce. €€

Biocenter [60 D4] C/ Pintor Fortuny 24; ☎ 933 01 45 83; w restaurantebiocenter.es; ⏰ 13.00–23.00 Mon–Sat, 13.00–16.00 Sun. A vegetarian restaurant (& shop) that's been going since 1980. Salads, veggie versions of Catalan classics, soups, veggie burgers & more. €

Elisabets [85 A2] C/ Elisabets 2; ☎ 933 17 58 26; w elisabets1962.com; ⏰ 12.30–17.30 Mon–Sat. Nothing much has changed here since it opened in 1962, & it remains as popular as ever for its hearty Catalan dishes & great-value set menu. €

Granja M. Viader [85 A2] C/ Xuclà 4–6; ☎ 93 38 34 86; w granjaviader.cat; ⏰ 17.00–20.30 Mon, 09.00–13.30 & 17.00–20.30 Tue–Sat. A lovely old-fashioned *granja* (milk bar), where you can enjoy hot chocolate (the owner invented the Cacaolat bottled chocolate milk back in the 1930s) & other local treats. €

SEASIDE BARCELONA
Restaurants

Can Majó [61 G5] C/ Emília Llorca Martín 23; ☎ 932 21 54 55; ◙ canmajo; ⏰ 13.00–16.30 Tue & Sun, 13.00–22.30 Wed–Sat. Traditional place right on the beach, serving divine seafood. Try the *suquet* (fish stew with monkfish, hake & mussels). €€€

Can Solé [61 G5] C/ Sant Carles 4; ☎ 932 21 50 12; w restaurantcansole.com; ⏰ 13.00–16.00 & 20.00–23.00 Tue–Sat, 13.00–16.00 Sun. Established in 1903, with photos of famous guests

all over the walls, this serves excellent paella & seafood dishes. €€€

Tapas bars and cafés

Bar Jai Ca [61 G5] C/ Ginebra 7–9; ☎ 933 19 50 02; w barjaica.com; ⏰ 08.00–23.00 Tue–Fri, 09.00–23.00 Sat–Mon. Friendly neighbourhood tapas bar with a small but much-coveted pavement terrace. €

Cova Fumada [61 G5] C/ Baluard 56; ☎ 932 21 40 61; w la-cova-fumada.res-menu.com; ⏰ 09.00–15.00 Tue–Fri, 09.00–14.30 Sat. This offers a glimpse of old Barceloneta, right down to the sawdust on the floor. €

Vaso de Oro [61 G5] C/ Balboa 6; ☎ 933 19 30 98; ⏰ noon–midnight daily. A narrow atmospheric bar that can get packed but worth it for the tasty tapas – from *patatas bravas* to more elaborate shellfish creations. €

THE EIXAMPLE
Restaurants

Alkimia [60 D4] Rda de Sant Antoni 41 (inside the Moritz brewery); ☎ 932 07 61 15; w alkimia.cat; ⏰ 13.00–15.30 & 20.00–22.00 Mon–Thu, 13.00–15.30 Fri. Exquisite, experimental cuisine by Michelin-starred chef Jordi Vilà in a chic modern setting. €€€€€

Besta [60 C3] C/ Aribau 106; ☎ 930 19 82 94; w bestabarcelona.com; ⏰ 19.00–22.30 Tue–Wed, 13.00–15.30 & 19.00–22.30 Thu–Sun. Superbly inventive Spanish cuisine from a pair of remarkable young chefs, who combine unusual flavours in ways that will dazzle your palate. Choose from 2 set menus: 9 courses €72, 12 courses €95. €€€€€

Cinc Sentits [60 C5] C/ Entença 60; ☎ 933 23 94 90; w cincsentits.com; ⏰ 19.00–22.00 Tue–Fri, 13.30–14.30 & 20.30–21.30 Sat. With 2 Michelin stars, chef Jordi Artal artfully prepares contemporary cuisine to seduce the '5 senses' in a sleek, pared-down dining space. €€€€€

Disfrutar [60 C3] C/ Villarroel 163; ☎ 933 48 68 96; w disfrutarbarcelona.com; ⏰ 13.00–14.30 & 20.00–21.30. 3 former chefs who trained at Ferran Adrià's legendary El Bulli restaurant are behind Disfrutar; for sheer creativity, there's nowhere like it. €€€€€

L'Olivé [108 A4] C/ Balmes 47; ☎ 934 52 19 90; w restaurantlolive.com; ⏰ 13.00–16.00 & 20.00–23.30 daily. A deservedly popular restaurant serving traditional Catalan cuisine with a modern twist. €€€

La Bodegueta [108 A2] Rambla de Catalunya 98; \ 932 15 48 94; w labodeguetarambla.com; ⊕ 09.00–23.00 daily. Join the rest of Barcelona down in this cellar for a well-priced, home-cooked meal or some tapas. €

Tapas bars and cafés

Casa Alfonso [61 E3] C/ Roger de Llúria 6; \ 933 01 97 83; w casaalfonso.com; ⊕ 08.00–midnight Mon–Fri, noon–midnight Sat. A charmingly old-fashioned tapas bar with hanging hams. €€€

Cervecería Catalana [108 A3] 4 C/ Mallorca 236; \ 932 16 03 68; ◻ cerveceria_catalana; ⊕ 08.30–01.00 Mon–Fri, 09.00–01.00 Sat–Sun. A dazzling array of tapas line the curved bar. Expect queues. €€

PLAÇA ESPANYA AND MONTJUÏC

Terraza Martínez [61 E7] Ctra de Miramar 38; \ 931 06 60 52; w martinezbarcelona.com; ⊕ 13.00–midnight Mon–Thu & Sun, 13.00–01.00 Fri & Sat. A fashionable haunt high on Montjuïc, where you can enjoy cocktails, paella & a dazzling view of the city twinkling at your feet. €€€€

✳ **Quimet i Quimet** [60 D6] C/ Poeta Cabanyes 25; \ 934 42 31 42; w quimetiquimet.com; ⊕ noon–16.00 & 18.30–22.00 Tue–Sat. With its

bottle-lined shelves & standing room only, this is the place to come for *montaditos* – delicate canapés with a host of delicious toppings. €€

OUTSIDE THE CENTRE
Restaurants

Botafumeiro [60 C2] C/ Gran de Gràcia 81; \ 932 18 42 30; w botafumeiro.es; ⊕ noon–01.00 daily. A prestigious & atmospheric Galician seafood restaurant, with superb old-school waiters in long white aprons. €€€€

Aranda's Grill [60 B1] Avda Tibidabo 31; \ 934 17 01 15; w asadordearanda.net; ⊕ 13.00–midnight Tue–Sun, 13.00–16.00 Mon. Traditional Castilian cuisine, including their signature roast lamb & suckling pig, in a beautiful Modernista setting. €€€

Tapas bars and cafés

Bar Tomás [60 A2] C/ Major de Sarrià 49; \ 932 03 10 77; w eltomasdesarria.com; ⊕ 12.30–16.00 & 18.30–22.00 Mon–Sat. Come to this unassuming bar to find out for yourself whether their *patatas bravas* really are the best in town, as widely claimed. €

La Nena [60 C1] C/ Ramon y Cajal 36; \ 932 85 14 76; ◻ granjalanena; ⊕ 08.00–21.00 daily. A popular, rustically decorated café for homemade cakes, quiches & more. It's a hit with families, thanks to its child-sized seats & piles of toys & games. €

ENTERTAINMENT AND NIGHTLIFE

Barcelona has always been a great city after dark. Unless you speak Spanish or Catalan and can take in the city's very lively theatre scene or a film (although some cinemas regularly show movies in their original language; page 52), your night out will probably involve music. Check out listings in English on **Barcelona Metropolitan** (w barcelona-metropolitan.com), the city's **BCN Guide** (w guia. barcelona.cat) and **We Barcelona** (w webarcelona.net). Pick up same-day, half-price theatre tickets at the Palau de la Virreina (page 83).

The Catalan national dance, the community-enhancing sardana (page 27) is the polar opposite to the soulful, exhilarating transport of flamenco. But a million-plus residents of Andalucian descent living in Barcelona have made this city a flamenco hotspot (even as Catalan locals look down their noses at this imported art form). Many of the flamenco clubs put on two or even three performances (*tablaos*) of pounding guitars, dancing and singing nightly, either with a drink or with dinner (around €60). All have online bookings.

CINEMAS

Cinemas Girona [60 D2] C/ Girona 175; w cinemesgirona.cat. Shows a mix of indie & art-

house films, along with major releases – all in VO (Versió Original).

FESTIVALS AND EVENTS

Barcelona has a packed calendar of events, starting on 5 January with **The Three Kings Parade** (w barcelona.cat) when The Magi arrive by sea and join a magical 3-hour-long parade through the streets. **Guitar BCN** (w guitarbcn. com) features guitar concerts of all kinds in various venues (Feb–Sep) while the patron saint of broad beans, **Sant Medir** (w santmedir.org), gets a big party in Gràcia with a parade of horse-drawn floats, thousands of sweets tossed to kids and **castellers** (human towers) in early March.

St Jordi, Barcelona's patron saint, sees lovers exchange books and roses on 23 April, and at the end of the month into early May the city's large Andalusian population host a **Feria de Abril** with flamenco, food and fun fair at the Fòrum. **Corpus Christi** is celebrated with L'Ou com Balla, the ritual of the 'dancing egg', in fountains all around the Barri Gòtic, including the cathedral cloister, around the same early June dates of **Primavera Sound** (w primaverasound. com), a hugely popular festival of contemporary music. This is followed by the even bigger three-day **Sónar** (w sonar.es) music, creative and technology fun fest in mid-June. **ALMA Barcelona** (w almafestival.info) sees some of the world's biggest names in popular music appear in the Poble Espanyol in June and July. The **Festival Grec** (w barcelona.cat/grec/en), the city's biggest cultural festival, runs from late June to early August featuring a spectacular line-up of Catalan and international performers. In mid-August is the **Festa Major de Gràcia**, an exuberant neighbourhood festival, with awards for the best street decorations; 11 September is the big marches for Catalan National Day **Diada Català**. In late September, the fantastic **Festa de La Mercè** says farewell to summer in four days around **24 September**, with more than 600 events, from outdoor concerts to *castellers*, and an alternative music festival **BAM**, all culminating in a frenzied *correfoc*. Next up is the **Jazz Festival** (w jazz.barcelona), held from October to December and in December the **Fira de Santa Llúcia**, the Christmas market in front of the cathedral, with a huge selection of *caganers* (page 17).

Filmoteca de Catalunya [85 A4] Pl Salvador Seguí 1; \935 67 10 70; w filmoteca.cat. Catalan film institute, showing art & cult films, always in VO.
Sala Montjuïc [60 D7] Castell de Montjuïc; w salamontjuic.org. Outdoor films in the former castle moat, with live music before the screening; book a deckchair & bring a picnic. One of the nicest ways to beat the summer heat.

CLUBS
Jamboree [85 B3] Pl Reial 17; \933 04 12 10; w jamboreejazz.com; ⏲ 16.00–midnight (jazz), midnight–05.00 (club) daily. A jazz club that converts into a hugely popular nightclub after the concerts are over.
Luz de Gaz [60 B3] C/ Muntaner 246; w luzdegas.com; ⏲ midnight–06.00 Thu–Sat. Rococo décor, jazz, rock, soul concerts & nightclub.

Moog [85 B4] C/ de l'Arc del Teatre 3; \933 19 17 89; w moogbarcelona.com; midnight–05.00 daily. Smallish, long-running club for tech & electronic music. Gets jam-packed around 02.00.
Opium [61 H4] Pg Marítim 34; \655 57 69 98; w opiumbarcelona.com; ⏲ noon–midnight (restaurant), midnight–05.00 (club) daily. Fancy beachfront restaurant & nightclub, with strict dress code & international DJs.
Razzmatazz [61 G2] C/ de Pamplona 88; w salarazzmatazz.com; ⏲ 00.30–05.30 Thu–Fri, 01.00–06.00 Sat–Sun. 5 rooms in a Poble nou warehouse with a massive variety of music in one of the biggest clubs in Spain.
Sala Apolo [61 E6] C/ Nou de la Rambla107; \934 41 40 01; w sala-apolo.com. Concerts & DJs by the Paral·lel.

3

FLAMENCO

Flamenco Palau Dalmases [85 D2] C/ Montcada 20; 660 76 98 65; w flamencopalaudalmases.com; ⏲ see website for show times. Shows in a beautiful Gothic-Baroque palace.

Grand Gala Flamenco 933 01 06 60; w grangalaflamenco.com; ⏲ see website for show times. They present *tablaos* at the Palau de Música Catalana (page 102) & at the Teatro Poliorama at La Rambla 115.

Los Tarantos [85 B3] Pl Reial 17; 933 04 12 10; w tarantosbarcelona.com. Founded in 1963, this is the oldest (& one of the least expensive) *tablaos* in the city; 4 half-hour shows nightly.

Tablao Cordobés [85 B3] La Rambla 35; 933 17 57 11; w tablaocordobes.es. Founded in 1970, one of the most prestigious in Barcelona.

Tablao de Carmen [60 B7] Poble Espanyol (page 118); 933 25 68 95; w tablaodecarmen. com. Young troupe named after famous dancer Carmen Amaya, who performed for King Alfonso XIII at the opening of the 1929 International Exhibition.

JAZZ

Casa Figari [60 C1] C/ Torrent de l'Olla 141; 930 04 99 75; w casafigari.com; ⏲ 20.00–02.00 Tue–Thu, 20.00–02.30 Fri–Sat. Funky neighbourhood bar with live jazz, great cocktails & DJ sessions.

Harlem Jazz Club [85 C3] C/ Comtessa de Sobradiel 8; 933 10 07 55; w harlemjazzclub. es; ⏲ 20.00–03.00 Tue, Thu–Sun. A classic, this unpretentious & long-running venue is one of the city's best for jazz, blues, soul & R&B.

Jamboree [85 B3] Pl Reial 17; 933 04 12 10; w jamboreejazz.com; ⏲ box office 17.00–23.00 daily; see website for concert/club times. An institution on Pl Reial since 1960, it's seen the neighbourhood go down & back up again. It becomes a nightclub after the concerts are over.

Jazz Club (Hotel Casa Fuster) [60 C2] Pg de Gràcia 132; 932 55 30 00; w hotelcasafuster. com/en/jazz-club. Live jazz in the Modernista Café Vienés every Thu from 21.00 to 23.00.

OPERA, CLASSICAL MUSIC AND DANCE

L'Auditori [61 F2] C/ Lepant 150; 932 47 93 00; w auditori.cat. Classical, jazz, pop & rock in a contemporary venue.

Liceu [85 B3] La Rambla 51–59; 934 85 99 00; w liceubarcelona.cat. Temple of opera, ballet & classic music (page 83).

Mercat de les Flors [60 C6] C/ Lleida 59; 932 56 26 00; w mercatflors.cat. The city's main venue for its flourishing contemporary dance scene.

Palau de la Música Catalana [61 E4] C/ Palau de la Música 4–6; 932 95 72 00; w palaumusica. cat. Inimitable Modernista (page 102) venue, this often features choral music by the prestigious **Orfeó Català,** as well as traditional, gospel, flamenco guitar & chamber music.

SHOPPING

Barcelona claims to have the highest ratio of shops to residents in Europe. The main central shopping areas are the Barri Gòtic and the Raval for trendy streetwear, vintage and secondhand clothes, interesting junk and antiques; and the centre of the Eixample (Rambla de Catalunya, Passeig de Gràcia and Avinguda Diagonal) for good-quality clothes and jewellery. Most of the popular chains – Zara, Mango, H&M, etc – can be found along the Carrer Portaferissa and the Avinguda del Portal de l'Àngel (in the Barri Gòtic) and the Passeig de Gràcia. The Eixample is best for slick interior-design shops. Serious shoppers hit Barcelona in January and July, when everything's on sale.

BOOKS

Hibernian Secondhand English Bookshop [60 C1] C/ Verdi 66; 932 17 47 96; w hibernianbooks.com; ⏲ 10.30–14.00 & 17.00–20.30 Mon–Sat. Barcelona's go-to for used English-language books, with

fiction, non-fiction, kids' books & more, all at budget-friendly prices.

Llibreria Altaïr [60 D4] Gran Via de les Corts Catalanes 616; 933 42 71 71; w altair.es; ⏲ 10.00–14.00 & 16.30–20.30 Mon–Sat. A huge bookshop on 2 floors dedicated to travel, from

TO MARKET, TO MARKET

Barcelona's fantastic municipal food markets – almost 40 of them – are not to be missed, with colourful stalls heaped with fresh fish, meat, fruit and vegetables. They're ideal for picking up gourmet goodies for picnics or gifts to bring home, and stallholders will vacuum pack local cheeses, ham, charcuterie and olives, among many other regional delicacies. And it's not just a feast for the senses: many markets put on all sorts of different activities, from cooking classes to kids shows.

While the Boqueria on La Rambla is easily the most famous, visit the markets in other neighbourhoods to avoid the tourist hordes. The gorgeously restored Sant Antoni market in the Eixample, the Santa Caterina market in the Born and the Mercat de la Llibertat in Gràcia are all excellent.

For more information, visit w ajuntament.barcelona.cat/mercats/en/markets/food-markets.

maps & guidebooks to inspiring travel literature in several languages.

Llibreria Finestres [108 B4] C/ de la Diputació 249; 933 84 08 09; w llibreriafinestres.com; ⏰ 10.00–21.00 Mon–Sat. Arguably the most beautiful bookshop in Barcelona, this has a wide selection of books in several languages, as well as a chic café & reading area with velvet sofas. At their equally stylish branch across the street (no. 250), they have art books, comics & graphic novels.

FASHION

Lullaby Vintage [60 D5] C/ de la Riera Baixa 22; 934 43 08 02; 🖼 lullaby_vintage_boutique; ⏰ 14.00–19.00 Tue, noon–20.00 Wed–Fri, noon–19.00 Sat. This street, along with nearby C/ Tallers, is the best for vintage finds. This colourful little boutique has a fabulous collection of dresses, bags, shoes & more from the 1920s to the early 2000s.

✳ **Picnic** [60 C1] C/ Verdi 17; 930 16 69 53; 🖼 picnicstorebcn; ⏰ 11.00–21.00 Tue–Fri, 11.00–14.30 & 17.00–21.00 Sat. The Gràcia neighbourhood is great for independent boutiques, particularly along C/ Verdi. Picnic has a carefully curated selection of fashion & accessories for men & women.

Sita Murt [108 A3] C/ Mallorca 242; 932 15 22 31; w sitamurt.com; ⏰ 10.30–20.30 Mon–Sat. Upmarket, beautiful fashion for women, with a creative twist.

Soruka [60 C1] C/ Astúries 50; 935 25 64 61; w soruka.com; ⏰ 10.30–15.00 & 16.00–21.00 Tue–Wed, 10.30–21.00 Sat, Mon & Thu, 10.30–15.30 & 16.00–20.00 Fri & Sun. Fun, colourful

bags, backpacks, wallets & footwear made from recycled leather, all designed in Barcelona. This is their outlet, with affordable prices.

FOOD AND DRINK

✳ **Casa Carot** [85 G2] C/ Daguería 16; 🖼 casacarot; ⏰ 11.30–14.00 & 17.00–20.30 Tue–Sat. Choose from a wonderfully pungent array of cheeses from independent producers around Catalunya. Also does cheese & wine tastings.

Casa Gispert [85 D2] C/ Sombrerers 23; 933 19 75 35; w casagispert.com; ⏰ 09.30–20.00 Tue–Sat. This beloved local institution has been roasting nuts, coffee & spices for over 170 years: worth a visit for the intoxicating aroma alone.

Entre Latas [60 D1] C/ Torrijos 16; 930 15 47 25; w entrelatas-bcn.com; ⏰ 11.00–14.00 & 18.00–21.00 Tue–Fri, 11.00–14.30 & 18.00–21.00 Sat. The Spanish prize *conservas* (gourmet tinned goods), & this shop has a fabulous range, all exquisitely packaged.

La Colmena [85 G2] Pl de l'Àngel 12; 933 15 13 56; w pastisserialacolmena.com; ⏰ 09.00–21.00 daily. Delicious sweets & cakes displayed in a charmingly preserved historic pastry shop that dates back to 1849.

Reserva Ibérica [108 B4] Rambla de Catalunya 61; 932 15 52 30; w reservaiberica.com; ⏰ 09.30–21.00 Mon–Fri, 10.00–21.00 Sat; ⏰ 11.30–20.00 Sun. A smart deli dedicated to the very finest acorn-fed Iberian ham, with tables where you can try their wares.

Vila Viniteca & La Teca [85 D2] C/ Agullers 7; 937 77 70 17; w vilaviniteca.es; ⏰ 08.30–

20.30 Mon–Sat. Vila Viniteca has long been one of the best places in town for Catalan & Spanish wines; just across the street at No. 9 is their deli, La Teca (✆ 93 310 19 56), selling delicious Catalan regional produce, plus a small bar & tasting area.

HANDICRAFTS AND DESIGN

B de Barcelona [61 E1] Avda Gaudí 28; ✆ 936 03 50 06; w bdebarcelona.cat; ⏱ 10.00–14.00 & 17.00–20.30 Mon–Sat. Colourful collection of Barcelona-themed keepsakes & gifts, from bags to notebooks, all by local designers.

Bon Vent [85 C2] C/ de l'Argenteria 41; ✆ 932 95 40 53; 📷 bonventbarcelona; ⏱ 10.00–20.30 Mon–Fri, 10.00–21.00 Sat. A treasure trove of lovely things from around the Mediterranean: ceramics, textiles, jewellery, straw baskets & more.

Doméstico Shop [60 C3] Avda Diagonal 419; ✆ 933 19 39 36; w domesticoshop.com; ⏱ 10.30–14.30 & 16.30–20.30 Mon–Sat. Contemporary design shop with decorative objects from Spanish & international designers.

La Manual Alpargatera [85 B3] C/ Avinyó 7; ✆ 933 01 01 72; w lamanual.com; ⏱ 10.00–

20.00 Mon–Sat. Traditional, handmade, Catalan rope-soled shoes (*espadrilles*) sold here since the 1940s.

Magatzems del Pilar [85 B2] C/ Boquería 43; ✆ 933 17 79 84; w adelpilar.com; ⏱ 11.00–19.00 Mon–Tue & Fri, noon–19.00 Wed–Thu, 10.00–14.00 Sat. Fans, mantillas, shawls & flamenco outfits in a historic shop from 1886.

Mister Andreu [85 E2] C/ de la Palla 9; ✆ 931 82 69 62; w misterandreu.com; ⏱ noon–20.00 Mon–Sat. Enchanting prints, postcards & more of Barcelona landmarks from the quirky imagination of Mister Andreu.

ONE-STOP SHOPPING

El Corte Inglés [61 E4] Pl de Catalunya 14; ✆ 932 81 50 13; w elcorteingles.es; ⏱ 09.30–21.30 Mon–Sat (Jun–Sep 09.30–22.00). A huge department store with a great supermarket & gourmet food shop.

Maremagnum [61 F6] Moll d'Espanya; ✆ 930 12 91 39; w maremagnum.klepierre.es; ⏱ shops 10.00–21.00 daily (see website for opening hours for eateries). Waterfront mall with everything from fashion chain shops to restaurants & tapas bars. Open every day of the year.

SPORTS AND ACTIVITIES

Barcelona is a fantastic city for sports and outdoor activities, and the balmy weather means you can enjoy them all year round. From watersports to cycling, yoga to skateboarding, there are facilities for pretty much anything you fancy. When it comes to spectator sports, football is king: legendary FC Barcelona plays at the newly remodelled Camp Nou; or you can catch their less famous rivals FCD Espanyol at their stadium just outside town.

For information on all the municipal sports facilities in the city, as well as special events such as the annual marathon, visit w ajuntament.barcelona.cat/esports.

FOOTBALL

FC Barcelona Camp Nou [60 A4] Avda Aristides Maillol; ✆ 934 96 36 00; w fcbarcelona. com. Try buying tickets online or through Ticketmaster to see one of the world's greatest football teams play in their newly remodelled & expanded stadium, the Camp Nou (page 128).

RCD Espanyol Avda Baix Llobregat 100, Cornellà de Llobregat; ✆ 932 92 77 00; w rcdespanyol.com. It's easier to get tickets to see Barcelona's other football team, which also plays in La Liga: buy online or purchase on the day.

HIKING, MOUNTAIN-BIKING AND RUNNING Head to the **Parc de Collserola** [60 A1] (page 127) in the hills behind Barcelona for the best hiking & mountain-biking routes within the city. The **Carretera de les Aigües** (take the funicular from the FGC stop, Peu del Funicula) is a panoramic path in Collserola that overlooks the entire city & is very popular for running & biking, but can be very busy at w/ends. The **seafront promenade** is also a favourite for running & rollerblading, with 5km of flat paths along the beach.

HORSERIDING

Escola Municipal d'Hípica La Foixarda Avda Montanyans 1; ☎ 935 97 06 63; w hipicalafoixarda. es; ⊕ office 09.00–14.00 & 16.00–19.00 Mon–Fri. The municipal riding school on Montjuïc offers pony rides & lessons for adults & children.

ICE SKATING

Pavelló Pista Gel Camp Nou C/ Aristides Maillol 12; ☎ 934 96 36 00; w fcbarcelona.com/ en/entradas/pista-de-hielo; ⊕ temporarily closed while the Camp Nou is being renovated. Check website for details. The skating rink in the FC Barcelona complex has 2 skating sessions a day & also offers classes.

SWIMMING POOLS

CEM Marítim Pg Marítim 33; ☎ 932 24 04 40 93; w claror.cat; ⊕ 07.00–23.00 Mon–Fri, 08.30–21.00 Sat, 09.00–16.00 Sun. Large sports complex near the beach, with indoor pool, plus a huge gym with sea views & a host of classes (aerobics, yoga, dance, etc).

Club Natació Atlètic Barceloneta Pl del Mar; ☎ 932 21 00 10; w cnab.cat; ⊕ 07.00–23.00 Mon–Sat, 08.00–20.00 Sun. Indoor & outdoor pools by the beach, plus a gym.

Piscina Municipal de Montjuïc Avda Miramar 31; ☎ 681 90 77 03; Jun–early Sep 11.00–19.00 Mon–Thu, 11.00–20.30 Fri–Sun. Constructed for the Olympic diving competitions, this outdoor pool has breathtaking views over the entire city but no other facilities. Open summer only.

Piscines Picornell Avda de l'Estadi 30–38; ☎ 934 23 40 41; w picornell.cat. Municipal pool & gym complex on Montjuïc, with indoor & outdoor pools.

TENNIS

Centre Municipal de Tenis Pg Vall d'Hebron 178–196; ☎ 934 27 65 00; ◙ cmtvallhebron; ⊕ 08.00–23.00 Mon–Fri, 08.00–20.00 Sat–Sun. Rent courts by the hour at the municipal tennis centre at Vall d'Hebron on the outskirts of the city. Rackets are available for rent.

WATERSPORTS

Base Nàutica Municipal Avda Litoral, Platja Mar Bella; ☎ 932 21 04 32; w basenautica.org; ⊕ 10.00–19.00 daily. Kayaks, windsurfs & paddle boards for rent, plus sailing courses, at this city-run sailing club.

Centre Municipal de Vela Moll de Gregal, Port Olímpic; ☎ 932 25 79 40; w velabarcelona.com; ⊕ 09.00–21.00. The municipal sailing club offers classes – catamaran, Laser dinghies, kayaking, SUP & windsurfing.

Escola Catalana de Surf C/ Rocafort 188 (office only); ☎ 937 10 64 30; w escolacatalanadesurf. com; ⊕ office 09.00–17.00 Mon–Fri. Surfing & SUP lessons & equipment hire.

Sea You Pg del Mare Nostrum 14; ☎ 661 67 37 02 (WhatsApp only); w seayoubarcelona.com; ⊕ see website. Classes & equipment hire for wing foil, surfing, surfskate, windsurfing, SUP yoga & more. They also run tours, including a sunrise SUP tour.

YOGA

Ocean Breath Avda del Litoral 86; ☎ 673 18 02 20; w oceanbreathbarcelona.com; ⊕ see website. Watch the sun rise as you practise yoga on the beach. Also runs workshops & retreats in breathwork, meditation & more.

YogaOne w yogaone.es. This company offers 15 centres across the city, with a choice of classes.

OTHER PRACTICALITIES

You'll find **banks and ATM terminals** all over the city, including at the airport and main train stations. The **main post office** [85 D3] (*correus* in Catalan, *correos* in Spanish; w correos.es; ⊕ 08.00–20.00 Mon–Sat) is at Plaça d'Antonio López, at the bottom of the Via Laietana.

The main public hospitals are **Hospital Clínic** [60 C3] (C/ Villarroel 170; ☎ 932 27 54 00; 🚇 Hospital Clínic), **Hospital Santa Creu i Sant Pau** [61 E1] (Avda Sant Antoni Maria Claret 167; ☎ 932 91 90 00; 🚇 Hospital de Sant Pau) and **Hospital del Mar** [61 G4] (Pg Marítim 25–29; ☎ 932 48 30 00; 🚇 Ciutadella-Vila Olímpica). There are **pharmacies** on every block, signed with an illuminated green or red cross: the pharmacy '*de guardia*' (open out of hours) will be posted at each of them. The **Farmàcia Clapés** [85 B3] (La Rambla 98) is open 24 hours a day, every day.

If you need **to report a crime**, you can go to any Guàrdia Urbana station (they are all listed on the city website w bcn.cat/guardiaurbana), but the most central is at La Rambla 43 [85 B3] (℡932 56 24 77; ⊕ 24hrs). However, you will need to go to the Mossos d'Esquadra station at C/ Nou de la Rambla 76–80 (℡933 06 23 00) to get a police report for your insurance.

WHAT TO SEE AND DO

LA RAMBLA AND AROUND It's the 'most beautiful street in the world', according to Lorca. It is also one of the busiest: day and night the Rambla is crowded with natives and visitors from every continent. Tacky souvenir shops line its length. Catalan Elvis impersonators, unicyclists and 'human statues' use it as a stage, although in 2022 the city embarked on an ambitious project to widen and 'detouristify' it and give it back to the locals, a project due to be completed in 2030.

Rambla means 'sand' in Arabic, and long ago this is what it was: a sandy gully of the river that drained the Collserola mountains, and eventually carried so many less pleasant effluents that it became known as the Cagallel, the turd-taker. In the 13th century, when Jaume I built the first set of medieval walls, they used the Cagallel as a moat. By 1366 the torrent was paved over, and, at the end of the 18th century, it was decided to make the Rambla a park lane. In 1859 the first of the plane trees was planted and thrived so well that, when something prospers, the Barcelonins say 'it grows like a tree in the Rambla'.

The Rambla is, in fact, five 'rambles', which all run together in one unbroken, tree-lined stretch between the port to the Plaça Catalunya.

La Rambla de Santa Mònica
This, the lowest rambla, was from the 15th to 18th century a major producer of artillery, most notably of a colossal cannon named 'Santa Eulàlia' cast in 1463, which blew up into smithereens when fired for the first time. The bleakly modern **Arts Santa Mònica** [85 B4] (℡935 67 11 10; w artssantamonica.gencat.cat; ⊕ 11.00–20.30 Tue–Sun; free) was created by Albert Viaplana and Helio Piñón from the cloisters of the 17th-century monastery of Santa Mònica and shows a wide range of contemporary creations, including video art, installations and more.

Just off Rambla Santa Mònica at Passatge de la Banca, a stately 19th-century Neoclassical mansion houses the **Museu de Cera** [85 C4] (℡933 17 26 49; w museocerabcn.com; ⊕ 10.00–19.30 Mon–Fri, 10.00–20.00 Sat–Sun; €21), where everyone is an imposter. This was the brainchild of the city executioner, Nicomedes Méndez, a quiet bachelor who lived with his pet rabbit. Noting the crowds that gathered to watch famous Anarchists meet the garrot vil, Méndez had the idea of prolonging the thrill by displaying waxworks of its victims. The city vetoed this, although it found nothing wrong with displaying other cities' famous criminals. These days the criminals have been replaced by the likes of Taylor Swift, Messi, Picasso and characters from *Star Wars*.

Rambla dels Caputxins and the Plaça Reial
The next Rambla, Rambla dels Caputxins, defines the heart of Barcelona's old theatre district. The first wooden playhouse was built in 1579 by the Hospital de la Santa Creu (page 95) after Felipe II granted it a monopoly on dramatic spectacles to raise revenue; the site today is occupied by the **Teatre Principal** (1850) [85 B4] (w teatreprincipal.com), the city's oldest theatre, with drama, dance and musical performances, including family-friendly events. The Capuchins who lent their name to this Rambla had a convent

here that had the dubious distinction of being the first to be burned in the first church-burning fury in 1835.

When the rubble was cleared, the land was auctioned off, and in 1848 Francesc Daniel Molina won the competition to design the **Plaça Reial** [85 B3], modelled after Madrid's Plaza Mayor. Molina enclosed it in harmonious Neoclassical residences with ground-floor shops and cafés. After hitting rock bottom as a playground for muggers, addicts and prostitutes, Plaça Reial was given a facelift in the early 1980s and planted with palms (although it's still wise to keep a sharp eye on your belongings). The palms chaperone the late 19th-century iron **Font de les Tres Gràcies** [85 B3] splashing in the centre and two flamboyant **Modernista lamp posts**. These are Gaudí's earliest known works (1878), designed in his student days and covered with emblems of Hermes, the god of commerce. Today it's one of the city's liveliest nightlife venues.

At the head of the Rambla dels Caputxins stands one of Barcelona's proudest institutions: the **Gran Teatre del Liceu** [85 B3], inaugurated in 1847 in place of a Trinitarian convent burned in 1835. Gutted by fire in 1861, it was rebuilt by Josep Oriol Mestres on an even grander scale, with 4,000 seats (second only to Milan's La Scala). As a symbol of the elite, the Liceu was the target of a notorious Anarchist attack, on 7 November 1893, when two bombs were hurled from the gallery, killing 22. In 1994, the Liceu burned to the ground again during last-minute work on the set for *Turandot*. A campaign to replace it began immediately, and, by late 1999 the prima donnas were back again.

The new theatre is a clone of Mestres' much-loved old building, only updated. The lobby has the opulent grandeur of yore and a wide marble staircase leading up to the dazzling Salon of Mirrors. The auditorium, one of the largest in Europe, is a great whirl of gilt and red velvet; the theatre's signature red velvet chairs reappear in the fantastical ceiling paintings by Perejaume.

Back on the Rambla, the **Pla de la Boqueria** [85 B3], with a colourful ceramic mosaic by Miró (1976), marks the medieval gate of Santa Eulàlia, where fairs and markets took place. Matching Miró's mosaic for exuberance is the **Casa Bruno Quadros** (1896) [85 B2], a former umbrella-makers, defended by a swirling dragon holding a brolly, designed by Josep Vilaseca. This stretch of the Rambla also features a more sombre memorial, dedicated to the victims of the 2017 terrorist attack, which features the words '*Que la pau et cobreixi, oh ciutat de pau*' (May peace shield you, city of peace) etched into the pavement.

Rambla de les Flors

Pla Boqueria marks the beginning of the Rambla de Sant Josep, known as Rambla de les Flors ever since the first flower stalls sprang up during the Corpus Christi celebrations in 1853. The flower girls were once a main attraction: the Modernista painter Ramon Casas was surely not the first or last to have fallen in love with, and married, one.

On the left, a large Modernista neo-Gothic arch beckons you into the food-filled wonderland of Mercat de Sant Josep, better known as **La Boqueria** [85 A2]. Founded in 1830 on the ruins of yet another burned monastery, La Boqueria had the first permanent stalls in the city and was roofed over in 1914. Just up from the market, the ivory-coloured Neoclassical **Palau de la Virreina** [85 A2] was built in 1778 by the Viceroy Manuel Amat of Peru with loot skimmed off the fabulous silver mines of Potosí. He laid on the marriage of the century then promptly died in 1782, leaving it all to his 19-year-old widow. Now it houses the **Centre de la Imatge** (933 16 10 00; w ajuntament.barcelona.cat/lavirreina; ① 11.00–20.00 Tue–Sun; free) featuring exhibits dedicated to contemporary art and culture, often photography and often linked somehow to the city.

Rambla dels Estudis The next rambla was named after the Estudi General, or university, founded by Martí the Humane and suppressed by Felipe V. The pride of its 18th-century Jesuit church, the **Església de Betlem** [85 A2], is a fancy Churrigueresque portal, but its once equally lavish Baroque interior was incinerated in 1936. Next to it, the old Jesuit College was replaced in 1880 with the Philippines Tobacco Company (No. 109), which was run, like much else in Barcelona, by Eusebi Güell, and supplied most of Spain's cheap smokes. It's now a swish hotel. Opposite, the arcaded 18th-century **Palau de Moja** [85 A2] was once the home of poet Jacint Verdaguer, and is now the headquarters of the Catalan government's Department of Culture.

Rambla de les Canaletes The uppermost segment is named after the magical **Font de les Canaletes** [85 A1] which promises that all who drink of it will stay in or return to Barcelona. Barça fans come here to celebrate after a victory.

Plaça Catalunya [85 A1] At the top of the Rambla extends the Plaça Catalunya, Barcelona's hub of human and pigeon life. The present square, as designed by Francesc Nebot, was inaugurated in 1927. During the Civil War, one building, the former Hotel Colón, was the PSUC headquarters and draped with enormous portraits of Lenin, Marx and Stalin. When Franco took the city in 1939, the offending portraits were stripped away and the square was renamed Plaza del Ejército, or Army Square. Thirty-eight years later, 250,000 Barcelonins gathered here on 11 September 1977 for the first post-Franco Catalan National Day.

Transport lines converge in Plaça Catalunya, and department stores occupy the fringes: El Corte Inglés, a cross between a ferry boat and a radiator; and the dull Triangle mall. Its hotchpotch of art includes the upside-down stair on a pedestal that is Subirachs' *Monument to Francesc Macià*, Republican president of the Generalitat in 1931. It's a Piranesiesque hulk that looks ready to crush *The Goddess*, an older, wistful sculpture by Josep Clarà.

THE BARRI GÒTIC On the map, you can see it at once: the 'egg yolk' from which Barcelona sprang as Roman Faventia Julia Augusta Paterna Barcino, in the loop between the curving Carrer dels Banys Nous, Carrer d'Avinyó and Via Laietana. Its lofty walls may have failed to keep out the Visigoths in AD415, but for the next 1,000 years they held tight to Barcelona's heart. Gentle Mons Tàber was the acropolis, and here the institutions of medieval Barcelona took root over their Roman predecessors. When the city burst out of its girdle of walls into the Eixample in 1870, it left behind a 14th-century time capsule, the most extensive Gothic city centre in the world, remarkably intact and sunny-side up.

Roman Barcino The best introduction to the area is **Plaça Àngel** [85 G1], just outside the **Portal Major**, or main gate. Originally this was the Plaça del Blat, or 'wheat square', where the city's grain was bought and sold. In the 9th century it witnessed a miracle: as Santa Eulàlia's relics were being ceremoniously moved from Santa Maria del Mar to the cathedral, the body, when it reached the square, became too heavy to carry. An angel appeared and pointed accusingly at an official, who confessed that he had pocketed Eulàlia's toe. He replaced it and the procession continued.

The streets around Plaça de l'Àngel have Barcino's best-preserved **Roman walls**, with towers as high as 14m, making cameo appearances in a mesh of medieval building, especially along Carrer de Sots-tinent Navarro. More walls, just up Vía

BARCELONA
Ciutat Vella (Old City)

Barri Gòtic

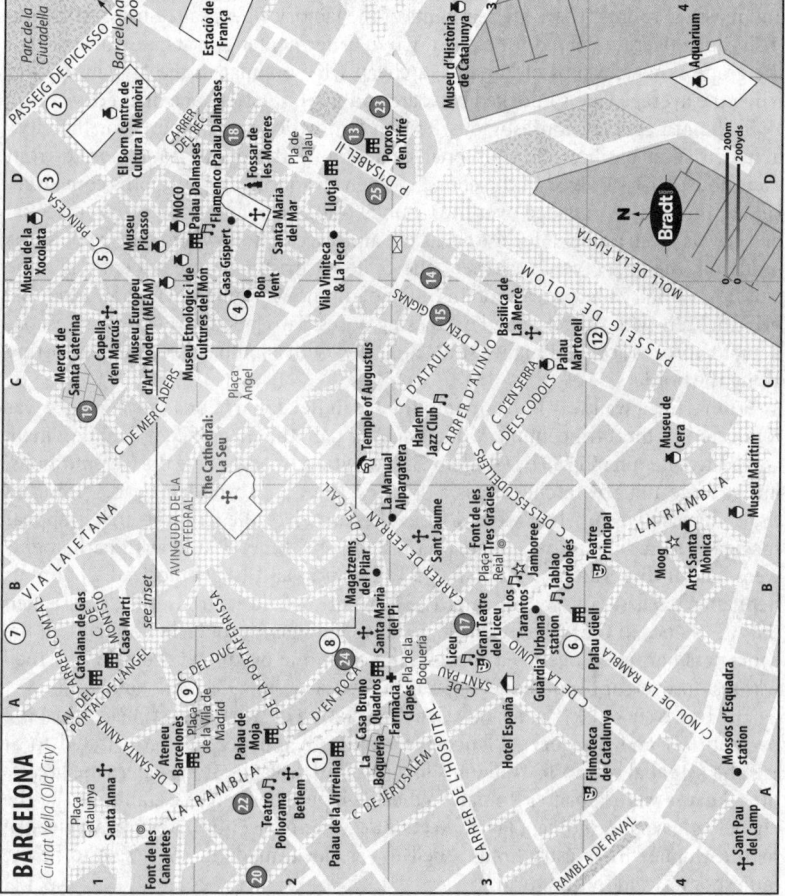

Parc de la Ciutadella

PASSEIG DE PICASSO

Barcelona Zoo

Estació de França

El Born Centre de Cultura i Memòria

CARRER DEL REC

Museu de la Xocolata

Museu Picasso

MOCO
Palau Dalmases
Flamenco Palau Dalmases

Fossar de les Moreres

Pla de Palau

Ponts den Xifré

Santa Maria del Mar

Lloija

C D'ISABEL II

Casa Gispert

Mercat de Santa Caterina

Capella d'en Marcús

Museu Europeu d'Art Modern (MEAM)

Museu Etnològic i de Cultures del Món

Casa Martí

C DE MERCADERS

Bon Vent

Vila Viniteca & La Teca

Plaça Àngel

Temple of Augustus

C D'ATAÜLF

C D'EN SERRA

C DELS CODOLS

Basílica de la Mercè

Palau Martorell

PASSEIG DE COLOM

Museu de Cera

Museu Marítim

LA RAMBLA

MOLL DE LA FUSTA

Aquàrium

The Cathedral: La Seu

AVINGUDA DE LA CATEDRAL

see inset

VIA LAIETANA

Harlem Jazz Club

La Manual Alpargatera

C D'AVINYÓ

CARRER D'AVINYÓ

CARRER DE FERRAN

C DE FERRAN

Sant Jaume

Font de les Tres Gràcies

Plaça Reial

Los Tarantos

Jamboree

Tablao Cordobés

Teatre Principal

Moog

Arts Santa Mònica

C DE LES ESCUDELLERS

C DELS ESCUDELLERS BLANCS

CIGNAS

AV DEL PORTAL DE L'ÀNGEL

CARRER COMTAL

Catalana de Gas

C DEL DISÓ
C MONISO
Casa Calvet

Ateneu Barcelonès

Palau de la Virreina

Plaça de la Vila de Madrid

Palau de Moja

La Casa Bruno Quadros

Santa Maria del Pi

Magatzems del Pilar

Santa Maria del Pi

Farmàcia Clapés

Pla de la Boqueria

Gran Teatre del Liceu

Liceu station

Palau Güell

Guàrdia Urbana

C D'EN ROCA

C DEL DUC

C DE SANTA ANNA

Plaça Catalunya

Font de les Canaletes

Santa Anna

LA RAMBLA

Teatro Poliorama

Betlem

Palau de la Virreina

C DE JERUSALEM

CARRER DE L'HOSPITAL

RAMBLA DE RAVAL

Sant Pau del Camp

C NOU DE LA RAMBLA

Hotel España

Filmoteca de Catalunya

Mossos d'Esquadra station

C DE L'UNIÓ
SANT PAU

Barri Gòtic (inset)

The kiss mural

Collegi d'Arquitectes

Plaça Nova

Casa de l'Ardiaca

Casa del Gremi dels Sabaters

Casa del Gremi de Calderers

Mister Andreu

Museu Diocesà

Museu Frederic Marès

AVINGUDA DE LA CATEDRAL

The Cathedral: La Seu

Capella de Santa Llúcia

Palau Episcopal

Sant Felip Neri

Plaça Sant Felip Neri

MUHBA El Call

Sinagoga Mayor

Palau del Lloctinent

Palau de la Generalitat

Plaça Sant Jaume

Ajuntament

Plaça de Ramon Berenguer III

Plaça del Rei

Museu d'Història de Barcelona (MUHBA)

Plaça Àngel

La Colmena

Casa Carot

Sants Just i Pastor

Palau Moxó

Palau Requesens

Museu d'Història de Catalunya

Bradt

N

0   200m
0   200yds

0   100m
0   100yds

3

85

Laietana in the **Plaça de Ramon Berenguer III el Gran** [85 G1], overlook Josep Llimona's equestrian statue of the count who married Barcelona to Aragon in 1137 and brought the city a royal crown.

Handsome **Plaça del Rei** [85 F1] started off as the courtyard of the Palau Reial Major, begun in the 10th century for the Counts of Barcelona and expanded when they became the Kings of Aragon. The square, with its picturesque fan of steps, would make a perfect setting for an opera, and once witnessed real drama, when Fernando the Catholic (never a favourite in Barcelona) narrowly escaped having his throat cut by a disgruntled peasant. The sculpture resembling a giant safe is Eduardo Chillida's *Topos* (1985).

Museu d'Història de Barcelona [85 G1] (MUHBA; Pl del Rei; ☎ 932 56 21 22; w barcelona.cat/museuhistoria; ☉ 10.00–17.00 Tue–Sat, 10.00–20.00 Sun; adult/reduced/under 16 €7/5/free)

A 15th-century Gothic merchant's palace was painstakingly moved to Plaça del Rei in 1931, but, while digging its foundations, workers uncovered a surprise: the remnants of Roman Barcino, now the largest underground excavations of any ancient city in Europe.

Traces of indigo dye still stain the stone vats of the dyeing workshops, which were later incorporated into the baths, fully and luxuriously equipped with a gymnasium and massage rooms. There are remnants of the factory where salted fish and garum (fish sauce) were prepared for export. Circular fermentation vats are pocked with the grape skins and pips of Laitania, a cheap wine popular in the 1st century BC, when the average Gaius knocked back around three-quarters of a litre a day.

In the 4th century, a prestigious Roman family donated property for the city's first Christian basilica and episcopal palace; note the pretty floor mosaic from their house that survived in the church. When the occupying Visigoths converted, Ugnes, the bishop, presided over the Council of Barcelona in AD599. The episcopal palace was given a facelift for the occasion, and a secret hollow for storing relics was hidden in the altar; even back then, one's fellow Christians were not entirely to be trusted. A small gallery area contains busts of unknown Romans who now resemble prize fighters with their chipped or missing noses. Two faded early-Gothic frescoes depict a procession of knights (c1265–1300), with fabulous creatures cavorting along the borders.

From here, a walkway leads up into the **Palau Reial**. Barcelona's royal palace was renovated in the 14th century, when its great hall, the magnificent **Saló de Tinell**, was added. Begun in 1359 by Guillem Carbonell, architect to Pere the Ceremonious, its six huge rainbow arches cross a span of 17m, with wooden beams filling in the ceiling between; when viewed from the corner of the hall, the arches appear magically to radiate from a single point. Banquets, funerals and even parliaments were held in the Saló de Tinell; in 1493 Fernando and Isabel received Columbus here after his first voyage, and later the Inquisition held its trials here, so dreaded that the stones in the walls were said to move if a suspect told a lie. After 1714, the room was baroqued over as a church, and everyone presumed the Saló de Tinell was lost forever, until someone dug under the plaster in 1934, and voilà.

The hall is linked to the narrow **Capella Palatina de Santa Àgata**. Begun in 1302 by Jaume II and his queen Blanche of Anjou, the chapel was rededicated to St Agatha by papal bull in 1601, thanks to a precious relic: the stone where the breasts of St Agatha were laid after Roman soldiers snipped them off in Catania, Sicily. The chapel's glory is the golden, lavish *Retaule del Conestable* (1466), the masterpiece of Jaume Huguet. The vestry holds a bell-tower clock, made in 1575, said to be the largest of its kind in the world.

A narrow, almost hidden, staircase leads out to the curious skyscraper that rises over the square – five storeys of galleries built by Antoni Carbonell in 1557 and anachronistically named the **Mirador del Rei Martí** after the popular humane king, to hide the unpleasant truth that it was really a spy tower for the hated viceroy, or Lloctinent, a position set up by Fernando the Catholic.

To the left of the Palau Reial is the **Palau del Lloctinent**, also by Carbonell, and beautifully restored in 2008. It contains the Archives of the Crown of Aragon, one of the world's greatest collections of medieval documents. Peek into the fine courtyard to see the magnificent coffered ceiling over the stair.

Museu Frederic Marès [85 F1] (Pl Sant Iu; ☎ 932 56 35 00; w barcelona.cat/museufredericmares; ⏰ 10.00–19.00 Tue–Sat, 11.00–20.00 Sun; adult/under 16 €4.20/free, free 1st Sun of the month)

Fernando the Catholic donated part of the royal palace to another of his great gifts to Barcelona, the Spanish Inquisition. Now it's home to the sublime and ridiculously amassed collection of sculptor and hoarder extraordinaire Frederic Marès (1893–1991). On the ground floor, you'll find armies of tiny Iberian ex-votos, followed by Roman, Greek and Iberian busts, coins and tombs. Then comes the largest collection of sculpture in Spain: an astonishing array of 12th–14th-century polychrome wood sculptures of sweet-faced Virgins and stylised crucifixes. The basement has more, plus an impressive 13th-century portal, capitals and columns, and tombs, including that of a 14th-century knight bearing a lovingly sculpted hawk on his left hand.

There is more gore on the first floor, with flayed and bleeding medieval saints punctured with arrows (although note one of the best pieces here, a 12th-century relief of the *Vocation of St Peter*). Nineteenth-century Baby Jesuses have real hair and

FREE MUSEUM ENTRY

Many of Barcelona's museums offer free admission either once a week or once a month.

Saturdays *Free from 15.00*
MACBA
Museu Nacional d'Art de Catalunya

Sundays *Free from 15.00*
Castell de Montjuïc
CCCB
Jardí Botànic
MUHBA Plaça del Rei
Museu de Ciències Naturals
Museu del Disseny
Museu Etnològic i de Cultures del Mon
Museu Marítim
Museu de la Música

First Sunday of the month *Free all day*
Castell de Montjuïc
Jardí Botànic

Monestir de Pedralbes
MUHBA Plaça del Rei
Museu d'Arqueologia de Catalunya
Museu de Ciències Naturals
Museu d'Història de Catalunya
Museu del Disseny
Museu Etnològic i de Cultures del Mon
Museu Frederic Marès
Museu de la Música
Museu Nacional d'Art de Catalunya
Museu Olímpic i de l'Eport
Museu Picasso de Barcelona
Pabellón Mies Van der Rohe

Thursday afternoon
Museu de la Música (free from 18.00)
Museu Picasso de Barcelona (free from 16.00)

dolly faces, intermingling with Catalan iron, Montserrat memorabilia and colourful plaques of the Dance of Death, showing the Grim Reaper reeling with ladies, monks and peasants. In the cool, vaulted courtyard by the entrance, orange trees overlook a charming outdoor café (☉ summer only), perfect for dizzy museum victims.

The Cathedral: La Seu [85 F1] (Pl de la Seu; ☏ 933 42 82 62; w catedralbcn.org; ☉ 09.30–18.30 Mon–Fri, 09.30–17.15 Sat, 14.00–17.00 Sun; adult €14 inc virtual audioguide & Diocesan Museum, see opposite; €28 evening visit & roof) Barcelona's huge Gothic cathedral, which, with its fat apse, octagonal towers and spires, is hard to miss. This is the third church to stand here; the first was flattened in al-Mansur's raid in AD985; of the second, a Romanesque one built by Count Ramon Berenguer I, only two doorways remain.

The earliest bit of the current model is the right transept, built in 1298 by Jaume II; its **Portal of Sant Iu** (St Ives) has carvings of St George and Barcelona's first count, Wilfred the Hairy, fighting a dragon and griffon, respectively. The **main façade**, based on the 1408 plans by a French master named Carli, was only begun in 1882. Catalan Gothic is famous for its conquest of space: although La Seu has only three aisles, the architects made it look like five, part of a rich and atmospheric interior that was one of the very few to escape the attentions of Barcelona's Anarchists.

The first chapel on the right, the star-vaulted **sala capitular**, contains the lucky crucifix borne by Don Juan on the mast of his flagship at the Battle of Lepanto in 1571; the S-shaped twist in Christ's body came about, they say, when it dodged a Turkish cannonball. The adjacent baptistry has a plaque that records the baptism here of the first six native Americans, brought over by Columbus, in 1493; the beautiful stained-glass scene of the *Noli me Tangere* is based on drawings by Bartolomé Bermejo.

The **choir** is enclosed in the middle of the nave behind a fine Renaissance screen by Bartolomé Ordóñez. The richly sculpted stalls of the 14th to 15th centuries were given fancy canopies and painted in 1514 with the arms of the kings of France, Portugal, Poland, Hungary, Denmark and England, when Emperor Charles V summoned them as Knights of the Golden Fleece to Barcelona, a proto-session of the United Nations before all were plunged into war; Henry VIII's seat is directly on the emperor's right. The fanciest carving of all, by Pere Sanglada, is on the **pulpit** (1403).

The choir faces the elegant, daringly low-vaulted **crypt** with an enormous keystone, designed by the Mallorcan Jaume Fabre, who was in charge of the cathedral works from 1317 to 1339. It holds the relics of the co-patroness of Barcelona, Santa Eulàlia, in a beautiful 14th-century alabaster sarcophagus. Eulàlia, the daughter of a merchant of Sarrià, threw dirt on the altar of Augustus and refused to worship Rome's gods, and the scenes on her tomb show the 13 grisly trials designed to change her mind, including being thrown naked into a vat of starving fleas and a seduction attempt by the handsome son of the Roman commander. Nothing could sway her, and her martyrdom ended when her torturers lopped off her breasts and crucified her. Her original 9th-century sarcophagus is set in the back of the crypt.

After the virtuoso crypt, the **altar** is an anti-climax, supported on two Visigothic capitals, with a bland bronze crucifix by Frederic Marès behind. To the right of this, the founders of the Romanesque cathedral, Ramon Berenguer I and his wife Almodis, lie in the velvet-covered wooden sarcophagi against the wall.

The door here leads into the sacristy and the **treasury**; holding pride of place is a late 14th-century gem-encrusted monstrance, and a silver-plated processional cross by Francesc Villardel, of 1383. Of the chapels radiating from the ambulatory, the fourth one on the right, dedicated to **Sant Joan Baptista i Sant Josep**, has the best art: the minutely detailed altarpiece of the *Transfiguration* by Bernat Martorell

(1450). On the far left side of the ambulatory you'll find the **lift to the roof** with grand views over the old city, and glimpses of the famous gargoyles – more than 200 of them, including an elephant and a unicorn.

What people tend to remember most fondly about the cathedral is the charming green oasis of the **cloister**, begun in 1385. Its iron-grilled chapels were once dedicated to the patron saints of Barcelona's guilds ('Our Lady of Electricity' is still going strong) and many leading guild masters are buried in the floor. A pretty pavilion holds the **Font de Sant Jordi**, with a figure of St George rising from a mossy green blob. At Corpus Christi, flowers are wound around the fountain and a hollow egg is set to dance in the jet of water (*l'ou com balla*). The egg placers don't have to look far for one, because 13 **white geese** natter away next to the fountain. They have been there since anyone can remember, symbols of Santa Eulàlia's virginity or a memory of the geese that saved Rome, or (most likely) just because. Also note the **Romanesque doorway** into the church, the only surviving bit of Ramon Berenguer I's cathedral, cobbled together out of Roman stones and capitals.

A chapel in the cloister houses the tiny **Cathedral Museum**, with its retired retables and reliquaries. The *Pietà* (1490) by Bartolomé Bermejo is his masterpiece and one of the first Spanish oil paintings; there's a beautiful altarpiece by Jaume Huguet, painted for the guild of the esparto grass workers, and the **organ cabinet door** paintings (1560) by the Greek Pere Serafí, named 'Peter of the Seven Ps' for his 'Peter Piper' slogan *Pere Pau pinta portes per poc preu* (Peter Pau paints doors for bargain prices).

Museu Diocesà [85 F1] (Pla de la Seu 7; ☎ 933 15 22 13; w museudiocesa.esglesia. barcelona; ⏰ 09.30–18.30 daily; combined admission with the Cathedral: adult/ reduced/under 12 €8/6/free) Works of sacred art from the diocese have been pensioned off in this excellent museum in the Pia Almoina, headquarters of a charitable foundation set up in 1009, although the current building, incorporating part of a Roman tower and its prophylactic head of Medusa, dates from 1423.

Among the treasures are the Sienese-inspired *Taula de Sant Jaume*, by Arnau and Ferrer Bassa; a reliquary of Sant Cugat (1312); and Romanesque frescoes of the Apocalypse from the apse of Sant Salvador de Polinyà (1122), a precursor of Picasso's *Guernica*. The *Custodia de Santa Maria del Pi* (1587) by Llàtzer de la Castanya is a masterpiece of the goldsmith's art, and there are retables by Bernat Martorell and the Portuguese Pere Nunyes. A startling 15th-century anonymous *Retaule de Sant Bartomeu* is a candidate for the goriest in Barcelona (although it has plenty of competition). Upstairs are alabaster Virgins, including one by Pere Joan, and Gil de Medina's huge *St Christopher* (1545).

Plaça Nova and around [85 E1] This lively square in front of the cathedral fills up with an antiques market every Thursday. It's framed by two Roman towers, renovated in the 12th century, along with an arch of the Roman aqueduct reconstructed in 1958. Huge iron letters, erected by the poet Joan Brossa in 1994, spell out 'Barcino'. Here too is the **Collegi d'Arquitectes** (1962) [85 E1], a poor advert for the architectural trade, but its façade is decorated by a sketchy frieze of popular celebrations by Picasso – he sent the designs from France for his only piece of public art in Barcelona. Just around the corner, on Carrer dels Capellans, you can join the queues lining up for their Insta shot in front of **the kiss mural** (official title: *El món neix en cada besada*, which means 'the world is born in every kiss'), made of more than 4,000 photo mosaics and created by photographer Joan Fontcuberta in 2014.

3

Nearby, at Carrer de Santa Llúcia 1, is the 12th–14th-century **Casa de l'Ardiaca** [85 F1] (of the Archdeacon), now home to the city's historical archive. In 1902, when the building was owned by the lawyers' college, Domènech i Montaner was called upon to install a postal slot. The swallow and tortoise expressed his opinion of lawyers – the swallows with wings to soar into the realms of truth, the tortoise plodding at the pace of court procedures. He also created a charming tiled courtyard, with a lofty palm and pretty Gothic fountain. Opposite is the Romanesque **Capella de Santa Llúcia** (1268) [85 F2], founded by Bishop Arnau de Gurb, whose tomb is within. Long, straight Carrer del Bisbe separates the Casa de l'Ardiaca from the medieval **Palau Episcopal** [85 E1], the bishops' palace, built on the Roman wall.

Just down Carrer del Bisbe, **Plaça Garriga i Bachs** is dedicated to five heroes of 1809, who attempted to take Montjuïc Castle from the Napoleonic occupiers; three hid in the cathedral organ for three days before they were hanged or garrotted. The church here is **Sant Sever**; like the cathedral, this church was protected by armed guards during the Civil War and is one of the few to preserve its frothy Baroque interior, with an altar in a trompe l'œil setting.

The lane next to the Palau Episcopal, Carrer de Montjuïc del Bisbe, leads back to the pretty, nearly enclosed **Plaça Sant Felip Neri** [85 E2], its melancholy air perhaps derived from its former role as the burial ground of the executed, whether prisoners or heroes. Its components are simple: one fountain, two trees and a church of **Sant Felip Neri** (1751), with a severe façade and a big Baroque altar inside. During the Civil War a bomb went off here (you can still see scars on the church), and in the 1940s, when the square was rebuilt, two handsome buildings were relocated here: the Renaissance **Casa del Gremi de Calderers** [85 E1], once headquarters of the coppersmiths' guild, and the **Casa del Gremi dels Sabaters** [85 E1], the shoemakers' guild, founded in 1202 under the sign of their patron St Mark.

Plaça Sant Jaume [85 F2] Carrer del Bisbe leads into the heart of civic Barcelona. Originally the Roman forum, it was recarved out of a warren of streets in the 1840s along with Carrer de Ferran, opening up an ongoing, face-to-face dialogue between the Catalan government (the Generalitat) and Barcelona's City Hall (the Ajuntament).

Palau de la Generalitat [85 F2] (⏲ by reservation only every 2nd & 4th Sat & Sun; book in advance at w presidencia.gencat.cat & bring your passport or photo ID; free) Created by Jaume I in 1249, the Generalitat was made up of representatives of the three Estates of the Catalan Corts (Church, military and civilian), and in 1359 it assumed fiscal responsibility for the realm, making it Spain's first real parliament. The palace was begun in the 15th century to give it a permanent seat. When Felipe V abolished the Generalitat in 1714, it was occupied by the Reial Audiencia, which rubberstamped Madrid's policies. But such is the Catalan virtue of *continuitat* that it resumed its function in 1977 – not something many secular medieval buildings get to do.

The façade on Carrer del Bisbe, designed in 1416 by Marc Safont, has some of the best gargoyles and modillions in Barcelona, topped by a superb rondel of St George by Pere Joan – a work that so pleased the Generalitat that they paid the sculptor double the agreed price. Carrer del Bisbe passes under a picturesque **Bridge of Sighs**, a much-maligned pseudo-Gothic touch added in 1928. What sighs, if any, are exhaled on the bridge are by the president as he leaves his official residence, the 16th-century **Casa dels Canonges** (the former canons' house), on his way to work.

The Gothic courtyard of the Generalitat is especially lovely: a carved exterior stair ascends on a daring stone arch to a gallery colonnaded with the slimmest of columns. The whole is crowned with pinnacles and gargoyles that resemble medieval Barcelonins. The **chapel** is entered by way of Marc Safont's Gothic portal (1436), flamboyant, vertical and ornate in a town that prefers its Gothic unadorned and broad in the beam. This, of course, is dedicated to Catalunya's patron, Sant Jordi, or George. When the Generalitat was enlarged in 1526, it added the orange-tree courtyard, the **Pati dels Tarrongers**, and beyond that the ceremonial **Golden Room**, with a 16th-century gilt ceiling. Here Flemish tapestries on the triumphs of Petrarch replace the Noucentista frescoes by Torres-Garcia, which fell out of favour under Primo de Rivera (his detached works are now in another room). The president and his ministers meet in the **Sala Antoni Tàpies**, with the eponymous master's painting based on the four medieval chronicles of Catalunya. The Generalitat is proud of its 40-bell carillon, which sounds every hour between 08.00 and 20.00.

Ajuntament [85 F2] (w ajuntament.barcelona.cat/en; ⊕ 10.00 Sun tour in English, arrive by 09.30; free) Jaume I sowed the seeds for the Ajuntament (city council) at the same time as the Generalitat, when he appointed a committee of 20 peers in 1249; by 1272 this had evolved into the annually selected Consell de Cent (Council of a Hundred), who ruled the city until 1714. It proved to be one Europe's most successful representative governments, partly through its unusual flexibility: tradesmen as well as patricians served, and the number 100 was not set in stone, but varied as circumstances saw fit. The Ajuntament's Neoclassical façade, added in the 1840s, is cold potatoes, but like the Generalitat it preserves a Gothic façade, on Carrer de la Ciutat, watched over by Santa Eulàlia. The oldest part of the Ajuntament, the **Saló de Cent** by Pere Llobet (1372), has round ribs reminiscent of the Saló de Tinell; it was restored by Domènech i Montaner in the 1880s, and Gothic bits were added in 1914. The **Saló de las Cròniques** is lined with bravura golden murals on the glories of Catalan history, by Josep Maria Sert (1928).

Temple of Augustus [85 C2] (⊕ 10.00–14.00 Mon, 10.00–19.00 Tue–Sat, 10.00–20.00 Sun; free) From the Plaça Sant Jaume, narrow Carrer de Paradís leads to the summit of Mons Tàber, marked by an ancient millstone in the pavement. Here, just inside the Gothic courtyard of the Centre Excursionista de Catalunya, are four impressive Corinthian columns and part of the podium from the 1st-century AD Roman Temple of Augustus, trapped like an exotic orchid in a hothouse.

East of Plaça Sant Jaume From the north (Gothic) side of the Ajuntament, Carrer d'Hèrcules leads to the Plaça Sant Just and two palaces: **Moxó**, adorned with sgraffito, and **Palau Requesens** [85 G2] (Palau de la Comtessa de Palamós). The latter, housing a Gallery of Illustrious Catalans, was the grandest private address in medieval Barcelona, built in the 13th century. Here, too, is the parish church of the count-kings, **Sants Just i Pastor** [85 G2] (Pl de Sant Just; ☏ 933 01 74 33; w basilicasantjust.cat; ⊕ 10.00–13.00 daily & 19.00–20.30 Mon, Wed, Thu & Sat; free) founded according to tradition by Louis the Pious in AD801. It is the last church in Spain to preserve its ancient privilege of Testament Sacramental bestowed by Louis himself, which gives any citizen of Barcelona the right to make a will, orally, without a notary or writ, if said before the altar of Sant Feliu.

MUHBA El Call [85 F2] (Placetade Manuel Ribé; ☏ 932 56 21 22; w barcelona.cat/museuhistoria; ⊕ 11.00–14.00 Wed, 11.00–15.00 & 16.00–19.00 Sat–Sun; adult/

3

under 16 €2/free) This fascinating little museum, part of the main Barcelona history museum (MUHBA), occupies a modern building constructed over the remnants of the medieval house of a veil weaver, and tells the story of Barcelona's ghetto (El Call, from the Hebrew qahqal or 'meeting place') from the earliest times to the present.

In the Middle Ages, the entrance to El Call was just to the left of the Generalitat, on modern Carrer del Call. No-one knows when the first Jews moved to Barcelona, although the Visigoths bear the ignominy of passing Spain's first anti-Semitic law, in AD694, which made all Jews enslaved people. By the 11th century, the Call was a well-organised community-within-a-community that was also the intellectual centre of Catalunya, home to its finest schools, hospitals, translators, poets, astronomers and philosophers.

It was here that the Girona-born mystic Moshe ben Nahman debated in the famous 'Disputation of Barcelona' in 1263. In 1243, however, Jaume I had ordered that the Call be walled off, and that Christians not be allowed to enter except when goods were displayed for sale; Jews were also compelled to wear cloaks with red or yellow bands. Much of this segregation was actually to protect Jews from persecution by Reconquista fanatics; Jews expelled from other territories in Spain were made welcome here by the count-kings, who depended on the community as bankers, ambassadors and interpreters (especially to Arab courts).

El Call began to incite a dangerous amount of envy. In 1391, a group of Castilians spread rumours that the Black Death had been brought by Jews from Navarre; a mob attacked the Call, brutally wiping out most of the community. King Joan I had the instigators put to death but could not halt the growing tide of anti-Semitism. In 1424, with the Castilians on the throne of Aragon, the Jews were expelled from the Call. In 1492, Fernando and Isabel compelled all the Jews in Sepharad (Hebrew for Spain) to convert or leave.

Over four centuries later, in 1925, Primo de Rivera granted the Sephardim around the world citizenship and protection under Spanish consulates. Not long after, Barcelona rediscovered its role as a haven, as 7,000 Jewish refugees moved into the city in the 1930s. Franco, for all his many faults, never persecuted Jews.

On tiny Carrer de Marlet, off Carrer de Sant Domènec del Call, the remnants of the medieval **Sinagoga Mayor** [85 F2] (C/ de Marlet 5; \ 933 17 07 90; w sinagogamayor.com; ⊕ 10.30–17.30 Mon–Fri, 10.30–14.30 Sun; adult €5), which may be one of the earliest synagogues in Europe and date back to the 3rd century, have been painstakingly preserved. Further down Carrer de Marlet, a stone remains poignantly in place along one wall, inscribed in Hebrew: 'Sacred foundation of Rabbi Samuel Hassareri, of everlasting life. Year 692.'

West of Plaça Jaume
Carrer de Ferran links the Plaça Sant Jaume to the Rambla; along it stands the little church of **Sant Jaume** [85 B3], which was built over a synagogue in 1394 by a confraternity of converted Jews and dedicated to the Trinity. In 1876 it was rededicated to St James the Moor-slayer, and topped in 1876 with a strikingly late, if not very politically correct, relief of the same. Here, in a Parisian-style arcade called **Passatge de Crédit**, Joan Miró was born in 1893. On Carrer d'Avinyó, where Picasso once had a studio, several old palaces were converted into brothels around the turn of the 20th century; note the fine *esgrafiados* that embellish the houses at Nos. 26 and 30.

Around the Plaça del Pi
Carrer dels Banys Nous, extending north of Carrer d'Avinyó, follows the curve of the Roman walls and was named after its 'new' Jewish baths, new in 1160 at any rate. It leads to the **Barri del Pi**, one of the

PICASSO'S DEMOISELLES D'AVIGNON

The 19-year-old Picasso had a studio near Carrer d'Avinyó at Carrer dels Escudellers Blancs, and he had the local ladies in mind when he painted *Les Demoiselles d'Avignon* (1907), his unfinished manifesto of Cubism. The painting was so incomprehensible even to other artists that it wasn't displayed publicly until 1937. In an interview in 1933 Picasso explained the name: '*Les Demoiselles d'Avignon*! How that name gets on my nerves! It was coined by Salmon [André, poet and friend]. You know at first it was called *The Brothel of Avignon*. You know why? Avignon has always been a familiar name for me, a name connected with my life. I lived only a few steps from the Carrer d'Avinyó. There I bought my paper and watercolours. Then, as you know, Max Jacob's grandfather was a native of Avignon. We were always making jokes about this picture. One of the women was supposed to be Max's grandmother...'

first medieval 'new towns' built outside the Roman walls; its name comes from a majestic pine that once stood in Plaça del Pi, in front of **Santa Maria del Pi** [85 B2] (**w** basilicadelpi.cat; ⊕ 10.00–18.00 Mon–Sat, 13.00–18.00 Sun & hols; adult/ reduced €8/6). Founded in the 10th century and rebuilt in 1322, Santa Maria del Pi is a textbook example of Catalan Gothic – austere and wide, but with a rose window said to be the largest in the world. The interior was gutted during the Civil War, but the choir, built with a stone arch even shallower than the vault in Santa Eulàlia's crypt in the cathedral and rebuilt in the 19th century, is remarkable, and everyone hopes it will last, because no-one knows how to build the like today.

Barri de Santa Anna By the 12th century Barcelona was too big to fit in its Roman walls and overflowed to the north and east, an area that Jaume I enclosed in his 13th-century walls to form the Barri de Santa Anna. One landmark, at Carrer de Montsió 3, is the **Casa Martí** (1895) [85 B1], the first building by Josep Puig i Cadafalch, a Modernista fantasy combining elements of Catalan and northern Gothic. Eusebi Arnau sculpted the *St George and the Dragon* on the corner, a motif that Puig would make his own.

The building is renowned as the home of **Els Quatre Gats** ('The Four Cats', slang for 'Just a few guys'), the bohemian taverna that once provided much of the impetus for the city's cultural life. Founded in 1897 by four former habitués of Montmartre – painters Santiago Rusinyol and Ramon Casas, puppeteer Miquel Utrillo (father of the Parisian painter Maurice Utrillo) and the eccentric Pere Romeu, who abandoned painting to devote himself to cabaret and cycling – it soon became the informal late-night meeting place for writers, artists, journalists and musicians. The Quatre Gats published its own art review, held avant-garde shadow-puppet shows, presented recitals and put on exhibitions, including Picasso's very first, while Romeu ran things after a fashion, having a screaming fit if anyone touched a cobweb. Six years later, he closed the taverna to devote himself entirely to his bicycle, and the place, ironically, was taken over by Gaudí and Llimona's pious Catholic Cercle de Sant Lluc, founded in reaction to the blasphemous tomfoolery of Casas and Rusinyol. But now there's a new Quatre Gats, an expensive reproduction of the original, but minus Romeu's precious cobwebs.

Turn left at the end of Carrer de Montsió for shop-lined **Avinguda del Portal de l'Àngel**. Its landmark is the Modernista **Catalana de Gas** [85 B1] at No. 20 (1895), an eclectic structure by Josep Domènech i Estapà, controversially converted

3

into an outpost of an international fashion chain. Another landmark is the **giant thermometer**, marking Cottett, one of the city's oldest opticians.

A row of simple 2nd–4th-century AD Roman tombs in **Plaça de la Vila de Madrid** [85 A2] were discovered under a burned-out convent in 1957. Such tombs once lined the roads out of the city; you can see how much the ground level has risen in 1,600 years. At Carrer de Canuda 6, the **Ateneu Barcelonès** [85 A1] was founded in 1836 as a literary and cultural club, and occupies an 18th-century palace. It's got a good restaurant and hosts regular exhibitions and concerts. From here, Carrer de Santa Anna leads to the simple Romanesque church of **Santa Anna** [85 A1] with its elegant double-decker Gothic cloister. Founded by the Knights Templar in the early 12th century, the church hosted the Corts held under Fernando the Catholic – the last parliament before Catalunya was tacked on to Castile.

EL RAVAL South of the Rambla, the *barri* of El Raval (Arabic for 'an area outside the walls') was originally covered with orchards and gardens; the Raval gradually found its role as a haven for the city's rejects – its unpleasant trades, its criminals, but mostly its poor and diseased. When it was joined to the Barri Gòtic by the 14th-century walls, convents and monasteries moved in to fill up the gaps.

And so it marinated quietly in its own juices until Spain's industrial revolution was born here. Soon, workers were cramming into tenements pressed up next to the factories, and by the 1850s the Raval was perhaps the unhealthiest neighbourhood in Europe. The streets towards the sea became a crowded den of misery, prostitution and crime known as the Barri Xinès – Chinatown. It owed its name to journalist Àngel Marsá, who was inspired by the lurid descriptions of Chinatowns in America, and its denizens were painted by Isidre Nonell and by the young Picasso, who used the district's poor as the subjects for his Blue Period.

Much to the disgust of proper Barcelona, the notoriety of the Barri Xinès brought thousands of tourists to peep up the city's skirts when they should have been in the Eixample, admiring its fancy dress. In recent years, the Barri Xinès has been so decaffeinated that neither Genet nor Picasso would recognise it today. Since a massive clean-up before the Olympics, old blocks of flats were restored; new ones are being built. The lower part, the old Barri Xinès, is still pretty rough around the edges, and not a place to linger alone after dark; but gentrification is slowly taking hold of the upper Raval, by the gleaming Museu d'Art Contemporani, where there are lots of arty galleries, bars and fashion stores.

Palau Güell [85 B3] (C/ Nou de la Rambla 3–5]; \934 72 57 75; w palauguell. cat; ◷ Apr–Oct 10.00–20.00 Tue–Sun, Nov–Mar 10.00–17.30 Tue–Sun ; adult/reduced/ages 10–17/under 10 €12/9/5/free) In 1886, when everyone else of means was moving into the Eixample, the great industrialist Eusebi Güell asked his new protegé, Antoni Gaudí, to build him a home in the Raval. The young architect finished it in 1888, at enormous cost, to coincide with the Universal Exhibition. For all the expense, the Güells spent little time here, although the house had an interesting afterlife: in 1937 it was used by the Communists as a prison for members of the POUM, who had supported the Anarchists.

The **façade** is restrained for Gaudí, with the exception of the swirling ironwork incorporating the Catalan coat of arms splayed across the tympanum of the two main arches. Güell's coaches passed into a **courtyard** vaulted with Gaudí's signature bare-brick parabolic arches, from where a marble-columned staircase ascends to the first floor. Columned galleries overhang the street, expanding the interior space. The **visitors' gallery** has a particularly elaborate ceiling; among the dense, Moorish designs are secret spyholes that enabled the Güells surreptitiously to hear their guests' conversations.

At the heart of the house is the lofty **salon**, overlooked by galleries and culminating in a magical three-storey-high parabolic cupola, a honeycombed beehive pierced with silvery shafts representing a constellation topped by the moon; this was Güell's Montsalvat, the castle where the Grail was kept in Wagner's *Parsifal*. The salon has perfect acoustics and was used for concerts, and the wide upper stairway formed a convenient musicians' gallery.

The richest materials were reserved for the **family chapel**: 4.8m panels of rare hardwoods and ivory sheathed in white tortoiseshell fold back to reveal an alcove that once held a sculpted altarpiece of tortoiseshell and wood, destroyed during the Civil War. Some furnishings survived the war by being moved elsewhere, including a huge Japanese-style fireplace, guarded by scaly wooden serpents, and the enormous dining table, purchased from Güell's heirs.

The upper floors contain the family's apartments. Above them, a narrow staircase leads out on to an amazing rippling **roof**, the best feature of the house. One of Gaudí's personal missions was to make roofs as interesting as the rest of his buildings, and here, in a space few people would actually see, he let his imagination run wild to create a forest of 20 chimney sculptures, each organic and covered in *trencadís*. In the centre, the beehive dome of the salon is contained in a spire with a row of parabolic windows, topped by a lightning rod and an eerie bat.

Around the Rambla de Raval Just up from the Palau Güell, several blocks of dilapidated housing were demolished in 2000 to make way for this wide, tree-lined Rambla, now chock-full of cafés and restaurants. Fernando Botero's bronze sumo wrestler Gat (1981) is a favourite with the local kids. Head down Carrer de Sant Pau to find the landmark **Hotel España** [85 B3] at No. 9. In 1902–03, Domènech i Montaner redesigned the ground floor of this hotel, and the well-preserved Modernista dining room is still decorated with a mural of sea creatures and mermaids with scuba flippers by Ramon Casas.

Sant Pau del Camp [85 A4] (C/ de Sant Pau; ☎934 41 00 01; w stpaudelcamp. blogspot.com; ⏰ 10.00–17.00 Mon–Fri; adult/under 12 €6/free) 'St Paul's in the Field', is the best of the few surviving Romanesque churches in Barcelona, and was probably founded by the son of Wilfred the Hairy, Count Guifré-Borrell (d911), whose tombstone is here. Subsequently destroyed in the Moorish raids in 985 and 1115, Sant Pau was rededicated in 1117. In 1528, the monastery became a Benedictine priory linked to Montserrat. Sant Pau's façade looks its age, decorated with blind arcading and archaic reliefs of the hand of God, the symbols of the Evangelists and bizarre little masks. Inside, three apses are crowned by an octagonal tower – the rest burned in the Setmana Tràgica in 1909. Best of all is the tiny cloister with its paired columns and triple-lobed Moorish arches and a garden, one of old Barcelona's most magical corners.

Antic Hospital de la Santa Creu [60 D4] (C/ de l'Hospital 56) One of the oldest hospitals in the world, it was founded in 1024 and rebuilt here in 1401, with the aim of concentrating all Barcelona's diseases in one place. In the 16th century it had 500 beds; in the 17th century there were 5,000, and in 1926, not long after Gaudí died here, it moved, after 900 years, to Domènech i Montaner's Modernista hospital near the Sagrada Família. The hospital's long vaulted halls now shelter books instead of patients: it's now the **National Library of Catalunya**, and is only open to visitors on 23

April, the day of St Jordi (Catalunya's patron saint). The former Gothic chapel now functions as a gallery, **La Capella**, with exhibitions by young artists.

Just down Carrer de l'Hospital from the library, the woebegone 18th-century church of **Sant Agustí** in Plaça Sant Augustí with its knobbly stone spikes colonised by pigeons, was never finished. It does, however, hold a place in Barcelona's heart, since in 1971 it became the birthplace of the Asamblea de Catalunya, a broad-based opposition movement that called for liberty of expression and the re-establishment of the 1932 Statute of Autonomy.

Mercat de Sant Antoni [60 D5] (w mercatdesantantoni.com)

In the old days, Carrer de Sant Antoni, off the west end of Carrer de l'Hospital, led to the gate that linked Barcelona to the rest of Spain, a scene of grand entrances and royal processions now occupied by this lively market. Designed in 1882 by Antoni Rovira i Trias (author of the losing plan for the Eixample), this Modernista cathedral of spuds and carrots remains one of Barcelona's most impressive iron structures, shaped like an X with four long naves extending crossways to each chamfered corner. Recently beautifully restored, it's become the focal point of one of Barcelona's most attractive new 'superblocks' (*superilles*), part of the city's efforts to combat pollution and prioritise people over cars, with semi-pedestrianised streets, dotted with benches and little gardens.

Museu d'Art Contemporani [60 D4]

(MACBA; Pl dels Angels 1; \934 81 33 68; w macba.cat; ☉ 11.00–19.30 Mon & Wed–Fri, 10.00–20.00 Sat, 10.00–15.00 Sun; adult/adult off-peak/student €12/10.20/9.60 (off-peak hrs: 13.30–15.00 Mon, Wed, Thu & Fri, 10.00–11.00 Sat–Sun), over 65 & under 18 free) Looming over the northern Raval is the glowing white shrine to contemporary art designed by American architect Richard Meier and completed in 1995. The building almost overwhelms the collection: all the glassed-in space in front is devoted to ramps (you can't help but wonder how the skateboarders outside in the square would love to have a go at them).

It is a vibrant and varied gathering, nonetheless; the core includes such lights as Tàpies, Calder, Dubuffet, Barceló, Klee, Oldenburg, Rauschenberg and Christian Boltanski. Tàpies is represented by a number of pieces, among them *Pintura Ocre* (1959), and Joan Brossa has some delightful 'poem-objects'. In Perejaume's *Postaler* (1984), the artist took a tall cylindrical frame fitted with angled slotted mirrors into different landscapes and photographed it with its shimmering reflections. There are several unsettling pieces, poised between horror and laughter, including the *Training Table for Reconverted Communists* (1991) – an elongated ping-pong table with guns laid at each end instead of bats, by Francesc Torres.

Centre de Cultura Contemporània de Barcelona [60 D4]

(CCCB; C/ de Montalegre 5; \933 06 41 00; w cccb.org; ☉ 10.00 – 20.00 Tue–Sun; adult/reduced €6/4 (1 exhibition), €8/6 (2 exhibitions)) Around the corner from MACBA, the former Casa de Caritat at first built in 1362 was remodelled over the centuries to do duty as a cloister for Franciscan nuns, seminary, hospital and, after 1802, as a workhouse for the poor. Then in 1987 the Maremagnum architects, Piñon and Viaplana, dipped it in a postmodernist solution, and it emerged as the CCCB. The dilapidated north courtyard was replaced by a huge glass and steel block that tilts forward; the south façade was also replaced, to make way for the MACBA. The entrance is by way of the pretty 18th-century Pati de les Dones, with mosaic decoration. The CCCB hosts imaginative exhibitions with urban themes.

Universitat Central [60 D4] (Pl de la Universitat) Barcelona's university is the heir of the Estudi d'Arts i Medicina, founded by King Martí in 1401. Planned and built between 1860 and 1873, the architect, Elias Rogent i Amat, was a disciple of Viollet-le-Duc, and used the Romanesque idiom to evoke Catalunya's roots. The courtyard to the left of the entrance, the Pati dels Lletres, with its orange trees and arcades, is especially pretty. Like most totalitarians, Franco was keen to get students and their ideas out of the city centre, and in the 1950s most of the university was relocated to Pedralbes.

LA RIBERA In 1907, the **Vía Laietana** was laid out, cutting the Barri Gòtic off from La Ribera, the old maritime and business district, also known as El Born. In the days before the building of Barceloneta, the sea washed up to what is now Avinguda Marquès de l'Argentera, and there was a constant bustle as goods were ferried to and from waiting ships. When the Rambla was still a sewer, the Born was the throbbing heart of Barcelona, surrounded by artisans and their shops, while medieval tycoons wheeled and dealed in the Llotja, the hub of western Mediterranean commerce in the 13th and 14th centuries.

Then came the lean centuries, and the traumatic amputation of half of La Ribera for the Ciutadella in the early 1700s. And then Barcelona spread into the Eixample and took most of La Ribera's trade with it. Today the neighbourhood is back in fashion, a transformation that began with the rehabilitation of Carrer Montcada, the finest medieval street in Barcelona.

Museu Europeu d'Art Modern [85 C1] (MEAM; C/ de la Barra de Ferro 5; ⟍933 19 56 93; w meam.es; ⊕ 11.00–19.00 Tue–Sun; adult/reduced/under 10 €13/10/ free) Just off Vía Laietana, this museum run by the Barcelona Academy of Art occupies the 18th-century Palau Gomis. Its collection of 20th- and 21st-century figurative and realist art will throw up some surprises. They frequently host special exhibitions and concerts.

Museu Picasso [85 D1] (C/ de Montcada 15–23; ⟍ 932 56 30 00; w museupicassobcn.cat; ⊕ 10.00–19.00 Tue–Sun (May–Sep 10.00–20.00); book timed tickets online: adult/reduced/under 18 €12/7.50/free; adult €14 with a special exhibition) Today, the once-secret palaces along Carrer Montcada are nearly all museums or galleries, thanks to an initiative taken in 1963 to restore the loveliest of them all, the 15th-century Palau Aguilar (with a courtyard by Marc Safont) and four adjacent palaces, in order to house the Museu Picasso. This remains one of the best places in Spain to see the works of a Spaniard acclaimed as the greatest artist of the 20th century. The core of the collection was donated in 1963 by Picasso's friend and secretary Jaume Sabartés, whom he met in Barcelona in 1899. After Sabartés' death it was augmented by Picasso himself, who, in spite of his refusal to have anything to do with Franco's Spain, had a special place in his heart for the city.

The collection begins with the drawings and doodlings of an eight-year-old in Málaga, kept by his doting mother and sister Lola; Picasso was so precocious that people believed he was a reincarnated grand master. Also here is his first major academic painting, *Science and Charity*, painted in 1897 under pressure from his father to find himself a wealthy patron. Picasso spent a year in Madrid, heading daily to the Prado to study the grand masters who 'breathed down my neck' as he put it. He then spent a few months in Horta de Sant Joan (see page 268) where he painted assured, fluid landscapes. On his return to Barcelona, his work became more eclectic and his style more personal. After a sprinkling of works from the Blue

3

Period (1901–04) – the eerie *Madman* (1904) and the touching, helpless mother and child of *Desamparados* (1904) – and others of the Pink Period in Paris (1905), we skim forward to the celebrated *Harlequin* of 1917. By this time, Picasso was back in Barcelona, collaborating with Diaghilev and his Ballets Russes, and falling headlong for dancer Olga Kokhlova. It was to be his last period in Barcelona.

The collection quietly skips four decades here, and then explodes with the extraordinary series donated by Picasso to the museum. Between 1954 and 1962, he embarked on a series of interpretations of three major paintings – Delacroix's Les *Femmes d'Alger*, Manet's *Le Déjeuner sur l'Herbe* and Velázquez's *Las Meninas*. Painted in intense seclusion between 17 August and 30 December 1956, each element in Las Meninas was meticulously pored over and re-evaluated, and developed 'like the characters and storyline of a serial novel'. Finally come paintings from his last years near Cannes, and ceramics donated by his last wife, Jacqueline.

The upper galleries contain a curious collection of etchings entitled *La Suite 156*, a surreal combination of the erotic fantasies of an old man and a personal interpretation of the history of art, with sly digs at grand masters from Raphael to Matisse, the same who used to breathe down his neck.

Along Carrer Montcada In 1148, Ramon Berenguer IV gave the land on what is know the Carrer Montcada to a rich merchant named Guillem Ramon de Montcada in return for financing the reconquest of Tortosa. Montcada sold lots to nine of his buddies, all 12th-century merchant tycoons, and they created a medieval Millionaires' Row. Most of their Gothic embellishments have disappeared, but lovely interior courtyards remained intact. The presence of money and the old Roman road led to the founding of the *correus volants* – 'flying runners', the origin of the *correos*, the Spanish postal service, which is first mentioned in 1166. This early Catalan pony express was headquartered at the northern end of the street, by the tiny Romanesque **Capella d'en Marcús**, where they would ride in to be blessed before setting out.

Nearly every palace on Carrer Montcada has a story. The 16th-century Gothic **Palau dels Marquesos de Llió** at No. 12 is now the Montcada branch of the excellent **Museu Etnològic i de Cultures del Món** [85 D1] (☏ 932 56 23 00; w barcelona.cat/museu-etnologic-culturesmon; ⊕ 10.00–19.00 Tue–Sun (Apr–Sep 10.00–20.00); adult/reduced/under 16 €5/3.50/free) on Montjuïc (page 117)). Renovated from a Gothic original, the 17th-century **Palau Dalmases** [85 D1] at No. 20 is the finest Baroque palace in Barcelona; don't miss the flamboyant courtyard stair, carved with the Rape of Europa, while Neptune and Amphitrite race up the waves in defiance of gravity. Today it's the venue for flamenco (page 78). Opposite, the 16th-century **Palau dels Cervelló** has four severe gargoyles guiding the rainwater away from the solarium and now houses the **MOCO** [85 D1] (C/ de Montcada 25; ☏ 936 29 18 58; w mocomuseum.com; ⊕ 10.00–20.00 daily, 10.00–21.00 Sat–Sun; adult/reduced €18.95/14.95), a branch of Amsterdam's modern and contemporary art museum featuring both the famous and rising stars in the art world.

Santa Maria del Mar [85 D2] (Pl de Santa Maria; ☏ 933 10 23 90; w santamariadelmarbarcelona.org; ⊕ 10.00–20.30 Mon–Sat, 13.30–17.00 Sun; adult/under 10 €5/free; guided tours in English inc the towers & crypt €10 – book online) This, the most beautiful of all Catalan Gothic churches, occupies an ancient holy site: the first church was built in the 4th century over the tomb of Santa Eulàlia. When Jaume I conquered Mallorca in 1235, he promised a temple to Mary, Star of the Sea, but his promise remained unfulfilled until Alfons III took Sardinia.

Alfons laid the first stone in 1329 and entrusted the design to sculptor Berenguer de Montagut. As Catalan maritime interests expanded, so did La Ribera's population of sailors, porters, tradesmen and merchants. Santa Maria del Mar was to be their church, and all able-bodied men in the parish donated their labour to build it, completing it in 50 years – a supersonic speed in those days, which accounts for its rare stylistic unity.

The **exterior** is almost startlingly simple, a great, austere mass of plain sandstone masonry. The façade, on Plaça Santa Maria, has a rose window framed by a pair of plain buttresses and twin octagonal towers. Two small 15th-century bronze figures of huddled stevedores, who loaded ships, decorate the main door in honour of the ordinary people who provided their labour to build the church. Yet just behind this fortress-like front waits a miracle, a sublime **interior** of airy spaciousness and light, ironically revealed by the Anarchists, who in 1936 started the fire that devoured all the Baroque fittings. The current lack of decoration emphasizes an absolute minimum of interior supports: the octagonal piers of the nave stand 12.8m apart, a distance unsurpassed in any medieval building. Two lofty aisles, half the width of the nave, have only simple niches for chapels between the buttresses. The raised altar is set in a transcendent crescent of slender columns that transform the apse into a glade in an enchanted forest. The stained glass dates from every century; the best, from the 1400s, shows the Ascension and Last Judgement. A visit to the roof terrace offers sublime views over the old city's rooftops and spires.

Along the southern flank of Santa Maria, a low wall and the fan-shaped **Fossar de les Moreres** (Cemetery of Mulberry Trees) marks the mass tomb of those who resisted the Bourbon troops of Felipe V in 1714. Some 3,500 bodies were brought here; all who fought on the Catalan side were buried within a now vanished ring of mulberry trees, and all who fought for the Bourbons were buried without. In 1989 the cemetery was made into a small square, the heroic dead memorialised with a sculpture holding an eternal flame.

Around Santa Maria del Mar

On the map, Santa Maria resembles a big beetle caught in an intricate web of streets, each bearing the name of the medieval trade. In the days of mass illiteracy, shops would identify themselves by hanging out a model of their goods; all that remains now are the stone female faces you see here and there that marked the brothels. Carrer dels Sombrerers along the side of the church was the realm of hatters; busy Carrer de l'Argenteria was the silversmiths' street. On Carrer de les Dames, ladies' street, hopeful spinsters gathered after bad storms; unmarried sailors often vowed to marry the first single woman they saw on shore if they survived.

Passeig del Born

The wide Passeig del Born extends from Santa Maria's apse. Born means tournament and it was used for jousting in the Middle Ages, as well as for the Inquisition's autos-da-fé. It was also the place to see and be seen before the Rambla stole its thunder, but now trendy shops and bars are bringing the wandering Barcelonins back.

The end of the Born is closed off by the **Mercat del Born** (1876), a striking iron structure with a patterned roof, by Josep Fontseré. In 2003, renovation work started to convert the building into a national library – when builders found the remains of streets and homes from the time when Felipe V ordered half of La Ribera demolished for the building of the Ciutadella (page 100). Today it's the **El Born Centre de Cultura i Memòria** [85 D1] (Pl Comercial 12; 932 56 68 51; w elbornculturaimemoria.barcelona.cat; 10.00–20.00 Tue–Sun (Nov–Feb 10.00–

19.00); free), with a host of workshops and exhibitions on the area's history and a viewing platform where you can gaze down on the preserved ruins.

Pla de Palau [85 D2] Once the site of the viceroy's palace, this graceful 19th-century square has a fountain of the Catalan Spirit as its centrepiece, topped with a spirit holding up a star who started life naked and has been dressed and undressed according to the sensibilities of the age for the past 150 years.

The other is the **Llotja** [85 D2] (w llotjademar.cat) or exchange, which was the secular cathedral of Catalan capitalism. Financed by a 3% tax on imports and exports, it was built by Pere Arbei for Pere III the Ceremonious in 1380, after the navy of Peter the Cruel of Castile damaged a more modest building. Although remodelled over the years and slapped with a bland Neoclassical facelift, the magnificent Gothic **Saló de Contractacions** with its 14m-high ceilings was left untouched; until Barcelona's bourse moved to the Passeig de Gràcia in 1996, it was the oldest continuously operating stock exchange in Europe. After 1775 it was used as a school of fine arts, the Reial Acadèmia Catalana de Belles Arts de Sant Jordi; Picasso's father taught here and Picasso attended classes until he quit out of boredom. Today the Chamber of Commerce hires it out for exhibitions and conferences.

Opposite the Llotja, on Passeig d'Isabel II, the **Porxos d'en Xifré** (1840) are two Neoclassical blocks built by moneybags Josep Xifré i Casas (1777–1856), who made his pile in Cuba's slave-worked sugar plantations. On the arcades are portraits of explorers and conquistadors, and terracotta reliefs of charming putti in cheerfully bowdlerised allegories of Cuban trade. It's the address of one of Barcelona's oldest restaurants, the **7 Portes** (page 74), founded in 1839 and still going strong.

Estació de França [85 E2] (Avda Marques de l'Argenteria) The old station for trains to France was erected in 1929 for the International Exhibition and built on a curve in the tracks, lending the iron structure an unusually sensuous beauty. Opposite, walk up the Passeig de Picasso to see Antoni Tàpies' *Homenatge a Picasso* (1983) – a glass cube in a pool that contains household items impaled by steel bars, perpetually splashed by jets of water.

Parc de la Ciutadella [61 F4] In 1714, that bitter date in the annals of Barcelona, the besieged city fell to the troops of Felipe V after an extraordinary, heroic, 11-month resistance. Barcelona knew if it fell it would lose all its vestiges of independence, and so it did. But there was worse to come: half of La Ribera was wiped off the map to construct, at Barcelona's own expense, the Ciutadella, one of the largest fortifications ever built in Europe, which could accommodate 8,000 soldiers.

Before leaving, the 5,000 evicted residents were compelled to tear down their homes stone by stone, and there was never any illusion about the Ciutadella's purpose: the army of occupation kept its cannons aimed at the city. When the progressive Catalan General Prim took power in 1869, he gave the fort to the city, designating 150 acres for a park, and declared that the heirs of original property owners should be compensated.

A competition was held for the park's design, and the winner was Josep Fontseré, an able architect and spotter of talent – his design team included two then unknowns, Domènech i Montaner and Gaudí. The trees Fontseré planted were just beginning to produce shade when Barcelona's buoyant mayor, Francesc de Paula Ruis i Taulet, announced that it was the chosen location for the 1888 Universal Exhibition, to be opened in a mere 11 months' time.

Fontseré protested, Fontseré was fired, and the project lurched full speed ahead in spite of doomsday predictions; Barcelona in the 1880s was in the grip of another recession and the mood was glum. Although it left the city deeply in debt, the exhibition was in fact the key event that kept Barcelona from sliding irrevocably into provincial backwaters. Like all good exhibitions, it also served as a stage for innovation – think of London and the Crystal Palace in 1851, or Paris and the dazzling ironwork of the Eiffel Tower of 1889. Barcelona in 1888 presented the world with Modernisme. It also gave the city a Dizzy Gillespie-size taste for tooting its own horn.

The Ciutadella also contains **Barcelona Zoo** [61 G4] (✆ 902 45 75 45; w zoobarcelona.cat; ⏰ winter 10.00–16.30 daily, summer 10,00–20.00 daily; check website), where, despite a shift towards conservation, the animals (lions, hippos and primates among them) are kept in diminutive enclosures. Nearby is the Plaça d'Armes, the old parade ground and now a formal garden. The square has the only surviving buildings from the Ciutadella: the chapel, Governor's Palace and Arsenal, designed by Prosper Verboom, with trumpet-mouthed gargoyles. This was converted into a royal residence, then into an art museum, and during the Republic, with a nice sense of irony, into the seat of the **Catalan Parliament**.

The Parc de la Ciutadella is well used, especially at weekends, when families come to paddle in little boats in the lake opposite Josep Fontseré's **Cascada**. This superbly ugly pile of stone is set in a monumental stair inspired by the Palais Longchamps in Marseille, with lashings of mythological allusions: four spitting dragons, Venus emerging from her half-shell, and the Quadriga of Aurora. Gaudí, they say, arranged the boulders of the grotto.

Many of the buildings built for exhibition survive, but none are open. Fontseré redeems his Cascada-splashed reputation with his pretty **Umbracle**, a cast-iron greenhouse for shade plants, with a wooden lattice roof, next to Josep Amargós' iron-and-glass **Hivernacle** winter greenhouse, recently beautifully restored after decades of neglect. In between, the neo-Pompeiian building was opened in 1882 as Barcelona's first public museum, the Museu de Geología.

Best of all the park's buildings is the great brick **Castell dels Tres Dragons**, designed by Domènech i Montaner as the Universal Exhibition's café-restaurant, although it wasn't finished in time to sell a single *pa amb tomàquet*. It did, however, herald Modernisme, with its innovative use of exposed plain brick and iron, crowned with whimsical ceramic decoration. It was nicknamed the 'Castle of the Three Dragons' after a poem by Frederic Soler. Fontseré designed the broad **Passeig Lluís Companys** outside the northern gate as the park's salon, although all but one of his bronze statues of Catalan heroes were melted down under Franco to make the giant Virgin presiding over the dome of the church of La Mercè.

At the top of the promenade stands the entrance to the 1888 fair, the **Arc de Triomf** by Josep Vilaseca. With no triumph in particular to commemorate (besides getting the exhibition ready on time!), Vilaseca's ensemble of mudéjar-style ceramic brickwork topped with four crowns manifests, if nothing else, the eternal Catalan longing to be different.

Around the corner, the **Museu de la Xocolata** [85 D1] (Chocolate Museum; C/ de Comerç 36; ✆ 932 68 78 78; w museuxocolata.cat; ⏰ 10.00–19.00 Tue–Sat, 10.00–14.00 Sun; adult/reduced/under 7 €6/5/free) is dedicated to its history, art and preparation of chocolate with state-of-the-art, multilingual, interactive exhibitions. And of course there's a gift shop.

BARRI SANT PERE For as long as anyone can remember, Barri Sant Pere was Barcelona's textile centre. In the 18th century, when the city couldn't ship enough calico to Spain's colonies, much of the medieval fabric was replaced with factories and housing for merchants and workers. The neighbourhood grew up in the 11th century on land owned by **Sant Pere de les Puelles** [60 F3] (Pl de Sant Pere; w parroquiadesantperedelespuelles.org; ⊕ 10.00–noon Mon–Sat, 11.00–18.00 Sun; free) a church founded outside the Roman walls by the Visigoths, then refounded in AD945 by the counts of Barcelona as a Benedictine convent. The puelles were the strictly cloistered young nuns, who enjoyed a great reputation for their beauty. When al-Mansur's troops burst in in AD985, the women cut off their own noses, hoping to avoid a fate worse than death; in disgust the Moors chopped off the rest of their heads. The church was rebuilt in 1147, and when the nuns left in the 19th century their cloister became a prison. After a burning in the 1909 Setmana Tràgica, it was given its fortress façade; after more arson in 1936, only a few columns and capitals remain (the best are in the MNAC).

Lively **Carrer de Sant Pere Més Baix** is the district's shopping street, lined with medieval and 18th-century palaces. The **Farmàcia Padrell** [61 F4] at No.52, the oldest in Barcelona, dates back to 1561; in 1890 it was given a pretty Modernista facelift. Farther south (backtrack a bit to Carrer de Freixures) is the big neighbourhood market, the **Mercat de Santa Caterina** (1847) [85 C1], renovated according to plans by the late Enric Miralles, architect of the Scottish Parliament, and capped with an undulating roof of multicoloured tiles.

Palau de la Música Catalana [61 E4] (C/ del Palau de la Música 4–6; ☏938 55 57 31; w palaumusica.cat; ⊕ 09.30–15.30; adult €18 self-guided, €20 guided tour, under 11 free)

There's an old joke: one Catalan starts a business, two start a corporation and three start a choral society. No-one can deny that this gruff, taciturn, capitalist tribe has a musical soul, and in the 1850s Renaixença fervour an ardent Republican named Josep Anselm Clavé founded the first workers' choral groups. There were 85 of them by 1861. The most important, the Orfeó Català, was founded in 1891 by Clavé and Amadeu Vives, and soon became an important representative of Catalan ideals and culture in Spain.

Flushed with success, in 1904 the Orfeó gave Lluís Domènech i Montaner a brief to create a 'Temple of Catalan art, a palace to celebrate its renaissance'. The idea warmed the cockles of Domènech's nationalist heart, and he delivered in spades, subcontracting the most accomplished artists of the day to create a Modernista garden of delights. But the Barcelonins are fickle folk. A decade after the palace won the city's prize for the best building of 1907, opinion had swung violently against it: Noucentista architects were calling for the destruction of the 'Palace of Catalan Junk'. Needless to say it survived all these insults to celebrate its glorious centenary in 2008, but some remodelling has been necessary over the years, the most recent a sympathetic restoration and extension by Oscar Tusquets. No-one has really managed to fix the famously bad acoustics.

In the narrow streets, the Palau resembles a bouquet stuffed in a cupboard: the site simply wasn't big enough. The decoration on the façade is a rapturous allegory of Catalan music and the music Catalans loved. Busts of Wagner (a big favourite), Beethoven, Bach and Palestrina by Eusebi Arnau decorate the second floor. Miquel Blay, a disciple of Rodin, sculpted the huge corner group that projects like a figurehead on a ship, with a knight and damsel emerging from a cloud of legendary figures. Mosaics by Lluís Bru along the top of the façade show the Orfeó performing in front of the Catalan Mount Sinai, Montserrat.

The lavish **lobby** is a cleaner's worst nightmare. The ceiling is decorated with a ceramic trellis adorned with plump clusters of roses, while the banisters are encased in smoky topaz glass and surrounded with blooms and vines. The starring role goes, of course, to the **auditorium**, an epiphany of stained glass and ceramics. Domènech wanted to bring in as much light as possible, and he dematerialized the walls' Gothic style, but with modern technology and a steel frame, making this the first curtain-wall building in Spain. Rainbow-coloured sunlight streams in through Antoni Rigalt's huge stained-glass **skylight**, filling the jewel-like glass box.

The **stage set** is composed of 18 unforgettable half-tile, half-3D-ceramic maidens by Eusebi Arnau, each brandishing a musical instrument before a background of *trencadís*. The proscenium is dramatically marked by flowing sculptures designed by Domènech, executed by Didac Masana and finished by Pau Gargallo: Beethoven and galloping, wild-eyed Valkyries confront Josep Clavé smiling serenely under a tree, while maidens below him act out his perennial choral hit song, *The Flowers of May*.

SEASIDE BARCELONA In the 13th and 14th centuries, Barcelona's dominance in the Mediterranean was such that her sailors boasted that 'not even a fish would dare to appear without the quatre barres', the flag of Catalunya. Endowed by nature with only a mediocre port, Barcelona's success came by way of sheer determination and mercantile savvy. The sea, however, was a strictly business proposition, leaving no room for any Venetian-style monuments or razzmatazz.

The change began in 1980: with the same determination that made the mess in the first place, the Ajuntament swept the freighters and containers away into the Zona Franca, and turned Barcelona into a Mediterranean playground, bobbing with yachts (including some of the world's biggest super yachts) instead of rubbish, buzzing with clubs, bars, restaurants and shops instead of flies. The 2024 America's Cup saw another wave of renovation, with €136 million spent on rehabilitating historic buildings like the pretty 19th-century customs house, the Portal de la Pau, expanding the Maremagnum entertainment mall, and the construction of a new promenade which juts into the sea behind the sail-shaped Hotel W.

Around the Drassanes

To begin where it all began, start in the Drassanes, the best-preserved medieval shipyards in the world. The first Arab *darsena*, or shipyards, were enlarged and improved between 1283 and 1328, and in 1388 the Drassanes took their present form. Thirty galleys could be built in their long bays at the same time. The Spanish navy took them over in 1663, then in 1941 gave them back to the city to restore and make into a museum on Catalunya's shipfaring past.

Museu Marítim [85 B4] (Av de les Drassanes; \ 933 42 99 20; w mmb.cat; ⏰ 10.00–20.00 daily; adult/reduced €10/5, free after 15.00 Sun) Although the architecture steals the show – the vaults are long enough to melt into shadows – the exhibits offer much to ponder. There's a display on medieval cartography when Mallorca's Jewish community had Europe's most advanced school of map-making. Displays illustrate ancient and medieval ship construction, with models (some in ivory, some in bottles, and instructions on how to get them in there); there are figureheads, seamen's chests painted with biblical warnings of women's wiles, and a copy of Jaume the Conqueror's famous *Llibro del Consolat de Mar*, medieval Europe's first maritime code.

The most dramatic exhibit is a full-scale replica of *La Real*, Don Juan's flagship at Lepanto, built in 1971 in honour of the 400th anniversary of the battle. Down at the port, you can also visit the museum's beautiful old schooner, the *Santa Eulàlia* (1918).

3

Monument a Colom [61 E6] (Pl Portal de la Pau; ℡932 85 38 34; ⊕ 08.30–14.30 daily; adult/reduced €8/6) Barcelona's original 225-tonne seaside bagatelle, a 50m cast-iron column made of melted cannons from the castle of Montjuïc and topped with a statue of Columbus, was erected at the foot of the Rambla for the 1888 Universal Exhibition. You can ascend into the crown under Columbus' feet for the view over the sea and Ramblas by taking the lift – the first one, according to Barcelona's tireless boasters, to be installed inside a column.

This Columbus is the biggest monument to the admiral anywhere in the world, and the irony of honouring the one man who led to Barcelona's decline, as Spain turned to the Atlantic and Seville took over as premier port, was not lost on the citizenry. Note that he has his back to Castile, and points not to America but towards Italy (where Barcelona's merchants wish he had stayed!).

Actually the intention in 1888 was to 'Catalanise' Columbus. Since Catalan, along with Portuguese and Castilian, were among the languages the admiral wrote (rather than Italian), and because he always went to great lengths to cover up his origins, there was a nationalist faction that claimed that he was really the Catalan Joan Colom from Girona (Gerona), which could easily be confused by a slip of the pen with Genoa (Genova). Others say he was from a Jewish family in Mallorca who had fled the bigotry by emigrating to Genoa. Mallorca was famous for its maps, which would explain where Columbus and his brother picked up their considerable cartographic skills.

Barcelona does have some authenticated Columbus associations, all of which are celebrated in the statuary around the base of the pillar. He met Fernando and Isabel here in 1493 after his first voyage, when he received the title of Admiral of the Ocean Sea and an annual stipend that kept the wolf from the door in his later years, when the Catholic Kings reneged on all their other promises. On his second voyage he took along a Catalan priest, Bernat de Bol, who became the first bishop in the New World. Today Catalan nationalists are more likely to disclaim him altogether: a replica of his *Santa Maria* moored nearby was burned by militants in 1989, and events celebrating the 500-year anniversary in 1992 were boycotted – even the choral societies refused to sing.

Next to Columbus, the **Duana Nova**, or New Customs House, is a silly neo-Renaissance wedding cake by Enric Sagnier (1902). Beyond this extends the **Moll de Barcelona** [61 F6], where I. M. Pei's huge semi-circular **World Trade Center** [61 F6] spearheads Barcelona's ambition to become the Mediterranean's container port capital as well as its busiest cruise port. If you aren't on a big cruise boat, you can catch a little one, a **Golondrina** ('swallow') for a tour of the port and coast at the Moll de les Drassanes under Columbus. Or take the jaunty new nautical bus service, the Bus Nàutic (w alsa.com/en/web/bus/touristic-services/bus-nautic; €1.90 one way), which crosses the port from Drassanes to the Llevant dock by the Hotel W.

Port Vell [61 F5] The flashy redevelopment of the Port Vell, or old port, is crossed by a handsome wooden bridge of high undulating arches, the Rambla de Mar, which rotates to let sail boats through. The old Moll's occupants include a huge glass and chrome shopping mall called **Maremagnum** [61 F6] and the **Aquàrium** [85 D4] (℡932 21 74 74; w aquariumbcn.com; ⊕ 10.00–19.00 Mon–Fri, 10.00–20.00 Sat–Sun, later in summer; adult/ages 5–10/ages 3–4 €25/18/10) was the largest in Europe until arch-rival Valencia stole its thunder. Best here is the vast central tank, encircled by a 68.5m viewing tunnel equipped with a slow human conveyor belt and serenaded by gentle New Age music; the patterns of silvery fish and sharks swimming all around are remarkably soothing. The old IMAX cinema is slated for demolition and will be replaced by a new outpost of the Liceu Opera House (page 83).

On the landward side of the Port Vell, the Moll de la Fusta is overlooked by Mariscal's 6m fibreglass *Prawn*, and Roy Lichtenstein's colourful *Barcelona Head* (1992). The old warehouses, the Magatzems Generals, have been reincarnated as the Palau de Mar, home to restaurants and the **Museu d'Història de Catalunya** [85 E3] (Pl Pau Villa 3; ✆932 25 47 00; w mhcat.cat; ◷ 10.00–19.00 Tue–Sat, 10.00–20.00 Wed, 10.00–14.30 Sun; adult/reduced €6/4). Designed to give an overview of Catalan history, the emphasis is on kid-friendly interactive devices, and there's a huge glass-topped relief that lets you tramp like Gulliver across Catalunya. The rooftop café is a treat with views over the port.

Around the Carrer Ample The palm-lined Passeig de Colom was widened when the sea ramparts were razed – in 1882, it became the first street to get electric lighting. Two streets in from here is the Carrer Ample, 'wide street' – wide enough for carriages, which in the 16th century was good enough to make it the city's most aristocratic address, hosting the likes of Emperor Charles V and the kings of Hungary and Bohemia.

Now better known for tapas than kings, the street ends at Barcelona's temple of letters, the **Correus** (1927), the post office designed for the 1929 Exhibition. Further along is the **Basílica de La Mercè** [85 C3] (Pl de la Mercè; ✆933 15 27 56; w basilicadelamerce.com; ◷ 09.00–13.30 & 16.30–20.00; free). Our Lady of Mercy joined St Eulàlia as co-patroness of Barcelona when she appeared to Jaume the Conqueror, asking him to found an order devoted to the deliverance of Christians held by Barbary pirates. The church was built in 1267, then rebuilt to fit Counter-Reformation ideals; its concave façade was transplanted from a demolished Baroque church. The fittings are Baroque, too, and there's a fine Gothic statue of the Virgin (1361) by Pere Moragues. She saved Catalunya from a plague of locusts in 1687 and, when Barcelona was besieged in 1714, she was made commander of the army, although unfortunately the Bourbons proved to be tougher than the insects. As if to emphasize the point, her statue on the dome, destroyed in the Civil War, was recast in 1956 from melted-down bronze statues of Catalan heroes. Among the Virgin's devotees are members of FC Barcelona, who sing a hymn of thanks whenever the team wins an important match.

The grand Neoclassical **Palau Martorell** [85 C3] (C/ Ample 11; ✆680 709 373; w palaumartorell.com; ◷ 10.00–14.00 & 15.00–19.00 Wed–Sun; adult/reduced €8/6) is one of the city's newest museums, with a huge stained-glass skylight and three floors of temporary exhibitions showcasing the works of artists such as Basquiat, Alexander Calder and Tamara de Lempicka.

Barceloneta In 1718, the destruction of 61 streets and 1,262 homes in La Ribera to build the Ciutadella left many people in makeshift shelters on the beach. The misery continued until 1753, when a French military engineer with the delicious name of Prosper Verboom designed a neighbourhood for the displaced (or at least their children) on this 25-acre triangle reclaimed from the sea. Following the most progressive planning ideas of the time, the streets of Barceloneta were laid out in a grid, with a market in the central square and long, narrow blocks of houses, permitting every room to have a window. As all houses were allowed only one upper floor, all had access to sunlight and air. Verboom's height prohibition was modified in 1837 and ignored ever since, turning the straight narrow streets into mini canyons.

Barceloneta is still vibrant, filled with seafood restaurants, edged by the city's oldest beach. The central **Plaça de la Font** is the site of the market (rebuilt in 2007) and of a pair of original two-storey houses at Nos. 30 and 32. On Plaça de la Barceloneta, the little 18th-century Baroque church of **Sant Miquel** [61 G5] is dedicated to Barceloneta's patron saint.

The neighbourhood is also an outdoor art museum; Mario Merz's *Crescendo Appare* (1992) along the Moll de la Barceloneta consists of the numbers of the Fibonacci series embedded under glass in the pavement. The beach is decorated with Rebecca Horn's lofty *Homage to Barceloneta* (1992), a swaying, stacked iron column that echoes the narrow old buildings of the *barri* and the famous but long-disappeared seafood shacks. In Plaça de Mar, towards the tower of the aerial cableway, is the most mysterious *A Room Where it Always Rains* (1992) by Juan Muñoz.

Nearby, the Torre de Sebastià supports the **Telefèric del Port** [61 E–G6] (aerial cableway; Pg Joan de Borbó; \934 30 47 16; w telefericodebarcelona.com; ⊕ 11.00 until dusk; €12.50 one way, €20 return) that crosses the sea to Montjuïc. Strung up for the 1929 fair, it offers sensational views that are well worth the vertigo.

Vila Olímpica [61 H3]

Until the late 1980s, the seafront between Barceloneta and the River Besos was occupied by decrepit textile factories, warehouses and train yards. Even if you could get to a beach, the water stank. The need to house 15,000 athletes for the Olympics propelled the Ajuntament in 1986 to undertake Barcelona's biggest urban-renewal project of the last century. Coastal train tracks were relocated, and 500 acres of Poblenou were expropriated and flattened to create the **Parc de Mar**, opening up 5km of new public beaches, and the Vila Olímpica, a district as rigidly planned as Barceloneta, but in many ways its antithesis. Each building was commissioned from a past winner of the FAD Architecture prize, and each ducked the occasion. Even the opportunity to make something interesting out of the deluxe Hotel Arts and the Torre Mapfre, at the time Spain's tallest buildings, was declined, leaving two boring boxes by the beach.

This is the one area of Barcelona clearly more friendly to cars than people, with car parks along the marina and big desolate spaces between the traffic. Needless to say, it's all fantastically popular, especially the **Port Olímpic** [61 H4], a confluence of shops, restaurants, beachside cafés and clubs, topped with the enormous headless bronze *Peix* (Fish) by Frank Gehry, a glistening hunk of postmodernist bait.

Poblenou

Adjoining the Port Olímpic is the Poblenou neighbourhood, a once run-down industrial area still dotted with a few 19th-century factories and chimney stacks among the boxy new towers. This area is the focus of the city's ambitious plans for an 'innovation district', called **22@** (w 22barcelona.com), and design studios, tech companies, artisan coffee shops and concept stores are popping up like mushrooms. Back in the 1980s, Javier Mariscal and other artists took over a dilapidated textile factory, **Palo Alto** [61 H2] (C/ dels Pellaires 30–38; \931 58 95 55; w paloalto.barcelona), and established a creative hub with artists' workshops and design studios. It would spearhead the transformation of Poblenou into Barcelona's foremost design district. The charming secret garden is a haven – except during the monthly markets (w palomarketfest.com), complete with food trucks and DJs.

Another old factory, which dates back to the late 18th century, is home to **Can Framis** [61 G1] (C/ de Roc Boronat 116; \933 20 87 36; w fundaciovilacasas.com/ en/museum/can-framis-museum-barcelona; ⊕ 11.00–18.00 Tue–Sat, 11.00–14.00 Sun; adult/reduced €8/4), a museum of contemporary painting, with a focus on

Catalan and Spanish artists. Extensively remodelled, not much survives of the original factory except its tall chimney. There are excellent temporary exhibitions and all kinds of activities, from guided visits by artists to family workshops.

At the end of Avinguda d'Icària, the **Cementiri de l'Est** [61 H2] was the city's first monumental cemetery, founded in 1773 when all the old graveyards in the choked, walled town were turned into squares and building sites. It, too, is choked, with a surreal accretion of monuments to the fathers of Barcelona industry, a preview of the lavish postmortem paraphernalia in Montjuïc's Cementiride Sud-Ouest. Madrid is proud of its sculpture of Satan in the Retiro park, but here Barcelona has something just as fey in its *Kiss of Death*. Jean Nouvel's contemporary **Parc del Poblenou** [61 H3], opened in 2008, offers a leafy retreat from the bedlam of the nearby seafront.

Parc del Fòrum [61 H2] After the Olympics, Barcelona wanted to keep its economic momentum going by holding another exposition, so then-Mayor Maragall proposed something called a Universal Forum of Cultures. The juiciest part of the plan, to the Catalan politicians, was that it gave them an excuse for another expensive building project. Hence the **Fòrum**, the brobdingnagian, triangular convention centre on stilts that Barcelonans call the 'floating blue cheesecake'. It houses the city's natural history collections, with lots of interactivity for the kids, in the **Museu de Ciències Naturals** [61 H2] (\ 932 56 60 02; w museuciencies.cat; ⊕ Oct–Apr 10.00–17.00 Tue–Fri, 10.00–19.00 Sat, 10.00–20.00 Sun; May–Sep 10.00–19.00 Tue–Sat, 10.00–20.00 Sun; adult/reduced €6/2.70, free 1st Sun of each month, & Sun after 15.00).

THE EIXAMPLE Barcelona's Eixample ('ay-sham-play'), like the world's other great one-offs, came about through a rare combination of factors, in this case a blank slate to build on, and the talent, skill, quirkiness, imagination and money to make it something thoroughly unique, with Anarchist bombs providing a restless basso continuo in the background and Gaudí off in his corner trying to save their souls by building the Sagrada Família. And, perhaps most intangibly, it's all thoroughly Catalan.

The Passeig de Gràcia and the Fairest of Discords
The greatest concentration of Modernista masterpieces is along the Eixample's most elegant boulevard, the **Passeig de Gràcia**, north of the Plaça Catalunya. In the late 18th century, the old road to Gràcia was the 'Elysian fields' of dance halls, theatres, beer gardens and amusements. The first trees were planted in 1827, and by 1872 it had its first horse-drawn trams.

If you love architecture, though, duck into Carrer de Casp, where at No. 48 stands the **Casa Calvet** (1898) [108 D4], Gaudí's first apartment building – the ironwork detail, the two crosses and the decorative elements presage his future masterpieces. The most dazzling stretch of the Passeig de Gràcia, between Carrer de Consell de Cent and Carrer d'Aragó, the so-called *Mançana de la Discòrdia* – or the 'block of discord'. Here, any passer-by can play the role of the Trojan Paris and award the prize to the fairest of these three wildly contrasting Modernista beauties.

Casa Lleó Morera [108 B3] (Pg de Gràcia 35; not open to the public) The first, the Casa Lleó Morera at No. 35, was built in 1864. Between 1902 and 1906, the owner let Domènech i Montaner have his way with it, and the result is his most lavish residential project, the corner crowned with an ethereal ceramic cupola, the whole frosted with decoration inside and out. For Barcelona's elite, wealth wasn't

3

BARCELONA
Passeig de Gracia

Casa de les Punxes,
Casa Comalat

For listings, see from page 72

🛏 **Where to stay**

1 Claris...............................B2
2 Gran Via.........................D4
3 Hostal Oliva...................C4
4 Hotel Palace..................D3
5 Jazz.................................D4
6 Mandarin Oriental........C3
7 Margot House................B3
8 Paseo de Gràcia.............A2
9 Praktik Èssens...............C4
10 Sir Victor.......................A1

✖ **Where to eat and drink**

11 Cervecería Catalana.......A3
12 L'Olivé............................A4
13 La Bodegueta.................A2

AVINGUDA DE LA DIAGONAL
CARRER DE PROVENÇA
CARRER DE MALLORCA
CARRER ROGER DE LLURIA
CARRER DE PAU CLARIS
CARRER D'ARAGÓ
PASSEIG DE GRACIA
CARRER DE MALLORCA
CARRER DE VALÈNCIA
CARRER D'ARAGÓ
CARRER BALMES
RAMBLA DE CATALUNYA
PASSEIG DE GRACIA
CARRER DE LA DIPUTACIO
CARRER ROGER DE LLURIA
CARRER DE LES CORTS CATALANES
CARRER DE PAU CLARIS
GRAN VIA DE LES CORTS CATALANES
CARRER DE LA DIPUTACIO

Palau Baró de Quadras
La Pedrera (Casa Milà)
Casa Thomas
Palau Ramon Montaner
Sita Murt
Museu Egipci
Fundació Antoni Tàpies
Casa Batlló
Casa Amatller
Casa Lleó Morera
Reserva Ibérica
Casa Calvet
Llibreria Finestres
Museu del Modernisme Barcelona

Bradt
N

0 ———— 100m
0 ———— 100yds

the only thing to flaunt on a façade: the family's interests, social status, business connections and hobbies were advertised as well.

As the ground floor of the Casa Lleó Morera was destined to house a photographer's studio, Arnau covered it with nymphs and reliefs relating to electricity and cameras, all sacrificed in 1943 by Loewe of Madrid, of leather goods fame, for larger shop windows. On the second floor, however, the nymphs survived the ruthless leather-goods-mongers. A gorgeous stained-glass bay window of happy roosters in the country by Joan Rigalt provides both a glamorous screen and a voluptuous rush of colour, while the walls are covered in delightful ceramic mosaic portraits by Gaspar Homar; the furnishings he designed for the room are now in the Museu Nacional d'Art de Catalunya.

Casa Amatller [108 B3] (Pg de Gràcia 41; ☏ 934 61 74 60; w amatller.org; ⊕ 10.00–20.00 daily; book timed tickets online from €15 with an audio guide, children ages 7–12 €9.50, under 7 free; guided tours from €17/12) Two doors down, Casa Amatller was called 'the apotheosis of decorative arts' when it was completed in 1898. Antoni Amatller i Costa, the Willy Wonka of Catalan chocolate, started the redecorating trend on the block when he hired Puig i Cadafalch to give his existing house a Gothic makeover. Puig's Gothic, however, is like no-one else's: the façade, decorated with ceramic plaques and discreet sgraffito, culminates in a remarkable stepped gable, richly aglitter with blue, pink and cream tiles.

The façade, in fact, is one big allegory of Amatller's life and passions, one of which was Catalan nationalism. Between the two doorways, we see St George battling the dragon; soulful figures represent painting, sculpture and music; monkeys hammer away at iron while rabbits stow the finished product, in a vignette of happy industrious workers. A bespectacled donkey engrossed in a book while his friend twiddles with a camera are references to Amatller's love of reading and his new photographic interests.

Perhaps Amatller spent too much time on his hobbies, because his wife ran off with an opera singer before the façade was finished; as a consequence, the *tribuna*, which in the best houses was used to show off the latest fashions to hoi polloi in the

THE MAKING OF THE EIXAMPLE

Barcelona was one of the first cities in Spain to industrialise and, by the early 19th century, it was among the most densely populated in Europe. Hemmed in by the medieval walls, Barcelona's buildings grew taller, the streets narrower, and open spaces fewer, as factories and workshops began to proliferate. . The city fathers endlessly petitioned the government in Madrid to remove the walls, but permission was only finally granted in 1854, during one of Spain's brief interludes of liberalism. When word reached Barcelona, wild celebration filled the streets as every man, woman and child started hacking at walls. Once the lid was off, the city in 1859 sponsored a competition for the plan of the 'extension', or Eixample.

The finalists were both Catalans. The Ajuntament chose the plan of municipal architect Antoni Rovira i Trias, who proposed exciting prospects and boulevards fanning out of the old city, respectful of its axes and origins, an organic translation between old and new. To Barcelona's dismay, Madrid intervened and imposed the losing scheme (to this day no-one knows why) by a Socialist engineer named Ildefons Cerdà, whose plan had nothing whatsoever to do with the old city in its modular waffle grid of uniform wide streets, with its distinct chamfered corners (*xamfrans*) to allow the new steam trams to turn more easily.

Cerdà's visions were utopian: his pure abstract plan would eliminate social classes – there was no reason why one block should be better than another – and there would be gardens in the centre of each block, with light, air and windows for all.

It's hard not to feel sorry for Cerdà, who spent his life and fortune on his vision. Few city plans have had their intentions as gleefully sabotaged. Barcelona quintupled in size over the next 50 years, but key elements of Cerdà's plan – the height and density restrictions, the parks and social services – soon went by the wayside; buildings and car parks filled in the blocks instead of gardens. Nor did Cerdà's ideas on equality make it off the blueprints. The Right Eixample (Dreta de l'Eixample), where Modernista architects created fabulous palaces for their wealthy clients, became more desirable than the Left Eixample (Esquerra de l'Eixample).

If the Barri Gòtic is Europe's largest medieval neighbourhood, the Dreta de l'Eixample (or to be more precise, the Quadrant d'Or between the Barri Gòtic, Diagonal, Carrer de Roger de Flor and Carrer de Muntaner) holds the greatest trove of 19th-century architecture, with over 150 listed Modernista buildings.

3

street, was built to one side, near the bedroom of Miss Amatller, the new lady of the house. The window decoration culminates in an almond tree, a play on the family name, with a curling letter 'A'.

The same motif is found on the grand staircase, along with a stern eagle and a lovely stained-glass skylight. The original elevator still wheezes its way between floors, and the *piano nobile* retains most of its rich decoration by Eusebi Arnau and Gaspar Homar.

Casa Batlló [108 B3] (Pg de Gràcia 43; ☎ 932 16 03 06; w casabatllo.es; ⏱ 09.00–22.00; book time-stamped tickets online for self-guided tours with augmented reality starting at €29, under 12 free) In stark contrast to Casa Amatller's sharp right angles is the absolutely extraordinary Casa Batlló, the block's third 'apple of discord'. This too was an older building, belonging to textile tycoon Josep Batlló, who basically wanted to outdo the Joneses next door and in 1904 commissioned Gaudí to give the house a facelift. Gaudí turned it into Barcelona's biggest allegory of St George and the Dragon, covered with a rippling blue skin of ceramic plaques and *trencadís* – the architect would stand in the middle of the Passeig de Gràcia to 'paint' the façade, directing workmen in the arrangement of the colours, which shimmer and change according to the light.

Gaudí's great collaborator Josep Maria Jujol topped it with an equally sublimely coloured roof for the dragon's scaly back. The pinnacle with its bulb dome and cross is St George's lance, piercing the dragon and placed to one side to complement the symmetry of the Casa Amatller; the *trencadí*-covered chimneys are the dragon's multi-spiked tail.

The first floor is the dragon's lair; the first balcony depicts the rose that grew from its blood, while the other balconies hint at the skulls and tibia in its larder. Or so it seems. Some have seen other visions in the façade – a representation of the sea, with soft blues and greens and bubbling windows hollowed out by the waves, the balconies of delicate wrought iron like fishing nets being tossed in the air. Or is it an allegory of the Venice Carnival, with a pert Harlequin, balconies forming masks and a dappled, confetti-strewn façade?

The first-floor apartment, completely redesigned for Batlló, is just as stunning: there isn't a straight line in the whole place, and it contains what must be the most sensuous staircase in the world, based on the curve of the dragon's tail. Note the magnificent blue ceramic light-well, which imperceptibly avoids the effect of light glaring down a pit by means of colour, using dark tiles at the top, gradually introducing lighter ones until reaching white at the bottom. The back of the house is covered in a skin of multicoloured *trencadís*, visible from an undulating terrace scattered with ceramic fountains and sculpted ponds.

Fundació Antoni Tàpies [108 B3] (C/ d'Aragó 255; ☎ 934 87 03 15; w fundaciotapies. org; ⏱ 10.00–19.00 Mon–Sat, 10.00–15.00 Sun; adult/reduced €12/8) Round the corner from the Mançana de la Discòrdia is the headquarters built by Domènech i Montaner for his brother's publishing company (1880–85), a prototype of Modernisme, as well as an early example of the architect's love for honest Catalan brick and iron. It was Barcelona's first domestic building with an iron frame, and the elaborate brick patterns are a reference to the Moorish-influenced mudéjar work of medieval Spain. Tàpies himself loved everyday materials, which he used for the *Núvol i Cadira* (Cloud and Chair) hovering over the building like a giant steel-wool pad.

Born in 1923 to a bourgeois family in Barcelona, Antoni Tàpies was a sickly child who relished days spent in bed, sketching and gathering a fund of images that would insinuate themselves into his later works. Like his friend Miró, he sought the extraordinary within the ordinary, while colouring much of his work with a pervasive self-referential and sometimes oblique film: graffitied walls recall those of the old Barcelona of his childhood; the recurring motifs of mirrors and wardrobes echo the images thrown back at the young invalid. These pieces, bleak and yet hauntingly spiritual, were created from found objects, scraps of paper and rags. In 1984 he set up this foundation for the study of contemporary and non-Western art; there is a selection of Tàpies' art and changing exhibitions by others.

Museu Egipci [108 B2] (C/ de Valencia 286; \934 88 01 88; w museuegipci.com; ⏲ 10.00–14.00 & 16.00–20.00 Mon–Fri, 10.00–15.00 & 16.00–19.30 Sat, 10.00–14.00 Sun; adult/reduced/ages 6–14 €13/9/5) Millionaire enthusiast Jordi Clos' excellent private collection of Egyptian art takes up three floors of an Eixample townhouse, including reconstructions of tombs and a choice collection of masks, ceramics, jewellery, statuettes and mummies, including a baby crocodile that looks like a pencil and other swaddled animals, complete with X-rays.

La Pedrera (Casa Milà) [108 A2] (Pg de Gràcia 92; \93 21 42 57; w lapedrera. com; ⏲ Mar–Oct 09.00–20.30 daily, Nov–Feb 09.00–18.30 daily; book time-stamped tickets online from adult/reduced/ages 7–12/under 7 €28/19/12.50/free, with audio guide; guided night tours year-round 21.00–23.00 with light shows, cava and treats €38, €29 and €22.50) Gaudí's Casa Batlló (page 110) created such a sensation that some even richer people, Pere Milà, a member of the Spanish parliament, and his wife from Reus, Gaudí's home town, immediately hired Gaudí to outdo himself a few blocks up the Passeig de Gràcia. Here he was given a virgin *xamfrà*, and the result, the Casa Milà (1905–10), was just what the couple ordered: the most extraordinary, singular apartment building ever built, nicknamed La Pedrera, 'the stone quarry'.

As much sculpture as building, the stone façade (supported by a complex steel armature and hammered to give it the desired rough texture) undulates around the bevelled corners of the intersection like a cliff sculpted by waves and wind, pierced by windows that seem to be eroded into the stone, underlined by Jujol's fantastical balconies of forged iron seaweed spilling over the edges and culminating in a roof of cresting white sea foam – or icing. Newspaper cartoons compared the building to a gooey cake. The colour-drenched interior **courtyard** is as striking as the façade, with its two irregular circular patios open to the sky, enclosed in winding ramps; Gaudí had wanted residents to be able to drive to their doors, but settled for Europe's first underground car park.

The ticket includes a visit to a recreated **apartment,** which is chock-full of the then-latest modern gadgets – electric lights, time-saving domestic appliances and telephones. Because Gaudí dispensed with interior load-bearing walls, no two apartments are alike. The first people to move in complained snootily that none of their furniture fitted in the swirling rooms; Santiago Rusinyol joked that residents would have to have snakes for pets, instead of cats and dogs.

Even the Casa Milà's **attic** is no ordinary attic, but a great wavy tunnel of catenary parabolic arches resembling the ribcage of a dragon – what the princess would have seen had not St George arrived on time. It contains a small museum, offering an overview of the man's work through models, photos, drawings and videos.

Steps lead up to the **roof.** Gaudí's installations have been called the precursors of Surrealism, Expressionism and Cubism, and you can wander around this beautiful if troubling garden of chimneys and ventilators shaped like bouquets of visored

3

knights in reddish stone (baptised the *espantabruixes*, or 'witch-scarers'), who keep company with four fat swirls of whipped cream holding the stair exits, coated in white *trencadís*. Perhaps the most extraordinary thing about the roof is what it is missing. Gaudí saw La Pedrera as a pedestal for a 12m statue of the Virgin Mary and a pair of angels, an idea the Milàs prudently vetoed after the 1909 Setmana Tràgica left Barcelona smouldering in a bout of church burnings. Gaudí was furious, left an assistant to finish the job, vowed he would never work for the bourgeoisie again, and devoted the rest of his life to trying to expiate the church-torching sins of his fellow Catalans by building the Sagrada Família.

Other Modernista highlights Just beyond La Pedrera, Avinguda Diagonal slices across the waffle of the Eixample. If in the Mansana de la Discòrdia you gave the prize to Puig i Cadafalch, two of his principal works astonish just to the right of La Pedrera. The **Palau Baró de Quadras** (1904) [108 A1] (Avda Diagonal 373; ⊕ guided tours in English at 10.00; book at w casessingulars.com; adult/reduced/under 30 €16/14/8) is his most flamboyant Gothic palace, its projecting first-floor windows covered with a Flemish Plateresque menagerie of fabulous creatures, plus George and the Dragon designed by the indefatigable Eusebi Arnau. At Nos. 416–420, Puig's massive neo-Gothic apartment block, the **Casa de les Punxes** (1903–05) [108 C1], or 'House of Spikes', bristles with the pointiest witch's-hat roofs ever, as needly spires rise out of its brick gables. Head just a bit further down to Diagonal 442 to see the remarkable **Casa Comalat** (1911) [108 C1] by Gaudí follower Salvador Valer, with a second even more curvaceous façade on Carrer de Còrsega 316, inspired by the Casa Batlló.

If, in the Mansana de la Discòrdia, you gave the apple to Domènech i Montaner, be sure to follow Carrer de Mallorca, running to the right off the Passeig de Gràcia to see the **Casa Thomas** [108 B2] (C/ de Mallorca 291; 1898), which has the earliest examples of his decorative ceramic appliqués – strange hybrid creatures, half-carnation, half-lizard. The **Palau Ramon Montaner** [108 B2] at Carrer de Mallorca 278, home of Domènech's publisher brother, was begun in 1889 by Josep Domènech i Estapà in a sober eclectic style. However, it was finished with pizzazz by Lluís, who frosted the top floor with mosaics by Gaspar Homar and showered decoration on the grand stair, with a lovely skylight by Joan Rigalt and sculptures by Eusebi Arnau – if you're wondering where the dragons are lurking, they're at the bottom of the steps. The building is now the seat of the Delegació del Govern a Catalunya – Madrid's representatives in the autonomous region.

For an overview of the Modernista movement beyond the buildings themselves, head to the **Museu del Modernisme Barcelona** [108 B4] (C/ de Balmes 48; ☏ 932 72 28 96; w mmcat.cat; currently closed for renovation), which exhibits a painstakingly curated collection of artworks and furniture from the period.

Sagrada Família [61 E1] (C/ de Mallorca 401; ☏ 932 08 04 14; w sagradafamilia.org; ⊕ Nov–Feb 09.00–18.00 Mon–Sat, 10.30–18.00 Sun; Mar & Oct 09.00–19.00 Mon–Sat 10.30–19.00 Sun; Apr–Sept 09.00–20.00 Mon–Fri, 09.00–18.00 Sat, 10:30–20.00 Sun; book timed tickets online €26, under 10 free but need a ticket; timed ascents into either the Nativity and Passion towers for a vertiginous dreamlike ramble high over the city and the basilica is €36; note that you can't purchase tower tickets once you're inside) George Orwell, writing of the church burnings during the Civil War in his *Homage to Catalunya*, wondered ruefully why there was one that the arsonists spared, 'the ugliest building in the world', with spires 'shaped like hock bottles'. These 107m bottles, of course, belong to Gaudí's great, unfinished Sagrada

Família. Occupying an entire block of the Cerdà plan, the Expiatory Temple of the Holy Family is surely the most compelling, controversial building site in the world, the symbol of Barcelona and of the scale of its extraordinary ambition.

History The church was begun on a cheap plot in 1882, the brainchild of bookdealer Josep Bocabella Verdaguer, founder of a society dedicated to St Joseph (the 'Josephines') and devoted to preserving the family values that he felt were being eroded throughout society. For the design, Bocabella hired Francesc del Villar (one of Gaudí's professors), who planned a typical neo-Gothic church. He got as far as the crypt in 1883 when disagreements led to his replacement by Gaudí – who was only 31 and had hardly built anything, but he was pious, and that was enough for Bocabella.

Gaudí finished the crypt and worked on the project off and on for the next 43 years. At first there was plenty of money, and the building survived the Setmana Tràgica arson in 1909, probably because it employed 300 workers. But the Setmana Tràgica gave Gaudí a new purpose: the temple would also expiate the sins of Catalunya. By then it had become Gaudí's full-fledged obsession, and in 1912, after the death of his collaborator Francesc Berenguer, he accepted no other commissions.

When money ran low, he sold everything he owned for the project, and in 1925 moved into a hut on the construction site, increasingly unkempt, living on bread, water, fruit and vegetables, soliciting funds, even going door to door for handfuls of pesetas. People crossed the street at the sight of the mad old genius with the piercing blue gaze. Fashion had moved on, away from Modernisme and Josephine piety.

Gaudí planned three façades, dedicated to the Birth, Passion and, the main one, Glory; each would have four towers, symbolising the 12 Apostles. Four higher towers rising over the crossing would be dedicated to the Evangelists, with a tower of the Virgin over the apse while in the centre a truly colossal 175m tower would symbolise the Saviour.

Although it was Gothic in plan, the architect promised that it would go beyond Gothic, using the system of inclined columns and parabolic arches that he used at the Güell Crypt (page 143). There would be no buttresses, or 'crutches', as he called them. He fussed over every detail and, when a bishop asked him why he worried about the tops of his towers, Gaudí replied: 'Your Grace, the angels will see them.'

On beyond Gaudí Gaudí started on the Birth Façade and completed one tower in 1926, then absent-mindedly wandered in front of a streetcar. He died three days later in a public ward in the medieval Hospital de la Santa Creu. By 1935, his followers had completed the other three towers of the Birth Façade according to his models. But Orwell was wrong when he wrote that the Anarchists never damaged the Sagrada Família: they hated everything it represented, and in 1936 they broke into the workshops and set fire to every plan and model they found, hoping to stop further work.

According to the philosopher Ferrater i Mora, four elements define the Catalan character: *seny* (wisdom, good sense), measure, irony and *continuitat*, which means not only continuity of tradition, but also the urge to finish a job once begun. In the case of the Sagrada Família, this fourth element is proving more powerful than the other three combined. In 1954, the Josephines (who are answerable to neither the city nor the Church) raised enough money to continue the project in 'the manner of Gaudí', instructing architects to guess the master's intent from the photos of a few surviving drawings. Their work has offended purists, who believe the temple should have been left alone as a memorial to the man's unique genius; they also point out that Gaudí never even followed his own models but was forever improvising, which gave his work its unique dynamism.

The Josephines, however, insist that Gaudí wished the Sagrada Família to be like the cathedrals of the Middle Ages, built over the generations – he himself estimated it would take 200 years to complete, but 'my client is not in a hurry'. As interest in Gaudí grows and money pours in, the pace of building has accelerated. Whatever reservations the city once had about the project have gone by the wayside, as the Sagrada Família has proved its value as a tourist attraction – it is already the most visited site in Catalunya, with over 4.7 million annual visitors, whose tickets are the main source of funding. And whatever you think of the aesthetics, it's impossible not to admire the devil-may-care momentum the project has gathered.

The Josephines hoped to complete the work by the centenary of Gaudí's death, in 2026, and – despite delays caused by the Covid-19 pandemic – they are still on track: all the towers except the Jesus tower are now complete. However, one façade has not even begun: Gaudí intended to nudge the main Glory Façade into Carrer de Mallorca, with a wide stair cascading into the next *xamfrà*, but in 1979 an apartment building was built in the way. The decision on whether to demolish it to make way for the new façade has been mired in legal wrangles for decades.

The façades Gaudí's personal touch is visible on the **Birth Façade**. He based the sculpture on photographs of everyday people, using a 33-year-old worker for Christ on the Cross and a six-toed barman for a Roman soldier. He made plaster casts of plants, flowers, people and a live donkey (which survived the ordeal); if you look closely you may even see a figure of a bomb-tossing Anarchist. The new sculpture here is by the Japanese sculptor Etsuro Sotoo, who was so overwhelmed when he saw the Sagrada Família that he immediately converted to Catholicism.

Gaudí finished one 120m tower with its bright ceramic finial, and the other three were built according to his models. Sculptor Josep Maria Subirachs, an avowed atheist born exactly nine months after Gaudí died, took on the job of the Passion Façade on the condition that he lived on the site and had complete artistic freedom. He proved to be sufficiently thick-skinned to survive all pleas from artists, architects and religious conservatives that he stop. He completed the façade in 1998, three years ahead of schedule, using synthetic stone of reinforced concrete with resin-bonded finishes. He decorated this with robotic sculptures, including centurions derived from the 'witch-scarers' on La Pedrera, a controversial naked Christ on the Cross, a figure of Gaudí and a magic square based on the number 33.

Whereas the Birth Façade has Gaudí's unmistakable textured style, resembling primordial growth – a 'terrifying, edible beauty', as Dalí described it – Subirachs' façade is mechanical, sinister and kitsch, as purposely brutal as its subject matter. The sculptor himself has stated that it 'has nothing to do with Gaudí'. Finishing touches include the great bronze door inscribed with 8,000 letters from a page of the Gospel, four huge travertine statues of the apostles and a 7.6m metal Christ, placed on a bridge between the two central towers.

The breathtaking **nave**, which Gaudí intended to resemble 'a forest of stone', is completed, with its 45m flat brick vaults and unique tree-like columns. New technology has helped architects to calculate the thrusts and build as Gaudí wanted, without buttresses, and to precision-cut each stone offsite, saving time. The apse alone is big enough to swallow the church of Santa Maria del Mar whole, and is flooded with rainbow-coloured light from the huge stained-glass windows.

In the **crypt**, you can visit Gaudí's tomb and the Museu de la Sagrada Família, with photos, diagrams, models, bits of sculpture and Gaudí's astonishing catenary model, made of chains and small sacks weighted in proportion to the arches and the load they would have to bear, which he used to build the Güell Crypt (page 143).

Hospital de la Santa Creu i Sant Pau [61 E1] (C/ de Sant Antoni Maria Claret 167; ☏ 935 11 78 76; w santpaubarcelona.org; ⊕ Apr–Oct 09.30–18.30 daily, Nov–Mar 09.30–17.00 daily; self-guided adult/reduced €16/11.20, with audio guide €20/14, under 12 free) Avinguda Gaudí leads from the Sagrada Família to another, completed and useful, if almost as gargantuan, Modernista work: Lluís Domènech i Montaner's Hospital de la Santa Creu i Sant Pau (1902–30), covering nine blocks of the Eixample, the world's most beautiful hospital.

Domènech i Montaner conceived the hospital as a garden city of 26 pavilions on a human scale, connected by underground service tunnels. The project was only a quarter built in 1911 when the money dried up, so it was decided to merge with the medieval Hospital de la Santa Creu in Raval, which provided the needed cash. Domènech worked with his son, who took over when his father died in 1923, and finished it in 1930.

The grounds invite aimless wandering, becoming an alternative universe at twilight, each brick pavilion different, topped with fantastically tiled roofs and encrusted with mosaics, lavishly decorated with sculptures by Eusebi Arnau and Pau Gargallo and their workshops. Rich stained glass and elaborately wrought lamps cast strange shadows. The large administration building (1910) has the most ornate interior and views from the upper floors.

Along the Gran Via de les Corts Catalanes The Eixample's main northeast–northwest artery has several monuments, beginning with a surprising one in Plaça Tetuan: Josep Llimona's **Monument to Dr Bartolomeu Robert** Dr Robert became the first Catalanist mayor of Barcelona in 1899, and sanctioned the bank strike that year: Madrid had raised taxes on banks to cover its losses in the 1898 war and, rather than pay, Barcelona's banks shut down. Gaudí may well have designed the base support of the 18 bronze Rodinesque figures.

Plaça de Braus de la Monumental [61 F2] (Grand Via 749) The only Modernista bullring in Spain, designed in 1916 by Ignasi Mas Morell and Domènec Sugrañes Gras. Made of brick, covered with blue and white azulejos and *trencadís*, the arena is laced with parabolic arches and punctuated with towers supporting huge yellow, white and blue ceramic dinosaur eggs. The Beatles played here in 1965, a landmark event in Franco's regime; today it's occasionally used for concerts.

Around Plaça de les Glòries Catalanes Cerdà's vision that the 'Square of Catalan Glories'– where the Diagonal, Meridiana and Gran Vía de les Corts Catalanes meet like the Union Jack – would be the throbbing centre of Barcelona was sabotaged by its conversion into a hideous giant elevated roundabout which stood for decades. Finally demolished, the square has recently inaugurated a string of walkways, gardens, play areas and fountains (the main roads have been pushed into underground tunnels) that have turned this once-grim area of grey anomie into a new favourite playground for locals.

Mercat dels Encants [61 F1] (Pl de les Glòries; w encantsbarcelona.com; ⊕ 09.00–20.00 Mon, Wed, Fri & Sat; auction at 08.00 Mon, Wed & Fri) Barcelona's

flea market has been around since the 14th century, and was here long before all the redevelopment. The stalls are now gathered under a striking new mirrored roof. Best to arrive in the morning when all the 300 vendors are present; early risers can compete for treasures in the auction. Just beyond it is the **Teatre Nacional de Catalunya** (TNC), an updated Parthenon by Ricardo Bofill, which has none of the elegance of Rafael Moneo's sleek Auditori (page 116), located just across the Carrer de Padilla.

Museu de la Música [61 F2] (C/ de Lepant 150; ☎932 56 36 50; w ajuntament. barcelona.cat/museumusica; adult/reduced/under 12 €6/4.50/free) Barcelona keeps its fascinating collection of antique and exotic instruments from the 16th century onwards, including one of Adophe Sax's original saxophones in the **Auditori** (1994), architect Rafael Moneo's austere antithesis of the Palau de la Música Catalana, containing an acoustically flawless auditorium clad in Canadian maple.

Torre Glòries [61 G1] (Av Diagonal 211; ☎935 47 89 82; w miradortorreglories. com; ⊕ Apr–mid-Oct 10.00–21.00 daily, mid-Oct–Mar 09.30–18.30; book online adult/reduced/under 5 €15/12/free (€18/15 at the ticket office), Mirador + Cloud adult/reduced €25/22) The beacon here is Jean Nouvel's skyline-changing 142m tower built in 2005. It is reminiscent of London's 'Gherkin' and quickly dubbed 'the Suppository' by the scatological Catalans, although Nouvel says its form was inspired by the towers of the Sagrada Família; 4,500 LED luminations give it a colourful nocturnal shimmer. There are great views from the mirador on top, and you can even climb above that to the *Cloud Cities Barcelona*, an immersive sculpture by Tomás Saraceno of 113 'cloud spaces' suspended in a dome over the Mirador on high tension cables.

Disseny Hub [61 G1] (Pl de les Glòries 37–38; ☎932 56 67 00; w dissenyhub. barcelona; ⊕ 10.00–20.00 Tue–Sun; adult/reduced/under 16 €6/4/free) Nicknamed the 'Stapler' this cantilevered hub for all things design was built by Bohigas, Martorell and Mackay, and combines research, exhibitions and museums under one roof – including Decorative Arts, devoted mostly to Spanish industrial design, ceramics from the Crown of Aragon – Paterna, Teruel, Manises, Barcelona – as well as from 13th-century Arab-Catalan Mallorca, and some by Picasso and Miró. There are also graphic arts, with items dating back three centuries, textile arts and a wonderful collection of historic fashion along with 20th- and 21st-century product and fashion design. The museum is the focal point of the annual **Llum BCN** art festival (w barcelona.cat/llumbcn), which sees the whole area lit up with dazzling light sculptures in early February.

Esquerra de l'Eixample and Sants
There are far fewer sights on the Left Eixample. Modernisme fans may want to seek out **Casa Golferichs** [60 C5], a Modernista Moorish medieval family townhouse (now a cultural centre), with a rare garden by the side. It was designed in 1901 by Gaudí collaborator Joan Rubió i Bellver while still in his twenties, but already demonstrating his trademark – expressive brick- and stonework, often in angular volumes (as in the wide eaves), and attention to detail. The interior was inspired by Gaudí's bishop's palace in Astorga. Another good one is the **Casa de Lactància** (1913) [60 C5] at Gran Vía 475, a late-Gothic Modernista public-welfare building by Pere Falqués and Antoni de Falguerra, crowned with a relief showing an allegory of Barcelona helping the unfortunate by Eusebi Arnau. It's now a retirement home; ask to step inside to see

the enchanting covered courtyard. Just off the Diagonal, look for the **Universitat Industrial** [60 B4] at Carrer del Comte d'Urgell 173–221, built in 1895 on the site of the former Batlló ceramics factory. In 1927–31, Joan Rubió i Bellvé designed the university's Escola del Treball, which includes a superb entrance hall of huge parabolic arches.

Sants

Sants The Sants district, on the far left of the Eixample, grew up along the Carrer del Creu Coberta, the old Roman road to the rest of Spain. It was home to giant textile mills in the 19th century, including Güell's Vapor Vell (now a public library) with its tremendous brick chimney, at Carrer de Galileu 51. Sants also has Barcelona's main train station; near it, the **Plaça dels Països Catalans** (1981–82) [60 A5] was originally a traffic intersection, and the architects, Helio Piñon and Albert Viaplana, were given a difficult brief: they could not build or plant anything because of train tracks below. Their response was to create a minimalist playground dotted with metal pole 'trees'.

On the south side of the station is **Parc de l'Espanya Industrial** [60 A5], named after the huge mill that once stood here. This is far more convivial, with a boating lake and *St George and the Dragon* (1985), by Andres Nagel, the largest of all dragon and Jordi sculptures in Barcelona, and the most popular with the small fry, thanks to its gigantic slide. The nearby **Plaça d'Osca** [60 A5], a charming square full of terrace cafés and tapas bars, is a popular spot for a weekend *vermut* in the sunshine.

PLAÇA D'ESPANYA AND MONTJUÏC

PLAÇA D'ESPANYA AND MONTJUÏC The south end of Barcelona is closed off by the 215m slope of Montjuïc, Barcelona's grandstand and showcase. Its name is derived either from 'Mons Jovis' – the mountain of Jove – or from the 'mountain of Jews' for the Jewish cemetery discovered by the castle. Barcelona lost its count-kings before they had a chance to lay out any palatial gardens or hunting preserves – the source of the great parks of Madrid and other European capitals.

But in compensation there was Montjuïc, and for centuries it provided a place to breathe for a city suffocating inside its walls. In 1914, the entire northern slope was beautifully landscaped by Jean-Claude Forestier and Nicolas Rubió i Tudurí, who went on to become the Johnny Appleseed of Barcelona's parks, adding a dozen new green spaces to the city. The driving force, of course, was a show, although, unlike in 1888, politics and economics kept intruding, and it wasn't until 1929 that the International Exhibition was under way. It bequeathed a permanent fair to the city and provided homes for its collections. Then, in 1992, it was all dusted off and crowned with an Olympic ring.

Buses 55 and 150 take in most of the park: the 55 goes from Plaça Catalunya via Poble Sec to the Museu Etnològic and MNAC, while the 150 runs from the Plaça Espanya up past the Poble Espanyol, the Olympic Stadium and the Fundació Miró to the castle. A funicular to Plaça Dante from the Paral·lel metro station connects with the **Telefèric de Montjuïc** cable car up to the Castell de Montjuïc [60 D7] (w telefericdemontjuic.cat; ⊕ daily Jun–Sep 10.00–21.00, Mar–May & Oct 10.00–19.00, Nov–Dec 10.00–18.00; one-way adult/child/under 4 €17/11/free). There's also an aerial cable car, the Telefèric del Port, that runs from Barceloneta to the beaches (page 106).

Plaça d'Espanya

Plaça d'Espanya [60 B6] This is the big doughnut gateway to Montjuïc, with its six radiating streets and fountain in the centre. Its Moorish-style **Les Arenes** (w arenasdebarcelona.com) the older of Barcelona's bullrings, was converted by Richard Rogers into a domed shopping and leisure centre, with a 12-screen cinema and more than a dozen restaurants. Next to it at Carrer de Llançà 20 is a remarkable block of flats, the **Casa de la Papallona** (1912) [60 B5] by Josep Graner, who built five workmanlike floors, then, overcome by whimsy, stuck an enormous *trencadí*-covered butterfly on top. It sets the tone for the **Parc Joan Miró** behind the bullring, featuring Miró's last major work, the *Dona i Ocell* (Woman and Bird), a 21m bowling pin or phallus with a horned cylindrical head. Miró intended to plant a whole forest of these, but death intervened, and dwarf palms have taken their place.

CaixaForum [60 B6] (Av Francesc Ferrer 6–8; ☎ 934 76 86 00; w caixaforum. org; ⏰ 10.00–20.00 daily; €6 for most exhibitions, under 16 free, prices vary for other activities) Just off Plaça d'Espanya, it's hard to miss Puig i Cadafalch's Fábrica Casarramona (1911), a striking Modernista brick and iron cotton-thread mill; the two towers disguise water tanks. Used after the Civil War as a police barracks, it's been spectacularly restored by the Fundació La Caixa to display the bank's ever-expanding art collection, along with some of the biggest international travelling exhibitions. It's a vast, glassy place with concert halls, a library, bookshop, café-restaurant and galleries.

Mies van der Rohe Pavilion [60 B6] (Av Francesc Ferrer 7; ☎ 932 15 10 11; w miesbcn.com/the-pavilion; ⏰ Mar–Oct 10.00–20.00 daily, Nov–Feb 10.00–18.00 daily; adult/reduced/under 16 €9/5/free) In contrast to the nearby CaixaForum stands this cool, elegant pavilion designed by the famous Bauhaus architect for Germany's exhibit in the 1929 fair. Mies, a stickler for fine materials and craftsmanship (unlike many of his disciples), once said, 'I would rather be good than original,' but here he was both, although his sleek horizontal work of travertine, onyx, glass and chrome, sited over a pair of reflecting pools, went unnoticed by most fair-goers.

But Barcelona's more perceptive architects were intrigued, among them Rubió i Tudurí: 'It just encloses space,' he marvelled. The original was demolished after the fair, and the present replica was reconstructed by the Ajuntament in 1986; inside, the prize exhibit is Rohe's perhaps all too familiar Barcelona Chair, denizen of a million waiting rooms.

Poble Espanyol [60 B7] (Av Francesc Ferrer 13; ☎ 935 08 63 00; w poble-espanyol.com; ⏰ 10.00–midnight Tue–Sun, 10.00–20.00 Mon; adult/reduced €15/11 (€13.50/10 if bought in advance online) ages 4–12 €9, under 4 free, family (2 adults, 2 children) €40) Another survivor of the 1929 fair, the 'Spanish Village' was conceived as an anthology of Spanish architecture, replicas of 117 buildings and streets across the country were cunningly arranged. There's live music, crafts, **Tablao de Carmen** flamenco (page 78) restaurants, arts and crafts workshops, kids' activities, and the **Fundació Fran Daurel** (w fundaciofrandaurel.com) housing works by Miró, Picasso, Dalí and others, including a sculpture garden.

Fira de Montjuïc [60 C6] (w firabarcelona.com/en/montjuic) Two semi-circular buildings cupped around Plaça d'Espanya mark the entrance to the 1929 International Exhibition, next to twin St Mark's campaniles standing there like souvenir salt and pepper shakers from Venice. Today the promenade is used as the Montjuïc fair. Beyond the towers, pompous palaces line up for inspection, including the twin Baroque-Moderne **Palau de Victòria Eugènia** and **Palau d'Alfons**

XIII, which were built according to Puig i Cadafalch's plans after he was dismissed from the project in 1923.

Further up, one of the star attractions of 1929, the **Font Màgica**, still performs aquatic ballets of colour and light to the rhythms of Tchaikovsky and Abba, while blue searchlights radiate a peacock's tail of beams from the hilltop Palau Nacional in unforgettable cheesy splendour.

Museu Nacional d'Art de Catalunya [60 C7] (MNAC; Parc de Montjuïc; \936 22 03 60; w museunacional.cat; ⊕ Oct–Apr 10.00–18.00 Tue–Sat, 10.00–15.00 Sun; May–Sep 10.00–20.00 Tue–Sat, 10.00–15.00 Sun; adult/under 16 and over 65 €12/free) A sun-baked never-ending stair and outdoor escalators ascend to the shamelessly bombastic Palau Nacional, which survived the Exhibition when it found a new role as Catalunya's chief art museum.

Romanesque gallery This contains the world's foremost collection of Romanesque murals, rescued in the 1920s from deteriorating chapels in the Pyrenees – and also from the wealthy American collectors who wanted to buy them. Barcelona's Ajuntament intervened, bought many and brought them here: Catalan art would remain in Catalunya, thank you very much. Above all, the murals demonstrate just how wealthy Catalunya was in the 11th and 12th century, when over 90% of business was transacted in gold.

The money attracted some of the top artists of the day, who translated Byzantine iconography and illuminated Catalan Bibles into strikingly bold, expressive figures, sharply outlined and filled in with flat rich reds, greens and golds. Even in the gloom of their original settings, in the flickering candlelight of almost windowless stone churches, these saints and martyrs would stand out, staring with their riveting dark eyes, red circled cheeks, stylised stringy hair and hands that look like flippers. One of the first, from the 12th-century **Sant Joan de Boí**, shows jugglers along with the *Stoning of St Stephen*, in which the hand of God descends from heaven to zap sainthood on Stephen with a laser beam. The more graceful paintings of the **Pedret circle** are attributed to an itinerant painter from Lombardy, whose frescoes from the Mozarabic **Sant Quirze de Pedret** show a familiarity with the art of Ravenna, notably in the Byzantine dress of the *Seven Foolish Virgins*. On the other hand, the artist of the strange and childlike 11th-century **Sant Miquel de Marmellar** could hardly draw a face, although like the others he struggled to depict seraphim just as the Bible described them, with six wings and 1,000 eyes.

In the apse of **Sant Climent de Taüll** (1123), the famous *Christ in Majesty* is one of the most commanding, direct images in medieval art. Painted by an artist with a precocious sense of foreshortening and expressive line, the powerful atmosphere of watchfulness is emphasized by angels and other wide-eyed figures. **Santa Maria de Taüll**, in which the Virgin holds pride of place, has a striking *Last Judgement* with nasty scenes of hell, peacocks and a wonderful surreal *David beheading a Goliath* with a sausage body.

Beyond are fine sculpted capitals, a room full of polychrome Virgins, and a harrowing *Deposition* from Santa Maria de Taüll, in which the Christ has moveable arms and dead, staring eyes. The *Majestat Batlló* portrays the crucified Christ, not in the exquisite agony but dressed like a king, open-eyed and serene, in the beautiful blue tunic of a sultan, symbolising the triumph over death. At the end of the Romanesque section is the ceiling of the **chapterhouse of Sigena** in Aragon (1200), damaged by fire in 1936 but still beautiful, its Old and New Testament figures inspired by English miniatures and Norman Sicilian mosaics.

3

Gothic art Cross into the Gothic section and the atmosphere changes at once to the decorative, courtly and elegant style of chivalry, knights, ladies and dragons. Unlike the Romanesque, this is primarily urban art, commissioned during Barcelona's heyday, and appropriately enough begins with the 13th-century murals from the Palau Caldes (now the Museu Picasso) of Jaume I's *Siege of Mallorca*, with its curious Arabic motifs in the upper section. The Second Master of Bierges' vivid *Life of St Dominic* has a great scene of a young scholar falling about with his books. Where Romanesque Virgins stare, their gracious Gothic counterparts, in wood, stone, ivory and alabaster, smile and relax. Among the best are those by Jaume Cascalls (active 1345–79).

One room has 14th-century Florentine and Sienese paintings that came to Catalunya by way of Avignon and influenced local painters, especially brothers Pere and Jaume Serra in the new International Gothic style, as in Lluís Borrassà's *Retaule de Guardiola* (1404). Joan Antigó, his contemporary, was a master of tender expressions, as in the beautiful *Annunciating Angel*; less tender, the Mestre d'Ail's altarpiece of *SS Catherine and Barbara* shows Catherine stepping on the king as if he were a worm. The masterful *Virgin of the Councillors* (1445) is the only certain surviving painting by Lluís Dalmau, who went to Bruges and then painted this for the Ajuntament's chapel. Inspired by Van Eyck, Dalmau realistically depicts the five pious city councillors in an elaborate but naturalistic Gothic setting.

Although the influential Bernat Martorell is represented only by his *Retable de St Vincenç*, his great follower Jaume Huguet fills up a big room on his own. Best of all is the central panel of his triptych of a very young and serious-looking *St George and the Princess*. By the mid 15th century, Flemish realism became the rage in Barcelona, visible in Bartolomé Bermejo's memorable *Resurrection from Limbo*.

Renaissance and Baroque galleries The museum runs out of Catalans at this point. The Renaissance and Baroque galleries are devoted to two spectacular bequests. The Cambó collection has superb paintings by the Master of Frankfurt, Pedro Berruguete, Giovanni de Ser Giovanni, Sebastiano del Piombo, Giandomenico Tiepolo, Goya (a lush and luminous *Amor and Psyche*), Velázquez, Zurbarán, Quentin Metsys, Quentin de la Tour and Lucas Cranach.

Although Madrid received the bulk of the Baron's collection, his Catalan beauty-queen wife made sure that 72 of his paintings settled in Barcelona. The Thyssen-Bornemisza Collection includes works by Italian masters such as Lorenzo Daddi, Lorenzo Monaco and Fra Angelico, whose sublime, ephemeral *Madonna of Humility* steals the show. Other works are by Titian, Tintoretto, Veronese, Giambattista and Giandomenico Tiepolo, Guardi, Canaletto and an excellent portrait by Velázquez of *Mariana de Austria* with her Habsburg face.

Modern art In this case 'modern art' means Catalan art from 1850 to 1920 (the city's patricians never gave a fig for collecting paintings, so local talent is all there is). The earliest works are by Marià Fortuny (1838–74): his enormous *Battle of Tetuan* (1863) honours the 500 Catalan volunteers who fought under General Prim. There are street scenes by Ramon Martí i Alsina, and rural idylls by the Olot School, especially by Joaquim Vayreda (1843–94), and bright seascapes by Joan Roig i Solé and Arcadi Mas i Fontdevila.

Then come the Modernistas. Ramon Casas' famous *Tandem Bike Self-Portrait* painted for Els Quatre Gats is here, and his remarkable, almost photographic, *Corpus Christi Procession Leaving Santa Maria del Mar* (1898). Other works are by his friend Santiago Rusinyol, who liked to shock the bourgeoisie, but more in his life than his painting. The leading sculptors – Josep Llimona, Miquel Blay and Eusebi Arnau – are represented, although Arnau left his best works scampering about on buildings.

There's beautiful furniture designed by Gaudí and Puig, and exquisite pieces by Gaspar Homar. Later Modernistas are shown too: Isidre Nonell, Francesc Gimeno and Joaquim Mir (see his voluptuous stained-glass screen), followed by the more classical Noucentistas: Joaquim Sunyer, Joaquim Torres-Garcia and Josep Clarà. The whimsical Pau Gargallo is here, along with the iron art by Juli González and Salvador Dalí's famous *Portrait of His Father*, one of his few works in Barcelona. Works by Picasso have also been added to the expanding collection of modern art, including *Woman with Hat and Fur Collar* (1937), one of his many portraits of Marie-Thérèse Walter, his lover from 1927 to 1935.

Art and the civil war The newest exhibition rooms focus on a whole host of objects – from paintings and sculpture to pamphlets, propaganda posters and money – relating to the Civil War. It's a fascinating collection, and includes photography by Robert Capa and Agustí Centelles, paintings by Angela Nebot and Juana Francisca Rubio, which highlight the changing role of women in a time of war; and some of the lesser known works shown at the Pavilion of the Spanish Republic at the 1937 Paris International Exhibition, for which Picasso painted his masterful *Guernica* (displayed in Madrid).

Afterwards you can head up to the rooftop (*terrat*) for wonderful views, enjoy an excellent lunch at the museum restaurant, or take a rest in the delightful nearby **Jardí Botànic Històric** (entrance just off MNAC's car park).

Museu Etnològic [60 C7] (Pg de Santa Madrona 16–22; ✆ 932 56 23 00; w barcelona.cat/museu-etnologic-culturesmon; ⏰ May–Sep 10.00–20.00 Tue–Sun, Oct–Apr 10.00–19.00 Tue–Sat, 10.00–20.00 Sun; adult/reduced €5/3.50 same ticket valid for the Montcada branch, page 98) This curious hexagonal building houses fascinating rotating exhibitions, with a permanent exhibit on Catalunya and the Pyrenees.

Steps lead down to a former quarry, now beautified with Montjuïc's oldest garden, **La Rosaleda**, which contains the **Teatre Grec**, used for the summer theatre festival; and the pretty **Jardins Laribal** with the **Font del Gat** ('cat fountain'), where a spring spills down a series of steps and there's a charming café.

Museu d'Arqueologia de Catalunya [60 C6] (Pg de Santa Madrona 39–41; ✆ 934 23 21 49; w macbarcelona.cat; ⏰ 09.30–19.00 Tue–Sat, 10.00–14.30 Sun; adult/reduced/under 16 €7/5/free) This museum holds copies of the Catalunya's Palaeolithic cave paintings of hunting and battle scenes; Bronze Age jewellery, including a magnificent headband and bracelets of beaten gold; and primitive fertility sculpture and the beautiful Carthaginian *Dama de Ibiza*. The ancient Iberians check in with vases and votives and a skull with a huge nail driven into it (evidence of posthumous rites, says the reassuring explanation). There are fine mosaics and an ivory gladiator in a wacky mask, and a reproduction of a room in Pompeii, filled with fine glass. The Visigoths left mosaic belt buckles, gold crosses studded with gems and a curious crown.

The Anella Olímpica Within the Anella Olímpica, or Olympic ring, are the principal venues of the 1992 games, including the Olympic Stadium, now the **Estadi Olímpic Lluís Companys**, a relic of the 1929 fair. Barcelona had bid to host

3

the 1936 games here, but lost out to Hitler's Berlin; in defiance it planned a 'People's Olympics', only the party was spoiled by another fascist named Franco, whose revolt began the Civil War the day before the games were to open. The interior was rebuilt for the 1992 games, while preserving the façade and bronzes by Pau Gargallo. Barcelona memorably beat Hollywood at its own game by igniting the Olympic cauldron with a flaming arrow.

The adjacent **Palau Sant Jordi**, by Japanese architect Arata Isozaki, was the architectural marvel of the 1992 games. The enormous space-frame roof seems to hover, undulating over the surrounding portico. The Barcelonins say it resembles a sleeping dragon. Nearby, the elegant 120m white needle-in-a-loop, death to any passing Zeppelin, is the **Torre de Telefònica** (1991), designed by Santiago Calatrava. The mast was aligned with the earth's axis so it can also be used as a sundial after the collapse of electronic civilisation; the curving base clad in *trencadís* is a nod to Gaudí.

Museu Olímpic i de l'Esport [60 C7] (Av de l'Estadi 60; ☎ 932 92 53 79; w museuolimpicbcn.cat; ⊕ Apr–Sep 10.00–19.00 Tue–Sat, 10.00–14.30 Sun, Oct–Mar 10.00–18.00 Tue–Sat, 10.00–14.30 Sun; adult/reduced/under 7 €5.80/3.60/free)

The multimedia museum devoted to all the Olympics (but especially Barcelona's) and the history of sport, dedicated to Joan Antoni Samaranch, the local who brought the games to his home town.

Fundació Joan Miró [60 D7] (Av de Miramar; ☎ 934 43 94 70; w fmirobcn.org; ⊕ 10.00–19.00 Tue–Sun; adult/reduced/under 15 €15/7/free)

Miró (1893–1983) wanted his native Barcelona to have his own collection of art, and in 1972 asked his friend Josep Lluís Sert to design its home. The white building, bathed in natural light, is a bookend to Sert's earlier Maeght Foundation in St-Paul-de-Vence, and in 1986 it was enlarged in the same style by Sert's collaborator, Jaume Freixa, to contain the growing collection. The core, of course, is an excellent sampling of Miró's paintings, sculptures, textile works and drawings made between 1917 and the 1970s.

Miró's early pre-Paris paintings reveal a fascination with Cézanne and the Cubists: geometric landscapes, still lifes and portraits, which glow eerily in bright, mad colours. When he moved to Paris in 1919 he joined André Breton's Surrealist movement, only to go a step beyond the other Surrealists by evolving his own playful language to express the dream reality of the creative unconscious. Central to all art is the tension between abstraction and representation. Miró claimed that this duality came from the *seny i rauxa* (common sense/wisdom/practicality and uncontrolled passion) opposition at the heart of the Catalan identity, of which he was always intensely proud.

The turning point from perceptual to conceptual came in the early 1920s when he painted a series of objects, as in *Still Life I* and *Still Life II*, in a single-minded search for the extraordinary in the commonplace. By 1930, he was, on Matisse's advice, experimenting with automatic painting, allowing his hand to guide him unconsciously, drawing great motifs in black paint and filling in the colour later.

Miró was invited to contribute a painting to the Spanish Pavilion in the 1937 World's Fair in Paris, along with Picasso's *Guernica* and Alexander Calder's *Mercury Fountain*. Miró's passionate *The Reaper* (Catalan Peasant in Revolt) disappeared almost immediately after the exhibition, but Calder's lissom sculpture-fountain, dedicated to the mercury-mining towns of Almadén, has been remounted here. The red circle spiralling slowly above the fountain could have been lifted from Miró's own peculiar sign language, honed throughout his life; the circle, for example, repeatedly appears with a tall, inclined crescent shape, clearly phallic, which represented what Miró described as 'le bonheur conjugal'. Another favourite in his vocabulary is the asterisk, recalling the merrily perverse and pervasive Catalan fascination with arseholes, either of caganers (page 17) or Barça fans, the culés.

Most of the works here are from Miró's final two decades. Among the most startling is the brilliant white *Solarbird* (1968), a sensuous, undulating sculpture in flight against a deep blue wall, and the funniest is the bronze *Ladder of the Evading Eye* (1971), with a staring eyeball poised at the top of a wobbling ladder. Some of his mature works are marked by a desire to isolate the language of signs and refine the colours in order to create a state of mind that would 'go beyond painting'; one of the loveliest is *The Day* (1974), a dark, inky swoop culminating in a vermilion circle. There's also a permanent collection of works made by artists honouring Miró, including Chillida's luminous *Homage to Miró* (1985).

Gardens East of the Fundació Miró
The **Jardins Mossèn Jacint Verdaguer** [60 D7] (Av Miramar 30) are especially pretty in spring, when water trickles lazily down the stepped terraces and the flowers burst into colour. The adjacent **Jardin Joan Brossa** have musical activities for pipsqueaks and lots of play areas, while the **Jardins de Mossèn Costa i Llobera** (Ctra de Miramar) overlooking the container port, provide a surreal wonderland of succulents from around the world.

Castell de Montjuïc
[60 D7] (Ctra de Montjuïc 66; ☎ 932 56 44 40; w ajuntament. barcelona.cat/castelldemontjuic; ⊕ Nov–Mar 10.00–18.00 daily, Apr–Oct 10.00–20.00 daily; adult/reduced/under 8 €12/8/free, includes audio guide; guided visits in English at 13.00 Sat–Sun) For centuries, fires would burn on the brow of Montjuïc to guide Barcelona's fishing fleet home. In 1640, during the Reapers' War, the old beacon tower was hurriedly converted into a castle in 30 days as the army of Felipe IV approached, before Barcelona was starved into submission.

The rest of the castle's history is just as unhappy. After the siege of Barcelona in 1714, Bourbon troops blew up the old castle, and in 1759 rebuilt it with another that would specialise in torturing political prisoners. In 1896, after the Corpus Christi bombing, Anarchists, and anyone in Barcelona who looked like one, were herded up here to be tortured. In 1909, the Anarchist founder of Barcelona's secular Modern Schools, Francesc Ferrer, was executed here after a sham trial following the Setmana Tràgica, raising a storm of protest throughout Europe.

The castle functioned as a military prison until 1960. Work has begun on its transformation into a Peace Centre, which may put its demons to rest. Next to the castle, the Fossar de la Pedrera is the old stone quarry where Republicans were shot and buried in a communal grave after the Civil War, marked by a memorial of 1985 and stone columns listing the known dead (an estimated 10,000 Republicans were executed in Barcelona in the first month, and 20,000 over the next two decades). One was the Catalan president Lluís Companys, who was captured by the Gestapo in Belgium in October 1940 and handed over to Franco, who had him taken here and shot. Companys' last request was to take off his shoes so that he could feel his homeland under his feet as he died.

In summer, the castle's moat hosts the Sala Montjuïc outdoor film screenings, where you can rent a deckchair, have a drink from the bar and catch a live concert before watching the film (page 77).

OUTSIDE THE CITY CENTRE
On the map, the ragged edges of the Eixample's grid mark its contact with older, once independent towns such as Gràcia. The Collserola foothills to the north, the Zona Alta, once held the summer retreats of the noble

3

and rich, but the trams attracted moneyed Barcelona in the early 20th century, leaving some fine works by Gaudí, especially the sublime Park Güell. And above the rich suburbs rises the city's mountain girdle, with fun Tibidabo and the utterly delightful Collserola Park, with views down on the city that bring home Barcelona's uniquely privileged position.

Gràcia A vortex for 19th-century liberals, Gràcia saw Anarchists, feminists, vegetarians, Protestants and Republicans flourish, form movements, and publish progressive periodicals, including one in Esperanto. In 1898 the town was annexed to Barcelona, not altogether willingly, and in the 1960s it once again became a centre of alternative left-wing ideas (as much as such things were allowed under Franco). Today Gràcia's laid-back narrow streets wander between compact squares, offering a nice contrast to the Barcelona of big art and monuments. Gràcia begins just north of the Diagonal.

At Passeig de Gràcia 2, the street narrows when it meets the massive **Casa Fuster** (1908–11) [60 C2], now a posh hotel, the last residential project of Domènech i Montaner. A right turn on to Carrer de Goya will take you to the spiritual heart of Gràcia, **Plaça de la Vila de Gràcia**, dominated by the 38m **Torre del Rellotge** [60 C2]. The square is flanked by Gràcia's **town hall**, embellished with florid lamps and the town's coat of arms, built in 1905 by Francesc Berenguer.

At the end of Carrer de Siracusa is **Plaça John Lennon**, added in 1993 with a record-shaped plaque inscribed 'Give peace a chance'. **Plaça del Sol** is the centre of Gràcia's nightlife, despite being soullessly revamped in 1987. It is surrounded with lively bars, restaurants and cafés, with chairs and tables spilling into the square on warm summer nights. Berenguer was responsible for many of the homes around here, including the **Casa Rubinat** [60 C1] on Carrer de l'Or 44, embellished with shimmering mosaics and brickwork.

Gaudí's first house, finished in 1885, was the **Casa Vicens** [60 B1] (C/ de Carolines 18–24; ☏932 71 10 64; w casavicens.org; ⊕ Nov–Mar 09.30–18.00 daily, Apr–Oct 09.30–20.00; adult/reduced/under 12 €18/16 reduced/free; see website for themed tours). A clean break from academicism, it was one of the first colourful buildings in Barcelona, covered with brickwork and chequerboard patterns of green and white tiles. (Senyor Vicens was a tile merchant, but even so the price of the house nearly bankrupted him.) The interior is as colourful as the exterior, and as usual there is some spectacular ironwork, notably in the palm frond fence.

The **Rambla del Prat** is Gràcia's showcase for Modernista architecture, where buildings retain fanciful façades, painted ceilings, wood-panelled staircases and elaborate ironwork. The oldest part of Gràcia is sandwiched between Carrer de Gran de Gracia and Vía Augusta, with the lively **Mercat de la Llibertat** (1893) [60 C2] at the centre, capped with a wrought-iron roof.

Park Güell [60 B1] (C/ d'Olot; ☏934 09 18 31; w parkguell.barcelona; ⊕ Nov–Feb 09.30–17.15, Apr–Oct 09.30–19.15; buy time-stamped tickets online well in advance as daily numbers are limited; park only adult/reduced €18/13.50, under 7 free although they too need a ticket; with the Casa Museu Gaudí €24/19.50) Perhaps the 20th century's greatest evocation of the infinite variety and magic of life, Gaudí's masterpiece occupies one of Barcelona's great balconies, 'Bald Mountain', Mont Pelat. The park, at once Surrealist – it was a major source of inspiration for Miró and Dalí – and abstract *avant la lettre*, owes its existence to Eusebi Güell, who bought two farms here in 1902 to lay out an exclusive English garden suburb (hence the English 'K' in Park).

To attract buyers Güell gave his pet architect free rein to design amenities: a grand entrance, a pair of lodges, a central market area and terraced drives. As a property development it was a flop; only three houses were ever built, but Güell was too rich to care. After his death in 1918, his family donated the park to the city.

In the midst of the bland, not-so-hoity-toity housing that actually was built on Bald Mountain, the Park Güell glows like a mirage. As in most of Gaudí's work, there are layers of symbolism in every aspect of the park. There's the usual Catalanism, but also, according to the Gaudí scholar Josep M. Carandell, much more: Masonry, Rosicrucianism, alchemy and all the garam masala of mysteries that fascinated the fin-de-siècle elite.

On either side of the gate are two **pavilions** as bright as candy, possibly inspired by a staging in 1900 of Engelbert Humperdinck's opera *Hansel and Gretel*. Both are crowned by superb sloping roofs of swirling coloured mosaics, cupolas, mushroom forms (a magic Amanita muscaria on the wicked witch's house) and Gaudí's signature steeple with its double cross. The **grand stair** swoops around the most jovial **salamander** imaginable, clinging to the fountain and covered with brightly coloured *trencadís* that symbolise fire. Above the salamander is a tripod with a stone representing the omphalos, navel of the universe: a reference to Delphi as the seat of wisdom. The bench above resembles a Greek tragic mask.

The remarkable, cavernous **Sala Hipóstila** was planned by Gaudí as a covered market. Known as the Hall of a Hundred Columns (actually, there are only 86 – a number that recurs in other measurements in the park), its Doric columns in their thick forest are cleverly hollow inside, allowing rainwater to run down into a vast cistern below, designed to store water for emergencies or irrigation. The shallow vaults of the ceiling look as if they were soft as marshmallow, covered with white *trencadís* and beautiful plafonds, representing four large suns (the four seasons), the phases of the moon and spiralling shapes, designed by Gaudí and brilliantly executed by Josep Maria Jujol.

The scalloped roof of the hall is rimmed with a snaking ceramic collage that also serves as the back of the **serpentine bench**. It is a masterpiece of three-dimensional art, a Surrealist, Cubist collage that predates Surrealism, Cubism and collages. To form the mould of the seat, Gaudí got a naked man to sit in wet plaster, while the *trencadí* design was the work of Jujol, who was so inspired that he broke up his own cupid-painted dinnerware for the project. The bench's seemingly random patterns of colour, and simple and abstract designs, offer new delights with each turn; the restorers discovered with some consternation that they had to match 21 different tones of off-white. Among the figures are crabs and symbols of the zodiac, and Catalan or Latin graffiti, inscribed in the clay and so well hidden that the words weren't discovered until the 1950s. No-one knows what's going on here; some believe the words form a mystic dialogue, perhaps with the Virgin Mary, who trampled the serpent, symbolised by the bench.

Then there are Gaudí's extraordinary **porticoes** and **viaducts**, 3km of them, sloping in and out of the hillside. All are made of stone found on the site and fitted together to form magical, sinuous passageways with walls like curling waves and fanciful stone tree-planters with aloes growing on top. They drove Dalí wild. None of the viaducts are alike; one has a column that resembles Carmen Miranda holding a pile of rocks on her head, called La Bugadera – but Carandell suspects she is really 'Sister Mason'.

There is more weirdness off the path leading to the nub of the hill: a six-lobed, truncated stone tower called the **Chapel**, shaped like a Rosicrucian rose, but

3

hermetically sealed. There are three stone crosses on the chapel, esoterically pointed on top like arrows; look towards the east and the three merge to form a single arrow.

Gaudí, a confirmed bachelor, lived for 20 years with his father and niece in the Torre Rosa, one of the park's three houses. It's a rosy-pink cottage with a morel-shaped chimney covered with *trencadís* and a garden filled with flowers wrought from bits of cast-off fencing. Now the **Casa Museu Gaudí**, it contains plans and examples of the beautiful organic furniture that Gaudí designed. Upstairs is Gaudí's simple bedroom, with a narrow bed and a framed copy of his prayer book and death mask.

Parc de la Creueta del Coll [60 B1] (Pg de la Mare de Déu del Coll 77) Up

from the Park Güell, this was created in 1981–87 from an abandoned quarry, with a popular palm-rimmed swimming lake (⊕ summer only) with an island and beach. The de rigueur public art is here as well: a piece by Ellsworth Kelly, and Eduardo Chillida's giant gentle claw, the *Elogi de l'Aigua* ('water eulogy').

Parc del Laberint d'Horta [60 B1] (Pg dels Castanyers 1 (metro Mundet, then a

10-min walk); ☎931 53 70 10; ⊕ Apr–Oct 10.00–20.00, Nov–Mar 10.00–18.00 daily; adult/reduced €2.23/1.42 no cash, Sun & Wed free) When Barcelona expanded in the 20th century up the hills, many of the lavish estates here were demolished. Fortunately, this one escaped the bulldozers. Originally occupying 133 acres (now reduced to 17), this beautiful, atmospheric park was the brainchild of the Marques de Alfarràs, a son of the Enlightenment. He designed the master plan in 1791 on the theme of Love and Disappointment and hired Italian architect Domenico Bagutti to lay out the gardens, lake, waterfalls, pavilions, statuary and a not-so-easy cypress maze, its centre marked by a statue of Eros. His descendants added a romantic garden and, in 1967, sold the park to the city.

Tibidabo [60 A1] Towering just west of the city, Mount Tibidabo's name, peculiar

even by Catalan standards, comes from St Matthew, who quotes Satan trying to tempt Christ while he fasted in the desert: '*Haec omnia tibi dabo si cadens adoraberis me*' ('All this I will give to you if you will fall down and worship me'). Purists might claim the incident took place in the Sinai, but a Catalan would counter, 'Just what's so tempting about a rocky desert?' Whereas the view from 550m Tibidabo, encompassing all Barcelona, Montserrat, the Pyrenees and even Mallorca, is a pretty seductive offer.

The FGC Avinguda del Tibidabo will get you as far as Plaça de John F Kennedy; the landmark here is the brightly coloured, dainty mosaic filigree Modernista tower and cupola of **La Rotonda** (1918), designed by Adolf Ruiz i Casamitjana. From here the Tramvia Blau (closed for renovation at the time of writing: take bus 196) ascends Avinguda Tibidabo to link up with the funicular. It passes, on the left at No. 31, the Casa Roviralta (1913), by Joan Rubió i Bellvé, a striking mudéjar fantasy with white stucco and elaborate, corbelled, angular brickwork; the lavish interior is the **Aranda Grill** restaurant, where Madonna was once famously entertained by a male stripper. Just up at No. 56 is Rubió's **Casa Casacuberta** (1907), now a school.

The old Funicular del Tibidabo has been replaced by the speedy new **Cuca de Llum** (Pl Dr Andreu; every 30mins when the Parc d'Atraccions is open), which creaks up to the summit and its crowning glory – the huge, spiky, expiatory temple of **Sagrat Cor** built in atonement for the Setmana Tràgica of 1909. A lift sweeps you up to the roof for staggering views. Stop for a cocktail at one of the panoramic bars, best in the late afternoon on a clear day, as the lights begin to twinkle in the great city below. Tibidabo's **Parc d'Attraccions** (✆ 932 11 79 42; w tibidabo.cat; ⊕ see website for opening hours; adult €35, children (90–120cm) €14, includes the Cuca de Llum funicular; adult €19 for the Cuca de Llum and classic rides of the Panoramic Area) is the oldest (and highest!) funfair in Spain and is still going strong, offering all the usual thrills – a wicked House of Horrors, funhouse mirrors, a log flume, roller coaster, and a museum of automatons. The **Panoramic Area** has a charming, little red aeroplane ride, the Avió, which dates back to 1928, and is said to be the first flight simulator in history, and one of the most panoramic Ferris-wheel rides imaginable.

Torre de Collserola
[60 A1] (Ctra de Vallvidrera al Tibidabo; ✆ 932 11 79 42; w torredecollserola.com; ⊕ Wed–Sun noon–15.00, but check website as opening hours are erratic; adult/reduced €5.60/3.10) A 10-minute walk south of the Parc d'Attraccions rises Norman Foster's slender and dynamic 244m telecommunications tower built for the Olympics, 'pure sculpture', as Sir Norman himself describes it. A glass lift shoots up to the tenth-floor observation deck for giddily vertiginous views 560m up.

CosmoCaixa (Museu de la Ciència)
[60 A1] (C/ d'Isaac Newton 26; ✆ 932 12 60 50; w cosmocaixa.org; ⊕ 10.00–20.00 daily; adult/under 16 €8/free) The older building was designed as an asylum by Josep Domènech i Estapà in 1894, while the brand new one next to it houses enough hands-on science exhibits to keep most children entertained for at least a couple of hours.

Torre Bellesguard
[60 A1] (C/ de Bellesguard 20; ✆ 932 50 40 93; w bellesguardgaudi. com; ⊕ 10.00–15.00 Tue–Sun; €9, reduced €7.20 self-guided tours; guided tours in English €16, book online) Barcelonins have been playing country squire at the foot of Collserola at least since 1400, when King Martí the Humane built a summer residence at Bellesguard. Some 500 years later, Gaudí was commissioned to build the Torre Bellesguard by its ruins and created a tall, neo-Gothic castle (1905), with his trademark four-armed cross at the top of the pinnacle. The interior has impressive, imaginative vaults and brickwork, mosaics and ironwork.

Collserola Park
[60 A1] It is hard to believe that bold, brassy Tibidabo forms part of one of the loveliest urban parks in Europe: made up over 16,000 acres of undulating forests, Collserola Park, dotted with fountains, forgotten villages, churches and old farmhouses, all seemingly a world away from the city at their feet. From the Peu de Funicular train stop, you can take the funicular up to the pretty hilltop and very wealthy village of **Vallvidrera**, with lovely views over the big city. Alternatively, take the train to the next stop, Baixador de Vallvidrera, a 5-minute walk from the park information centre, and an outpost of the Barcelona history museum, **MUHBA Vil.la Joana** in the charming, 18th-century, honey-coloured farmhouse covered with twisting wisteria. This was the home of the Miralles family, who invited the impoverished tuberculosis-stricken poet-priest Jacint Verdaguer (page 213), author of the great Catalan epic poems *L'Atlàntida* (1876) and *Canigó* (1886), to spend his last weeks in the fresh air. The museum is dedicated to the poet and his works, with manuscripts, books and personal objects.

Sarrià
The last independent township to be annexed to Barcelona, Sarrià is slightly schizophrenic: the new part is full of smart homes, but old Sarrià hasn't changed much at all. The main street, Carrer Major de Sarrià, strings along small

squares with a lazy, village atmosphere. A church has stood on Plaça Sarrià for more than a millennium, although the present Sant Vicenç dates only from the early 20th century. Just off the square is a lively, red-brick Modernista market (1911).

Farther up, Plaça Sant Vicenç is surrounded by a higgledy-piggledy collection of narrow, arcaded houses, all painted different colours. Gaudíphiles won't want to miss his **Col.legi de les Teresianes** (1890), a private school built by Gaudí in 1890. Although constrained by finances, he endowed the building with elaborate wrought-iron details and defined the corners with his favourite cross-crowned steeples.

Palau Reial de Pedralbes [60 A3] (Av Diagonal 686; ⊕ park daily 10.00–16.00)

On the south end of Sarrià, the Palau Reial de Pedralbes was a rather nice present to Alfonso XIII from Eusebi Güell's heirs to thank him for making dad a count. It became headquarters of the Republican government at the end of the Civil War; from here President Azaña and La Pasionaria joined the rest of Barcelona on 29 October 1938, tearfully cheering as the last 12,673 members of the International Brigades marched down the Diagonal towards France and away from a hopeless cause. Franco made the palace his residence in Barcelona, and the former king Juan Carlos' daughter, Christina, held her wedding banquet here in 1997.

Leafy trees shade the **palace's park**, dotted with lily ponds and secret bowers laid out in 1925 by Nicolas Rubió i Tudurí. Tucked away in a tiny bamboo forest is the little **Hercules fountain** by Gaudí, only discovered in 1983 under the ivy, with shape of a dragon spewing water from curling jaws.

Pabellones Finca Güell [60 A3] (Av de Pedralbes 7; ☎ 933 17 76 52; w rutadelmodernisme.com; ⊕ 10.00–16.00 Sat–Sun; adult/reduced/under 6 €6/3/ free)

Just behind the park is a fence and gate guarded by one of Gaudí's first and most formidable ironworks, the **Pedralbes Dragon** (1884). Spanning 5.4m the dragon whips its scaly tail and roars, baring long, pointy teeth. It also incidentally guarded Eusebi Güell's own orange grove and country house, to which Gaudí contributed the exotic, Hindu-inspired, corbel-roofed gatehouse and stable (1884–87), which were also the first to be decorated with his signature *trencadís* and cross.

Monestir de Pedralbes [60 A3] (Bda del Monestir 9; w monestirpedralbes.

barcelona; ⊕ Oct–Mar 10.00–14.00 Tue–Fri, 10.00–17.00 Sat–Sun; Apr–Sep 10.00–17.00 Tue–Fri, 10.00–19.00 Sat, 10.00–20.00 Sun; adult/reduced €5/3.50, under 16 & Sun after 15.00 free) At the top of the Avinguda de Pedralbes, a cobbled lane leads up to this handsome Gothic convent founded for noble ladies by Queen Elisenda, the fourth wife of Jaume II, in 1326. It is a rare time capsule of Catalan Gothic, built quickly and scarcely altered since. The three-storey **cloister** with its delicate columns, garden and fountains is serene and lovely, surrounded by the Poor Clares' tiny prayer cells.

The small, irregular **Capella de Sant Miquel** houses perhaps the finest Gothic fresco cycle in Catalunya, Ferrer Bassa's *Seven Joys of the Virgin and the Passion*, painted in 1346, two years before the Black Death killed the painter and a third of the population of Barcelona. The **church** contains stained glass by Mestre Gil and the lovely alabaster tomb of Queen Elisenda, sculpted in 1364 and before her death – she wasn't taking any chances on getting a good likeness. There is also a lovely medieval kitchen garden, with vegetables, herbs and medicinal plants.

Camp Nou [60 A4] (Museum entrance on Av Aristides Maillol; ☎ 934 96 36 00; w fcbarcelona.com; ⊕ daily 10.00–18.00, but check times on the website) Barça

ELEVEN MEN WITH ONE BALL BETWEEN THEM

Barça...mes que un club ('Barça...more than just a club'). First there were a few bored Englishmen getting up a game on turnip fields outside town. Then they formed clubs, as expats do: the Hispania Football Club and the Barcelona Football Club, or Barça. The Barcelonins were intrigued and began to play too, encouraged by the news from the city's hygienists that football was good therapy for the ills caused by the industrial revolution. Hispania (now Espanyol) was supported mainly by pro-Hispanic residents of Barcelona (nicknamed the *periquitos*), but Barça became linked with Catalan nationalism.

Immigrants were fairly impervious to the choral societies and the Renaixença of Catalan verse, but most of them adored football, and Barça became the prime vehicle for them to identify with the Catalan cause. Politics, as usual, was never far away, and in times of trouble matches turned into mass political rallies. In 1936 the president of the club had the misfortune to be in Castile, where he was caught and executed by Franco. When Barcelona was occupied in 1939, Franco ordered that the club be purged – saying it had been infiltrated by the Communists, Anarchists and Catalan Nationalists.

Yet, in spite of a Spanish Football Federation run by Falangists, Barça won five cups in the early 1950s. They offered the best alternative to the invincible machine of Real Madrid, a club pumped full of money by the old dictator until it became the best in the world. Supporting Barça became an act of protest against the regime. It was the 'unarmed army' of the Catalans, forbidden even to speak their own language, and one of the few outlets available to express national unity.

or FC Barcelona, the city's beloved football club, is magnificently headquartered in Europe's largest stadium at Camp Nou, in the Les Corts district. It's currently being expensively (€900 million) and massively remodelled to expand capacity to 105,000. At the time of writing, Barça are playing at the Olympic Stadium in Montjuïc, but are due to return to the Camp Nou for the 2025/26 season.

Originally built in 1957, the money was raised by fans paying their fees up to five years in advance – a first act of architectural self-affirmation of Catalan will after the Civil War. The museum is as popular as the Museu Picasso, and yet, despite the crowds, it maintains a reverent silence, akin to that in any great cathedral. While construction is underway, there are no stadium tours, although you can see the works taking shape. Today Barça has more members than any club in the world; even Pope John Paul II, visiting in 1982, accepted membership.

3

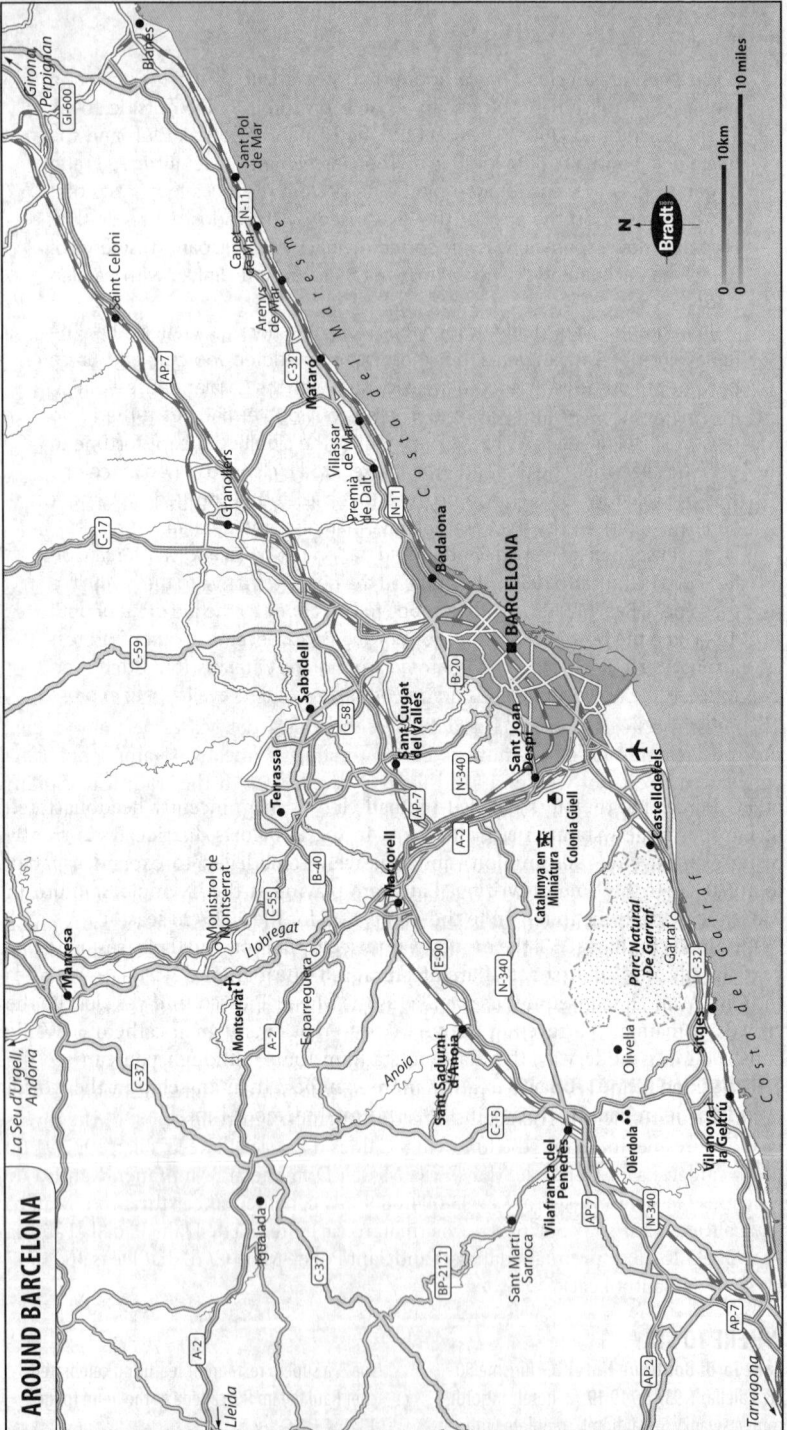

AROUND BARCELONA

Girona/Perpignan
Gi-600
Blanes
Sant Pol de Mar
N-11
Canet de Mar
Sant Celoni
AP-7
Arenys de Mar
C-32
Mataró
C o s t a   d e l   M a r e s m e
Villassar
Premià de Dalt
N-11
C-17
Granollers
Badalona
C-59
BARCELONA
B-20
Sabadell
C-58
Sant Cugat del Vallès
AP-7
Terrassa
N-340
Sant Joan Despí
A-2
Colònia Güell
Monistrol de Montserrat
B-40
Martorell
Catalunya en Miniatura
Castelldefels
C-55
Llobregat
E-90
N-340
Manresa
Montserrat
A-2
Esparreguera
Parc Natural De Garraf
Garraf
C-32
C-37
Anoia
N-340
Olivella
C o s t a   d e l   G a r r a f
La Seu d'Urgell, Andorra
Sant Sadurní d'Anoia
C-15
Sitges
Igualada
Vilafranca del Penedès
Olèrdola
Vilanova i la Geltrú
C-37
Sant Martí Sarroca
BP-2121
AP-7
N-340
A-2
Lleida
AP-2
AP-7
Tarragona

N
Bradt

0   10km
0   10 miles

4

Around Barcelona

As in many great cities, there's a dark secret lurking out here on the outskirts of Barcelona. While the immaculately kept centre glistens with money and taste, large parts of the hinterlands are just plain awful, not the first place you'd choose to go touring in. But the buses and trains can easily whisk you to any of the oases within it.

Foremost among these is Montserrat, the Catalans' holy mountain, its surreal peaks sitting incongruously amid the sprawl. Another of the oases is resolutely urban; the surprising city of Terrassa reminds us that the industrial age is part of our history and culture too. Just as surprising is the Penedès, the quiet wine region that supplies the Catalans with their bubbly cava. There are two wild nature reserves here too, along with some Modernista panache from Gaudí and Jujols, and the beach blanket Babylon of Sitges.

NORTH OF BARCELONA: THE COSTA DEL MARESME

The 72km between Barcelona and Blanes, the Costa del Maresme, may not be the most glamorous of Catalunya's costas ('maresme' means 'swamp') but it's a convenient stretch of weekend sand for city-dwellers, with the train line (Spain's first, built in 1848) right behind the beach. Much of the coast was transformed beyond recognition in the 1960s by a mass invasion of cement-mixers, and most of these former fishing villages are now low-key resorts, popular with Catalan families. Still, there are pockets of charm to discover among the apartment blocks – narrow old lanes and whitewashed cottages, fishing boats in the harbours and a sprinkling of Modernista villas built by returning 'Indianos' in the late 19th century.

Badalona is on the L2 metro line. Commuter trains (*rodalies*) depart every 30 minutes from Barcelona-Sants & Plaça Catalunya and stop at all the coastal towns. Buses for the same depart from the Estació Barcelona Nord.

TOURIST INFORMATION For information on the whole Maresme region, visit w turismemaresme.cat. There are tourist information centres in most of the towns of the Maresme, including the following: Caldes d'Estrac (Pl de la Vila; ☎937 91 00 05; w caldetes.cat), Canet de Mar (Casa Museu Domènech i Montaner, Xamfrà de les rieres Gavarra i Buscarons; ☎93 794 08 98; w canetdemar.cat/turisme), Mataró (C/ La Riera 123, ☎937 58 26 98; w visitmataro.cat), Premià de Dalt (Pl de la Fàbrica 1; ☎936 93 15 15; w premiadedalt.cat) and Sant Pol de Mar (C/ d'Abat Deàs 36; ☎937 60 45 47; w santpol.cat).

🏠 WHERE TO STAY

Sant Jordi Boutique Hotel C/ Turisme 80– 88, Calella; ☎937 66 19 19; w hotelsantjordi. com. A swanky 5-star hotel, complete with spa & a superb restaurant featuring celebrated chef Raül Balam Ruscalleda at the helm (page 132). €€€€

Dormsy C/ Esglesia 65, Arenys de Mar; ☏ 649 97 85 06; w dormsy.cat/apartamentos. Set in a charmingly converted old townhouse, these 4 apartments for between 1 & 5 people pair designer furnishings with vaulted Catalan ceilings & exposed brick walls. €€€

Vila Arenys Riera del Bisbe Pol 89, Arenys de Mar; ☏ 937 95 88 86; w hotelvilaarenys.com. This crisp, modern hotel offers 16 comfortable rooms, a good restaurant & a roof terrace with plunge pool & bar – but really stands out for its exceptionally helpful staff. €€€

Hotel Gran Sol N-2, km 664, Sant Pol de Mar; ☏ 937 60 00 51; w hotelgransol.info. There are few accommodation options in Sant Pol de Mar but this modest, mid-sized hotel offers immaculate rooms, some with sea views; it's part of a local hospitality school, & the students serve remarkably good food at reasonable prices in the restaurant. €€

Hotel Mitus Riera de la Torre 20, Canet de Mar; ☏ 937 94 29 03; w hotelmitus.com. You'll get a good welcome at this family-run, 1-star hotel, which has simple, AC & spotlessly clean rooms near the beach. €

� WHERE TO EAT AND DRINK

Restaurante El Drac by Raül Balam

Ruscalleda C/ Turisme 80–88, Calella; ☏ 937 66 19 19; w hotelsantjordi.com; ⏰ 20.30–22.00 Thu–Fri, 13.30–15.00 & 20.30–22.00 Sat, 13.30–15.00 Sun. This elegant restaurant on the ground floor of Calella's fanciest hotel has become a gourmet hotspot since famous chefs Raül Balam Ruscalleda & Brazilian chef Murilo Rodrigues Alves took over at the helm. Expect sublime, creative renditions of Catalan favourites: choose from the 2 served tasting menus (€84/63) or go à la carte. €€€€€

Hispania C/ Real 54, Arenys de Mar; ☏ 937 91 04 57; w restauranthispania.com; ⏰ 13.00–16.00 Mon, Wed, Thu & Sun, 13.00–16.00 & 20.00– midnight Fri & Sat. One of the oldest restaurants in the area, which has attracted celebrity guests from Robert de Niro to the Spanish king over the last 70 years, this serves up excellent, classic Catalan cuisine, including mouthwatering seafood. €€€€

Portinyol In the port, Arenys de Mar; ☏ 937 92 00 09; w elportinyol.com; ⏰ 09.30–16.30 Thu– Mon. Grand old place by the fishing port, with light-filled dining areas & a terrace; splurge for the freshest shellfish & lobster. (Their sister restaurant, Bei Pepe w beipepe.com, in Malgrat de Mar is also recommended.) €€€€

✳ Cuina Sant Pau C/ Nou 10, Sant Pol de Mar; ☏ 937 60 06 62; w cuina-santpau.cat; ⏰ 13.00– 15.30 & 20.00–22.30 Wed–Sat, 13.00–15.30 Sun. Legendary chef Carme Ruscalleda earned

3 Michelin stars at the restaurant which once occupied this building: now her son, Raül Balam Ruscalleda & Brazilian chef Murilo Rodrigues Alves (who also run El Drac, see left) offer delicious bistro cuisine using fresh seasonal produce. Try the house speciality, *croquetes de canelons*. €€

✳ Lasal de Vareda Pg Marítim 190, Mataró; ☏ 931 14 05 80; w lasaldelvarador.com; ⏰ Oct, Nov & Mar–May 10.00–17.00 daily, Jun–Sep 10.00–midnight daily (closed Dec–Feb). Delicious, organic cuisine prepared with the freshest local ingredients – including spectacular paellas & tasty tapas – in a simple, seafront *xiringuito* that shows its commitment to sustainability with no plastic, & the use of solar power, etc. €€

La Queixalada C/ Castanyer 18, Canet de Mar; ☏ 937 94 06 20; ✉ laqueixalada_canetdemar; ⏰ 12.30–16.00 Mon–Thu, 12.30–17.00 & 19.30–23.30 Fri–Sat, 12.30–17.00 Sun. Get there early to beat the crowds at this informal place specialising in *coques* (Catalan flatbread with different toppings), salads & tapas with a creative twist. They also serve a great value set lunch menu. €€

Restaurant del Santuari Parc del Santuari, Canet de Mar; ☏ 937 94 10 07; w restaurantelsantuari. com; ⏰ 10.00–18.00 Wed–Mon. Modernista restaurant designed by Puig i Cadafalch, by the Misericordia sanctuary, serving seafood & desserts featuring local produce. €€

WHAT TO SEE AND DO Badalona (Roman Baetulo), with a long beach and palmy Rambla, is a major industrial centre and 'the cradle of Spanish basketball', and now has one of the great ethnically mixed populations of greater Barcelona. The **Museu de Badalona** (Pl de l'Assemblea de Catalunya 1; ☏ 933 84 17 50; ⏰ 10.00–14.00 & 15.00–20.00 Tue–Sat, 10.00–14.00 Sun; adult/reduced/under 17 €6.60/5.30/free; w museudebadalona.cat) was built in 1966 over Baetulo's Roman baths to shelter the small but exquisite marble torso of the *Venus of Badalona*, along with Iberian stelae (stone slabs) and Roman mosaics.

In 1848 the first train in Spain chugged from Barcelona to **Mataró**, and in 1867 the town gave birth to one of the brightest stars in the Modernista constellation, Josep Puig i Cadafalch, who designed the Ajuntament and several other buildings here. In the hills behind the small resort town of **Premià de Mar** is **Premià de Dalt**, a sleepy time-capsule village set in vineyards and pine forests, while **Villassar de Mar** is a chic enclave for Barcelonin second-homers, dotted with Modernista villas. The hot springs at **Caldes d'Estrac** drew Barcelonins in the 19th century, and they covered the piney hills with attractive villas. One who came later was writer, poet and art critic Josep Palau, a good friend of Picasso and world-renowned expert on his work, so much so that, when art dealers asked Picasso to authenticate a piece, he would send them to Palau, saying 'Palau knows my work better than I do'. He left his private collection of Picassos (including a startling self-portrait) and other 20th-century Catalan artists to the **Fundació Palau** (C/ Riera 53; ✆937 91 35 93; ⏱ 10.30–14.00 Tue–Wed & Sun, 10.30–14.00 & 17.00–19.00 Thu–Sat; adult/reduced/under 12 €7/3.50/free; **w** fundaciopalau.cat).

Over 2 miles of sand link Caldes d'Estrac to **Arenys de Mar**, the main fishing port on this stretch of coast, where a lively fish auction is held every afternoon at the harbour from Monday to Friday. The town's museum, the **Museu d'Arenys de Mar** (C/ Església, 43; ✆937 92 44 44; ⏱ 10.00–13.30 Tue–Fri, 10.00–13.00 Sat, 11.00–13.00 Sun; adult/reduced/under 12 €3.50/2/free; **w** museu.arenysdemar.cat), has collections of every known type of lace, and rocks and minerals from around the world in adjoining buildings. **Canet de Mar**, next up the coast, was a favourite spot of Domènech i Montaner, and in 1918–20 he built a house, now the **Casa Museu Lluís Domènech i Montaner**. It's all rather restrained compared to his Barcelonin flights of fancy, but is packed full of memorabilia and architectural drawings. Various guided tours start at the house, one taking in Montaner's other buildings: the **Ateneu Obrer** (1887) and pointy, ornate **Casa Roura** at Riera Sant Domènech, as well as the other Modernista villas built by the 'americanos'.

The most charming town along this stretch of coast is **Sant Pol de Mar**, long a favourite weekend getaway for wealthy Barcelonins, which has a bijoux old quarter of steep narrow streets spilling down to a picturesque harbour.

INLAND FROM BARCELONA: SANT CUGAT DEL VALLÈS TO MANRESA

Well within day-trip distance of Barcelona, there are superb Romanesque and Visigothic churches, Modernista mansions and factories, and a mellow old monastery in Sant Cugat del Vallès (known simply as Sant Cugat). There are **tourist information** offices in all the major towns of this area, including Sant Cugat (Pl d'Octavià 10; ✆936 75 99 52; **w** visit.santcugat.cat), Terrassa (Pl de Josep Freixa i Argemí 11; ✆937 39 70 19; **w** visitaterrassa.cat) and Manresa (Pl Major 20; ✆938 78 40 90; **w** manresaturisme.cat).

GETTING THERE AND AROUND Commuter train services around Barcelona are provided by the FGC (**w** fct.cat), run by the Catalan government (services are prefaced with an 'S'), as well as the state-run *rodalies* (**w** rodalies.gencat.cat/es/inici), with services prefaced by an 'R'). Note that the FGC lines depart from a different section of the Plaça Catalunya station than the *rodalies* lines. Sant Cugat is about 20 minutes from Barcelona's Plaça Catalunya on the S5 FGC train line. For

Sabadell, take the S2. For Terrassa, the R4 line goes to the central station from Sants and Plaça Catalunya, & the S1 line of the FGC takes you there (Terrassa-Rambla station) from Plaça Catalunya. The R4 carries on to Manresa.

WHERE TO STAY

Hotel Petit Luxe C/ Teatre 3, Terrassa; 935 14 12 21; w hotelpetitluxe.cat. Central, smart & modern, with 9 spacious rooms & suites, most of which have a balcony or terrace. €€€

Món St Benet Camí de Sant Benet, Sant Fruitós de Bages; 938 75 94 04; w monsantbenet. com/en/hotel-mon. A large, modern hotel with 87 stylish rooms with huge private balconies overlooking the monastery & Parc Natural. There's an outdoor pool & a pair of excellent restaurants (see below). €€€

Arrahona Sabadell Ctra de Barcelona 446, Sabadell; 937 20 53 20; w sercotelhoteles. com/es/hotel-arrahona-sabadell. Set in a fabric factory from the 1950s, this large modern hotel

has a mix of rooms & apartments, an outdoor pool, restaurant & gym here – all for a very reasonable price. €€

L'Hotelet Pg Pere III 38, Manresa; 938 72 37 51; w hoteletmanresa.com. Occupying the 2nd floor of a handsome Modernista building, this boutique hotel has 7 rooms, which have been thoughtfully restored to preserve original details, a shared sitting room with complementary coffee, & a delicious rooftop terrace. €€

Hotel Els Noguers Av Països Catalans 167, Manresa; 938 74 32 58; w hotelelsnoguers. cat. A modern 2-star hotel in the city centre, with slightly dated rooms but generous b/fasts, a decent restaurant & very welcoming staff. €

WHERE TO EAT AND DRINK

L'O (Món Benet) Camí de Sant Benet, Sant Fruitós de Bages; 938 75 94 29; w monsantbenet.com/en/restaurants; ⏲ 13.30–14.30 & 20.30–21.30 Fri–Sat, 13.30–14.30 Sun. This is the flagship restaurant at Món Benet, with a Michelin star for its refined contemporary cuisine €€€€€. There are 2 other excellent & more affordable restaurants here, both featuring produce from their own kitchen garden: El Món (€€€), with sophisticated Catalan dishes (⏲ 07.00–10.00 & 20.00–22.30 Mon–Fri, 08.00–11.00 & 13.00–15.30 & 20.00–22.30 Sat–Sun), & La Fonda, which offers set daily menus (€24.50 w/days/€35 w/kends for 3 courses; ⏲ 13.00–15.30 daily, plus bar service 11.00–17.00).

❋ **Aligué** Ctra de Vic - El Guix 8–10, Manresa; 938 3 25 62; w restaurantaligue.cat; ⏲ 09.30–18.00 Mon–Fri, 10.00–15.00 Sat–Sun. Famous since 1957 for its 'esmorzars de forquilla' (literally, 'fork breakfasts'), which are hearty Catalan

dishes like *botifarra amb mongetes* (sausage with beans) or *cap i pota* (beef head & trotters), this is a wonderful place to try authentic regional cuisine. €€

Rauxa C/ Tres Creus 15, Sabadell; 936 79 96 25; w rauxabodega.com; ⏲ 13.00–16.00 & 20.00–23.00 Tue–Sat, 13.00–16.00 Sun. Catalan cuisine is reimagined at this stylish, 'contemporary bodega': try the fennel, green bean & pine nut salad, or fillet of cod with Mediterranean herbs & green curry mayonnaise. €€

Taverna 1913 Pl Major 13, Manresa; 938 72 47 40; ◙ taverna1913_manresa; ⏲ 18.00–23.30 Tue–Wed, 18.00–midnight Thu, 18.00–01.30 Fri, 11.30–15.00 & 18.00–01.30 Sat, 11.30–16.00 Sun. With tables out on the city's handsome main square, this serves up tasty tapas, juicy burgers, platters of regional cheeses & charcuterie, all accompanied by their wonderful selection of wines. €

SANT CUGAT DEL VALLÈS Just over the Collserola hills northwest of Barcelona, Sant Cugat del Vallès is a leafy commuter suburb with a handsome Modernista train station. Originally the Roman Castrum Octavianum, it has a suburb centrepiece in the **Reial Monestir de Sant Cugat** (Pl Octavia 1; 936 75 99 52; w visit.santcugat.cat/horaris-del-monestir-sant-cugat; ⏲ Oct–May 10.30–13.30 & 16.00–19.00 Tue–Sat, 10.30–14.30 Sun; Jun–Sep 10.30–13.30 & 17.00–20.00, 10.30–14.30 Sun; free).

Founded by Louis the Stammerer in AD878, it became the most powerful Benedictine house in the county. The church was rebuilt in the Gothic style with a huge rose window and Lombard tower. The Romanesque cloister is the star of the show, with 144 capitals depicting scenes from the New and Old Testaments sculpted by the monk Arnau Cadell in the 1190s; one capital with an inscription even shows him at work in a rare moment of medieval non-anonymity. In the chapter house, the **Museu de Sant Cugat** houses another masterpiece, the golden *Retaule de Tots Sants* by Pere Serra (1375). The **MercAntic** (Avda Rius i Taulet 120; ☎936 74 49 50; w mercantic.com; ⊕ 10.00–19.00 Tue–Fri, 10.00–15.00 Sat–Sun) is an antiques market that is hugely popular at weekends, when it has food trucks, live music and *vermut* (vermouth, the classic Catalan aperitif).

SABADELL Sabadell is the bitter arch-rival of Terrassa, the Manchester to its Leeds, a sprawling city of big banks. It was making woollen cloth on a large scale by the 15th century, and, when the industrial revolution took off, the population soared from 2,000 in 1800 to 218,000 today, making Sabadell Catalunya's fifth-largest city.

Near the FGC train stop at La Rambla you can walk along Carrer de l'Indústria, passing two fine Modernista buildings by Juli Batllevell, the **Hotel Suisse** at No. 59 and the **Lluch Offices** at No.10. A bit further up, in the peaceful historic centre, the 19th-century mayor's residence is now the **Museu d'Història de Sabadell** (C/ Sant Antoni 13; ☎937 27 85 55; w museus.sabadell.cat/museu-historia; ⊕ 17.00–20.00 Tue–Sat, 11.00–14.00 Sun), with changing exhibitions. The **Casa Fàbrica Turull**, which was both textile factory and home to the wealthy Turull family, was built in 1819, once hosted the Spanish queen, Isabel II, and is now the city's **Museu d'Art** (C/ Doctor Puig 16; ☎937 25 71 44; w museus.sabadell.cat/museu-art; ⊕ 17.00–20.00 Tue–Sat, 11.00–14.00 Sun; free). Best of all is the headquarters of one of Spain's biggest banks, the **Caixa de Sabadell** (1905–1915), at Carrer de Gràcia 17, by Jeroni Martorell, a temple to Mammon tricked out to the gills.

TERRASSA In Terrassa they told us that their city doesn't get a lot of tourists. If you've ever tried to drive there you'll find out why. The city is stuck in the most craptastic corner of all Catalunya, where a pall of smoke hangs over industrial wastelands. And even if you want to get there you might not be able; road signs to the city centre usually lie, and it's all too easy to cruise in circles until life seems a cruel joke.

Which is a pity, because Terrassa, if you ever find it, is a pretty nice town. Catalunya's fourth-largest city was built by industry, lives for industry, and isn't ashamed to say so. They're proud of their hard work and their history, which goes back a mere million years or so. Their accomplishments are many; after Barcelona, they may have the biggest collection of Modernista architecture anywhere.

History Excavations in 1997–2012 along the Vallparadís, the ravine that runs through the city, have unearthed evidence of human habitation from 800,000–1,000,000 years ago, among the oldest anywhere in Europe. Terrassa only enters history as a Roman town called Egara. By the time of the Visigoths it was an important bishopric, and they left the wonderful complex of pre-Romanesque churches that is Terrassa's great landmark today.

The Moorish occupation began in AD718, and lasted for an uncertain period. There must have been trouble, for somewhere along the way old Egara became Terra Rasa – 'wasteland'. Terrassa got back on its feet by the 13th century, but it didn't make a splash until 1833 when the first steam engine in Catalunya was installed here. A minor town grew into a city, and filled up with factories. The first boom was followed by a bigger one in the 1950s. Since then the population has increased five-fold, to over 225,000.

Like Reus, Terrassa is a town where they left the old brick smokestacks standing when the textile mills and foundries of a century ago were demolished. They're quite elegant, and they make perfect symbols for the city. Terrassa today considers itself the jazz capital of Catalunya. There are no points for guessing what its politics are like: not far from the Visigothic churches you can stand on the corner of Equality Street and Human Rights Square.

What to see and do

Around Plaça Vella The closest thing to a centre is the shady Plaça Vella. It has the nondescript **Catedral del Sant Esperit** (1593) which contains an excellent alabaster *Burial of Christ* (1540) by Italian-trained Martí Diez de Liatzasoloi, and an outlandish parabolic-arched **chapel** by Terrassa's most renowned Modernista architect, Lluís Muncunill. The cathedral's neighbour is the imposing **Torre del Palau**, the only part remaining from the castle that once occupied this square.

A block north up Carrer Cremat, Plaça Raval de Montserrat has the odd pseudo-medieval **Ajuntament** (1902), an early work of Muncunill; peek inside to see the grand stairwell. The city fathers sacked Muncunill as city architect right after the Ajuntament was finished, and that, finally, gave him a chance to show he was capable of something more than eclectic pastiches. Just around the corner on Carrer Joan Coromines is his **Societat General d'Electricitat** (1908). It's a very modest brick building (now used as a restaurant) but an exceptional one. The architecture has less in common with Catalan Modernisme than with international trend-setters such as Louis Sullivan or Hendrik Berlage, putting it right up with the mainstream avant-garde of the time. It practically screams Modernity, a symbol of a new world full of possibility as much as the electricity once generated inside it.

Just to the west on the city's promenade, the **Rambla d'Egara**, is another Modernista monument, the elegant **Mercat de la Independència** (1908), where the architecture makes a perfect setting for the gorgeous produce inside.

Museu de la Ciència i la Tècnica de Catalunya (mNACTEC) (Rbla d'Ègara, 270; ☎ 937 36 89 66; w mnactec.cat; ⊕ mid-Sep–mid-Jun 09.00–18.00 Tue–Fri, 10.00–14.30 & 15.30–19.30 Sat, 10.00–14.30 Sun; mid-Jun–mid-Sep 10.00–14.30 Tue–Sat; adult/reduced/under 16 €6/4/free) Muncunill's best-known factory in Terrassa was the big Vapor Aymerich Amat i Jover, now the main seat of Catalunya's Museum of Science and Technology. Industrial history is very important in Catalunya, and mNACTEC runs 29 other former industrial sites in the region, including mines, foundries, car and rail museums, a cement plant and a cork factory (most are mentioned in this book). Here, the building itself is the star exhibit, a magnificent interior space under a saw-tooth roof of brick arches and glass (Muncunill's invention) that floods the building with light. The exhibits

---

'EL PASSEIG DELS MUSEUS' DISCOUNT PASS

Ask at the tourist office (in the Masia Freixa building) for the 'El Passeig dels Museus' pass, which gives you entry to all Terrassa's main sights (mNACTEC, Museu Tèxtil, the Seu d'Ègara, the Castell Cartoixa de Vallparadís and the Casa Alegre de Sagrera) for €8.

detail technology from Neolithic times onward, with working antique machinery, collections of cars, aircraft, motorcycles and all kinds of gadgets – you can even cook snacks on their big solar reflector.

After the museum, take a detour across the Rambla for a few blocks to see Terrassa's splashiest Modernista building, the **Masia Freixa** (1907) in the Parc de Sant Jordi on Carrer de Volta. Muncunill originally designed it as a factory for industrialist Josep Freixa i Argemí, but Freixa liked the result so much, he had the architect turn it into a house for his family. It's quite a folly, surrounded by porticoes of parabolic arches and undulating brick domes.

West of the centre You have seen how Terrassa made its money; to the east, you can see how it spent it. The posh side of town contains such flashy landmarks as the **Teatre Principal** (1911) on Plaça Maragall, and Muncunill's **Gran Casino** (1920) on Carrer Font Vella.

Most of the bosses lived in this part of town, within walking distance of their factories, but you'd never pick out their mansions; sober, austere façades were the rule – probably sound policy when your working class was mostly Communists and Anarchists. A typical example is the **Casa Alegre de Sagrera** (C/ Font Vella 29; ☎937 31 66 46; w visitaterrassa.cat/casa-alegre-de-sagrera; ⊕ 10.00–13.00 & 16.00–19.00 Tue–Sat, 11.00–14.00 Sun; adult/reduced/under 16 €6/4/free). Francesc Alegre i Roig, an arriviste textile magnate, married into an old-money family and turned its 18th-century home upside down, with Modernista-influenced stained glass, paintings and wrought iron. Besides the furnishings and garden, the attractions here include a room full of Chinese art, with porcelains and ivories going back to the T'ang dynasty, and another with views of old Terrassa made in the 1920s and '30s by a very talented local artist named Mateu Avallaneda.

Seu d'Ègara (Pl del Rector Homs; ☎937 83 37 02; w seudegara.cat; ⊕ 10.00–13.00 & 16.00–19.00 Tue–Sat, 11.00–14.00 Sun; adult/reduced/under 6 €5/2/free) This trio of small churches is one of Spain's greatest early-medieval monuments, a little Brigadoon hidden away just outside the heart of industrial Terrassa. The way in is down Carrer de la Creu, from near the Teatre Principal, and then over the Torrent de les Bruixes ('Witches' Creek') on a picturesque medieval bridge called the **Pont de Sant Pere**.

The three churches stand in a row, on a height between two narrow ravines. It was a habit in Visigothic Spain, as in northern Italy, to sometimes build not one big metropolitan church, but an ensemble of smaller ones. Here Santa Maria was the seat of the bishop, with an adjacent episcopal palace that is now lost; Sant Miquel was for baptisms; and Sant Pere served as the parish church. This is the only such church complex in Spain to have survived in something like its original form.

A plaque in **Santa Maria** dates the consecration to 1112, although what we see is a reconstruction of a building that may go back to the 5th or 6th centuryAD. The surviving original work includes the apses and the pretty pavement of coloured stone. The apse retains some faded 10th- or 11th-century paintings, and some excellent later medieval frescoes, including a cycle of the *Life of St Thomas of Canterbury* – Thomas à Becket, always a popular saint in Spain.

In the middle stands the exquisite little **Sant Miquel**, built, like many pre-Romanesque churches, in a Greek-cross plan. Note the 'Moorish' horseshoe arch above the portal and window; this trademark feature of Islamic architecture in Spain really isn't Moorish at all, but Visigothic in origin. Inside, the columns holding up the cupola re-use Roman capitals. Underneath is an unusual three-lobed

4

crypt, dedicated to the truly obscure Sant Celoni. **Sant Pere**, also a reconstruction of a Visigothic-era church, contains remnants of faded medieval frescoes, and a glorious 15th-century altarpiece by Jaume Huguet, tucked away on a side wall.

Parc de Vallparadís Right in front of the three churches, the Torrent de les Bruixes and Torrent Monner come together to form the ravine called the Torrent de Vallparadís. Old Terrassa grew up on the edge of this ravine. Cleaned up and landscaped as the 3.5km-long Parc de Vallparadís, it is a refreshing focal point for locals, with gardens, ponds and walking trails. It's also become the city's main venue for all kinds of festivals and traditional events, from carnival parades to jazz concerts. Families love it, as there are lots of play areas and picnic spots, an outdoor swimming pool and even a miniature railway.

On the fringes of the park is the **Museu Tèxtil** (C/ Salmerón 25; ☏937 31 52 02; w cdmt.cat; ⏰ 10.00–13.00 & 16.00–19.00 Tue–Sat, 11.00–14.00 Sun; free), which exhibits fabrics and clothing from all over the world, with examples going back to earliest times. Next to it is the **Castell Cartoixa de Vallparadís** (C/ Salmerón s/n; ☏937 85 71 44; w terrassa.cat/ca/castell-cartoixa-vallparadis; ⏰ 10.00–13.00 & 16.00–19.00 Tue–Sat, 11.00–14.00 Sun; adult/reduced/under 6 €3/2/free), a 12th-century castle converted to a Carthusian monastery in 1344, housing a municipal museum with sculptures, ceramics and 19th-century paintings.

MANRESA Like Terrassa, Manresa is a surprisingly pleasant place to spend a day, an oasis on the edge of the Barcelona industrial belt. It's much smaller, though, with only 78,000 people; you can see open country from the top of town. Manresa blossomed in the Middle Ages, but its decline followed the rest of Catalunya's under Spanish rule. The town was sacked in the War of the Spanish Succession, and partly destroyed by Napoleon's troops in 1808, but started its comeback soon after as one of Catalunya's early industrial towns.

What to see and do
Col·legiata Basilica de Santa Maria (La Seu) (C/ Baixada de la Seu; ☏938 72 15 12; w seudemanresa.cat; ⏰ 10.30–13.30 & 16.00–19.00 Tue–Fri, 10.30–14.00 & 16.00–19.00 Sat, noon–14.00 & 17.00–19.00 Sun; adult/reduced/under 16 €5/3/free) Originally there was an Iberian village on the Puigcardener, a hill overlooking the confluence of the Cardener river and the Llobregat. Now, it holds the city's landmark, locally known simply as 'La Seu'. It's a stout and worthy example of Catalan Gothic, with rows or buttresses and pinnacles that give it an alert and military air.

Inside, the attraction is a wealth of 14th-century painted altarpieces that managed to escape being carted off to Barcelona's MNAC museum. The greatest of these, Pere Serra's magical *Retaule de l'Esperit Sant* (1394), is considered this important painter's masterpiece. It tells the whole Christian story from the creation to the Crucifixion, with the emphasis on the presence of the Holy Spirit in the miracles of scripture. Among the other altarpieces is the *Retaule de Sant Marc* (1346) by Arnau Bassa, a work that looks as if its author might have had a trip to Tuscany (Catalans call this period of their art 'Italogòtic'). Some bits of the original Romanesque church survive, including parts of the cloister and the lovely, unusually stylised Portal of Santa Maria, from the 13th century.

Manresa Modernista Like Terrassa, Manresa's first century of industry left it with a good collection of Modernista buildings, most concentrated around the central Carrer Sant Miquel. For an introduction, there's the charming **Farmàcia**

Esteve (1912) on Plaça de l'Om. Continue down the pedestrian Carrer Born, past the **Sastreria Tuneu** (1906) to Plaça Sant Domènec for the **Casa Torrents** (1905), an imposing home built by Manresa's own Modernista architect, Ignasi Oms; nearby, don't miss the prettiest thing in town, a little **kiosk** (now a tourist information point) built in 1917 after a design by Puig i Cadafalch.

Modernista magic continues along the city's elegant and urbane rambla, **Passeig de Pere III**. First, on the right, is the **Casal Regionalista** (1918) by another local architect, Alexandre Soler i March, and then, a little further along on the left, the two finest works of Ignasi Oms: the **Casa Lluvia** (1908; just around the corner on C/ Oms) and the absolutely glorious **Casino** (1906).

Santa Cova de Sant Ignasi

(Camí de la Cova 17; 938 72 04 22; w covamanresa. cat; 10.30–13.00 & 16.00–19.00 Mon–Sat, 10.00–11.00 Sun; donation requested, guided visits adult/reduced/under 16 €8/6/free) Íñigo López de Recalde, the Basque from Guipuzcoa who would one day become St Ignatius of Loyola, founder of the Jesuit Order, found his spiritual vocation as he spent a year recovering from the wounds he suffered fighting in the Battle of Pamplona in 1521. As soon as he was well enough, he exchanged clothes with a beggar and set out on a pilgrimage to Montserrat. After that he ended up in a monastery in Manresa, where he spent a very ascetic year fasting, performing menial labour, having visions and writing his Spiritual Exercises, the foundation of his later missionary work.

For most of that time he was living in a cave on the edge of the city, one with a view of Montserrat. This Santa Cova ('holy cave') is the seed from which an enormous complex has grown. The cave itself has become a shrine, sumptuously decorated in mosaics, alabaster reliefs and stained glass. There's also a small museum, and an audiovisual show on Ignatius' life. Perhaps the best part of the complex is the church, with a delightful rococo façade.

Below the Santa Cova is another landmark that appears on all the postcards. The camel-back, 113m **Pont Vell** has been carrying people over the Llobregat for 700 years and it's still in good nick.

Museu del Barroc de Catalunya

(Pl de Sant Ignasi 14–16; 938 74 11 55; w museudelbarroc.cat; 10.30–13.00 & 16.00–19.00 Mon–Sat, 10.00–11.00 Sun; donation requested, adult/reduced/under 16 €8/6/free) Opened in 2024, in the remodelled Neoclassical Col·legi de St Ignasi, this is Catalunya's first museum dedicated to Baroque art. Highlights include paintings of Saint Francis of Assisi by the most renowned Catalan artist of the age, Antoni Viladomat (1678–1755), as well as works by local painters such as Joaquim Juncosa and Francesc Tramulles Roig. The experience is designed to be immersive, with Baroque music providing a soothing backdrop to the almost 200 artworks on display and audiovisuals that explain the Baroque movement and how it developed in Catalunya.

While new exhibition spaces are being created in the same building for the local history museum, you can also see a small exhibition of treasures from the **Museu Comarcal de Manresa** (10.00–14.00 Tue–Fri; free), including late Roman mosaics from local villas, and colourful ceramics that were manufactured here in the 14th century.

Món de Sant Benet

(Camí de Sant Benet, Sant Fruitós de Bages; 938 74 11 55; w monsantbenet.com; see website for different experiences and prices) Just northeast of Manresa, the Sant Benet monastery was not one of Catalunya's luckier religious houses; the Moors sacked it twice and what was left burned up in a fire in 1633. It was

4

abandoned and cannibalised until 1907, when Elisa Carbó, mother of painter Ramon Casas, converted part of the monastery into a cosy Modernista family home. In 2000, a private foundation purchased the lot and restored the church, its enchanting cloister and Modernista rooms, and then added a hotel and restaurants (page 134). It also offers tours, wine tastings and other experiences. The monastery overlooks the **Parc Natural de Sant Llorenç del Munt i de l'Obac** – two ranges of coastal hills and cliffs between the Llobregat and Ripoll rivers, covered in holm oaks and pines.

MONTSERRAT

Uncanny, mystical Montserrat, the 'Dream turned Mountain' and spiritual heart of Catalunya, is visible from just about anywhere from within the Barcelona province. This isolated, fantastical 10km 'serrated mountain' made of jagged, pudding-stone pinnacles rises precipitously over deep gorges and shallow terraces. It is so different from the surrounding countryside, heaven itself may have dropped it there. Geological upheavals 10 million years ago left the mountain to be sculpted by the wind and rain into a hedgehog of phallic peaks with names like the 'Potato', 'Bishop's Belly', 'Salamander', and a hundred others.

HISTORY Montserrat's human history is just as fantastical: St Peter supposedly came here to hide an image of the Virgin carved by St Luke in a cave; in another grotto, the good knight Parsifal discovered the Holy Grail – a legend used by Wagner for his opera. In AD880, not long after Christians regained the region, the statue of the Virgin (hidden by someone before the advance of the Moors) was discovered on Montserrat and, as is so often the case in Christian legend, it stubbornly refused to budge beyond a certain spot. Count Wilfred the Hairy built a chapel to house it, and in AD976 this was given to the Benedictines of Ripoll. Throughout the Middle Ages it was a magnet for pilgrims.

Independent and incredibly wealthy, Montserrat was favoured by Charles V (the old hypocrite visited nine times), and his son Philip II rebuilt the church. During the Peninsular War, Catalan guerrillas fortified it as a base, and in reprisal the French looted and sacked the monastery. As the Catalan Renaixença gathered steam, Montserrat became its symbol. In 1918, the first Bible in Catalan was printed here, and Verdaguer, Gaudí and Pau Casals were all fervent devotees of the Virgin. Under Franco, Montserrat was the only church permitted to celebrate Mass in Catalan, and couples flocked here to be married in their own language.

Even today Montserrat evokes the same image for Spaniards as Niagara Falls for Americans; it's a traditional honeymoon destination, to receive the blessing of the Moreneta ('the little brown one'), as the Virgin is affectionately called, before undertaking the supreme adventure of marriage.

GETTING THERE AND AROUND From Barcelona, there's a daily Juliá (w autocaresjulia.com) bus to Montserrat (⊕ Oct–May departure 09.15, return 17.00; Jun–Sep departure 09.15, return 19.00; ✆ 933 17 64 54) leaving from the bus station next to Sants train station. Alternatively, take an FGC train (line R5) from the station under the Plaça d'Espanya (⊕ departures every 30mins 05.36–22.30 daily; check w fgc.cat for timetables).

Get off either at the station Aeri de Montserrat for the *telèferic* (cableway; approx every 15mins; w aeridemontserrat.com; adult/reduced/child 4–13/under 4 €9.30/8.15/4.90/free) or at the next stop, Monistrol de Montserrat, for the *cremallera* (rack-and-pinion railway; ⊕ every hour 08.48–17.48, more frequently in summer;

check **w** turistren.cat/trens/cremallera-i-funiculars-de-montserrat for timetables; return tickets adult/reduced/child 4–13/under 4 €14/12.60/7/free). Both offer free parking at the base. If you're coming from Barcelona you can buy combined tickets for the train and cableway or *cremallera* at Plaça Espanya station, or you can purchase an all-inclusive ticket called the Tot Montserrat (€69.90, available online at the city's tourist information website, **w** bcnshop.barcelonaturisme.com), which includes return train, cableway or *cremallera*, unlimited use of the funiculars on Montserrat, entrance to the Basilica (no need for prior booking or joining the queue), as well as entrance to the museum and lunch at the self-service café.

If you want to hike up from Monistrol, the **Camí de les Aigües** pilgrimage path is a steep but rewarding climb linking Monistrol to the Montserrat complex (approx 1.5hrs).

TOURIST INFORMATION Montserrat's tourist information office, on the main square of the complex, Plaça de la Creu (📞938 77 77 77; **w** montserratvisita.com;

HEINRICH HIMMLER COMES TO MONTSERRAT

Is the Grail a chalice, a dish or a stone? And is it somewhere in Glastonbury, or Rennes-le-Château, or Valencia, or in the Cloisters Museum? Why not here in Catalunya? In truth, people have been asking that question for centuries. A recurring stream of mystical thought and legend associates the Grail and the Grail castle with the eastern Pyrenees. The German knight and poet Wolfram von Eschenbach, whose *Parzifal*, written in about 1198, is the most complete and most provocative account of the Grail legend, gives the name of the Grail castle as Munsalvaesche, which sounds like 'Montsalvat', an old name for Montserrat. Eschenbach's work inspired Wagner's opera *Parsifal*, which turned a great medieval epic into treacly pudding, but did a lot to renew interest in Grail matters. Interestingly, *Parsifal* had its first authorised performance outside Bayreuth at the Liceu in Barcelona.

Thanks perhaps to Wagner, the Nazis were obsessed with this aspect of the Grail story. In the 1930s Grail addict and future SS officer Otto Rahn poked all over the French Pyrenees for ruined castles or secret caverns where the Grail might be hiding. Under the occupation the Nazis were at it again. In 1940, while Hitler was having his famous conference with Franco on the French–Spanish border at Hendaye, a certain Heinrich Himmler checked into the Ritz in Barcelona. Next day, he paid a call to Montserrat.

The abbot, aware of Himmler's attacks against the Church, wouldn't see him, but referred him to the only monk who spoke a little German. He apparently told the Nazi big shot that he didn't know anything about any Grails, and Himmler had to go back to Berlin empty-handed. The story took a new twist with a 2005 book by a Canadian professor named Joseph Goering. In *The Virgin and the Grail*, Goering notes that 'grail' is an old Catalan word for a kind of serving dish, and he claims that Catalan art in the 12th century provides the first artistic representations of the Grail. In particular, he cites the frescoes of Sant Climent de Taüll (page 307); here, under the famous image of Christ Pantocrator, the Virgin stands holding something with radiating lines emanating from it that looks rather like a bowl of hot soup, but might indeed be a Holy Grail. All of which leaves Grail-hunters back where Grail-hunters are always left – at square one.

4

⏰ 09.00–18.30 Mon–Fri, 09.00–19.30 Sat–Sun) offers details on the many different combined tickets available, depending on your interests: you can also find the information on their website.

🏠 **WHERE TO STAY AND EAT** To get a feel for Montserrat, stay overnight, but be prepared: it can get quite cold even in summer. The monks run a *hostal*, apartments and a youth hostel. When you book accommodation, your return *cremallera* ticket is free.

An alternative to monkish hospitality is staying down in Monistrol de Montserrat, where the *cremallera* station is located. It has a small collection of rooms, restaurants and cafés; it's a good idea to book well in advance.

Abat Cisneros Pl del Monestir s/n; ☎ 938 77 77 01; w montserratvisita.com/es/donde-dormir/hostal-abat-cisneros-montserrat. Classically decorated rooms, some with mountain views, plus a restaurant & bar, right next to the Basilica. **€€€**
Cel·les Abat Marcet Montserrat Pl del Monestir s/n; ☎ 938 77 77 01; w montserratvisita.com/es/donde-dormir/celles-abat-marcet-montserrat. This has 92 modern apartments for between 1 & 4 people, complete with simple kitchenettes. **€€**
Alberg Abat Oliba Pl del Monestir s/n; ☎ 938 77 77 01; w montserratvisita.com/es/donde-dormir/alberg-abat-oliba-montserrat. A large, bland block in the heart of the monastery complex. Simply decorated dbls, family rooms & dorms with bunks for between 4 & 10 people. Dbls **€€**, bunks **€**
✳ **Casa Camí de les Aigues** ☎ 600 45 12 65; w casacamidelesaigues.com. A cosy little B&B, with charming, simply decorated rooms located right at the start of the Camí de les Aigües pilgrimage path that goes up to Montserrat. **€**
Guilleumes C/ Escoles 5, Monistrol de Montserrat; ☎ 938 28 40 65; w guilleumes.com. Rooms with a view of Montserrat, not from it. A friendly budget hotel, with basic, pristine rooms & a good restaurant (usually lunch only: check in advance if you want dinner). **€**

WHAT TO SEE AND DO The **Monastery** can hardly compete with the fabulous surroundings; after a lovely ride, the *cremallera* and *telefèric* leave you in a somewhat grim and business-like square of grey stone buildings. On the lower level are the enormous gift shops and the **Museu de Montserrat** (⏰ 10.00–17.45; adult/reduced/under 8 €8/6.50/free), which is usually empty, despite having a surprisingly good art collection that includes works by Catalan artists from Santiago Rusiñol and Isidre Nonell to Picasso and Dalí, French Impressionists, including Monet and Degas, and Old Masters, from El Greco to Caravaggio and Tiepolo. These is also a room of orthodox icons, and archaeological finds from Greece, Palestine, Mesopotamia and Egypt.

Behind the chilly façade of the **Basilica** (⏰ 07.00–20.00 main church, 08.00–10.30 & noon–17.45 Virgin Throne; adult/reduced €12/9. Mass is free to Spain residents and those lodging in Montserrat but you must still book your place in advance), there's a beautiful courtyard decorated in green *esgrafiat* work. Philip II's church lost most of its sumptuous furnishings to Napoleon's men, but the enthroned *Virgin of Montserrat* still presides over the high altar; the strange statue with a faraway look dates from the 12th century, though it is believed to be a copy, coloured black to imitate the original idol. There's always a queue lining up to touch the outstretched hand of the Virgin, holding an orb representing the universe, and which is said to bring healing and even miracles. Pilgrims still come to worship her in droves on 27 April, when she is celebrated as the patron saint of Catalunya, and 8 September, the feast of the Nativity of Mary.

The **Escolanía boys' choir**, founded in the 13th century – the oldest music school in Europe – still performs a *virrolei* and *salve* at 13.00 from Monday to Friday, and also sings at Sunday mass (note that prior reservation is required; see w escolania.cat).

Best of all, though, are the **walks** around the mountain. An easy walk (about 1.5km) called **Els Degotalls** takes in a wonderful view of the Pyrenees (it's signposted near the snack bar). There are two funiculars (for timetables and prices, see w turistren.cat/trens/cremallera-i-funiculars-de-montserrat) that depart from close to the Basilica: the **Funicular Santa Cova** descends to the **Santa Cova**, where a 17th-century chapel marks the exact finding place of the Moreneta; while the **Funicular Sant Joan** will take you up to a panoramic viewing platform and the **Hermitage of Sant Joan**. Several spectacular hikes depart from here, including one (which takes about an hour) up to the **Hermitage of Sant Jeroni** – traditionally the spot given to the youngest and most spry hermit. From the hermitage a short path rises to the highest peak in the range (1,253m), offering a bird's-eye view of the holy mountain and across to the Pyrenees.

Down on the southern slopes of the magic mountain, at **Collbató**, you can visit the **Coves de Salnitre** (Ctra de les Coves s/n; ☏680 53 60 63; w covesdemontserrat. org; ☉ tours (in Catalan) Sep–Jun 10.00, 11.30, 16.30 Sat–Sun, Jul–Aug 10.00, 11.30, 16.30 daily; adult/reduced/under 6 €8.50/7.25/free), a beautiful stalactite cave that reminds all the Catalans of Gaudí, and is just about worth the 244 steps you'll have to climb to get in.

DOWN THE LLOBREGAT RIVER: SOUTH OF MONTSERRAT

From Manresa all the way down to the sea, the Llobregat is a hard-working river. From the *cremallera* train up to Montserrat, you might have noticed the new factories popping up even around the skirts of Catalunya's holy mountain. The towns that follow the river along its way may be decidedly lacking in charm, but then, somebody has to do the work that keeps the world turning, no?

There is a **tourist information office** at the Colònia Güell (C/ Claudi Güell 6; ☏936 30 58 07; ☉ May–Oct 10.00–19.00 Mon–Fri, 10.00–15.00 Sat–Sun, Nov–Apr 10.00–17.00 Mon–Fri, 10.00–15.00 Sat–Sun).

GETTING THERE AND AROUND There are FGC trains (lines S3, S4, S8 and S9; w fgc. cat) from Plaça Espanya in Barcelona to Colònia Güell, which has its own stop. By car, if you can find your way to the Sant Vicenç dels Horts exit of the A2, it's signposted from there. Catalunya en Miniatura is easiest reached by car (just off the A2, exit 3) or by taking FGC train (R1, R4) from Plaça Espanya and then catching the Soler i Sauret bus (line 62; w solerisauret.com). You can buy a combined ticket (*bitllet combinat*), which includes train, bus and entrance to Catalunya en Miniatura (adult/reduced/under 4 €14/10/free; with Aventura Vertical adult/reduced/under 4 €22/17/free).

WHAT TO SEE AND DO
Esparreguera Esparreguera can offer a branch of Terrassa's mNACTEC (page 136); the **Colonia Sedó** (C/ Contínues s/n; ☏936 66 35 27; w museucoloniasedo.cat; ☉ 10:00–14:00 Sat–Sun, closed Aug; adult/reduced/under 16 €5/3/free) was a 19th-century model industrial village built around a cotton mill. Here, mNACTEC wants to show off the industrial organisation, the advanced water-power system that ran the mill, and a crazy corkscrew smokestack, a masterpiece of brickwork.

Colonia Güell and Gaudí's Crypt (BV2002, Santa Coloma de; ☏936 30 58 07; w gaudicoloniaguell.org; ☉ 10.00–17.00 Mon–Fri, 10.00–15.00 Sat–Sun; guided tour/with audio guide/reduced €13/10/7.50) Labour and class disputes in Barcelona

4

led magnate Eusebi Güell to consider a little adventure in paternalism in 1890. He closed his Barcelona textile mill, fired all his anarchist workers, and set off for a new start in what was then open country.

The Colonia Güell was planned as a pseudo worker's co-operative (Güell was still boss) around a cotton goods mill, with houses, a store, a school and other buildings for the workers designed by Gaudí's assistants, Francesc Berenguer and Joan Rubió Bellver. Almost all of it survives, as a peaceful and rather dreamlike neighbourhood set around a little square with the company shops, the **Ateneu**, or cultural centre, and a **statue of Joan Güell**, Eusebi's father and founder of the dynasty.

The original chapel on the estate was found to be too small, and in 1898 Güell asked Gaudí to design a larger church, set apart in a grove of trees. The sketches for this look like a cross between Coney Island and the Emerald City of Oz, but, once Güell died in 1918, funds for the church dried up, and only the **crypt** was completed.

Yet of all Gaudí's works, this magical, primordial avant-garde grotto is the most innovative – a marvel of virtuosity and engineering. It has no right angles and no straight lines; all the pillars bend at weird expressionist angles. Many critics consider it Gaudí's greatest work. It contains no religious painting or sculpture; the spirituality in it is expressed in architecture alone. Gaudí employed some of his mathematical magic here, as in the parabolic arches, but he also had something else modern architects don't have: Catalan bricklayers. There is no steel reinforcing anything, anywhere: the whole thing is made of rough-hewn stone and brick, primitive textures brightened with stained glass and *trencadí* collages. Robert Hughes' description of Gaudí's architecture as a 'womb with a view' fits it to a T.

Sant Joan Despí

While you're out here, bumming around in the miasmic suburbs looking for Modernista treasures, you can find two more just over the Llobregat in the little industrial community of Sant Joan Despí. Gaudí's disciple Josep Maria Jujol came here in 1913 to build a house for his aunt, and the result was the **Torre de la Creu** at Passeig de Canalies 12 by the train station. Locals call it the Torre dels Ous, the 'Egg Tower'; the building is a composition of six cylindrical towers topped by egg-shaped domes. It all seems symmetrical, but, when you look closely, it never is.

After working in Tarragona and the Alt Camp Jujol returned to complete a few more projects here, all within walking distance. The **Casa Negre** (1915–30) on Plaça Catalunya has a delightful curvy façade decorated in *esgrafiat* work, with a bay window in the shape of a rococo-era coach stuck incongruously in the centre. There's some beautiful decorative work inside; don't miss the quirky, spectacular chapel.

You can see four more from Jujol on nearby Carrer Jacint Verdaguer, including three houses in a row: the **Torre Jujol** (1932), **Torre Serra-Xaus** (1921) and **Can Rovira** (1926), and the interior decoration of the church of **Sant Joan Baptista** (1943).

Catalunya en Miniatura

(Can Balasch de Baix s/n; 📞 936 89 09 60; w catalunyaenminiatura.com; ⏱ 10.00–18.00 daily; models only: adult/seniors & children 3–12/under 3 €14.25/10.45/free; with adventure park: adult/children 8–12/children 4–7/under 4 €21.85/18.05/15.20/free) Torrelles de Llobregat is the biggest folly of its kind in Europe, and your chance to ride a miniature train and see the best monuments of Catalunya from the perspective of a Gulliver. Naturally, there's a special section devoted to Gaudí. The adjoining adventure park, with high ropes and zip lines through the trees, is a big draw for families.

ALT PENEDÈS

Wine and the Penedès have always gone together. According to archaeologists, vines have been growing in the shadow of Montserrat for at least 2,500 years, and the region's fortunes have risen or fallen with the grapes ever since. In the 18th century they were selling Penedès wine to the British and the Dutch. When it went out of fashion there, they turned it into brandy and shipped it to Latin America. That went like a bomb until phylloxera wiped out the vines in the late 1880s. But when it was time to replant on American rootstock, the winemakers realised they were just in time to cash in on the new fashion for sparkling wines, and the Penedès made its new cava a worthy competitor to champagne.

Some wine regions have a lush and idyllic air; broadly speaking, this isn't one of them (although there are little pockets of bucolic charm). It's small and intense, with a definite air of agribusiness about it (the power lines running through it don't help either).

GETTING THERE AND AROUND Nothing could be easier than hopping out from Barcelona to Sant Sadurní or Vilafranca for a day's wine excursion in the Penedès. You can reach both by the R4 train (see timetables at w rodalies.cat). In Sant Sadurní, the Freixenet cellars are right by the station, and in both towns many of the others are right in town, not in the country.

TOURIST INFORMATION There are tourist information offices in Vilafranca del Penedès (C/ Hermenegild Clascar 2; ☎ 938 18 12 54; w turismevilafranca.com; ⏰ 09.30–13.30 & 15.00–18.00 Mon–Sat, 10.00–13.00 Sun) and in Sant Sadurní (C/ de l'Hospital 23; ☎ 938 91 31 88; w santsadurni.cat/turisme; ⏰ 09.15–14.30 & 16.00–18.00 Mon–Fri, 10.00–14.00 & 16.00–18.00 Sat, 10.00–13.00 Sun). Both provide information on local wineries, tastings and guided visits.

🏠 WHERE TO STAY

✴ **Hotel Boutique Font de la Canya** Camí d'Avinyó 12, Avinyonet del Penedès; ☎ 621 19 06 99; w hotelfontdelacanya.com. A dreamy country hotel with just a handful of pretty rooms set amid olive groves & vineyards & with views of Montserrat. Outdoor pool, good restaurant (€€€) & attentive staff. €€€€

Bolet Casa Modernista BV-2117, km 15; ☎ 633 77 47 38; w boletcasamodernista.com. The Bolet family have been making wine on this estate (about 13km west of Vilafranca del Penedès) for 7 generations. Their beautiful Modernista mansion now offers 5 beautiful, spacious rooms, each

named after a different wine, & you can enjoy tastings & tours of their cellars. €€€

Hostal Sant Sadurní C/ Sant Antoni 99, Sant Sadurní d'Anoia; ☎ 938 91 43 35; w hss.com.es. Unassuming, basic hostal with immaculate rooms, all with AC & Juliet balconies. No restaurant or b/fast service, but there are plenty of cafés nearby. €

Pensio Restaurant Avenida C/ Eugeni d'Ors 48, Vilafranca del Penedès; ☎ 938 17 13 19; w restaurantelavenida.com. A good budget base in the centre of town, this has 6 clean & simple rooms above this popular local restaurant (€€), serving tasty traditional Catalan cuisine. €

✗ WHERE TO EAT AND DRINK

Cal Ton C/ Casal 8, Vilafranca del Penedès; ☎ 938 90 37 41; w restaurantcalton.com; ⏰ 13.00–15.30 Mon, 13.00–15.30 & 20.30–22.00 Thu–Fri, 13.00–16.00 Sat–Sun. A beloved local institution, serving reliably good local cuisine paired with an excellent wine list (of course). As well as à la

carte, you can choose from 3 tasting menus, which include a vegetarian option. €€€

La Cava d'en Sergi C/ València 17, Sant Sadurní d'Anoia; ☎ 938 91 16 16; w lacavadensergi.com; ⏰ 13.00–16.00 Tue–Fri, 13.00–16.00 & 21.00–23.00 Sat, 13.00–16.00 Sun. Sophisticated local

CAVA

'Cava', as you might have guessed, simply means a cellar. In the old days the better Catalan wines, those that were laid down, were called 'cava' wines, and somehow through the years that came to be the name given to Catalunya's beloved bubbly.

And beloved it is. Catalans don't save the cava for New Year's, but drink it as an aperitif, or an everyday tipple at the bar after work. We have seen bottles of cava emptied and left on door sills in back alleys. It is still de rigueur for celebrations, though, and sometimes it can be a symbol of Catalan nationalism. On the memorable night in 1975 when Franco died, they drained every last bottle in Barcelona.

The great European festival of fizz really got its start in the decadent, over-the-top Paris of the 19th century, when champagne first became synonymous with high times. In 1872, an aristocratic old Penedès vintner named Josep Raventós made a visit to Champagne to see how it was done, and decided to try it at home. That was the origin of cava, and the first great cava house, Codorníu. 'Champagne Catalan', as it was called before denomination laws came in, was a hit, and other producers soon followed.

Today, it's usually made from macabeo (viura), xarel·lo and parellada grapes; since the 1980s chardonnay has also become popular. There are also various varieties of rosé cava. The process is almost exactly the same as for champagne. At first the wine is almost colourless; some yeast is added for further fermentation, and the wine is bottled and given a metal cap like a beer bottle's. This second fermentation is when the carbon dioxide that makes the bubbles is formed, in an aging process that can last from nine months to four years.

Then comes the tricky bit, the remuage, or riddling. For a period, the bottles are tilted downwards and carefully rotated a fraction each day, to make the yeast settle out. Then they quickly freeze the necks where the sediment has collected; when the cap is removed, the pressure pops the frozen lees out. A little extra cava from the same vintage (the *licor d'expedició*), with a carefully measured content of sugar, is added to govern the flavour. And then, in goes the cork.

Penedès doesn't just make cava; Catalunya's biggest wine region produces still red and whites, some of great distinction, but nevertheless cava is its fame and its

dishes with a contemporary twist. The set lunch (€26) is great value for the quality on offer. €€€
Mil Nou-Cents – Bar à vins C/ Pi i Margall 4, Sant Sadurní d'Anoia; ✆ 930 42 81 60; ⌾ milnoucents_baravins; ⌚ 19.00–23.00 Wed– Fri, 13.00–16.00 & 20.00–23.00 Sat. A cosy wine bar, serving delicious plates to share along with more substantial dishes. They also sell all kinds of local goodies – wines, charcuterie, cheeses, premium tinned goods, & more. €€

VILAFRANCA DEL PENEDÈS AND AROUND This big sun-baked town is known throughout Catalunya not only for wine, but *castellers*; here they build their human towers ten storeys high. Vilafranca's parish church of **Santa Maria** (1285) was one of the first Gothic buildings in Catalunya; ask at the tourist office and they'll get you in to climb the bell tower for a view of the town.

Across Plaça Jaume from the church, a medieval palace and adjacent building have been restored to house the **Vinseum** (Pl de Jaume I; ✆ 938 90 05 82; w vinseum.cat; ⌚ 14:00–18:00 Tue–Wed, noon–22.00 Thu–Sat, noon–15.00 Sun; adult/reduced/under 13 €10/7/free), Spain's first museum dedicated to wine, prosperity. Wine-lovers who come for a visit may be a little disappointed; don't expect the kind of convivial wine tourism you can enjoy in other parts of Spain, or France and Italy. It's a little too close to the big city for that. Almost everywhere, you're expected to ring ahead for a reservation, and pay for admission; in the bigger estates a visit can be little more than a promotional film followed by a perfunctory tour and tasting.

In Sant Sadurní, the cava capital, a trip to **Codorníu** (Avda Jaume Codorníu; ☏ 935 05 15 51; w codorniu.com/en/visits) is definitely worthwhile, as much for the wine as for the remarkable Modernista complex of buildings (1915) designed by Puig i Cadafalch, with a museum and over a million square feet of cellars. Although it has become a multinational concern, Codorníu is still run by the Raventós family; its great rival **Freixenet** (Avda Joan Sala 2; ☏ 938 91 70 00; w freixenet.com/es/es), which has been making it only since 1914, is even bigger and much more corporate in spirit. Their advertising over the decades has made them almost as much of a consumer icon as Coca-Cola or Guinness. Among the others, **Antonio Mascaró** (C/ Casal 9, Vilafranca del Penedès; ☏ 938 90 16 28; w www.mascaro.es/es/visitas/enoturisme-by-mascaro-la-visita-bienvenidos-a-mascaro) also produces still wines and brandies.

Albet i Noya made the first organic cava for the Danish market in 1972, and they have gone all-organic since (Can Vendrell, Sant Pau l'Ordal; ☏ 938 99 48 12; w albetinoya.cat). **Ludens** (Masia Grabuac, Font-Rubí; ☏ 938 97 81 29; w cavaludens.cat) has another Modernista cellar. **Jean León** (Torrelavit, 7km north of Sant Sadurní; ☏ 938 17 76 90; w jeanleon.com), who went to America as a stowaway and eventually founded the famous Hollywood restaurant La Scala in partnership with James Dean, gave it up in the 1960s to make prize-winning wines in Penedès. His modern estate makes for one of the more interesting visits. Jean León is now owned by **Torres**, another global wine giant that began in Vilafranca with an 'Americano' who came back from Cuba in 1870 to start his wine empire here. Torres' huge estate outside Vilafranca can be visited too (w torres. es), though you'll want to get well sloshed before you go. There's an automated train trip through the vineyards and cellars, and a 'multimedia experience with vineyard aromas'. Oy!

founded in 1944. Today it includes a bit of everything else too, with collections of art, natural history and ceramics thrown in, all now displayed in spanking new galleries after a recent expansion. It offers a host of activities relating to wine, from talks to tastings, and was awarded Best Wine Museum in Europe in 2024 by the Council of Europe.

North of Vilafranca, the village of **Sant Martí Sarroca** grew up around a 10th-century castle called **La Roca** and the adjacent church of **Santa Maria**, which has a fine Romanesque choir and a 1421 painted altarpiece attributed to Jaume Cabrera. Further west, the next scenic road down towards the coast passes the impressive **Castell de Castellet** (☏ 938 14 45 06; ⊕ 10.00–14.00 for guided tours only (in Catalan); advance booking by phone required), long a hot spot on the Moorish-Christian border; parts of it date to the 10th century.

OLÈRDOLA (Castell d'Olèrdola s/n, Sant Miquel d'Olèrdola; ☏ 938 9 01 42; w macolerdola.cat; ⊕ Mar–May & Oct–mid-Dec 10.00–17.30 Tue–Sun, Jun–Sep

10.00–20.00 Tue–Sun, mid-Dec–Feb 10.00–16.00 Tue–Sun; adult/reduced/under 16 €7/5/free) South of Vilafranca, on a height overlooking the road to Sitges, was the big town in this region until the late Middle Ages. Lost in a forest of pines and palmettos, there isn't much left of it now, outside of the Conjunt Històric, maintained by the Barcelona Archaeological Museum; traces go back to the Iberians and the Neolithic era, and the ruins of a medieval church.

SANT SADURNÍ D'ANOIA
Sant Sadurní d'Anoia produces 90% of all Catalunya's cava. The giant producers Codorníu and Freixenet have their enormous operations on the outskirts, but many of the other 80 or so smaller cellars are right in the town. Sant Sadurní is where wine and Modernisme come together. As they rebuilt their business after the phylloxera crisis, the wine barons hired some of Catalunya's top architects, including Puig i Cadafalch, to build their homes and cellars. Outside of the Codorníu winery (page 147), none is particularly special in itself, but the tourist office offers guided tours of the 'Ruta Modernista' that includes a visit to Codorníu.

SANT PERE RIUDEBITLLES
If you're ever up in the hills north of Sant Sadurní, have a look at the Pont Nou aqueduct, 25m high and 80m long, built not by the Romans but the medieval Catalans (restored in 1721 after an earthquake). Why was such a huge work erected in an isolated rural setting? The answer is another secret from Catalunya's remarkable industrial past. Back in the 13th century, all that water was powering paper mills. The remains of some of these can be seen in and around the village, along with one impressive waterwheel.

COSTA DEL GARRAF

When Barcelonins want to sprawl on a beach they usually head south to the Garraf. This little patch of rugged mountains gives Barcelona some unspoiled green space on its doorstep, and it pushes right down to the coast, keeping it from being as frantic and overbuilt as the strip north of the city. Altogether, it's a coast thoroughly tamed to the ends of the metropolis; the commuter trains make it practically a Barcelona suburb. There are two big beach towns: sophisticated Sitges, very much a petal of the Fiery Rose of Anarchism that fluttered down to the sea; and the more workaday Vilanova i la Geltrú.

South of Barcelona, the coastline is taken up for over 20km by the airport and industry. The main highway hits the coast at **Castelldefels**, a big Barcelona suburb with a hugely popular, 5km-long, Blue Flag-certified, Wi-Fi-equipped stretch of sand. A dozen old watchtowers survive, relics from the 16th century when Turkish pirates were a constant menace. Castelldefels' council prides itself as a patron of the arts, and there's enough modern sculpture in its parks and roundabouts to fill a scrapyard. The town church, **Santa Maria**, is a right peculiar Modernista-neo-Romanesque-Byzantine work of 1903 with some paintings inside to match, supplied with a slight touch of Dalí by the Argentine-Catalan artist Josep Serrasanta. Casteldefells hosted many of the canoeing events in the 1992 Olympics, and you can take a turn in a boat or try other sports at the Canal Olímpic.

After Castelldefels, the coast and its nearly empty hinterland are enclosed in the **Parc Natural de Garraf** (w parcs.diba.cat/en/web/garraf). It's a dry, spare wilderness, kept empty by rugged terrain, but there's just enough water for pine forests and vines. There are no roads through the park, although hiking and cycling paths have been laid out; you'll find park information centres in Sitges and all the surrounding villages. Inland, at **Olivella**, one of the old *masies*, called **Palau Novella**, has become Spain's first Tibetan Buddhist monastery; they have a museum of Tibetan art and welcome visitors.

The coast south of Castelldefels is a busy place, squeezed under the Garraf peaks; there is a pretty sandy beach, lined with miniature, whitewashed, wooden beach cabins at the fishing port of **Garraf**, and several smaller and less crowded ones along the way. Garraf has another attraction, the **Celler Güell** (1895–1900) designed by Gaudí and Francesc Berenguer. Eusebi Güell had envisaged a hunting lodge here. Before it was finished, the plan got twisted around, and the hunting lodge turned into a winery with a gatekeeper's house. The result is as jaw-dropping as anything of Gaudí's.

SITGES

Wedged between the Garraf massif and a lovely long crescent of sand, Sitges has been Barcelona's favourite resort ever since the Modernistas flocked here at the turn of the century, led by painter and writer Santiago Rusinyol (1861–1931). Rusinyol, the son of a textile tycoon, was a Catalan original, a proto-Dalí in life if not in his art. His bohemian lifestyle and his Sitges Festes Modernistes and art exhibitions brought a little of Belle Epoque Paris to Catalunya. The little fishing village of Sitges would never be the same again. Even when the artistic buzz faded, it remained a devoted party town. Its wild carnival was the only one in Spain that Franco was never able to completely suppress. It attracts a big international crowd in summer, and during special events like the carnival and the film festival in October, you can barely squeeze in.

Sitges was probably a discreet gay rendezvous for decades before the post-Franco liberalisation brought things out into the open. There are not only gay bars and clubs, but gay beaches, gay hotels, even a gay laundry. There is no gay ghetto: Sitges is an utterly cosmopolitan, artsy resort with an interesting mix of folks from all over. Plus, it has 16 beaches, including eight with all the facilities in the town centre (including the Platja de la Bassa Rodona, the current gay muscle beach), along with a series of delightful coves stretching south linked by a cliff-top walk.

GETTING THERE AND AROUND R2 Sud commuter trains from Barcelona's Estació de Sants & Plaça Catalunya depart every 15–20 minutes for Sitges & Vilanova i la Geltrú via Castelldefels (the Castelldefels-Platja station is a minute from the beach) and Garraf; not all trains stop at all stations, so check before you board. You're certainly welcome in Sitges, but your car isn't. They already have far too many; street parking can be nearly impossible and the rates in the city-run car parks are extortionate.

WHERE TO STAY *Map, page 150*

Sitges isn't for the staid nor the economy-minded, nor for those without a reservation. Things calm down considerably in the off-season, when prices plummet and many hotels close down, but even then, be sure to call in advance.

Hotel Casa Vilella Pg Marítim 21; ☏ 935 24 02 00; w en.hotelcasavilella.com. A seafront charmer, with a dozen stylish rooms in an elegantly restored villa built in 1919, a garden with pool & a good restaurant (€€€). **€€€€**

Subur Maritim Pg Marítim s/n; ☏ 938 94 15 50; w hotelsuburmaritim.com. One of the better 4-star options, this large, modern hotel on the seafront has a big pool, Wi-Fi & free bikes; most rooms have sea-view balconies. **€€€€**

SITGES

Where to stay
For listings, see from page 149

1 Antonio's Hostal
2 El Xalet
3 Hotel Casa Vilella
4 La Santa Maria
5 Parrots
6 Romàntic
7 Subur Maritim
8 Termes

Where to eat and drink

9   Chai
10 El Pou
11 La Marinada
12 La Punta de Sitges
13 Maricel
14 Nem
15 Petit Bangkok

Off map
    Can Laury
    La Cupula

La Cupula
Can Laury

C/ D'EN POMPEU FABRA

C/ MARAGALL

Bar Voramar

Platja de
Sant Sebastià

C/ RAFAEL LLOPART

Cau Ferrat and
Museu Maricel
Palau Maricel

The Dutchess

Sant Bartolomeu
i Santa Tecla

Railway
station

C/ MAJOR

La Cocteleria
del Factor Vi

C/ BONAIRE

Bears
Bar

Museu Romàntic
Can Llopis

XXL   Man
       Bar

C/ DE LES
PARELLADES

Platja de
Ribera

AV. D'ARTUR CARBONELL

C/ DESPALTER

PG DE VILANOVA

AV SOFIA

PG DE LA RIBERA

Platja de
Sitges

PG DE VILANOVA

AVINGUDA DE NOSTRA SENYORA DEL VINYET

AV NAVARRA

C/ JOSEP CARBONELL I GENER

PG DE LA RIBERA

PG DE VILLAFRANCA

N

Bradt

300m
300yds
0
0

La Santa María Pg de la Ribera 52; 938 94 09 99; w lasantamaria.com. Mid-sized seafront hotel with bright, prettily furnished rooms & a little sun terrace with geraniums. Downstairs is a popular restaurant (€€€) with a terrace. €€€

Romàntic C/ Sant Isidre 33; 938 94 83 75; w mediumhoteles.com/hotel-medium-romantic. 3 atmospheric 19th-century villas with delightful, colourfully-tiled courtyard gardens, which are particularly popular with gay couples. All rooms are beautifully furnished with antiques. €€€

Antonio's Hostal C/ Parellades 11; 663 91 10 65; w antonioshostal.com. In the old town, with a handful of attractively decorated rooms, most

of which have balconies or a terrace, & a pretty courtyard terrace where b/fast is served. €€

El Xalet C/ Isla de Cuba 33–5; 938 11 00 70; w elxalet.com. Small hotel near the station with a dozen charming rooms in one of the prettiest Modernista houses in Sitges. €€

Parrots C/ Joan Tarrida; 938 94 13 50; w parrots-sitges.com. The brightly painted centre of gay life in Sitges, with 16 simple rooms, a terrace bar, restaurant (€€€) & sauna. €€

Termes Ptge Termes 9; 938 94 23 43; w hostaltermes.com. The 12 rooms (all with AC) are a bit of a tight squeeze, but clean & inviting; there's also a small 1-bedroom apartment available. Good value for this expensive town. €€

✕ WHERE TO EAT AND DRINK *Map, opposite*

Can Laury Pg del Port Aiguadolç 49; 938 94 66 34; w canlaury.com. A large, bustling restaurant with a huge terrace overlooking the marina, where you can enjoy excellent seafood & paella as you admire the glossy yachts. €€€€

Maricel Pg de la Ribera 6; 938 94 20 54; w maricel.es; 13.15–15.15 & 20.15–22.00 Wed–Mon. Classic upscale restaurant on the seafront, with tables clad in immaculate white linen, lots of wood panelling & paintings. The menu showcases exquisite Catalan cuisine including a choice of seafood & meat dishes. €€€€

La Marinada C/ Rafael Llopart 49; 938 11 08 01; lamarinada.sitges; 13.00–15.30 Wed–Thu, 13.00–15.30 & 20.30–22.30 Fri–Sat, 13.00–16.00 Sun. A long-established local favourite that serves spectacularly fresh seafood cooked over a wood-fire grill – try the turbot. They also serve excellent Mediterranean rice dishes, including paella. €€€€–€€€

La Cúpula Av Llorach 5, Garraf; 936 32 00 15; w lacupulagarraf.com; 12.45–17.30 Tue–Thu & Sun, 12.45–17.30 & 20.30–midnight Fri–Sat. Perfectly set on a low cliff overlooking the picturesque Garraf beach (1 train stop from Sitges or a 20-min drive), this romantic spot specialises in fresh fish & seafood. €€€

La Punta de Sitges C/ Sant Damià 14; 640 15 25 65; w lapuntasitges.com; 19.00–midnight Mon–Fri, 13.00–17.00 & 19.00–midnight daily.

Small restaurant near Platja de Sant Sebastià with a creative menu of 'plates to share' that change according to what's in season. €€€

※ **Nem** C/ Illa de Cuba 9; 938 94 93 32; w nemsitges.com; 13.00–17.00 & 19.30–23.00 daily. You'll need to reserve for a spot at this wonderful little restaurant, which has a regularly changing, short menu of '*platets*' (small plates). Unusual flavours & textures are combined into mouthwatering dishes such as sea bream sashimi with lime, cilantro, sweet potato & chilli or homemade yogurt ice cream with rosemary & lemon. Note that there are 2 lunch sittings & 3 evening sittings. €€€

Chai C/ Sant Pau 36; 938 11 46 59; w chaiindiancuisine.com; noon–16.30 & 19.00–23.30 Wed–Mon. This is the Sitges branch of a small chain of Indian restaurants (there is another in Vilanova i la Geltrú) serving excellent, authentic food, including veggie options. €€

El Pou C/ Sant Bonaventura 21; 930 13 47 98; w elpoudesitges.com; 20.00–22.30 Wed–Thu, 13.30–15.15 & 20.00–22.30 Fri–Sun. Delicious tapas & small plates to share, with a creative fusion of Catalan, Japanese & Peruvian flavours. €€

Petit Bangkok C/ Jesús 55; 613 01 28 88; w petitbangkok.com; 13.00–16.00 & 19.30–22.00 Tue–Sat. An outpost of the Barcelona original, this colourful little restaurant serves tasty Thai specialities prepared by Thai chefs. €€

ENTERTAINMENT AND NIGHTLIFE In town, the action is centred on bar-lined Carrer Primer de Maig, popularly known as 'Sin Street', and the narrow streets around the Plaça Industria, which is home to Parrots, a combination gay hotel, restaurant, sauna and bar that is a long-established institution and centre for people-watching (page 151).

Among the gay bars & clubs, there's **XXL** on Carrer Joan Tarrida, the **Bears Bar** on Carrer Bonaire, and the **Man Bar** on Carrer Sant Bonaventura. For more info, see **w** gaysitgesguide.com.

For cocktails, head to **La Cocteleria del Factor Vi** (C/ Bonaire 25) or **The Dutchess** (C/ Nou 4). **Bar Voramar**, on Sant Sebastià beach, is the city's oldest pub and has occasional jazz concerts.

WHAT TO SEE AND DO
Sant Bartolomeu i Santa Tecla
Sitges' picture-postcard view is the one framing its pretty parish church, on a terrace overlooking the beach. They only open it for Masses; Sitges is that kind of town. Don't miss the few narrow streets directly behind the church, calm and lovely and well-whitewashed, with some whimsical notices and painted azulejo tiles stuck here and there.

Cau Ferrat and Museu Maricel
(C/ Fonollar 7; ℡938 94 03 64; **w** museusdesitges. cat; ⊕ Mar–Oct 10.00–19.00 Tue–Sun, Nov–Feb 10.00–17.00 Tue–Sun; adult/ reduced/under 17 €12/8/free) Two of Sitges' best museums sit side by side on a narrow street behind the church. They share an entrance, and are linked internally, to provide a singular artistic experience. To the left is the Cau Ferrat, a pair of old fisherman's cottages joined together and magnified to a celestial folly by Santiago Rusinyol. Only in Spain! (Or as the Catalans would say, only in Catalunya!) There's more than a touch of madness in Rusinyol's hideaway. The house itself may be the star of the show, with its electric-blue-painted walls and acres of azulejos and enormous inglenook fireplace. The upstairs is a sort of great medieval hall, where Rusinyol would put on performances and exhibitions for his famous Festes Modernistes from 1892 to 1899.

Naturally, there's plenty of painting everywhere, by Rusinyol and many others, including an early Picasso (*La Cursa de Braus*) and two luminous El Grecos, of the *Magdalene* and *St Peter*. Rusinyol got these cheap in Madrid, and when he brought them back he hired a band and led them in a parade through the streets. Rusinyol was an avid collector of many things, and this great curiosity shop displays them all. Antique locks, keys and door-knockers were evidently closest to his heart, but there's a wonderful collection of glass work from the earliest times – the 8th century BC – up through the Romans to the artists of Venice and Bohemia.

Adjoining it is the Museu Maricel, built by the Chicagoan Charles Deering, heir to the International Harvester tractor fortune, and a man who made nearly as much an impact on Sitges as Rusinyol. With its big sea-view windows, this house would rate a visit even if it were empty. As it is, the city has stuffed it with more than 3,000 works of art collected by Jesús Pérez-Rosales. Who was Jesús Pérez-Rosales? The town gynaecologist; business must have been very, very good.

And he had a good eye. Some of the works come uncomfortably close to the kitsch barrier (lots of Bouguereau-style naked ladies invariably described as 'allegories'), and that perhaps has kept the collection from getting the attention it deserves. There are few big names here, but a lot that is first-rate. There is an exceptional room of 13th–15th-century Catalan painting and sculpture, notably a *Crucifixion* by the Aragonese Tomás Giner, court painter to King Fernando El Católico. The allegories don't stop. The best, perhaps, is the *Miracle of Saint Genevieve*, an entire room painted in weirdly compelling chiaroscuro by Josep Maria Sert depicting the famous *Battle of the Marne* in 1914. Upstairs, there is loads of aristocratic clutter. If you've never seen a writing desk in the shape of Paris's city hall before, here's your chance.

Across the street, Deering commissioned artist Miquel Utrillo to restore an unused hospital for his main residence, the **Palau Maricel** (C/ Fonollar s/n; 938 94 03 64; w museusdesitges.cat; guided visits only, 10.00 (English), 11.00 & noon (Catalan), 13.00 (Spanish) Sun; adult/reduced/under 16 €12/7/free). It's a gorgeous Noucentista building, especially the courtyard inside, full of lavishly tiled and gilded salons. Best of all is the lovely cloister, with glorious sea views, and the rooftop terrace.

Museu Romàntic Can Llopis (closed for renovation) in the centre of town, conjures up the elegance of the 19th century and its love of gadgets – not to be missed by music-box fans. There's also a huge doll collection, some dating back to the 17th century.

VILANOVA I LA GELTRÚ

If Sitges is too exciting, or too expensive, and you still want to have a good time on the beach, hop on the bus and slide over to Vilanova i la Geltrú, just 9km down the coast (or take the cliff walk from the end of the beach, which passes a series of heavenly coves, and takes about 1½hrs). This unusual three-headed town is many things, but exciting is not really one of them. La Geltrú is the original village. They say that in the Middle Ages the barons who ran it were so rough on La Geltrú's people that many of them moved to some land close by that he didn't control. Their new settlement, Vilanova, soon outstripped the mother village; the third head appeared only a century ago, when a resort strip grew up around the fishing port and nearby beaches.

The main **tourist information office** is at Parc de Ribes Roges, s/n (938 15 45 17; 10.00–14.00 & 16.00–18.00 Mon–Sat), with additional info points at Plaça de la Vila 11 and the railway museum.

WHERE TO STAY

Ceferino Pg Ribas Roges 2; 938 15 89 31; w hotelceferino.com. Vilanova's best, a swanky beachfront hotel, with 26 elegant rooms & huge suites, plus an excellent restaurant. €€€€€

Hotel Ribas Roges C/ Joan d'Austria 7; 938 15 03 61; w hotelribesroges.com. A friendly, family-run 2-star hotel with a dozen comfortable rooms close to the beach. €€

Solvi 70 Pg Ribes Roges; 938 15 12 45; w solvihotel.com. Another good, affordable option; many of the rooms at this mid-sized hotel have balconies facing the sea & there's a rooftop sun deck & bar (summer only). €€

WHERE TO EAT AND DRINK

Cal Purgat C/ l'Arquebisbe Armanyà 8; 938 14 21 45; noon–16.00 & 20.00–midnight Wed–Fri, 13.30–16.30 & 20.00–01.00 Sat, 13.30–17.00 Sun. Hearty classic Catalan cuisine & local wines served in an atmospheric old building; it's a big favourite with locals, thanks to the friendly staff & a convivial atmosphere. €€€

La Sal Pg Marítim 59; 660 93 91 67; la_sal_vilanova_i_la_geltru; 13.00–16.00 Tue–Sun.

A lovely, shady terrace is the perfect place to enjoy paella & other classic Mediterranean rice dishes or beautifully fresh seafood. €€€

* **La Taverna del Port** Pg Marítim 104; 938 10 12 05; 13.00–16.00 Tue–Sun. Small, cosy & inviting restaurant with delightful staff, tasty Catalan favourites with a modern twist. Call ahead if you're vegetarian & they'll whip you up something special. They

4

JUANITA THE CARP

Francesc Roig Toqués, a former boat-builder and fisherman, amassed a delightful collection of briny bric-a-brac and displayed it in his own museum of curiosities, But the museum's biggest attraction was Juanita the carp, a very small, goldfish-sort-of-carp, who had been taught by Mr Roig to eat from a spoon and drink from a wine *porró*. Her legend lives on in the local *correfoc* (page 47), where whirling, human-sized *porrons* and carps have now joined the standard fire-spitting devils and dragons in the parade.

also run movie nights, where you can enjoy dinner with a film. €€
L'Ombú Bistro Pg del Carme 48; ☎ 938 10 07 37; ◙ ombubistro; ⏰ 11.00–19.00 Tue–Thu, 11.00–23.00 Fri–Sun. A friendly spot with an eclectic menu that includes everything from brunch & tapas to more elaborate dishes (some veggie & vegan options too). Make sure you order the *vermut*, a pre-lunch classic in Catalunya. €

WHAT TO SEE AND DO A long, shady Rambla Principal connects workaday Vilanova with the seafront Barri Marítim. The beaches are even better than Sitges', though the scene is much calmer, even in summer, and everything's noticeably cheaper. It is notably hooked on museums, dedicated to everything from troubadours to trains.

Museu Victor Balaguer (Avda Victor Balaguer s/n; ☎ 938 15 42 02; w victorbalaguer.cat; ⏰ 10.00–14.00 & 17.00–19.00 Tue–Sat, 11.00–14.00 Sun; adult/reduced/under 12 €5/2.50/free) This museum commemorates its founder, a 19th-century poet-politician, the 'Troubadour of Montserrat' who won the first Jocs Florals (page 11). In an impressive Beaux-Arts building, the collection is mostly Catalan painting, with works by Rusinyol and Casas.

Museu del Ferrocarril (Pl Eduard Maristany; ☎ 938 158 491; w museudelferrocarril. org; ⏰ 10.00–14.30 Tue–Fri & Sun, 10.00–14.30 & 16.00–19.00 Sat; adult/reduced/ under 4 €8.50/6/free) A brilliant place to while away an afternoon, this has tons of memorabilia and what it claims is the biggest collection of steam engines in Europe, set in the old workshops. Among the painstakingly restored historic carriages is a futuristic Talgo train from 1950 and a 1948 reconstruction of the very first Spanish train that ran in 1848.

Espai Far (Pujada Far de Sant Cristòfol; ☎ 600 50 92 23; w espaifarvng.cat; ⏰ 10.00–14.00 Fri & Sun, 10.00–14.30 & 11.00–14.00 Sat; adult/reduced/under 12 €5/2.50/free) At the eastern end of the strip, the very picturesque old Sant Cristòfol lighthouse is now home to a maritime museum, recounting the town's long fishing tradition. A collection of curiosities gathered by beloved local eccentric, Francesc Roig Toqués have also found a berth here, along with tributes to his famously talented carp, Juanita (see above). There's a serious fishing port here, one of the biggest on Spain's Mediterranean coast, and you can see the auctions going on most days when the boats come in.

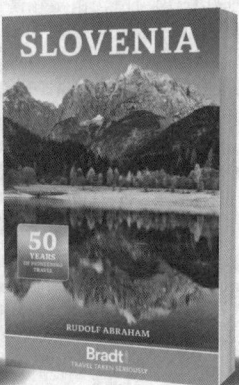

COSTA BRAVA

Perpignan

Banyuls-sur-Mer

Platja Borró
Portbou

Platja Grifeu
Llançà

Muga

N-260

GI-610

Porta de
la Selva

*Cap de
Creus*

Parc
Natural dels
Aiguamolls

GI-614

Cadaqués

Figueres

C-260

Roses

Cala
Montjoi

Cala Jóncols

**Castelló
d'Empúries**

Cala Rostella

Empuriabrava

L'Almadrava

Cala Murta

N-260

C-31

GIV-6216

Fluvià

Sant Pere
Pescador

*Gulf of
Roses*

E-15

GI-623

N-11

C-31

Sant Miquel
de Fluvià

Sant Martí
d'Empúries

Banyoles

L'Escala

GI-634

Verges

Ter

L'Estartit

*Illes
Medes*

C-66

C-252

**Torroella
de Montgrí**

Púbol

Ullastret

Madremanya

Corçà

Empúries

Platja de Pals

Sa Riera

Girona

Monells

Pals

Sa Tuna

Cruïlles

**La Bisbal
d'Empordà**

Begur

Aiguablava
Cap de Begur

GI-664

Aiguaxelida

Palafrugell

Tamariu

C-31

Llafranc

*Cap de
Sant Sebastià*

Llagostera

Palamós

Sant Antoni de Calonge

**Caldes de
Malavella**

C-31

Platja d'Aro

**Sant Feliu
de Guíxols**

Barcelona

GI-681

C-63

Tossa de Mar

Lloret de Mar

Blanes

N

Bradt

0		20km
0		20 miles

5

Costa Brava

At first it was simply the East Coast, the 'Costa del Llevant'. Then in 1908, journalist Ferran Agulló Vidal described it as the 'Costa Brava' (or Wild Coast), a name so apt it stuck. Then in 1949 another writer, Rose Macauley, came along and confirmed its reputation in her classic *Fabled Shore*, evoking the Costa Brava's fishing villages, cobalt bays, moon-like beaches and otherworldly light. It was well received. And it made the Franco government think that perhaps the world, then immersed in the Cold War, might be ready to forget the Civil War and give Spain a chance?

As the bit of Spain most accessible to European coach parties, the Costa Brava was chosen as the first foreign currency money-spinner; speculators were given the green light to throw up mazes of cheap hotels and cheap bars: the package holiday was born. Lloret de Mar became the 'abroad' holiday for millions of Brits. In the 1960s they could only take £50 out of the country, but that was enough for two weeks of sun, fun, and burgers and chips. With the advent of charter flights, it was a model followed by Benidorm, Torremolinos and the Balearics.

By 2000 the Costa Brava was yesterday's news. That was then. A kinder, gentler Costa Brava has come to the fore. Even in Lloret, the 18–30 club has moved on as the town tweaks its image to appeal to families. The northern beaches have opened up since low-cost flights came to Girona airport, but they've learned from past mistakes (and also because the wealthy Catalans who have long summered here want to keep it a secret). This part of the coast has always been ravishing, less trampled, less known: the Cap de Begur with its exquisite coves and coastal walks; the medieval villages just inland, where castles and *masies* have been converted into five-star hotels, *cases rurales* and *agriturismes*; wild, salty Cap de Creus and magical Cadaqués; the superb diving around the Illes Medes in L'Estartit, the wetlands at Aiguamolls, the biggest ancient Greek archaeological site in Spain at Empúries, and the anchovy paradise of L'Escala.

BLANES TO PALAMÓS

North of Barcelona, just beyond the Costa del Maresme (page 131), the coastline becomes more dramatic, with plunging cliffs clad in Mediterranean pine giving way to impossibly lovely coves. Some towns along this stretch have sold their souls entirely to tourism, but others have preserved time-capsule old quarters, like Tossa de Mar, or traditional ports, like Sant Feliu de Guíxols or Palamós, where you can still see the day's catch being auctioned off.

There are **tourist information offices** in all the towns along this stretch of coast including in Tossa de Mar (Av del Pelegrí 25; ☎972 34 01 08; w visittossa.com), Lloret de Mar (Av de les Alegries 3; ☎972 36 57 88; w lloretdemar.org), Blanes (Pl de Catalunya; ☎972 33 03 48; w blanescostabrava.cat), Sant Feliu de Guíxols (La Rambla 22; ☎972 82 00 51; w visitguixols.com), and Palamós (Pg del Mar 2; ☎972 60 05 00; w visitpalamos.cat).

5

GETTING THERE AND AWAY Trains from Barcelona frequently stop at Blanes and Lloret de Mar (take the R1 line from Plaça Catalunya; w rodalies.gencat.cat). Moventis SARFA buses (☏ 919 49 60 79; w compras.moventis.es) serve the Costa Brava from Girona and Barcelona's Estació del Nord; many resorts are served by direct Sagalés buses (w sagales.com) from Barcelona airport and Girona airport as well. Portbou and Llançà are most easily reached by trains to France (line R11 from Barcelona).

WHERE TO STAY Note that most hotels on the Costa Brava close between November and March and that prices often halve outside the peak summer season.

Eden Roc Hotel & Spa Platja de Sa Boadella, Lloret de Mar; ☏ 972 36 87 00; w hotel-edenroc. com. This large, luxurious cliff-top resort features all the 5-star trimmings, from plush rooms & suites with panoramic views of the Mediterranean to 3 swimming pools, an excellent restaurant (€€€€) as well as exclusive access to the secluded Sa Boadella cove below. €€€€€

Hotel La Gavina Pl Roserar s/n, S'Agaró; ☏ 972 32 11 00; w lagavina.com. The Costa Brava's most prestigious address since 1932, this iconic grand palace hotel offers sumptuous rooms, a magnificent seawater infinity pool & exquisite dining options (€€€€) plus its own private beach cove. €€€€€

La Malcontenta Paratge de Torre Mirona, Platja de Castell 12, Palamós; ☏ 972 31 23 30; w lamalcontentahotel.com. A wonderful 19th-century mansion has been converted into one of the coolest hotels on the Costa Brava. Set in elegant grounds with a lovely pool. €€€€€

Balneari Vichy Catalan Av Dr Furest 32, Caldes de Malavella; ☏ 972 47 00 00; w 1881hotelbalneariovichycatalan.com. Famous for its healing waters since 1881, this large thermal spa hotel occupies a magnificent Modernist building with spacious rooms, therapeutic mineral water pools & extensive gardens. €€€€

Casa Coco Boutique Hotel & Spa Av Vila de Tossa 28, Lloret de Mar; ☏ 972 36 58 62; w casacocolloret.com. A serene retreat from Lloret's party atmosphere, this has 22 boho-chic rooms, a small saltwater pool & garden spa, plus a rooftop bar. €€€€

Casa Indiana Hotel Boutique C/ Roig i Raventós 11, Blanes; ☏ 972 35 36 61; w casaindiana.com. An elegant, colonial-style boutique hotel just steps from the beach, this welcoming spot has 11 unique rooms, many with spectacular views, a charming garden patio & a panoramic rooftop terrace. €€€€

Hotel Boutique Mamma Mia C/ Sant Telm 8, Tossa de Mar; ☏ 972 34 11 83; w hotelmammamiatossa.com. This features a dozen bright, sea-themed rooms, an excellent Italian restaurant (€€€) & a sun-drenched rooftop terrace, perfectly positioned between the old town & the seafront promenade. €€€€

Hotel Mas Tapiolas Ctra C65 km 7, vecindario de Solius; ☏ 972 83 70 61; w hotelmastapiolas.com. About 10km inland from Sant Feliu de Guíxols, this mid-sized, sophisticated rural farmhouse complex has spacious, elegant rooms, a natural swimming pool & a wonderful spa with thermal circuit, all surrounded by 40ha of private forest with hiking trails & mountain views. €€€€

Park Hotel San Jorge Ctra Palamós s/n, Platja d'Aro; ☏ 972 65 23 11, w parkhotelsanjorge. com. Set on a cliff over a beautiful sandy cove, a superb renovation of a hotel from the 1950s with a swimming pool & spa, fabulous b/fast buffet & a charming restaurant (€€€). It's a bargain out of season. €€€€

Calèndula Hotel C/ Sant Domènec 1, Sant Feliu de Guíxols; ☏ 972 32 16 22; w hotelcalendula. es. Combining historic charm with contemporary comforts, this modest little hotel set in a 19th-century townhouse has a handful of individually designed rooms & a hidden courtyard garden. €€€

Diana Pl d'Espanya 6, Tossa de Mar; ☏ 972 34 18 86, w hotelesdante.com/en/home/hotel-diana. Delightful old villa with a pretty courtyard backing on to the seaside promenade & about 20 rooms. Inside there's an original Gaudí fireplace, Modernista frescoes & plenty of light from the glass roof. Closed in winter. €€€

Trias Pg del Mar 7, Palamós; ☏ 972 60 18 00; w hoteltrias.com. A century-old hotel by the sea (Truman Capote stayed here), but a short stroll from the middle of town. There's a pool & one of

Palamós' best restaurants (€€€€), famous for its rice served with fresh crab (*cranc*). €€€

Hostal Boutique Es Menut C/ Sant Josep 22, Tossa de Mar; ☏ 972 34 12 54; w hostalesmenut.

com. A charming stone-built boutique guesthouse with half a dozen stylish rooms, a delightful b/fast terrace & an unbeatable location in Tossa's historic centre, just moments from the beach. €€

✶ WHERE TO EAT AND DRINK

La Cuina de San Simon C/ Portal 24, Tossa de Mar; ☏ 972 34 12 69; w lacuinacansimon.com; ⏰ 13.00–15.00 & 20.00–22.00 Tue–Sun. You'll need to book to get one of the handful of tables at this cosy gourmet temple with a Michelin star, situated in a house built in 1714. Don't hesitate: splash out on the 6-course *menú degustació* (€118.50). €€€€€

Bahía Pg del Mar 19, Tossa de Mar; ☏ 972 34 03 22; w restaurantbahiatossa.com; ⏰ 09.00–16.00 & 19.30–22.00 daily. Since 1954, the place for good seafood & *cim i tomba*, the classic Tossan dish – a succulent fish stew made with monkfish, potatoes, tomatoes, herbs & garlic. €€€€

✶ **Can Roquet** Pl de l'Església 1, Romanyà de la Selva; ☏ 972 86 60 29; w canroquet.com; ⏰ 13.00–15.00 & 19.30–21.30 Wed–Sun. An enchanting spot in the heart of one of the loveliest little hamlets of the Empordà. Enjoy refined, beautifully presented & creative Catalan cuisine out on the terrace, under a canopy of vines, or in the cosy dining room covered in murals. €€€€

La Gamba Pl Sant Pere 1, Palamós; ☏ 972 31 46 33, w lagambapalamos.com; ⏰ 13.00–15.45 & 19.30–22.15 Thu–Mon, 13.00–15.45 Tue. Three generations of the Cuadrat family have put smiles on diners' faces with the freshest Palamós prawns & other shellfish at this spacious, classic restaurant with a large terrace near the port. €€€€

La Taverna de Mar Pg de Sant Pol, S'Agaró; ☏ 972 82 16 69; w latavernadelmar.cat; ⏰ 13.00–15.00 Mon, Tue, Thu & Sun, 13.00–15.00 & 20.00–22.00 Fri–Sat. A charming, seafront restaurant decorated in Mediterranean blue & white, this is a big local favourite for ultra-fresh seafood & shellfish (carnivores are also catered for), using traditional recipes but adding a creative twist. They also do a tasting menu for €75. €€€€

✶ **Sa Lola** Pg Pau Casals 59, Blanes; ☏ 972 35 52 19; w salolagastronomic.com; ⏰ 13.00–16.00 & 20.00–23.00 Wed–Sat. For Catalan cuisine at its most playful & inventive, don't miss this enticing little gastro bar, with quirky vintage décor & a laid-back feel. Chefs Rafa Salinas & Albert Mir,

who trained with the Adrià brothers, have created a 6-part tasting menu (just €48) which perfectly showcases their imaginative approach to Catalan flavours. €€€€

La Selvatana C/ de l'Allada, 5, Palamós; ☏ 972 31 41 48; ◙ laselvatanapalamos; ⏰ 12.30–15.15 & 20.00–22.15 Tue–Sat, 12.30–15.15 Sun. A relaxed, classic Catalan restaurant in the historic heart of Palamós that has been serving up generous & delicious paellas & other local specialities since 1960. €€€

Xiringuito Cala Bona Cala Sant Francesc, Blanes; ☏ 972 33 49 13; w restaurantcalabona.com; ⏰ Apr–Sep 08.00–16.00 daily. Come for the wonderful paellas & tasty local cuisine, & stay for the *havaneres* – sea shanties that date back to the 19th century, when locals headed for the Americas to find their fortune. The generous set lunches (€21.50 & €28.50) are excellent value. €€€

Cala Banys Bar Camí de Cala Banys, Lloret de Mar; ☏ 972 36 55 15; ◙ barcalabanys; ⏰ mid-Jun–Aug 10.00–01.00 daily; call ahead for hours rest of the year. Going since 1967, this boho-chic cocktail bar is perched above a tiny, pristine cove – it feels a world away from the hubbub of town, although it's only a 5-min walk along the cliff path from the main beaches. Perfect for a sunset cocktail, but note that there is no food. Cash only. €€

✶ **La Gàbia dels Mussols** Pg del Mar 8, Sant Feliu de Guíxols; ☏ 615 18 46 78; ◙ gabiadelsmussols; ⏰ May–Sep 09.00–23.00 daily. A hugely popular *xiringuito* (beach bar) in the middle of town, serving delicious tapas prepared with local ingredients, as well as coffee, drinks & cocktails. €€

La Proa C/ Cristòfol Colom 31, Sant Feliu de Guíxols; ☏ 872 02 75 32; ◙ laproarestaurant; ⏰ 09.00–16.00 Mon–Tue & Thu, 09.00–16.00 & 20.00–22.30 Fri–Sat. A classic, old-school seafood restaurant near the port that's been going for decades with a very loyal clientele. Perfectly fresh seafood straight from the port & traditional Catalan dishes like *butifarra amb mongetes* (sausage with white beans). The w/day set lunch (€17.50) is a bargain. €€

5

BLANES With a long beach and fishing fleet, Blanes is where it all begins. Uniquely, it's bookended by lush botanical gardens. To the south, by the pretty cove of Sant Francesc, German botantist Karl Faust planted the beautiful 10 acre **Jardí Botànic Marimurtra** (Pg de Carles Faust 9; ☎972 33 08 26; w marimurtra.cat; ⊕ Mar–May & mid-Sep–Oct 10.00–17.00 daily, Jun–mid-Sep 09.00–18.00 daily, Nov–Feb 10.00–14.00 Mon–Fri & 10.00–16.00 Sat–Sun; adult/under 4 €12/free) on the hill of Sant Joan, with some 3,000 species, including a unique selection of *Androcymbium* (related to lilies) and century-old *Araucarias* next to his villa, the very embodiment of the old Costa Brava elite. On the north end of Blanes, thousands of cacti, prickly pears and aloes grace the **Jardí Botànic Pinya de Rosa** (Camí de Santa Cristina s/n; ☎972 35 06 89; w pinya-de-rosa.es; ⊕ 10.00–16.00 Mon–Fri, 10.00–14.00 Sat–Sun; adults €5), planted in 1954 by Fernando Riviere de Caralt, a civil engineer.

LLORET DE MAR Ask any Catalan, and they'll say the best way to see Lloret de Mar is from a fast car speeding down the highway. The town has well over a hundred hotels, cheek-to-jowl with theme parks, go-karts, bars, burger stands, flashing noises and glaring lights and a casino to rake up any loose change, all radiating from a long beach set in lush cliffs. Once the Roman Loryma, Lloret in the 18th and 19th centuries was so poor that thousands sailed away to seek a better life in the Caribbean. At least some made it big (there's a poignant plaque on the seafront, remembering those who didn't) and returned as *indianos* to build villas and flaunt their wealth.

One of a handful of surviving villas on the waterfront now houses the **Museu del Mar** (Pg Camprodon i Arrieta 1–2; ☎972 36 44 54; w patrimoni.lloret.cat/es/moll-museo-abierto-de-lloret/museo-del-mar; adult/reduced/under 12 €4.10/2/free), dedicated to seaworthy things, with models, figureheads, films and interactive displays. In the attractive pre-mass-tourism village centre, Lloret's pretty church is also worth a look, with its party-coloured tiled dome and Modernista chapels.

There are great views from the landmark 10th–11th-century watchtower, the **Torre Sant Joan**, or from the dreamy **Jardí Santa Clotilde** (Paratge de Santa Clotilde; ☎972 37 04 71; w lloretdemar.org/en/cultura/santa-clotilde-gardens; ⊕ Apr–Oct 10.00–20.00 daily, Nov–Jan 10.00–17.00 daily, Feb–Mar 10.00–17.00 daily; adult/

CATALUNYA'S *CAMINS DE RONDA*: FROM SMUGGLERS TO SELFIES

The secret coastal footpaths where guards once kept watch for pirates and smugglers have been transformed over the last few decades into the glorious *camins de Ronda*, which stretch for about 200km from Portbou, by the French border, all the way down to Blanes, passing Mediterranean pine forests, impossibly perfect coves and jaw-dropping cliffs. Some, like the dizzying paths around the Cap de Creus, are little more than scrambly tracks, better for mountain goats and more experienced hikers, while others, such as the stretch between S'Agaró to Sant Feliu de Guíxols (about 5km), are elegant, well-maintained walkways carved into the cliff. This section, like those around S'Agaró and Calella de Palafrugell, can be accessed by wheelchairs and prams, and are popular with families for languid Sunday strolls. Some of the most popular sections include Begur to Calella de Palafrugell (about 11km) and the stretch between Tossa de Mar and Lloret de Mar (about 12km), both of which have been recently renovated. You'll find plenty of information on each individual *camí de Ronda* at the local tourist offices.

reduced €6.10/3.10), set on a cliff on the southern edge of Lloret, rising on a hill above a tidal wave of apartment blocks. The gardens were designed in 1919 by young Nicolau Rubió i Tuduri, who was inspired by the Renaissance gardens of Rome and Florence with terraces of fountains, statues and towering cypresses descending languidly towards the sea. You might recognise them from *House of the Dragon*, the *Games of Thrones* prequel – the tourist office sometimes runs themed guided visits pointing out the key locations.

The main beaches are crammed, but you can follow the coast path to several delightful little coves, like Cala Santa Cristina and Cala Treumal or the Cala Boadella (a nudist beach).

TOSSA DE MAR A pretty drive up the coast from Lloret – or, if you're feeling fit, a hike along the coastal path (about 12km) – Tossa de Mar was 'discovered' back in the 1920s by the first foreign visitors to the Costa Brava, but it has maintained considerably more charm. Roman Turissa shows its pedigree in the foundations and simple mosaic floors of the 1st-century BC **Villa Roma Els Ametller**, tucked up behind the tourist office (Av del Pelegrí 5–13; ☉ rarely open, but ask at the tourist office).

The picturesque old town or **Vila Vella**, tumbles over the cape – a maze of alleys, stone and whitewashed houses, embraced by 12th-century walls and seven towers overlooking Tossa's wide swath of beach. In its heart, the **Museu Municipal** (Pl Roig i Soler 1; ☏972 34 07 09; ☉ closed for restoration until 2026), has finds from the Roman villa, as well as a somewhat motley collection of paintings by artists who stayed in Tossa. One was Marc Chagall, who spent the entire summers of 1933 and 1934 here, and gave the town his painting *El Violinista Celeste* in gratitude. Nearby, a 16th-century Gothic house contains the **Museu de la Dona** (C/ Codolar 4; ☏972 96 46 33; w visittossa.com/en/cultural-heritage/art-and-culture/womens-museum; ☉ 10.00–13.00 & 16.00–20.00 Wed–Sun; adult/reduced €2/1), which offers an insight into Tossa life long before the tourist hordes from the perspective of the town's hard-working, resilient women.

At its highest point the Vila Vella had a castle, but this was knocked down for a lighthouse in the 19th century; the current **Far de Tossa** (Pg de Vila Vella; ☏97 234 33 59; w visittossa.com/en/cultural-heritage/art-and-culture/tossas-lighthouse; ☉ 10.00–14.30 Mon–Tue, 10.00–18.00 Wed–Thu, 10.00–14.00 & 15.00–18.00 Fri–Sat; adult/reduced/under 12 €3/1.50/free), built in 1917, has displays on lighthouses, and the lives of their keepers, from around the Mediterranean.

Tossa has more than its share of public art, including, along the **Passeig Marítim**, Spain's only statue to Joan Salvador Gavina (aka Jonathan Livingston Seagull), and a bronze, life-sized (but still petite) Ava Gardner gazing out from the Vila Vella's walls. The beautiful Ava fell in love with the Costa Brava while filming 1951's *Pandora and the Flying Dutchman*. According to rumours, she fell in love with a bullfighter too – rumours that brought the jealous Frank Sinatra flying over.

As well as the golden curve of the main beach, you can head up the coast – either by car or on the panoramic Camí de la Ronda coastal path) to find some of the prettiest coves on this whole stretch of coast, the **Cala Pola** and the **Cala Giverola**.

INLAND FROM TOSSA: LLAGOSTERA AND CALDES DE MÁLAVELLA From Tossa, the GI-681 to Girona climbs dramatically over the granite Cadiretes Massif to the Selva plain (selva means 'jungle') where the farming town of **Llagostera** just happened to produce one of the most successful poster and advertising designers in Paris in the 1920s and '30s. Emili Vilà i Gorgoll (1887–1967) may not be a household name, but you can fill in all the gaps in your knowledge at his house, now the **Museu Emili Vilà** (C/ Sant Pere 25; \669 41 19 40; w museuvila.com; ⊕ guided visits only; call or email e info@museuvila.com; adult/under 12 €5/free), with some 300 works by the master, including portraits of movie stars, dating from his days in Hollywood, as well as small works by Modigliani, Toulouse-Lautrec and Picasso.

Although the volcanoes in the Garrotxa (page 200) draw most of the attention, there was plenty of volcanic activity in these parts 30 million years ago as well. Their warmth lingers in the springs at **Caldes de Malavella**; used by the ancient Romans, they now gurgle up in a snazzy, colourful Modernista spa, the Balneari Vichy Catalan (page 158). The town's long history of thermal cures is related in the **Espai Aquae** (C/ Sant Grau; \600 37 26 10; w visitcaldes.cat/espai-aquae; ⊕ 10.00–13.00 & 17.00–19.00 Wed–Sat, 10.00–13.00 Sun; adult/reduced/under 6 €3/2/free). Geologists know the region best for its **Camp dels Ninots**, the 'field of figurines' – chunks of opal in curious shapes. The **Ruta Termal** (w viesverdes.cat/en/rutes_vies_verdes/thermal-greenway), one of Catalunya's wonderful Vies Verdes – old train lines that are now used for hiking and biking – runs through Caldes de Malavella, connecting with two more 'green routes'.

SANT FELIU DE GUÍXOLS AND AROUND
If you still have any doubts about the Costa's bravura, the 23km road from Tossa to Sant Feliu de Guíxols will cure them, with its legendary 365 bends, dotted with miradors along the way for admiring the vertiginous views of musclebound cliffs tumbling into the blue. After 7km, a side road winds up to the 19th-century **Santuari de Sant Grau**, where the vistas inspired Ferrán Agulló to give the coast its name. There are a few chances for a swim on the way, involving descents on tiny winding roads; keep an eye peeled for the turnoff at Rosamar.

Like Tossa, Sant Feliu de Guíxols was a big shot in the 10th century, when the Benedictine **Monastery of Sant Feliu** on the southern end of the modern town was one of the wealthiest in Catalunya. The huge complex, rebuilt after a sacking by the Moors in the 9th century, once had a moat and seven fortified towers before it was savaged in Catalunya's 1835 church-burning spree. Even so, its surviving walls, towers, Gothic church and Mozarabic Porta Ferrada are an impressive sight. It's now home to the **Espai Carmen Thyssen** (Pl Monestir s/n; \618 37 08 53; w espaicarmenthyssen.com; ⊕ Jul–Aug 11.00–13.30 & 17.00–20.30 daily; Sep–Oct 10.00–13.30 & 15.00–17.30 Mon–Fri, 11.00–13.30 & 17.00–19.00 Sat, 11.00–13.30 Sun; adult/reduced/under 16 €8/4/free), with changing exhibitions featuring world-class artworks from the vast collection of Carmen Cervera, former Miss Spain and wife of the late Baron Thyssen-Bornemisza.

Wander the palm-lined Passeig Marítim, lining the sandy beach, and stop for a drink at the pretty Modernista **Nou Casino de la Constància**. Or visit the old dolls and tin cars in the **Toy History Museum** (La Rambla 12–14; \972 82 22 49; w museudelajoguina.cat; ⊕ Jun–Sep 10.00–13.30 & 17.00–21.00 Mon–Sat, 11.00–14.00 Sun; Oct–May 10.00–13.30 & 16.00–19.00 Mon–Fri, 10.00–13.30 & 16.00–20.00 Sat, 11.00–14.00 Sun; adult/reduced/under 9 €6/5/free), featuring antique Spanish toys and fun model trains.

Sant Feliu's more intimate, prettier beach is 2.5km north at **Sant Pol**. Just beyond lies the exclusive enclave of **S'Agaró**, the brainchild of José Ensesa. In the 1920s, his now-legendary Noucentista hotel La Gavina (page 158) and surrounding villas overlooking the coves and pines rivalled Antibes among the Hollywood set. Then, in 1959, Elizabeth Taylor, Montgomery Clift, Katherine Hepburn and director Joseph Mankiewicz came to film Tennessee Williams' unsettling *Suddenly Last Summer* at

Sant Pol and S'Agaró. In summer, when the road to S'Agaró is blocked, park at Sant Pol (or try to!) and walk to the beaches on the magnificent seaside promenade.

Platja d'Aro is Lloret de Mar's younger sister, with a vast beach and even vaster assortment of hotels and holiday flats. Other beaches, less crowded, dot the coast to the north all the way to the little resort of **Sant Antoni de Calonge**, although parking is often problematic; be prepared for long walks and stairs down to the sea. A coastal walk (part of the Camí de Ronda) links Sant Antoni de Calonge to **Palamós**, in the Middle Ages the chief port serving Girona. It was one of many on the coast sacked by the pirate iral Barbarossa in 1543, which led to a rapid decline; Palamós recovered as a cork-exporting port, only to suffer grave damage and the loss of hundreds of houses in the Civil War. Today it's the most important commercial fishing port on the Costa Brava, specialising in red prawns (*Aristeus antennatus*) which are famous throughout Spain and found on every local menu.

The **Platja de la Fosca** is safe for the smallest child, and the **Cala Estreta**, a double cove divided by a sand bar, is as pretty as a picture.

Palamós also has an award-winning museum dedicated to fishing, the **Museu de la Pesca** (C/ Moll Pesquer s/n; 972 60 04 24; w museudelapesca.org; Jan–Feb 10.00–13.30 & 15.30–18.00 Tue–Fri, 10.30–14.00 & 16.00–19.00 Sat, 10.30–14.00 Sun; Mar, Nov & Dec 10.00–13.30 & 15.30–19.00 Tue–Fri, 10.30–14.00 & 16.00–19.00 Sat–Sun; Apr–Jun & Sep–Oct 10.00–13.30 & 15.30–19.00 Mon–Fri, 10.30–14.00 & 16.00–19.00 Sat–Sun; Jul–Aug 10.00–14.00 & 16.00–19.00 daily; adult/reduced/under 6 €5/2.50/free), which also has a pair of beautifully restored fishing boats in the harbour that date back to the early 20th century. The *llotja* (fish auction) takes place opposite the museum every afternoon or you can pick up your own ultra-fresh catch of the day from the stalls (16.30–20.00 Mon–Fri). Inland lie Platja Aro's medieval village 'descendants'. The most atmospheric is **Romanyà de la Selva**, built around the 10th-century church of Sant Martí, up in the heart of **Les Gavarres Natural Park**, the source of all that cork. To the east of Romanyà stands one of Catalunya's largest dolmens, the **Cova d'en Daina** (2700 BC), surrounded by a granite cromlech of smaller stones.

THE HEART OF THE COSTA BRAVA

The ancient Greeks had exquisite taste, and chose the stunning site of Empúries for their most important settlement in Spain. It has since evolved into Baix and Alt (Lower and Upper) Empordà, home to the Costa Brava's most scenic beaches, coves and landscapes, littered with handsome medieval towns and castles that recall the days of the Counts of Empordà, a feisty bunch of feudal lords set up to safeguard the lands conquered from the Moors. For centuries their history would be one of bloody politics. The Count Kings of Barcelona finally put an end to it in 1402, when the last of the local dynasties died off. In the intervening 600 years the Counts of Empordà built so many castles that some linguists think the name Catalunya derives from Castle-onia.

TOURIST INFORMATION You're never far from a tourist information office on the Costa Brava: find information on the whole region, including a comprehensive list of tourist offices at w costabrava.org. There are outposts in all the major towns and resorts, including Palafrugell (C/ Santa Margarida 1; 972 06 11 72; w visitpalafrugell.cat), L'Estartit (Pg Marítim; 972 75 19 10; w visitestartit.com), Begur (Avda de l'Onze de Setembre 5; 972 62 45 20; w visitbegur.cat), Tamariu (C/ de la Riera; 972 62 01 93; w visitpalafrugell.cat), La Bisbal d'Empordà (Pl del Castell; ✆972 64 51 66; w visitlabisbal.cat), Palafrugell (C/ de Santa Margarida 1; ✆972 06 11 72) and Calella de Palafrugell (C/ de les Voltes 6; ✆972 61 44 75; w visitpalafrugell.cat).

WHERE TO STAY Prices on the Costa Brava spike in August, when hotels fill up quickly. Most close between October/November and Easter (dates vary annually), so check in advance.

Aigua Blava Platja de Fornells, Begur; ✆972 62 45 62; w aiguablava.com. A charming, whitewashed complex tucked into the picture-postcard cove, with rooms, suites & apartments on different levels, more family-oriented than the parador, with its pool & tennis court. The restaurant (€€€€), with local specialities & especially good fish, is excellent. €€€€€

Mas de Torrent Afores de Torrent s/n, 4km from Pals at Torrent; ✆972 30 32 92; w hotelmastorrent. com. A sumptuous, 5-star Relais & Chateaux hotel set in an 18th-century country house with stylish rooms furnished with antiques, plus 20 secluded bungalows & a pool set in extensive gardens. It has all the luxury trimmings, including a fabulous restaurant (€€€€), spa, hammam & more. €€€€€

Parador Costa Brava Platja D'Aiguablava, Begur; ✆972 62 21 62; w parador.es. A modern white box filled with artworks, magnificently located on the cliffs surrounded by pines, boasting one of the finest views in Spain; each room faces the sea with a balcony. Pool & beach just below, & the wonderful Mar i Vent restaurant (€€€€), with its exquisite seafood. €€€€€

Aigua Clara C/ Sant Miquel 2, Begur; ✆972 62 32 86; w aiguaclara.com. This has 10 luminous, characterful rooms, with a smattering of antiques & old fixtures in a pretty pink-&-white mansion built in 1866. €€€€

El Convent Ctra del Racó 2, Begur; ✆972 62 30 91; w hotelconventbegur.com. In a quiet setting, a minute below Begur, this small hotel occupies a 17th-century convent set amid ancient terraces & Mediterranean forest. Rooms are prettily furnished, although some are small. Yoga classes are offered in the gardens in the summer, as well as massages, wellness treatments & a refreshing pool. €€€€

Hotel el Far Llafranc; ✆972 30 16 39; w hotelelfar.com. A stunner; converted from an 18th-century lighthouse & set amid the pines high over the sea. Just 9 delicious colour-soaked rooms, a beautiful patio, & fine restaurant (€€€€)

which is one of the best in the area. The only thing that might disturb the peace are wedding parties. €€€€

Molí del Mig Camí del Moní s/n, Torroella de Montgrí; ✆972 75 53 96; w urh-hoteliers.com/ en/moli-del-mig-by-urh. A combination of a 15th-century mill & a contemporary, eco-friendly structure set on 7ha of land, with a swimming pool, library museum & dedicated facilities for cyclists, including bike hire. €€€€

Casa Dos Torres C/ Chopitea 59, Calella de Palafrugell; ✆972 61 70 19, w casadostorres.com. Delightful Scottish-owned B&B with a handful of traditionally furnished rooms, fabulous buffet b/fasts, a pool, honesty bar & a shady garden. €€€

Hostalillo C/ Bellavista 22, El Tamariu; ✆972 62 02 28; w hotelhostalillo.com. A large white, modern hotel set on the cliffs above the beach, with a lovely, geranium-filled terrace. Most of the impeccable rooms have balconies, some boasting beautiful Mediterranean views. €€€

Hostal Sa Rascassa Aiguafreda, Begur; ✆972 62 28 45; w hostalsarascassa.com. Beautifully isolated by the sea in a gorgeous little cove, 5 lovely, award-winning rooms & delicious grilled fish at the restaurant (€€€) by candlelight. €€€

Hostal Sa Teula C/ Carudo 12, Llafranc; ✆872 98 85 89; w hostalsateula.com. A stylish little *hostal* in the town centre with 18 rooms decorated in soothing Mediterranean shades of sand & ochre, all with AC. Just 100m from the main beach. €€€

Hostal Sa Tuna Platja Sa Tuna, Begur; ✆972 62 21 98; w hostalsatuna.com. 5 delightful beachside rooms, a little on the small side but stylishly decorated with blue & cream linen, & an excellent restaurant (€€€) serving wonderful seafood & *arròs negre*. €€€

Llafranch Pg Cypsela 16, Llafranc; ✆972 30 02 08; w hllafranch.com. An old favourite from 1958, where Sophia Loren, Liz Taylor & Rock Hudson once hung out; one of the original owners, nicknamed 'the Gypsy', threw legendary parties. Rooms are classically decorated, & there's a lovely beach terrace & good restaurant serving old family recipes from cocktails to desserts. They also offer tours of the coast in their own boat. €€€

Mas Comangou C/ Ramon Llull 1, Begur; ✆972 62 32 10; w mascomangau.com. A medium-sized boutique hotel with classic rooms with beamed ceilings in a 19th-century stone *masia* on the outskirts of town & a lovely terrace & restaurant. €€€

Sant Roc Pl Atlàntic 2, Calella de Palafrugell; ✆972 61 42 50; w santroc.com. Opened in 1955, a large, pleasantly 'lived-in', family-run hotel on the headland overlooking one of the prettiest towns on the coast. Surrounded by gardens & a gorgeous terrace overlooking the bay. Closed Nov–Mar. €€€

El Cau del Papibou C/ Major 10, Peratallada; ✆972 63 40 18; w hotelelcaudelpapibou.com. A

handful of cosy & quiet rooms in a medieval house in the centre of one of the prettiest villages of the Empordà. Hearty, traditional b/fasts. €€

Hostal Barris C/ Pere Coll Rigau 10, Pals; ✆972 63 67 02; w hostalbarris.com. A family-run charmer in the historic centre of the medieval village of Pals, this has half a dozen simple, AC rooms prettily decorated in sunny yellow & blue. €€

Hostal L'Estrella C/ de les Quatre Cases 13, Palafrugell; ✆972 30 00 05; w hostalestrella. cat. A friendly mid-sized inn, which dates back to the 17th century, this has modest rooms with a choice of en suite or shared bathrooms, set around a quiet courtyard. No AC, but they do have fans, & the price is hard to beat on this glitzy coast. Closed Oct–Easter. €€

✕ **WHERE TO EAT AND DRINK** Always reserve in advance to ensure a table, and note that opening times vary wildly, depending on the time of year, the weather, etc. Many restaurants, particularly those right on the beachfront, close in winter (from around October/November to March/April).

In seafood restaurants, look for local classics such as *garoines* (sea urchins' eggs), *suquet de peix* (a sumptuous fish stew) and *arròs negre* (rice cooked in cuttlefish ink).

Cap Sa Sal C/ Cap sa Sal 24, Begur; ✆972 62 43 75; w capsasalrestaurant.com; ⏱ 13.00–15.30 & 19.30–22.00 daily. A favourite with fashionistas, this restaurant enjoys a spellbinding setting, with tables set on a series of terraces that overlook a stunning little cove. Modern, Catalan cuisine with a focus on seafood. It also has a handful of chic, minimalist rooms (€€€€€). €€€€

Can Bosch C/ Fora Muralla 5, Púbol; ✆972 48 83 57; w restaurantcanbosch.com; ⏱ 09.00–17.00 Wed–Thu & Sun, 09.00–17.00 & 20.00–22.00 Fri–Sat. A welcoming long-established classic near the Castell Gala Dalí, this serves excellent Catalan cuisine, including hearty stews, fresh meat & fish cooked on the grill & tasty local wines. Enjoy it out on the terrace in summer or in the cosy brick-walled dining room in winter. €€€

Can Quel, Ullastret ✆621 21 67 69; ⦿ canquel. ullastret; ⏱ 09.00–17.00 Tue–Thu & Sun, 09.00–17.00, 20.00–22.30 Fri–Sat. A wonderful, local restaurant that has been simply & elegantly renovated & serves delicious Catalan classics prepared with the freshest, locally sourced ingredients. €€€

Rostei C/ Concepció Pi, Begur; ✆972 62 42 15; w restaurant-rostei.com; ⏱ 19.30–23.00

Mon–Fri, 13.15–15.30 & 19.45–10.30 Sat–Sun. Seasonal menu with a strong emphasis on local fish, grilled vegetables & mushrooms in the autumn, & a good choice of dessert classics. The wine list includes those grown by the Rostei family on their estate. Ask for a table in the garden. €€€

Solimar Platja del Racó, Begur; ✆972 63 64 19; ⦿ restaurantsolimar; ⏱ 12.30–21.30 daily. A friendly, family-run, traditional seafood restaurant right on the beachfront, this is definitely one of the contenders for the best paella on the Costa Brava. €€€

✳ **Toc al Mar** Platja d'Aiguablava, Begur; ✆972 11 32 32; w tocalmar.cat; ⏱ 13.00–15.30 Wed & Sun, 13.00–15.30 & 20.00–22.30 Mon, Tue & Thu–Sat. The perfect Costa Brava experience: freshly caught fish sizzling on the grill, wonderful paellas, delicious local wines, all served up in a quirky, colourful restaurant right on the beach. €€€

Font de Sabruixa Urbanización Puigvermell, C/ Font de la Bruixa s/n, Pals; ✆628 60 48 33; w sivanabosc.com; ⏱ 19.00–23.00 Mon & Wed–Fri, 13.00–17.00 & 19.00–00.30 Sat–Sun. In the woods, just back from the beach – very simple, but legendary for its succulent meats grilled over charcoal. €€

5

Mas Oliver Avda Espanya, Palafrugell; ☎ 972 30 10 41; w guiacat.cat/restaurant/mas-oliver-palafrugell; ◷ 13.00–16.00 Mon, Wed, Thu & Sun, 13.00–15.30 & 20.00–23.00 Fri–Sat.

Restaurant in a restored *masia*, with a pretty garden; tasty, good-value set lunch menu, plus fresh fish, snails (a local speciality), stews & rice dishes. €€

SPORTS AND ACTIVITIES The **camins de Ronda** (page 160) overlap in several places with the magnificent GR92 coastal path, which extends along the whole Mediterranean coast. There is some information available at local tourist offices, from the Catalan tourist board (w catalunya.com/en/continguts/rutes-itineraris/gr-92-sender-mediterrani-24-1-44) or from the Federació d'Entitats Excursionistes de Catalunya (w feec.cat; in Catalan only), but serious walkers should invest in good, up-to-date maps.

GOLF
Golf Platja de Pals C/ del Golf 162; ☎ 972 66 77 39; w golfplatjadepals.com. One of the top 10 courses in Spain.

HORSERIDING
Panorama Trails Casa Rectoral 5; ☎ 689 30 30 92; w panorama-trails.com. A wide range of riding excursions are available, from riding holidays to half-day guided treks or self-guided trails.

HOT-AIR BALLOONS TRIPS
Globus Empordà Colomers; ☎ 620 84 67 42; w globusemporda.com. Rides over the countryside in a hot-air balloon.

WATERSPORTS
La Sirena Pg Marítim 2, L'Estartit; ☎ 972 75 09 54; w divingsirena.com. Long-established diving company, which runs snorkelling & diving trips around Montgrí, the Illes Medes & Baix Ter nature reserve.

Kayaking Costa Brava C/ Enric Serra 42, Tamariu; ☎ 972 77 38 06; w kayakingcostabrava.com. Offers fantastic sea-kayaking tours of the calas, caves & cliffs of Cap Begur & other locations along the Costa Brava.

Poseidon Nimrod Diving Platja Pelegrí s/n, Calella de Palafrugell; ☎ 972 61 53 45; w poseidoncalella.com. Diving courses, boat & snorkelling trips, plus paddleboard & surfboard rental.

PALAFRUGELL In medieval times, the deliciously named Palau Frugell (or Palace of Fruits) sheltered Norman raiders and pirates within its walls. Today old Palafrugell is a web of narrow, curiously anonymous streets converging on busy central Plaça Nova. It has a couple of claims to fame: as the birthplace of Catalunya's best-known journalist, Josep Pla (1897–1981), and home to Spain's one and only cork museum, the **Museu del Suro** (Placeta del Museu del Suro s/n; ☎ 972 30 78 25; w museudelsuro.cat; ◷ mid-Jun–mid-Sep 10.00–14.00 & 17.00–20.00 Mon–Sat, 10.00–14.00 Sun; mid-Sep–mid-Jun 10.00–13.00 & 16.00–19.00 Mon–Fri, 10.00–14.00 & 17.00–20.00 Sat,10.00–14.00 Sun; adult/reduced/under 12 €6/3/free). In the late 18th century, as the market for champagne took off, so did the demand for quality cork – and the surrounding Gavarres and L'Ardenya hills had some of the best. Palafrugell became a major manufacturer: the money was excellent compared to wages in Barcelona's mills, and far more certain than fishing. Most of the work was done by hand, while factory readers read aloud to pass the time. It wasn't long before the newly educated cork-workers were founding literary athenaeums and casinos (clubs) where they could meet, read and discuss the issues of the day. Most cork factories closed down with World War I but one, owned by an American firm, lingered on until 1970. The factory building itself is now the **Fundació Vila Casas en Can Mario** (☎ 972 30 62 46; w fundaciovilacasas.com; ◷ mid-Jan–mid-Jun & mid-Sep–mid-Nov 11.00–14.00 & 16.30–20.30 Sat, 11.00–14.00 Sun; mid-Jun–mid-Sep 11.00–

HAVANERES AND CREMAT

In summer Calella de Palafrugell lilts to Catalan-Cuban sea shanties called *havaneres*. The songs grew out of a cultural give-and-take that began in early colonial times, when Europe's *contradansa* (a fast-paced folk dance) was introduced to the New World; the Cubans added their own Caribbean beat and in the 19th-century the songs, accompanied by guitar and accordion, were brought back to Catalunya by returning emigrés and sailors. The first havanera score, *El amor en el baile*, was published in 1842; and the first worldwide hit, *La Paloma* by Basque composer Sebastián Yradier, came out in 1855. Yradier's other classic, *El Arreglito*, was borrowed by George Bizet for *l'Amour est un oiseau rebelle*.

Today in Catalunya over a hundred groups play *havaneres*. In 1967, the Amics dels Havaneres in Calella de Palafrugell started a festival that today draws some 30,000 fans in late June or early July. And the perfect traditional drink on a cool evening sitting by the sea? *Cremat*, a potent shot of burnt rum, flavoured with cinnamon, lemon and coffee beans. Be warned; it's an acquired taste.

13.30 & 17.30–20.30 Tue–Sun; closed mid-Nov–mid-Jan; adult/reduced €10/5), dedicated to contemporary sculpture, with both a permanent collection and temporary exhibitions.

Palafrugell's **beaches** are some of the most beguiling along the Costa Brava, at their best in September, when the water's still warm but the crowds have cleared off and parking isn't a nightmare (all the beaches are served by Moventis buses from Palafrugell's station).

The largest of these, at the end of an incongruous highway, is **Calella de Palafrugell**, an archetypal whitewashed fishing village – and now a chic weekend bolthole for well-heeled Catalans – tucked under Cap Roig, with a few of the traditional fishing smacks called *mallorquinas* bobbing in the bay.

CAP DE SANT SEBASTIÀ AND CAP DE BEGUR Cliffs pirouette to the sea between a series of gently shelving strands and lapis lazuli coves, while parasol pines cling to every ledge: these two capes are among the crown jewels of the Costa Brava. You can drive or bus down to most of the beaches, but walking along the shore is far more beautiful, while kayaking around the coast can get you to many places inaccessible by land.

The GR92 from Calella de Palafrugell meanders north to sheltered **Llafranc**, with a silvery crescent of sand and smart hotels and restaurants; this was probably Roman Cypsela, and in 1950 they say you could still find bits of wall, mosaic, pottery and coins lying around. From Llafranc's church the path continues to the **Cap de Sant Sebastià** (site of the **Can Mina dels Torrents** dolmen) and up 161 steps to the **Far de Sant Sebastià**, a lighthouse built in 1857; the reward for using up all your puff is a truly magnificent vista. Then continue north to **Tamariu** beach, enveloped in fragrant pines.

Next come **Aiguaxelida** and **Aiguablava**, with the Costa Brava's parador on the promontory hidden in the trees above. The beach at **Sa Tuna** has a whitewashed fishing village for a backdrop; **Sa Riera** is another Blue Flag beauty. **Begur**, on the hill above, is a pleasant hilly village gathered under a 10th-century fortress, built to shelter shore-dwellers from Norman raiders.

PALS Just inland medieval villages dot the slopes of the Gavarres mountains and the fertile plain between Begur and Girona, where zoning laws have helped to preserve the countryside from the worst of the sprawl. The striking walled ensemble of **Pals** was almost destroyed in the Civil War but has since been meticulously rebuilt to become a honeypot for coach tours. Sand dunes back the 6km-long **Platja de Pals**, framed by a great tree-topped chunk of rock and much frequented by German families.

LA BISBAL D'EMPORDÀ Historically the most important town in the area, this market town first recorded in AD901. Its attractive Romanesque castle, built by the Bishop of Girona ('Bisbal' comes from Bisbe, or 'bishop'), now houses the Baix Empordà historical archive. You don't have to be in town long to notice that it makes pots; the ceramics trade dates from the 17th century and a long street of shops does a brisk trade. La Bisbal can also boast of Catalunya's top sardana dance band, the Cobla Principal de la Bisbal, founded in 1888 and now the Generalitat's official cobla.

Nearby are two churches to seek out: Mozarabic **Sant Juliá de Boada** with horseshoe arches, off the road to Pals, and the lovely Romanesque **Sant Esteve at Canapost** on the road to Peratallada.

AROUND LA BISBAL Located northeast of La Bisbal, where the Gavarres mountains begin to rise, Peratallada's name means 'cut rock' – an accurate description, with its deep moat, Romanesque-Gothic castle and tangle of lanes carved in the rock. Just north, medieval **Ullastret** is near the even older Iberian settlement of Ullastret, where, in the 5th century BC, the Indiket tribe built their most important hilltop settlement in Catalunya, defended by enormous walls. Inside are the remains of houses, reservoirs, canals, and a main square. Lead plaques discovered here are among the most important records of Iberian scripts (and incidentally helped to disprove the theory that the Basque language descended from Iberian). Finds from the site are in an outpost of the **Museu d'Arquelogia de Catalunya (MAC) museum** (C/ Afores s/n; ✆972 17 90 58; w macullastret.cat; ☉ Oct–May 10.00–18.00 Tue–Sun, Jun–Sep 10.00–20.00; adult/reduced/under 16 €7/5/free) in a 14th-century hermitage.

Northwest of La Bisbal, there are more pretty villages: **Corçà** (if a tad over-restored); **Cruïlles**, with a striking 11th- to 12th-century donjon; atmospheric **Monells**, and walled **Madremanya**, with attractive townhouses. From here you can drive up to the **Convent de la Mare de Déu dels Àngels** (488m), jam-packed with picnickers at weekends, who come for strolls and to take in the stupendous views. Dalí and Gala were secretly wed here in 1958.

PÚBOL: THE GALA DALÍ CASTLE (Pujada del Castell 28; ✆972 67 75 05; w salvador-dali.org/es/museos/castillo-gala-dali-de-pubol; ☉ Jul–Aug 10.00–18.15 daily; see website for opening times the rest of the year. Closed Jan–Feb.)

Not long after Dalí met Gala in 1929, he promised her a palace. It took him until 1969, but he finally kept his word, purchasing and restoring the ruined 11th-century castle in Púbol, off the C66 towards Girona. Their rule was that Dalí could only enter if she invited him, which she very seldom did, preferring to entertain scores of young lovers.

In 1980, as she became increasingly senile, Gala accidentally mixed up Dalí's medicine and badly poisoned him, so he could no longer physically paint. When she died two years later, King Juan Carlos, who always had a soft spot for Dalí, made the 78-year-old artist the Marquis of Púbol. He moved into the castle, but, two years later, after being burned in a mysterious fire, he moved back to Figueres, where he spent the rest of his life. Opened to the public since 1996, the Gala Dalí Castle offers up Gala's throne room (after her death Dalí liked to sit on the throne for interviews) and plenty of kooky Dalíesque details, portraits, drawings and sculptures, Gala's haute-couture frocks, and a pool watched over by statues of Wagner.

TORROELLA DE MONTGRÍ AND L'ESTARTIT Once a royal town like Pals, Torroella de Montgrí is easy to spot from a distance, thanks to its enormous castle on the Montgrí massif. This was begun in 1294 by Jaume II as an outpost to keep tabs on the Counts of Empordà, and as their quarrel was settled before the castle was completed, he left it a great hollow shell.

Torroella, rather surprisingly, was once Girona's port. In 1178, a band of Moors sailed up and massacred the monks in a nearby monastery. Not long after, the Counts of Empordà, to spite the count-kings, diverted the course of the River Ter so successfully that the port silted up completely. Most of Torroella's magnificent walls were demolished in the 19th century.

Yet the town itself still wears its head high: laid out by royal planners in a grid, it has a Renaissance tower and gates, an arcaded **Plaça de la Vila**, and **Sant Genis**, a big 14th-century Gothic church. There's an Augustinian monastery with a beautiful Tuscan Renaissance-style cloister unique in Catalunya, which now serves as a viola school. In the heart of the old town, a Renaissance mansion houses the **Museu de la Mediterrània** with interactive displays and artefacts on both local history and human settlements in the wider Mediterranean. Another palace from Torroella's glory days, the 15th-century **Palau Solterra** is the home of the extensive Catalan photography collection of the **Vila Casas Foundation**.

Torroella's seaside extension **L'Estartit** has a 5km sandy beach. Yet its claim to fame is among divers, who come to pester the sea creatures around the seven little picturesquely lopsided **Illes Medes**, floating a mile off the coast. In the bad old days pirates used them as a base, and in the 15th century a fort was built on the largest, Meda Gran, though it eventually fell into the sea. The surrounding waters, full of caves, crags and shipwrecks going back to ancient times, have been designated a nature reserve (park information office: Pg del Port s/n, L'Estartit; ☏972 75 17 01; w parcsnaturals.gencat.cat/ca/xarxa-de-parcs/illes-medes) since 1990, and are among the richest in marine life in the western Mediterranean – providing a full larder for the estimated 14,000 yellow-legged gulls, shags and cormorants who make up the islands' population. If you're not a diver, there are glass-bottom boat cruises, snorkelling and sea kayak tours.

Just west, **Verges** attracts crowds on Holy Thursday nights, when men don luminous skeleton costumes and cardboard skulls to scamper about to the booming drums in a 'Dança de la Mort', their Halloween caperings a reminder of the Black Death.

THE GULF OF ROSES

5

The Gulf of Roses may be the name on the map, but foodies know this as the southern reaches of the Anchovy Coast, which extends north to Collioure in France: the waters here are cooler than elsewhere in the Mediterranean and rich in the plankton the anchovies love.

You're well served by **tourist offices**, with an outpost in every town and resort including L'Escala (Ctra d'Orriols a Viladamat; ☏972 77 06 03; w visitlescala.com),

Roses (Avda de Rhode 77; ☎902 10 36 36; w visit.roses.cat), Castelló d'Empúries (Pl dels Homes; ☎972 15 62 33; w castelloempuriabrava.com) and Sant Pere Pescador (Ctra de la Platja; ☎972 52 05 35; w visitsantpere.com).

⌂ WHERE TO STAY

Almadraba Park Platja de Almadraba, Roses; ☎972 25 65 50; w almadrabapark.com. The sleekest choice, a large, cliff-top hotel founded in 1969 by the Mercader family (owners of the Hotel Empordà in Figueres). Plush, AC rooms, with amenities including a fine, award-winning restaurant (€€€€), pool, sauna & tennis courts. **€€€€**

Cala Jóncols 12km north of Roses in Cala Jóncols; ☎972 19 90 28; w calajoncols.com. A mid-sized, sustainable hotel, this has white, fresh rooms deliciously isolated on the beach amid gardens & olive groves, with a pool & a diving club, canoes to hire for exploring the coast & good restaurant serving local cuisine. **€€€€**

Hostal Empúries Platja de Portitxol s/n, L'Escala; ☎972 77 02 07; w hostalempuries.com. A blissful, whitewashed charmer with a strong commitment to sustainability, which sits on a quiet beach near the Greco-Roman ruins. Serene, impeccably stylish rooms, a wonderful spa & a great restaurant (€€€) focusing on locally sourced ingredients. **€€€€**

Palau Macelli C/ Carboner, Castelló d'Empúries; ☎972 250 567; w palau-macelli.com. An elegant small hotel, set in a palace built in 1666, with charming gardens, a spa in the former carriage house & chic, minimalist but very comfortable rooms. **€€€€**

Canet Plaça Joc de la Pilota, Castelló d'Empúries; ☎972 25 03 40; w hotelcanet.com. Very friendly, family-run hotel in a 1920s building with plenty of quirky charm. There are 29 good value, simple rooms & an excellent restaurant (€€€) which offers traditional Catalan cuisine. **€€€**

Les Hamaques C/ d'Albons 6, Viladamat; ☎972 78 84 58; w leshamaques.com. A romantic little rural hotel with 5 stylish rooms in a peaceful village. There's a tranquil garden where you can drowse away an afternoon in a hammock or by the pool, plus wellness treatments & delicious, healthy b/fasts using fresh local produce. **€€€**

Mas la Torre Palau Saverdera; ☎609 32 58 52; w maslatorre.com. The perfect countryside retreat, this centuries-old *masia* (still a working farm) has 7 peaceful rooms only 2km from the beach. **€€€**

Riomar C/ del Riuet, Sant Martí d'Empúries; ☎972 77 03 62; w riomarhotel.com. On the beach, a large, peaceful family-oriented hotel, vintage 1969, but updated since, with a pool & restaurant. Tranquil & hugely popular with Catalan families. **€€€**

Taverna de la Sal C/ Santa Màxima 7, L'Escala; ☎972 77 62 78; w tavernadelasal.com. This lovely, intimate hotel has 6 pretty, whitewashed rooms overlooking the beach, along with a sunny roof terrace & a great seafood restaurant (€€) with a summer terrace. **€€€**

Nautilus Avda Nautilus 17, Roses; ☎972 25 62 62; w hotelnautilus.net. A surprisingly good bargain, this large, modern hotel near the beach has lots of facilities including a pool. **€€**

THE DALÍ OF THE KITCHEN: FERRAN ADRIÀ

The most famous restaurant, perhaps the most famous in the world for decades, Ferran Adrià's El Bulli was founded in 1964 and closed in 2011. Now Adrià has set up a culinary foundation and centre in its place (w elbullifoundation.com/elbulli1846), where you can explore its history and the experimental no-holds barred playfulness of molecular cuisine, from the first foam ('white bean espuma with sea urchins', created in 1994) to the spherical melon caviar (2003), which became emblematic of El Bulli's cuisine in later years. This revolutionary approach to cooking still influences top chefs in Catalunya and around the world. 'At El Bulli, we created a language that was not known by anyone,' as Adrià once explained. Just like surrealism.

YES, WITH ANCHOVIES!

Anchovies are key to Catalan cuisine, but don't mistake them for the grey slivers of salt that show up on our pizzas: the Catalan version is rosy-coloured, firmer and meatier. There are over a hundred species, but only one, the European anchovy – Engraulis encrasicolus or *seitó* – is commercially viable, sturdy enough to not be damaged in the nets.

Anchovy season runs from May to October, and traditionally they are bagged by night using a lamp that mimics the full moon the little fish love. Once unloaded in port, they are immediately beheaded and gutted, and layered with sea salt in large barrels and kept in cool rooms to ripen for at least three months – the art of the master-salter is to know exactly for how long. Afterwards the anchovies are cleaned in fresh water, manually deboned, laid out to dry overnight and packed in jars, tubs or cans and filled with sunflower oil.

Shops in L'Escala also sell them the way many Catalans prefer, whole and packed in salt, so they do the cleaning themselves. Family anchovy-salting factories survive in L'Escala and Collioure, but, since the 1980s, the catch in the Mediterranean (which connoisseurs prefer to the more common Atlantic anchovy) has declined, owing to warmer summer temperatures and the use of huge French ships that use nets so fine that they sweep up the baby fish before they have a chance to reproduce. Recent conservation efforts have been rewarded by some recovery in catch volumes, but they remain substantially lower than historical levels.

Most of the anchovies you see in supermarkets these days come from Morocco and are cured with cost-cutting methods – so you may do a double-take at the prices in L'Escala's anchovy shops. But great Catalan chefs will use no other.

✕ WHERE TO EAT AND DRINK

La Gruta C/ Pintor Enric Serra 44, L'Escala; ☎ 972 77 62 11; w restaurantlagruta.com; ⏰ 13.00–15.00 & 20.00–22.00 Tue–Sat. Artful, award-winning Franco-Catalan cuisine is offered at this welcoming, elegant restaurant. Choose from 3 set menus – a w/day lunch menu (€30), the Bistronómico (€42.50) or the Descubrimiento (€62.50). €€€€

Rafa C/ Sant Sebastià 56, Roses; ☎ 972 25 40 03; 🖂 rafas_restaurantroses; ⏰ 13.00–15.30 & 20.00–22.00 Tue–Sat, 13.00–15.30 Sun. Famous as Adrià's favourite restaurant – or at least that's what Rafa told Anthony Bourdain. There's no menu, only the day's catch (often including anchovies) personally chosen by Rafa, then perfectly grilled. €€€€

Cal Campaner C/ Mossen Carles Feliu 23, Roses; ☎ 972 25 69 54; w calcampaner.cat; ⏰ 13.00–15.00 Tue–Thu & Sun, 13.00–15.00 & 20.00–22.00 Fri–Sat. A beloved local classic since 1966. Tiny, hard to find, informal & serving nothing but deliciously prepared, spectacularly fresh seafood. €€€

Grop C/ Port 21, L'Escala; ☎ 972 05 95 50; w restaurantgrop.cat/en/restaurant-grop-en; ⏰ 13.00–15.30 & 19.30–22.30 daily. A relaxed, rustic-chic restaurant serving excellent local meat & fish dishes, as well as pasta & salads, all freshly prepared with a modern twist. Veggie & vegan options are available. €€€

✳ **Korpilombolo** Pl de l'Ajuntament, L'Escala; ☎ 972 77 32 95; 🖂 restaurantkorpilombolo; ⏰ 13.00–15.30 & 20.00–22.30 Thu–Sat, 13.00–15.30 Sun. Delicious, contemporary cuisine served as artistically presented 'small plates' to share in a tiny restaurant run by a Catalan-Swedish couple. Specialities change depending on what's freshest at the market, but are always mouthwateringly delicious. €€€

Pa i Raim C/ Torres i Jonama 56; ☎ 972 44 72 78; w pairaim.com; ⏰ 13.00–15.00 &

5

20.00–22.00 Thu–Sat, 13.00–15.00 Sun. An elegant restaurant where you'll find top-notch modern Catalan cuisine, prepared with seasonal, local produce, including wild mushrooms in autumn. €€€

Portal de la Gallarda C/ Pere Estany 14, Castelló d'Empúries; ✆972 25 01 52; 🔲 portaldelagallarda; ⏰ 12.30–15.00 Wed–Thu & Sun, 12.30–15.00 & 20.00–22.00 Fri–Sat. Reliable grilled meats & salads, just behind the

church by the 11th-century fortified gate to the city; pretty views from the terrace. €€€

Cal Patufet C/ Figueres 2, Castelló d'Empúries; ✆972 15 81 14; ⏰ 13.00–15.00 Mon, Wed & Sun, 13.00–15.00 & 19.30–22.00 Fri–Sat. Lovely, family-run & delightfully old-fashioned Catalan restaurant serving local classics including meat, fish & vegetables *a la brasa'* – cooked on a charcoal grill. The set lunch menu (available w/days) is a bargain. €€

L'ESCALA Founded in the 16th century by fishermen, L'Escala has several shops near the port sell nothing but anchovies caught by its fleet of traditional *tranynas* – and they're the world's finest, as any Catalan will tell you. You can study them in depth at the **Museu de l'Anxova de la Sal** (Av Francesc Macià, 1; ✆972 77 68 15; w museudelescala.com; ⏰ 10.00–13.00 Tue–Thu & Sun, 10.00–13.00 & 17.00–20.00 Fri–Sat). The locals are also proud of their Sardana; statues of complete sardana band play silently right in front of the town beach.

Ancient Empúries

The excavations of Spain's most important ancient Greek city of Empúries lie within the sound of the waves just north of L'Escala, in a peaceful garden setting dotted with parasol pines. It wasn't always so peaceful. Around 600BC, Greeks from Phocaea set up a trading counter here that they called Emporion, or 'market', on its little isthmus where an indigenous Iron Age settlement had existed since the 9th century BC. It traded with the Phoenicians, Etruscans and Greeks. When a second wave of Greek colonists settled a new site, a bit further south, the first settlement became known as Palaiapolis (the 'old city').

In 218BC, during the Second Punic War, Scipio captured Emporion in the first Roman action in Iberia; a Roman military camp set up in 195BC and the new Emporion evolved into a city ten times the size of the Greek one. Under Augustus the whole became the Municipium Emporiae. Pirate attacks beginning in the 3rd century AD made it less desirable. The Visigoths showed up to build a few churches, but it was completely abandoned not long after. Excavations began in 1908, and archaeologists reckon only 25% of the site has been revealed.

Behind the mighty walls of the Greek 'New Town' or Neapolis lie the foundations of sanctuaries to Asklepios, god of healing and the Egyptian god Serapis. There's an agora and stoa, the centre of any Greek city, cisterns, houses (with a few mosaics), a forge and a workshop from the 1st century BC used for salting anchovies, converted by the Romans into a factory for making their beloved fermented fish sauce, or garum.

A garden and road separate the Greek Neapolis from the Roman town. Only a fraction of the latter has been uncovered: two grand houses with fine mosaics, the forum, temples, part of a wall and gate, apartment houses, shops and an amphitheatre. The site's **museum** has as its prize a life-sized, 3rd-century BC statue of Asklepios with his snake, but there are other treasures as well: an unusual altar from the 2nd century BC painted with a cock and a pair of snakes, remains of a Roman catapult, and beautiful intricate mosaics – of fish, a partridge taking jewels out of a basket, and the Sacrifice of Iphigenia.

SANT MARTÍ D'EMPÚRIES

While Neapolis was abandoned, Palaiapolis evolved into this charming village. It was important enough in the 8th century AD to become the capital of the county of Empúries, although in the 11th century even that relocated to Castelló d'Empúries (see below), and the place has managed to stay out of history ever since. A seaside promenade links Sant Martí to L'Escala; along it you can see the huge stone jetty built by the Greeks just before the arrival of the Romans. There are beaches and dunes here, well known among local windsurfers, all the way to the little port resort of **Sant Pere Pescador**. Just inland, **Sant Miquel de Fluvià** has a fine Romanesque church of 1066.

PARC NATURAL DELS AIGUAMOLLS

North of L'Escala, the Ter, Fluvià and Muga rivers once flowed into ancient lakes. These were drained in the 18th and 19th century to create farmland and pastures, leaving only a strip of coastal wetland, which in 1983 was protected as the 478ha Parc Natural dels Aiguamolls. Migratory birds adore it; a network of walking and bike paths make it easy to spot the ospreys, storks, flamingos, great bitterns and purple herons among the 324 species here.

These wetlands were only protected after a chunk was turned into **Empuriabrava**, the 'biggest marina town in Europe', where residents park their boats in their backyards. If you want nightlife, Empuriabrava delivers, especially in summer; but year-round (especially at weekends) you'll find a lively strip of bars and clubs known as Los Arcos, just in from the beach.

CASTELLÓ D'EMPÚRIES

Empuriabrava is the offspring of this venerable, handsome medieval town that once served as the port and seat of the Counts of Empúries, occupying its own little island. In the 6th century the Visigoths built a church at the highest point in town; it was destroyed by the Moors and rebuilt in AD888 by Wilfred the Hairy. From the 11th to the 13th centuries, the Counts of Empúries, hoping to get their own bishop, rebuilt Wilfred's church the size of a cathedral.

The scheme failed to nab a prelate, but the **Basilica of Santa Maria** (Pl Mossèn Cinto Verdaguer; \688 33 10 94; w basilicasantamaria.com; ⏰ Nov–Apr 10.00–17.00 daily, May–Jun & Sep–Oct 10.00–18.00 daily, Jul–Aug 10.00–20.00 daily; adult/reduced/under 12 €2.50/2/free), known as 'the Cathedral of the Empordà', still impresses with a lavish marble portal, covered with statues of the saints and alabaster windows. One chapel holds the alabaster Gothic altarpiece by Vicenç Borràs (1435), while the Capella de la Mare de Deu dels Dolors of 1777 is an over-the-top gold and white confection; other bits are in the museum in the sacristy. The count's palace is now the Ajuntament, and there's also a once densely populated Call (Jewish quarter), in a network of little streets; remains of the New Synagogue can still be seen on Carrer Peixateries Velles. The **Eco-Museu Farinera** (C/ Sant Francesc 5–7; \972 25 05 12; w ecomuseu-farinera.org; ⏰ Oct–Mar 10.00–14.00 & 16.00–18.00 Tue–Sat, 10.00–14.00 Sun; Apr–Jun & Sep 10.00–14.00 & 16.00–19.00 Tue–Sat, 10.00–14.00 Sun; Jul–Aug 10.00–14.00 & 17.00–20.00 daily; adult/under 6 €1/free) occupies an old flour mill, where you can learn all about mid-19th-century technology. You can even visit the clink, the **Museu Cúria Presó** (Pl Jaume I; \972 25 08 59; w castello.cat/museu-dhistoria-medieval-de-la-curia-preso-s-xiv; ⏰ Nov–Mar 10.00–14.00 Tue–Fri & Sun, 10.00–14.00 & 16.00–18.00 Sat; Apr–Jun & Sep–Oct 10.00–14.00 Tue–Fri, 10.00–14.00 & 16.00–18.00 Sat–Sun; Jul–Aug 10.00–14.00 & 16.00–18.00 daily; adult/under 6 €1/free) of 1336, complete with prisoners' graffiti. Down by the car park, a picturesque cloister has a public wash-house in the centre.

ROSES

Domino stacks of high rises sprawling over the coastal hills and along the long sandy beach are what's coming up in Roses. Named after the Greek island of

Rhodes, home of the traders who founded it on a low hill in 776 BC, Roses grew into an important Hellenistic, Roman, Visigothic and medieval settlement, especially after the port at Castelló d'Empúries silted up. Ruins of old Roses and the medieval church of **Santa Maria** all lie within the embrace of the vast, brooding star-shaped **Ciutadella de Roses** built in 1543 by Emperor Charles V, after Barbarossa decimated the town; it also houses a museum on Roses' history.

One of the sweet things about Roses is a 23km-long footpath, the **Camí de Ronda** that follows the shore from the yacht marina along the port to the old tuna-fishers' cove of **L'Almadrava**, past the pretty calas of the wild Punta Falconera. One of the prettiest beaches to aim for is **Cala Rostella**, one of the few with any shade (park on top and walk down the path); another is **Cala Murta**, where swimsuits are optional. Beyond **Cala Montjoi**, you'll find a couple of other lovely coves before the road gives up at **Cala Jóncols**.

Roses was popular in Neolithic times, too: the town has set up a megalithic route towards Punta Flaconera. The funeral chamber of the **Casa Cremada** has two menhirs (4th–3rd millennia BC), slightly predating three large dolmens: the **Creu d'en Cobertella**, claimed the largest in Catalunya, topped by a massive; the **Llit de la Generala** and the **Cap de l'Home**.

CAP DE CREUS: CADAQUÉS TO PORTBOU

On the map it protrudes from the coast like a nipple on a frosty day, and up close Cap de Creus is just as fascinating. Its fabric is 450-million-year-old rock, shattered and upended when the Iberian peninsula collided with Europe to form the Pyrenees, then scoured and eroded into strange shapes by the *tramuntana* wind that blows so fiercely. Joan Maragell famously called Empordà the 'palace of winds'. Terraces laboriously carved over the ages are now abandoned: the phylloxera epidemic in the 1880s killed the vines, a devastating frost in 1956 killed the olives, and wildfires over the past couple of decades have left the rock prey to the elements. Dalí spent much of his life amid this 'grandiose geological delirium'; its brilliant light, coves and weirdly shaped rocks appear repeatedly in his paintings. In spite of all the disasters, the Cap de Creus is a nature reserve, boasting the largest stretch of undeveloped coast in Spain, a privileged home to rare flora and fauna on land and in the surrounding seas.

CADAQUÉS They call it the 'St-Tropez of Spain', and in many ways this jewel of the Costa Brava fits the bill. Cadaqués is just as hard to reach, at the end of long, tortuous roads over the Cap de Creus, and although it lacks St-Trop's big sandy beaches it boasts similar arty-celebrity credentials: not only Dalí and Lorca, but Picasso, Matisse, Man Ray, Max Ernst, Chagall, Marcel Duchamp, Albert Einstein, Walt Disney, Mick Jagger and a gaggle of film stars and millionaires have spent time here.

And it's easy to see why: with its whitewashed houses and cobbled streets clustered around a giant white mothership of a church and a bijou fishing port, Cadaqués is the most beautiful town on the coast. But although the young, the wealthy and the hip converge here, it's not posey like St-Tropez, but laid-back, like a Greek island.

The **tourist information office** (C/ d'es Cotxe 2; \972 25 83 15; w visitcadaques. org; ⊕ 09.00–21.00 daily) is tucked just back from the seafront near the Casino. The very helpful staff can give you information on everything from local festivals and events to boat rentals and yoga classes.

Getting there and away The **bus station** (C/ Sa Tarongeta 29) is located on the outskirts of town and has ticket machines, a ticket office and left-luggage lockers. There are regular services to Roses, Barcelona, Girona and Figueres, though timetables are reduced in the winter. Most services in this part of the Costa Brava are offered by Moventis (see timetables and purchase tickets at w moventis.es).

If you come **by car**, take the narrow, winding GI-614 road from Roses. Parking in the town itself is extremely limited, so best to leave your car in the pay-and-display car park by the bus station.

Where to stay Note that hotel prices skyrocket in July and August and you'll find much better rates in the shoulder season. Many hotels are closed or only open at weekends between November and March.

Villa Gala C/ Solitari 3; 872 22 80 00; w hotelvillagala.com. Just steps from the church in the old centre, this glamorous bolthole features contemporary rooms with designer furnishings & bold artworks, plus a chic courtyard oasis with sun loungers & a plunge pool. €€€€€

Hotel Sol Ixent Av de Sant Baldiri 10; 972 25 10 43; w hotelsolixent.com. Set in a quieter, residential neighbourhood, but only a 5-min walk to a couple of small coves, this medium-sized hotel offers crisp rooms in neutral shades, most with balconies, an excellent restaurant (€€€) & a lovely pool set in gardens. €€€€

Llané Petit C/ Dr Bartomeus 37; 972 25 10 20; w llanepetit.com. Perfectly located on a pretty beach, this medium-sized hotel has plush, comfortable rooms, some with views over the dazzling bay, as well as a good restaurant (€€€) & pool. €€€€

Blaumar C/ Massa d'Or 21; 972 15 90 41; w hotelblaumar.com. A lovely mid-sized peaceful hotel with airy rooms decorated in Mediterranean blue & white, some with balconies. There's a small pool in the garden, shaded by olive trees, & it's just a 10-min stroll to the centre or to Dalí's house. €€€

Hostalet de Cadaqués C/ Miquel Rosset 13; 972 25 82 06; w hostaletdecadaques. com. This friendly little inn hidden down a tiny, cobbled street offers great-value, immaculate, whitewashed rooms, all with AC, just steps from a choice of bars, shops & cafés. €€€

Port Lligat Platja de Portlligat; 972 25 81 62; w hotel-port-lligat.vivehotels.com. Long-established small hotel next to Dalí's house, with modest rooms offering fine views over the bay & a children's playground & pool. €€€

Tramuntana C/ de la Torre 9; 972 25 92 706; w tramuntanahotel.com. A small hotel in an elegantly converted townhouse, with simple but stylishly decorated rooms, a comfy lounge for relaxing & delicious b/fasts featuring homemade cakes. €€€

Where to eat and drink

Compartir Riera Sant Viçenc s/n; 972 25 88 56; w compartircadaques.com; 13.00–15.00 & 20.00–22.00 Tue–Sat. For a truly unforgettable experience, dine at this enchanting restaurant helmed by former chefs from legendary El Bulli. It only serves a set tasting menu (a vegetarian version is available), & each course is a work of art. Despite its stellar reputation, service is relaxed & unstuffy. €€€€€

Casa Anita C/ Miguel Roset; 972 25 84 71; casaanitacdq; 20.00–22.00 Mon, 13.00–15.00 & 20.00–22.00 Tue–Sun. In business for over 60 years, the legendary family-run restaurant has doodles by Picasso & Dalí. Delicious freshly fried fish & seafood *a la planxa*. €€€€

Cap de Creus Cap de Creus; 972 19 90 05; w restaurantcapdecreus.com; 10.00–23.00 daily. Right in the heart of the nature reserve, this occupies the old guardhouse next to the 19th-century lighthouse. The eclectic menu features everything from local favourites to excellent curries & the views will take your breath away. Also great for coffee & homemade cake after a hike. €€€

Casa Nun Pl de Portixó 6; 972 25 88 56; w casanun.com; 13.00–17.00 & 20.00–midnight Mon & Wed–Sun (Jul–Aug daily). Enjoy fresh seafood, paellas & Catalan rice dishes at this classic seafront restaurant, set in a narrow townhouse. There are heavenly views over the bay, particularly from the romantic balcony table. €€€

5

Lua C/ Santa Maria 1; ☎ 972 15 94 52; ◙ lua_
cadaques; ◷ mid-Jun–mid-Sep 13.00–15.30 &
20.00–22.30 daily; call ahead for opening times
the rest of the year. A colourful little charmer,

tucked down a steep cobbled street, this serves
up a tasty & inventive menu that tours the
globe. €€€

What to see and do The town's illustrious arty history gets a nod at the **Museu
de Cadaqués** (C/ Narcís Monturiol 15; ☎ 972 25 88 77; ◷ Jul–Aug 10.00–20.00
daily, Sep–Jun 10.30–17.30 Mon & Wed–Sat & 10.30–14.00 Sun), with rotating
exhibits that often relate in some way to the Surrealist maestro. For older art, visit
the outsized **Església de Santa Maria** (◷ 08.00–20.00 daily), built after the original
version was burned to the ground by the Ottoman pirate iral Barbarossa in 1543.
It has a show-stopping Baroque altarpiece sculpted and painted by Jacint Moretó
and Pere Costa, and occasionally hosts concerts, particularly in summer (ask at the
tourist office for details). There are spectacular views over the entire bay from the
viewing point in front of the church: look out for the curious, triangular-shaped
islet, **Es Cucurucuc**, a much-loved local symbol.

The steep narrow streets around the church, cobbled with the local grey slate
and awash with well-heeled, linen-clad visitors, are now lined with chi-chi art
galleries and boutiques. The whitewashed lanes spill down to the seafront, where
more shops, cafés and restaurants jostle for attention. Among them is the **Casino**
(also called the Societat L'Amistat, meaning 'The Friendship Society'), established
in 1870 as a social and cultural club for working people. Its large and airy café-bar,
refreshingly down to earth, is still the main meeting point for locals, particularly in
winter, when all the crowds have gone.

The slender **Platja Gran**, the main beach right in the centre of town, is a
favourite with families, thanks to its shallow waters, but a short amble in
either direction will bring you to plenty more enticing little coves. Among the
colourfully painted wooden boats ('*llaüts*') bobbing photogenically in the bay is a
beautifully restored fishing boat from 1925, the ***Sant Isidre*** (**w** chartersantisidre.
com), which operates tours around the Cap de Creus with a stop for swimming
in the crystal-clear waters.

DALÍ'S SCANDALOUS LAST YEARS

The one major exception to Dalí's no-guest rule at his home in Port Lligat
was the beautiful multilingual and possibly transsexual model, singer
and disco queen Amanda Lear, whom the artist met in a Paris club in
1965. Lear became Dalí's last muse, and, according to many, his greatest
creation. He introduced her to art; she introduced him to the Beatles and
the Rolling Stones.

Most biographers claim that Dalí in his last years fell into the hands of
corrupt advisors who forced him to sign countless forgeries and as many as
35,000 blank sheets of paper for future lithographs (others say he just wanted
to make money and signed them on his own). When his manager, 'Captain'
John Moore, was arrested in 1999 for altering Dalí's *Double Image of Gala*
(1969), police found 10,000 fake Dalí lithographs in his house in Cadaqués.
In 1970, Kirk Douglas visited Dalí during the shooting of *The Light at the Edge
of the World*, a thriller filmed on the Cap de Creus. Dalí, according to Douglas,
talked of erect penises and tried to snare him in a threesome before Douglas
managed to escape.

Dalí was one of the first painters to take a keen interest in film, and he collaborated with Buñuel on his two Surrealist classics, *Un Chien Andalou* (*An Andalusian Dog*; 1929) and *L'Âge d'or* (*The Golden Age*; 1930). Lorca, an Andalucian, took umbrage at *Un Chien Andalou* (rightly or wrongly believing that the title was an insult directed at him) and broke off his friendship with the pair. *L'Âge d'or* (originally titled *The Icy Water of Egotistical Calculation*) opens with scenes filmed on Cap de Creus with a cast of locals, and it too caused umbrage – and a riot – when it opened in Paris.

A 15-minute stroll will bring you to **Port Lligat**, with a sandy beach and the **Casa-Museu Salvador Dalí** (🖀 972 25 10 15; **w** salvador-dali.org; ⏱ 09.30–19.50 daily, exc Mon during Nov–Mar & 9 Jan–9 Feb; guided visits only, book well in advance; adult/reduced €15/12). In 1929, the Surrealist French poet Paul Éluard and his Russian wife, Gala, came to visit Dalí in Cadaqués. Gala was 11 years older than Dalí, but he was smitten, much to the disapproval of his father. Dalí senior booted him out; Dalí junior defiantly bought a fisherman's cottage in Port Lligat just down the coast. It was the first of four shacks the artist purchased and strung together.

Although exhibitionists in public, Dalí and Gala were intensely private at home. Once past the clutch of eggs on the roof and jewellery-encrusted stuffed polar bear at the entrance, his home turns out to be surprisingly restrained, a cosy labyrinth, filled with dried bouquets of immortelles gathered by Gala, who shared Dalí's obsession with immortality. A mirror was placed so that Dalí could be the very first person in Spain to see the sun rise each morning, without getting out of bed.

He always painted while sitting down, so invented a giant easel on pulleys that slid into the floor below, allowing him to work on large canvases from his armchair. For Gala he built an acoustically wonderful egg-shaped boudoir, which she filled with objects from Russia; the doors of her dressing room are covered with newspaper clippings about the couple. There are no guest rooms, but visitors were admitted to the charming patio, where olive trees grow in giant teacups, and where Dalí the voyeur could observe them through peepholes. The long phallic swimming pool – where visitors were allowed, and therefore wildly extravagant – is watched over by a statue of the Michelin man, a hot-pink bench in the shape of lips, and a couple of giant stuffed pythons.

Port Lligat is one of the access points to the wild and beautiful **Cap de Creus nature reserve** (**w** parcsnaturals.gencat.cat/en/xarxa-de-parcs/cap-creus), which covers this entire headland and boasts several rugged hiking trails (including a section of the GR11 trans-Pyrenean route) that link miniature, unspoiled coves. No vehicles are admitted in summer, but you can park in Port Lligat and make the 2-hour hike (or take a shuttle bus) up to the **lighthouse** perched high on the rocky tip of the cape. This is the easternmost point of Spain, the throne room of the 'palace of winds', and the views are superb. Of course, this being Catalunya, there's a good restaurant, too (page 175).

EL PORT DE LA SELVA Not as swanky as Cadaqués, but still oozing plenty of Mediterranean charm, **El Port de la Selva** is another whitewashed fishing village, where working boats bob among the pleasure craft. **Platja Gran** just south of town is

5

the busiest beach, but, if it's windy, a coastal path leads to the more sheltered pebble cove of **Tamariua**. Far fewer visitors make it up to the handsome fortified nucleus of **Selva de Mar**; there's a lovely path to an old watermill.

A steep but rewarding hike (about 5km) from Port de la Selva or short drive will bring you to the **Monestir de Sant Pere de Rodes** (Camí del Monestir s/n; t] 972 38 75 59; w patrimoni.gencat.cat/es/monumentos/monuments/conjunto-monumental-de-sant-pere-de-rodes; ⊕ Jun–Sep 10.00–20.00 daily, Oct–Mar 10.00–17.30 Mon–Thu, 10.00–19.00 Fri–Sun; adult/reduced/under 16 €6/4/free), a vertiginous Romanesque monastery, spectacularly located high above the coast. In her 1986 autobiography, *My Life with Dalí*, Amanda Lear describes how she and Dalí rode donkeys up to this enormous monastery to enquire whether or not they should be married. Perhaps ancient inhabitants did as well, when a Roman temple of Venus Urania stood here; in ancient times this was Cape Aphrodision, until St Helen, on her way back from the Holy Land in the 4th century, Christianised the temple of love and left it a piece of the Holy Cross.

Jump ahead to AD610, when enemies were at the gates of Rome. In a panic, Pope Boniface IV entrusted three monks with the Church's holiest relics – the head and right arm of St Peter – and told them to get out of town. The monks brought the relics to Cap de Creus, hid them in a safe place and returned to Rome, only to find the threat had passed. The pope sent them back to retrieve the relics, but the monks had hidden them only too well, and rather than return and face a furious pope, they founded a monastery on the site of the ex-temple. In AD979, Pope Benedict VII issued a bill saying that if a pilgrim physically couldn't make it to Rome, a trip to Sant Pere was just as good, thus beginning the monastery's heyday. In 1022 it was rebuilt in the new Romanesque style. By 1100 only Santiago de Compostela was a more popular pilgrimage destination in the western Mediterranean. The monks had estates throughout the Empordà; they carved terraces in the ancient rock and made the best wine in Catalunya. The great Master of Cabestany laboured for years in the cloister, carving capitals that were said to be the finest anywhere.

In 1348, the Black Death struck, leaving only 30 monks; in 1409, King Martí the Humanist, who had just gobbled up Empordà, took advantage of a temporary lack of abbots and took control. Luxury and immorality began to creep in. Abbots stopped living in the monastery. In 1708, French mercenaries under the Duc de Noailles pillaged its art and treasure, and destroyed what they could not carry, including the sculptures by the Master of Cabestany. The monks abandoned Sant Pere altogether by 1798 (which casts doubt on Amanda Lear's story, but never mind). Doors, windows and other bits were carted away.

The picturesque ruin is said to have inspired Umberto Eco's novel *The Name of the Rose*, but in 1998 Sant Pere suffered a final ignominy at the hands of restorers. All the original bits, outside of a couple of capitals and fragments of wall paintings, are now in museums. Even so, the location is breathtaking: the 27m belltower and little crypt, and lofty main body of the church are original, although the rest feels like a Piranesi-esque confusion of floors, stairs, cloisters and walkways.

Getting there and away Regular buses (check timetables at w moventis.es) connect El Port de la Selva with Portbou, Llançà and Figueres (all of which have train stations), with reduced frequency in winter. There is also a summer-only service (no. 32) to Cadaqués (about 30mins) and Roses. From El Port de la Selva, it's a 10-minute drive or about an hour and 15 minutes on foot (via a steep section of the GR11) to the monastery of Sant Pere de Rodes.

🏠 Where to stay and eat

Porto Cristo C/ Major 59; ☎ 972 38 70 62; w hotelportocristo.com. Set in a 19th-century townhouse just steps from the main beach, this mid-sized option has modern, comfortable rooms, some with balconies overlooking the sea, a minuscule spa with a jacuzzi & a couple of restaurants (€€–€€€). €€€€

Hs La Tina C/ Major 15; ☎ 972 38 71 49; w hostallatina.cat. In the village centre a stone's throw from the sea, this simple, old-fashioned hostal has basic but spotless rooms & studio apartments, plus a restaurant (€€) serving classic Catalan favourites. €€

Can Pepitu C/ Mar 20; ☎ 640 72 47 46; 📷 canpepitu. A colourfully painted boat is the centrepiece at this friendly tapas bar right on the seafront. The creative menu offers everything from the famous local anchovies to Asian-fusion dishes like pork bao bao. €€

La Perleta C/ Baix 16, Selva de Mar; ☎ 972 12 63 60; 📷 canperleta. This tiny, enchanting spot offers delicious tapas & plates to share in a pretty, stone-walled restaurant with a small interior garden. The list of daily specials might include stuffed peppers, smoked sardines or homemade *croquetas*. €€

LLANÇÀ TO PORTBOU At the frontier with France, the coast is no less *brava*. **Llançà**, the biggest town, was built a couple of kilometres inland to protect it from pirates, and conveniently concentrates its monuments in the Plaça Major: there's a 14th-century **Torre de la Plaça**, with exhibits on the town's history, and a 15th-century **Episcopal Palace**, and the **Arbre de la Llibertat** (Liberty Tree), planted in 1870 during the heady days when the Catalan general Joan Prim was seeking a constitutionally minded king for Spain. Here too is the **Museu de l'Aquarel.la** (Watercolour Museum; Pl Major 3; ☎ 972 12 14 70; w mda.cat; ⏰ 09.00–13.00 Mon, 09.00–13.00 & 17.00–20.00 Tue–Fri, 10.30–13.00 & 17.00–20.00 Sat, 10.30–13.00 Sun; adult/under 16 €2/free) featuring a nice array of watercolours mainly by local painter Josep Martínez Lozano. At 16.30 locals gather to see what the fishermen have brought into **Llançà Port**, the little harbour set on either side of the wild El Castellar headland, offering grandstand views of the town and the Pyrenees. The best beaches are 2km north, **Platja Grifeu** and the sandy curve of **Platja Borró**, and tiny coves further along.

Hemmed in by the final toss of the jumbly rock-dice of the Albera mountains at the tail end of the Pyrenees, **Portbou** is only 3km from Roussillon in France. For centuries it was a perfect smugglers' port, sheltered from the *tramuntana* wind; towards the end of the Spanish Civil War, it was one of the few ports that the Republicans could still use to bring in goods. Portbou sounds vaguely ghostly, and it can still send shivers down the spine of those old enough to have passed through its cavernous station, standing in long queues for passport inspections and customs and hefting bags across the tracks. Spain made her national rail gauge wider than France's to keep the French from invading by train. In 1995, the Schengen Accord threw 500 officials out of work. Now the modern high-speed train tracks have made even changing trains passé.

Portbou today isn't quite a ghost town, but off season it can seem like it. Poet Stephen Spender was here during the Civil War in 1936, but the place reserved its biggest nightmare for a visitor who arrived by foot: philosopher and culture critic Walter Benjamin (page 180), associate of Theodor Adorno, Max Horkheimer and Herbert Marcuse at the Frankfurt School for Social Research.

Getting there and away The most convenient way to reach Llançà and Portbou is by train, with regular services to Figures, Girona and Barcelona (timetables at w renfe.com). There are also buses (timetables at w moventis.es) to El Port de la Selva and Cadaqués, with dramatically reduced services in winter.

THE DEATH OF WALTER BENJAMIN

With the rise of the Nazis in the 1930s, Theodor Adorno and Max Horkheimer had relocated to New York and encouraged Benjamin to follow. Fatally he didn't, and lingered in Paris, lonely and impoverished, convinced that he needed the Bibliothèque Nationale for his research.

Benjamin had initially hoped that Communism would act as a potent weapon against fascism but, like many intellectuals, he was abruptly disabused of that notion when Hitler and Stalin signed their pact. In early 1940 he channelled his fury into *Über den Begriff der Geschichte* (*Theses on the Philosophy of History*), a bleak, searing critique of Marxism. He left the manuscript with his friend Hannah Arendt and fled from Paris to Lourdes the day before the Nazis arrived. Max Horkheimer managed to organise a provisional US passport and Spanish transit visa for him via the American consulate in Marseille. Benjamin hoped to reach Lisbon and fly to New York and, on 25 September 1940, he and two companions walked from Banyuls-sur-Mer (page 330) to Portbou.

Benjamin was only 48, but he was a heavy smoker and had a bad heart. He was carrying his last work in a briefcase. No-one knew what was inside, though he told everyone it was very important and to be saved at all costs. At Portbou, the Spanish frontier guards gave Benjamin the heartbreaking news that the rules of the game had been changed the day before: he now needed a French exit visa and would have to be deported back to France. Seeing he was unwell, the police allowed him to spend the night in the Hotel de Francia (formerly at C/ del Mar 5).

The next day Benjamin was found dead in his bed. He is known to have had morphine on him, and it was assumed that the terror of being deported had led him to take his own life, although the death certificate gives the cause of death as a brain haemorrhage. Henny Gurland, the woman travelling with him (and future wife of Erich Fromm), claimed Benjamin had given her two suicide notes to pass on to Adorno which she later destroyed. She and her son were allowed to go on to Lisbon the next day. Conspiracy theories have been woven.

There was enough money in the dead man's pocket to pay for a niche in Portbou's Catholic cemetery for five years. His bones were removed in the 1940s and placed in the communal ossuary, although you can see a plaque on the cemetery wall, put up after Franco's death with a quote from the *Theses on the Philosophy of History*: 'There is no document of civilisation which is not at the same time a document of barbarism.'

And the manuscript in Benjamin's briefcase? It was given to a fellow refugee who lost it on the train to Madrid. Benjamin is remembered, along with all the other 20th-century refugees who passed to and fro through Portbou, with an unsettling monument called *Passagen*, by Israeli sculptor Dani Karavan. A rusty metal chute of claustrophobic stairs descends from the cemetery to the sea, blocked by a plate of glass, evoking Benjamin's last surviving if unfinished work, the *Passagen-Werk* (the *Arcades Project*; published in 1982).

Where to stay and eat

La Goleta C/ Pintor Tarruella 22, Llançà; 972 38 01 25; w hotellagoleta.com. Overlooking the port, this family-run *hostal* has 28 pristine, whitewashed rooms, including family rooms, & a pretty courtyard chill-out area with a play corner for children. The restaurant (€€€) serves excellent fresh seafood & rice dishes. €€€

Hotel Comodoro C/ Méndez Nuñez 1, Portbou; 609 47 15 04. A 5-min walk from the beach, this friendly little B&B has old-fashioned, charmingly kitsch, guest rooms, many of which have balconies. B/fast includes homemade jams & can be served out on the plant-filled terrace. €€

La Florida C/ Floridablanca 23–25, Llançà; 972 12 01 61; w lafloridahostal.com. In the old part of town, with a dozen or so tidy rooms decorated in crisp blue & white, & a classic, old-fashioned café-bar. €€

Voramar Pg de la Sardana, Portbou; 972 39 00 16; w voramarportbou.com; 13.00–14.00 Mon & Thu–Sun. Portbou may seem an unlikely setting for this restaurant, where young chefs Guillem Gavilan & Pau Jamas are producing some of the most exciting contemporary cuisine on the Costa Brava (with a Michelin star to prove it). Choose from 1 of 2 set menus (€95/130) & expect your taste buds to be dazzled. €€€€€

5

6

Girona and Its Province

Girona is one jammy province. In many ways it's the California of Spain – the wealthiest province per capita, and one containing more than its share of good things. Its seafront is the spectacular Costa Brava (page 157), while the snow-capped winter and summer playground of the Pyrenees beckons on the horizon. Cork forests and olive groves decorate the coastal mountains; orchards and farms prosper in the rich volcanic soil. Girona itself is one of Spain's most atmospheric medieval cities, while the honest traveller is constantly waylaid by Neolithic dolmens, Iberian oppida, Greek and Roman relics, medieval villages, Romanesque churches and Gothic castles. The Modernistas were here, too, if somewhat few and far between, but so was a certain Salvador Dalí, who left behind Spain's second most popular museum (after Madrid's Prado) in Figueres, as well as his residences in Port Lligat and Púbol – duly promoted as the 'Dalí Triangle'.

This chapter stretches west to the Llobregat River, taking in part of northern Barcelona province. Altogether it makes up most of 'Old Catalunya', cradle of the new nation first consolidated in the Dark Ages by Guifré el Pilós (Wilfred the Hairy). It has some truly lovely countryside, perfect for long walks or lazy dawdling while staying in exquisite hotels or budget B&Bs in former monasteries, castles or traditional *masies*. From the beans of Santa Pau to sausages, truffles and wild mushrooms in Vic and Berga, this is also a region that takes food very, very seriously.

GIRONA

Girona is a serious, secretive and fascinating city, with an historical palette as varied as its much-photographed, ochre-hued houses hanging over the River Onyar. The medieval streets of the Barri Vell have been lovingly neglected, leaving intact an evocative neighbourhood of vaulted passageways, winding steps and tiny squares, crowned by a cathedral unique in Europe. It has a small but excellent collection of museums, including one devoted to what was one of the most important Jewish quarters in Spain. The intellectual torch is now held by the university – although students grumble that Girona has the worst nightlife in Spain. Oh, stop moaning and hop on a bike, Girona would say. The city is one of Europe's cycling capitals, surrounded by over 1,200km of mountain bike trails, 'Vies Verdes' converted from extinct rail lines, and a network of relatively empty, often stunning mountain roads.

HISTORY As a city, Girona was inevitable: there just had to be a city on this hill, at the confluence of four rivers, midway between the Pyrenees and the Mediterranean. The Iberians were here first, followed by the Romans who founded Gerunda on the Rome-to-Hispania Via Augusta. St James, they say, preached here, and the see was founded in AD247. Goths and Franks invaded, the walls were improved, and by the

5th century AD it was the seat of a bishop. The Visigoths held it briefly, followed by the Moors. In AD778 Charlemagne took it back and made it the seat of a county in the Hispanic Marches. The first Jews in the city were recorded in AD890.

The 12th century was a golden period, when Girona grew so quickly that it expanded on to the left bank of the Onyar River. It was contested throughout history. Its nickname, 'City of a Thousand Sieges', is a slight exaggeration; the real number is 25, but, by May 1809, when 18,000 French troops appeared at the gate for the third time in two years, it must have seemed like a thousand. The French controlled the rest of Catalunya by then, but Napoleon knew that as long as Spain controlled Girona, his army was in danger of being cut off. Girona was not particularly well defended. The medieval walls around the old town had not been improved, and the garrison numbered only 5,700 Spanish regulars and 1,100 local troops.

However, the surrounding hills were well fortified and Girona had a brilliant commander in Mariano Álvarez de Castro. The French fired some 20,000 shells and 60,000 cannon balls into the city, brought in reinforcements, and finally, in August, managed to capture the strategic castle of Montjuïc above the city. They thought Álvarez would soon surrender; instead, he built barricades and trenches inside the city and the fight, now urban warfare, continued into December. Supplies were exhausted, and after a last daredevil sortie Álvarez was so exhausted and ill that he handed over command and received his last rites. Two days later, on 12 December, the town capitulated.

It is estimated that in all 10,000 people, soldiers and civilians, had died inside Girona; the French lost some 13,000 men during the eight months of the siege, including many to disease. Yet even though the French won the battle, they lost the war: the terrible sieges of Girona and Zaragoza succeeded in pinning down, delaying and demoralising the French. 'Immortal' Girona became a rallying cry for Spanish resistance for the rest of the war.

During the Civil War, Nationalists bombarded it from air, Anarchists pillaged and burned the churches, and thousands of refugees tramped through on the way to France. In the 1960s, things began to pick up again: the city expanded into 'Greater Girona', devouring and incorporating satellite towns in its path; by the 1980s it was the wealthiest city per capita in Spain.

GETTING THERE AND AWAY

By air Girona-Costa Brava airport (↖972 18 67 08; w aena.es/en/girona-costa-brava.html) is 12km south of the city. **Buses** operated by Sagalés (↖902 13 00 14; w sagalesairportline.com) run from the airport to Girona (30mins) & Barcelona (around 70mins). Sarfa-Moventis buses (↖972 33 78 42; w moventis.es) service the Costa Brava. Another option, if you book at least 24 hours in advance, is Shuttle Direct (w shuttledirect.com), which will take you directly to your accommodation.

By train Girona's railway station [187 A5] is in Plaça d'Espanya. All trains between France and Barcelona stop here, including the regional lines (R11 and RG1; w renfe.com) as well as high-speed rail services. There are also direct trains to Tarragona, Lleida, Zaragoza and Madrid.

By bus Girona's bus station [187 A5] (↖972 20 15 91) is next to the train station. It's the main station for both local, inter-urban, national and international bus services.

By taxi Taxis in Girona are white with a blue band. Local companies include Radio Taxi (↖677 30 75 92; w radiotaxigirona.com) and GI Taxi (↖972 22 23 23).

6

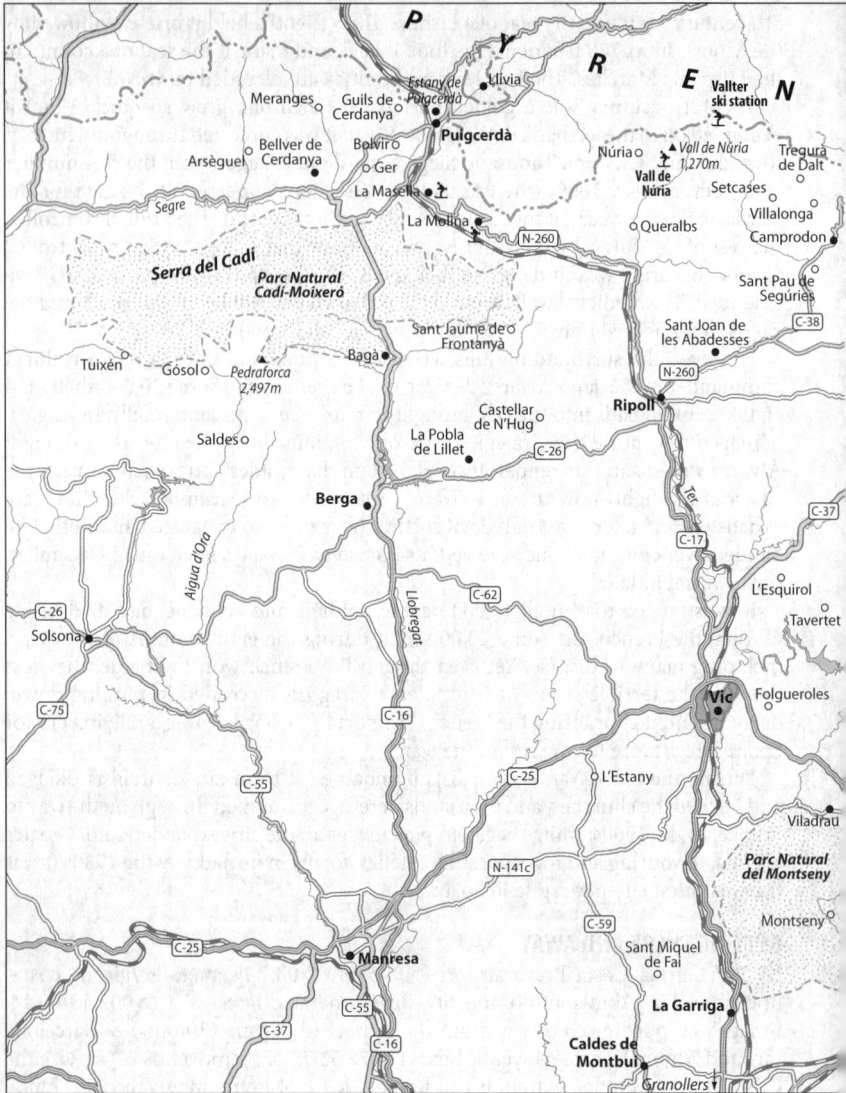

By car

For on-street parking (always difficult to find), note that spaces marked in green are exclusively for residents while those marked in blue are available to everyone. Pay at meters or using the Aparcar app. It may be more convenient to use one of the several underground garages in the new town (including one in Plaça de Jaume Vicens i Vives by the Pont de Sant Feliu) and walk over the bridge into the medieval core.

Car hire

All the usual companies have counters at the airport as well as offices in the city centre (including Hertz w hertz.es; Budget w budget.com; Europcar w europcar.com). These are mostly concentrated around the train station in the newer part of town.

GIRONA PROVINCE

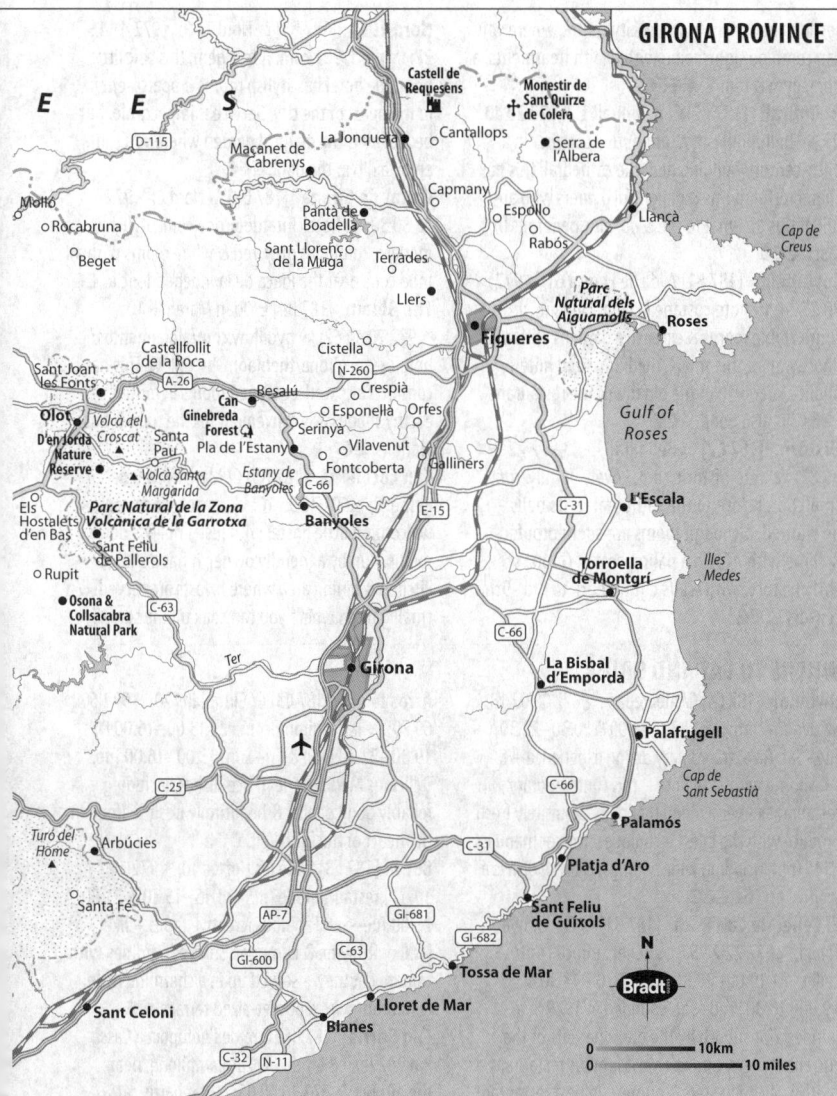

TOURIST INFORMATION The very friendly and helpful tourist information [187 C3] (Rbla de la Llibertat 1; ☏972 01 00 01; w girona.cat/turisme/eng/index.php; ⏱ 09.00–20.00 daily) is centrally located just by the Pont de Pedra at the entrance to the Barri Vell.

WHERE TO STAY

✳ **Hotel Palau Fugit** [187 C3] C/ Bonaventura Carreras i Peralta 4; ☏872 98 73 62; w palaufugit. com. Set in a splendid *palacete* tucked away near the cathedral, this exquisite small hotel is filled with artworks & boasts a serene patio

garden & individually decorated rooms that ooze style. €€€€

Mas Ferran [187 A5] Camí de la Bruguera s/n; ☏972 4 28 8 90; w masferran.com. Handsome stone 18th-century *masia* in a peaceful rural setting about 4km from the city centre, where you can combine sightseeing with health treatments, a pool, gym & tennis. €€€€

Bellmirall [187 C2] C/ Bellmirall 3; ☎972 20 40 09; w bellmirall.cat. A diminutive charmer in a 14th-century building near the cathedral, this has characterful rooms & delightful owners who are full of tips on what to see & do, plus generous b/fasts. €€€

Costabella [187 B1] Avda de França 61; ☎972 20 25 24; w hotelcostabella.com. Elegant, comfortable rooms & extensive gardens with a pool await at this smart, medium-sized hotel about 2km north of the old town. The restaurant (€€€) is also good. €€€

Històric [187 C2] C/ Bellmirall 4a; ☎972 22 35 83; w hotelhistoric.com. Lovely, family-run, small hotel close to the cathedral (& its bells – be warned, although rooms are soundproofed & come with AC), in a palimpsest of Girona's early history, with walls dating back to 3rd–9th century. €€€

Nord 1901 [187 B3] C/ Nord 7–9; ☎972 41 15 22; w nord1901.com. A real gem, this chic little boutique hotel has stylish rooms & apartments in the heart of the city. Service is impeccable, but best of all is the magical garden where you can enjoy a dip in the pool. €€€

Ciutat de Girona [187 B3] C/ Nord 2; ☎972 48 30 38; w hotelciutatdegirona.com. Stylishly modern, luminous grey, red & white rooms with all mod cons near the Plaça de la Independència. €€

The Bloom [187 B4] C/ Joan Maragall 10; ☎972 20 44 62; w bypillow.com/alojamientos/hoteles-en-girona/thebloom-by-pillow. This has comfortable, well-equipped rooms in muted, earthy shades & is convenient for the train & bus stations. €€

Can Cocollona [187 A5] C/ Mare de Déu del Remei 8; ☎607 40 96 10; w cancocollona.com. A welcoming little hostel with just 1 dbl & 3 dorm rooms. Run by a friendly owner, it has a shared kitchen & dining area where b/fasts are served, & a small garden where you can soak up the sun. €

✗ WHERE TO EAT AND DRINK

Divinum [187 C4] C/ Albereda 7; ☎872 08 02 18; w dvnum.com; ⏰ 13.30–15.00 & 20.30–22.30 Tue–Sat. An extraordinary dining experience – & a favourite with Joan Roca – this contemporary restaurant serves a menu that pairs exquisitely fresh produce with the latest techniques. The set menu is €145 (not including wine pairings) & every dish is a work of art. €€€€€

El Celler de Can Roca [187 B1] C/ Can Sunyer, Taialà; ☎972 22 21 57; w cellercanroca.com/celler; ⏰ 19.00–20.30 Tue, 12.30 –13.30 & 19.00–20.30 Wed–Sat. Founded in 1929 in a nondescript suburb by the grandparents of the current owners, Girona's most famous restaurant (with 3 Michelin stars & numerous 'best restaurant in the world' accolades) is run by the charming, highly skilled & unpretentious Roca brothers: Joan (head chef), Josep (sommelier) & Jordi (pastry chef) who pioneered the Roner system of cooking sous-vide. The contemporary dining room looks out over young maples, & a list of wines so vast that it comes to the table on wheels. Elegant takes on classic Catalan dishes are 'inspired by emotions, childhood memories, scents & the Catalan landscape'. The set menu, El Festival, is €225 (without wine pairings). You'll need to reserve at least 6 months in advance. €€€€€

Arròs i Peix [187 C3] C/ Ciutadans 20; ☎972 60 69 79; w larrosgirona.com; ⏰ 13.00–16.00 & 19.30–22.30 Mon & Fri–Sun, 13.00–16.00 Tue. Delicious Mediterranean rice dishes, including reliably good paella, & beautifully fresh seafood in the heart of the Barri Vell. €€€

8de7 [187 C3] C/ de les Hortes 10; ☎972 10 44 30; 📷 restaurant8de7; ⏰ 13.15–15.30 & 21.00–23.00 Tue–Sat. Fabulous, creative tapas – like lamb with wine & kumquat, smoked sardines with tomato chutney – served up in a charming little restaurant with a pocket-sized terrace. €€

Can Barris [187 B6] Ctra de l'Aeroport a Cassà, km 242 (exit 8 off the A7) at Campllong, near the airport; ☎972 46 10 05; w canbarris.cat; ⏰ 13.00–16.00 Tue–Fri & Sun, 13.00–16.00 & 20.00–23.30 Sat. This classic roadside inn is a local institution, where happy families come to slurp up industrial quantities of *cargols* – little snails in a rich, tomato sauce – along with other Catalan favourites. There's a big shady terrace for summer dining, & four large buzzy dining rooms inside. €€

Casa Marieta [187 C2] Pl de la Independència 5; ☎972 20 10 16; w casamarieta.com; ⏰ 09.00–22.00 daily. Girona's oldest restaurant, now run by the 5th generation of the founding family; generous helpings & hearty fare such as *botifarra amb*

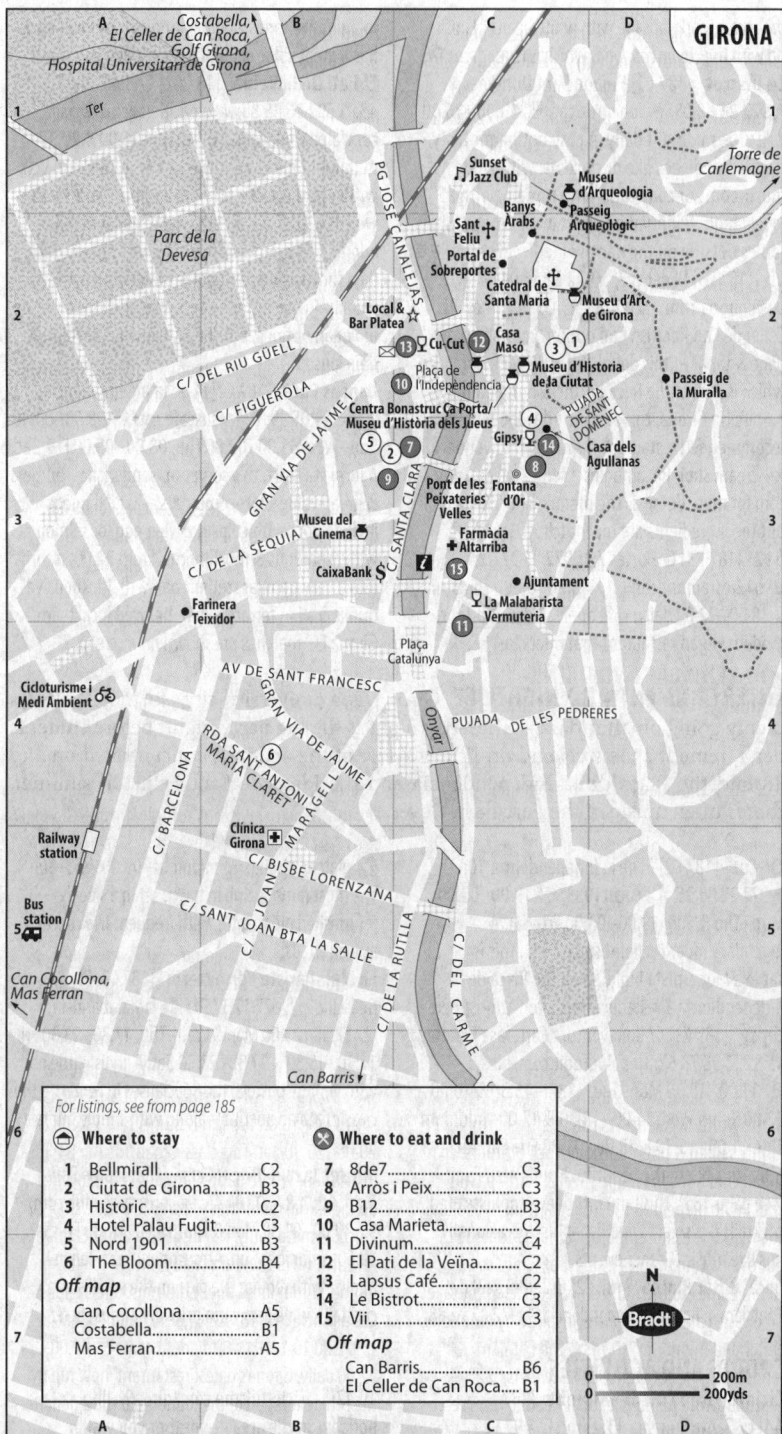

GIRONA

Costabella,
El Celler de Can Roca,
Golf Girona,
Hospital Universitari de Girona

Ter

Parc de la Devesa

PG JOSE CANALEJAS

C/ DEL RIU GÜELL

C/ FIGUEROLA

GRAN VIA DE JAUME I

C/ SANTA CLARA

C/ DE LA SEQUIA

Sunset Jazz Club

Banys Arabs

Sant Feliu

Portal de Sobreportes

Local & Bar Platea

Cu-Cut 13

12 Casa Masó

10 Plaça de l'Independència

Centra Bonastruc Ça Porta/
Museu d'Història dels Jueus

5 2 7

9

Museu del Cinema

CaixaBank

Farinera Teixidor

Museu d'Arqueologia

Passeig Arqueològic

Torre de Carlemagne

Catedral de Santa Maria

Museu d'Art de Girona

3 1

Museu d'Historia de la Ciutat

Passeig de la Muralla

PUJADA DE SANT DOMÈNEC

4

Gipsy

14

8

Casa dels Agullanas

Pont de les Peixateries Velles

Fontana d'Or

Farmàcia Altarriba

15

Ajuntament

La Malabarista Vermuteria

11

Plaça Catalunya

AV DE SANT FRANCESC

GRAN VIA DE JAUME I

PUJADA DE LES PEDRERES

Cicloturisme i Medi Ambient

RDA SANT ANTONI MARIA CLARET

C/ BARCELONA

6

Clínica Girona

C/ BISBE LORENZANA

C/ SANT JOAN BTA LA SALLE

C/ DE LA RUTLLA

C/ DEL CARME

Railway station

Bus station

Can Cocollona,
Mas Ferran

Can Barris

For listings, see from page 185

Where to stay

1 Bellmirall...................C2
2 Ciutat de Girona.......B3
3 Històric.....................C2
4 Hotel Palau Fugit......C3
5 Nord 1901.................B3
6 The Bloom................B4

Off map

Can Cocollona...............A5
Costabella......................B1
Mas Ferran....................A5

Where to eat and drink

7 8de7.........................C3
8 Arròs i Peix...............C3
9 B12...........................B3
10 Casa Marieta............C2
11 Divinum...................C4
12 El Pati de la Veïna.....C2
13 Lapsus Café..............C2
14 Le Bistrot.................C3
15 Vii...........................C3

Off map

Can Barris.....................B6
El Celler de Can Roca.....B1

N

Bradt

0   200m
0   200yds

6

mongetes (pork sausage with white beans). Finish up with the *crema catalana*, which is legendary. €€

Le Bistrot [187 C3] Pujada Sant Domènec; 📞 972 21 88 03; w lebistrot.cat; 🕑 13.00–16.00 & 19.30–midnight daily. A cosy option for tasty, traditional dishes like duck confit with wild mushrooms or cod gratin with tomato, with a lovely high-ceilinged dining room & a handful of tables outside on the narrow medieval street. €€

Vii [187 C3] Pl del Vi 7; 📞 972 21 56 04; w viigirona.com; 🕑 13.00–23.00 Thu–Mon. If Celler de Can Roca isn't an option, you can enjoy wine & tapas at this delightful little wine bar which is part of the Roca brothers' burgeoning empire (in Girona, this also includes the highly recommended restaurant Normal & the wonderful ice-cream shop Rocambolesc; see w cellercanroca. com for more details). The menu is short & classic, but the ingredients are top-notch. €€

B12 [187 B3] C/ Hortes 7; 📞 972 01 32 02; w b12restaurant.cat; 🕑 kitchen 13.00–15.45 & 18.00–22.00 daily; café open all day. A bright, modern vegan restaurant that offers tasty &

imaginative tapas, veggie burgers & more. It also has a great value set lunch on w/days. €

El Pati de la Veïna [187 C2] C/ Ballesteries 45; 📞 692 26 45 88; w elpatidelaveina.wixsite. com/elpatidelaveina; 🕑 12.45–16.00 & 20.30–midnight Mon–Sat. Tucked away in the Barri Vell, with lots of eclectic artworks & knick-knacks, as well as a graffiti wall that you're encouraged to add to, this offers a bargain 3-course menu each day, showcasing seasonal produce. There are usually 4 choices for each course, including veggie or vegan options, but they are always absolutely delicious. €

Lapsus Café [187 C2] Pl de la Independència; 📞 972 21 05 39; w lapsuscafe.cat; 🕑 08.00–00.30 Sun–Wed, 08.00–02.00 Thu, 08.00–03.00 Fri–Sat. A local stalwart, this serves up sandwiches, burgers & great-value 'plats combinats' – which might include pork with chips & a fried egg, or salmon with asparagus & mushrooms. From 22.00, it turns into a very popular student bar, with inexpensive drinks & a big terrace where beloved local team, Girona FC, matches are shown on a screen. €

ENTERTAINMENT AND NIGHTLIFE Girona is a university city, so there's always plenty going on after dark – Thursday night is the big party night, before students head home for the weekend on Friday. Most of the action is concentrated on and around the Plaça de la Independència and the Plaça de Sant Feliu. In summer, there's often music in the Parc de la Devesa.

Cu-Cut [187 C2] Pl de la Independència 10; 📞 972 22 85 25; 📷 cucut1983; 🕑 19.00–02.00 Mon–Thu & Sun, 19.00–03.00 Fri–Sat. A legendary meeting point since 1983, this is set in a Modernista building on the Plaça de la Independència & reliably offers a fun atmosphere.

Gipsy [187 C3] C/ Bonaventura Carreras i Peralta 4; 📞 872 98 73 62; w palaufugit.com/gipsy; 🕑 11.00–15.30 Mon–Tue, 11.00–15.30 & 16.00–22.00 Sun & Wed, 11.00–15.30 & 17.00–midnight Thu, 11.00–15.30 & 18.00–01.00 Fri–Sat. An ultra-chic bar in the beautiful Hotel Palau Fugit (see page 185), this has craft beers, sophisticated cocktails & a select wine list. It also occasionally has live music & other events.

Local & Bar Platea [187 C2] C/ Jeroni Real de Fontclara 4, near Pl Independència; 📞 972 22 72 88;

📷 platea_girona; 🕑 midnight–03.00 Wed–Sun. The most famous club in town, set in a sleekly refurbished old theatre, with frequent live concerts as well as DJs.

La Malabarista Vermuteria [187 C3] Pl Bell-Lloc 2; 📞 627 17 17 57; 📷 lamalabarinsta; 🕑 17.30–23.00 Mon & Wed–Thu, 17.30–23.30 Fri, 11.30–15.30 & 17.30–23.30 Sat. A stylish little bar with vintage posters, this specialises in *vermut* – the classic Catalan aperitif – along with simple but tasty tapas.

Sunset Jazz [187 C1] Club C/ d'en Jaume Pons Martí 12; 📞 872 08 01 45; w sunsetjazz-club.com; 🕑 19.00–01.30 Mon & Thu, 19.00–02.30 Fri–Sat, 19.00–midnight Sun. Atmospheric jazz club in a cellar with regular live gigs on the small stage, cocktails, wine & a warm, friendly atmosphere.

SPORTS AND ACTIVITIES

Cicloturisme i Medi Ambient [187 A4] C/ Santa Eugènia 11, Girona; 📞 972 22

10 47; w cicloturisme.com/giro. Cycling holidays in the area – whether you want

to pedal with the family for a day, or scale mountain passes for a week or more, as well as bike rental.

Golf Girona [187 B1] Santa Julià de Ramis; ✆972 17 16 41; w golfgirona.com. The most convenient course for the city.

OTHER PRACTICALITIES You'll see pharmacies on every street; they are marked with a green or red cross. The friendly **Farmàcia Altarriba** [187 C3] (Rbla de la Llibertat 18; ✆ 972 20 01 91; w canalfarmaciaonline.com/farmacia-altarriba; ⊕ 09.00–20.30 Mon–Fri, 09.00–14.00 & 16.30–20.00 Sat) is conveniently central and still has its original charming Modernista furnishings.

CaixaBank [187 B3] C/ Santa Clara 9–11. This ATM is handily located near the tourist office, but you'll find plenty all over the city.
Clínica Girona [187 B5] C/ Joan Maragall 26; ✆972 21 04 00

Hospital Universitari de Girona Doctor Josep Trueta [187 B1] Avda de Franç s/n; ✆972 94 02.00
Main post office [187 B2] Avda de Ramon Folch 2; ✆972 48 32 72; w correos.es; ⊕ 08.30–20.30 Mon–Sat

WHAT TO SEE AND DO
Catedral de Santa Maria
[187 C2] (Pl Catedral s/n; ✆ 972 42 71 89; w catedraldegirona.cat; ⊕ Nov–mid-Mar 10.00–17.00 Mon–Sat, noon–17.00 Sun; mid-Mar–mid-Jun & mid-Sep–Oct 10.00–18.00 Mon–Fri, 10.00–19.00 Sat, noon–17.00 Sun; mid-Jun–mid-Sep 10.00–20.00 Mon–Fri, 10.00–20.00 Sat, noon–17.00 Sun; (also includes to Sant Feliu) adult/reduced/under 8 €7.50/5/ free) Few cathedrals enjoy such a stupendous setting, high over the city and visible from miles around. Navigate the intimate lanes of the Barri Vell until you reach Girona's version of Rome's Spanish Steps – a majestic 18th-century stairway, with 90 steps waiting to test your piety before you reach the cathedral at the top. Its remarkable, nearly square façade pierced by its great rose window dates from the 18th century as well. The three tiers of figures are mostly replicas: the only ones spared by sentimental Anarchists are the allegories of Faith, Hope and Charity. Only one planned bell tower was ever built, topped by Girona's guardian angel – a bronze weathervane.

Yet the cathedral surpasses the grandeur of its stairs with its single nave, just under 30m across – a width surpassed only by St Peter's in Rome. Originally planned by architect Pere Sacoma as a typical three-aisled church, work began in 1347 – just in time for the Black Death, which not only killed some 1,000 Gironans, but set off a long period of decline. In 1404, the new master builder, Guillem Bofill, took over, and, as the apse was completed, he devised a money-saving improvement: to replace Sacoma's planned three naves with a single great nave. His proposal was so radical that in 1416 the bishop of Girona summoned all the leading architects of Catalunya to a council to solicit their opinions as to whether or not such a cathedral would actually stand. It did, and does, a survivor of so many sieges, now threatened by something the builders never dreamed of: nummulites, minute fossils of worms in the city's limestone. Whole blocks of stone have had to be replaced.

The colossal Gothic vault soars 22.8m above the floor, supported by its interior buttresses; the poet Joan Maragall called it the 'canopy of heaven'. Look out for a host of other details: the 11th-century alabaster **high altar**; a 14th-century masterpiece of silverwork, surmounted by an equally remarkable silver-plated **canopy**; the 11th-century 'Throne of Charlemagne'; the beautiful 14th-century **alabaster tomb of Countess Ermessenda** by Guillem de Morell; the exceedingly strange painting of the *Last Supper* by Perris de la Roca (1560), where St John seems to have been replaced

6

by a woman, tucked under Christ's arm, with what looks like Mount Canigou in the background.

The trapezoidal double-colonnaded Romanesque **cloister**, built in the 12th century, is unique, and has exquisitely carved capitals, sculpted with a mix of the sacred and secular.

Treasury The cathedral boasts some exceptional treasures, starring the 11th-century **Tapestry of Creation**, which, along with the Bayeux Tapestry, is the best surviving 1,000-year-old work in textile in the west. It records a magical view of Genesis, with the Creator surrounded by sea monsters, wind-bags, the seasons, and Eve popping out of Adam's side, and much more. Equally precious is the *Código del Beatus*, an illuminated commentary on the Apocalypse from AD974, one of the most beautiful books ever made with its richly coloured and fantastically imagined Mozarabic miniatures by the monk Emeterio and the nun Eude (one of the first recorded women artists). The small **coffer of Caliph Hisham II**, a Moorish work from the 10th century, is one of the finest in Spain.

Museu d'Art de Girona
[187 C2] (Pujada de la Catedral 12; 972 20 38 34; w museuart.com; May–Sep 10.00–19.00 Tue–Sat, 10.00–14.00 Sun, 10.00–20.00 Tue–Sat, 10.00–14.00 Sun; adult/reduced/under 16 €5/4/free) More medieval delights await right next to the cathedral in this museum in the former Episcopal Palace. Exhibits include a remarkable beam, the '**Biga de Cruïlles**' dated 1200, carved and painted with funny-faced monks lined up like a chorus line; a unique 16th-century glazier's table, used by the cathedral's stained-glass makers; a beautiful 15th-century catalogue of martyrs from Bohemia; a 10th-century portable altar from Sant Pere de Rodes and a *Calvary* by Mestre Bartomeu (13th century), with a serenely smiling Christ with a face like Shiva, ready to dance off the Cross.

There are a pair of exceptional 15th-century altarpieces: the *retable of Púbol* by Gothic master Bernat Martorell, and one from Sant Miquel de Cruïlles by Lluís Borrassà. Upstairs, there are rooms of 19th- and 20th-century Catalan paintings, with a selection of landscapes by Joachim Vayreda and others of the Olot school.

Portal de Sobreportes
[187 C2] Back down the 90 steps from the cathedral, turn right and pass through this medieval gateway flanked by two round towers. The huge stones of their bases pre-date even the Romans, and there's a niche hollowed out on top for a statue of 'Our Lady of Good Death' invoked by the unfortunates led through the gate on their way to execution.

Sant Feliu
[187 C2] (Pujada de Sant Feliu, 29; 972 20 14 07; w catedraldegirona. cat; 10.00–18.00 Mon–Sat, 13.00–18.00 Sun; (also includes entry to cathedral) adult/reduced/under 8 €7.50/5/free) This 13th–17th-century church stands at the summit of its own smaller flight of stairs. Like the cathedral, it only received one of its two planned towers – a stone filigree one that had its point knocked off by a streak of lightning. The church stands over an early Christian cemetery, where the city's first bishop and patron Saint Narcís 'of the Flies' suffered martyrdom in AD307. He is honoured in an 18th-century chapel, where a painting illustrates the origins of his unusual sobriquet: during the siege of 1285, when French invaders broke open his tomb, an angry swarm of monster flies emerged and bit the soldiers to death. It was a lesson the French never forgot in their subsequent 24 sieges of Girona – whatever they did, they didn't mess with Narcís – but Girona never forgot the saint's big moment, and you can still buy chocolate *mosques* (flies) in the local pastry shops.

Set inside Sant Feliu's presbytery walls are two Roman and six Palaeochristian **sarcophagi** with fine carvings: one shows a vigorous lion hunt, another Pluto carrying away Persephone into the depths of hell. There's a replica of Girona's most famous statue, the 12th-century **Leonessa**, in Plaça Sant Feliu, whose bottom needs to be kissed if you're considering a move here.

Banys Àrabs
[187 C2] (C/ Ferran el Catòlic s/n; ☎972 19 09 69; w banysarabs. cat; ◷ 10.00–18.00 Mon–Sat, 10.00–14.00 Sun; adult/reduced/under 8 €3/1/free) Turning right after the Portal de Sobreportes, a door in a wall leads to the 12th-century, best-preserved public baths in Catalunya, built by Morisco craftsmen, its beautiful tiled pool illuminated within by an elegant, eight-sided oculus on slender Roman columns. It functioned into the 16th century.

Museu d'Arqueologia
[187 C1] (C/ Santa Llúcia 8; ☎972 20 26 32; w macgirona. cat; ◷ 10.00–19.00 Mon–Sat, 10.00–14.00 Sun; adult/reduced/under 16 €7/5/ free) Across the Galligants River from the baths stand two attractive 12th-century churches: tiny **Sant Nicolau** with its three apses, and the elegant Monestir de **Sant Pere Galligants**, with a striking tower and a beautiful little Romanesque cloister, its capitals sculpted with plants, animals and scenes from the childhood of Christ. It's now a stunning setting for the city's archaeology museum, with Neolithic, Iberian, Greek and Roman finds displayed around the nave and cloister.

After visiting the museum, take a historic walk. The **Passeig Arqueològic** [187 C1] offers a stroll along the Galligants amid medieval walls, towers, springs and gardens to the pretty Vall de Sant Daniel, where Countess Ermessenda (who helped finance the building of the cathedral) founded a convent in the 11th century. Here the lofty 11th-century **Torre de Carlemagne** [187 D1] is one of several access points to the delightful **Passeig de la Muralla** [187 D2], a narrow walkway along the city ramparts once reserved for patrolling soldiers, which allows you stroll among the rooftops and towers of the Barri Vell.

Museu d'Historia de la Ciutat
[187 C2] (C/ de la Força 27; ☎972 22 22 29; w web2.girona.cat/museuhistoria/cat/index.php; ◷ May–Sep 10.30–18.30 Tue–Sat & 10.30–13.30 Sun, Oct–Apr 10.30–17.30 Tue–Sat & 10.30–13.30 Sun; adult/reduced/under 16 €4.20/2.10/free) This museum occupies a 15th-century townhouse that was later converted into a Capuchin convent; exhibits cover everything from prehistoric pots to Roman milestones and a lively mosaic of a chariot race (AD300), to paintings of the 1809 Siege and relics of the Civil War and Franco years. Other highlights include the Tarlà, a puppet version of a local man who during the Black Death, when the city was quarantined, went out and entertained children with bizarre dances on a beam suspended over the street.

El Call: Jewish Girona
Carrer de la Força defined the western border of Girona's Call. At its height, in the 1200s, this intricate little ghetto counted some 1,000 souls and the most important school of Jewish mysticism in the west. As in Barcelona and Tarragona, Girona's Call came under the direct authority of the crown, enjoying autonomy from the municipal council, the Jurats. The count-kings regarded the Jewish communities as a national resource and favoured them, but they also made use of these enclaves to meddle in city affairs.

This created no end of tensions over the years; the Jurats, egged on by a fanatical clergy and jealous debtors, isolated Girona's Call into an almost windowless ghetto with only one entrance. During Easter people would gather to throw stones on it

6

from the heights of the cathedral. During the persecutions of 1391, many Jews were killed; after a century of decline and restrictions culminating in the expulsions of 1492, the Call was built over and forgotten.

In the 1970s, when people began to return their attention to the Barri Vell, a local restaurateur bought up some of the buildings here, excavated the old stones and streets and discovered the *yeshiva* (learning centre) and had the Star of David laid on the patio. In 1987, the local authorities purchased the property, and made it into the **Centra Bonastruc Ça Porta** [187 C2]. The centre's **Museu d'Història dels Jueus** [187 C2] (C/ de la Força 8; ☏972 21 67 61; w girona.cat/call/eng/index.php; ⊕ Jul– Aug 10.00–19.00 Tue–Sat & 10.00–14.00 Sun–Mon; Sep–Jun 10.00–18.00 Tue–Sat & 10.00–14.00 Sun–Mon; adult/reduced/under 14 €4/2/free) charts the history of the Jews in Catalunya and houses an important collection of funerary stones. It is home to the **Institut d'Estudis Nahmànides**, dedicated to medieval Jewish studies.

The Call to the Rambla de la Llibertat
From the Call, follow Carrer de la Força and Carrer Peralita south to one of Girona's most photographed corners, the **Pujada de Sant Domènec**, a little poem of urban design where the beautiful Renaissance **Casa dels Agullanas** [187 C3] arches gracefully over the bifurcating steps; the elaborate façade atop the right-hand stair belongs to the 16th-century church **Sant Martí**. Above Sant Martí, the 14th-century **Dominican convent** is now used by university students instead of the militant friars who were proud to be known as the Domini canes, the 'hounds of the Lord'.

Further south, just off Plaça del l'Oli, in little Carrer del Sac, a star marks the house where, on 1 January 1900 Rumba King **Xavier Cugat** was born. His family moved to Havana five years later, and he attained fame and fortune in America while conducting his band with a baton in one hand and holding a chihuahua in the other. When Cugat died in 1990, he was brought home and buried in Girona.

Carrer dels Ciutadans, south of Plaça del l'Oli, was the fancy address of stately mansions: one, the enormous Romanesque-Gothic **Fontana d'Or** [187 C3], has a lovely garden courtyard usually open to the public. At the end of Carrer dels Ciutadans stands Girona's **Ajuntament** [187 C3] in handsome, arcaded Plaça del Vi, the former wine market, along with the 19th-century **Municipal Theatre**, where two Catalan *gegants* stand vigil, waiting for a holiday, when they're allowed to sally forth and menace the children. Most of the action, however, is concentrated in Girona's favourite street, the delightful porticoed **Rambla de la Llibertat** that runs parallel to the Onyar River, lined with bars and boutiques.

Riu Onyar
This river divides medieval Girona from its newer quarters on the left bank. In 1876, the Gustave Eiffel firm built the most striking of the footbridges that lace the city together, the **Pont de les Peixateries Velles** [187 C3] ('bridge of the old fishmongers') which even looks a bit like a fishnet in iron. From here, there's a beautiful view of houses in a dozen shades of ochre built up directly over the Onyar as if it were a Venetian canal. It wasn't always this way: the houses long served as an outer defensive wall to the river's moat. After the last siege people began to open windows, galleries and balconies in the walls, and in the 1980s local architects fixed them up and painted the façades with an Italian flair. One of them, the **Casa Masó** [187 C2] (C/ Ballesteries 29; ☏972 41 39 89; w rafaelmaso.org; ⊕ guided visits only, available Tue–Sat with flexible timings, book online; adult/reduced/under 16 €10/5/free), belonged to acclaimed Girona architect Rafael Masó (1880–1935), and has been beautifully restored and opened to the public. It's full of exquisite Noucentista furnishings and artworks.

The Onyar's fat carp glide under the nattering ducks, while the reflections lead to jokes about exactly which Narcissus is the city's patron – the saintly one 'of the flies' or the one in love with his own beauty.

Girona's left bank Even by the Middle Ages the city had begun to expand to the left bank, the Barri del Mercadal. In 1855, Girona demolished an Augustine monastery to create the handsome arcaded **Plaça de la Independència** [187 C2], a favourite place for people-watching, with a monument dedicated to the defenders of 1809 in the centre. Carrer Santa Clara is the main street here, lined with shops; two streets south of Plaça de la Independència, Carrer Obra leads to the **Museu del Cinema** [187 B3] (Tomàs Mallol Collection; C/ Sèquia 1; ✆972 41 27 77; w girona.cat/turisme/eng/museus_cinema.php; ◷ Jul–Aug 10.00–19.00 Mon–Sat, 10.00–14.00 Sun, Sep–Jun 10.00–18.00 Mon–Sat, 10.00–14.00 Sun; adult/reduced/under 14 €7/5.50/free). Filmmaker Tomàs Mallol not only collected equipment and memorabilia from the early days of cinema, but also the mirrors, shadow puppets, magic lanterns and other items used to illustrate stories, pre-celluloid.

The Barri Mercadal has a handful of buildings designed by Rafael Masó, Girona's most celebrated Noucentista architect, whose birthplace and home can be visited (page 192). His masterpiece, the **Farinera Teixidor** [187 A3], at Carrer de Santa Eugènia 42, behind the train station, has a curving roof and pinnacle clad in white ceramics to resemble the flour that was originally milled here. He also designed the **Casa de la Punxa** opposite, named after its pinnacle which wears a jaunty green ceramic wizard's hat.

Parc de la Devesa [187 A2] The park extends along the banks of the Ter, where you can often see cormorants diving in the water. With its neatly ordered grove of 2,500 plane trees, it's a delicious retreat on a hot day; in summer the park fills up with bars and restaurants, where there's often something musical or theatrical happening.

FIGUERES

As the birthplace of Dalí, Figueres (originally Roman Juncaria on the Via Augusta) could claim to be the world capital of Surrealism. It could have made his museum into a major tourist factory. Think of all the mileage Memphis gets out of Elvis. But Figueres doesn't do anything of the sort. Instead, it has fun being a kind of anti-Girona; in contrast to the medieval, romantic city of dark alleys, Figueres is youthful and a bit kooky from having its brainbox battered by the tramuntana, which blows 60 days of the year.

GETTING THERE AND AROUND
By train Regional trains from Barcelona to France (lines RG1 and RG11) stop at the station in the city centre (Pl Estació s/n; w renfe.com), while the high-speed lines stop at AV Figueres Vilafant (C/ de les Pedreres, Vilafant), 1.5km west of the centre. A shuttle bus service operates between the two stations.

By bus The bus station is located next to the regional train station (Pl Estació 17) and is the main hub for the bus network to the upper Costa Brava. Sarfa-Moventis buses (✆972 33 78 42; w moventis.es) run regularly from Figueres to Roses and Cadaqués.

By car Figures can be reached by the A-7 motorway or the N-260. On-street parking is difficult to find: spaces with green road markings are for residents, blue

6

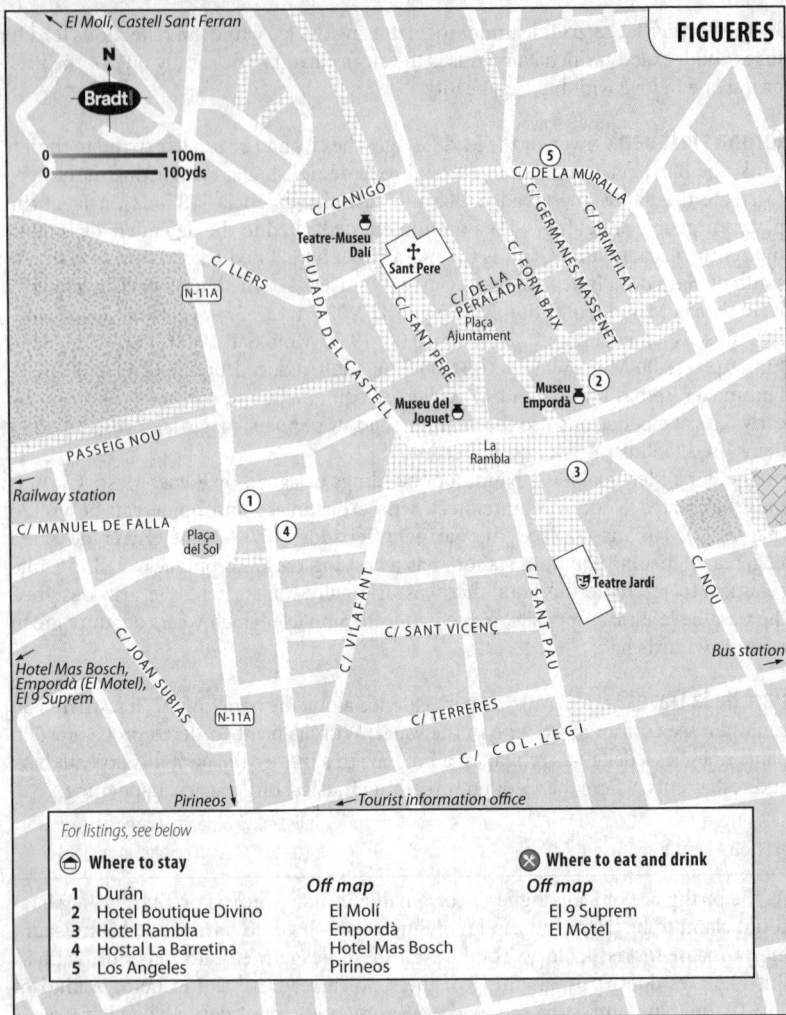

FIGUERES

El Molí, Castell Sant Ferran

Bradt

| 0 | 100m |
| 0 | 100yds |

C/ CANIGÓ

Teatre-Museu Dalí

Sant Pere

C/ LLERS

N-11A

PUJADA DEL CASTELL

C/ SANT PERE

C/ DE LA PERALADA

Plaça Ajuntament

C/ FORN BAIX

C/ GERMANES MASENET

C/ DE LA MURALLA

C/ PRIMFILAT

Museu del Joguet

Museu Empordà

La Rambla

PASSEIG NOU

Railway station

C/ MANUEL DE FALLA

Plaça del Sol

C/ VILAFANT

C/ SANT VICENÇ

C/ SANT PAU

Teatre Jardí

C/ NOU

Bus station

Hotel Mas Bosch, Empordà (El Motel), El 9 Suprem

C/ JOAN SUBIAS

N-11A

C/ TERRERES

C/ COL·LEGI

Pirineos

Tourist information office

For listings, see below

🛏 **Where to stay**

1 Durán
2 Hotel Boutique Divino
3 Hotel Rambla
4 Hostal La Barretina
5 Los Angeles

Off map

El Molí
Empordà
Hotel Mas Bosch
Pirineos

✖ **Where to eat and drink**

Off map

El 9 Suprem
El Motel

is for everyone. Pay at the meters. The underground car parks are usually the safest bet: the most central are at Plaça Catalunya and by the regional train station at Carrer de Joan Arderius 2.

TOURIST INFORMATION The main tourist information office (Pl de l'Escorxador 2; ☎972 50 31 55; w en.visitfigueres.cat; ⊕ 09.30–18.00 Mon–Sat, 10.00–15.00 Sun) occupies a Modernista building that was once an abattoir in the city centre. The friendly staff can provide info on the many guided tours they offer, with themes from local gastronomy to the Spanish Civil War.

🏠 **WHERE TO STAY AND EAT** *Map, above*
Hotel Mas Bosch 1526 Les Tres Cases s/n; ☎972 56 01 55; w hotelmasbosch1526.com. A tranquil country hotel set in a 16th-century *masia* about 3km west of the city centre, with about a dozen dreamy rooms, a romantic wine bar & a pool in the gardens. €€€€

Durán C/ Lasauca 5; ☎ 972 50 12 50;
w hotelduran.com. Right on the Rambla since
1855, the Durán offers 65 modern rooms furnished
in a classic style. Dalí, who loved good food, often
held court in the hotel's renowned restaurant
(€€€); try the *sarsuela amb llagosta* (fish stew
with lobster). €€€

Empordà 3km north on Ctra N11, Km763; ☎ 972
50 05 62; w hotelemporda.com. A mythic place,
overlooking pretty countryside on the road to
France. Founded in 1961 by Josep Mercader, the
great pioneer in the revival of gourmet Catalan
cuisine, the **El Motel** restaurant (€€€€), which
passed to the hands of his son-in-law Jaume
Subirós & grandchildren, remains one of the
best, acclaimed for its imaginative adaptations of
regional specialities. Game dishes are a speciality,
as are Mercader's original broad bean & mint
salad & *taps de Cadaqués* – delicious Champagne-
cork-shaped cakes. Rooms are spacious & well-
equipped, if rather bland. €€€

El Molí Ctra Pont de Molins a les Escaules
(just north of Figueres); ☎ 972 52 92 71;
w hotelelmoli.es. Rooms filled with heirloom
furniture in a 17th-century watermill on the
River Muga, which gurgles a lullaby for peaceful
slumbers. Good traditional Catalan restaurant
(€€€) too, under the stone vaults & with a
delightful terrace. €€€

✳ **Hotel Boutique Divino** C/ Enginyers 2;
☎ 972 98 00 66; w hotel-divino.com. An arty little
boutique hotel slap bang in the city centre, with
striking, individually decorated rooms & some
extraordinary, often Surrealist, artworks. Service is
exceptional. €€€

Los Angeles C/ Barceloneta 10; ☎ 972 51 06 61;
w hotelangeles.com. Simple, reliable mid-sized
hotel with traditionally furnished rooms only 5min
from the Teatre-Museu Dalí. €€

Hotel Rambla La Rambla 33; ☎ 972 67 60 20;
w hotelrambla.net. Fantastically central, right
on the Rambla, this mid-sized, family-run hotel
offers spacious, if rather dated, rooms & a warm
welcome. It also has handy lockers for storing
luggage & bikes.

Pirineos Avda de Salvador Dalí i Domènech 68;
☎ 972 50 03 12; w pirineoshotelfigueres.com. Crisp,
functional rooms & a good restaurant (€€) are on
offer at this modern hotel, handily located about a
10min walk from the Dalí museum. It doesn't ooze
charm, but it offers excellent value. €€

Hostal La Barretina C/ Lasauca 13; ☎ 972 67
64 12; w hostallabarretina.com. A simple, old-
fashioned guesthouse, with basic rooms & a classic
restaurant (€€) serving Catalan cuisine, just off La
Rambla. €

El 9 Suprem C/ Llobregat 4; ☎ 972 09 83 00;
📷 9suprem; 🕑 08.00–17.00 Mon–Sat. This
modern restaurant doesn't look too fancy, but the
food is consistently voted among the best by locals.
Delicious, creative Catalan cuisine, including an
excellent set lunch. €€€€

WHAT TO SEE AND DO
Teatre-Museu Dalí (Pujada del Castell 28; ☎ 972 67 75 00; w salvador-dali.org;
🕑 Jan–Mar, mid-May–Jun & Oct–Dec 10.30–18.00 Tue–Sun; Apr–mid-May & Sep
09.30–18.00 Tue–Sun; Jul–Aug 09.00–20.00 daily; Sep–Jun adult/reduced €18/15
or €26/23 with guided visit, Jul–Aug adult/reduced €21.50/17.50 or €29.50/25.50
with guided visit. There is a €2 surcharge for all tickets bought at ticket office rather
than online.)

Forget the Vatican: this is 'the spiritual centre of Europe' according to Dalí, who
opened this museum in 1974 in a merry reconstruction of Figueres' municipal
theatre, which had been badly damaged in the Civil War. The building itself is a
Surrealist work of art. Its landmark Galatea Tower wears a garland of eggs and is
covered in a meticulously tidy pattern of ceramic turds. St Peter's in Rome is topped
by statues of halo-ed saints; here they beckon with loaves of bread on their heads.

Expect surprises at every turn – and allow at least 3 hours to see it all. Giant
figures of Dalí and Gala rocket to the heavens on the trompe l'œil ceiling; Dalí's
1948 installation *Cadillac* has a system to sprinkle its snail-covered mannequin
occupants. In a more serious vein, it also houses some of Dalí's most iconic
paintings: the early light-filled *Port Alguer* (1924), *The Spectrum of Sex Appeal* (1932),
Soft Self-Portrait with Fried Bacon (1941), *Poetry from America, the Cosmic Athletes*

6

The difference between me and a madman is that I am not mad.

– Salvador Dalí

It's a shame that this outrageous megalomaniac, so obsessed with immortality, didn't live forever. Salvador Felipe Jacinto Dalí i Domènech was born in Figueres on 11 May 11 1904 at Carrer Monturiol 10, the son of a well-to-do notary. One might say even his conception and birth were surreal: he was born almost exactly nine months after the death of his two-year-old brother, who was also named Salvador, which left him convinced that he was his brother's reincarnation.

His precocious talent for art was encouraged by his father's best friend, artist Raymond Pixot, the father of Dalí's collaborator. Not long after Dalí's mother died in 1921, he was admitted to the Academia San Fernando in Madrid. He wrote in his diary of the time: 'The world will admire me. Perhaps I'll be despised and misunderstood, but I'll be a great genius, I'm certain of it.'

Gifted with an impeccable technique, endlessly creative, and capable of painting in any style he put his hand to, Dalí became the most famous of the Surrealists while still in his twenties, when he painted his first 'hand-painted dream photographs' of melting watches and human bodies fitted with sets of spilling drawers. During the Civil War he offered to go to Barcelona and run a Department for the Irrational Organisation of Daily Life (only to be told: thanks anyway, it already exists).

(1943), *The Bread Basket* (1945), and *Atomic Leda* (1949), and larger works, such as the wonderful *Face of Mae West Which Can Be Used as an Apartment*, plus Dalí's collection of works by other artists.

The old wizard lived his final years in an apartment in the Torre Galatea, at the side of his collaborator Antoni Pixot, who remained museum director until 2015. After his death, Dalí was embalmed in a fluid guaranteed to keep his body intact for two centuries, and buried – controversial to the bitter end – under the glass dome in the museum, not far from the toilets. Dalí began designing gold and precious gems back in 1941. An annexe to the museum, **Dalí-Joies**, contains 39 exquisite pieces.

Sant Pere (C/ Sant Pere 8; ☎ 972 50 03 25; ⊕ 09.00–18.00 daily; free) Opposite the museum, this tall, startling clean-looking Gothic church was built by King Pere the Ceremonious in 1378, but much reconstructed after being pillaged and burned by Anarchists and bombarded by Franco in the Civil War. In its day it witnessed a royal wedding: in 1701, King Philip V married Maria Louisa of Savoy here. It later witnessed the baptism, first communion and funeral of Dalí.

Along La Rambla Little survives of medieval Figueres, but a short walk down from the museum you'll come to the town's handsome Rambla, built like Barcelona's over a foul-smelling stream in 1832 and lined with towering plane trees. Monuments honour the city's famous sons: Dalí's face is reflected in a funhouse mirror of a bright lipstick-like tube, and an elaborate Noucentista memorial by Enric Casanovas honours Narcís Monturiol i Estarriol (1819– 85), who invented the first, partially working combustion-powered submarines.

There are several Modernista buildings in Figueres: one of the prettiest is the **Teatre Jardí**, one street back from La Rambla, in Plaça Josep Pla.

He and his wife Gala would later move to the United States, living there full-time from 1940 to 1948. If other Surrealists drew their inspiration from the irrational well of the unconscious, Dalí claimed his came from 'critical paranoia' – a carefully cultivated delusion, a conscious suspension of rational thought, a way of art and life. Part of his paranoia came from his fear of madness – his grandfather, reportedly driven mad by the wind, took his own life. Some have argued that the public bluster, provocation and showmanship was only a screen that allowed Dalí the space back in Port Lligat to investigate his personal obsessions and anguish (he was apparently impotent) with remarkable candour. When not at work, he went about offending everyone, not worrying that the art world considered him a publicity-mongering, money-grubbing buffoon (André Breton, the 'pope' of Surrealism, famously excommunicated him).

Essentially apolitical, he was the one Catalan artist to get along with Franco, but on the whole Spain's conservatives didn't like him much. Like a gadfly, he broke art taboos right and left – cheerfully painting religious kitsch (all the while arguing that Jesus Christ was made of cheese), 'selling out' by doing some very funny television commercials, designing the logo for Chupa Chups lollipops; he may even have been behind forgeries of his own work (page 176). As a posthumous insult to Catalunya, he left everything to the Spanish state. Although with this museum, the house at Portlligat, and the castle at Púbol, the arty anchors of Costa Brava's rejuvenation, Catalunya didn't do too badly.

Museu dels Joguet (Toy Museum) (C/ Sant Pere 1; ☎972 50 45 85; w mjc.cat; ⏰ mid-Mar–Jun & Sep–Dec 10.30–18.00 Tue–Fri & 10.30–19.00 Sat, Jul 10.30–19.00 daily, Aug 10.30–19.30 daily; adult/reduced €8/6.50) This fascinating and enjoyably interactive museum houses some 4,000 toys, including some once played with by Lorca, Miró and Dalí, plus an impressive collection of *caganers*.

Museu Empordà (Rbla 2; ☎972 50 23 05; w museuemporda.org; ⏰ 10.00–19.00 Tue–Sat, 10.00–14.00 Sun; adult/reduced €5/2.50, free with entry to Teatre-Museu Dalí) Handsomely remodelled in 2025, this museum displays Catalan painting from artists including Miró, Tàpies and Dalí in glossy new galleries, plus archaeological and historical items (ceramics from ancient Empúries, Roman glass, capitals and more from Sant Pere de Rodes) fill the halls.

Castell Sant Ferran (Pujada del Castell s/n; ☎972 50 60 94; w castellsantferran. com; ⏰ Jul–Aug 10.00–20.00 daily, Sep–Jun 10.30–18.00 Tue–Sun; adult/reduced €5/3.50. Note that, given the size of this fortress, visits are divided into three areas: the interior, the subterranean waterways (includes a boat trip) and the exterior (a 4x4 trip with guide around the moat). You must reserve in advance for the latter two by phone: ☎972 50 60 94 or 667 699 702.) On a hill above the Dalí museum sprawls the jumbo pentagonal Castell Sant Ferran, Europe's second-largest fort. Although the Treaty of the Pyrenees established the frontier with France at Pertús in 1659, King Fernando VI still didn't entirely trust the French and ordered the construction of this fort in 1753. The story goes that his courtiers once found the king in his gardens in Madrid, staring towards the northeast; when asked what he was looking at, he replied that, given the money he was spending, he reckoned he should be able to see the fort from Madrid!

6

It didn't even keep the French out – Napoleon's armies grabbed it twice. During the Civil War, it served for a week in 1939 as the last bastion of the Spanish Republican government, when for a brief while Figueres was the capital of Republican Spain.

THE ALT EMPORDÀ

The country around Figueres is pure Mediterranean, an idyll of vines, cork oaks, cypresses and olives, and astonishingly unspoiled – 99% of people driving to Spain barrel down the motorway and never get off. Signs on rutted tracks lead up to dolmens, which are exceptionally plentiful, as are bodegas where city-slickers come to stock up on wine. Quite a few foreigners have fixed up farms and houses in the nearly abandoned villages of the **Serra de l'Albera**, giving them a fresh lease on life. The Serra itself is a nature reserve – based in Figueres, you can easily spend a day or two exploring.

WHERE TO STAY

Hotel Peralada C/ Robertí, Peralada; 972 53 88 30; w hotelperalada.com. With vast, stylish rooms in a soothing palate of cream & grey, a spa inspired by the Empordà wines (it has its own winery in a Pritzker-prize-winning building), outstanding restaurant (€€€) with a Michelin star, a pool in the extensive gardens & even its own golf course, this ultra-luxurious country resort has everything you need for a pampering break. €€€€

Can Xiquet Afores s/n, Cantallops; 972 55 44 55; w hotelcanxiquet.com. Comfortable hotel & excellent restaurant (€€€) & gorgeous views from the rooms, a wide range of activities: outdoor pool, gym, excursions in the Albera nature reserve, cooking courses & tastings, & much more. €€€

Hotel & Spa la Central Antiga Carretera de Darnius, Maçanet de Cabrenys; 972 53 50 53; w hotelspalacentral.com. A pretty Modernista chalet with stylish rooms in a gorgeous setting, overlooking a lovely, tree-shaded river. It offers spa treatments & plenty of suggestions for excursions, & hires out boats, bikes & fishing tackle. The restaurant serves delicious modern Catalan cuisine & local wines. €€€

Hotel Castell de Vallgornera Camí de Vallgornera, Peralada; 651 14 61 71; w castelldevallgornera.com. This enchanting little rural hotel is set in a castle that dates back to the 12th century, with views over vines & rolling hills. There is just a handful of romantic, tastefully decorated rooms & a shady garden with a pool. €€€

Hotel Restaurant Els Caçadors Urbanización Casa Nova, Maçanet de Cabrenys; 972 54 41 36; w hotelelscassadors.com. There are 17 impeccable rooms at this inviting hotel, but the real draw is the excellent restaurant (€€€), where you can enjoy creative Catalan cuisine prepared with the finest local produce. €€€

La Fornal dels Ferrers C/ Major 31, Terrades; 972 56 90 95; w lafornal.com. The antique-filled 18th-century 'Smithy's Smith' offers 4 romantic rooms & a lovely restaurant (€€€) with a garden, & a special cherry menu in season. €€€

Can Garriga C/ Figueres, 3, Garriguella; 610 92 31 62; w can-garriga.com. Peaceful little B&B in a traditional stone house; 3 antique-filled bedrooms & 3 apartments sleeping 4–8 people. €€

Hotel de la Font C/ Baixada de la Font 15–19, Peralada; 972 53 85 07; w hoteldelafont.com. Comfortable little hotel with 12 rooms, occupying a former convent & its pretty cloister. €€

Hostal Rural Can Xicu Pl del Fort 12, Capmany; 659 08 49 66; w momentsrurals.com. An ancient stone house now contains this small guesthouse, with stylish rooms set around a wonderful Gothic courtyard. There's a garden where you can relax & continental b/fasts are served. €€

WHERE TO EAT AND DRINK

Ca la Maria C/ Unió 5, Mollet de Peralada; 972 56 33 82; w restaurantcalamaria.net; ⏱ 12.45–15.00 Mon & Thu–Sun. Since 1960, one of the most popular restaurants in the Alt Empordà, set in an 18th-century cellar & serving big helpings of rabbit, kid, duck & pork dishes. €€€

Carles Antoner Pl Major 2, Lladó; ☎972 55 37 11; 📷 carlesantonerrestaurant; ⏰ 09.00–17.00 Mon, Thu & Sun, 09.00–17.00 & 20.00–22.30 Fri–Sat Small, rustic, creative Catalan cuisine based on the daily market in the heart of a medieval village. Dishes might include secret of pork with truffle, or smoked aubergine with squid ink pasta. €€€

Can Tenli C/ Dómines 11, Maçanet de Cabrenys; ☎972 54 40 51; w cantenli.com; ⏰ 09.00–16.00 Tue–Fri & Sun, 09.00–16.00 & 20.00–22.00 Sun. A beloved local favourite, which has been serving up excellent, traditional cuisine since 1977. Their star dish is cod (*bacallà*), prepared according to a family recipe passed down from Grandma Maria. €€

WHAT TO SEE AND DO

Peralada In 1270 Peralada was the birthplace of the medieval chronicler Ramon Muntaner. Muntaner joined the Almogàvers, a feared and ruthless band of mercenaries who dressed in animal skins and fought under the command of former German-Italian Knight Templar Roger de Flor in 1302, stirring up all kinds of trouble in Sicily and the Eastern Mediterranean. Muntaner survived to retire and record his *Crònica*, one of the main sources of Catalan medieval history. He would have known Peralada's 13th-century Dominican monastery, of which only the cloister survives.

The village's main focus, however, is the 16th-century **Castell de Peralada** of the Rocabertí family, former Counts of Empordà, with its two round crenellated fairytale towers smothered in ivy. It houses a casino and hosts a major music festival in July and August. Nearby, the former Carmelite convent contains the **Castell de Peralada Museum** (Pl del Carme s/n; ☎972 53 81 25; w museucastellperalada.com; ⏰ guided tours only, which are held Jun–Sep 10.00, 11.00, noon, 15.30, 16.30 & 17.30 Mon–Sat, 10.00, 11.00 & noon Sun; Oct–Mar 10.00, 11.00, noon, 16.00, 17.00, 18.00 & 19.00 Mon–Sat & 10.00, 11.00 & noon Sun. There are separate tours of the museum & the park; adult/reduced/under 10 €11/7/free) which includes a library famous for a thousand editions of Don Quixote, an atmospheric wine museum, and a museum of glass, with enamels and delicate pretty pieces going back to Roman times. The castle is also a leading maker of DO Empordà wines and excellent cavas and offers a variety of tastings and tours.

Serra de l'Albera This Serra is one of the last native habitats for the Hermann's tortoise in Spain; north of Peralada in Garriguella, you can visit the **Centre de Reproducció de Tortugues de l'Albera** (Santuari de la Mare de Déu del Camp; ☎972 55 22 45; w tortugues.cat; ⏰ mid-Mar–Jun & Sep–Oct 10.00–13.00 Tue–Sat, Jul–Aug 10.00–15.00 daily; adult/under 4 €7/free) and learn all about them. The area also has an important concentration of dolmens – **Espollo** even has a dolmen fountain, as well as the **Albera Nature Reserve's Centre d'Informació** (C/ Amadeu Sudrià 3; ☎972 54 50 79; w parcsnaturals.gencat.cat/ca/xarxa-de-parcs/albera/inici/index.html; ⏰ 09.00–14.00 Mon–Thu, 09.00–14.00 &16.00–19.00 Fri, 10.00–14.00 & 15.00–19.00 Sat–Sun; free) where you can learn the locations of two dozen other megaliths around the village and nearby **Sant Climent Sescebes**. Sant Climent also has something you don't see every day: a falconry school (Escola de la Falconeria).

The landmark at **Rabós**, further up the GI603, is an impressive fortified church, but an even more impressive one waits further up the road, in the wild dolmen-dotted **Serra de la Mala Veína**, the fortified **Monestir de Sant Quirze de Colera** (not currently open to the public, but occasionally used to host concerts) consecrated in AD935 and renovated in 1123. The Benedictines here once held extensive estates and vineyards in Empordà and Roussillon; the basilica has three naves and barrel vaulting with traces of frescoes, and stands next to the 11th-century abbot's house and scant remains of the cloister. There's a restaurant in the former stables.

6

Pretty little **Capmany** to the west is a wine centre, with another important group of dolmens. It's close to the bustling frontier town of **La Jonquera**, the last motorway stop in Spain, as busy these days as Portbou is empty, brimful of car parks, restaurants, petrol stations and allegedly the two biggest brothels in Spain. As it's illegal for big rigs to circulate on Sundays in France, it becomes a huge festival of trucks every weekend.

A side road, however, leads up to another world altogether: the medieval village of **Cantallops** and the romantic **Castell de Requesens** rising high above a lush green cork forest on the French border. The first castle was built on the site by the Empordà counts in the 9th century AD, and, a thousand years later, the Count of Peralada rebuilt it as a summer retreat; it suffered decades of depredations as a Guardia Civil barracks, but is fascinating nonetheless, even in its funky state.

Northwest of Figueres: Llers and around There isn't much shaking these days in **Llers**, but that wasn't always the case; although flattened by the Nazi Condor Legion during the Civil War, the village still has the raggedly jumbled ruins of one of Catalunya's most notorious castles, belonging in the 1170s to Count Guifré Estruc – who may well have been the world's oldest vampire. The story goes that he set out to convert the last local pagans to Christianity, only to earn himself their curses instead. And, unlike the outcome one expects in pious stories, this time the bad guys won; Count Estruc returned home to Llers, terrorising the locals, sucking their blood and raping their women and fathering monsters. In the end, an old nun courageously went into the cemetery, dug up his body and drove a stake into his heart.

These days Llers prefers to promote its cherries, and holds a festival in early June dedicated to its sweet red beauties; **Terrades**, 6km west, boasts 100,000 cherry trees. There's a 14th-century castle, partially converted into a *masia* just south at **Vilarig**, while **Cistella** has a medieval core. The artificial lake, the **Pantà de Boadella**, has rarely been full in recent years (in 2024, at the peak of the latest drought, it was down to just 14% of its capacity), but it enjoys a beautiful setting, and the surrounding villages are a popular weekend destination. The old walled town of **Sant Llorenç de la Muga** has a very picturesque, fortified 14th-century bridge, and **Maçanet de Cabrenys**, set in cork oak forests, boasts a striking menhir, the **Pedra Dreta**, on the edge of town.

NORTHWEST OF GIRONA: LA GARROTXA

Gironans are fortunate in their choice of weekend destinations: if they don't fancy a Costa Brava beach, or Barcelona, or the Pyrenees, they can make a short hop just northwest of the city to the arcadian landscapes of the Pla de l'Estany and La Garrotxa, dotted with some 30 well-preserved volcanic cones that last flipped their lids some 11,500 years ago. People come to walk around the craters, or fly over them in balloons and eat in the excellent restaurants.

GETTING THERE AND AWAY No train lines run in this area.

By bus The Olot bus station is at Carrer Bisbe Lorenzana 15 (◊972 26 01 96). The principal bus operator in this region is Teisa (◊972 20 48 68; w teisa-bus.com), which runs buses from Girona roughly every 30 minutes to Banyoles, Besalú and Olot. Teisa also run the local bus, el Transversal, every hour between Castellfollit de la Roca, Sant Joan les Fonts and Olot. It also operates Rumbus, a special sustainable

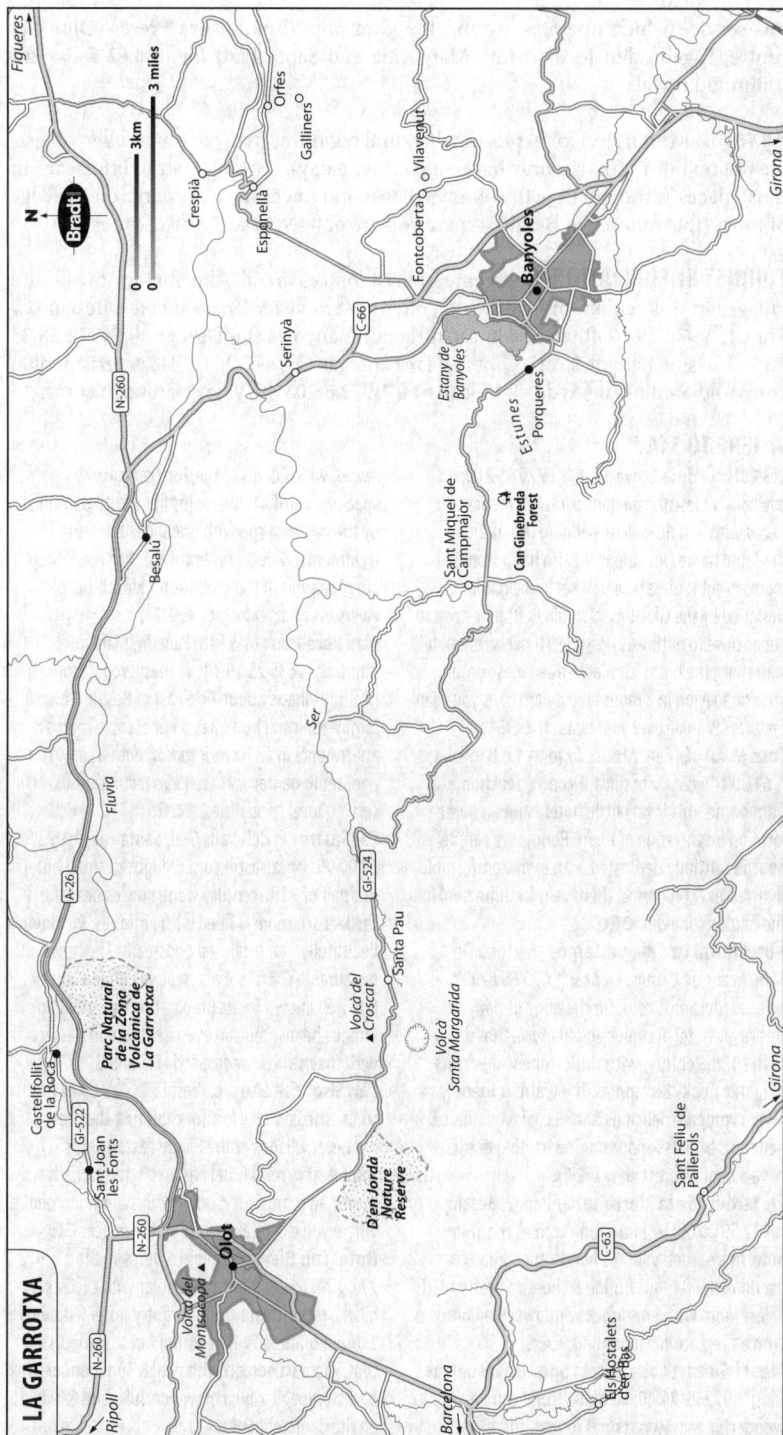

LA GARROTXA

N

Bradt

0 3km
0 3 miles

Figueres

Girona

Orfes
Galliners
Crespià
Espanella
Vilavenut
Fontcoberta
Banyoles
Serinyà
C-66
Estany de
Banyoles
Estunes
Porqueres
N-260
Besalú
Sant Miquel de
Campmajor
Can Ginebreda
Forest
Ser
Fluvià
A-26
Parc Natural
de la Zona
Volcànica de
La Garrotxa
GI-524
Volcà del
Croscat
Santa Pau
Volcà
Santa Margarida
Castellfollit
de la Roca
GI-522
Sant Joan
les Fonts
N-260
D'en Jordà
Nature
Reserve
Olot
Volcà del
Montsacopa
N-260
Sant Feliu de
Pallerols
C-63
Girona
Ripoll
Barcelona
Els Hostalets
d'en Bas

6

bus service which operates around the Olot area (linking Les Preses, Olot city centre, Fageda d'en Jordà, Santa Margarida and Santa Pau) for just €2 a day for unlimited travel.

By car A car is useful for exploring this rural region, as many of the smaller villages are not on bus routes (or only have one service a day). Parking is straightforward in most places, although note that many villages and towns have car parks on the edge of town (for example in Besalú) where you are obliged to leave your car.

TOURIST INFORMATION There are tourist offices in all the major towns and villages in this region, most of which offer guided visits. These include Besalú (C/ Pont 1; ☏ 972 59 12 40; w besalu.cat/turisme), Banyoles (Pg Darder 30; ☏ 972 58 34 70; w turisme.banyoles.cat), Olot (C/ Dr Fàbregas 6; ☏ 972 26 01 41; w turismeolot. com) and Santa Pau (Avda de Volcans 14; ☏ 972 68 03 49; w visitsantapau.com).

⌂ WHERE TO STAY

Les Cols C/ de la Canya, Olot; ☏ 972 26 92 09; pavilions w lescolspavellons.com. This medieval *masia* with a multi-award-winning restaurant of the same name (see opposite) also has 5 stunning rooms in cubic glass pavilions set in the gardens. Designed by the Olot-based studio RCR) that strive to get as close to nature as possible; showers resemble waterfalls, the baths, similar to a Japanese onsen, are akin to lying in a mountain stream, & as you lie in bed stars twinkle over your head. €€€€

Casa Maui C/ Pere Alsius i Torrent, 17, Banyoles; ☏ 613 08 46 85; w mauicasa.com. A real home from home, this lovely little hotel enjoys a quiet location on the edge of town. Rooms are simple, but thoughtfully decorated with extra comfortable mattresses & pillows, & there's a refreshing pool in the garden for a dip. €€€

Hotel Rural La Sala de Camós Rectoria De Sant Vicenç de Camós, Camós; ☏ 629 65 87 64; w lasaladecamos.com. On the edge of Banyoles, this rustic hotel occupies an old *masia* that dates to the 12th century, with thick stone walls & lots of quirky nooks & crannies. The warm & friendly owners prepare delicious home-cooked dinners & generous b/fasts for guests. The inviting gardens have a pool & forest views. €€€

Els Jardins de la Martana C/ Pont 2, Besalú; ☏ 972 59 00 09; w lamartana.com. A charming hotel in a garden villa. 11 handsome rooms overlook the famous bridge & there's a pretty tiled b/fast room with enormous windows, & a library with a fireplace for snuggling. €€€

Mas El Guitart Casa Rural i Spa Mas El Guitart, Olot; ☏ 972 29 21 40; w guitartrural.com. A wonderful, family-run rural retreat, this old stone *masia*, which dates to the 16th century, has spacious, comfortable rooms filled with paintings by the owner, a spa with massages & beauty treatments, & delicious home-cooked food. There are play areas in the grounds for kids, & bucolic views over hills & forests. €€€

Mas Pere Pau Mas Pere Pau s/n, Maià de Montcal; ☏ 635 25 19 38; w masperepau.com. In a tiny village about 7km east of Besalú, this family-run rural hotel has 5 impeccable rooms & 2 apartments in an historic *masia*, with a seawater pool set in gardens, as well as a restaurant (€€€) serving local specialities. €€€

Cal Sastre Pl dels Valls 6–9, Santa Pau; ☏ 972 68 00 95; w calsastre.com. Delightful small hotel in a pair of 15th-century stone houses near the castle. Each room is filled with antiques, including beautifully hand-painted bedsteads. The hotel restaurant (€€€) serves creative Catalan cuisine, & is well known for its preparation of Santa Pau's famous beans. You can even get them in dessert with the *menú de degustació* (€55). €€

Can Sisó Can Sisó s/n, Crespià; ☏ 628 60 41 88; w cansiso.com. Perfect for exploring the pretty medieval villages of the Pla de l'Estany, this comfortable rural hotel has just 3 traditionally furnished rooms & a garden with swimming pool where you can relax & soak up the peace. €€

Hotel Can Blanc Parajes La Deu s/n, Olot; ☏ 972 27 60 20; w canblanc.es. Popular with cyclists & hikers, this blissfully quiet country hotel with only a dozen rooms sits in beautiful forest just outside Olot. There's a garden with pool & sun loungers, bike storage, & a host of wonderful walks & rides on the doorstep. €€

Hotel L'Ast Pg Dalmau 63, Banyoles; ☎972 58 48 79; w hotelast.com. A mid-sized, modern hotel near the lake, with a pool, café, restaurant (€€€) & terrace. Spotless, functional rooms. €€
Hotel 3 Arcs C/ Ganganell 15, Besalú; ☎972 59 16 78; w hotel3arcs.com. The location – right in the heart of medieval Besalú – can't be beaten. Rooms are bright, spotless & air-conditioned, & there's a café for b/fast downstairs. €€

La Fustana C/ Girona 22–24, Maià de Moncat; ☎972 59 04 79; w lafustana.com. Eco-friendly, contemporary rural hotel located in charming village 5km east of Besalú. Very reasonably priced, tasty dinners (available on request) as well. €€
Borrell C/ Nònet Escubós 8, Olot; ☎972 27 61 61; w hotelborrell.com. Good, small, functional hotel with clean, comfortable rooms & friendly, helpful staff right in the city centre. €

✖ **WHERE TO EAT AND DRINK** A number of restaurants specialise in 'volcanic cuisine' based on ingredients from La Garrotxa's rich soil: Santa Pau beans (*fesols*), potatoes from the Vall d'en Bas, black turnips, *piumoc* cured sausage and *recuit*, a fresh cheese made with goat's milk.

Les Cols C/ de la Canya, Olot; ☎972 26 92 09; w lescols.com. This beautifully restored 13th-century house is the ancestral home of award-winning (including 2 Michelin stars) chef Fina Puigdevall, whose market-fresh, imaginative cuisine elevates the finest Garrotxa ingredients to new heights. You could also stay in their magical, glass-cube pavilions in the gardens (see opposite). €€€€
Hostal dels Ossos C/ Santa Pau s/n, km2, Batet de la Serra; ☎972 26 61 34; w hostaldelsossos. cat; ⏲ 08.30–15.30 Mon–Wed & Fri, 09.00–15.00 Thu, 8.30–16.00 Sat–Sun. A popular restaurant in a *masia* with a vine-covered terrace, famous for its succulent grilled meats (*carn a la brasa*), *guisats* (stews) & 'volcanic cuisine'. €€€
La Deu Ctra La Deu, Olot; ☎972 26 10 04; w ladeu.es; ⏲ 13.00–16.00 & 20.00–22.30 Mon–Tue & Thu–Sat, 13.00–16.00 Sun. Huge restaurant & founding member of the 'volcanic cuisine' group, specialising in the good things of the earth. The w/day set lunch (€18.80), featuring local specialities, is a bargain. €€€
Pont Vell C/ del Pont Vell 24, Besalú; ☎972 59 10 27; w restaurantpontvell.com; ⏲ 13.00–15.00 Wed–Thu & Sun, 13.00–15.30 & 20.00–21.30 Fri–Sat. An elegant restaurant in a pretty stone house that dates back to the 11th century, with a terrace overlooking the famous bridge, serving sophisticated Catalan cuisine accompanied by a fine wine list. €€€
Can Guix C/ de les Mulleras 3, Olot; ☎972 26 10 40; w canguix.cat; ⏲ 08.00–16.00 & 20.00–22.30 Mon–Tue & Thu–Sat, 08.00–16.00 Wed. Popular, family-run restaurant that has been serving up heaping portions of traditional dishes at low prices for more than half a century. €€

Can Roca C/ Carles Fortuny, Esponellà (10km north of Banyoles); ☎972 59 70 12; w restaurantcanroca.cat; ⏲ 13.00–15.30 Wed–Thu & Sun, 13.00–15.30 & 20.00–22.00 Fri–Sat. A local favourite for traditional cuisine, with meat cooked traditionally on a wood-fired grill, succulent stews & specials in season, like the stuffed artichokes in spring or wild mushrooms in winter. €€
Can Turó Mas Can Turó, Sant Privat d'en Bas; ☎972 19 62 44; ✉ restaurant_can_turo; ⏲ 13.00–15.00 Mon, 13.00–15.00 & 20.00–22.00 Fri–Sat, 13.00–16.00 Sun. Run by an enthusiastic young couple, this stone *masia* in a lovely old village is a picturesque setting for delicious, creative Catalan cuisine based on local produce. The menu is short but changes monthly, to reflect whatever is in season, & they also offer an excellent set lunch (€16.80). A real charmer. €€
Can Xabanet C/ Carmen 27, Banyoles; ☎972 57 02 52; w canxabanet.com; ⏲ 13.00–16.00 Mon–Wed & Sun, 13.00–16.00 & 20.30–23.00 Fri–Sat. A popular local spot near the lake, with generous portions of traditional cuisine & a breezy outdoor terrace. The set lunch menu (€18, available on w/days) is a bargain, & the service is warm & friendly. €€
✱ **Primera Planta Green Kitchen** C/ Verge del Carme 8 (inside the Núria Espai Social), Olot; ☎621 27 03 24; ✉ primera_planta_kitchen; ⏲ 12.30–16.30 Mon–Fri. Whether you're vegan or not, it's hard to resist these delicious, creative vegan dishes, including curries, salads, stews, all lovingly prepared. They offer a set lunch menu (€17) with 4 options in each course to choose from, as well as gorgeous homemade cakes. €

6

SPORTS AND ACTIVITIES
Hiking and biking Olot lies in the centre of two beautiful cycling/walking paths: the **Girona–Olot Via Verde del Carrilet I** and **Ripoll–Olot Via Verde del Ferro i Carbó** (start in Ripoll if you want to go downhill). It's also on the Pirinexus Route, which loops for 340km around Catalunya. For more information see **w** viesverdes. cat. Bikes, including electric bikes, can be rented through Garrotxa Amb Biki (Avda de l'Estació 10, Olot; ****972 69 20 23; **w** garrotxambici.com).

Horseriding and hot-air balloons
The Garrotxa region is very popular for hot-air ballooning, and there's no better way to see the volcanic landscape than from a basket high in the sky. There are several providers, including **Vol de Coloms** (Ctra del Volcà Croscat s/n, Santa Pau; ****689 47 18 72; **w** voldecoloms.cat). These lovely, verdant slopes and woods can also be explored on horseback: the **Can Genassa Riding Club** (Maià de Montcal; ****667 35 17 11; ◙ hipicacangenassa), offers horseriding classes as well as day treks around the region.

BANYOLES Before there was the town of Banyoles, there was the Benedictine **Monestir de Sant Esteve**, founded in AD812 at the end of Carrer Nou; if it's open (a rare event: ask at the tourist office) you can admire a beautiful Gothic altarpiece of 1437 by Joan Artigo and a cloister with tombs of medieval abbots. The parish church in the centre, the 13th-century **Santa Maria dels Turers**, is one of the first examples of Catalan Gothic, with good stained-glass windows. The vortex of daily life is the lovely porticoed 13th-century **Plaça Major**.

There are two museums to visit: the **Museu Darder d'Història Natural** (Pl dels Estudis 2; ****972 57 44 67; **w** museusdebanyoles.cat/darder; ⊕ Sep–Jun 10.30– 13.30 & 16.00–18.30 Tue–Sat, 10.30–14.00 Sun; Jul–Aug 10.30–13.30 & 16.00– 19.00 Tue–Sat, 10.30–14.00 Sun; adult/reduced/under 16 €3/1.50/free) honours adopted son Francesc d'Assís Darder i Llimona, the first zoo-keeper in Barcelona, who came to Banyoles in 1910 to fish, and introduced new species into the lake. His taxidermic skills are on display, but what was once the most famous exhibit is missing: the 'Negre de Banyoles', a bushman mummified by French taxidermists in the 1830s and acquired by the museum in 1916, who became something of Banyoles' mascot. No-one said a word about it until 1991, when a local politician of Haitian origin wrote to the mayor of Banyoles, asking him to remove it. Locals protested. African nations threatened to boycott the Olympics. Even Kofi Annan got involved before El Negre was removed and sent off to Botswana for a decent burial.

No whiff of scandal has tarnished the **Museu Arqueològic Comarcal** (closed for restoration, due to reopen in late 2025) housed in the old Gothic almshouse. Banyoles, it turns out, has been populated since the cows came home – there's a copy of the unique and famous (in Palaeontological circles at any rate) 80,000-year-old Neanderthal Jaw of Banyoles, found in 1887 by the chemist Pere Alsius i Torrent, one of Catalunya's pioneer prehistorians. There are finds from the Palaeolithic caves at Serinyà, Roman artefacts from the Vila Romana de Vilauba, and Iberian and Visigothic finds from Porqueres. The only Neolithic lake settlement in Iberia was discovered here in 1990: the Parc Neolític de la Draga dates back to 5000BC – older than most of the similar settlements in the Alps and northern Italy.

ESTANY DE BANYOLES No-one thinks of lakes when they think of Catalunya, but Banyoles has a very pretty one. It's not big, covering only a square kilometre, but it's unique, located at the confluence of two subterranean rivers flowing down from the Alt Garrotxa. Over the millennia the rushing water ate at the karstic crust above and caused it to collapse, forming the lake. For years, it slumbered peacefully, a favourite of carp fishers, until it was chosen as the site for rowing events during the 1992 Olympics, and developments sprang up along its shores – but nothing too drastic. There are bikes, row boats, and canoes to hire.

PLA DE L'ESTANY This is the area around the lake, the triangle formed by Besalú, Figueres and Girona, a gently rolling region of farms, *masies*, second homes and Romanesque churches. In **Porqueres**, across the lake from Banyoles, don't miss the beautiful church of **Santa Maria** (1182), with a barrel-vaulted roof, an intriguing frieze of symbols, heads and animals in medallions arched over the door, exquisitely carved capitals, and triumphal arch.

Just west of Porqueres, off the GI524 to Sant Miquel de Campmajor, are the striking landscapes of **Estunes**, giant slabs of limestone cracked into massive fissures by earthquakes, and the **Can Ginebreda Forest** (Ctra de Mieres, km 25.5; \972 58 25 38; w canginebreda.cat; ⊕ 09.00–18.00 daily; €4, cash only) where since 1972, sculptor Xicu Cabanyes has created an unusual erotic sculpture garden and restaurant, a vortex of counter-culture life in the Garrotxa.

You can spend a couple of peaceful hours exploring the other churches and villages of the Pla de l'Estany: **Esponellà**, **Crespià**, **Orfes**, **Galliners**, **Vilavenut** (with ruins of a Roman villa) and **Fontcoberta**. Or explore where the owner of Banyoles' famous jawbone might have resided, in Serinyà's **Parc de les Coves Prehistòriques** (C-66; \972 59 33 10; w plaestany.cat/les-arees/promocio-economica-i-turisme/parc-de-les-coves-prehistoriques-de-serinya; ⊕ Mar–Jun & Sep–Nov 10.00–13.00 Tue–Sun, Jul–Aug 10.00–15.00, Dec–Feb closed; adult/reduced/under 6 €8/4/free) with its Neanderthal cave shelters and the lovely cave Reclau Viver.

BESALÚ Set at the confluence of the Fluvià and Capellada rivers, the walled town of Besalú is irresistible, one of Catalunya's purest, most dreamlike medieval ensembles. First a Roman and Visigothic settlement, it had its glory days as a little feudal capital; Louis le Debonair captured it from the Moors in AD800. Wilfred the Hairy freed it from the control of Girona, and, from the year 1000, Besalú (pop. 800) was the seat of the County of Cerdanya-Besalú, thanks to its most famous count, Bernat Tallaferro (990–1020), who fought the Moors in Córdoba and earned the favour of the pope. In 1111, it was all inherited by the County of Barcelona.

After that, time stood still in Besalú. Its pride and joy is a remarkable 11th-century **dog-legged fortified bridge**, made of eight irregular arches with a tax-collecting tower at the bend, last rebuilt after it was damaged in the Civil War. The town itself is a medieval stage set, but to have a peek behind the façades, you'll need to join one of the tourist office's guided tours. There are two churches from Besalú's 11th-century heyday: the large **Monestir de Sant Pere**, finished by Bernat Tallaferro and decorated by a pair of stone lions triumphant over evil, and **Sant Vicenç** (1018), its entrance prettily decorated with floral motifs. There's an 11th-century hospital, and the **Casa Cornellà** furnished with antique tools and furnishings.

Like Girona, Besalú had an important **Call**, centred around Carrer Comte Tallaferro and Carrer Rocafort. In 1964, a 12th-century **Miqvé** (a ritual bathhouse) (Baixada de la Mikweh; \972 59 12 40; ⊕ by appointment only; ask at the tourist information office) was discovered next to the ruins of the synagogue when a local dry cleaner tried to dig a well; as the last Jews left Besalú in 1436, they sealed and hid the entrance. It's the only one ever found in Spain.

6

OLOT After an earthquake in 1427, the Garrotxa's bustling capital Olot was rebuilt in an attractive Renaissance grid around a bijou **Plaça Major**. But it was Olot's outskirts, the dappled beech and oak forests and lush volcanic cones illuminated by a diaphanous light, that drew Catalan landscape painters, beginning in the late 18th century and leading to the founding of the **Escola de Belles Arts d'Olot**, now housed in the beautiful Renaissance Claustres del Carme just east of the Plaça Major.

Some of their paintings are in the **Museu de la Garrotxa** (C/ Hospici 8; \972 27 11 66; w museus.olot.cat/visita/museu-de-la-garrotxa; ⏰ 10.00–13.00 & 15.00–18.00 Tue–Fri, 11.00–14.00 & 16.00–19.00 Sat, 11.00–14.00 Sun; adult/reduced €3/1.50). Located in the massive stone building of the former hospice, it displays one of Ramon Casas' most famous paintings, *The Charges* (of the Guardia Civil routing a crowd of strikers in Barcelona), sculpture by Josep Clarà and Miquel Blay, and a collection of Cigarillos París posters.

The large parish church of **Sant Esteve** has a couple of Baroque altarpieces, and an El Greco in its parish museum. Nearby, the **Casa Museu Can Trincheria** (C/ Sant Esteve 29; \972 27 11 66; w museus.olot.cat/museus/#casa_museu_can_trincheria; ⏰ 10.00–13.00 & 16.00–19.00 Tue–Fri, 11.00–13.00 & 16.00–19.00 Sat; free) has its original furnishings, typical of an 18th-century bourgeois family, as well as a remarkable, enormous *pessebre* (Christmas crib), made by the house's obsessive owner and his servant.

In the 19th century, swells from Barcelona followed the artists to Olot and built a handful of Modernista mansions; two of the best are **El Drac** (now a bookshop) opposite Sant Esteve, by Alfred Paluzie (1901) and the **Casa Solà Morales** (1915), a pretty confection by Domènech i Montaner on the Passeig d'en Blay, covered with lavish floral designs and a pair of caryatids by Eusebi Arnau.

PARC NATURAL DE LA ZONA VOLCÀNICA DE LA GARROTXA

On the south edge of Olot, the **Casal dels Volcans** (Avda Santa Coloma 47; \972 26 60 12; w parcsnaturals.gencat.cat/ca/xarxa-de-parcs/garrotxa) overlooks the beautiful old oaks and botanical gardens of the **Parc Nou**. It contains the park information office for the Garrotxa Volcanic Zone, where you'll find lots of maps and info. But, for the most exciting introduction to the region's explosive geology and the impact of the devastating 1427 eruption, head back into town to find the **Espai Crater** (C/ Macarnau 55; \972 27 91 32; w espaicrater.com; ⏰ Jul–Aug 10.00–14.00 & 16.00–20.00 Tue–Sun; Sep–Jun 10.00–14.00 & 15.00–18.00 Tue–Fri, 10.00–14.00 & 15.00–19.00 Sat, 10.00–14.00 Sun; adult/reduced/under 4 €7.50/5/ free). This is Olot's newest and glossiest museum, with lots of interactive exhibits. Four dormant volcanoes surround Olot; only 500m north of the centre you can walk up to the **Volcà Montsacopa**, with a hermitage on top and fine views over Olot.

Around 5km north of Olot, **Sant Joan les Fonts** offers two lovely walks: one along a stretch of the ancient Roman Via Annia, or **Via de Capsacosta**, passing several Romanesque chapels; the second, a 2-hour circuit (No. 16) beginning in the Plaça Major and passing curious basalt columns left by the volcanic flows. Sant Joan's 12th-14th century **Castell Estada Juvinyà** (C/ Juvinyà; \972 29 03 80; w turismesantjoanlesfonts.com/ca/monuments/castell-de-juvinya; ⏰ 16.30–19.30 Mon–Tue, 10.00–14.00 & 16.30–19.30 Wed–Fri, 10.00–14.00 Sat; free) is now a library, which also has displays on local history.

A favourite subject for painters, **Castellfollit de la Roca** is just east, built on a startling 40m basalt escarpment over the River Fluvià; its medieval buildings and narrow streets are paved with the dark volcanic rock.

South of Olot off the road to Santa Pau, the **D'en Jordà Nature Reserve** is a huge beech forest growing on ancient lava flow: the changing leaves put on a stunning show in autumn. Next is **Santa Pau**, a little charmer with a 13th-century castle, medieval lanes and arcaded square, the Fira dels Bous, scene of the old cattle market. There are lovely views from the walls, and restaurants and shops cooking or selling its famous *fesols de Santa Pau*, or white beans.

The surroundings offer lovely walks, including a steep hike up to the Garrotxa's largest crater, the verdant **Volcà Santa Margarida**, 350m across, with a 13th-century chapel in its former crater. Another, the **Volcà del Croscat**, has a neat slice quarried out of its side, as if it were a giant chocolate cake. Another dozen walking trails surround medieval **Sant Feliu de Pallerols** further south, a handsome town with medieval bridges and mills. Just to the northeast, little **Els Hostalets d'en Bas** has an extremely photogenic street, **Carrer Teixeda**, lined with houses with old wooden balconies.

INTO THE CATALAN HEARTLAND

In the 9th century AD, the river valleys and small mountain ranges north of Barcelona were Count Guifré el Pilós' front lines; by the time of his death Catalunya extended as far west as the Llobregat. The Hairy One founded and lavishly endowed three important monasteries to anchor his claim – at Vic, Ripoll and Sant Joan de les Abadesses – which helped immensely in getting the power of the literate on his side. Montseny, Barcelona's bucolic playground, is just beyond the collar of sprawl, and the dramatic Collsacabra peaks east of Vic are great places for walks and dotted with striking, if sometimes twee, medieval villages.

GETTING THERE AND AROUND
By train Renfe's R3 regional line (w renfe.com) runs from Barcelona to La Garriga, Figaró, Vic, Ripoll, Ribes de Freser and La Molina (the ski resort) before culminating at Puigcerdà. Granollers is on regional lines R2 and R8.

The *cremallera* (rack-and-pinion railway) between Ribes de Freser and the Vall de Núria is operated by FGC (✆ 972 73 20 20; w turistren.cat/es/trenes/cremallera-de-nuria; ⊕ check website for timetables; return ticket adult/reduced/4–13/under 4 €33/28/21.50/free).

By bus Teisa (✆ 972 20 48 68; w teisa-bus.com) operates bus services between Barcelona, Girona, Figueres and Vic, Ripoll, Sant Joan de les Abadesses and Camprodon. It is the principal bus operator in this region.

Sagalés buses (✆ 902 13 00 14; w sagales.com) runs an express bus service between Barcelona and Vic. It also operates a SkiBus from Barcelona to La Molina. Teisa provides a SkiBus service between Girona and Vallter. These SkiBus services include a one-day ski pass.

By car A car is useful for visiting some of the smaller villages in this area, and parking is usually easy to find except in the bigger towns and cities.

By bike This region is a hugely popular cycling destination, with a host of excellent trails, including the wonderful Vies Verdes (converted former railway lines). Many hotels cater to cyclists with bike storage. More information at w viasverdes.cat.

TOURIST INFORMATION
There are tourist information offices in all the major towns and cities. In the smaller villages, the Ajuntament (town hall) will provide

6

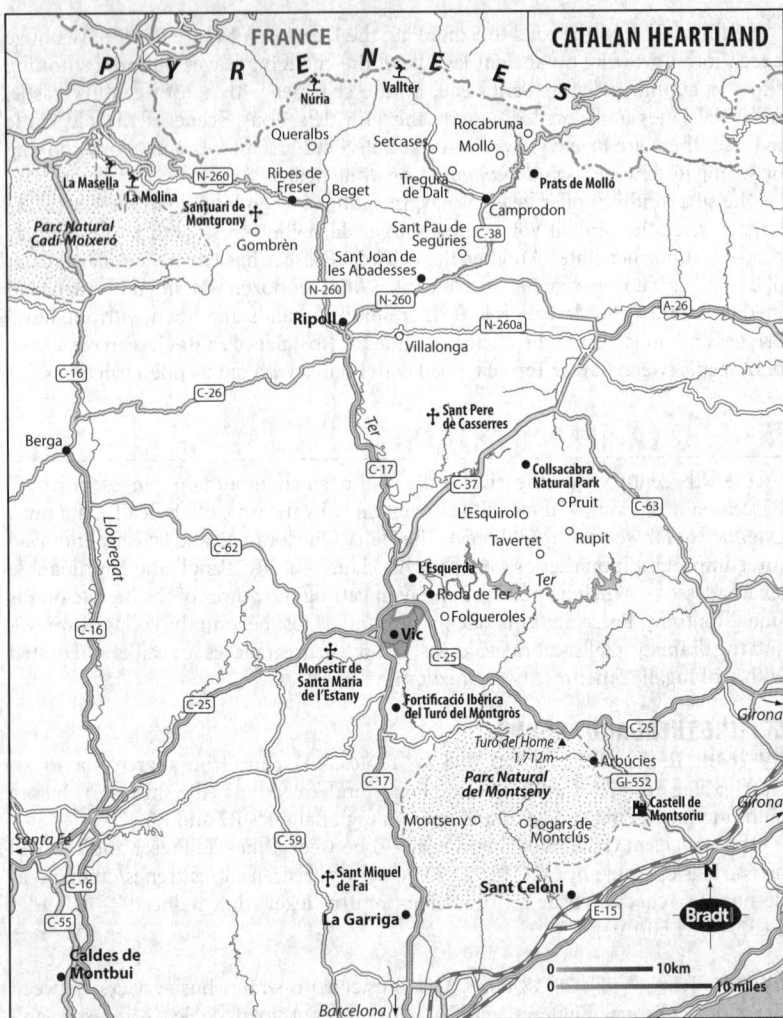
CATALAN HEARTLAND

information on guided tours or opening times or even hand out the key to churches or other sights.

Caldes de Montbui Pl Font del Lleó 20; 938 65 41 40; w visiteucaldes.cat
Granollers C/ Anselm Clavé 2; 938 79 49 80; w visitgranollers.com

Ripoll Pl de l'Abat Oliba s/n; 972 70 23 51; w visit.ripoll.cat
Sant Joan de les Abadesses Pl de l'Abadia 9; 972 72 05 99; w santjoandelesabadesses.cat
Vic Pl del Pes s/n; 938 86 20 91; w victurisme.cat

WHERE TO STAY

Can Barrina Ctra Palautordera km 12.7, Montseny; 938 47 30 65; hotelcanbarrina. There are 14 peaceful rooms in this family-run hotel, set in a *masia* built in 1620, surrounded by

forests; there's a pool & an excellent restaurant (€€€) serving game & mushroom dishes. €€€
Hostal Estrella Pl Bisbe Font, Rupit; 938 52 20 05; w hostalestrella.com. Beautifully refurbished

stone mountain inn, run by the same family for 4 generations. The 16 rooms have been elegantly updated, preserving all the original details, & they can provide lovely picnic baskets to take on a romantic walk. Excellent restaurant serving modern Catalan cuisine. €€€

Hotel Rural-Spa Resguard Dels Vents Camí De Ventaiola s/n, Ribes de Freser; 972 72 88 66; w hotelresguard.com. A handsome hotel with crisp, contemporary design & blissful views over the surrounding mountains, spacious rooms & suites, a spa & wellness area, restaurant serving traditional Catalan dishes with a modern twist (€€€), & blissful views over the surrounding mountains. €€€

Mas Albereda Avda Sant Llorenç 68, Sant Julià de Vilatorta; 938 12 28 52; w masalbereda.com. There are 20 elegant rooms & suites at this country hotel, set in a historic house in a garden with a pool. Celebrity chef Nandu Jubany is at the helm of the restaurant (€€€€), which serves creative Catalan cuisine, including a *menu de degustació* (€55) as well as à la carte options. €€€

Sant Marçal Montseny Ctra GIV between Viladrau-Santa Fe km 6.5, Montseny; 931 98 25 15; w santmarcalmontseny.com. Charming rooms of character in this mid-sized hotel, with lots of exposed stone, & a good restaurant (€€€) in a restored Romanesque monastery in a lush mountain pass. Wonderful service gives it an edge over others in the region. A favourite for weddings. €€€

Vall de Núria Estació de Montaña Vell de Nuria, Núria; 972 73 20 30; w hotelvalldenuria.cat. Set in the grim-looking sanctuary, but with nicely furnished rooms & a decent restaurant serving mountain meals. They offer lots of packs on their website – adventure, astronomy, etc – which are good value. €€€

Ca la Manyana Avda Verge de Montserrat 38, Sant Julià de Vilatorta; 938 12 24 94; w calamanyana.com. Homey welcome in the spacious rooms & one of the best-known (& best-value) restaurants (€€) in the area, with a wide choice of seasonal dishes. €€

Calitxo El Serrat s/n, Camprodon; 972 74 03 86; w hotelcalitxo.com. A mid-sized, chalet-style hotel with cosy rooms, balconies & lovely views into the Pyrenees: it has a good restaurant (€€) & an outdoor pool in the garden. €€

Camprodon Pl Dr Robert, Camprodon; 972 74 00 13; w hotelcamprodon.com. Central, pink Modernista classic from 1916, with pleasant gardens overlooking the river & a pool. The restaurant (€€), with chandeliers & oil paintings, serves up classic Catalan mountain cuisine. €€

Catalunya C/ Sant Quintí 37, Ribes de Freser; 972 72 70 17; w catalunyaparkhotels.com. Mid-sized hotel near the train station with stylish, modern rooms & a warm welcome from the family owners. Guests have access to the pool & garden in its pricier sister hotel, Catalunya Park, nearby. €€

Maristany Pg Maristany 20, Camprodon; 972 13 00 78; w hotelmaristany.com. 10 modern rooms in a typical mansion along the town's prettiest street with a pool. €€

Parador de Vic-Sau Paraje el Bac de Sau, Ctra de Tavèrnoles km 10; 938 12 23 23; w paradores. es/en/parador-de-vic-sau. Some 14km from Vic, this modern parador is a charming idealisation of a Catalan *masia*, or country house, in a pine grove & overlooking the Sau Reservoir. €€

Xalet Coromina Ctra de Vic 4, Viladrau; 938 84 92 64; w xaletcoromina.com. In the centre of the Parc Natural del Montseny, 8 snug rooms in an ivy-covered mansion, set in a little garden with lovely mountain views. The restaurant (€€€) features imaginative cuisine. €€

Cabrerès Hostal C/ Major 26, Cantonigròs; 938 56 50 22; w cabrereshostal.com. A simple inn in the middle of a tiny village, with 8 dbl rooms, a café-bar & bike hire for exploring the remarkable Collsacabra. €

Els Caçadors C/ Balandrau 24; Ribes de Freser; 972 72 70 01; w hotelsderibes.com. Since 1919, a mid-sized, comfortable country inn, with a choice of rooms & self-catering apartments. Best known for its excellent restaurant (€€€) that specialises in tasty dishes using mountain ingredients. €

Hostal Can Nogué C/ del Mig 2, Tavertet; 938 56 52 51; w hostalcannogue.com. 6 cosy rooms in an old stone *masia* & succulent grilled meats served on the terrace at the enormously popular restaurant (€€); be sure to book in summer. Rooms available with full or half board. €

Hostal El Forn Beget; 972 74 12 30; w elforndebeget.com. 4 comfortable, if rather dated, dbls in a characterful 16th-century inn filled with an eclectic mix of paintings & old tools & lovely owners. The restaurant (€€) has delicious Catalan cuisine, with a beautiful terrace overlooking the river. €

6

Hostal La Plaçeta Pl Carme 9, Camprodon; 972 74 08 07; w laplacetacamprodon.com. Family-run, small traditional hotel in the centre, with warm & friendly owners & a popular restaurant (€€) serving up mountain classics. €
Pic de l'Àliga Núria; 934 83 83 63; w xanascat. gencat.cat. The youth hostel, with dorms for 3–18 people, enjoys a spectacular setting right at the top of the ski-centre's cable car. €
Santuari de Montgrony Gombrèn; 608 57 34 88; w santuaris.cat/santuari/santuari-de-nostra-senyora-de-montgrony. Peaceful, 8-room stone *hostal* amid the rocks under the sanctuary, with stunning views & an excellent restaurant (€€). €

✖ **WHERE TO EAT AND DRINK** A big lure is the food: Vic is famous for its pork sausages and charcuterie, truffles and wild mushrooms. Heading up towards the Pyrenees, you'll also find mountain trout, lamb and artisan cheeses on the menu. Camprodon is known for its sweets and biscuits.

Ca l'Ignasi C/ Major 4, Cantonigròs; 938 52 51 24; w calignasi.com; ⊕ 13.00–15.30 Thu–Sun. Simply spectacular creative mountain cuisine by Ignasi Camps. Dishes might include scrambled eggs with mushrooms, asparagus & black pudding, or oven-baked cod with potato & vegetable cream. €€€
El Pont 9 Camí de la Cerdanya 1, Camprodon; 972 74 05 21; w restaurantelpont9.com; ⊕ 13.00–15.30 Wed & Sun, 13.00–15.30 & 20.00–22.00 Thu–Sat. Bright dining room with fine views over the Romanesque bridge & tasty market cuisine. €€€
Fonda Xesc Pl del Roser 1, Gombrèn; 972 73 04 04; w fondaxesc.com; ⊕ 13.30–15.30 Thu & Sun, 13.30–15.30 & 20.30–21.30 Fri–Sat. Friendly, stone-built, old-fashioned inn founded in 1730, in a tranquil village, this restaurant is famous for its refined interpretations of classic Catalan cuisine. It also has a handful of simple rooms (€€). €€€
✳ **Insòlit** C/ Corretgers 4, Vic; 722 76 20 55; w insolitrestaurant.com; ⊕ 13.00–15.30 Mon, Tue, Thu & Sun; 13.00–15.30 & 20.00–22.00 Fri–Sat. Chef Nuria Sanuy & Montse València (front of house), who have worked at some of the most exciting Catalan restaurants including Disfrutar (Barcelona) & Compartir (Cadaqués), have created their own extraordinary hotspot of culinary fireworks in Vic. Expect the unexpected in this welcoming & unstuffy restaurant with a pretty interior courtyard. The set lunch menu (€22) is superb. €€€
La Competència C/ Sant Miquel de Sants 21–23, Vic; 691 52 18 99; ▣ lacompetencia.bar; ⊕ 13.00–15.30 Tue, 13.00–15.30 & 20.15–22.30 Wed–Sat. Sophisticated, creative Catalan cuisine in an elegant, minimalist dining room: every dish is a miniature work of art, showcasing the finest local produce but often with a fusion twist. €€€
Reccapolis Ctra Sant Joan 68; 972 70 21 06; w reccapolis.com; ⊕ 13.00–15.15 Mon & Thu–Sun. Ripoll's best restaurant is 2.5km from the centre, in a handsome mansion; lots of lovely mushroom dishes in season, & creative combinations of fruits, nuts & meats. Go for the tasting menu (€40), which might include dishes like pork tenderloin & *canamillana* (a kind of mountain bubble & squeak). €€€
Can Po Ctra Beget s/n, Rocabruna; 972 74 10 45; ⊕ 13.00–16.30 Mon, 13.00–16.30 & 20.30–22.30 Fri–Sun. One of the best restaurants in the area, serving a mix of traditional & creative dishes. There's a wonderful open fire in winter & an outdoor terrace in summer. €€
Casa Rudes C/ Major 10, Sant Joan de les Abadesses; 972 72 01 15; w restaurantcasarudes.com; ⊕ 09.00–16.00 Tue–Sun. A village institution for over a century. The food is good rather than great, but portions are generous & the rustic setting is charming. €€
El Petit Vegà C/ Sant Roc 4, Camprodon; 972 74 05 21; ▣ elpetitvega; ⊕ 12.30–15.00 & 19.30–22.00 Tue–Sun. Pep & Laura have created a delightful little oasis in this miniature restaurant, where they serve up wonderful vegan dishes like homemade *croquetes* with calçots & shitake mushrooms, vegetable *canalones* & scrumptious desserts. €€
Restaurant Mas Les Feixes Ctra de Olot s/n; 647 65 54 30; w maslesfeixes.com; ⊕ 13.00–17.00 & 20.30–11.30 Sat, 13.00–17.00 Sun. A cosy little restaurant on the road out of town towards Olot that specialises in mountain dishes, from lamb chops to homemade *canelones*, cooked over a wood-fired grill. €€

SPORTS AND ACTIVITIES You'll find comprehensive information for **skiing** at w turismoencatalunya.es/en/ski-resorts-Catalonia.html. All these resorts are also popular in summer, particularly for hiking and mountain biking.

La Molina Alp; ℡972 89 20 31; w lamolina. cat. This is the oldest ski resort in Spain (1909) although it only got its first lifts in 1942. It has 68 runs over 71km. Along with La Masella, with which it is linked by ski lifts, it forms the Alp 2500 ski area.
La Masella ℡972 14 40 00; w masella.com. This has 65 runs, covering 74km, and has one of the longest ski seasons in Spain. It's also one of the best for night skiing, with illuminated pistes.

Núria ℡972 73 20 20; w valldenuria.cat. This has 10 pistes – a couple over 4km long – & two teleskis, plus a wide range of activities for children, including a huge toboggan run.
Vallter Setcases; ℡972 13 60 57; w vallter. cat. A small resort, this is set in a cirque at around 2,000–2,500m; it has 13 runs, covering 20km, & a snow park for the kids.

PARC NATURAL DEL MONTSENY The highest of Catalunya's pre-coastal mountains, the massif of Montseny – 'Mount Signal' (1,706m) – earned its name from the times when travellers used the mountains to orientate themselves and judge distances. Only 55km from Barcelona, Montseny is a deep green oasis of peaks and valleys, high plains and abrupt cliffs, springs and rivers, majestic beech, oak and fir forests, a collage of landscapes and climates ranging from Mediterranean to subalpine, home to over 200 vertebrates of all kinds. The main gateways to the Parc Natural del Montseny lie off the AP-7 (exit 11), and at **Sant Celoni**, which has the grandest sgrafittoed façade in the region, on the church of **Sant Martí** (1703).

From here the road (BV-5114) ascends to **Santa Fé** near the summit of Montseny's highest peak, **Turó del Home**, reached by a 1.5-hour walk. The reward is a view over most of Catalunya across to the Pyrenees; an easier 2.5-hour green-marked path goes through the forest around a reservoir. A second route just to the west, the BV-5301, follows the Tordera River into the mountains, where you can pick up information at the Natural Park Office at **Fogars de Montclús** (Masia Mariona, Ctra BV-5119, km 2.5, Mosqueroles, Fogars de Montclús; ℡938 47 51 02; w parcs.diba. cat/es/web/montseny; ◷ 09.30–15.30 daily).

The village of **Montseny** is further up, in a lovely setting, with the remains of the 13th-century monastery of Sant Marçal. Nearby El Brull has the mighty walls of the 5th-century BC **Fortificació Ibèrica del Turó del Montgròs**. **Viladrau**, an old spa town on the northern edge of the park, is another exceptional area for walks.

Arbúcies to the east is set in a lush valley bubbling with springs. In its picturesque streets are the **Plaça de la Vila**, shaded by a huge plane tree planted to celebrate the first short-lived Spanish Republic (1873), and a Modernista building, the sgrafittoed **Granja Royal** on Carrer Francesc Camprodon. The **Museu Etnològic del Montseny La Gabella** (C/ Major 6; ℡972 86 09 08; w museuetnologicmontseny. org; ◷ 10.30–14.00 & 16.30–19.30 Tue–Fri, 10.30–14.00 Sat–Sun; adult/under 6 €4/free) covers the inhabitants and customs of Montseny, and runs excellent workshops and walks (usually in Catalan only). There are exhibits on local legends – many places have 'witch' (*bruixa*) in their name, recalling the benighted years of 1617 and 1627, when 22 local women were sent to the gallows, accused of causing the violent storms that destroyed the local crops. The nearby 13th–14th-century **Castell de Montsoriu** (Camí del Castell de Montsoriu; ℡972 01 19 60; w montsoriu. cat; ◷ book guided tours in advance on the website), is one of the finest surviving Catalan Gothic castles, and has huge views over the valley, and there are several Romanesque churches for the keen to seek out.

6

GRANOLLERS TO VIC The C-17 runs just to the west of the Montseny Natural Park, skirting **Granollers**, Catalunya's breadbasket and most important agricultural market town; its Thursday market, first recorded in 1040, is still going strong. The city's iconic Renaissance **Gran Porxada** (1586) grain market is in its handsome square, next to the pink neo-Gothic **Ajuntament** (1904) designed by Simó Cordomí; other good buildings are the Gothic **Casa del Condestable** in C/ Sant Roc and the **Hospital de Sant Domènec,** now used as a public library. The **Museu de Granollers** (C/ Anselm Clavé 40–42; ☏938 42 68 40; w museugranollers. cat; ⏰ Apr–Oct 18.00–21.00 Tue–Fri & Sun, 11.00–14.00 & 17.00–21.00 Sat; free) has archaeological finds, medieval paintings and sculpture, bridal chests, glass and ceramics.

If you aren't in any hurry to get to Vic, there are some tempting detours off the highway. To the west of Granollers, **Caldes de Montbui** has steaming hot springs that made it a popular resort in Roman times and again in the 1890s; a bevy of Modernista villas mark its second heyday. **Thermalia** (Plaça de la Font de Sant Lleó; ☏938 65 41 40; w visiteucaldes.cat; ⏰ Jun–Aug 10.00–14.00 & 17.00–20.00 Tue–Sat, 10.00–14.00 Sun, Sep–May 10.00–14.00 & 16.00–19.00 Tue–Sat, 10.00–14.00 Sun; adult/reduced €3/2.25) doubles as a tourist office and museum housing the still-usable Roman baths, historical artefacts, and sculpture. **La Garriga**, north of Granollers, is another spa town, site of the glamorous **Balneari Blancafort** (1876) where many leading figures of the Renaixença came to ease their aches and pains. Nearby C/ dels Banys has several lovely Modernista buildings, but the best, four townhouses built around 1910 by Manuel Joaquim Raspal, are concentrated in a block known as the **Illa Raspall**. There's a fine Gothic retable in the **Església de la Doma**; the hermitage of **Santa Maria del Camí** dates from the 10th century and contains the tomb of Xixilona, daughter of Wilfred the Hairy.

West of La Garriga, a narrow road climbs from Sant Feliu de Codines to one of Catalunya's beauty spots, **Sant Miquel de Fai**. In AD997, the Counts of Barcelona donated the spot to a pious lord named Gombau to build a little monastery. A Gothic priory was added. But it's the setting, surrounded by cliffs and grottoes, waterfalls and lakes, that brings the weekend day-trippers and wedding parties.

VIC Midway between Barcelona and the Pyrenees, Vic is a lively little university city. Originally Ausa, the capital of the Ausetani Iberians, it survived into Visigothic times, only to be destroyed in AD826 when it rebelled against the Franks. In 878, Wilfred the Hairy, hoping to repopulate the area, refounded the town on the site of an old suburb, Vicus Ausonae, now capital of the comarca of Osona.

Wilfred's scholarly great grandson Oliba (c971–1046), was the Count of Berga, but renounced worldly things to become abbot of Ripoll and Cuixà (in Roussillon) in 1008, and then bishop of Vic in 1018. Oliba was one of the most important churchmen in his day: besides fostering learning at Ripoll (page 215), he promoted the movement of Peace and Truce of God, setting aside certain days when no-one could quarrel; his assemblies of Peace and Truce would eventually evolve into the Catalan Corts.

Vic's first markets took place in Oliba's day in the vast **Plaça Major**, encompassed by an attractive mix of Baroque and Modernista buildings, all with porticoes. One is the **Ajuntament**, housing a collection of works by Josep Sert (page 213), including fragments from the first cathedral murals. The medieval core occupies a hilly triangle just behind: on the highest point, in Plaça del Pare Xifré, the cella of a 2nd-century AD Roman temple survives as part of the 11th-century **Palau Montcada**.

Cathedral (C/ Cloquer 5; ☎ 938 86 44 49; w www.bisbatvic.org; ⏰ 10.00–13.00 & 16.00–19.00, Espai Sert closed on Sun & Mon, no visits during mass; adult/reduced/under 18 €5/4/free) Bishop Oliba's aluminium statue stands in front of the cathedral he reconstructed. In 1781 Vic saw fit to knock it all down (except for the bell tower and crypt) and replace it with a massive neoclassical pile. In the early 20th century, the bishops, perhaps feeling a bit guilty, led the campaign to restore Catalan monasteries and use Catalan in sermons, and hired Josep Maria Sert (1874–1945) to cover the interior of the cathedral with golden chiaroscuro murals, the largest series in the world, a job Sert completed in 1929. He went on to decorate Barcelona's Ajuntament and New York's Rockefeller Center but then received the news that the cathedral was set on fire in 1936, and the murals were irreparably damaged. Yet, in what must be a world record of some kind, the no-longer-young Sert returned, and reapplied an acre or so of gold leaf before his death in 1945. Robert Hughes called him 'the Tiepolo of the dictatorship', but, whatever his politics, his heroic murals are astonishing, turbulent, painted with a personal iconography that often seems to have little to do with religion.

The Romanesque **crypt and treasury** contain works which managed to escape the restoration and the flames: the painted alabaster retable (1427) on the *lives of Mary and St Peter* by Pere Oller, a beautiful gold processional cross of 1397 by

THE CATALAN HOMER: JACINT VERDAGUER

Like many a bright younger son from peasant backgrounds, Verdaguer was enrolled in a seminary where he could get a good education – in this case, Vic, where he was a mediocre student and angered his teachers by writing secular poetry. But his poetry was very good. In 1866, his *Ode to Rafael Casanovas*, on the Barcelonin hero of the 1714 siege, won a prize in the Jocs Florals, Barcelona's poetry competition. The poem not only impressed the judges with its refreshingly direct, vivid use of the Catalan language, but Verdaguer impressed them as well, a handsome young peasant in his rough clothes and *barretina*, the red Phrygian cap. Both the man and his art seemed to perfectly embody the spirit of the new national Renaixença.

But Verdaguer also took the priesthood seriously, and at the age of 25 he was ordained and served as a country priest at Vinyoles north of Vic. In 1874 he became ill, and when the doctor recommended a sea voyage he took a job as a ship's chaplain sailing back and forth from Cádiz to Havana. During his journeys he wrote what has become the best-loved poem in the Catalan language, *L'Emigrant*, and an epic, *L'Atlàntida*, recounting how the submersion of Atlantis created the Atlantic ocean separating Spain and Latin America, and how the Spanish discovery of America reunited the two lands.

It was the beginning of a meteoric rise to fame. *L'Atlàntida* won first prize at the Jocs Florals. The poet was declared a 'Mestre en Gai Saber'. He went to Rome to meet the pope to discuss the poem, and travelled widely and luxuriously, writing among other works the *Ode to Barcelona* and, in 1885, a second epic, *Canigó*, about the mythic origins of Catalunya in a Pyrenean monastery, earning him the title of 'Poet of Catalunya' and the 'Catalan Homer'. His delight in nature and deep love for Catalunya, combined with an extraordinary gift for imagery have kept him on his pedestal, even if other aspects of his poetry, its sentimentality and religious fervour, may not at first glance appeal to modern tastes.

6

Joan Carbonell, and a chain made from the melted gold recovered from Sert's original murals.

Across the square from the cathedral, the outstanding **Museu d'Art Medieval** (Plaça Bisbe Oliba; ☎938 86 93 60; w museuartmedieval.cat; ⊕ Apr–Sep 10.00–19.00 Tue–Sat, 10.00–14.00 Sun, Oct–Mar 10.00–13.00 & 15.00–18.00 Tue–Fri, 10.00–19.00 Sat, 10.00–14.00 Sun; adult/reduced/under 10 €8.50/5.50/free) contains one of the largest and finest collections of Romanesque and Gothic art in Europe. Works include a marvellous array of 12th-century altar frontals, a famous stylized wooden *Descent from the Cross* from Erill la Vall, *majestats* and polychrome Virgins from glamorous Madonnas to stodgy matrons; surreal Gothic drawings of the Last Supper from La Seu d'Urgell, a baldachin from the Ribes Valley, beautiful paintings by Jaume Huguet, Pere Serra, Ferrer Bassa, Jaume Ferrer, Lluís Borrassà, Ramon de Mur and sweet works by Joan Guascó and his son Perot of the local Vic school.

The wide, languid curl of Vic's Ramblas follows the old city walls. Well signposted, off the Rambla del Carme, a former convent houses the **Museu de l'Art de la Pell** (C/ Arquebisbe Alemany 5; ☎938 83 32 79; w museuartpellvic.cat; ⊕ 10.00–13.00 & 16.00–19.00 Tue–Fri, 11.00–14.00 Sat–Sun; free) with a thousand objects all made of leather assembled by local tanner Andreu Colomer Munmany, including gilt leather altar frontals, bags, armchairs, saddles, masks, and shadow theatre puppets. The Sala Sert in the **Edifici el Sucre** has Sert's paintings on the *Wedding of Camacho*, the same that grew into murals in the dining room of New York's Waldorf Astoria. It's now used by the chamber of commerce for events, but can occasionally be visited by guided tour (ask at the tourist office).

AROUND VIC: THE OSONA AND COLLSACABRA NATURAL PARK
Once you get past the sprawl, the Osona region has its share of wild forests, picture-postcard villages and country houses. If you're keen on the Romanesque, there's a treat in remote little L'Estany southwest of Vic; take the Manresa road to exit 164, and follow the signs. The **Monestir de Santa Maria de l'Estany** (Pl del Monestir 2, L'Estany; ☎938 30 30 40; w monestirestany.cat; ⊕ May–Oct 10.00–14.00 Wed–Sun, Nov–Apr 10.00–14.00 Wed–Fri & Sun, 10.00–14.00 & 15.00–19.00 Sat; adult/reduced/under 18 €5/4/free) was founded in 1080 by Augustian canons and rebuilt in the 12th and 13th century; the church is handsome but the best bits are the 72 capitals in the luminous cloister, sculpted by several different hands with animals, biblical scenes (the Slaughter of the Innocents), hunting scenes, floral subjects, mermaids and elephants.

The main attraction is to the east of Vic: the villages and stunning landscapes along the Ter, its reservoirs and craggy Collsacabra mountains. First to the east, however, is **Folgueroles**, birthplace of Jacint 'Mossèn Cinto' Verdaguer in 1845. The **Casa Museu Verdaguer** (C/ Major 7; ☎938 12 21 57; w verdaguer.cat; ⊕ Apr–Oct 10.00–14.00 Tue–Fri & Sun, 10.00–14.00 & 17.00–19.00 Sat; Nov–Mar 10.00–14.00 Tue–Sun; adult/reduced/under 12 €3/2.50/free) not only has memorabilia but is also the seat of the Verdaguer foundation and can direct you to other sites around town related to the poet.

Northeast of Folgueroles, the Counts of Osona founded the Benedictine monastery of **Sant Pere de Casserres** (C/ BV-5213, Les Masies de Roda; ☎937 44 71 18; w santperedecasserres.cat; ⊕ Feb–Apr & Sep–Dec 11.00–16.30 Wed–Sat, 11.00–15.00 Sun; May–mid-Jul 11.00–17.00 Wed–Sat, 11.00–15.00 Sun; mid-Jul–Aug 11.00–18.00 Wed–Sat, 11.00–17.00 Sun; Jan closed; adult/reduced/under 7 €5/3/free) in 1005. King Philip II later gave it to the Jesuits: there's a massive basilica and a little cloister, with well-worn capitals. It's a beautiful setting for an annual music festival, held at the end of April/early May. On the northwest bank of the Sau Reservoir, **Roda de Ter** was long a hotbed of banditry; when Catalunya's market for mercenaries collapsed in the 16th century with its decline in the Mediterranean, banditry was one of the few career options left for the unemployed. (In *Don Quixote*, there's a passage where Sancho Panza remarks that they must be near Barcelona, because the trees are full of hanged bandits.) Roda's predecessor, the Ausetani Iberian-medieval town of **L'Esquerda**, is gradually being excavated, and finds are housed in the newly revamped **Museu Arqueològic de l'Esquerda** (Avda Pere Baurier s/n; ☎938 54 02 71; w lesquerda.cat; ⏱ 10.00–14.00 Tue–Fri, 10.30–13.30 Sat–Sun; free).

Further east lies the medieval village of **L'Esquirol**, where a road winds up into the Collsacabra to **Tavertet**; here, a clutch of 17th- and 18th-century houses and the Romanesque church of **Sant Cristòfol** are dwarfed by the remarkable sinuous 213m cliff the village stands on, high over the Ter Valley. There are stunning hiking routes in this area, including to the 50m-high Salt de Molí Bernat waterfall.

Back along the road to Olot, amid more splendid Collsacabra crags and cliffs, are a pair of picturesque villages from the same era with oddly anagrammatic names: **Pruit**, with a fine collection of *masies*, and **Rupit**, famous for its wooden 'hanging bridge' rebuilt in the 1990s, but packed with tourists at weekends. Hike out (about 2hrs round-trip) to the vertiginous **Salt de Sallent**, a 115m-high waterfall.

Ripoll
Mallards quack merrily at the confluence of the Ter and Freser rivers in the centre of Ripoll, 'the Cradle of Catalunya' but the rest of the town just seems to shuffle along. In AD589, the Visigothic king Recaredo founded the first church here after converting from Arianism to Catholic orthodoxy, and in AD888 Count Guifré el Pilós (the Hairy One, again) and his wife Guinedell refounded it as a Benedictine monastery, now considered one of the greatest jewels of Romanesque architecture in Spain.

Santa Maria de Ripoll
(Pl de l'Abat Oliba s/m; ☎972 70 42 03; w monestirderipoll. cat; ⏱ Apr–Sep 10.00–14.00 & 16.00–19.00 Mon–Sat, 10.00–14.00 Sun; Oct–Mar 10.00–13.30 & 15.30–18.00 Mon–Sat, 10.00–14.00 Sun; adult/reduced/children 5–18/under 5 €7.50/5.50/3.50/free) As first Count of Barcelona, Guifré designated the monastery of Santa Maria de Ripoll as the pantheon of his dynasty (a role later taken over by Poblet, page 251). In the 11th century, its scholarly abbot Oliba directed the monks in the scriptorium to translate Arabic manuscripts into Latin, making it one of the great diffusers of learning in the West, filling Ripoll's vast library with Classical texts. Oliba rebuilt the church in 1032, and in the next century Santa Maria reached its apogee; Count Bernat II of Besalú funded the great west portal, and Ripoll's scriptorium produced the *Gesta Comitum Barcinonensium* (Deeds of the Counts of Barcelona). The *Gesta* was medieval Catalunya's foundation myth, complete with some fact-adjusting justifications for its independence from France as well as explaining how Guifré got his name: 'he had hair in places where other men did not'.

The roof of Oliba's church collapsed in the earthquake of 1428, but it suffered an even worse fate in the 1820s when it was rebuilt in a Neoclassical idea of what a basilica should look like, although the monks got little joy from it; a decade later, the monastery was suppressed and set alight. In the 1880s, in the first wave of Catalan nationalism, it was soullessly restored. Today an enormous Catalan flag flaps over the tower.

6

The **alabaster portal**, one of the greatest works of Romanesque sculpture in Spain, has become weathered and damaged over the years but is now glassed in to protect it from the elements. In over a hundred individual scenes, it is a great 'Bible in stone' with the Pantocrator on top that encompasses much of scripture, the tales told with vigour, verve and imagination, with the Zodiac, Labours of the Months, and some monsters thrown in for good measure.

Inside, light filters into the cold, pious grey spaces through alabaster windows, while banners designed by Puig i Cadafalch hang in the nave. In the left transept, you can pay your respects to the modern (1985) tomb of Guifré el Pilós, whose bones were discovered in the cloister. The cloying mosaic altarpiece was a gift from Pope Leo XIII.

The enchanting **cloister** (1171–1205) has paired columns crowned by a delightful medieval bestiary of dragons, dogs, monsters, mermaids, pigs and musicians – everything, in fact, except scenes from scripture.

Across the main square, the former municipal hospital now houses the **Museu Etnogràfic de Ripoll** (Pl de l'Abat Oliba s/n; ☏972 70 31 44; w museuderipoll.org; ⏲ 10.00–13.30 & 16.00–18.00 Tue–Sat, 10.00–14.00 Sun; €4), with displays on the town's history and popular culture, and an exhibit on the scriptorium with facsimiles of some of the masterpieces made by the monks (fortunately, the abbot had sent all of its treasures to the archives in Barcelona before the monastery was wrecked in the 1830s).

Iron was key to Old Catalunya's fortunes, and, until it closed down in 1978, the **Farga Palau** (Pg de la Farga Catalana 16; ☏972 70 31 44; w museuderipoll.org; ⏲ 10.00–13.30 & 16.00–18.00 Tue–Sat, 10.00–14.00 Sun; included in admission to Museu Etnogràfic, see above) was a rare surviving 17th-century foundry famous for its nails (Ripoll once produced most of Spain's supply), firearms and railings. A system of ponds and channels from the River Freser supplied the hydraulic power behind the forge's mighty drop hammers; it was so noisy that most of the workers were deaf by the time they retired.

Balancing all of Ripoll's piety and industry are the legends of wicked Count Arnau, who was said to have sold his soul to the devil. He lived in Gombrèn up in the mountains to the west, where the **Museu de Comte Arnau** (C/ Carbasser 4; ☏972 73 03 00; w gombren.cat/turisme/altres-serveis-i-equipaments/museu-del-compte-arnau; ⏲ 11.00–14.00 Sun; free) has finds from the Castell de Mataplana, the count's supposed residence. A few kilometres further on is the wonderfully scenic 9th-century **Santuari de Montgrony**, reached by steep steps that the dastardly Count Arnau is said to have ordered his unhappy serfs to carve out of the rock before cheating them of their pay.

SANT JOAN DE LES ABADESSES

East of Ripoll, you can drive or walk the Ruta de Ferro i Carbó (a paved path through the pretty countryside, replacing the old rail line which once transported coal from the Ogassa mines) to Sant Joan de les Abadesses on the River Ter, a medieval town planned on a tidy grid in the 13th century around a bijou Plaça Major.

Monastery of Sant Joan de les Abadesses

(Pl de l'Abadia s/n; ☏972 72 23 53; w monestirsantjoanabadesses.cat; ⏲ Jun 10.00–13.00 & 16.00–18.00 Mon & Wed–Sat, 10.00–13.00 Sun; Jul–Aug 10.00–13.00 & 16.00–18.00 Mon–Sat, 10.00–13.00 Sun; Sep–May 10.00–13.00 Mon & Wed–Fri, 10.00–13.00 & 16.00–18.00 Sat, 10.00–13.00 Sun; adult/reduced/under 12 €5/3/free) This monastery, which gives the town its name, was founded by Guifré el Pilós in AD878 for his daughter Emma, the first abbess. In 1017, the abbess and her nuns were given the boot due to the machinations of Bishop Oliba and Count Bernat Tallaferro of Besalú, who went to Pope Benedict VII and claimed that the convent was full of 'parricides and whores of Venus'. Monks moved in, and it came under the control of Besalú. The complex was mostly rebuilt in the 12th century, and again after the 1428 earthquake brought down the roof.

It was spared rebuilding and remains atmospherically dark, austere and mysterious, an aura heightened by the very unusual but moving 13th-century wooden *Deposition*, known as the Santíssim Misteri but nicknamed Les Bruixes – the witches – for the stiff weirdness of its wooden figures. Apparently a communion wafer survived for seven centuries wedged in the forehead of the figure of Christ. The **museum** has a good collection of art dating back to the 11th century, including richly decorated gold and silverware, rock crystal crucifixes, fabrics, sculptures and paintings. The handsome abbot's palace next to the church houses the tourist office.

The fountain in nearby **Plaça de l'Abadessa Emma** was a gift from Mexico, thanking local composer Jaume Nunó, who composed the Mexican national anthem. Not much survives of the ruined 12th-century **Església de Sant Pol**, once the villagers' church, but it's worth a look for its tympanum sculpted with Christ, SS Peter and Paul. The **Pont Vell** over the Ter dates from 1140; it was destroyed in the last fight in the Civil War in February 1939 and rebuilt in 1970.

CAMPRODON AND ITS VALLEYS
Continuing up the Riu Ter, the water becomes cleaner, the scenery grander. **Sant Pau de Segúries** is proud of a picturesque stretch of ancient Roman road, and has a bike path along the old rail line to **Camprodon**.

Thanks to the trains, Camprodon became a summer resort in the 19th century, promoted by Dr Bartolomeu Robert who set up the first summer camp. Today, it's a pretty, if rather worn mountain town with houses overhanging the river. Camprodon's medieval roots show in its Romanesque monastery **Sant Pere**, founded in the 10th century by Guifré II, grandson of the Hairy One, and in its stone bridges, especially the 12th-century **Pont Nou**. Its most famous son was the composer Isaac Albéniz (1860–1909), whose bust presides in front of the parish church of Santa Maria and whose memory is evoked in the mid-July to mid-August Albéniz Music Festival; there's also a **Museu Isaac Albéniz** (C/ Sant Roc 22; ✆972 74 00 10; w museuisaacalbeniz.org; ⊕ Oct–May 10.00–14.00 & 17.00–19.00 Mon–Sat, 10.00–13.00 Sun; Jun–Sep 10.00–14.00 & 17.00–20.00 Mon–Sat, 10.00–13.00 Sun; free) with memorabilia donated by descendants. As a composer he was inspired by traditional Spanish tunes: his famous 'Leyenda' from the *Suite Española* was used in The Doors' 'Spanish Caravan' and played at French president Nicolas Sarkozy's inauguration, in honour of his then wife Cécilia, Albéniz's great-granddaughter.

Northwest of Camprodon the road climbs to **Villalonga**, **Tregurà de Dalt** and **Setcases**, where many of the old stone houses are now holiday homes, and then to the **Vallter** ski station. The **Ulldeter refuge** is a pretty 30-minute walk up on the GR11 from the car park. The original refuge, another hour up, was the first one on the Iberian peninsula, but was ruined in an avalanche. Just above the ruin, a path leads to the source of the Riu Ter.

Northeast of Camprodon, you can follow the Ritort up to **Molló**. Its striking Romanesque church, **Santa Cecília**, has an ornate portal decorated with animal modillons and the seven deadly sins. In 1936 Republicans took down its bells to make ammunition, and banged on them for three days trying to break them into pieces, driving everyone mad until a villager finally told them to fill them first with sand. Up towards the French border are the soft green meadows of **Prats de Molló**.

6

Alternatively, follow the road towards the Garrotxa by way of **Rocabruna**, with its ruined castle, and the medieval village of **Beget** with its 12th-century tower and Romanesque church **Sant Cristòfol**, the only one in the area the Republicans didn't ransack. Inside, it still has a superb 12th-century 2m wooden *Majestat*, a Romanesque font, and a Gothic alabaster altarpiece, made by the sculptors at Sant Joan de les Abadesses.

RIBES DE FRESER AND NÚRIA Up the River Freser from Ripoll, Ribes de Freser is a rather refreshing, ordinary market town where most people stop only for the extraordinarily vertiginous journey up to the top of the Pyrenees by the *cremallera*. This rack-and-pinion railway, built in 1931, rises over 1,000m in 12.5km, stopping by way of the attractive grey stone village of **Queralbs** with a very pretty marble porch on its 10th-century church.

Beyond are dramatic canyons of the **Núria** and many tunnels before the *cremallera* emerges in the Vall de Núria (1,270m), a beautiful, lofty, bowl-shaped valley with a rather grim sanctuary, rebuilt in the 1880s and 1950s. It houses the 11th-century *Virgin La Mare de Déu de Núria*, reputedly carved by St Gil, the patron of local shepherds. Apparently there was once a menhir in the valley that infertile women would hike up to and rub against, in the hopes of becoming pregnant; today couples more decorously pray before the cross, put their heads in the sacred pot and ring the bell. It apparently works quite often, and, if they have a girl, the grateful parents are likely to name her Núria.

The Virgin is officially the patroness of winter sport, and fittingly, Núria has a ski station, while in summer there are lovely walks that skirt the edges of precipitous chasms; the most popular is the 4-hour walk down to Queralbs on the GR11. Elsewhere in the valley, the big news is the twinned ski resorts of **La Molina** and **La Masella**.

INTO THE PYRENEES

The two Catalunyas, Old (lands conquered under Wilfred the Hairy in the 9th century) and New (conquered in the 12th century) are generally divided by the Llobregat River. Besides the superb scenery, there are some memories of the French Cathars who fled here during the early 13th-century Albigensian Crusade.

BERGA'S LA PATUM

A Masterpiece of the Oral and Intangible Heritage of Humanity according to UNESCO, La Patum takes place from Wednesday night to the Sunday of Corpus Christi in late May or June. The festival grew out of medieval plays on the battle between good and evil, and over four days La Patum features ancient songs, processions, dances and mock battles, surrounded by swirling crowds of people dancing and singing along. There's the crowned L'Àliga (The Eagle); Turks and Cavallets (Little Horses), a battle of Maces, Giants and Dwarves. A relative newcomer to La Patum, the La Guita Xica is a long-necked fire-spewing dragon, a good protective spirit that evolved from a demonic mule.

The climax of La Patum is one of the great displays of Catalan *rauxa*: the wild dance of the 'Plens', masked men covered partly in green foliage with Roman candles sticking out of their heads like antennae, streaming golden sparks while fireworks blast just overhead.

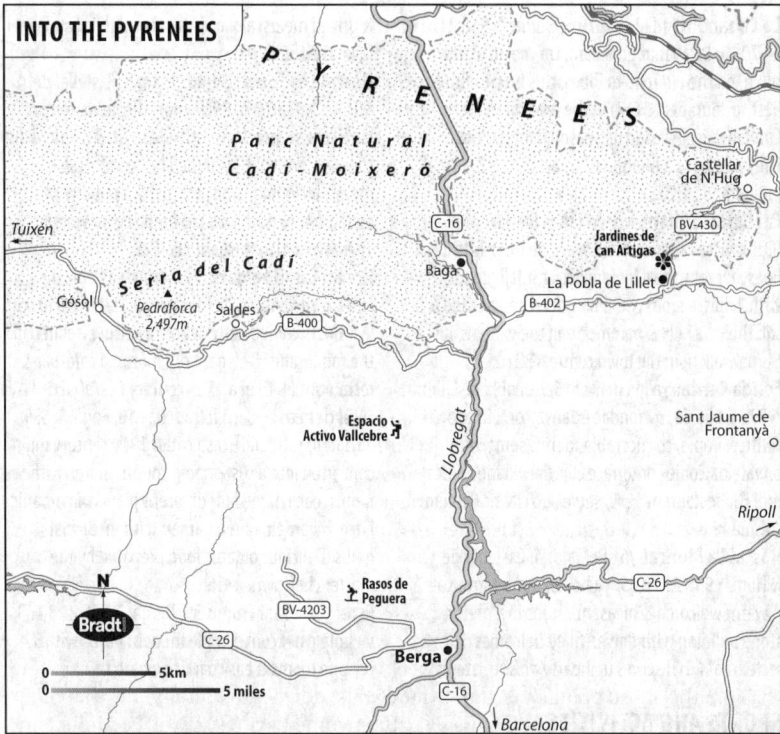

As all over Catalunya, you'll find helpful **tourist information offices** in almost every town and village. Particularly in smaller villages, they hold the keys to churches or other sights that are often not visited enough to be open all the time. The main tourist offices in the region are in Berga (C/ Àngels 7; ↘938 21 13 84; **w** turismeberga.cat), Bagà (C/ Raval 18; ↘619 74 60 99; **w** turismebaga.com), La Pobla de Lillet (Estación del tren; ↘687 99 85 41; **w** turismelillet.cat) and Castellar de N'Hug (↘938 25 70 77; **w** turismecastellardenhug.cat).

GETTING THERE AND AROUND
By bus Alsa (↘902 42 22 42; **w** alsa.es) operates an express bus line from Barcelona to Berga and Llívia via Manresa. It also runs local buses in the area, with services between Guardiola de Berguedà to La Pobla de Lillet and Castellar de N'Hug. **Mir** (↘972 70 30 120; **w** autocarsmir.com) runs buses between Ripoll and La Pobla de Lillet. Note that there are few services to smaller towns and often no service at all on Sundays.

By car From Barcelona, the E-9/C-16 motorway swoops up to Berga, continuing on to the Pyrenees via the Cadí tunnels. A car is very useful for exploring this sparsely populated region, which is not well served by public transport. Off this main road, the country roads are winding and narrow and often hair-raisingly high, so drive with care.

WHERE TO STAY AND EAT Most of the traditional old inns in this region have reliably good restaurants.

La Cabana C-1411z km 79.5, Berga; \938 21 04 70; w lacabanaberga.com. On the outskirts of town, on the old road to Ribes, this is one of the best restaurants (€€€) in the area for modern Catalan cuisine based on seasonal ingredients. They also have a handful of smart rooms & a small indoor pool. €€€

Cal Barraca Travessera Coforb 5, Berga; \609 71 09 30; w calbarraca.com. Lovely, peaceful little rural house for rent, ideal for families or small groups, with 2 dbls, a room with bunks for 4 people, and a sgl. There's a pool & hammocks in the gardens, just a 5-min walk from the town centre. €€

Fonda Cerdanya Pl del Fort 5, La Pobla de Lillet; \772 54 26 63; w fondacerdanya.com. In the centre, simple, comfortable rooms, some with private balconies or terraces, in the village's oldest inn. The restaurant (€€) serves up classic Catalan cuisine. €€

Hostal La Muntanya Pl Major 4, Castellar de N'Hug; \938 25 70 65; w hostallamuntanya.cat. A warm welcome & pleasant rooms in a pretty stone building with flower-filled balconies. The restaurant (€€) serves up hearty *guisats* (stews)

& grilled meats, along with other classic Catalan favourites. €€

Hostal Les Fonts BV-4031, km 8, Castellar de N'Hug; \938 25 70 89; w hostallesfonts.com. A large, classic hotel, just outside town & overlooking the river, with old-fashioned but comfortable rooms, including family rooms, & a popular restaurant (€€) with a big fireplace in winter. There's a pool in the gardens. €€

Hostal Rural Falgars 7km from La Pobla de Lillet, Ctra Santuari de Falgars s/n; \937 44 10 95; w falgars.com. Utterly peaceful setting isolated in the mountains; 8 elegant dbl rooms, a café-bar & restaurant (€€) in a 17th-century *hostal*. €€

Molí del Caso Barri Terradellas 10, Bagà; \639 31 11 04; w molidelcaso.cat. A 19th-century mill converted into a sustainable country hotel, with 5 rooms, each named for different plants, an organic kitchen garden, plus a garden with medicinal herbs. Delicious organic food prepared by the master chef-owner. €€

Estel Ctra Sant Fruitós 39, Berga; \938 21 34 63; w hotelestel.com. Simple modern hotel, with 32 pristine rooms & easy parking nearby. €

SPORTS AND ACTIVITIES

Skiing Rasos de Peguera (\ 938 21 13 08; w rasos.net) Only 125km from Barcelona, near Berga in Castellar del Riu-Montmajor, it has 14 ski runs, two cross-country trails and five lifts. It's a small resort with no difficult runs, making it good for families, first-timers, and one-day skiers. In summer, it has biking and hiking trails.

Climbing and canyoning The Berguedà region is popular for climbing, canyoning amd other adventure sports. Many are concentrated in the Espacio Activo Vallcebre (\650 85 34 79; w espaiactiuvallcebre.cat). There are numerous local providers who can rent out equipment and offer classes (see the website for a comprehensive list).

BERGA The base of the Serra del Cadí (the southern confines of the vast mountain plain of the Cerdanya) has a pleasant if unremarkable historic centre. But what it lacks in monuments it more than makes up for with an extraordinary festival, La Patum (page 218).

Two churches, just outside of Berga, stand out. A narrow road from the Plaça de Guernica leads eastwards to the Romanesque **Sant Quirze de Pedret** (C/ C-16 km 96; \664 56 75 81; w elbergueda.cat/ca/pl266/cultura/romaniC/id642/sant-quirze-de-pedret.htm; ⊕ guided visits in Catalan, Apr–mid-Dec 10.00, 11.00 & noon Sat–Sun; free). Although its famous artworks are now in the National Museum of Catalan Art in Barcelona (page 119) and in Solsona, a restoration in 1995 uncovered some fascinating murals which date back to around 1100.

Just west of Berga, the 18th-century **Santuari de La Mare de Déu de Queralt** (BV-4242 10; \938 22 23 80; w santuarideQueralt.cat; ⊕ 08.00–20.00 daily; free) the

'Balcony of Catalunya', is balanced on a narrow mountain ridge (a funicular makes the trip up from the car park daily except Monday, or there are steps if you have sufficient puff). Inside, its rather unusual 14th-century figure of Virgin and Child has a swallow resting on the Virgin's hand and a weasel underneath her foot. Of late Queralt has been promoted as the end of an eight-day walk, the **Camí dels Bons Homes**, from Montsegur, retracing the steps of the Cathars who fled this way from France. The same road, the BV-4142, heads north to the **Rasos de Peguera** ski station.

SERRA DEL CADÍ To the northwest, the scenic B-400 follows the southern edge of the stunning, unspoiled Serra del Cadí, a chain that includes one of Catalunya's biggest national symbols, the iconic 2,497m, twin-peaked **Pedraforca** (pitchfork stone, supposedly the devil's own fork, or some say his cloven hoof), a favourite challenge of trekkers and daring rock-climbers who ascend its sheer walls; it's so popular that the mountain has its own information centre (Pl Pedraforca s/n; ☎938 25 80 05; w parcsnaturals.gencat.cat/ca/xarxa-de-parcs/pedraforca; ⏲ 09.00–14.00 daily) in **Saldes**.

In **Gósol**, to the west, Picasso and his lover Fernande Olivier stayed in the only inn for three months in 1906. The artist (who by then was living in Paris and deep in his Blue Period) painted villagers and landscapes, seeking his pagan Mediterranean roots – just before he invented Cubism. There is a wonderful exhibition describing his stay in Gósol, along with copies of paintings from this period, in the Ajuntament's **Centre Picasso de Gósol** (Pl Major 1; ☎973 37 29 77; w centrepicasso.art; ⏲ Jul–Aug 10.00–14.00 & 15.00–19.00 Tue–Sat, 10.00–14.00 Sun; Apr–May & Sep–Oct 10.00–14.00 & 15.00–19.00 Wed–Sat, 10.00–14.00 Sun; Nov–Mar 10.00–14.00 & 15.00–19.00 Fri–Sat, 10.00–14.00 Sun; free).

Tuixén, further west, is famous for its *trementinaires* – literally the 'turpentiners' – women who gathered medicinal mountain herbs, and who travelled across Catalunya for several months at a time. There's an annual festival in their honour every May, as well as a **Museu de les Trementinaires** (C/ de 25717; ☎973 37 00 30; w trementinaires.org; ⏲ 10.00–14.00 & 16.00–19.00 Sat, 10.00–14.00 Sun; free) along the road to La Seu d'Urgell, and a **Jardí Botànic de les Trementinaires** planted with the herbs they grew.

More grand scenery awaits to the east up the Llobregat. At Guardiola de Berguedà turn east to pretty **La Pobla de Lillet** ('field of lilies') with a pair of medieval bridges and a statue of Eusebi Güell, the area's great benefactor (page 24). A life-sized 12th-century *Majestat* holds pride of place in the parish church, transferred here from the Romanesque **Monestir de Santa Maria de Lillet** (ask at the tourist office for keys), 2km from the centre and next to a curious round chapel dedicated to St Miquel.

There are numerous springs in the area; and, along the River Llobregat and the little train line that once linked La Pobla de Lillet to El Clot de Moro (page 222) there's a surprise: Gaudí's lush **Jardines de Can Artigas** (C/ Ferrocarril s/n; ☎687 99 85 41; w turismelillet.cat/tour-item/jardins-artigas; ⏲ contact the tourist information office to book a guided tour in advance; adult/reduced/under 5 €5/4.50/ free), designed for his patron Güell's industrialist friend Joan Artigas. Gaudí drew out plans and sent two workers from the Park Güell to oversee the project, but the gardens fell into disrepair when the nearby Artigas factory was burned in the Civil War. In 1994 they were restored. As in the Park Güell, the emphasis was on local stone, in sinuous walls and terraces and bridges and fountains; statues of the symbols of the four Evangelists figure prominently. Gaudí also designed the **Xalet**

6

Catllaràs in 1901 (it's in the meadows beyond the Santuari de Falgars, reachable only by 4x4) for workers in the local coal mines.

Up the road towards Castellar de N'Hug is another Modernista work: the remarkable **El Clot del Moro** (1904), a cement factory designed by Rafael Guastavino. Built for Eusebi Güell, it was the first in Catalunya to produce Portland cement and it functioned until 1975; it's now the **Museu del Ciment Asland** (Paratge del Clot del Moro s/n; ☏ 938 25 70 37; w museuciment.cat; ⏰ April–mid-Dec, check website for opening times; adult/reduced/under 16 €8/4/free). Some believe that the fairy-tale chalet of the manager was by Gaudí as well. **Castellar de N'Hug** itself, with its cobbled streets and rural houses, is a popular resort; Catalans love to visit the never-failing **Fonts de Llobregat**, the source of Barcelona's river, which gushes from the rocks in a waterfall. The village's 12th-century church of **Sant Vicenç de Rus** has kept some of its original mural paintings; another good one is south in **Sant Jaume de Frontanyà**, proud to be the smallest municipality in Catalunya (pop. 26).

Back on the C-16 to Puigcerdà, little **Bagà** was the home to the ancient Pinós family of barons. The pretty porticoed **Plaça Galceran de Pinós** recalls a knight who was rescued from a Moorish prison in Almería by the miraculous intervention of a silver Byzantine cross. It was reputedly brought over from the First Crusade and is now kept in the handsome Transitional church of **Sant Esteban** (1339). The medieval Palau de Pinós contains the tourist office and the **Centre Medieval i dels Càtars** (Pujada de Palau 7; ☏ 619 74 60 99; w turismebaga.com; ⏰ Jul–Aug daily, guided visits at 10.30, other times check with the tourist office; free), which has several rooms dedicated to local history and the area's link with the Cathars.

Bagà is one of the access points of the **Parc Natural Cadí-Moixeró**, the biggest nature reserve in Catalunya. Made up of densely forested limestone mountains, it has Spain's greatest population of chamoix and offers some serious trekking for experienced walkers and paths for mountain bikes. Pick up maps and information at Bagà's Centre de Documentació del Parc (C/ de la Vinya 1; ☏ 938 24 41 51; w parcsnaturals.gencat.cat/ca/xarxa-de-parcs/cadi; ⏰ 09.00–14.00 Mon–Thu, 09.00–14.00 & 16.00–18.00 Fri, 09.00–16.00 Sat, 09.00–13.00 Sun).

PUIGCERDÀ AND THE CERDANYA

The lofty Cerdanya plateau-valley covers 419 square miles of the bed of a prehistoric lake. Once all part of Catalunya, it was divided equally between Spain and France by the Treaty of the Pyrenees in 1659, Spain getting the valley of the Segre. Guifré el Pílós' third son, Miron, was count of Cerdanya, and his descendants remained players in the stew of Old Catalan politics until the line died out in 1117 and it passed to the count of Barcelona.

Although it produces potatoes and pears (it gets more sun than anywhere in the Pyrenees) tourism is the Cerdanya's main money-spinner: alpine and cross-country skiing, snowshoeing and dog-sledding, riding and hiking, golf and balloon rides, trekking and mountain biking are all on offer. Yet it's hardly crowded: this is one of the least densely populated areas in Europe. Catalan is lingua franca on both sides of the frontier, although an even older language is behind the bizarre place names such as Er, Pi, Ro, Ix, and Ur.

GETTING THERE AND AROUND

By train Renfe's regional train line (R3) runs from Barcelona to Puigcerdà via Vic. Some services continue on to La Tor de Querol Enveig (in French, Latour-de-Carol-Enveitg) where you can make connections for Toulouse or catch Le Train Jaune de Cerdagne (page 359) to Villefranche-de-Confluent, with links to Perpignan.

By bus   Alsa (✆902 42 22 42; w alsa.es) operate bus services from Barcelona, Berga, Bellver and Manresa to Puigcerdà and Llívia. Teisa buses (✆972 20 48 68; w teisa-bus.com) link Puigcerdà to Girona, Llívia, Ribes de Freser, Ripoll, Sant Joan de les Abadesses and Olot.

TOURIST INFORMATION   Puigcerdà's helpful tourist office is handily located right in the centre of town (Pl de Santa Maria s/n; ✆972 88 05 42; w puigcerdaturisme. cat). There are also tourist information offices in Llívia (C/ dels Forns 10; ✆972 89 63 13; w llivia.org/en.html) and Bellver de Cerdanya (Pl Major 12; ✆973 51 00 16; w bellver.org/turisme).

🏠 WHERE TO STAY

Torre del Remei   Camí Reial s/n, 4km outside Puigcerdà, in Bolvir; ✆972 14 01 82; w torredelremei.com. For a real treat, head for this stunning Modernista palace, now a 5-star hotel with 24 exquisite rooms & suites, extensive gardens, a pool, a large, elegant terrace & plenty of activities including golf, hiking & skiing close by. The restaurant (€€€€), easily the finest in the region, serves refined Cerdanyan cuisine. €€€€

Hotel Villa Paulita   Avda Pons i Gasch 15, Puigcerdà; ✆972 88 46 22; w villapaulitahotel. com. Stylish boutique hotel in a pretty pink mansion (& an annexe), with a garden, a fancy spa & a gourmet restaurant (€€€€) with lovely views over the lake. €€€

Cal Marrufes   C/ Ripoll 3, Age; ✆972 14 11 74; w calmarrufes.com. About a dozen rooms & apartments in a beautifully restored old farmhouse in a tiny hamlet, just east of Puigcerdà. €€

Can Borrell   C/ Retorn 3, Meranges; ✆972 88 00 33; w canborrell.com. Peaceful rooms in an old stone farmhouse far from the hurly-burly, with an excellent creative restaurant (€€€), with dishes based on local ingredients. €€

Hotel Bernat de So   (C/ Cereja 5, Llívia; ✆972 14 62 06; w hotelbernatdeso.com. In one of the oldest properties in Llívia, comfortable, sustainable design, friendly owners & a pool in the gardens. €€

Hotel del Lago   Avda Dr Piguillem 7, Puigcerdà; ✆972 88 10 00; w hotellago.com. Large, modern hotel, with well-equipped rooms (some with private fireplaces), a garden, indoor & outdoor pools & small spa. €€

Hotel del Prado   Ctra de Llívia s/n, Puigcerdà; ✆972 88 04 00; w hoteldelprado.cat. Delightful, mid-sized chalet-style hotel on the edge of town, & an excellent restaurant (€€€). It's popular with families, & has a large garden with pool & a play area. €€

Hostal Rusó   Pujada de l'Església 2, Llívia; ✆972 14 62 64; w hostalruso.es. Cosy, pristine, if small, rooms in an old stone building with a courtyard in the historic centre. A traditional Catalan b/fast is included. €

🍴 WHERE TO EAT AND DRINK

La Formatgeria de Llívia   Pla de Ro s/n, Llívia; ✆972 14 62 79; w laformatgeria.com; ⏱ 13.00– 15.30 & 20.00–22.00 Sun, 13.00–15.00 Mon, 13.00–15.00 & 20.15–22.00 Thu, 13.00–15.00 & 20.15–22.30 Fri–Sat. Stylish glass dining room with views & wonderful dishes from the Cerdanya, prepared with a creative touch, in this old cheese factory, along with excellent wines. €€€

El Pati de la Tieta   Ctra dels Ferrers 20, Puigcerdà; ✆972 88 01 56; w elpatiodelatieta. com ⏱ 12.30–15.30 & 19.30–22.30 Thu–Sat, 12.30–15.30 Sun. Tasty local meat cooked on a wood-fired grill, as well as pizzas. There's a pretty vine-covered terrace for summer. €€

Pizzeria Taller   Rbla Josep Maria Martí 6, Puigcerdà; ✆972 88 03 10; 📷 fabianmartin_ pizza. The headquarters of Fabían Martín, former boxer, famous for his excellent & highly unusual pizzas with wildflowers or edible gold (it's in the balsamic vinegar), & also for his pizza acrobatic skills. €€

6

✳ **Tap de Suro** C/ Querol 21, Puigcerdà; ☎678 65 59 28; ◙ tapdesuro; ⏱ 19.00–23.00 Tue–Sun. Delightful wine bar, serving up delicious, creative tapas which are paired with a thoughtful selection of wines from all over the region. €

SPORTS AND ACTIVITIES

Golf For those who enjoy a round of golf, **Golf Sant Marc** (Camí de Sant Marc, Puigcerdà; ☎689 20 06 05; w golfsantmarc.com) offers a scenic 18-hole course with mountain views.

Hiking Puigcerdà and the Cerdanya region are popular for hiking, with several routes, including demanding long-distance routes like the GR11 and GR4, as well as easier, shorter walks that are suitable for families or less experienced walkers.

Mountain biking The Cerdanya is a major mountain biking hub. The Centre de BTT de la Cerdanya (BTT Centre of La Cerdanya; w cerdanya.org/en/what-to-do/ routes/bike-routes/btt) has established a number of trails for cyclists of all levels, which are well maintained and signposted.

Skiing and snowshoeing These resorts are also popular in summer, when visitors come to enjoy hiking and other outdoor activities.

Guils Fontanera Guils de Cerdanya; ☎972 19 70 47; w guils.com. Cross-country ski resort, often site of the Spanish National Championships. 45km of tracks.

Lles de Cerdanya Cap del Rec, Lles de Cerdanya; ☎973 29 31 00; w lles.net. Cross-country skiing & snowshoeing.
Aransa El Fornell s/n, Aránser; ☎679 98 71 30; w aransaski.com. Cross-country skiing.

PUIGCERDÀ The one urban patch is right on the border with France. The town has been the capital of the Cerdanya ever since it was founded in 1117; now a bustling resort town ringed in by holiday apartments, it had considerably more character before it was badly bombed in the Civil War. Somehow the bombs missed its landmark, the lofty 13th-century octagonal **bell tower**, while destroying the rest of the church of Santa Maria. Nearby in Plaça dels Herois is one of the town's most striking buildings, the eclectic pink **Casino Ceretà**, home to Puigcerdà's cultural society. Around the corner in Passeig 10 d'Abril, the Dominican monastery church of **Sant Domènec** has frescoes from 1362, showing brutes dealing the saint a splitting headache.

The town's lake, **Estany de Puigcerdà**, is a feat of medieval engineering from 1260, bringing water by aqueduct to irrigate local farms and provide ice. In the 19th century, when the rail line was extended to town, wealthy Barcelonins built summer houses overlooking the water. The romantic 19th-century **Parc Schierbeck** around the lake was the work of Danish consul German Schierbeck, who was fond of the place.

In the Treaty of the Pyrenees Spain gave France 33 villages of Upper Cerdanya – but not the 'towns'. Hence the anomaly of **Llívia** (pop. 1,500), an islet located 6km from Puigcerdà inside France. An Iberian oppidum called Kerr, later Julia Libyca on the Roman highway Strata Ceretana, Llívia was the ancient ('and logical', it sniffs) capital of the Cerdanya. Its little medieval core is home to the **Farmàcia Esteva**. Dating from 1415, this pharmacy is said to be the oldest in Europe – and owned by the Esteva family from 1660 to 1926. It was purchased by the government of Girona in 1965 on condition that it always remains in Llívia. The medicines are stored not in cabinets, but ornate shrines, veritable retables of drugs – all now part of the eclectic **Museu Municipal** (C/ dels Forns 10; ☎972 89 63 13; w museullivia. net; ☉ 09.30–14.00 & 15.30–18.30 Wed–Fri, 10.00–14.00 & 15.30–19.00 Sat, 09.30–14.30 Sun; adult/reduced/under 6 €4/3/free).

Up a small road northwest of Puigcerdà, **Guils de Cerdanya** has a popular cross-country ski resort. Other sights are west of Puigcerdà off the N260 which follows the Riu Segre across a giant meadow. This was also one of the roads to Santiago de Compostela; at **Bolvir** the little church of El Remei has displays on the pilgrims. Just after **Ger** you can turn up the winding road to **Meranges**, a small stone hamlet famous for carving clogs. You can see how they did it at the **Museu de l'Esclop** (Pl Major 1; ☎635 57 79 23; closed for renovation). It's also the base for the popular walk to the small Malniu lakes, legendary rendezvous for witches in the 16th and 17th centuries.

Down in the valley, **Bellver de Cerdanya** is surrounded by a bevy of tiny hamlets. The 10th-century **Santa Eugènia** in **Nerellà** keeps its bells in the startling 'Leaning Tower of the Cerdanya'. Towards Le Seu d'Urgell, on the road south of Martinet you can visit a relic of the bad old days – part of Franco's secret defences across the Pyrenees, consisting of 2,000 bunkers thrown up in the 1940s in case the Allies were angry enough to invade. The Cerdanya was considered particularly vulnerable and had the greatest concentration: you can explore some at the **Parc dels Búnquers**. On a lighter or at least more musical, note, tiny **Arsèguel** might tempt you to stop with its **Museu de l'Acordió** (closed indefinitely) with a collection of accordions from the Pyrenees and its lovely tangle of steep medieval alleyways. La Seu d'Urgell (page 298) waits at the end of the road.

6

7

Tarragona and Its Province

Everyone knows Girona and the Costa Brava. Now it's time to come to terms with the other side of Barcelona. Once the northern coast had made the touristic big time, this one had to have a name too, and Spain's indefatigable tourist bureaucracy eventually came up with 'Costa Daurada'. Don't expect the 'Golden Coast' to be an endless sandy tourist trap; in fact there are only a few small patches of overbuilt beaches, and these are close to the big city, Tarragona. The tourist promoters should have left it alone. Tarragona and its province have enough character and interest; they don't really need a contrived nickname. The coast isn't even the major attraction: there's a wonderful diversity of landscapes here, a little bit of everything packed into a small space.

Over half the province's people live in the two-headed urban conglomeration that contains Tarragona, once a great Roman provincial capital, and the modern industrial city of Reus, along with the major resorts of Salou and Cambrils. Just inland are the rugged Prades mountains, with a trio of glorious medieval monasteries on one side, including the famous Poblet, where Catalunya once buried its kings. On the other side is one of the world's great wine regions, Priorat. Further south, the tail end of the Costa provides some quiet beaches, on the way to the Ebro Valley, the northernmost spot where citrus fruits will grow, and the Ebro Delta, one of the Mediterranean's most important wetlands.

TARRAGONA

Imagine, if you can, a period when Barcelona was merely provincial, when its citizens had to travel to a great metropolis down the coast for a good time. Two thousand years ago that must have seemed the natural order of things for the people of Colonia Iulia Urbs Triumphalis Tarraco, the capital of Hispania, one of the few places in the empire a sophisticated Roman official wouldn't have minded getting posted to.

History has taken Tarragona down a peg, but left it a gracious city of palm trees and well-worn ruins that is a delight to visit. It has a striking setting, a natural rampart 70m above the sea; locals and tourists alike love to come down to watch the ships and enjoy the sea breezes at the 'Balcony of the Mediterranean'. Now that the *tarragonins* are freed from the joint burdens of governing Hispania and conjugating Latin verbs, they can devote all their time to the important things: drinking coffee and eating tapas. We wouldn't want to leave the impression that Tarragona is only a party town. Despite the laid-back Mediterranean air and the packs of tourists inspecting the Roman relics, the 141,00 *tarragonins* really do work for a living. Their city is one of Spain's biggest ports, and an increasingly important industrial centre.

TARRAGONA PROVINCE

Lleida

AP-2

Santuari de Montserrat

C-12

Vallbona de
les Monjes

C-37

L'Espluga
de Francolí

Montblanc

Santa Maria
de Poblet

AP-2

Santes
Creus

Zaragoza

Prades

Valls

Vilafranca del
Penedès

A-27

Escaladei

N-340

Montferri

Vistabella

El Vendrell

Villa de
Centcelles

La Secuita

Coma
Ruga

Ebre

Riba-Roja

Bellmunt
del Priorat

Falset

N-420

Riudecanyes

Els Pallaressos

Pont del
Diable

Torredembara

Reus

Tarragona

Corbera
d'Ebre

Monestir de
Sant Miquel
d'Escornalbou

E-15

Castell de Tamarit

Altafulla

Torre de los Escipiones

N-420

El Pinell
de Brai

Miravet

Pratdip

Mont-roig
del Camp

PortAventura World

Gandesa

Benifallet

C-44

Cambrils

Salou

Coll de
Moro

Miami
Platja

Horta de Sant Joan

*Parc Natural
dels Ports*

C-12

El Perelló

L'Ametlla
del Mar

Tortosa

L'Ampolla

*Punta del
Fangar*

TV-3454

*Estany de
l'Encanyissada*

Deltebre

*Parc del
Delta d
l'Ebre*

N

Encanyissada

Bradt

Sant Carles
de la Ràpita

0 ——— 10km

0 ——— 10 miles

Alcanar

Valencia

HISTORY Before Tarragona was Roman it was an Iberian town; in fact, it may have been the most important town the Iberians ever built; on the fortifications, underneath the work of Roman and medieval times, you'll see the foundations of huge 'cyclopean' stones that the natives somehow manoeuvred into place. According to ancient historians, the natives called the place something like 'Kesse', which is probably the same as the name of the Iberian tribe that inhabited the area, the Cessetani.

The Romans made it a prime objective in the Second Punic War, with Gnaeus Cornelius Scipio seizing the town in 218BC. Their rebuilt and resettled version, now called Tarraco, was soon filled with immigrants from Italy and the Greek east. It would be the base for the long and difficult Roman conquest of Spain and the capital of the vast province of Hispania Citerior.

Tarraco was the most elegant city on the Iberian peninsula; the poets Martial and Pliny praised its superb climate, fertile fields and delicious wines, and Augustus relaxed here after his 26BC campaign in the north of Spain. By the 2nd century AD it had 30,000 inhabitants. A Christian community existed from an early date; a local legend has it that St Paul preached in Tarraco. The Visigoths made it one of Spain's leading bishoprics in the 5th century AD; St Hermenegild, a Visigoth prince who

7

converted to Catholicism, led the city in a revolt against the Arian heresies of his father, King Leovigild, who had him martyred.

By then Tarraco was only a shadow of its former self. Fires, invasions and the silting up of its harbour whittled the population down, and those who remained gradually moved up into the old Roman citadel, within the safety of its impressive walls. As home to an archbishop, it continued to be a seat of authority, and important churches were built, all now vanished. With the coming of Moorish rule after AD713, the city lost its political raison d'être and almost disappeared.

A much-reduced Tarragona – probably little more than a village – is said to have been almost entirely Jewish. Its second chance came after it was taken by Ramon Berenguer III in 1118. The count gave it to the Archbishop of Barcelona, who in turn handed it over to a Norman mercenary named Robert Bordet. Norman rule only lasted until 1171, but it laid the foundation for the city's revival. They began the 'king's castle' and the new cathedral. Tarragona got a city government of its own in 1336. After playing a full part in Catalunya's imperial adventure in the Middle Ages, the city once again declined into a backwater under Spanish rule.

Tarragona was besieged in the War of the Spanish Succession, and twice in the Napoleonic Wars, including a particularly brutal siege at the hands of the French in 1811: after the French forced their way in, they butchered 2,000 of the townspeople. Now, a modern city has spread far beyond the hilltop walled enclosure, building one of the most spacious and urbane *eixamples* (extensions) of any Catalan city. The economy has been growing apace, thanks to its port, which ships out the products of industries in the suburbs as well as the majority of Catalunya's agricultural exports, and the booming tourism industry. Greater Tarragona, counting its twin city Reus, now has a population of over half a million.

Visualising Roman Tarraco

Usually, it isn't hard to tell how a Roman city looked, even when a modern one is piled on top of it; its bones are still warm – a neat grid of streets, though maybe worn and kinked a bit over the centuries – and there's often a square where the old forum used to be. Tarragona is different, and, if you mean to wander around town looking at the widely scattered Roman remains, you'll have to know the layout to make sense of it. The plans and reconstructions in the Archaeological Museum (page 233), or the great model (*maqueta*) of the city in Plaça del Pallol (page 234), will help.

The ancient *tarragonins* must have taken their horse racing pretty seriously, because the track was set in the very centre of town: the circus filled all the space between the Rambla Vella and Carrer Ferrers. The north side of Plaça del Font was roughly the line of the spina, the centre strip of the racecourse, lined with monuments, statues and perhaps an obelisk or two. Tarraco's circus overlooked an equally imposing amphitheatre. In the Roman Empire, only cities in the west had amphitheatres. The Greek east wasn't so impressed with staged combats and mass slaughters of exotic animals (or occasionally people), but colonials like the Celts, North Africans and Iberians lapped it up.

Tarragona's **Part Alta** ('upper part'), the colourful old town, probably had very little population at all in Roman times. Its mighty walls were built to shield an administrative city, the seat of the provincial government. All that space held nothing but soldiers and bureaucrats, working in offices set around two huge forums. On the other side of the circus lay the real, workaday city, in the area bisected by the delightful Rambla Nova today. Everything here went to seed in the Dark Ages, as the surviving *tarragonins* took shelter inside the administrative city's stronger walls, and this area remained open country until the 19th century.

TARRAGONA

Bradt

N

0   300m
0   300yds

For listings, see page 231

Where to stay

1 B&B Hotel Tarragona
   Centro Urbis
2 H10 Imperial Tarraco
3 Hostal 977
4 Plaça de la Font
5 Tarragona Hostel

Off map

Hotel Mas La Boella
Làpety Hotel

Where to eat and drink

6 Bar El Cortijo
7 Bufet el Tiberi
8 El Crank
9 El Cup Vell
10 El Terrat
11 Les Coques
12 Racó de l'Abat

Off map

Restaurant Ca l'Eulàlia

Làpety Hotel

VIA AUGUSTA

PG DE SANT ANTONI

Santa Maria
del Mirade

Platja del
Mirade

PASSEIG MARÍTIM RAFAEL CASANOVA

Passeig
Arqueològic

Casa Canals

Cathedral

PART ALTA

C/ DE SANT PAU

C/ DE LA
MERCERIA

Plaça del
Fòrum

Museu d'Art
Modern

Museu
Arqueològic

Volta Pallol
(Mapping i
Maqueta de Tàrraco)

C/ MAJOR

C/ CAVALLERS

Circ Romà
& Pretori

Amfiteatre
Romà

VIA DE L'IMPERI ROMÀ

C/ DE LA MARIA CRISTINA

RAMBLA VELLA

Balcó del
Mediterrani

Railway
station

PG DE ESPANYA

RAMBLA NOVA

Teatre
Metropol

C/ DE LA UNIÓ

C/ D'APODACA

EIXAMPLE

Plaça de
Corsini

CaixaBank

Fòrum de
la Colònia

Teatre
Romà

C/ LLEIDA

Farmàcia
Fullana Fiol

Mercat
Central

RAMBLA NOVA

AVDA PRAT DE LA RIBA

C/ MALLORCA

C/ PERE MARTELL

C/ REIAL

C/ DEL MAR

MOLL DE LA COSTA

Bus station

Museu del
Port de Tarragona

Tinglado 4

AV RAMON Y CAJAL

N-340

Necropolis
de Tàrraco

C/ PERE MARTELL

C/ CARDENAL VIDAL I BARRAQUER

EL SERRALLO

PG DE LA INDEPENDÈNCIA

Hotel Mas La Boella,
Hospital Universitari de
Tarragona Joan XXIII

Restaurant Ca l'Eulàlia

7

Now, ancient foundations lie under blingy skyscraper apartments, and remains of its praetorium and forum are kept up as little parks. Of course, the great Roman roads that connected the cities were part of the same unified style of urbanism. If you leave Tarragona along the coast to the north, the main N340 follows the Roman Via Augusta. Romans used the roads outside their cities as a setting for important tombs and monuments, as along Rome's famous Appian Way. On the Via Augusta you'll see a triumphal arch, and the Tomb of the Scipios, the brothers who inaugurated the conquest of Spain for Rome. No Roman town would be complete without an aqueduct, and Tarragona has one of the grandest survivors, the Pont del Diable out in the woods 7km north of town (page 237), and worth the trouble it takes to find it.

GETTING THERE AND AWAY

By air Tarragona is served by the small Reus airport (w aena.es/en/reus. html), 12km away. Local bus L50, operated by Reus Transport (℡ 977 30 00 66; w reustransport.cat) links the airport with Reus, and Monbus services (℡ 900 92 91 92; w monbus.es) link it to Tarragona and Barcelona; Plana (℡ 977 55 36 80; w empresaplana.cat) services link it to La Pineda, Salou, and Cambrils on the Costa Daurada. All the main car rental companies have a booth at the airport, as well as offices in the city centre (including Hertz w hertz.es; Budget w budget; Europcar w europcar.com).

By train Tarragona is linked frequently to Barcelona (regional lines R16 and R17) and Lleida (R14): for timetables, see w rodalies.gencat.cat. Renfe operate services to Zaragoza and Valencia by rail several times a day (w renfe.com). The RENFE station is just below the Balcó del Mediterrani. The high-speed AVE trains can take you to Lleida (31mins) or Madrid (2.5hrs), but note that the AVE station, called Tarragona Camp, is out in the country 12km north of town (off the N240 near Peñafort) and connected to the main station by local buses.

By bus The Estació de Autobuses (℡ 977 22 91 26) is at Plaça Imperial Tàrraco, the big circle on the western edge of the Eixample. The bus, operated by Alsa (℡ 902 42 22 42; w alsa.es) is the easiest way to get to Barcelona; there are connections for all other major Spanish cities. Within Tarragona, bus services are operated by EMT (w emtanemambtu.cat), and Plana (℡ 977 55 36 80; w empresaplana.cat) run regular services to Salou, Cambrils, Port Aventura, Reus, and other towns in the province.

By car Parking is tricky in the city centre, with on-street parking spaces hard to find. Road markings define the different zones: you can park for up to 2 hours in blue zones and for up to 24 hours in orange zones. Green zones are for residents, but non-residents can park in available spaces for up to 2 hours. For convenience, consider leaving your car at the big underground car park (w pavapark.com/ parkings/parking-balco-del-mediterrani-tarragona, centrally located by the Balcó del Mediterrani on Rambla Nova.

TOURIST INFORMATION The city tourist office (C/ Major 39; ℡ 977 25 07 95; w tarragonaturisme.cat; ⊕ 10.00–14.00 & 15.00–18.00 Mon–Sat, 10.00–14.00 Sun) is very centrally located close to the cathedral. The Catalan Tourist Board also has an information office, just off the Rambla Nova (C/ Fortuny 4; ℡ 977 23 34 15; w catalunya.com; ⊕ 09.30–17.00 Mon–Fri, 10.00–14.00 Sat), which can provide info on the city as well as across the entire region.

🏠 WHERE TO STAY *Map, page 229*

Hotel Mas La Boella Autovia T-11, Salida 12, La Canonja; ☎ 977 77 15 15; w laboella.com. Blissfully set amid olive groves & manicured gardens about 6km from the city centre, this handsome *masia* has been converted into a gorgeous boutique hotel, with 13 spacious rooms & suites across 2 buildings, a fine restaurant (€€€) & an outdoor pool. €€€€

Làpety Hotel Camí de la Cuixa 19; ☎ 977 13 13 17; w lapetyhotel.com. Just 8 lovely rooms, some with private terraces, in a beautiful villa that dates back to 1910. Set in large, landscaped gardens, it's an oasis of peace just a 5-min walk from the beach & about 10min to the Part Alta. €€€€

H10 Imperial Tarraco Rbla Vella 2; ☎ 977 15 66 07; w h10hotels.com/en/tarragona-hotels/h10-imperial-tarraco. A bit of Miami Beach modern, this huge white hotel is beautifully sited on the Balcó del Mediterrani & most rooms have stunning views. It's handy for the old town & has a pool. €€€

B&B Hotel Tarragona Centro Urbis Pl de Corsini 10; ☎ 977 24 01 16; w hotel-bb.com/es/hotel/ tarragona-centro-urbis. Large, modern hotel which has bright, immaculate rooms with AC, some with large balconies, which is nicer on the inside than it looks on the outside. Despite the name, b/fast is not available, but there are plenty of cafés nearby. €€

Hostal 977 C/ Cavallers 4 bis; ☎ 977 21 66 51; w hostal977.com. Cosy little charmer tucked down a narrow street in the Part Alta, with 5 quirky but stylish rooms featuring lots of exposed brick & wooden beams & a sitting area where you can enjoy a coffee or a glass of wine. €€

Plaça de la Font Pl de la Font 26; ☎ 977 24 61 34; w placadelafont.hoteltarragona.net/en. A small hotel with about 20 rooms on this pretty square. Bright, attractive rooms, some with balconies overlooking the square. €€

Tarragona Hostel C/ de la Unió 1; ☎ 637 54 54 84; w tarragonahostel.com. This basic backpacker hostel is handily located in the Part Alta & offers a dozen inexpensive dorm rooms as well as dbls with private or shared bathrooms, a courtyard garden & shared kitchen. €

🍴 WHERE TO EAT AND DRINK *Map, page 229*

El Cup Vell C/ d'en Ventallols 8; ☎ 636 85 82 43; 📷 elcupvell; ⏱ 13.45–15.00 & 20.45–22.00 Wed–Sat, 13.45–15.00 Sun. There's no sign & no menu at this tiny & very charming gastro hotspot, tucked away down a narrow street, but whatever creative dishes you will be served straight from the open kitchen will be exquisitely fresh & delicious. €€€€€

El Terrat C/ Pons d'Icart 19; ☎ 977 24 84 85; w elterratrestaurant.com; ⏱ 13.00–15.30 & 20.30–21.30 Wed–Thu, 13.00–15.30 & 20.30–22.30 Fri–Sat, 13.00–15.30 Sun. Imaginative chef Moha Quach suffuses Mediterranean cuisine with flavours from Morocco, while focusing on locally sourced produce. Definitely a place to push the boat out on one of the 2 tasting menus (€85/115) if you want an unforgettable meal. €€€€€

Restaurant Ca l'Eulàlia Pl Bisbe Bonet; ☎ 977 21 50 75; w caleulalia.com; ⏱ 13.30–15.30 Mon–Sat. One of the best places near the harbour to enjoy beautifully fresh fish, along with classic Mediterranean rice dishes like their excellent paella. €€€€

El Crank C/ Sant Pere 33; ☎ 877 07 27 68; w elcrank.cat; ⏱ 13.45–15.00 & 20.45–22.00 Wed–Sat, 13.45–15.00 Sun. Buzzy, fashionable, stylish gastrobar set a couple of streets back from the port, with tasty cuisine that puts a modern twist on popular local favourites. €€€

Les Coques C/ Sant Llorenç 15; ☎ 977 22 83 00; w les-coques.com; ⏱ 13.00–15.45 Wed–Thu & Sun, 13.00–15.45 & 20.30–22.00 Fri–Sat. Pretty, rustic-style restaurant that serves up market-fresh Catalan cuisine with a modern twist. €€€

Racó de l'Abat C/ de l'Abat 2; ☎ 625 71 59 01; w abatrestaurant.es. A wonderfully old-fashioned restaurant, where you can enjoy fish & meat cooked on a wood-fired grill (a la brasa), as well as traditional tapas in a vaulted dining room with wooden beams. €€€

Bar El Cortijo C/ Rebolledo 27; ☎ 977 22 48 67; 📘; ⏱ 07.30–16.30 Mon–Sat, 08.00–noon Sun. A classic, wonderfully old-fashioned tapas bar, renowned for its delicious, authentic dishes prepared to time-honoured recipes. €€

Bufet el Tiberi C/ Martí d'Ardenya 5; ☎ 977 23 54 03; ⏱ 13.00–16.00 Mon–Sat. A long-standing favourite, this popular neighbourhood local serves all the traditional favourites – canelons, stuffed chicken, rices, stews – buffet-style, so you can eat as much as you want. €€

7

OTHER PRACTICALITIES

Banks There are several ATMs and banks around the Plaça de la Font and the Plaça Nova in the city centre, including CaixaBank at Rambla Nova 100.

Medical There are lots of pharmacies in Tarragona, marked with a red or green cross. The **Farmàcia Fullana Fiol** (C/ Cristòfor Colom 1; ✆ 977 21 45 17; w farmaciafullana.com; ⊕ 08.30–21.30 daily), just off the Rambla Nova, is conveniently central and open daily. The city's largest hospital is the **Hospital Universitari de Tarragona Joan XXIII** (C/ Dr Mallafré Guasch 4; ✆ 977 29 58 00).

Post office The main post office in Tarragona is located at Plaça Corsini s/n (✆ 977 25 19 46; w correos.es; ⊕ 08.30–20.30 Mon–Sat).

WHAT TO SEE AND DO
Old Tarragona

Balcó del Mediterrani As in Barcelona, Tarragona's main promenades are called *rambles*: the Rambla Vella and the parallel Rambla Nova, both decorated with Modernista buildings. Both begin at the 'Balcony of the Mediterranean', its famous 97.5m belvedere overlooking Tarragona's port and beautiful beaches. Looking the other way, punctuating the end of the Rambla Nova, is a wonderfully cinematic statue of King Pere III's great admiral-privateer **Roger de Llúria**, the man who conquered Sicily for the Crown of Aragon.

The Balcó, with its fountains and palm trees and panoramic views, is the gathering place of the *tarragonins*, especially on Sunday morning. Down below, besides the sea and the port, you can see the ruins of the Roman amphitheatre (page 236).

Circ Romà and Pretori (Pl del Rei; ✆ 977 24 22 20; w tarragona.cat/patrimoni/museu-historia; ⊕ Apr–Oct 09.00–20.45 Tue–Sat, 09.00–14.30 Sun; Nov–Mar 09.00–20.00 Tue–Fri, 09.00–20.30 Sat, 09.30–14.30 Sun; adult/under 12 €5/free) Just behind the Balcó, north of the Rambla Vella, you can climb over the remains of the southern curve of the **Circ Romà** (Roman Circus), with the vaulting that held up some of the banks of seats. Far as they were from the finish line, these weren't the cheap seats. If it worked like Rome's Circus Maximus, seats weren't numbered, so it would have been first come first served. Domitian, that most sporting of emperors, built the circus in the 1st century AD. Adjoining the circus, and linked by an underground passage, is the 1st-century BC **Pretori** (Praetorium), where some finds from the circus are displayed. It's popularly called the 'Castle of Pilate' (Tarragona perversely liked to claim Pontius Pilate as a favourite son), but it's really a medieval palace built over a Roman one; it hosted Augustus and Hadrian, and later the Kings of Aragon. The French destroyed much of it in the siege of 1811, but one defence tower survives.

COMBINED TICKET FOR TARRAGONA'S ROMAN SITES

You can pay individually at each of the sites (adult/reduced/under 12 €5/2.50/free), or purchase the joint admission ticket for the five Roman sites in Tarragona that are run by the city's history museum.

The price is €15 (reduced €7.50, children under 12 go free) and includes entry to Passeig Arqueològic, Circ-Pretori, Fòrum de la Colònia (currently closed for restoration), Amfiteatre and the Casa Canals.

Museu Arqueològic (Closed for renovation until end 2026; highlights are on view in El Serrallo at Tinglado 4, page 236) Next to the Praetorium, the Archaeological Museum has an exceptional collection of everything Roman. It's been closed for renovation since 2018 and is expected to reopen at the end of 2026. Until then, some of the biggest highlights of the collection are on display at a warehouse by the port (page 236).

Based on the museum's displays pre-2018, expect to see a quorum of statues of emperors and togaed local worthies (the heads are largely missing; as elsewhere in the empire, cities would often knock them off when an emperor died and replace them with the visage of the new man). Some rare mural paintings from the interiors of houses have been moved here, including a lively hunting scene, and plenty of mosaics, including one lovely fountain with mosaics of fish at the bottom of the basin, designed to be seen through the water. Another mosaic shows nearly every variety of seafood available in Tarragona's waters in precise detail. Besides making us hungry for lunch, it also serves as a prelude to the many rooms of everyday objects: candlesticks, cosmetics and jewellery, lamps, and lots of kitchen equipment. These help make old Tarraco come alive, even if you can't puzzle out the Catalan explanations.

There's some genuine art here too: a chubby, charming baby Hercules with his club, or a remarkable giant marble medallion bearing the image of Zeus Ammon with his ram's horns. There's nothing in Tarragona that would look out of place in Rome itself. Artists and architects in Gaul developed their own unique variations on the Classical styles, but Hispania was so completely a colony that its art often betrays a wish to out-Italy Italy.

In the back streets around the museum, you can see what remains of Tarragona's **Jewish quarter**, in the narrow arched lanes around Plaça dels Àngels, where the synagogue once stood.

Casa Canals (C/ d'en Granada 11; ☎977 24 28 58; **w** tarragona.cat/patrimoni/museu-historia; ⊕ Apr–Oct 09.00–20.45 Tue–Sat, 09.00–14.30 Sun; Nov–Mar 09.00–18.30 Tue–Fri, 09.00–18.30 Sat, 09.30–14.30 Sun; adult/reduced/under 12 €5/2.50/free) The Canals family home, which dates from the 18th century, was remodelled handsomely to host Carlos IV in 1802, when he came to open the Tarragona port. The Canals family lived here right up until the 1990s, when they ceded it to local government. There are lots of gilded salons, stuffed with paintings and portraits of people we probably wouldn't enjoy knowing, and a rather scrubby garden to explore.

Museu d'Art Modern (C/ Santa Anna 8; ☎977 23 50 32; **w** dipta.cat/mamt; ⊕ Jun–Sep 10.00–20.00 Tue–Fri, 10.00–15.00 & 17.00–20.00 Sat, 11.00–14.00 Sun; Oct–May 10.00–18.00 Tue–Fri, 10.00–14.00 & 16.00–18.00 Sat, 11.00–14.00; free) Set in a trio of 18th-century townhouses, this museum displays the work of 19th- and 20th-century artists, including Santiago Rusiñol and Ramon Casas, as well as a large collection by Tarragonin sculptor Julio Antonio, but the highlight is Joan Miró's vibrant *Tarragona Tapestry* (*Tapís de Tarragona*, 1970).

Plaça del Forum This pretty square, with lots of terrace cafés, has a tiny fraction of the remains of the tremendous Roman Provincial Forum, headquarters of the government. This gives on to the 14th-century arcaded **Carrer Merceria**, where, at no. 17, you'll find the **Antigua Casa Corderet**, the very first shop in Catalunya when it began selling candles in 1751, which is still going strong. Beyond it, where the street meets Carrer Major, you'll see the fine 17th-century **Casa Consistorial**.

7

Cathedral (Pla de la Seu s/n; ☎ 977 23 62 09; w catedraldetarragona.com; ⊕ Jul–Aug 11.00–20.00 Mon, 09.30–19.00 Tue–Sat, 14.00–20.00 Sun; Nov–Feb 11.00–17.00 Mon, 09.30–17.00 Tue–Fri, 09.30–18.00 Sat, 14.00–18.00 Sun; Sep–Oct & Mar–Jun 11.00–19.00 Mon, 09.30–19.00 Tue–Sat, 14.00–19.00 Sun; adult/reduced/7–12/under 7 €12/8.50/5.50/free) A stairway from Carrer Major ascends to Tarragona's tremendous cathedral of Santa Tecla, a masterpiece of the Transitional style, begun in the 12th century and completed in the 15th. The cathedral complex almost exactly covers the spot once occupied by the upper square of the Provincial Forum, with the governor's offices and a temple to the deified emperors – a religious and political continuity of over 2,000 years.

The principal façade, though incomplete, presents a very French-Norman air, with a magnificent rose window and fine 13th-century statues. Inside, more than the other great Catalan cathedrals, Tarragona has preserved its mystical gloom – which makes it difficult to see the magnificent wood and alabaster *Retaule de Santa Tecla* in the **Capilla Mayor**, a 1430 work by Pere Johan honouring Tarragona's patron saint. In the predella the details become increasingly minute and include tiny spiders and butterflies, as fine as filigree. Santa Tecla was a girl from Konya, Turkey, who was converted by St Paul and followed him for a long time thereafter, dressed as a boy. Her legendary story consists largely of fighting off cads and miraculously escaping tortures, as you can see on the retable.

To the right of the altar stands a starkly realistic **tomb effigy of Archbishop Joan d'Aragó**, made by a 14th-century Italian artist. There's a mudéjar **sacristy** from the same era, a 16th-century organ and the 14th-century Gothic **Chapel of Santa Maria dels Sastres** (of the tailors), a profession wealthy enough here to have endowed the cathedral's finest chapel.

The enormous **cloister** is decorated with 12th-century sculpture that alone would make the trip to Tarragona worthwhile. Moorish influences are evident in the geometric panels that fill the spaces below the arches. The scenes over the door are especially robust and, among the fanciful capitals, don't miss the one just to the right as you enter, depicting two scenes from the medieval fable of the clever cat who feigns death to outsmart the cautious mice hiding in the rafters. Note also the *mihrab*, the little niche in the wall orientated towards Mecca. What's this doing in a Christian cloister? If they know, the *tarragonins* aren't saying. The cathedral **museum** is just off the cloister, with an archaeological collection and some fine Gothic painting and sculpture from parish churches. Among the highlights are a Roman sarcophagus, a carved Arab archway, and a 15th-century tapestry.

Just across Carrer Coques from the cathedral complex stands the **Hospital de Santa Tecla**, a rare and remarkable example of a workaday medieval building. It has a charming Romanesque arcade over the pavement, and the well-worn air of a building that has seen it all over its 800 years.

Volta Pallol (Mapping i Maqueta de Tàrraco) (Pl del Pallol; ☎ 977 24 22 20; w tarragona.cat/patrimoni/museu-historia; ⊕ shows at 10.00, noon, 16.00, 17.00, in Catalan, Spanish, English & French; adult/under 12 €5/free) Near the end of Carrer Cavallers is the picturesque Plaça del Pallol where vaulted Gothic buildings were built over the western end of the huge Provincial Forum. One of these, the Volta Pallol, now holds an impressive, complete architectural model of the ancient city, which is the centrepiece of an immersive mapping installation, projected all around the vault.

Passeig Arqueològic (Avda Catalunya s/n; ☎ 977 24 22 20; w tarragona.cat/patrimoni/museu-historia; ⊕ Apr–Oct 09.00–20.45 Tue–Sat, 09.00–14.30 Sun;

Nov–Mar 09.00–18.30 Tue–Fri, 09.00–18.30 Sat, 09.30–14.30 Sun; adult/reduced/ under 12 €5/2.50/free) The Passeig Arqueològic, an archaeological promenade that encircles much of the old town, begins at the **Portal del Roser**, one of the six city gates (note the double axes and Iberian letters carved into the cyclopean blocks of the lower stones). The path, with manicured gardens and panoramic viewing points, winds between the ancient walls – rugged Iberian blocks at their base, tidy Roman stone added by the Scipios on top – and the Baroque-era walls put up by the English during the War of the Spanish Succession. The best part is near the **Minerva Tower**, where a bronze **statue of Augustus**, donated by Mussolini just before the Civil War, looks on authoritatively.

Lower Tarragona

Plaça de la Font Situated between old Tarragona and new, the Plaça de la Font is the closest thing this city has to a centre, home of the Ajuntament and ringed with bars and restaurants. The buildings on the southern side of this square are built over the vaults of the **Roman circus**; you'll find plenty of other bits of the circus sticking out from the houses on the surrounding streets.

The **Ajuntament**, which once was a Dominican monastery, conceals a real surprise within, one that fills a courtyard. Lluís Domènech i Montaner was called on in 1906 to create a bit of colossal, over-the-top Modernisme for the **Tomb of Jaume I**. This is a great canopy over a marble ship, encrusted with glittering mosaics and meant to carry heavenward the remains of the greatest of the Catalan count-kings. Jaume, unfortunately, isn't in it. He was buried at the monastery of Poblet (page 251) and, when the place was sacked and looted in 1835, grave-robbers left him lying in pieces on the floor. A priest gathered up the remains, which eventually found their way to Tarragona cathedral. Franco moved them back to Poblet in 1952, and now Domènech's grand tomb sits empty, waiting for some new count-king to fill it.

The Eixample From Plaça de la Font, head south across the Rambla Vella and enter modern Tarragona, a sharp, elegant district full of high-rise apartments, and a touch of Modernista architecture here and there. The **Rambla Nova** is the main drag, connecting the Balcony of the Mediterranean with the grandiose Plaça Imperial Tàrraco.

Among the Modernista monuments on the Rambla are Bernardí Martorell's massive brick **Theresian Convent** at Carrer Assalt (1922), and three early works by Tarragona's own Modernista architect Josep Maria Pujol: the **Teatre Metropol** (1908), **Casa Bofarull** (1920) at Carrer Sant Agustí, and the **Casa Aleu** (1927) at Carrer Ixart.

From the Casa Aleu, cross over the Rambla and head south on Carrer Cañellas for more Pujol. There's a grand and glorious **Mercat Central** (1919) and, across Plaça Corsini, the striking **Casa Porta Mercadé**. A block further south, behind the main post office, you will see the columns and foundations of Roman Tarraco's porticoed **Fòrum de la Colònia** (closed for restoration, but you can see it from the street); the excavated section includes a basilica, possibly used as law courts, a bit of a temple and some adjacent streets and buildings. Carry on another two streets, to Carrer Caputxins, for the scanty remains of the **Roman Theatre** (Teatre Romà, C/ Sant Magí 1), which was built into the hillside overlooking the port.

Necròpolis de Tàrraco (Av Ramón y Cajal, 84; ☎ 977 25 15 15; w mnat.cat/ necropolis-de-tarraco; ⊕ closed for restoration) At the western edge of the

Eixample, on the banks of the Francolí River, the city's gargantuan, garish shopping mall, **Park Central**, makes a noisy neighbour for the city's early Christian cemetery. This was unearthed during the construction of a tobacco factory – that huge hulk now standing forlorn and empty behind the excavations. After the burial of the bishop St Fructuosus, martyred in AD259, this area became a place of pilgrimage and a popular spot for burials. As the city dwindled, the cemeteries became overgrown and forgotten. The necropolis is the richest yet discovered in Spain, producing funerary monuments and mosaics, from the pagan Romans to the Visigoths. Two interesting crypts remain in situ.

All the best artefacts from the necropolis are displayed in the adjacent **museum**. Note the strange Lions' Sarcophagus, a 4th-century ivory doll, and the mosaic of Optimus. When Park Central was going up, the builders found that the Necropolis stretched out on to the site. After some negotiations and excavations this part is now, weirdly enough, on display in the shopping mall's basement car park.

Beaches   You've already seen everything down under the cliffs, in the panoramic view from the Balcony of the Mediterranean. The city's mile-long beach, the **Platja del Miracle**, is paralleled by the main rail line for Barcelona (if you need a quieter beach, there's a good one that's usually less crowded at **Arabassada**, 1.5km to the north).

Amfiteatre Romà   (Parc de l'Amfiteatre romà; ☎977 24 22 20; w tarragona.cat/patrimoni/museu-historia; ⊕ Apr–Oct 09.00–20.45 Tue–Sat, 09.00–14.30 Sun; Nov–Mar 09.00–18.30 Tue–Fri, 09.00–18.30 Sat, 09.30–14.30 Sun; adult/under 12 €5/free) Behind the railway and just under the Balcony stands the 2nd-century AD Roman amphitheatre. By the standards of Rome's Colosseum it's a midget, but with seating for 14,000 bloodthirsty provincials this is still an impressive civic ornament. St Fructuosus, along with his deacons Augurius and Eulogius, were burned here in AD259, and a 5th-century bishop built a basilica in their honour right over the ruins, on the exact spot of their execution. That church fell into a Dark Age ruin, and the medieval one that replaced it, the 12th-century **Santa Maria del Miracle**, hasn't fared too well either.

On the other side of the train station sprawls Tarragona's bustling **port**, where, under the gaze of a stately Neoclassical clocktower, container cargo ships jostle for space with Catalunya's biggest fishing fleet, car ferries for the Balearic Islands, and some startlingly opulent yachts.

El Serrallo   At the end of the port area you'll come to Tarragona's venerable fishing quarter, El Serrallo. It's a dense urban neighbourhood now, and a bit of a disappointment when the crumbling, picturesque cottages turn out to be mostly apartment blocks from the 1950s. Still, they are painted in pretty colours and there are plenty of good spots along the quay for seafood and tapas, as well as ships' chandlers and antiques shops.

While the main archaeology museum (Museu Arqueològic, page 233) is being renovated, some of the highlights from the collection are on show in the old port passenger terminal: **Tinglado 4** (Moll de Costa; ☎977 23 62 09; w mnat.cat/en/tinglado-4-in-the-port-of-tarragona; ⊕ Jun–Sep 09.30–20.30 Tue–Sat, 10.00–14.00 Sun; Oct–Apr 09.30–18.00 Tue–Fri, 09.30–14.00 & 15.00–18.00 Sat, 10.00–14.00 Sun; adult/reduced/under 16 €4/2/free). The star of the collection is the arresting mosaic of the Medusa from the 3rd century AD, a little ivory doll, complete with articulated arms and legs, from around the same period, and the marble bust of handsome Emperor Lucius Verus (AD161–169) who was co-regent with Marcus Aurelius.

There are ship models and maritime paraphernalia to inspect at the nearby **Museu del Port de Tarragona** (Moll de Costa, s/n; ☏977 25 94 34; w porttarragona. cat/en/port-city/port-museum; ⊕ Jun–Sep 10.00–14.00 & 17.00–20.00 Tue–Sat, 11.00–14.00 Sun; Oct–Mar 10.00–14.00 & 16.00–19.00 Tue–Sat, 11.00–14.00 Sun; free), which brings the port's working history to life with lots of interactive exhibits. They've installed an intriguing, 4km-long path, the **Ruta Patrimonial del Port de Tarragona**, which takes in the most important historic sights around the port, from cannon to cranes. If that sounds like too much hard work, you can take a cruise around the harbour with a fish dinner on the **Tarragona Blau** (w tarragonablau. com), which leaves from the Serrallo end of the port.

The Roman Environs of Tarragona

Aqüeducte de les Ferreres The aqueduct at Segovia may be bigger, but Tarragona's **Aqüeducte de les Ferreres** (better known locally as the **Pont del Diable**), located about 3km from the city centre (off the AP7 motorway, or take bus no. 5 or 18 from Pl Imperial Tàrraco) certainly makes an impression. This graceful golden beauty, one of three Tarraco built, supplied the city with water from the Francolí River.

The effect is heightened by the aqueduct's isolated position, lost in the woods outside the city. From the car park, pass through the crumbling ornate gate, follow the path for about 5 minutes and it will appear. The aqueduct bridge, 26m high and 249m long, may have been the biggest expense in the builders' budget, but the real art of the Roman engineers lies in the things you can't see.

Consider that this aqueduct begins 25km away, and that the channel that carries the water, most of it just underground, has to keep a constant slope of precisely 0.04%. Bridges are necessary only when the aqueduct has to cross a valley or ravine. This one, lovely as it is, also provides a lesson in plain, no-nonsense Roman engineering, rather like one of the great Victorian-era railroad viaducts. With a tape, you could see how every measurement in it works out to a simple multiple or fraction of a Roman foot (about 30cm).

Villa de Centcelles (C/ Afores s/n, 6km from Tarragona; ☏977 52 33 74; w mnat. cat/en/roman-complex-of-centcelles; ⊕ Jun–Sep 10.00–13.30 & 16.00–20.00 Tue–Sat, 10.00–14.00 Sun; Mar–Apr & May–Oct 10.00–13.30 & 15.00–18.00 Tue–Sat, 10.00–14.00 Sun; Nov–Feb 10.00–13.30 & 15.00–17.30 Tue–Sat, 10.00–14.00 Sun; adult/reduced €4/2) After all these Roman marvels, Tarragona saves perhaps the best for last. In the 4th century AD, when the Roman world was falling apart, the wealthy had largely given up on the decayed cities, and they spent most of their time in great private villas, home to the very small number of noble families that had come to own nearly everything in Roman society.

Relatively little of this one has yet been excavated; the fascinating bit is a mighty domed chamber that survived thanks to its conversion into a church in early medieval times. From the outside, it's only a plain and unassuming stone building. Once within, you're looking up at a 10.7m dome – the biggest (and only) ancient dome surviving in Spain, built in the same ingenious double-dome architecture as the Pantheon in Rome. The dome was built as a mausoleum, entirely covered with some of the most important mosaics of early Christendom.

Only fragments remain, but enough to create a magical world in tawny-coloured stone and glass tesserae. As is common in the earliest Christian art, Classical and

7

scriptural images co-exist side by side. Down at the bottom are hunting scenes; above, scenes from both Testaments, including Noah's Ark and Daniel in the lions' den; for some of these, the versions here are the oldest known representations in mosaic. These are accompanied by allegories of the Four Seasons, interspersed with what were probably ceremonial scenes from the Imperial court, now mostly lost.

In the hunting scene, note the dominant, centrally placed figure with portrait features. He's the boss, the scholars say – the man for whom this mausoleum was built. But who was he? One intriguing possibility is that he is no less than Emperor Constans I, son of Constantine the Great, who was assassinated just over the Pyrenees at Elne in AD350. That's still a matter of dispute, but in Centcelles we have one of few examples anywhere outside Rome of the beginnings of official Christian art and iconography.

THE COSTA DAURADA NORTH FROM TARRAGONA

North of Tarragona, a trio of Roman monuments are a reminder that the traffic-choked N-340 follows the Via Augusta, which once swept all the way down the Mediterranean coast from the Pyrenees to Gades (modern Cádiz) in the south. Much of this stretch of the Costa Daurada is intensively developed, but you can find respite in a sprinkling of smaller, quieter resorts where the pace is gentler than in the headline destinations further south and where Catalan and Spanish are still more commonly heard than English and German. Among them are Altafulla, with its fine sandy beach and elegant old quarter, and El Vendrell, birthplace of cellist Pau Casals. Torredembarra, Coma-Ruga and Calafell mix up broad seafront promenades and sweeping, family-friendly beaches with plenty of nightlife, if not a lot of charm.

TOURIST INFORMATION There are tourist offices all along this popular stretch of coast, incuding in Altafulla (Via Augusta 34; ☎977 65 14 26; w visitaltafulla.cat), Calafell (C/ Sant Pere 29; ☎977 69 91 41; w visit.calafell.cat), Torredembarra (Pg de Rafael Campalans 10; ☎977 64 45 80; w turismetorredembarra.cat) and El Vendrell (Av Balneari 3; ☎618 57 14 78; w elvendrellturisme.com).

🏠 WHERE TO STAY

Le Méridien Ra Beach Hotel & Spa Avda del Sanatori 1, El Vendrell; ☎977 69 42 00; w marriott.com/en-us/hotels/reumd-le-meridien-ra-beach-hotel-and-spa. Extravagant resort hotel in a charming villa-style building that dates back to the 1920s which sits right on the beach. It has all the 5-star trimmings, including lavish rooms & suites overlooking the Mediterranean, an award-winning spa, plus pools, gym & a fine restaurant (€€€€). €€€€€

Hotel Gran Claustre C/ del Cup 2, Altafulla; ☎977 65 15 57; w granclaustre.com. Up in Altafulla's lovely little historic heart, this romantic hotel occupies an 18th-century townhouse. There are 39 individually decorated rooms & suites, a courtyard garden with plunge pool & an excellent restaurant, **Guadium** (€€€), with fresh, market cuisine. €€€

May Altafulla Beach Boutique Hotel Camí del Prat 58–60, Altafulla; ☎877 99 02 32; w mayboutiquehotel.com. A mid-sized, modern beach hotel with pretty rooms decorated in blue & white with wicker accents. There's a roof terrace with sun deck, pool & bar, plus a good restaurant (€€€) serving tasty Mediterranean food. €€€

Hotel Antiga Pl Catalunya 29, Calafell; ☎977 69 06 38; w antiga.info. In the atmospheric old town, this mid-sized hotel has compact but well-equipped rooms, a leafy garden with pool, & a traditional restaurant (€€) where you can enjoy local specialities. €€

Hostal Coca C/ Antoni Roig 97, Torredembarra; ☎977 64 00 55; w hostalcoca.com. This friendly inn has been going since 1820. Guests come back year after year for the good-value, simple rooms

& the cosy restaurant (€€) serving up delicious Catalan home cooking. €€

Hotel Paradís C/ Camí del Moro 65, Torredembarra; ☎977 64 06 37; w hotelparadis.es. You'll get a warm welcome at this simple, family-run 1-star hotel, which has 10 basic but pristine rooms, including dbls, trpls & family rooms, all with AC & private bathrooms. It's about a 10-min stroll to the beach. €€

La Masieta Avda del Dr Pujol 16, Creixell; ☎977 80 10 11; w lamasieta.es. An old masia has been converted to contain this welcoming small hotel, which has pretty, rustically furnished rooms, including a suite on the top floor with its own terrace with hot tub, a plant-filled patio garden with a small pool, & one of the best restaurants in the area, **Mediterraneum** (€€€). €€

✕ **WHERE TO EAT AND DRINK** People around here are wild for *xató*, the traditional Catalan sauce made with almonds and hazelnuts, garlic, maybe tomatoes and…well, every village has its own prized recipe. It's usually served with a salad of endives, tuna, cod, olives and anchovies, and restaurants are measured by how well they do it.

Esencia C/ Montserrat 15; ☎877 64 03 49; ◻ esenciaelvendrell; ⏲ 13.00–16.00 Tue & Sun, 13.00–16.00 & 20.00–23.00 Wed–Sat. A popular local institution, this elegant restaurant is a place of pilgrimage for its fresh, modern Mediterranean cuisine with an international twist, including dishes like marinated duck with couscous, swordfish with coconut, & vegetable tempura. €€€

L'Estany C/ Mercé Rodoreda 20, Calafell-Platge; ☎977 69 26 50; w restaurantlestany.com; ⏲ 13.30–15.45 Mon–Tue & Thu, 13.00–15.45 & 21.00–22.30 Fri, 13.30–15.45 & 21.00–22.30 Sat, 13.30–16.00 Sun. Excellent fresh seafood (& much more, including outstanding xató) at a good price in a classic restaurant with blue-&-white décor, just two blocks from the beach. It also does calçots in season. €€€

La Cuina de la Marga Pg Marítim Joan Reventós 50, El Vendrell; ☎640 69 29 09; w lacuinadelamarga.com; ⏲ 13.00–15.45 Tue–Thu, 13.00–15.45 & 20.15–23.00 Mon &

Fri–Sun. A charming restaurant right on the beachfront, with a stylish interior & an outdoor terrace offering sea views. Enjoy delicious fresh seafood & meat cooked on a wood-fired grill (*a la brasa*), along with paella & other Mediterranean rice dishes. €€€

Aromatic Via Augusta 21, Altafulla; ☎977 65 19 54; w aromaticrestaurant.com; ⏲ 13.30–15.30 & 19.30–22.30 daily. Delicious, fresh seasonal cuisine, with the emphasis on international vegan & vegetarian dishes (although some fish & meat options are also available) served up in a pretty, plant-filled garden. €€

Taverna del Quatre C/ de Dalt 57, Altafulla; ☎620 20 58 63; ◻ tavernadelquatre; ⏲ 08.00–16.00 & 19.00–23.00 Mon & Fri–Sat, 08.00–16.00 Thu & Sun. Tasty tapas from *croquetes* & *patates braves* to platters of Catalan charcuterie & fresh local specialities prepared with whatever is in season (the artichokes in spring are fantastic), & good company at this popular tavern. €€

ALONG THE ANCIENT VIA AUGUSTA You may have had your fill of ruins in Tarragona, but the Romans aren't done with you yet. Along the coast east from Tarragona, the ancient Via Augusta is now the N340 for Barcelona. Along its way it passes three other Roman monuments. At the 6km mark stands the impressive 9m **Torre de los Escipiones**, once fancied to be a funerary monument to the two famous Scipio brothers, Publius and Gnaeus, who died fighting the Carthaginians in 212 BC; the two figures in relief represent a popular military deity, the Anatolian god Attis. At 8km, a tall, strange monolith marks the centre of a Roman stone quarry, the **Cántara del Médol**. At 20km the **Arco de Barà**, a triumphal arch, spans the ancient road, erected for some forgotten victory in the 1st century BC.

ALTAFULLA If only the Romans could see their Via Augusta now. All their monuments on the N340 are pretty much lost in the boiling traffic. This stretch of

7

coast, part suburb of Tarragona and part resort strip, has been intensively developed. Charming it ain't, though the beaches are splendid. One oasis amid it all is Altafulla, with a lovely, well-restored walled centre and a small fishing port. The remains of another wealthy Roman villa, with some of its mosaics and other art, have been found here in the **Villa de Els Munts** (Pg del Fortí s/n; ☎ 977 65 28 06; w mnat. cat/en/the-roman-villa-of-els-munts; ☺ Jun–Sep 10.00–13.30 & 16.00–20.00 Tue–Sat, 10.00–14.00 Sun; Mar–Apr & May–Oct 10.00–13.30 & 15.00–18.00 Tue–Sat, 10.00–14.00 Sun; Nov–Feb 10.00–13.30 & 15.00–17.30 Tue–Sat, 10.00–14.00 Sun; adult/reduced €4/2), which was first excavated in the 16th century. It was large and lavish enough that it is thought that Emperor Hadrian may have stayed here during his visit to Tarraco in AD122–23.

The landmark on this part of the coast is the **Castell de Tamarit** restored by Charles Deering before he moved on to Sitges (page 149). Once it housed a fabulous hoard of art, but Deering eventually sent it all back home to Chicago.

CALAFELL AND AROUND Neighbouring **Torredembarra** and **Coma-Ruga** are even bigger and more intense than Altafulla. So is Calafell. This village which consists of an old centre and a beach strip on opposite sides of the motorway, has a famously haunted castle, the **Castell del Calafell**, that attracted so many goblins, witches and storms that the locals built a *comunidor* inside it (a magical, four-sided shrine or building, open to the four winds). You'll see these all over Catalunya. Not all of them are ancient; this one dates from the 18th century. Calafell also has the remnants of a Roman villa (Ruïnes Romanes Vilarenc), built in the 1st century AD. It's always open and signs are posted recounting what little is known about its origins.

EL VENDRELL Near Calafell, the busy town of El Vendrell seems to exist largely to honour its famous son, the great cellist Pau Casals. There's a statue in the central Plaça Nova, a year-long schedule of concerts in the Auditori Pau Casals, his **Casa Nadiua** (birthplace) (C/ Santa Anna 2; ☎ 977 18 18 19; w museus.elvendrell.net/ casa-nadiua-de-pau-casals; ☺ Jul–Aug 10.00–14.00 & 18.00–20.00 Tue–Fri, 11.00–14.00 & 18.00–20.00 Sat,11.00–14.00 Sun; Sep–Jun 10.00–14.00 & 17.00– 19.00 Tue–Fri, 11.00–14.00 Sat–Sun; adult/reduced/under 8 €8/6/free) and the house near the beach on Avda Palfuriana where he lived 1909–39, now the **Museu Pau Casals** (Avda Palfuriana 67; ☎ 977 68 42 76; w paucasals.org; ☺ 10.00–14.00 & 16.00–18.00 Tue–Fri, 10.00–14.00 & 16.00–19.00 Sat, 10.00–14.00 Sun; adult/ reduced/under 8 €8/6/free). Casals, born in 1876, was an international star by 1899. A fervent Republican, he left Spain at the end of the Civil War and vowed never to return until democracy was restored and died in 1973, two years before Franco; one of his greatest legacies is the festival he founded just over the border in Prades in 1950 (page 355).

El Vendrell has no end of strange little museums including the **Museu Déu** (Pl Nova 6; ☎ 977 68 42 76; w museus.elvendrell.net/museu-deu; ☺ Jul–Aug 10.00– 14.00 & 18.00–20.00 Tue–Fri, 11.00–14.00 & 18.00–20.00 Sat, 11.00–14.00 Sun; Sep–Jun 10.00–14.00 & 17.00–19.00 Tue–Fri, 11.00–14.00 & 17.00–19.00 Sat, 11.00–14.00 Sun; adult/reduced/under 8 €8/6/free), dedicated to art, bric-a-brac and oriental rugs, and the **Fundació Apel·les Fenosa** (C/ Major 25; ☎ 977 15 41 92; w museuapellesfenosa.cat; ☺ mid-Apr–mid-Oct 11.00–14.00 & 18.00–20.00 Thu– Sat, 11.00–14.00 Sun; mid-Oct–mid-Apr 11.00–14.00 & 17.00–19.00 Thu–Sat, 11.00–14.00 Sun; adult/reduced/under 8 €6/3/free), dedicated to the sculptor friend of Picasso (1899–1988). Why not skip them all and head straight for **Aqualeon** (Les Basses s/n, Albinyana; ☎ 977 68 76 56; w aqualeon.es; ☺ summer only, see website for times; adult/reduced & children aged 5–10/children aged 3–4/under 2 €33/24/13/free), where there are giant waterslides and wave pools?

REUS

It was a strange fate that cast Reus and Tarragona together as twin cities, the two centres of one sprawling conurbation, like a fried egg with two yolks. The yolks must have come from different roosters; they couldn't have less in common. Tarragona with its palms and Roman columns and seafood tapas seems a world away from modern, glossy, hard-working Reus, a town that didn't get going until Tarragona had already been rebuilt twice. In Tarragona, they come for the ruins and museums. In Reus, they go shopping.

Reus's history won't take long to tell. There seems to have been a village on the site in Roman times, but Reus as Reus only appears in the wake of the Reconquista: a Norman named Roberto de Aguiló founded the town in 1150. The archbishops of Tarragona gave it the right to hold a trade fair, and Reus grew rapidly.

From the 1600s it fell victim to a really horrible run of bad luck: the plague hit it 15 times in that century, and three more in the next. That was accompanied

NATURE'S ARCHITECT

'Nature, who is always my teacher…' In the Gaudí Centre (in the same building as the tourist office), they'll show you a model of the pinnacles of the Sagrada Família, along with a photo of the little *crespinell*, a pretty flowering succulent that is common in the meadows of Catalunya. The crespinell gave the architect the idea for the pinnacles' shape. Gaudí wasn't the first architect to spend a lot of time looking at flowers. Back in medieval Paris, the carved decoration for Nôtre-Dame and the Sainte Chapelle was provided respectively by two of France's most common spring flowers, the celandine and the lowly buttercup. To Gaudí, as to the medieval builders, the columns in a cathedral recalled the trees in a forest. A constant attention to the forms of nature was something that he and the builders of the Middle Ages had in common. In his case, it could lead to extremes (and usually did).

Gaudí's devotion to nature was also one of things that made him so hard for his contemporaries to understand. As the principal of the School of Architecture in Barcelona had reflected when Gaudí graduated in 1878, he didn't know if he was giving a degree to a genius or a madman. One of the most enduring lessons he learned was that nature does not like straight lines, and in architecture the straight line is always the easiest solution. So Gaudí, quite alone, went off in the opposite direction.

Nature's forms, along with his profound knowledge of mathematics, taught him to make parabolic and hyperbolic arches, and virtuoso tricks like the breathtaking convex vaulting used in the Colonia Güell crypt. Studying forms in nature and in mathematics, one puzzle often seems to lead to another, deeper one, and the same is true with Gaudí, who left scores of little mysteries in his works for others to ponder. Gaudí's deep religious faith is the other big difference between his architecture and everyone else's. It required that every work, large or small, sacred or secular, be designed as praise for the Creator. To the Great Perfectionist, this devotion had to be extended to the tiniest detail in everything. No shortcuts. Not ever.

7

by economic decline, and political troubles. The city came under rough French occupations in 1640 and again in 1723. Reus's fortunes picked up with the rest of Catalunya when Madrid permitted the American trade to reopen in 1778. Almost at once, this led to an industrial boom in the town; Reus was soon sending its textiles all over the world, a little Catalan Manchester that grew to be the second-largest city after Barcelona.

While the creative juices were flowing and money was plentiful, Reus contributed two of the central figures of the Catalan cultural renaissance: the painter Mariano Fortuny, and the architect Antoni Gaudí. Reus's collection of Modernista buildings is one of the main reasons for visiting the city today, and to commemorate their most famous son they've just cleared one the most prominent corners of the old centre and dropped down the shiny, startling Gaudí Centre on it. There aren't a lot of other sights, but Reus is a bright, urbane, attractive city. It's worth a day when you're in the neighbourhood.

TOURIST INFORMATION The tourist information office is located right on the main square (Pl del Mercadal 3; 977 01 06 70; w reusturisme.cat; 09.30–14.00 & 16.00–19.00 Mon, 10.00–20.00 Tue–Sat, 10.00–14.00 Sun), and shares the space with the Gaudí Centre.

WHERE TO STAY

Hotel NH Ciutat de Reus Avda de Marià Fortuny 85; 977 34 53 53; w nh-hotels.com/en/hotel/nh-ciutat-de-reus. A large, modern, glassy business hotel, which makes up for what it lacks in charm with a very central location & sparkling rooms, many with balconies. Like most business hotels in Spain, prices drop considerably in summer. €€€

Mas Passamaner Camí de la Serra 52, La Selva del Camp; 977 76 63 33; w maspassamaner.com. This 1922 villa designed by Domènech i Muntaner is now a rural boutique hotel, with about 20 spacious rooms & suites as well as 2 private villas. There's a garden with pool plus a spa & wellness area. €€€

Sant Jordi Avda de Sant Jordi 24, Montbrio del Camp; 977 82 67 19; w hotel-santjordi.es. Warm & welcoming, this medium-sized country hotel, about 10km southeast of Reus, has a choice of rooms & self-catering apartments in a sleepy village. There's a pool in the grounds, along with facilities for cyclists who come for the many bike routes in the area. €€€

Hotel Centre Reus C/ Hospital 6; 977 12 64 14; w hotelcentrereus.com. A good, central choice, with impeccable, airy rooms & a rooftop bar with wonderful views just a 3-min walk from the main square & the Gaudí Centre. €€

WHERE TO EAT AND DRINK

Vítric C/ Santa Anna, 24; 977 43 36 73; vitricrestaurant; 13.15–15.15 & 20.30–22.00 Tue & Thu, 13.15–15.15 Wed, 13.15–16.30 & 20.30–00.30 Fri–Sat. Come to this chic but delightfully unstuffy 'gastronomic tavern' to enjoy spectacular, incredibly imaginative cuisine – such as red shrimp tartare with white asparagus cream or lamb stew with couscous & cauliflower – from a very talented young chef. The w/day lunch menu (€30) is a steal. €€€€

Terraza de Gaudí Plaza del Mercadal 3; 977 49 42 04; terrassa_gaudi; noon–01.00 Wed–Thu, noon–02.00 Fri–Sat, noon–18.00 Sun. On the 4th floor, with a terrace offering gorgeous views, this might seem like a tourist haunt but is hugely popular with locals. Come for fresh, good-value market cuisine, the excellent set lunch (€25, w/days only) or just a cocktail on the terrace. €€€

Le Bistrot C/ Santa Anna 18; 977 17 48 43; w lebistrot.es; 13.00–15.00 & 20.30–22.30 Mon & Thu–Sat, 13.00–15.00 Tue. One of several bars & restaurants on this lively, narrow street, this charming spot offers market-fresh Catalan dishes with a French twist – like the Morbier cheese gratin with wild mushrooms, ham & potatoes. Everything is prepared with Km0 (locally sourced) produce wherever possible. €€

Mesón Les Tines   C/ Casals 3; ☎ 977 34 46 14; ◼ MesonLesTines; ⏰ 09.00–23.30 Mon–Sat. This wonderfully old-fashioned tavern, with barrels & exposed brick walls, is famous for its roast meats (*graellada*) as well as a great choice of traditional tapas, all served up in a cheerful neighbourhood atmosphere. €€

Rosa del Vents   Pl de Peixateries; ☎ 977 34 54 37; ⏰ noon–midnight daily. Sweet little restaurant tucked under the arcades of one of the city's prettiest squares, this has tasty Catalan favourites like *canelons* & roast lamb & a good set lunch (€15.50, available w/days). €€

WHAT TO SEE AND DO
Plaça Mercadal and the Gaudí Centre   This elegant pedestrian square was the centre of medieval Reus. The market may be gone, but you can still have a look at one of Reus's finest Modernista buildings, the richly ornate 1902 **Casa Navàs** of Lluís Domènech de Montaner.

It offers all the contrast in the world to the gleaming **Gaudí Centre** (Pl del Mercadal 3; ☎ 977 01 06 70; ᴡ reusturisme.cat/ciutat-de-gaudi/gaudi-centre; ⏰ Jun–Sep 10.00–20.00 Mon–Sat, 10.00–14.00 Sun; Oct–May 10.00–14.00 & 16.00–19.00, 10.00–14.00 Sun; adult/reduced/children 9–14/under 9 €11/7/7/ free). The architecture doesn't look entirely right here, with its black louvres and stainless-steel trim – more of a high-tech radio than a building. But don't be afraid, push right in. A lot of cleverness went into this museum; not only does it entertain, but it teaches us non-specialists a lot about the mathematical tricks and brilliant emulation of nature that made Gaudí so special.

The ground floor contains the city's tourist office (where you can get the brochure to do the Modernista tour later) and a rather posh music shop, besides the entrance. Once you get inside, the atmosphere is less Gaudí and more Flash Gordon. Sliding doors open and close mysteriously and lights constantly blink on and off. Do take the audio headphones; they're almost indispensable. Exhibits include models of the pinnacles of the Sagrada Família, and contraptions that demonstrate some of Gaudí's fascinating solutions to engineering problems, using working models to explain the natural ventilation system of Casa Batlló and the water storage system that is the secret purpose of the Park Güell.

Another model explains the ingenious upside-down system of hanging chains that Gaudí used to work out the advanced mathematics of his 'catenary' vaults and arches. The exhibit that really fills out the picture of this endlessly fascinating character, though, is the reproduction of Gaudí's dusty, cluttered workshop, stuffed full of books, drawings and natural models. The Sagrada Família and every excruciatingly planned and executed detail in it were made for the glory of God – so were his apartment buildings, though their inhabitants probably never dreamed it. Here, in contrast, are the table and chair Gaudí built for himself, knocked together out of scraps from the work sites.

Around Reus   Ask the average inhabitant of this end of Catalunya what Reus is famous for, and chances are they won't mention Modernista architecture or even Gaudí, but shopping. There's plenty of swank and glitter in the shops here, especially on **C/ Monterols**, the pedestrianised shopping street that runs northwards to the lovely and shady **Plaça de Prim**, a bustling square decorated by a ferocious equestrian statue of another local hero, General Joan Prim i Prats, a successful general in Morocco and later a major figure in Spanish politics. If you have a chance while you're in Reus, take in an opera or a concert at the **Teatro Fortuny** (1882), a monument to Reus's golden years and one of the most lavish opera houses in all Spain.

7

Reus has two more museums: the **Museu Salvador Vilaseca** (Raval de Santa Anna 59; ☎977 01 06 60; w museudereus.cat/col·leccio/arqueologia; ⊕ 10.00–14.00 & 17.00–20.00 Tue–Sat; free), with an absorbing collection of finds, including funerary objects dating back to the 3rd millennium BC from the cave of Cau d'en Serra, in Picamoixons, and a **Museu d'Art i Història** (currently closed indefinitely for renovation) on Plaça de la Llibertat, with a good helping of Catalan art, including several works of Reus's own artist, Mariano Fortuny.

You might take the time to follow the tourist office's **Ruta del Modernisme** and see all the Modernista buildings in town. The standout is the **Casa Navàs** (Pl del Mercadal 5–7; ☎977 71 06 70; w casanavas.cat; ⊕ guided visit only; visits at 11.00, noon, 13.00, 16.00, 17.00 & 18.00 Mon–Fri; 11.00, noon, 13.00, 14.00, 16.00, 17.00, 18.00 & 19.00 Sat; 11.00, noon, 13.00 & 14.00 Sun (see the website for special themed visits); adult/reduced/under 8 €13/10/free), nicknamed 'La guapa de la Mercadal' ('The Beauty of Mercadal Square'), which was designed by Domènech i Montaner in 1901. Relatively subdued on the outside but a floral extravaganza within, its exuberant interior has been preserved intact for more than a century. There are more Domènech i Montaner buildings – the **Casa Gasull** and **Casa Rull** – along the **Carrer Sant Joan**, Reus' showcase street.

But his biggest Modernista gift to the city, however, lies just outside town, signposted off the CN420 for Falset. The **Institut Pere Mata** (Ctra de l'Institut Pere Mata s/n; ☎977 01 06 70; w reusturisme.cat/joia-modernista/institut-pere-mata; ⊕ Jun–Sep 11.00–14.00 & 16.30–18.30 Mon–Sat, 11.00–14.00 Sun; Oct–May 11.00–14.00 & 16.00–18.00 Mon–Sat, 11.00–14.00 Sun; adult/reduced/under 8 €9/8/free) was a highly progressive and modern psychiatric hospital when it was completed in 1912, one that covers over 40 acres. For Domènech i Montaner, it was practice for one of his greatest works, the even bigger Hospital de la Santa Creu i Sant Pau in Barcelona (page 115). Here, the decoration is more restrained, but the Arab-influenced details and wealth of stained glass and blue and white azulejos make it one of the most beautiful hospitals you'll ever see.

NORTH OF TARRAGONA

Tarragona has always owed some of its prosperity to the fertile plain that surrounds it, the Camp de Tarragona. This is down-to-earth farming country, rich in Catalan folk traditions, but here too, surprisingly, are two of the greatest works of Modernista architecture outside Barcelona. At its northern edge, the Camp climbs up to the comarca called the Conca de Barbera; here you can see some beautiful countryside, and one of the province's biggest attractions, the 'Cistercian Triangle' of opulent medieval monasteries, as well as the walled medieval city of Montblanc. To the west, there's a very small patch of very big mountains, the Muntanyes de Prades, which slope down to the serious wine country of the Priorat.

GETTING AROUND
By train Regular *rodalies* trains (line R13 from Barcelona via Valls and R14 from Tarragona; for timetables, see w rodalies.gencat.cat) stop at L'Espluga de Francolí, Montblanc and Valls.

By bus Plana (☎977 55 36 80; w empresaplana.cat) operates bus services between Poblet and Tarragona via Valls, Montblanc and L'Espluga de Francolí, along with services between the smaller towns of the region, including between Valls and the Monestir de Santes Creus. Monbus (☎ 900 92 91 92; w monbus.es) runs buses between Tarragona and Lleida that stop at Poblet, Valls, Montblanc and L'Espluga de Francolí.

By car While public transport to the larger towns in this region is good, a car is handy to explore the smaller villages. There is no train service or regular bus service to Vallbona de les Monges, so a car is essential.

TOURIST INFORMATION All the main towns, including those listed below, have tourist information points. There is also a regional tourist booth at the Santa Maria de Poblet monastery (Pg Abat Conill; ☎ 977 87 12 47; w concadebarberaturisme.cat).

L'Espluga de Francolí Pl del Mil·lenari 1; ☎ 977 87 12 20; w esplugaturisme.cat

Montblanc Muralla de Sta. Tecla 56; ☎ 977 86 17 33; w montblancmedieval.cat

Valls C/ de la Cort 3; ☎ 977 61 25 30; w visitavalls.cat

🏠 WHERE TO STAY

Cal Maginet Pl de Catalunya 16, Vilaverd; ☎ 693 06 97 33; w calmaginet.cat. Blissful little country guesthouse in a sleepy village about halfway between Valls & Poblet. Comfortable rooms with wooden beams & a cosy restaurant (€€) for traditional Catalan dishes. It's a great base for cycling & hiking. €€

Fèlix Ctra N-240 km 17, Valls; ☎ 977 60 90 90; w felixhotel.net. Big, modern hotel set in pretty gardens about 3km from the town centre, with a pool & tennis courts, & spacious rooms in the main building or in bungalows; a favourite for weddings & *calçotades* (page 246) in the lovely restaurant (€€€). €€

Hotel Cal Blasi C/ Alenyà 11, Montblanc; ☎ 977 86 13 36; w calblasihotel.squarespace.com. A perfect little home-from-home within Montblanc's famous walls, this has 9 prettily decorated rooms, delightful staff & delicious b/fasts. €€

Hostatgeria de Poblet Pl de la Corona D'Arago 11, Vimbodí i Poblet; ☎ 977 30 03 50; w hostatgeriadepoblet.cat. The very best way to soak up the special atmosphere of Poblet is to stay at this large, modern hotel built of honey-coloured stone to match its surroundings. Rooms are plain but well-equipped, & guests can attend mass to hear the monks sing. €€

Rural Jorda C/ Sant Antoni 5, Rodonyà; ☎ 629 01 42 31; w ruraljorda.cat. A few charming, rustically furnished rooms in a quiet, country village just a 5min drive from the Santuari de la Mare de Déu de Montserrat. There's a courtyard garden with pool, a games room & outdoor barbecues you can use in summer. €€

Ca L'Estruch Raval de Vimbodí 8, Vallclara; ☎ 616 23 68 07; w calestruch.com. Located in a pretty, stone village about 12km southeast of Poblet, this family-run & friendly *casa rural* has a handful of rooms & a small apartment for 3–4 people. €

Hostal del Senglar Pl Montserrat Canals 1, L'Espluga de Francolí; ☎ 977 87 04 11; w hostaldelsenglar.com. A village institution, with 22 simple, old-fashioned rooms, all with AC, & a big garden. The restaurant (€€€) is where everybody goes in L'Espluga, & serves stewed boar & other game. €

L'Ocell Francolí Pg Cañellas, L'Espluga de Francolí; ☎ 977 87 12 16; w ocellfrancoli.com. Modest, old-fashioned inn with a dozen basic rooms & a very good, traditional restaurant (€€€) which vies with the Hostal del Senglar (see above) as the best in town. €

✕ WHERE TO EAT AND DRINK

Art Camí Clos s/n, Espluga De Francolí; ☎ 977 87 18 71; w artrestaurant.es; ⏰ 13.00–15.30 daily. Elegant, Catalan cuisine that's based on traditional recipes but given a contemporary twist.

This award-winning spot on the edge of town is a favourite with locals, & off the tourist path. €€€

Masia Bou Ctra Lleida, km 21.5, Valls; ☎ 977 60 04 27; 🄵 masiabou; ⏰ 11.00–18.00 Thu–Sun.

Like Felix (page 245), Masia Bou is famous for its atmospheric *calçotadas*. Put on your bib & get stuck in to these delicious spring treats. The rest of the year, you can enjoy more tasty local favourites, including meat & fish cooked over a wood-fired grill (*a la brasa*). €€€

Molí del Mallol Muralla Santa Anna, Montblanc; ☎977 86 05 91; w elmolidelmallol.com; ◷ 13.00–16.00 Mon–Thu & Sun, 13.00–16.00 & 20.30–23.00 Fri–Sat This elegant restaurant, in an old stone building that dates back to the 12th century, serves refined Catalan cuisine. The speciality is snails – *caragols* – which are served in dishes like *butifarra negra I caragols* (black sausage with snails), or you could go for the roast suckling pig with tomato chutney & saffron. €€€

Casa Nostra C/ Sant Miquel, L'Espluga de Francolí; ☎658 94 75 25; ⓕ pizzeriarestaurantcasanostra; ◷ 20.00–23.00 Mon & Fri, 13.00–15.30 & 20.00–23.00 Tue–Thu

& Sat–Sun. A pleasant surprise, this modest little hole-in-the-wall serves delicious pizzas & pastas – as well as a perhaps unexpected range of classic local dishes, such as excellent stuffed baby squid or pork loin with almond sauce. €€

Cúmul C/ Ducat 1, Montblanc; ☎633 49 44 06; ◎ cumul___; ◷ 12.30–17.00 & 20.00–midnight Thu, 13.00–17.00 & 20.00–midnight Fri, noon–17.00 & 20.00–01.00 Sat, noon–17.00 Sun. A buzzy, quirky tapas bar set in an old pharmacy, with a selection of very creative small plates to share. It's always full so get here early for a table. €€

Fonda dels Àngels Pl dels Àngels, Montblanc; ☎977 86 01 73; w fondadelsangels.com. A time-honoured old inn in a building that dates back to the 13th century, this popular restaurant has been in the same family since 1930. It dishes up generous portions of classic Catalan cuisine, prepared with ingredients from its own kitchen garden. €€

LA RUTA JUJOL: VISTABELLA TO MONTFERRI You saw some of the early and minor work of Josep Maria Jujol in Tarragona's Eixample. North from the city, in a string of out-of-the-way villages, you'll find the buildings that, along with his Barcelona collaborations with Gaudí, established Jujol's name among the greatest of Modernista architects.

Heading up into the plain called the **Camp de Tarragona**, just off the N240 beyond Tarragona's Roman aqueduct, the first stop is **Els Pallaressos**, where the

CALÇOTADA: A RITE OF WINTER

Forget all the fancy-pants heirs of El Bulli. For a genuine Catalan soul feast there's nothing like heading outdoors, donning a bib and slurping grilled spring onions, or, as they're properly known, *calçots de Valls*, a protected brand in Catalunya since the 1990s. The Spaniards like their onions – they grow more than any country in western Europe and they eat the most as well, demolishing an average of 7kg annually per capita.

But *calçots* are something special, barbequed on vine cuttings until charred and black on the outside, but tender and sweet inside and served to diners who strip off the sooty outer layers (a messy business, necessitating bibs) and drench them in a sauce made from toasted almonds and locally grown hazelnuts, roast tomatoes, roast garlic, local olive oil, red pepper, salt and parsley. Then the *calçot* is suspended over the mouth, white side down, and dropped.

In the old days, the traditional meal included artichoke omelettes, fruit and coffee; today it's plenty of bread, grilled sausages and lamb chops. The season extends from later January to early spring; the biggest Calçotada festival, in Valls, takes place in late January, when mountains of *calçots* are served to 30,000 happy slurpers. You'll get your chance too; plenty of restaurants in the province have *calçots* on the menu for starters.

The traditional Catalan *sardana* dance is a communal rite and an affirmation of Catalan identity and unity PAGE 27

above
(MP/S)

Every local festival features dancing *gegants*, giant figures of wood and papier-mâché which are supported by someone in the skirts PAGE 46

below left
(VK/S)

The streets of many Catalan towns are transformed with intricate floral carpets to celebrate Corpus Christi PAGE 48

below right
(S/D)

above left (V/D) Dalí's Theatre-Museum in Figueres is a surreal celebration of his art and gift for theatrical flair PAGE 195

above right (T/S) Rainbow-coloured light streams in through the vast skylight in the Palau de la Música, a Modernista masterpiece PAGE 102

below (JBC/D) The Modernistas transformed even factories and mills with decorative brickwork and colourful tiling, such as this flour mill in Vic PAGE 212

The Masia Freixa building in Terrassa displays the swooping, parabolic arches beloved by the Modernistas PAGE 137

above (RB/S)

The Casa Vicens, designed by a young Antoni Gaudí for a wealthy tile manufacturer, was inspired by mudejar forms PAGE 124

above right (OS/S)

The Casa Batlló's fantastical façade and swirling organic forms exemplify Gaudí's vision at its most playful PAGE 110

below (TP/S)

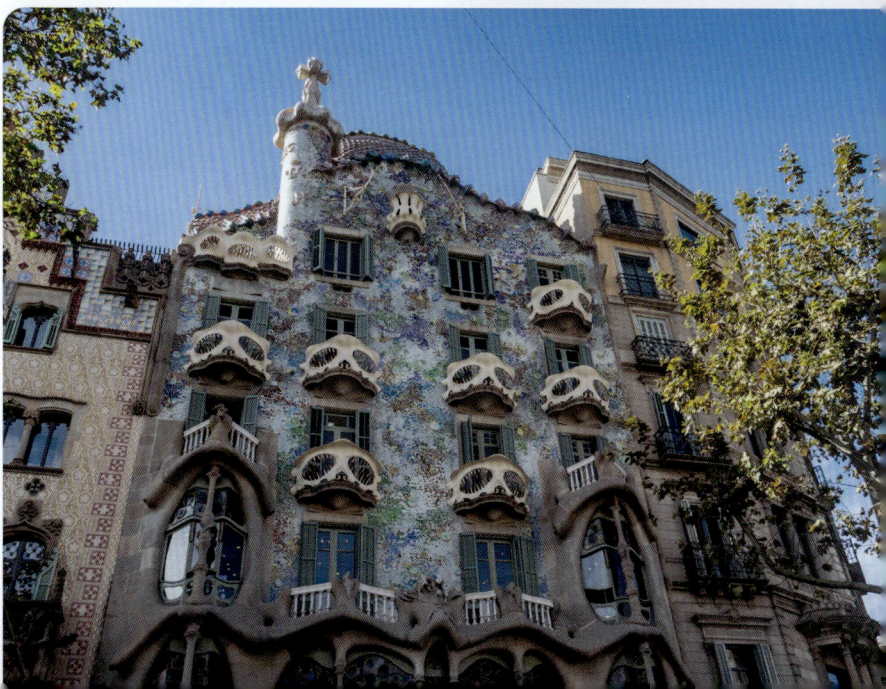

above left (H36/D) — The Catalan Pyrenees are studded with tiny mountain towns like Beget, huddled together against the harsh winters PAGE 218

above (T/S) — The Greeks and Romans developed an ancient Mediterranean port at Empúries, where atmospheric ruins gaze out over the sea PAGE 172

below (IAR/S) — Besalú is a beautifully well-preserved historic town, accessed by a picture-postcard medieval bridge PAGE 205

Girona's enchanting old town is tightly clustered around an enormous cathedral and ringed by medieval walls PAGE 182

above
(OB/D)

Perched dramatically on a basalt cliff, Castellfollit de la Roca is a favourite with painters PAGE 206

below
(G/D)

above
(AG/S)

Stunning Pyrenean peaks, glassy lakes and breathtaking hikes are found in the Parc Nacional de Aigüestortes i Estany de Sant Maurici PAGE 308

below
(FV/S)

The Costa Brava is a paradise for cyclists, with pine-fringed trails and glorious Mediterranean views PAGE 157

The Ebro Delta serene wetlands shelter abundant birdlife and preserve age-old Catalan traditions PAGE 261

above (GG/S)

The sunniest valley in the Pyrenees, the Cerdanya is home to a wide array of wildlife PAGE 222

right (L/D)

The sun glows on the famous Penedès vineyards, with the sacred mountain of Montserrat as a backdrop PAGE 145

below (MV/S)

above
(MU/D)

Basking on the banks of the Ebro River, arty little Miravet is crowned by a vast Templar castle PAGE 270

left
(MT/S)

Art and culture thrive in Sitges, particularly in the handsome Palau de Maricel museum overlooking the sea PAGE 149

below
(MT/S)

Whitewashed Cadaqués has long inspired artists with its beautiful light and wild setting at the easternmost tip of Spain PAGE 174

Jujols family lived. It has several buildings he remodelled early in his career, and also the wonderful and outlandish **Casa Bofarull** (1914–31).

Further north, near **La Secuita** lies the hamlet of **Vistabella**. Here Jujol designed a church that many consider to be his masterpiece, **El Sagrat Cor** (1918–23). It was done on a shoestring; Vistabella at the time counted only 128 inhabitants, and they spent a lot of time collecting stones from their fields to make this church possible. Still, despite a tiny construction budget, the final effect is stunning, a complex play of interlaced geometric forms that seems almost Islamic in inspiration, under a cupola made of parabolic ('catenary') arches topped with a needle-sharp belltower. Jujol was a painter too, and he did some of the lovely decoration inside; this is still being restored, after Anarchists set it on fire in the Civil War.

Further north, across the valley of the little River Gaiá, you'll see what seems to be a fairy-tale castle atop a distant hill. This is the 'little Sagrada Família', the **Santuari de la Mare de Déu de Montserrat** (Partida Corralot s/n; \621 22 38 15; w montferri. altanet.org/santuari-mdd-montserrat; ⊕ 10.00–14.00 & 16.30–19.00 daily; guided visits in Catalan available on prior request, call to reserve; adult/reduced/under 12 €5/3/free), located just north of the village of **Montferri**. Begun in 1921, funds ran out five years later and the church was completed only in the 1990s. Working for Gaudí, Jujol had contributed much of the design and decoration in the Park Güell, and it shows in this exquisite, playful building. Like El Sagrat Cor, the Santuari was designed for a small village with a very limited budget, and everything in it is made of the simplest materials. But if the materials are plain, the geometry in the design is as mind-spinningly complex as a Bach fugue. The bulbous parabolic vaults around the central tower were meant to recall the mountain pinnacles of Montserrat. Inside, an octagon of parabolic arches holds everything up.

VALLS The capital of the Alt Camp comarca is a modern, busy place. It hasn't much to attract the visitor, but it is the homeland of two of the great Catalan fetishes, symbols of the national identity. One is the humble *calçot* (page 246). The other is the *castell*. Valls was the birthplace of the fine art of building human towers, and it is still famous throughout Catalunya for the daring and skill of its *castellers*, who are honoured by a monument in the town centre, a 13.7m obelisk decorated with scenes of some of the more famous castells made here. Valls has three *casteller* clubs, including the celebrated *Colla Xiquets de Valls*. The best times to see them are the festivals of Sant Joan on 24 June, and Santa Úrsula on the third Sunday in October.

Valls' **Call**, the Jewish quarter, is still reached via its medieval arch and still well preserved; also worth a look are the Gothic church of **Sant Joan Baptista** and the Chapel des Roser, with a 17th-century portrayal in azulejos of the Battle of Lepanto, the great 1571 sea fight in which the Spaniards and their allies finally stopped the tide of Ottoman Turkish expansion in the Mediterranean. The **Museu de Valls** (Pg dels Caputxins 18; \977 60 66 54; w valls.cat/museu-de-valls-visites; ⊕ 17.00–20.00 Tue, 11.00–14.00 & 17.00–20.00 Wed–Sat, 11.00–14.00 Sun; free) on Passaig dels Caputxins has archaeological finds and a large collection of Catalan painting.

SANTES CREUS (Pl Jaume el Just s/n; \977 63 83 29; w patrimoni.gencat.cat/en/ monuments/monuments/royal-monastery-of-santes-creus; ⊕ Jun–Sep 10.00–19.00, Oct–Mar 10.00–17.30; adult/reduced/under 16 €6/4/free) The first of the region's three great monasteries is just north of the village of Aiguamúrcia. This one isn't nearly as crowded as Poblet in summer, and, since there are no monks in residence, you get to see everything. More importantly, perhaps, you aren't obliged to tag along on a guided tour. Instead, you'll get a flashy, prize-winning audiovisual show.

7

THE CISTERCIAN EMPIRE

Strategically located between Tarragona and Lleida, at the centre of the 'New Catalunya' conquered from the Moors, stand three huge and magnificent Cistercian monasteries, the most impressive in all of Spain. They are: Santes Creus, east of Valls; Poblet, in the mountains to the west; and Vallbona de les Monges, built for women, further north towards Tàrrega. As the Catalans, Aragonese, Templars and their allies reclaimed this distant outpost of al-Andalus in the mid 12th century, the monks of the Cistercian order were marching right behind them. Never believe for a minute that anything that happened in the Middle Ages was just a feudal muddle. This expansion of medieval Christendom was a highly planned operation, one that mobilised men and women from all over Europe. Conquering a country requires a lot of blood and treasure. The Cistercians, among others, were here not only to Christianise the conquest, but to make it pay. And that, above all the other monastic orders, is where the Cistercians excelled.

This order, founded only in 1098, was then in the midst of a wave of expansion that contemporaries found almost miraculous. The Cistercians' great leader, St Bernard of Clairvaux (d1153), had built it into a model of intelligence and efficiency while shoring up Christian theology and earning himself sainthood and status as a Doctor of the Church. (On the other hand, Bernard was a damn rotter who persecuted Peter Abelard and free scholarship, burned books, promoted attacks against the Cathars and anyone else he saw as heretical, and generally made life miserable for people he suspected might be having a good time.)

The Cistercians began as an attempt to restore the original, strict monastic rule of St Benedict. When Bernard's Cistercians weren't praying, they were working, and – here's the new twist – when they stopped working they were dreaming up ways to work more effectively. Cistercians pioneered improved methods in agriculture and husbandry. They built trading networks that stretched across Europe. Where there were swamps, they drained them; where there was ore, they mined it and smelted it. They were behind many of the technological innovations that made the Middle Ages such an economic boom time, notably the use of water power, which they employed to run big workshops that are seen as the precursors of the modern factory system.

It's a little mystery why the three big Cistercian installations in Catalunya should have been placed so close together. But it would be a mistake to think

Santes Creus was founded in 1158, devastated with the dissolution of the monasteries in 1835, and has been carefully restored since. The monastery reached the height of its influence in the 14th century, when its abbots were friends and counsellors to kings, though in this respect it was gradually eclipsed by Poblet. In 1317, after the dissolution of the Templars, the Abbot of Santes Creus was permitted to start the Order of Manresa, which was similar in purpose and organisation, and took in many former Templars as members.

The **church**, begun in the 1170s and completed in 1221, has an especially austere façade, with crenellations that give it a military look that is carried on inside, down a nave lined with plain, massive pillars. There is no pretence of austerity at all, though, in the big Baroque retable or in the **royal tombs**, which include those of Jaume II, Blanche of Anjou and Pere III, along with the great admiral Roger de Llúria. Perhaps the best part of Santes Creus is the lovely **cloister** (1313–41), in which the Cistercian prohibition of figurative decoration was somehow suspended of them as purely local institutions. Each held lands and farms and workshops spread across the Kingdom of Aragon and beyond. Royal patronage was important to all three from the start, as evidenced by the Aragonese kings buried inside.

When you visit one of these Cistercian houses, remember that this was a branch of an international conglomerate, closely bound to the centres of political and economic power. Cistercians didn't care much for poetry or art, but they had a terrible weakness for architecture. Even in Bernard's day, they made sure they picked the best available architects and workmen for the new monasteries they were building across Europe. At the same time, the ethos of austerity that lay at the heart of everything Cistercian required a whole new aesthetic.

The classic Cistercian abbey church is Gothic at its grandest – the order and the Gothic style were practically born together – but without the elaborate decoration of a city cathedral; the fantastical figurative ornaments that so enlivened the capitals and portals of the Romanesque was strictly forbidden. Abbey church façades are often nothing more than an unadorned portal underneath plain lancet windows, with sometimes a small rose window on top; it was architectural Protestantism, four centuries before the Reformation.

The three churches here have little in common with the stout, quirky Catalan Gothic of Barcelona; just as the order was an international movement, its architecture was a mature international style, which took its inspiration from France. To compensate for the lack of frills, Cistercians insisted on sheer perfection in conception and proportions. And they usually got it; their churches are acclaimed as some of the most elegant productions of the Middle Ages.

In truth, Cistercian austerity fades proportionally with time, and with distance from the order's home at Cîteaux, in Burgundy. In each of the three monasteries here you can see how the original stern and solid Romanesque gave way to delicate Gothic soon after building had commenced. The gorgeous rib vaulting and window traceries of Catalunya's three houses would be the envy of any metropolitan cathedral.

The **Ruta del Cister ticket**, available online at w patrimoni.gencat.cat/en/la-ruta-del-cister/cistercian-route-pass, costs €15 and includes entry to the three monasteries.

to allow some charming carvings on the capitals, the work of an Englishman whose name has come down as Reinart Funoll.

MONTBLANC From Santes Creus to Poblet, you'll pass into the comarca called the Conca de Barberà, an agricultural region known for its DO Conca de Barberà wine. The 'conca' is a broad natural basin, running roughly from Barberà to Tàrres, that creates some striking scenery as you descend into it from the surrounding hills.

The comarca's capital is Montblanc, an attractive walled town with an air of distinction; in the late Middle Ages it was the seat of a dukedom, and the Catalan Corts (parliament) sat here four times. They'll tell you that Saint George, or rather Sant Jordi, killed his dragon here – he's the patron of Catalunya as well as England. A plaque marks the spot at the **Porta de Sant Jordi**, and the feat is re-enacted every April during Montblanc's Medieval Festival.

7

The 14th-century **walls** (Portal de Sant Francesc; ☎ 977 86 17 33; w montblancmedieval.cat/see-do/monuments/military/walled-enclosure; ⏰ mid-Jun–mid-Sep 10.00–14.00 & 17.00–19.00 Wed–Sat, 10.00–14.00 Sun; Oct–Mar 10.00–14.00 & 16.00–18.00 Thu–Sat, 11.00–14.00 Sun; adult/reduced/under 13 €3/1.5/free), which survive almost completely intact, along with their 34 towers, are still impressive today. Outside them, a little 12th-century **bridge** survives too, in a neglected part of town over the River Francolí. On the Raval de Santa Anna, have a peek inside the medieval **Hospital de Santa Magdalena**, now the town archives, for its charming little courtyard and fountain. The **Carrer Major**, the main street of the old town, used to be covered with medieval arches. Side streets to the right lead to the picturesque town centre: the **Plaça Major** with the town hall, and the adjacent **Plaça Santa Maria**, a picture-postcard setting for the Catalan Gothic parish church **Santa Maria** and its elegant Baroque portal, which replaced an original destroyed in the Reaper's War.

Across from the church, the 14th-century Casal dels Josa is now the main building of the **Museu Comarcal** (C/ Josa 6; ☎ 977 86 03 49; w mccb.cat; ⏰ 09.00–14.00 Tue–Thu, 09.00–14.00 & 17.00–19.00 Fri, 11.00–14.00 & 17.00–19.00 Sat, 11.00–14.00 Sun; adult/reduced €4/3), with a motley collection that includes local archaeological finds, a collection of nativity scenes, and works of art donated by the sculptor Frederic Marès. Behind the church, the **Centre d'Interpretación d'Art Rupestre** (C/ Pedrera 2; ☎ 977 86 21 77; w mccb.cat; ⏰ 09.00–14.00 & 16.00–18.00 Mon–Fri; adult/reduced €4/3) is dedicated to the scores of prehistoric painted caves that have been discovered in this part of Catalunya. None is currently open to visitors, but here you can see reproductions of some striking art.

Back on Carrer Major is the ruggedly primitive 12th-century church of **Sant Miquel**. It's hard to believe that the Catalan parliament met here twice (in 1307 and 1370). The streets behind, around **Carrer dels Jueus**, were once the Jewish district. Carrying on down Carrer Major through the western city gate, you'll come to the ruined **Monastery of Sant Francesc**, with a large 14th-century church that was long used as a winemaker's warehouse. Nowadays the wine is kept in the **Cèsar Martinell Cooperativa** (1922) outside the walls on Carrer Santa Tecla. The Montblanc area grows many Conca de Barbera and other wines, but the co-operative here is mostly known for cava, named Pont Vell after the medieval bridge.

North of Montblanc in the Conca, **Sarral** is a village known for centuries for mining and working alabaster. It has reproduced a 1917 workshop, with demonstrations of how it was done. There are a handful of workshops in the village, and they turn out some quite artistic works.

L'ESPLUGA DE FRANCOLÍ
Just west of Montblanc, on the way to Poblet, L'Espluga de Francolí gets its name from the enormous cave (or *spelunca*) that lies underneath its centre, called the **Cova Museu de la Font Major** (Avda de Catalunya s/n; ☎ 977 87 12 20; w covesdelespluga.info; ⏰ by guided visit only, 10.30, 11.15, noon, 12.45, 16.30 & 17.30 Sat–Sun; adult/reduced/5–14/under 5 €8.50/7.65/5.50/free). The town carried that name for centuries without knowing why; the cave was only rediscovered in 1853. Though an impressive 2½ miles in length, this isn't a pretty stalactite cave, but Espluga tries to make up for that with a merciless guided tour (in Catalan, but audioguides in other languages are provided) and a ton of information on its geological formation and archaeological finds; that's why it is a 'cova museu'.

Espluga has other attractions, including the 12th-century Gothic **Sant Miquel Arcàngel**, a town **library** that once was a hospital of the Knights Hospitallers, and a remarkable institution called the **Casal de l'Espluga**, founded by Lluís Carulla, a hugely successful businessman and town benefactor. You can't miss its big complex of buildings on the edge of town – behind the picnic ground with the house shaped like a gigantic barrel. It's a very Catalan idea, dating from the Franco years, when Carulla began it to help keep Catalan language and culture alive. That remains its purpose today, and it acts as a kind of social and cultural club for all the people of the town. There are gardens and meeting halls, a theatre company, a literary circle, sports clubs and courses; you can learn anything from quilting to judo here. Maybe every town should have one (the Casal also includes a restaurant).

Carulla also set up a museum of rural life in the villa in which he was born, which has recently moved to a shiny new home on the edge of town: the **Museu Terra de la Fundació Carulla** (Ctra de Montblanc 45; ☏977 87 05 76; w museuterra. cat; ⏱ 10.30–18.30 Tue–Sat, 10.30–14.00 Sun; adult/reduced/under 18 €6/4.50/ free). One of many museums about farming life in the old days scattered across Catalunya, it is perhaps the most interesting, a serious attempt to present the history of the region through the articles of everyday life, with plenty of interactive exhibits to keep kids entertained.

If you'd like to pick up some of the many local delicacies grown or produced in the region, head to the **Agrobotiga de Poblet** (Pl Ramon Berenguer IV 4; ☏977 87 09 58; w fetalaconca.cat) to find a wonderful selection of wine, olive oil, charcuterie, cheeses, chocolate and more.

SANTA MARIA DE POBLET (Pl de la Corona d'Aragó, Vimbodí i Poblet; ☏977 87 00 89; w poblet.cat; ⏱ mid-Jun–mid-Sep 10.00–12.30 & 15.00–18.30 Mon–Sat, 10.30–12.30 & 15.00–18.30 Sun; mid-Sep–mid-Jun 10.00–12.30 & 15.00–18.00 Mon–Sat, 10.30–12.30 & 15.00–18.00 Sun; adult/reduced/under 7 €9.50/free) From L'Espluga de Francolí, it's only 5km to the famous Cistercian monastery of Santa Maria de Poblet, founded by Ramon Berenguer IV in 1151 to commemorate the end of the Reconquista in Catalunya. For centuries Poblet was its most powerful and privileged monastery, and it shows. Architecturally, it is the richest of the three Cistercian sisters, and the view through the traceries of its golden tower takes in blue mountains, behind gorgeous rolling hills covered in vines.

This is a house built for gentlemen. That, of course, is exactly what most of the monks were. Even before Pere III made the monastery a pantheon for the Kings of Aragon, Poblet was already the Catalan aristocratic retreat par excellence, even possessing a royal palace for visiting kings. Openly dissipated and corrupt in later years, Poblet was so despised that, when the monks were suspected of harbouring Carlist sympathies at the time of the dissolution in 1835, the locals found an excuse to avenge centuries of maltreatment. In their fury they wrenched apart the buildings and torched its famous library.

The ruins of Poblet stood overgrown with wildflowers until the 1940s, when a band of Italian Cistercians reclaimed and beautifully restored it (about 30 monks currently live in Poblet). At the ceremonial entrance, the **Porta Daurada**, stands a little Plateresque jewel, the freestanding **Capella de Sant Jordi**, built in 1442 by King Alfons V (better known to us as Alfonso the Magnanimous) in thanks for his conquest of the Kingdom of Naples. The Porta Daurada was completed in 1493, to commemorate a visit of Fernando and Isabel, and it bears the arms of newly united Aragon and Castile over the arch.

The gate leads to the **Plaça Major**, with the 13th-century **Capella de Santa Caterina**, one of the oldest parts of the complex. The façade of the church and the rest of the monastery is enclosed behind yet another wall, the **Porta Reial**, dripping with Baroque decoration.

7

The **church**, although begun almost when Poblet was founded, took another two centuries to be completed, with plenty of modifications in style along the way. At the end of the heavy Romanesque nave stands a glistening Renaissance altarpiece, carved in alabaster by the Valencian sculptor Damián Forment. Poblet was known as 'Catalunya's Escorial' for its many **tombs of the Kings of Aragon**, on both sides of the high altar, which were wonderfully restored by sculptor Frederic Marès. Among the many are Alfons I el Batallador (d1134) and Jaume I 'the Conqueror' (d1276), who finally made it back here in 1952 after his long posthumous exile in Tarragona (page 226). When he came back he had two skulls, and they're still trying to figure out which one's really his. The exquisite effigy is carved wearing a simple monk's habit; Jaume asked to become a Cistercian of Poblet just before he died.

Outside is a richly sculpted **cloister**, with a lovely fountain in a little pavilion at its centre that could be an image from a medieval illumination. The guided tour will lead you on to the huge vaulted wine cellar, the fine Gothic chapterhouse, the dormitory, the refectory and kitchen, and the **Palace of King Martí l'Humà** (Martin the Humanist) from 1397; the kings came to Poblet so often, eventually they built themselves a proper home here. This handsome building now houses a small museum, with some charming carved medieval wooden sculpture, architectural fragments, paintings and ceramics.

VALLBONA DE LES MONJES (C/ Major s/n; ☏ 973 33 02 66; w monestirvallbona. cat; ☺ guided visits in Catalan or Spanish at 10.30, 11.30, 12.30, 16.00, 17.00 Tue–Sat, 10.30, 11.30, 12.30, 16.00 Sun; also self-guided visit with audiovisual 18.00 Sat & 17.00 Sun; €8) Vallbona, the third member of the Cistercian trio lies 30km up in the hills, just over the border in Lleida province. It was built for nuns, and located far away from anything else so they wouldn't be distracted. Nevertheless, a village eventually grew up around the convent. In 1573, the Church decided to ban convents for women in isolated places, and Vallbona languished. Like Poblet, it has been restored and repopulated only in this century.

The architecture differs little from Poblet and Santes Creus: four-square Cistercian Romanesque laid on with a frosting of delicate Gothic, bits and pieces of everything else, most of it unfinished, all topped with a lovely octagonal Gothic tower. The **church** has a few royal tombs, including those of Violant of Hungary, the wife of Jaume I, and their daughter Sança. In a chapel on the right, note the beautiful Gothic statue of the *Mare de Déu del Cor* (Our Lady of the Choir) by Guillem Seguer, a sculptor from Montblanc. This Virgin Mary is one of many at Vallbona. Another fine one, by an unknown artist, can be seen in the chapterhouse, the *Mare de Déu del Claustre*. There are so many other noble tombs on the floor in the church and chapterhouse that Vallbona has been called a 'museum of Catalan heraldry'. There's also a delightful old **pharmacy**, with lots of blue-and-white ceramic jars and utensils dating back centuries: although convents were ordered to close their pharmacies by the Council of Trent in 1545, to avoid being accused of practising dark arts, the nuns here carried on preparing their herbal remedies right up until the 19th century. The charming **cloister** dates from the 12th–15th centuries.

THE PRADES MOUNTAINS AND PRIORAT

Between Poblet and Reus, there's a patch on the road maps where all the roads are lined with green for scenery. It looks enticing on the map, but you'll find that the Prades mountains, however green, can be downright unreasonable. Entering this pocket massif is an adventure from any direction, like storming a castle; the most spectacular of the roads leading in, perhaps, is the one from Reus through Vilaplana: a hundred hairpin turns taking you almost 1,070m straight up, with breathtaking views over the sea.

TOURIST INFORMATION This region has a number of very efficient tourist information offices, which can provide a wealth of information on everything from bodega tours to hiking routes. You'll find them in Prades (C/ Muralla 3; ☎977 86 83 02; w prades.cat/en) and Falset (Pl de la Quartera 1; ☎977 83 10 23; w turismefalset. cat & w turismepriorat.org).

There's a small information booth that covers the Serra de Montsant nature reserve and villages like Siurana in Cornudella de Montsant (C/ Comte de Rius s/n; ☎977 82 10 00; w turismesiurana.org).

🏠 WHERE TO STAY

Gran Hotel Mas d'en Bruno Polígono 5 Parcela 71, Torroja del Priorat; ☎877 67 60 70; w masdenbruno.com. An award-winning, ultra-luxurious boutique hotel, with 24 exquisite suites gazing out over vine-clad hills, & every possible 5-star luxury trimming, including a private wine cellar, a spa in the old olive-oil mill, infinity pool & exceptional restaurant, **Vinum** (€€€€). €€€€€

✳ **El Palauet del Priorat** C/ de les Eres 7, Cornudella de Montsant; ☎670 96 14 64; w elpalauetdelpriorat.com. An enchanting rural hotel, set amid endless vines just outside the little town, with 7 spacious rooms & suites in an old stone house, all elegantly decorated. They produce their own excellent Montsant wines, & you can tour the bodega & enjoy delicious gourmet cuisine. €€€

Balcó de Priorat C/ Bonrepos 18, La Morera de Montsant; ☎609 94 76 05; w elbalcodelpriorat. com. Located on a street that means 'good rest', this is exactly what you'll get at this small, friendly

inn. Rooms are traditionally furnished, simple & excellent value. The excellent restaurant (€€€) serves lovingly prepared local cuisine cooked with the freshest seasonal produce. €€

Cal Llop C/ de Dalt 21, Gratallops; ☎977 83 95 02; w cal-llop.com. A smart boutique hotel at the heart of the village, with 10 spacious rooms, some with private balconies, & a wine bar where you can try the best local vintages. €€

Hostal Sport C/ Miquel Barceló 6, Falset; ☎977 83 00 78; w hotelpriorat-hostalsport.com. Built in the 1920s & handsomely remodelled; this large hotel boasts attractive rooms & apartments, & a very popular traditional restaurant (€€€). €€

Cal Pons C/ Sant Llorenç 12, Prades; ☎658 56 94 51. A small, old-fashioned guesthouse with a few traditionally furnished rooms in the heart of the village. They can store bikes & also rent them out too. (They don't have a website, so you'll have to book by phone, through the tourist office or on a booking platform.) €

🍴 WHERE TO EAT AND DRINK

Restaurant Brichs Falset; ☎690 25 12 06; w brichsrestaurant.com; ⏰ 13.30–15.15 Wed & Sun, 13.30–15.15 & 20.30–22.15 Thu–Sat. A sleekly designed glassy restaurant, with a terrace offering wonderful views over the town, this is a good spot for modern Catalan dishes that are based on traditional recipes but given a contemporary twist. €€€

✳ **La Cooperativa** C/ Unió, Porrera; ☎977 82 83 78; ◙ restaurantlacooperativa; ⏰ 13.00–14.30 Mon–Sat. A delightful restaurant set in the village's wine co-operative. Surprising dishes from cod to curries, made with largely organic & Km0 (local)

produce, & plenty of wine from the vines you see out the window. €€

✳ **La Morera** C/ de la Bassa 10, La Morera de Montsant; ☎667 44 29 04; ◙ restaurantlamorera; ⏰ 13.30–15.30 Fri–Sun. This little restaurant hidden down a narrow street has become a place of pilgrimage for local foodies, thanks to its consistently excellent cuisine based on traditional recipes. The whole family have been roped into this venture, a real labour of love, & their passion for what they do is evident in every bite. €€

Quinoa C/ Miquel Barceló, Falset; ☎977 83 04 31; ◙ quinoa_restaurant_falset; ⏰ 13.30–15.30 Mon, Wed, Thu & Sun, 13.30–15.30 & 21.00–23.30

7

CATALAN QUINTESSENCE: PRIORAT AND MONTSANT WINES

A monastery, a land, a wine – it's all tied together. The three make up everything you need to know about this little region, scarcely 50km wide. The prior was the man who held the keys to the Charterhouse of Scala Dei, which owned just about everything here. The wine his monks learned to make is still the Priorat's very identity, and has become one of Catalunya's finest.

The Priorat's growers had been winning medals back in the 1880s and 90s, before the phylloxera hit. For decades afterwards, there wasn't much ambition left, and much of the old knowledge and techniques were lost. Things began to change radically in the 1970s and 80s. As in so many other ways in those fizzy post-Franco years, the Catalans were waking up in a hurry. A new generation of vintners rebuilt the medieval terraces, planted new stock, and hit the books, trying to recapture the old Carthusian magic. They did their work so well that nowadays the best Priorats are counted among the finest wines in the world. In fact, Priorat has been awarded Spain's highest classification, DOQ (Denominació d'Origen Qualificada), which it shares only with Rioja.

It all began when the monks arrived from Provence in the 12th century, bringing the first grenache grapes with them. Long before chartreuse was invented, even before their Baroque-era slide into high-living decadence, Carthusians knew a thing or two about drink. It started innocently enough, with the order's vocation in medicine and pharmacy. One medieval Carthusian scholar wrote of alcohol as the fifth element, the quintessence, and sovereign against any imbalance in the body's humours.

No-one knows how they ended up in the Priorat, but we might suspect that someone tipped them off, that some wine-bibbing monkish scout sent a note to the Charterhouse saying that here, in these obscure hills lately reclaimed from the Moors, was the perfect soil for wine. What makes it special, they say, is the slate bedrock, which pushes up a layer of chips on the surface to keep the roots moist while it gives the soil an extra helping of useful minerals. Catalan vintners call this

Fri–Sat. Delicious, traditional Catalan food with a modern touch, like their wonderful *arròs de mar y muntanya* – a type of paella with seafood & meat. It also does one of the best-value set lunches in the area (€17 w/days, €27 w/ends). €€

Calaix de Sastre Wine Bar Pl de la Quartera 39, Falset; ✆615 82 99 52; ☑ calaixdesastre_ winebar; ⏱ 09.00–15.00 Mon–Tue, 09.00–16.00 Thu, 09.00–16.00 & 19.00–23.00 Fri, noon–16.00 & 19.00–23.30 Sat, noon–16.00 Sun. Sample local wines along with platters of charcuterie & cheeses, & other delicious tapas. It's also the perfect place to enjoy a *vermut* – the classic Catalan aperitif – in good company. €

SPORTS AND ACTIVITIES This beautiful, rural region is a popular spot for all kinds of outdoor activities, including hiking, cycling and rock climbing. The Priorat website (w turismepriorat.org/en/what-do) lists some of the best hiking and biking routes, many of which follow different themes – for example, a *pedra seca* (dry wall) route or an olive oil route. It is also a good resource for information on climbing in the Montsant Massif (w turismepriorat.org/en/climbing-montsant-massif) with maps of the main routes and sites, including Siurana and the abandoned village of La Mussara.

PRADES The biggest village up here is nicknamed 'La Vila Vermella' from the striking red colour of the local stone, used in the medieval walls and many of the stony soil *llicorella*, and the stuff it produces can be drunk young, or put away for amazingly long periods. It also makes the Priorat one of the world's most potent wines – some labels go up to 24%, although 14–16% is more common.

They are complex blends, often using five or more different varieties of grape. Garnacha (Grenache) was the original, and Cariñena (Carignan) the first new variety to be planted after the phylloxera decimated the original vines after 1900. Now, besides these, Cabernet Sauvignon and Syrah are also common.

Many of the famous names of the Priorat are small, artisanal operations, some only 10ha or less. Getting great wine out of stony soil, in a climate that tends to extremes, is an art. They baby their low-yielding vines, and then they hand-pick the grapes. In 2020, the region adopted a new classification system, Els Noms de la Terra (The Names of the Land), which reflects the increased emphasis on single-vineyard wines highlighting specific terroirs within Priorat.

Many of the best-known producers are around the village of Gratallops, where the Priorat wine revolution began. These include **Clos Mogador**, **Clos Erasmus** and the current superstar of the Priorat, **Álvaro Palacios**, whose l'Ermita wine has won top prizes all over the world (some of their other labels, such as Les Terrasses, are a little more affordable).

In addition to Priorat, this little corner of Catalunya also produces **DO Montsant** wines, red and white, in a doughnut-shaped area that neatly surrounds the very small kingdom of Priorat. Montsant, made by about 60 producers, uses the same grapes; the difference is in the soil. DO was granted in 2002 and this has become a well-established denomination, with many organic and biodynamic producers. Some Montsant labels are getting rave reviews and commanding high prices, but most are still considered among the best-value wines in Spain. The pioneering co-operative **Celler Capçanes** (977 17 83 19; w cellercapcanes.com) in the village of that name makes a variety of quality-focused wines and offers a range of visitor experiences, including tastings and tours.

buildings. In the centre of the pretty, arcaded **Plaça Major** stands the odd, spherical **Fountain of Prades** from the 1500s. The source of the fountain is unknown, but it has never in known memory run dry.

SIURANA On the road to Cornudell, Siurana is a romantic spot, with its Arab castle perched atop a cliff known as 'the Balcony of Priorat', ancient stone-built houses, and a primitive 12th-century **church** with an unusual and finely carved portal down by the river gorge. The **castle** was the Moors' last stronghold in Catalunya, where they held out until 1153. Siurana lies on the edge of the Priorat wine region, but this village has its very own DO status, for its high-quality and intensely fruity olive oil, considered among the finest in Spain. It's easy to see how the Moors held on so long; Siurana hangs over 600m in the air. Down below, you can go kayaking on the reservoir, the **Embassement de Siurana**, which almost dried up during the recent drought – the worst ever recorded in Catalunya – but is now, thankfully, on its way to being replenished.

7

FALSET The modern capital of the Priorat, Falset is an attractive village with a castle and an ensemble of medieval and Renaissance buildings around its arcaded plaça. The popular Fira del Vi, held every May, brings crowds from all over Catalunya to celebrate. Like so many villages of western Catalunya, it has a lovely Modernista **Bodega Cooperativa** by Cèsar Martinell (1888–1973).

Martinell was one of the great architects of Catalunya's golden age. He studied with Gaudí, and worked with him on the Sagrada Família, but the gods of architecture had a most peculiar destiny reserved for him. Martinell ended up spending much of his life designing bodegas – over 40 of them, mostly in the villages of Tarragona province. That was the hand he was dealt, and, like the true artist he was, he made them the most beautiful, most functional wine cellars ever built. Architectural historians and winemakers note how cleverly and efficiently he arranged the interior spaces, but, for us non-specialists, the striking thing will be the soaring parabolic arches he learned from Gaudí, built in brick with an ingenious system of supporting columns.

AROUND FALSET Once you're out of Falset and on to the back roads, you'll see just how peculiar a place the Priorat really is. Those back roads are narrow, and they tend to meander about as if they've had a little too much Priorat wine. Here and there, outcrops of the metamorphic slate stick up between the vineyards, and sometimes the striations are as twisty as the roads. Villages perch high in the air, and if you manage to get inside them there's no place to park.

What do you do in the Priorat besides drink? Choices are limited. Hiking is becoming increasingly popular, and there is a movement to clear and mark the area's ancient pathways. Or you might drive over to **Bellmunt del Priorat** and its **Museu de les Mines** (Ctra de la Mina s/n; ℑ626 38 47 06; w minesbellmunt.com; ⊕ you must reserve visits in advance by phone or email e museu@minesbellmunt. cat, Jul–Aug 11.00, noon & 17.00 Tue–Sat, 11.00 & noon Sun; Sep–Jun 11.00, noon & 17.00 Sat, 11.00 & noon Sun; adult/reduced/under 8 €8/5/free), where they'll take you down for guided tours of the 9 miles of tunnels where they once mined lead.

There isn't a lot left of the old charterhouse, the **Cartoixa d'Escaladei** (Camí de la Cartoixa s/n; ℑ977 82 70 06; w patrimoni.gencat.cat/en/monuments/monuments/ carthusian-monastery-of-escaladei; ⊕ May–Sep 10.00–19.00 Tue–Sat, 10.00–15.00 Sun, Oct–Mar 10.00–17.00 Tue–Sat, 10.00–15.00 Sun) in the village of **Escaladei** but it's worth a visit for the stunning, isolated setting under the Montsant cliffs. After the dissolution of Spain's monasteries in 1835 it was abandoned and eventually fell into ruin. The local people were delighted to be rid of the monks, along with their rents and tithes, and they helped themselves to most of the stones. The monastery got its name, the story goes, when a shepherd had a vision of a stairway with angels ascending to heaven. Scala Dei was the first Carthusian establishment in Spain, and the head of all those that followed.

Lone arches still stand, along with part of the church façade and remnants of three delicate cloisters, to give an idea of what sumptuous digs this once must have been. One of the original Carthusian cells has been recreated for visitors along with a pretty little kitchen garden, where the monks grew their vegetables and medicinal herbs.

THE COSTA DAURADA: SOUTH FROM TARRAGONA

Spain's 'Golden Coast' continues on past Tarragona out towards the delta of the Ebre. While its beaches are often long and even gold coloured, they lack that most elusive quality, charm. This side (at least once you get past Cambrils) isn't nearly as intense as the other side of Tarragona. The scenery is siesta-sleepy, and the resorts attract older folks enjoying the sun and tranquillity, and families with young children who require nothing more than good castle-building sand, shallow sea, and their peers for a perfect holiday (most of the visitors are Spanish and French).

Beginning from Tarragona, the first few steps aren't so promising. The first attraction is a Mordor-like skyline of smokestacks and petroleum towers at the enormous industrial area at **Vila Seca**. Just inland is PortAventura World, the Catalan answer to Disneyland, with a watery annexe called **Caribe Aquatic Park** and, its glitziest attraction, Ferrari Land.

TOURIST INFORMATION As you'd expect in one of the most popular tourist destinations on the Med, you'll never be more than a stone's throw from a tourist information office. Some of the main ones include Salou (Pl d'Europa; ↘977 35 01 02; w visitsalou.eu), Cambrils (Pg de les Palmeres 1; ↘977 79 23 07; w cambrils-turisme.com) and L'Ametlla del Mar (Av Amistat Hispano Italiana s/n; ↘977 45 64 77; w visitametllad
emar.com).

WHERE TO STAY This is package-tour country, jam-packed with two- and three-star establishments, all relatively new and all pretty much alike. You don't want to be here in the summer madness, especially in Salou or Cambrils, but the rest of the year – and many hotels do stay open – either of these towns can be a pleasant stopover.

Instants Boutique Hotel C/ Galceran Marquet 1, Cambrils; ↘977 79 53 64; w instantsboutiquehotel.com. A refreshing break from the standard resort hotels, this is a mid-sized, chic retreat from the crowds – & the kids (it's adults only). Rooms are whitewashed & airy, & there's a sun deck by the saltwater pool where you can drowse the afternoons away in peace. €€€€
San Diego C/ Penedès 23, Salou; ↘977 38 07 16; w besthotels.es/destinos-y-hoteles/best-san-diego.html. Typical package hotel, a huge white complex, but a good one, especially if you have kids; mini club, playground & pool, all just 5mins from the beach. €€€€
Can Solé C/ Ramon Llull 19, Cambrils; ↘977 36 02 36; w cansole.es. A few blocks from the beach & the restaurant strip, with 27 simple, rather old-fashioned rooms at a decent price. Friendly, talkative folks. €€€
Hotel Bon Repòs C/ Llibertat 49, l'Ametlla de Mar; ↘977 45 60 25; w hotelbonrepos.es. This

medium-sized, modest but delightful hotel has pristine rooms & apartments, a courtyard garden with pool & bar serving drinks & tapas. €€€
L'Alguer C/ Mar 20, L'Ametlla del Mar; ↘977 49 33 72; w hotelalguer.net. A 5-min walk from the beach, this mid-sized modern hotel has rather dated rooms, but friendly staff; ask for a room with a sea view. €€€
✳ **Mas Aguiló** C/ Lluna 17, Miami Platja; ↘621 19 54 64; w masaguilo.com. This is a new, small hotel with just 4 stylish & spanking-new rooms in a thoughtfully renovated stone house that dates back to the 18th century. Charming owners & a leafy courtyard garden. €€€
Rovira Avda Diputació 6, Cambrils; ↘977 36 09 00; w hotelrovira.com. This large, family-run hotel has been going since 1952, keeping guests happy with freshly renovated rooms in soothing Mediterranean colours, generous b/fasts, a pool in the gardens & a very good seafood restaurant (€€€). €€€

✕ WHERE TO EAT AND DRINK
Can Bosch Rbla Jaume I 19, Cambrils; ↘977 36 00 19; w canbosch.com. A culinary landmark in the region, which earned its Michelin star back in 1984, in a central & elegant location. Creative cooking from a father & son team & a big wine list; for a memorable splurge there's a €115 *menú degustació*. Or, if you want to push the boat out yet

further, you can book their special lobster tasting menu (price depends on market). €€€€€
Delirante C/ Levant 7, Salou; ↘977 38 09 42; w deliranto.com; ⊕ 13.30–14.30 & 20.30–21.30 Wed–Sat. This restaurant burst on to the culinary scene relatively recently but chef Pep Moreno has already won a Michelin star among many other

7

accolades. Conceived as a spectacle from start to finish, this is glorious, contemporary cuisine at its most theatrical. The 18-course set menu is €125 (€195 with wine pairings). €€€€€

Miramar Pg Miramar 30, Cambrils; ↘977 36 00 63; w miramar-cambrils.com; ⏱ 13.00–15.00 & 20.00–23.00 Mon & Wed–Sun. This chic restaurant has been going strong for 6 decades & is still one of the best places for an excellent seafood dinner on the waterfront. €€€€

La Morera C/ Berenguer de Palou 10, Salou; ↘977 38 57 63; ◻ morera_pabloyester; ⏱ 13.30–15.00 & 20.30–22.00 Tue–Sat, 14.00–16.00 Sun. You'll enjoy some of the best & most authentic Catalan cuisine at this elegant, glassy restaurant, all prepared with the freshest produce & beautifully presented. They also have a lovely terrace for summer dining. €€€

Bar del Pòsit C/ Pescadors 27, Cambrils; ↘977 13 12 74; w elposit.com; ⏱ 12.30–23.30 daily. A wide range of tapas, plus more substantial dishes – including fresh fish, Mediterranean rice dishes & veggie options – prepared, as much as possible, with Km0 (local) produce. Lively, laid-back & good value. (They also have a slightly more formal restaurant at Pl Mossèn Joan Batalla 3.) €€

Sisters Café C/ Girona 9, Salou; ↘877 06 74 20; ◻ SistersCafeRestaurant; ⏱ 13.00–17.00 Mon & Wed–Sun. Sweet little restaurant, decorated with simple charm, which serves up hearty portions of local fare at good prices. €€

Cala Cris C/ Major 4, L'Ametlla de Mar; ↘877 91 61 88; ◻ calacrisametllademar; ⏱ noon–midnight daily. *Vermut*, wine, tapas, art & live music – what more could you want? This is a popular gathering place for locals & always has a great atmosphere. €

SALOU After the promontory of Cap Salou, you're at the southern end of the Tarragona-Reus conurbation, specifically in the tastefully landscaped roundabouts of Salou, the biggest and brashest package-tour ghetto on the Costa Daurada. You wouldn't guess it, but there is an old settlement here. Jaume the Conqueror sailed off from Salou in 1229 to do some conquering, in this case the island of Mallorca.

He wouldn't know the place today. Turn a corner, and behind a long wall of plate-glass windows a thousand English and Scandinavian ladies are playing bingo. Around the next bend, another seafront palace opens to vistas of waltzing blue-rinse battalions. Salou is a family kind of place; it is an agreeable and civilised city by the sea, though the air of a tourist bubble is unmistakable.

A city it undeniably is, with a bit of old town, built around a 1530s blockhouse called the **Torre Vella**, which now houses a small museum of enamelwork from around the world. Beyond that is a huge modern **Eixample**, a long and attractive beachfront promenade named for King Jaume, a market district with a busy weekly street market on Via Roma, and a lovely fountain with an impressive colour and light show called the **Font Lluminosa**, designed by Carles Buigas, the mad genius who created Barcelona's Font Màgica.

PORTAVENTURA WORLD (Avda Pere Molas s/n, Vila-seca; ↘ 977 77 90 90; w portaventuraworld.com; ⏱ see website for opening times; tickets start at €70 for 2 days/2 parks, but there are numerous options available. Discounts when booked online in advance) This, the 'Biggest Theme Park in the Med', is divided into six zones, connected by boats and Mickey-Mousey steam trains. In the **Mediterranean Zone** there's an ever-so-charming fishing village and the explosive Furios Baco ride, based on a fictional wine experiment gone wrong, though if you step on a boat you're likely to end up in **China**. In this zone, they'll bundle you on an ultra-modern, ultra-speedy rollercoaster called the Dragon Khan that looks as if it was designed by a delirious Santiago Calatrava with a little help from Dr. Seuss, or the even taller and faster Shambhala, where you might lose your lunch on Europe's biggest rollercoaster drop (78m). Climb back on the boat or the steam train and the hallucinations multiply. You can cruise under the **Polynesian** seas with a friendly talking dolphin to guide you, or experience a simulated buffalo stampede in the **Wild West**. Best of all perhaps is the **Mexico Zone**, which seems to be based on some brooding Aztec ritual of human sacrifice, possibly yours. Here, after the Templo del Fuego funfair, you will be invited to the indigenous ceremony of the Plumed Serpent, which (surprise!) involves being whirled at indecent speeds around the Sacred Totem Pole. If all that sounds too dizzying, you can meet Big Bird and friends in **SésamoAventura**, with rides, pools and play areas for the littlest kids.

Each zone contains a playground, restaurants, shows, boat rides and souvenir shops, all tarted up to some stereotype from the prevailing theme. It's enough to make any normal parent gag, but Port Aventura redeems itself with the pure kitsch hilarity of it all.

Over in **Ferrari Land**, where no opportunity is missed to slap on a Ferrari logo, the rides include Red Force, Europe's tallest (112m) and fastest (180 km/h) rollercoaster (there's a junior version, too), racing simulators and a whole host of exhibits about the history of Ferrari, plus smaller rides for younger kids.

CAMBRILS Everyone in Cambrils will tell you that Cambrils is a much nicer resort: less frenetic, smaller, more convivial. That's about half true, Cambrils is an old fishing village (with one of Catalunya's biggest fleets) that luck has made into an overspill suburb of Salou. Its old town has another old defence tower, a lot of very good fish restaurants, a mile or two of *urbanizacions* (housing estates), and another endless beach beyond the old fishing harbour, where you can watch the return of the fishing boats (Mon–Fri at around 17.00, except May & June).

The **Museu d'Història** (Via Augusta 1; ☎977 79 45 28; w cambrils.cat/museu; ⊕ 11.00–14.00 & 17.00–20.00 Sat, 11.00–14.00 Sun; adult/reduced/under 12 €2/1/ free) on Via Augusta is built in an old watermill, which has been restored to grind flour once again. There's a small archaeological collection in this location, but this ambitious little museum is really spread all over Cambrils. They'll direct you to the other sites; the **Torre de l'Hermita**, a medieval watchtower with exhibits on medieval Cambrils, the **Torre del Port** in the centre of the waterfront, which shows temporary exhibitions, and an **Agricultural Museum**, all with the same hours and admission.

The Marques de Marianao, from a local family that had most of its interests in Cuba, built Cambrils' other attraction, the **Parc Samà** in 1882. This is a large botanical garden, designed to recapture some of the beauty of the Caribbean island that was then the jewel in Spain's empire. Some of the plants, though, come from as far afield as Brazil and Australia; highlights include parterres of palms, cypresses and orange trees and a 2-acre lake studded with fantasy islands.

About 7km outside Cambrils in Mont-roig del Camp – sadly now tucked next to the motorway – is the **Mas Miró** (Finca Mas Miró s/n; ☎977 17 91 58; w masmiro. com; ⊕ mid-Jun–mid-Sep 10.00–14.00 & 17.30–20.00 Tue–Sat, 10.00–14.00 Sun; mid-Sep–Oct & Easter week–mid-Jun 10.00–14.00 & 15.30–18.00 Tue–Sat, 10.00– 14.00 Sun; Nov–Easter week 10.00–14.00 Tue–Fri, 10.00–14.00 & 15.30–18.00 Sat, 10.00–14.00 Sun; adult/reduced/under 8 €10/8/free), the old country *masia* where Joan Miró summered as a young man. It was here in 1911, while convalescing after a breakdown and serious illness, that Miró decided to dedicate himself fully to painting. This rural landscape and the Mediterranean light were formative influences on Miró and the *masia* and surroundings appeared in several famous early works, including *La Masia* (1921–22) and *Mont-roig, l'església i el poble* (1919).

It's a large, whitewashed complex, complete with chapel and enormous henhouse, drowsing amid olive groves and fields. The tour includes some of the

7

family rooms and bedrooms, with some of the original furnishings, as well as Miró's painting studio. There are few paintings and drawings, almost all of which are reproductions, but it does provide a wonderful insight into how this landscape shaped his artistic vision.

RIUDECANYES About 15km inland from Cambrils is the pretty village of Riudecanyes, where the seven medieval streets were named after the seven days of the week. The only reason for coming up here though is the fortified hilltop **Monestir de Sant Miquel d'Escornalbou** (Ctra d'Escornalbou s/n; ℅ 677 56 04 97; w patrimoni.gencat.cat/en/monuments/monuments/castle-and-monastery-of-escornalbou; ⏲ Jun–Sep 10.00–20.00 Tue–Sun, Oct–mid-Dec & Mar–May 10.00–17.30 Tue–Sun, mid-Dec–Feb 10.00–16.00 Tue–Sun; adult/reduced/under 8 €8/6/free) with a 12th-century church, a collection of prints and ceramics that belonged to the last owner, and a lovely belvedere with views down to the sea.

MIAMI PLATJA Back on the coast, heading south, the next town tried to drum up some notoriety by dubbing itself 'Miami Beach'. Despite its name, you couldn't ask for a more anonymous, innocuous resort; Interpol will never find you here. Something worse might: up in the hills above Miami you can visit **Pratdip**, and learn about the *dips*, spectral vampire dogs that used to terrorise the countryside, sucking the blood from their human and animal victims. There's one figured on the

HELL ON THE EBRO

All the vines and olives have been carefully replanted, and all the blasted tanks and trucks long ago hauled off for scrap. It's almost impossible to tell that decades ago these hills witnessed the biggest battle of the Spanish Civil War. By the summer of 1938, Republican Spain was in dire straits. Franco's Nationalists had taken the Basque lands, and pushed their way to the coast south of the Ebro, cutting the area controlled by the legitimate government in two. The Republican leadership in Valencia, largely in the hands of the Communists, decided on one big roll of the dice. They would give General Juan Modesto the best divisions the Republic had left, and make one big push to drive Franco from the Mediterranean, reunite the two Republican zones, and perhaps change the course of the war.

It began 15 minutes after midnight on Sant Jaume's Day, 25 July 1938, when Republican volunteers swam across the river and established beachheads on a broad front that extended from Amposta all the way to Mequinenza, near Lleida. At first the Loyalists advanced, in a slow and bloody fashion. Massive bombardments from the German Condor Legion eventually slowed them down. The Germans blew up all the bridges over the river, and Franco, who commanded the front personally, ordered all the dams upstream to release water, which raised the river level and made repairing the bridges more difficult.

Gandesa was the first objective of the attack, but the Republicans never quite made it even this far. The Nationalists began their counter-offensive on 1 August, as soon as the ever-cautious Franco could get enough reinforcements in place. This part of the Republican front was under the command of a bitter Communist apparatchik with little military experience, Enrique Lister, who gave an order that anyone who attempted to retreat would be shot.

village coat of arms, and some more on a retable in the church. In some versions of the legend they are hellacious uncanny beasts with glowing eyes, in others they seem more like Border collies gone radically wrong. You'll always know one if you see it; they're black and white, with one lame front leg.

L'AMETLLA DEL MAR After Miami Beach is a long, empty stretch of coast, ending in this modest little charmer at the end of the Costa Daurada. Like Cambrils, L'Ametlla del Mar is a working fishing village. Unlike Cambrils, it's still small and peaceful, and not yet overbuilt. People come for the tranquillity, and to tour around the attractive shoreline on foot or by boat. There is no big beach of the kind that has attracted so much development to other parts of the Costa, but maybe something better: about two dozen little coves, linked by a lovely coastal footpath.

Ametlla goes back only to the 1770s when some families of fishermen from Valencia settled, bringing new life to a stretch of coast that had become abandoned due to marauders and malaria. Down by the fishing port there is a pair of modest hotels, and tapas are never in short supply.

THE EBRO DELTA

It's time to introduce the Ebro (Ebre in Catalan), Spain's most voluminous river if not quite its longest. The Ebro starts far to the west in the Cantabrian mountains.

The battles would last for 116 days. Although the Republicans had lost the initiative and would never regain it, they had no choice but to hold on; for his part, Franco saw his chance to break the Loyalist army once and for all. Slowly through August, September and October, the front inched back towards the Ebro. On one single day near the climax, 30 October, 17,000 tons of shells and bombs fell on the Serra de Cavalls east of Gandesa.

The Battle of the Ebro was the last stand of the International Brigades, the young idealists who had come from all over the world to fight fascism in Spain. The government in Madrid cynically tossed them all into the front lines, where they bore the brunt of the casualties, and then, when little was left of the Brigades, Prime Minister Negrín announced their dissolution before the League of Nations, in a vain attempt to convince Britain and France to do something to force Franco to reciprocate, by getting rid of his German and Italian helpers. The last broken Loyalist forces crossed back over the Ebro at Flix on 18 November (with them was war correspondent Ernest Hemingway).

It had all been for nothing. The Nationalists lost only 23,000 men in total casualties, the Republicans 70,000. Their army was finished as a fighting force and, although the war dragged on for another four months, now there was no longer any doubt of the outcome. In January 1939 Franco's men would march into Barcelona.

The Battle of the Ebro is the kind of thing that most Spaniards are happy to forget, but it came back at them in February 2008, when 88-year-old Faustino Olivera of Barbastro, in Aragon, asked his doctor to remove what he thought was an old cyst in his shoulder that had begun to give him pain. It turned out to be the last bullet of the Spanish Republic still on the job. Olivera, a Nationalist conscript, took the shot while defending a position on the Ebro and somehow carried it with him unawares for 70 years.

7

The Romans called it Iberus Flumen, and from that we get the name of Iberia. Until the Romans pushed the Carthaginians out of Spain in the Second Punic War, this river was the Roman-Carthaginian border. It became a border again for a while in 1938 – between Nationalist and Republican Spain, and the long struggle over its course made for the biggest battle of the Civil War (page 260).

The Ebro isn't much good for navigation; Spain's dry climate makes it too shallow in summer. But it's still great for fishing; some of the biggest catfish and carp in Europe live in the Catalan and Aragonese stretches of the river.

However, the Ebro Delta faces urgent threats from climate change, with coastal erosion advancing rapidly: projections suggest it could shrink by up to 70% by the end of the century. When Storm Gloria hit in 2020, it tore through the delta, turning large swathes into temporary islands.

In response, the Ebro Delta Natural Park (Parc Natural del Delta de l'Ebre) is ramping up protection for this extraordinary ecosystem, home to over 300 bird species and a vital stop for migratory flocks. UNESCO acknowledged its global significance by designating it a Biosphere Reserve in 2013.

Agriculture, particularly in the delta's rice fields, is also adapting. Farmers are embracing more sustainable practices, from cutting back on pesticides to using smarter water management techniques that help preserve both wildlife habitats and local livelihoods.

With droughts worsening across Spain, environmental groups are pushing for bold solutions: controlled sediment flows, natural barriers to guard the coast, and smarter land-use planning. The Ebro Delta has become a global bellwether, showing what's at stake in the fight to protect coastal wetlands from a changing climate

TOURIST INFORMATION There are tourist information offices in all the larger towns and villages, including in L'Ampolla (C/ Ronda del Mar 12; ☏977 59 30 11), Sant Carles de la Ràpita (Parc de Garbí s/n; ☏977 05 10 60), Alcanar (C/ de Lepanto; ☏977 73 76 39) and Ulldecona (Pg de l'Estació 6; ☏619 77 08 69). There are park information offices for the Delta de l'Ebre in Deltebre (Ecomuseu, C/ Dr Martí Buera 22; ☏ 977 48 96 79; w parcsnaturals.gencat.cat/es/xarxa-de-parcs/delta-ebre (Catalan or Spanish only) or w atraccionatural.cat) and near the Estany de l'Encanyissada lake (page 264) (Casa de Fusta, Estany de l'Encanyissada; ☏977 26 10 22; wesite same as above), both of which have leaflets with different walks and bike rides, among lots of other information about the area.

🏠 WHERE TO STAY

Miami Mar Pg Marítim 18, Sant Carles de la Ràpita; ☏977 74 58 59; w miamicanpons.com. A large, modern hotel right on the beach, with a pool, & spacious rooms with balconies. A family establishment that grew out of a great restaurant, **Can Pons** (€€€), located within the hotel. €€€

Tancat de Codorniu N-340, km 1059, Alcanar; ☏977 73 71 94; w tancatdecodorniu.com. You'll find 17 smart, stylish rooms overlooking endless groves of orange trees, & expansive grounds with 2 pools at this elegant country retreat. There are 2 restaurants: one serving Mediterranean cuisine in the gardens (€€€) & another, the magnificent

Citrus (€€€€€), which was recently awarded a Michelin star. €€€

Delta Avda del Canal, Camí de la Illeta, Deltebre; ☏717 71 57 75; w deltahotel.net. This hotel, with 24 wood-panelled rooms, is set in extensive grounds with a lagoon on the edge of town. There's a pool, a play area for kids & maybe the best restaurant (€€€) around. €€

Juanito Platja Pg Marítim s/n, Sant Carles de la Ràpita; ☏977 74 04 62; w juanitoplatja.com. Delightful, simple beach hotel run by the same friendly family since 1960. All 35 rooms enjoy blissful sea views & there's also a good restaurant (€€) to feast on local specialities. €€

✳ **L'Hotelet del Delta** C/ Riu Ebre 31, Deltebre; 📞638 10 42 47; w hoteletdeldelta.com. Charming, whitewashed, small hotel with a handful of individually decorated rooms with views overlooking the river & a little courtyard garden with a plunge pool & little nooks for relaxing. €€

Mas Masdeu Camí de la Cablanca, L'Aldea; 📞600 24 02 46; w masmasdeu.com. A quiet, rural 19th-century farmhouse in the little village of L'Aldea, this has 5 pretty rooms with exposed stone walls & wooden beams. The lovely owners prepare delicious home-cooked dinners on request. €€

Rull Avda Esportiva 155, Deltebre; 📞977 48 77 28; w hotelrull.com. Plain but very comfortable mid-sized functional hotel outside Deltebre, with a pool & restaurant (€€€). €€

Agustí Hostal C/ Pilar 22–24, Sant Carles de la Ràpita; 📞977 74 04 27; w hostal-agusti.amenitiz.io. First-rate bargain *hostal* in the town centre, with pristine rooms with AC, as well as studios & apartments & very friendly staff. Bike storage is available. €

Bon Lloc Ctra de Vinaròs s/n, Ulldecona; 📞977 57 30 16; w hotelbonlloc.es. A small & rustic country inn with a pool & an excellent restaurant (€€): good farm cooking & local wines. €

✕ WHERE TO EAT AND DRINK

Les Moles Ctra La Sénia, Ulldecona; 📞977 57 32 24; w lesmoles.com. The area's prize-winning restaurant, with a Michelin star among other accolades, which prepares imaginative dishes with vegetables from their biodynamic garden, along with other sustainably sourced produce. There are several tasting menus (including a vegetarian one, €145, & another, Terra Incognita, €125, which showcases local specialities) & an excellent set lunch for €47.90. €€€€€

Casa Ramón C/ Arsenal 16, Sant Carles de la Ràpita; 📞977 74 23 58; w casaramon.cat. Reasonably priced seafood, including a set menu for €89 for 2 people, which will fill you up with all the local specialities, including frog's legs, eels & paella – & a good wine list. Also has inexpensive, although dated, rooms (€). €€€

Nuri Cr s/n, Riumar; 📞977 48 01 28; w restaurantnuri.com. At the end of the road east from Deltebre, this is a classic restaurant in a converted barn, where everyone piles in for a paella

& some mussels before taking a boat trip around the delta (see below) from the quay just opposite. €€€

Olmos C/ Unió 165, Deltebre; 📞977 48 05 48; w cruzerosdeltadelebro.es. Olmos, which runs the boat tours (see below), will fill you up with river eels & other local specialities in a happy, laid-back bar-restaurant right by the quay. €€€

Racó del Port Pg Marítim, Les Cases d'Alcanar; 📞977 73 70 50; 🅵 /p/Racó-del-Port-100052005943877. Les Cases is a little fishing village just outside Alcanar. Here by the port is an unpretentious seafood spot that's been going strong for half a century, thanks to its beautifully fresh fish & shellfish. €€€

Avi Agustí Ctra Poble Nou, Km3 43540, Sant Carles de la Ràpita; 📞659 37 20 79; w muscleraaviagusti.com. 'Grandad Agustí' grows mussels & oysters out on a large wooden platform in the bay of Alfacs; you can be picked up by boat in Sant Carles de la Ràpita & whisked out to enjoy them fresh from the sea. €€

SPORTS AND ACTIVITIES Birdwatching, biking and hiking are the most popular activities in the Delta de l'Ebre. The park boasts an incredible diversity of birdlife (the flamingos are its most famous residents) and there are several viewpoints ('*miradors*') where you can watch them (listed here w turismeamposta.cat/en/birdwatching-4). The bike and walking paths are clearly marked with green signs and the park information office (page 262) can provide pamphlets with instructions for each itinerary. There are several bike rental outfits in the area, including Deltacleta (Ctra TV-3451 km 3, Masia de la Torra, Deltebre; 📞648 72 58 62; w deltacleta.cat), which specialises in electric bikes but also rents out all kinds of other bikes (gravel, fat tyre, tandems, etc.), and also runs guided tours. If you prefer to take in the scenery in from the water, you can take a boat tour with Creuers Delta de l'Ebre (departing from Final Pas Illa de Buda s/n, Deltebre; 📞629 53 47 57; w creuersdeltaebre.com) and Olmos (departing from C/ Unió 147; 📞625 10 07 07; w cruzerosdeltadelebro.es).

7

EBRE DELTA   As deltas go, the Ebre's isn't very old. Back in Roman times the town of Amposta was a busy port; now it's marooned some 30km upstream. Ironically, the natural wetlands the environmentalists are struggling to save are themselves the product of a manmade ecological disaster. A thousand years ago, the vast Iberian plateau was almost entirely under trees, and it was said that a squirrel could travel from Extremadura to the Pyrenees without touching the ground.

Deforestation began during the Reconquista as Castile, Léon and Aragón were settled by a burgeoning Christian population. Then, during the mad, violent scramble for booty and power that Spain still calls its 'Golden Age', in the 16th–18th centuries, enormous areas were cleared for land speculation, to make money to replenish the eternal deficits of kings and princes. This deforestation created the wasted, empty landscapes we see all over central Spain today, and much of the Iberian plateau's best topsoil ended up in a mushrooming Ebre Delta, where it now grows rice for Spain's paellas.

A century ago this delta was a desolation cursed by malaria; today, over 60% of it is under rice paddies, dotted with new villages that look a little rough, but prosperous and happy.

Parc Natural del Delta de l'Ebre
Although paddies and rice-processing plants occupy the centre of the delta; everything around the edges is devoted to the waterfowl – some 300 species of them – and the tourists who come to see them. Since the 1980s, the fringes of the delta have been protected in this park

The park's headquarters and information office lies at the entrance to the village of **Deltebre** right in the middle of the delta. This includes an **Ecomuseu** (C/ Dr Martí Buera 22; \977 48 96 79; w parcsnaturals.gencat.cat/ca/xarxa-de-parcs/delta-ebre; ⊕ 10.00–14.00 & 15.00–18.00 Mon–Sat, 10.00–14.00 Sun; adult/reduced/under 7 €2/1/free) with an interesting little aquarium and exhibits on the delta's flora and fauna, its traditional life and work, and the ecological issues related to its upkeep and survival. Deltebre itself, the delta's little capital, is a new raw sort of place, with the only accommodation around.

Among the places of interest in the park is the **Estany de l'Encanyissada**, a lagoon and major bird area with bike paths, and two park information offices, including one in the **Casa de la Fusta** in Amposta. This is the place to visit if you mean to do any serious birdwatching; there are exhibits on many of the species that call the delta home. The **Punta de la Banya** is a small island near **Encanyissada**, connected to the southern tip of the delta by a sand spit, part of a string of beaches that line the delta's southern edge.

There are more beaches on the northern side, notably at **Punta del Fangar**, where sunny summer days sometimes produce mirages over the water. The next lagoon east, **El Canal Vell**, is where you're most likely to see flamingos. The coastal road (N340) here marks the landward boundary of the delta; following it, you'll pass through a string of villages that marked the shoreline before the delta was born.

L'Ampolla and around
At the northern end of the delta, L'Ampolla is a fishing village that has grown into a fair-sized town, and is still famous for oysters (the ones grown here are Japanese oysters, *casostrea gigas*, and pretty tasty too). There's nothing picturesque about L'Ampolla, and it won't trouble you with sightseeing, but it's a good place for a seafood dinner, or an afternoon on one of the little beaches and coves around its strip of coast.

In the hills above L'Ampolla, **El Perelló** has some Roman remains, including a long surviving stretch of the Via Augusta, and also a painted cave called **Cabrafeixet**, decorated with hunting scenes similar to those at Ulldecona (see below). **Amposta** was a port in ancient times; now it's a lively and noisy place with a little suspension bridge over the Ebro built in 1918 and a local history museum, the **Museu de les Terres de l'Ebre** (C/ Gran Capità s/n; ✆977 70 29 54; w museuterresebre.cat; ⏲ 11.00– 14.00 & 17.30– 20.00 Tue–Sat, 11.30–14.00 Sun; adult/reduced/under 7 €2/1/free).

Sant Carles de la Ràpita
At the southern end of the delta, this town is splendidly located on one of Europe's largest natural harbours, the **Port dels Alfacs**. In 1780 Charles III wanted to take advantage of nature's gift and make this a great seaport, to replace marooned Amposta as a port and bring some economic life to the area. Little came of it, but today Sant Carles is a busy resort in summer, popular with Barcelonins, although of no special charm, except around the old fishing port, where boats are still made the old-fashioned way.

ALCANAR AND AROUND
The southernmost town in Catalunya, Alcanar has a beach, and above the road north to Ulldecona you'll see a bowl-shaped hill crowned with what was the ancient town of **La Moleta del Remei**. Occupied in the 7th–2nd centuries BC, La Moleta belonged to the Iberian tribe called the Ilercavons.

Up in the hills, across the motorway from Alcanar, **Ulldecona** is a well-kept little town with a castle begun by the Moors, a bit of a medieval centre with a Catalan Gothic church, and a few Modernista buildings, including three by Cèsar Martinell. Today, however, Ulldecona is best known for its cave art, discovered only in 1975. This consists of 13 caves in the Godall hills north of town, of which only two can be visited right now, by guided tours from the **Centre d'Interpretació d'Art Rupestre** (Ermita de la Pietat, Ctra Ulldecona-Tortosa, km 4.5; ✆977 57 33 94; w visitmuseum. gencat.cat/en/museum/centre-d-interpretacio-d-art-rupestre-abrics-de-l-ermita; ⏲ Jun–Sep 10.00–14.00 & 16.00–19.00 Tue–Sat, 10.00–14.00 Sun, Oct–Mar 10.00– 14.00 & 16.00–18.00 Tue–Sat, 10.00–14.00 Sun; museum only adult/reduced/under 9 €3/2/free, museum & Rock Shelter I adult/reduced/under 9 €7/5/free, museum & Rock Shelter I & IV adult/reduced/under 9 €10/7/free), which also has a museum. The caves (called 'Abrics' in Catalan or 'Rock Shelters') are not nearly as old as the famous Palaeolithic cave art in Cantabria or southwest France – only around 8,000 years. Neither are they as artistically sophisticated. Still, they are vigorous, colourful works, mostly hunting scenes with deer and other animals along with stick-figure representations of hunters, some with bows.

TORTOSA AND AROUND

Tortosa suffered greatly in the Civil War, when the Battle of the Ebro was raging nearby, and much of its old town was razed to the ground. It languished for decades, but has recently prettied up its biggest monuments and renovated the riverfront with parks and cafés. Its efforts were rewarded in 2021, when it was chosen as Capital de la Cultura Catalana.

Publius Cornelius Scipio (father of Scipio Africanus) wrecked the place in 215BC in the Punic Wars, then refounded it and gave it the new name Dertusa, 'city of stones'. It knew some good days as the capital of a Muslim *taifa*, and enjoyed some prosperity under the Christians too, as evidenced by its impressive Gothic cathedral. Medieval Tortosa had a large and sophisticated Jewish community and an important Templar commandery. It flourished in the 16th century, when the splendid Reials Col·legis were constructed, one of the finest Renaissance buildings in all Catalunya, but then its fortunes faded once again. Still, now that much of the

7

Civil War damage has finally been repaired, the city's new optimism is celebrated with the lively Festa del Renaixement (Renaissance Festival) in late July, which brings out thousands of locals in period costume for a giant street party.

TOURIST INFORMATION The very helpful Tortosa tourist information office (Rbla Felip Pedrell 3; ☎ 977 44 96 48; w tortosaturisme.cat); ⊕ May–Sep 10.00–14.00 & 16.00–19.00 Mon–Sat, 10.00–13.30 Sun, Oct–Mar 10.00–13.30 & 15.30–18.30 Mon–Sat, 11.00–13.30 Sun) is conveniently located in the same building as the Museu de Tortosa right in the centre of town. It does double duty, as it is also the information point for the whole Terres de l'Ebre region. The information centre for the Parc Natural dels Ports is in Roquetes (C/ Val de Zafan; ☎ 977 50 40 12; w parcsnaturals.gencat.cat/ca/xarxa-de-parcs/ports/inici), across the river from Tortosa. There are also tourist information points in Horta de Sant Joan (C/ Pintor Pablo Ruiz Picasso 18; ☎ 977 43 50 43; w turismehortadesantjoan.cat), Benifallet (Avda Lluís Companys 6; ☎ 977 46 23 34; w turismebenifallet.cat) and Gandesa (Avda Catalunya 3–5; ☎ 977 42 09 10; w gandesa.cat/turisme).

🏠 WHERE TO STAY

Hotel Villa Retiro C/ Molins 2, Xerta; ☎ 977 47 38 10; w hotelvillaretiro.com. The perfect luxury oasis for a gastronomic break, this 5-star boutique hotel with about 20 rooms & suites occupies a thoughtfully renovated Modernista villa set in gorgeous gardens with every possible luxury including its famous Michelin-starred restaurant, **Xerta** (€€€€€). **€€€€**

Parador Nacional Castell de la Suda C/ Castillo de la Zuda s/n, Tortosa; ☎ 977 44 44 58; w paradores.es/en/parador-de-tortosa. There's nowhere better to stay in town then this large parador. Considering the destruction in 1938 the restorers did a terrific job: the palatial rooms have tremendous views, & there is a good restaurant (€€€), gardens & a pool. **€€€**

Casa Barceló Avda Generalitat, Horta de Sant Joan; ☎ 977 43 53 53; w casabarcelo.com. A warm, country inn, with 11 cosy & rustically furnished rooms, plus a good restaurant (€€) serving up local favourites. **€€**

Casa Rural La Torre del Prior Camí de la Casella s/n, Tortosa: ☎ 652 93 15 11; w torredelprior.cat. A peaceful rural guesthouse about 3.5km north of the city centre, this old stone house with a 12th-century watchtower has just 7 pretty rooms with views over orange trees & fields of wheat. **€€**

Hotel Restaurant Pepo C/ Piscines 1; ☎ 977 46 22 00; w restaurantpepo.com. There are 9 immaculate, simple rooms & a traditional restaurant (€€) serving up tasty local specialities right in the heart of this charming village. **€€**

Mas de Taniet Camí de Móra s/n, Benissanet; ☎ 977 40 76 04; w mastaniet.com. 8 simple rooms in a restored country house 5km from Miravet, with a pool & restaurant (€€) that serves produce from its own kitchen garden. **€€**

Miralles Avda Generalitat 19–21, Horta de Sant Joan; ☎ 977 43 55 55; w hotelmiralles.com. Good, simple rooms in this mid-sized guesthouse, with views over the village Picasso painted & the lovely countryside, & a fine restaurant (€€) where the speciality is *crestó* – mountain goat in escabeche (not poached from the park; they raise their own!). **€€**

Palau de Miravet C/ Palau 28, Miravet; ☎ 656 26 63 98; w palaudemiravet.com. Charmingly furnished, traditional house in the village run by a pair of artists, with a gallery & a handful of inviting & peaceful rooms & suites. They also have an apartment for rent. **€€**

Piqué Avda Catalunya 68, Gandesa; ☎ 977 42 00 68; w hotelpique.com. Gandesa doesn't get many visitors, & there's nothing special here, but this is a good, honest, inexpensive hotel with 50 pristine rooms & a smart restaurant (€€). **€**

✖ WHERE TO EAT AND DRINK

El Parc Avda de la Generalitat 72, Tortosa; ☎ 977 44 48 66; w restaurantelparc.cat. Beautifully set in a park on the riverfront, here you can tuck into modern Catalan & international cuisine & then retire to the outdoor lounge area for coffee. There are often concerts in summer. €€€

La Fusteria C/ Montcada 9, Tortosa; ✆977 51 01 98; w sites.google.com/view/bar-restaurant-la-fusteria; ⏲ 07.00–17.30 Mon, Wed–Fri, 08.30–17.30 Sat, noon–17.00 Sun. Classic local favourite for reliably good, traditional Catalan cuisine & one of the best-value set lunches (€14) in town. €€

Los Banys C/ Ricard 57, Tortosa; ✆977 44 36 44; w losbanys.es; ⏲ noon–16.30 & 19.00–midnight daily. Set in the remnants of the medieval Arabic baths, this is now a lively spot for creative tapas, such as prawn carpaccio, as well as burgers & wraps. €€

El Rebost de l'Estel Pl Major 2, Miravet; ✆605 10 80 29; 🖵 rebostestel; ⏲ 08.00–23.30 daily. Friendly, simple spot on the main square, with platters of local cheeses & charcuterie, good tapas, as well as burgers & pizzas. €€

Molí de Xim C/ Major, Miravet; ✆977 40 77 58; w molidexim.cat. Classic home cooking, in a restored old olive-oil mill, with lovely views. €€

SPORTS AND ACTIVITIES There are lots of opportunities for hiking and biking in this region, including along the Via Verde (w terresdelebre.travel/en/que-fer/turisme-actiu/via-verda), a 27km trail for hikers, bikers and horses that has been created from an abandoned rail line through some pretty countryside between Arnés and Pinell de Brai.

WHAT TO SEE AND DO One of the best things about Tortosa is its **market**, an early Modernista work (1887) covering an entire block along the Ebro. From here, look up and you can see **La Suda**, the dramatic citadel that was a Roman-Iberian acropolis, an Arab palace and a Templar castle before getting blown to smithereens in 1938. After the war the government picked up the pieces and reassembled them as a parador (page 266). Look out over the river, and you'll see a bizarre rusty column covered with inscrutable figures; this is the **Monument to the Battle of the Ebro**, the largest surviving Francoist monument in Catalunya, unveiled by the dictator himself in 1966. Although long slated for removal, works have been put on hold for court wrangles: some locals can't wait to see the back of it, while others argue that there is a value to remembering the horrors of the Civil War and the lives that were lost. Further upstream, you'll see a bright red bridge (**Pont Roig**), built for trains in the 19th century, and now a delightful section of the Via Verde, with a wide path for walking and biking,

Underneath La Suda is the **Catedral de Santa Maria de Tortosa** (Porta de Palau 5; ✆977 44 61 10; w cataloniasacra.cat/llocs/catedral-de-santa-maria-de-tortosa/63/l_ca; ⏲ May–Sep 10.00–14.00 & 16.00–19.00 Tue–Sat, 11.00–14.00 Sun; Oct–Apr 10.00–14.00 Tue–Fri, 10.00–14.00 & 16.00–18.00 Sat, 11.00–14.00 Sun; adult/reduced/under 10 €5/4/free), one of Catalunya's largest. A jumble of old buildings has been cleared in front of the cathedral, opening up an airy square that looks out over the river and gives the incredible façade room to breathe. Although mostly from the 18th century, it can't decide whether it wants to be Neoclassical or perhaps Mexican Baroque. Behind it, though, there's a soaring Gothic interior with a beautiful apse, a pretty cloister with a fountain at its centre, and some fine chapels, especially that of the city's patroness, Nostra Senyora de la Santa Cinta. A small **museum** in the old canon's house outlines the cathedral's history with art and antiquities spanning a thousand years, from Roman and Visigothic finds to a 16th-century carved choir.

During the restoration works, remnants of the Roman walls, the 6th-century Visigothic basilica, the Muslim settlement and even some Restoration-era steps were discovered and are now preserved in **Cota 0** (C/ Costa de Capellans 2; ✆977 44 96 48; w tortosaturisme.cat/en/lugar/tortosa-cota-0; ⏲ May–Sep 10.00–13.30 & 17.30–19.30 Tue–Sat, 11.00–13.30 Sun; Oct–Apr 10.00–13.30 & 16.30–18.30 Tue–

7

Sat, 11.00–13.30 Sun; free), a small ultra-modern museum cleverly slotted in under the cathedral square. It's a palimpsest of 15 centuries of history, the ruins brought to life by a glossy audiovisual show.

Behind the cathedral, the **Museu de Tortosa** (Rbla Felip Pedrell 3; ☏ 977 51 01 46; w museudetortosa.cat; ⊕ May–Sep 10.00–13.30 & 17.30–19.30 Tue–Sat, 11.00–13.30 Sun; Oct–Apr 10.00–13.30 & 16.30–18.30; adult/reduced/under 14 €3/2/free), set in an old Modernista slaughterhouse, has a charming, magpie collection that spans everything from Roman amphorae to paintings by local artists.

Further up, near La Suda, Tortosa's back streets hide a Renaissance jewel, the **Reials Col.legis** (Royal Colleges) (C/ Sant Domènec 12–23; ☏ 977 44 46 68; w tortosaturisme.cat/en/lugar/the-royal-colleges-and-the-permanent-exhibition-about-the-city-and-the-renaissance-festival; ⊕ May–Sep 10.00–14.00 & 16.00–19.00 Tue–Sat, 09.30–13.30 Sun; Oct–Apr 10.00–13.30 & 15.30–18.30 Tue–Sat, 09.30–13.30 Sun; adult/reduced/under 14 €3/2/free), founded by Emperor Charles V himself in 1544. The complex features three buildings, all of which retain their splendid Renaissance portals. The College of Sant Jaume has a glorious arcaded courtyard, with a lavish frieze depicting the different monarchs of the Crown of Aragon. Nearby, the church of Sant Domènec houses an exhibition on the city's history and another highlighting its famous Renaissance Festival. Little survives of the third building, the College of Sant Jordi i de Sant Domènec, originally the university, except its monumental doors.

PARC NATURAL DELS PORTS South of Tortosa, the Ebro Valley is lush and green, lined with gardens and even orange groves. North of the city, though, it climbs into some dramatic scenery, rugged, forested mountains with streams and waterfalls where human habitations are few and far between. There aren't any bridges for 30km north of the city. If you take the west bank, roads leading up into the hills will try to entice you into the Parque Natural dels Ports, set around the slopes of 1,447m **Mount Caro** on the borders of Catalunya, Aragon and Valencia. The park is only beginning to be developed for tourism, which makes it ideal for serious hikers and for the Spanish mountain goat. The park information office and **Ecomuseu** (C/ Pintor Pablo Ruiz Picasso; ☏ 977 43 56 86; w hortadesantjoan.cat/ecomuseu-els-ports; ⊕ 09.30–13.30 & 16.00–18.00 Sat, 09.30–13.30 Sun; free) is located in Horta de Sant Joan.

HORTA DE SANT JOAN Horta, a little labyrinth of rugged stone streets, is an attractive, typically Catalan village. The Templars once ruled here too, and they began the interesting **Convent de Sant Salvador,** 2km outside town, with a church and cloister still in good shape.

Horta's current fame, though, is that it briefly served as the home of Pablo Picasso, in 1898 and again in 1909. Of course, every place where Picasso spent more than half an hour has tried to make a cottage industry out of it, but the artist does seem to have been greatly influenced by this village and its rural life. 'Everything I know I learned in Horta,' he is recorded as saying. The paintings of the village he finished here on his second trip are landmarks in the development of Cubism. You can learn about them at the **Centre Picasso** (C/ Hospital; ☏ 977 43 53 30; w centrepicasso.cat; ⊕ 09.30–13.30 & 16.00–18.00 Sat, 09.30–13.30 Sun; free), which occupies a much-restored 16th-century hospital.

BENIFALLET If you take the east bank of the Ebro north from Tortosa, you'll pass **Tivanys**. Here another Iberian settlement can be inspected on the hills above the modern village. Further on comes Benifallet and the **Coves de Benifallet**. There are a number of caves here, including the **Cova de Cullas**, with some Neolithic-era paintings, but the main attraction is two beautiful stalactite caves, the **Cova Meravelles** and the **Cova del Dos** (Barranc de Sant Jordi s/n; ✆977 26 78 00; w turismebenifallet. cat; ⏰ hours vary, check with the tourist information office; adult/reduced/5–13/ under 5 €8/7/free), which are the only two open for visits. Benifallet is an attractive, lively little town, which has become a hub for outdoor activities.

GANDESA Like everything else in this part of the Ebro Valley, Gandesa was once Templar property. That's about the whole of its history, save for a few terrible months in 1938 when this village of 2,600 was in the world's headlines every day, as the focal point of the Battle of the Ebro, the climactic battle of the Spanish Civil War. As the main objective of the last great Republican offensive, Gandesa took a lot of blows, and it had to be almost completely rebuilt.

A number of relics do remain though, from what must have been a rather genteel past. The **church of L'Assumpció** is a dull 18th-century building, but it retains a fascinating portal from its medieval predecessor, decorated with minute, precise carvings of scenes and figures that have had the Romanesque experts guessing for a long time. Next to it stands a Renaissance town hall, the **Casa de la Vila**, and nearby is the modest Templar commandery, the **Palacio del Castellà**, for centuries the local jail.

Gandesa is a wine centre, home of the Terra Alta denomination, which includes a number of wines made mostly from macabeo and garnacha (grenache) grapes. Gandesa's **Bodega Cooperativa**, built in 1919, is one of the first and most spectacular of the many designed by Cèsar **Martinell**, with soaring brick parabolic arches and 'Catalan' vaulting, ideas that the architect developed here.

Near the modern village of **Corbera d'Ebre**, northeast of Gandesa, you can visit the ruins of old Corbera (the 'poble vell') up in the hills, abandoned after Nationalist artillery and the German Condor Legion blasted it to bits. It's an eerie place, looking pretty much as it did when the villagers left it. Most visitors to this area are interested in the war, and they get all they can use at the **Centre d'Interpretació 115 dies** (C/ Freginals 18; ✆977 42 15 28; w batallaebre.org/115-dies-corbera-debre; ⏰ 10.00– 14.00 & 16.00–19.00 Tue–Sat, 10.00–14.00 Sun; adult/reduced/under 12 €4/2/ free) in Corbera d'Ebre. This is one of five interpretation centres, two memorials and 20 historic sites related to the battle run by the Democratic Memorial of the Generalitat de Catalunya, and offers the best overview and introduction to this terrible 115-day battle. Exhibits include arms and relics from the battle, posters, and even a reconstruction of a Republican trench. Military historians say one of the reasons the Republic lost was its leaders' inability to understand modern warfare. While the Germans and Italians were teaching Franco how to fight with air power and armoured blitzkrieg, the Republicans were still fighting World War I-style, with trench lines and murderous frontal infantry assaults.

The high-water mark of the Republican advance was a line roughly from Xerta to Gandesa and on to Fayón. Almost all of the fighting took place between that line and the Ebro – not a very large space for 36,500 men to die in. After the war Franco's government did nothing to clean up the battlefield, or give the Republican soldiers who died there a decent burial. Even today, big storms still wash bones out from the hill slopes. Much of the area was wasteland for decades, and now it draws a strange breed of war tourists, armed with metal detectors, hunting for relics.

Coll de Moro, where Franco made his headquarters during the battle, has yet another Iberian village under excavation. **El Pinell de Brai**, on the way to Benifallet,

7

is a wine town, with another, less grandiose co-operative building by Martinell, adorned with a frieze of azulejos depicting the grape harvest and drunken hunters by jovial Xavier Nogués.

MIRAVET We have been mentioning the Templars here and there, and you can see what's left of their headquarters at the **Castle of Miravet** (Camí del Castell s/n; \ 977 40 73 68; w patrimoni.gencat.cat/en/monuments/monuments/miravet-castle; ⊕ Jun–Sep 10.00–20.00 Tue–Sun, Oct–mid-Dec & Mar–May 10.00–17.30 Tue–Sun, mid-Dec–Feb 10.00–16.00 Tue–Sun; adult/reduced/under 16 €5/3/free). When the order helped Ramon Berenguer IV seize the lower Ebro from the Moors in the 1150s, the king granted them vast lands that they would hold for the next century and a half. They rebuilt the Moorish castle here to oversee it all. After the order was outlawed, Miravet became one of the last Templar redoubts, falling in 1308 after a year-long siege.

Luxurious as it must have been in its heyday, there's little to see inside but the fine view over the parapets. In the deathly silence that hangs over the place you can explore the Templars' Romanesque chapel, with a spiral stair to the tower, the dormitory and refectory – although, curiously, no-one has ever found a trace of a chimney or kitchen. The upper patio is called the **Patio de la Sang**; here, in 1308, the last Templars of Miravet were beheaded.

Miravet village, spilling down from the castle to the river, is a very charming little place, with its ancient steps and alleyways, its artisan potters who recreate Moorish designs, and a ferry across the Ebro.

Not many intrepid visitors press any further up the Ebro Valley. Past **Riba-Roja** the working stretch of the Ebro begins, with a string of dams and reservoirs that get some use for watersports and fishing. Here we're already on the border with the region of Aragon, and the landscapes are looking sparser and stranger, on the edge of the weird little salt and gypsum desert called **Els Monegres** that stretches all the way to Zaragoza.

8

Lleida, the High Pyrenees and Andorra

How exciting is it? Not the right question, really. This western end of Catalunya is decidedly lacking in coastal corniches and spectacular seafood, Modernista palaces and Surrealists. Its one great age of art was 800 years ago, and most of that has been carted off to the museums of Barcelona and New York. So why come? For starters, there's the surprising city of Lleida, with its hilltop cathedral, one of the forgotten treasures of Spain. Lleida and its plain full of orchards lie at one end, the High Pyrenees with ski resorts and mountain scenery at the other. And in between are some delightful places you've probably never heard of.

In between Lleida and the High Pyrenees are sweet and lovely towns like Solsona, Cervera and Balaguer, the remote and very medieval never-never land of the Llobregós, and pre-Pyrenean massifs like Montsec that are very attractive places for hiking and outdoor sports. Prices are low, the food's good and the people friendly. It's a low-key province, without a lot of crowds and bustle and hustle, and a perfect spot for a kind of understated, informal tourism that many people find very enjoyable. Instead of frantic sightseeing, it offers a place to relax a bit and get to know a little rustic corner and its people and traditions well. If you have time to spend and an eye for detail, you'll discover it is a rich region indeed.

LLEIDA

When you first come to Lleida (Lérida in Castilian), you might not think much of it at all. First you pass through miles of orchards, then the busy outskirts full of warehouses stacked with crates of fruit, a reminder that Lleida has always made its living from apples, peaches and pears. When you get inside the city, it seems a hopeless jumble of big boulevards that don't lead anywhere and all look the same. But persevere; hidden down by the river is a fine old historic centre with lots to see and do. The place grows on you. After taking some hard knocks from history Lleida is on its way back again, slowly and carefully, and once you get to know it you'll find it a lively and quite likeable town.

HISTORY Lleida lies along the River Segre in the midst of Catalunya's most extensive plain. It begins with the Ilergetes, the Iberian tribe that occupied the plain. About 425BC, they decided to found a capital for themselves on the height over the Segre called the Roca Sobirana. Its name was Iltirta. Two centuries later, after the Second Punic War, the bosses up in the citadel were Roman, and they called their refounded city Ilerda. Ilerda consisted of a fortified governmental forum similar

LLEIDA, HIGH PYRENEES AND ANDORRA

to Tarragona's, up where the Seu is now, and a small grid of streets on the slopes to the west and south, with another forum near the bridge over the Segre, roughly where the Pont Vell stands today. The city became famous in the Roman world when Julius Caesar defeated Pompey's generals here in 49BC.

Ilerda fell to the Visigoths in the 5th century AD, and to the Moors in AD719. Little is known about it in these periods, but the Reconquista and the settling of 'New Catalunya' gave the city a chance to make a brilliant comeback. After Ramon Berenguer IV took it in 1148, the three powers behind the Catalan Reconquista – the landowning nobles, the Templars and the Church – each played their part in assuring that Lleida would be New Catalunya's metropolis. The cathedral was begun in 1203; the city got the right to self-government in 1264, and in 1300 the Estudi General became the first university in the Kingdom of Aragon. For centuries Lleida was indeed the 'capital on the land', the most important Catalan city after Barcelona.

Its downfall came in the 18th century, during the Wars of the Spanish Succession. As a fervently anti-Bourbon stronghold the city was bound to suffer, but the victorious King Philip was determined to make a special example of it. The university was closed and moved to Cervera, while the king razed the entire area around La Seu Vella to build a new fortress to keep watch on the Lleidans. Further indignities came in the Spanish Civil War, when Lleida was repeatedly bombed by the Nationalists.

Today, after languishing for decades, the city's economy is thriving again. Traditionally Lleida was a place where fruit from the plain was shipped throughout Spain and Europe. Now, that has turned into an important food-processing industry. A restored university helps keep Lleida a bustling place; the population has reached 145,000, about a quarter of whom are immigrants from over a hundred countries.

GETTING THERE AND AROUND
By air The Aeroport de Lleida-Alguaire (w aeroportlleida.cat) is linked to Ibiza, Menorca and Mallorca with Iberia's regional Air Nostrum (w airnostrum.es). It's also used by charter airlines in winter for ski holidays.

By train Regional train lines R14 (via Valls) and R14 (via Tarragona) run from Barcelona to Lleida (w rodalies.gencat.cat), which is also served by high-speed AVE services (w renfe.com). The glorious 19th-century RENFE station is Lleida-Pirineus on Avinguda Francesca Macià on map at the end of the Rambla Ferran. There are also FGC (w fgc.cat) train services from Lleida to Balaguer (RL1) and to Pobla de Segur (RL2). FGC run a special tourist train along the route, the Tren dels Llacs (page 287) using refurbished old steam and diesel trains.

By bus The big bus station is on the Avda Blondel by the river, which is handy for the town centre. You can get just about anywhere by bus: services around the Lleida region are mainly run by Moventis (w moventis.es), which also runs services to Tarragona and Barcelona. Alsa (w alsa.es) has also regular connections to Valencia, Huesca, Zaragoza & many other towns.

By car The city introduced an LZE (ZBE in Spanish and Catalan) in 2025, which limits entrance to the old city centre, depending on the vehicle type. Check up-to-date details before arrival; in English at w urbanaccessregulations.eu/countries-mainmenu-147/spain/Lleida or in Catalan/Spanish at w paeria.cat/ca/serveis/zona-de-baixes-emissions-de-lleida. Given that Lleida is relatively small, the easiest option is to park outside the historic centre and walk or take public transport. Parking is as horrible as anywhere else in Spain: one tip for finding a space is to head up to the Seu and the streets around it, where you can usually find a place, and then take the walkway and lift down to Plaça Sant Joan. There are large underground car parks near the train station and the Seu, where you can drop the car if you can't find on-street parking.

TOURIST INFORMATION The helpful tourist information office is right in the centre at Carrer Major 31 (✆973 70 03 19; w turismedelleida.cat; ⏱ 10.00–14.00 & 16.00–19.00 Mon–Sat, 10.00–14.00 Sun). There's an outpost of the Catalan tourist information service in the Seu, too (✆973 23 82 46; w catalunya.com; ⏱ 10.00–14.00 & 16.30–19.30 Mon–Sat, 10.00–15.00 Sun).

8

LLEIDA

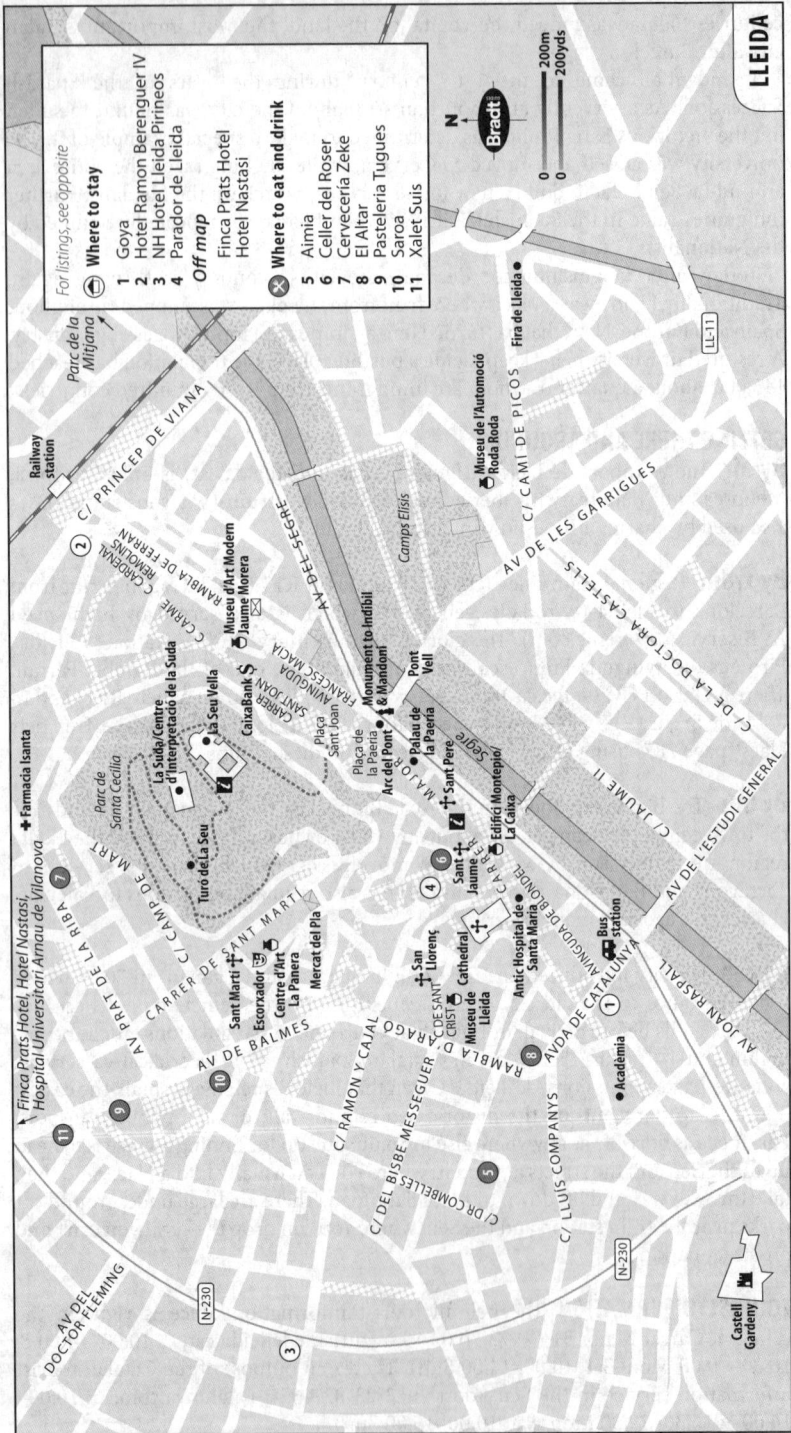

For listings, see opposite

Where to stay
1 Goya
2 Hotel Ramon Berenguer IV
3 NH Hotel Lleida Pirineos
4 Parador de Lleida

Off map
Finca Prats Hotel
Hotel Nastasi

Where to eat and drink
5 Aimia
6 Celler del Roser
7 Cerveceria Zeke
8 El Altar
9 Pastelería Tugues
10 Saroa
11 Xalet Suis

0 — 200m
0 — 200yds

🏠 WHERE TO STAY *Map, opposite*

Why are hotels in this town so breathtakingly cheap? Nobody seems to know. Just enjoy it; stay an extra day.

Finca Prats Hotel N-240, km 102.5; ☎ 973 25 48 14; w fincaprats.com. Fancy 5-star golf resort with ultra-modern rooms, an excellent spa, top-notch restaurant (€€€) & outstanding service – all at a surprisingly affordable price. The one drawback is the location, just off the motorway. €€€

✴ **Parador de Lleida** Pl Sant Antoni Maria Claret; ☎ 973 00 48 66; w parador.es. This is a gorgeous parador set in a 17th-century convent, with 28 elegant rooms arranged a beautiful triple-decker cloister. There's a great restaurant (€€€) in the church, serving modern Catalan cuisine – including *caragols a la llauna*, the classic local snail dish, of course. €€€

Hotel Nastasi Avda Rovira Roure 214; ☎ 973 24 92 22; w hotelnastasi.com. A modern, rather eccentric hotel (for a start, there's an elephant to greet you at the entrance) on the edge of town, with spacious, quirkily decorated rooms with different themes, a small spa & indoor pool. €€

NH Hotel Lleida Pirineos Gran Pg de Ronda 63; ☎ 973 27 31 99; w nh-hotels.com. A large, modern, extremely comfortable hotel on the edge of the town, with a good, international–Catalan restaurant (€€€) but note that it is closed Fri. €€

Goya Alcalde Costa 9; ☎ 973 26 67 88; w hotelgoyall.wixsite.com/hotelgoya. A simple, 1-star, family-run hotel with 17 traditional, slightly dated rooms & a warm welcome. €

Hotel Ramon Berenguer IV Pl Ramon Berenguer IV 3; ☎ 973 23 73 45; w hotelramonberenguerlleida.com. Large, well-equipped hotel with some old-fashioned charm, right across from the train station: pleasant rooms at very reasonable prices. €

✖ WHERE TO EAT AND DRINK *Map, opposite*

Aimia C/ Doctor Combelles 67; ☎ 973 261 618; w aimia.cat; 🕐 13.30–15.30 & 20.30–22.30 Wed–Sat, 13.30–15.30 Sun. Chef Jordi Pallàs has been cooking up some of the most delicious cuisine in Lleida since 2012. There are 2 menus to choose from: the Aimia (€40) with 3 starters, a main course & dessert, or the Alma de Aimia (€60) with 8 delectable dishes that showcase the chef's creativity. ('Aimia' means 'beloved woman' in the songs of old troubadours.) €€€€

Saroa C/ Torres de Sanui 12; ☎ 973 09 17 01; w saroarestaurant.com; 🕐 13.00–17.30 Mon–Wed & Sun, 13.00–17.30 & 20.45 –01.00 Thu–Sat. Even in a city as enamoured with food as Lleida, Saroa stands out. It's an elegant, white-on-white restaurant where you'll find refined Catalan cuisine with a contemporary twist, all prepared with whatever is freshest & in season & exquisitely presented like works of art. €€€€

Celler del Roser C/ Cavallers 15; ☎ 973 23 90 70; w cellerdelroser.cat. An institution in the historic centre, set in a 17th-century cellar. Long famous for snails, also *bacallà* (cod) & dishes with wild mushrooms. €€€

Xalet Suis Avda de l'Alcade Rovira Roure 9; ☎ 973 04 12; w xaletsuis.com. The charming, rustic surroundings – all wooden beams & geranium-filled balconies – are a delightful, if unlikely, setting for top-notch Catalan dishes prepared with creative flair. €€€

Cervecería Zeke Av Prat de la Riba 42; ☎ 973 22 55 51; 🕐 12.45–17.00 & 19.45–midnight Mon–Sat. A local favourite for its *ous estrellats* (scrambled eggs with ham) & other tapas & *racions*. The menu is short, but changes regularly – & usually offers some wonderful cheeses (including one with truffle). €€

El Altar Avda de Catalunya 26; ☎ 973 09 66 62; 📷 elaltar_tapas; 🕐 18.00–midnight Tue–Sat. Hugely popular, central tapas bar with a little terrace where locals come to tuck into excellent *patatas braves*, tasty *montaditos* (canapés) with different toppings & a host of different daily specials. €

Pasteleria Tugues Avda Alcalde Rovira Roure 5; ☎ 973 24 87 66; w tugues.com; 🕐 08.30–20.30 Tue–Fri, 08.30–14.30 Sat–Sun. This bakery-café is the perfect spot for b/fast pastries or for afternoon coffee & cake. €

ENTERTAINMENT AND NIGHTLIFE There is a collection of bars around Carrer Humbert Torres, a little pedestrianised street off Avda Prat de la Riba that is a great place to go for a drink and some tapas in the evening (Zeke, page 275, is a great choice).

For nightlife, look south, along Carrer Bonaire, and to the west, on Avinguda d'Alcalde Rovira Roure. Younger folks also frequent the collection of bars and cafés along Carrer Bisbe Messeguer, off the Rambla d'Aragó behind the big University building. Thursday night tends to be the biggest night for going out, as most students return to their home towns and villages at weekends.

OTHER PRACTICALITIES

Banks There are several banks and ATMs in the city centre, particularly around Plaça de la Sal and Avinguda Prat de la Riba. A centrally located branch is CaixaBank at Plaça de la Sal 5–6.

Medical You'll find plenty of pharmacies in Lleida, which are marked with a red or green cross. The **Farmacia Isanta** (Avda Alcalde Porqueres 76; ✆973 23 33 59) is a handy, centrally located option. The main city hospital is the **Hospital Universitari Arnau de Vilanova** (Avda Alcalde Rovira Roure 80; ✆973 24 81 00; w icslleida.cat).

Post office The main post office in Lleida is located at Rambla de Ferran 16 (✆973 24 82 00; w correos.es). Opening hours are typically 08.30–20:30 Monday to Friday.

WHAT TO SEE AND DO

Turó de La Seu (Turó de la Seu Vella; ✆973 23 06 53; w turoseuvella.cat; ⊕ May–Sep 10.00–14.00 & 16.30–19.30 Tue–Sat, 10.00–15.00 Sun; Oct–Apr 10.00–13.30 & 15.00–17.30 Tue–Sat, 10.00–15.00 Sun; adult/reduced/under 7 €7/5/free) As in many Catalan towns, Lleida's hill (*turó*) is a sort of acropolis that has witnessed a remarkable historical continuity as a religious and political centre since Iberian times. However, after the Bourbons destroyed the area in the early 18th century (page 273), Lleida became a very different city indeed, and a confusing one. Now, what once was the centre is largely dead space of parks and quiet residential streets, leaving Lleida a sort of doughnut-shaped city where the action isn't in the middle, but everywhere around it.

Up on top stands **La Seu Vella**. Tremendous in scale, with lots of panache, this is one of the great monuments of Spain. After the Iberians and Romans, the Moors built a castle from which to rule the little kingdom that appeared after the fall of the Caliphate, and a mosque that occupied the site where the Seu is now.

A church, probably converted from the old mosque, existed here from the Christian conquest, but the Seu as we see it now was not begun until 1203; it may have been conceived as a personal monument to Jaume the Conqueror. Although consecrated in 1278, the Seu was not completed until 1431, when the last stones of the **belltower** were hoisted into place. This majestic 70m tower forms Lleida's landmark skyline, with the help of the church's huge octagonal cupola and the smaller tower intriguingly called the 'tower of exorcisms'.

Soon after the belltower was completed, it acquired its famous occupants, two venerable ladies who have been watching over the city's fortunes now for about 600 years. These are **Silvestra (1418)** and **Mónica (1486)**, the bells, which respectively strike the hours and quarter-hours. Mónica was a little cracked for a while, but is now happily back in her spot after a cure in Austria; the two were joined in the 20th century by five modern bells.

The entrance to the complex is through the **Porta del Lleó** (1826), a monumental gate in the walls festooned with the arms of the Seu's Bourbon nemeses. Disaster came for Lleida and for the Seu with the Wars of the Spanish Succession. The troops of the Bourbon claimant, Philip V, took the city in 1707, and as in Barcelona, the new king ordered a fortress built to overawe the Lleidans. The height on which the Seu and the old Moorish castle stood was the logical place; the works must have destroyed the city's oldest neighbourhoods and monuments. The Seu itself narrowly escaped; Philip had ordered it razed, but somehow it never happened, and it would be used first as a barracks, later as a powder magazine and a barber shop. Its return to the church, and the beginnings of the restorations, date only to 1949.

You'll have to nearly circumnavigate the vast bulk of the church to get in, passing first the **Baluard de la Reina**, with views over the city. The church has no less than four portals, of which the southern **Porta de l'Anunciata** is the oldest, and the only place in the Seu where some fragments of the mosque that preceded it survive. The northern **Porta de Sant Berenguer** is also Romanesque in style, while the other two are impressively decorated with the sculptural work of the 'School of Lleida', including the grand main **Porta dels Apòstols** which leads into the cloister, and the **Porta dels Fillols** ('of the children') on the south.

Considering its sad history, there isn't much left inside, although what is there has been cleaned up in recent years: original alabaster windows, the remains of 13th–14th-century frescoes in the apse and some of the chapels, and fragments of tombs of the Montcada, the medieval clan from Barcelona who were powerful here, and helped build the Seu to hold their family pantheon.

Cloister The cloister was built for the cathedral chapter, and your first thought on entering it might be, where do I sign up? This is the most spectacular cloister in Spain, perhaps anywhere, and the Lleidatans also claim it as the biggest. It occupies the site of the old mosque courtyard. The unusual plan, with a campanile separated by an open courtyard from the church, is Moorish in origin; the Great Mosque in Córdoba is laid out the same way.

The cloister was built in the 14th century, when famous Catalan sculptors such as Guillem Seguer and Jaume Cascalls were in charge of the works. Its glory is the 17 enormous and beautiful Gothic windows. No two are alike. Note the delightful carved decoration on the capitals, some of the finest work of the Lleida school; much of it is modern restorations, after the damage sustained while the cloister was part of a barracks. Best of all, there's a feature almost no other cloister has. On one side, called the **mirador**, the windows open out to splendid views over Lleida. It's a perfect medieval fantasy setting; you could sit here all day.

Up above the church to the north stands **La Suda**, the Roman-Moorish-Catalan castle that suffered a lot over the centuries, most recently in the Napoleonic Wars and the Spanish Civil War. Painstakingly restored, it now contains the **Centre d'Interpretació de la Suda**, with info panels and an audiovisual presentation. It is located in what was once the palace's throne room, where six-year-old Jaume I, who would become known as 'el Conqueridor' (the Conqueror), was crowned in 1214. There's a summer café-bar on the rooftop, which offers tremendous views over the whole city.

On the northern slope of the hill is the lovely **Parc de Santa Cecília**, laid out in memory of those who died during the siege of 1640 during the Reapers War, and which ended on 22 November, the feast day of Saint Cecilia.

Down the Eix Today, the centre of the action is the long main street, which changes its name several times (C/ Cardenal Remolins, C/ Carme, C/ Sant Joan, C/ Major) as it passes from the train station underneath the Seu, paralleling the river.

8

People in Lleida call the whole thing the Eix, or 'axis' (pronounced 'aysh' rhyming with 'day-shh').

It's a great street, closed to traffic for its entire length and lined with shops and palaces and Modernista monuments. Starting from the station, the first square is busy **Plaça Sant Joan**, with the big, clumsy church of the same name. This was the site of the Roman-era forum, and the main temple stood where Sant Joan is now. The big stairway off to the right leads up to a lift to the Seu.

The next square, **Plaça de la Paeria**, announces itself, with a bit of Catalan whimsy, 'the most beautiful street sign in the world', painted in 1931 to cover a blank wall adjoining Lleida's town hall, the **Palau de la Paeria** (Pl de la Paeria 1; \973 70 03 00; w paeria.cat; ☉ guided visit only, ask at the tourist office). This is a word unique to Lleida and some of the towns in its province. *Paeria*, the city government, and the title of the mayor, *paer*, come from the Latin *patiarii*, 'men of peace', and they have kept these titles since Jaume I granted self-government in 1264. The building was begun in the 13th century as a private residence and, though much restored since, it is one of the notable surviving works of medieval Catalan secular architecture.

The parts of the Paeria that can be visited include the chapel, which has a glorious gilded retable by Jaume Ferrer (1451), the *Verge dels Paers*, showing the Virgin Mary and archangels Michael and Gabriel receiving four of Lleida's mayors. The **Municipal Archive** has two of the city's treasures on display, the Carta Pobla, the original charter of the city's settlement, and the Llibre dels Usatges, the famous 14th-century charter of Catalan rights. Downstairs, the old dungeon, **La Morra**, has some interesting graffiti from prisoners who sat here awaiting their executions. On the front of the building, note the little plaque commemorating the first eight-storey *castell* (human tower, page 46) in Lleida, made here on 6 April 2008. The *castellers* always rate a plaque when they perform a really good one; you'll see them all over Catalunya.

A detour along the river Back behind the Paeria, the 15th-century **Arc del Pont** is the only part of the city wall left standing. Near it is the **Monument to Indíbil and Mandoni** (Estàtua d'Indíbil i Mandoni), two chiefs of the Iberians who fought the Romans during the Second Punic Wars. Rome in those days won its victories through clever diplomacy nearly as often as on the battlefield. These two handsome dupes let the Romans trick them into giving up their alliance with Carthage. Once the legions had polished off the Carthaginians, it was Indíbil and Mandonio's turn; they both fell in Rome's final victory in 205BC.

Here on the Riu Segre, on the right is the **Avinguda de Blondel**, the riverfront promenade with some of Lleida's best Modernista buildings, and also, most conspicuously, the **Edifici Montepio**, the city's modest ten-storey skyscraper. Spaniards in general have been wild for skyscrapers since the 1920s, and even if they never got very tall, they certainly had style. This one now belongs to a foundation run by **La Caixa**, Catalunya's giant savings bank, and it puts on some interesting art exhibitions in their gallery just behind the tower (w lacaixafoundation.org/en/caixaforum-cosmocaixa-centres). In the opposite direction begins Lleida's shady **Rambles** (Av Francesc Macià and Rbla de Ferran), which have been elegantly restored in recent years. A key part of the recent revamping of this area was the expansion and renovation of the **Museu d'Art Modern Jaume Morera** (Rbla de Ferran 13; \973 70 04 19; w morera.paeria.cat; ☉ Jun–Sep 10.00–14.00 & 17.00–19.00 Tue–Sat, 10.00–14.00 Sun; Oct –May 10.00–14.00 & 16.00–18.00 Tue–Sat, 10.00–14.00 Sun; adult/reduced/under 16 €5/2.50/free), with a collection of modern and contemporary Catalan art, including landscapes from the eponymous painter and Surrealist sculptures by Leandre Cristòfol, one of the most prominent Spanish artists of the 20th century.

Back on the Eix The next sight is the church of **Sant Pere**, with a pretty Churrigueresque portal. Americans from the Golden State might want to drop in and pay their respects at the tomb of Gaspar de Portolà, first governor of California. A little further down, the 14th-century Gothic chapel of **Sant Jaume** marks the spot where according to local legend the apostle James (Santiago) had to stop on his way from the Holy Land to Santiago de Compostela when he got a really nasty thorn in his toe; angels came down from heaven to pull it out for him.

Off to the right, **Carrer dels Cavallers** leads up into the oldest neighbourhoods of Lleida, passing the 18th-century **Convent des Rosers**, now the elegant parador (page 275). Continue down the Eix and you'll meet the graceless hulk of an 18th-century Neoclassical **cathedral** (Pl de la Catedral; \973 26 94 70; w bisbatlleida.org; ⊕ for services; free) that Lleida built to replace the ruined Seu.

Antic Hospital de Santa Maria (Pl de la Catedral; \973 27 15 00; w iei.cat; ⊕ Jun–Sep 10.00–14.00 & 18.00–20.30 Mon–Fri, 10.00–14.00 & 19.00–21.00 Sat, 10.00–14.00 Sun; Oct–May 10.00–14.00 & 17.30–20.30 Mon–Sat, 10.00–14.00 Sun; free) Just across the Eix from the cathedral, this was built in the 15th century to consolidate the city's hospitals. Now it contains a cultural centre which holds special exhibitions and has a small archaeological collection. It's worth a look any time for the gorgeous arcaded courtyard with its sweeping staircase, one of the glories of medieval Catalan architecture.

Museu de Lleida (C/ Sant Crist 1 \973 28 30 75; w museudelleida.cat; ⊕ Jun–Sep 10.00–14.00 & 17.00–19.00 Mon–Sat, 10.00–14.00 Sun; Oct–May 10.00–14.00 & 16.00–18.00 Mon–Sat, 10.00–14.00 Sun; adult/reduced/under 16 €5/2.50/free) Behind the cathedral, you can find your way through some of the oldest streets in Lleida to its main museum, set in a huge, white, boxy building that was designed to accommodate all the small collections that had been scattered around town in a single exhibition space. There's a little bit of everything here, from the beginnings of Lleida and its province up to the Renaissance. From the Palaeolithic, there are reproductions of some of the many cave paintings in the area, followed by Neolithic finds, and fine Roman mosaics.

The Middle Ages are represented by some fascinating art. A reconstructed ensemble of altar furnishings from various churches gives an unexpected idea of how the interior of a Romanesque church looked in its time – like a Classical Greek temple, it's more wild and colourful than you might have expected. Also here are the famous Àger chessmen (page 280), one of the oldest sets ever found in Europe. There are works of the medieval 'School of Lleida', the sculptors who worked on the Seu, and a wealth of painting gathered from churches and monasteries around the province. The altarpieces by the late 14th-century Bartolomeo de Robió and his workshop stand out, vigorous, naturalistic works similar to the new painting that was happening then in Florence. Among the others, don't miss the wonderful scene of the medievals at dinner, from the refectory of the Seu.

Sant Llorenç (Pl de Sant Josep 6; \973 26 79 94; w www.turismedelleida.cat/en/explore/heritage/esglesia-de-sant-llorenc; ⊕ 09.30–12.30 & 17.00–19.00 Mon–Fri, 11.00–12.30 & 17.00–19.00 Sat, 11.00–12.30 Sun; free) Behind the museum, this church looks like a smaller version of the Seu, and it is, begun about the same

8

THE ÀGER CHESSMEN

Just how did princes and barons while away those dreary Dark Age Sunday afternoons? From the 9th century on, at least, the cleverer ones were playing the new game that was sweeping Europe – chess. Chess had already come to the Islamic world through Persia, and made its way to Europe through Byzantium, through Spain, and up the Volga, brought to Russia and Scandinavia by Viking traders from the Middle East. Judging from the number of surviving sets, Spain is where it caught on the strongest. Many, like the one here, were probably made in Egypt, where rock crystal carving was an established trade.

Typically for Islamic chessmen, the pieces are simple and abstract: the king is represented by his throne, the rook by a bit of crenellation. Note the piece with the slightly hooked top. That would be the bishop, except there weren't any bishops yet, or queens either. In medieval chess, there was only a slow-moving minister to keep the king company and defend him, and instead of a speedy and slyly oblique bishop you'd be stuck with a clumsy, diagonal-hopping *alfil*, or elephant, who also stayed close to the king. Like real medieval warfare, medieval chess put the emphasis on defence. Ever wonder how things end up in museums? These little lumps of crystal have a story to tell. They belonged to none other than that doughty knight of the Reconquista, Mir de Tost (page 290); 96 chessmen are mentioned in his will.

The Monastery of Àger got them and, when that closed in 1857, a few of them went to the bishops of Lleida. They kept them in the episcopal bedroom until one finally donated them to this museum. All the best ones spent a long time in the parish church of Àger, which auctioned them off in 1907. Later on they would be picked up by the Emir of Kuwait, looted by the Iraqis in 1991, before finding their way back to the Emir. They now form part of the al-Sabah Collection, on display at the Kuwait National Museum.

time by the same builders and sculptors. The lovely octagonal belltower has been restored and, inside, Sant Llorenç is one of the rare Catalan churches that still has most of its original artwork, including four Gothic retables.

For centuries after the Conquest of 1149 this part of town was known as the Moreria for its surviving Moorish population, which somehow managed to remain until the 1600s; ironically enough, it has become home to many North Africans once again. A little further into the neighbourhood, on Carrer de Sant Martí, there's the Mercat del Pla, the city's **market**, and beyond that the rough and rugged church of **Sant Martí**, which should give an idea of how the Catalans were building in the first generations of the Reconquista. For centuries this was the chapel of Lleida's university. Close by, the **Centre d'Art La Panera** (Pl Panera; ⟍973 26 21 85; w lapanera.cat; ⊕ 10.00–14.00 & 17.00–19.00 Tue–Sat, 11.00–14.00 Sun; free) occupies a medieval exchange and granary, and features usually excellent temporary exhibitions of contemporary art displayed next to thousand-year-old columns.

Outside the centre Most Lleidatans live in their modern and busy streets outside the centre, though there isn't a lot to see there. The **Escorxador**, not too far from the Museu de Lleida, was originally a slaughterhouse by Lleida's best-known Modernista architect, Francesc de Paula Morera i Gatell, and has been restored as a theatre. Just around the corner to the south, on Carrer de l'Acadèmia is the

Acadèmia Mariana. Monumental religious art may have been dead in 1870 but no-one told the Catalans, hence this colossal tribute to the Virgin Mary, combining frescoes, stained glass, Greek marble and some wonderful wrought ironwork in a frothy, kitsch extravaganza.

Across the Riu Segre, just over the Pont Vell from the city centre, Lleida, like Paris, has its own Elysian Fields. The **Camps Elisis** is a gracious park with avenues of plane trees. At its eastern end, it merges into the **Fira de Lleida**, the home of the city's annual trade exhibition, which retains a number of pretty pavilions from the period 1880–1920, including the Café Chalet and a Modernista building that was once an aquarium. A languid stretch of the **Camí del Riu** ('River Path'), a 15km-long walking and biking path that follows the Segre River, also runs through the park. If you follow it upstream for a couple of kilometres, you'll find the **Parc de la Mitjana**, a tranquil nature reserve which is a favourite with locals.

Just behind the Camps Elisis on Carrer de Santa Cecilia, the **Museu de l'Automoció Roda Roda** (Avda Blondel 64; ☎973 70 03 93; w cultura.paeria.cat/ca/equipaments/museu-roda-roda; ☉ 11.00–14.00 & 17.00–20.00 Tue–Sat, 11.00–14.00 Sun; free) has a collection of antique cars, including some luscious pre-war luxury models: a 1925 Rolls-Royce Phantom and something that in its day was even classier than a Roller, a Hispano-Suiza, made in Barcelona. The *Biscuter*, a cute little tin can on wheels from the impoverished 1950s, is at the other end of the spectrum.

Finally, on a hill (*turó*) overlooking the city from just outside the ring road (Gran Pg de Ronda) on the southwest, the **Castell Gardeny** (Turó de Gardeny; ☎973 70 03 93; w castellgardenylleida.com; ☉ end Jun–Sep 09.00–14.00 Wed–Sun, Oct–end Jun 10.00–16.00 Wed–Fri; adult/reduced/under 12 €3/2/free) was one of the Templars' major installations in Catalunya, along with Miravet (page 270). The Templars built their castle, really a small fortified commandery, almost as soon as Lleida was taken from the Moors. They weren't really worried about the Moors coming back. A Templar commandery handled loads of cash from the rents and profits on its far-flung lands, and a building like this was fortified to protect it.

After the War of the Spanish Succession, Philip V turned it into a modern artillery-proof fortress, with a low wall around the original Templar building. Although the city promotes this as one of the major sights, there isn't a great deal to see. Still, they make the most of what is there to discover with a rousing audiovisual show, and special guided visits in costume (see website for details). The views over the whole city are tremendous.

OUTSIDE LLEIDA
Raïmat Everyone knows that the restaurants of this village, 16km northwest of Lleida, are famous for rabbit. It's their speciality, and also a little joke. When villagers started growing wine grapes around 1914, so many bunnies appeared that they ate all the vine shoots, so making a casserole out of them was the only sensible solution.

Raïmat today produces a variety of wines, including some well-regarded reds, made from cabernet sauvignon, shiraz or tempranillo; you can visit the **bodega**, run by Codorníu, on the Lleida road (w 15bodegas.com). The older part of the bodega was built in 1918 by the Modernista Joan Rubió i Bellver; it was the first reinforced concrete building in Spain.

Roca dels Moros South of Lleida, in the comarca called Les Garrigues, there are millions of olive trees but not much else, though the countryside becomes increasingly pretty as it climbs up towards Montsant and the Priorat (page 252). In Roca dels Moros, you can visit some 9,000-year-old cave paintings

8

at the **Centre d'Interpretació d'Art Rupestre de la Roca dels Moros del Cogul** (Camino de El Cogul a Albagés, km 1; ✆ 672 445 990; w patrimoni.gencat.cat/en/monuments/monumentos/el-cogul; ⏲ 10.00–14.30 Wed–Sat; adult/reduced/under 16 €4/2/free). There's plenty of other, much more recent painting, including some accompanied by Iberic and Latin graffiti; other subjects are much like the other caves further south: various animals, hunters and elegant ladies in their long skirts.

Arbeca (31km east of Lleida) Here you can see the ruins of a **castle** that once belonged to the Dukes of Cardona, and a pre-Iberian village, **Els Vilars**, consisting of a circle of houses built around a well, one of the few such villages not sited on a defensible height. This area is wonderful in spring, when the orchards erupt in a sea of pale pink almond blossom.

EAST OF LLEIDA

East of Lleida, the landscape opens into the broad plains of the Urgell region, a rural patchwork of wheat fields that glow gold in late summer and orchards that burst into clouds of pale blossom in spring. There is a scattering of small but historic towns to explore, including Bellpuig with a striking Renaissance church, quiet little Anglesola, and lively, arty Tàrrega, once an important Jewish centre. The belle of them all is Cervera, with an 18th-century university and a beguiling old town.

GETTING THERE AND AROUND Like much of rural Catalunya, a car is very handy for getting around and reaching the more remote villages. On-street parking can be tricky in some bigger towns, but there are always car parks on the edge of town.

Regional **rail** lines RL3 and RL4 (✆ 912 32 03 20; w rodalies.gencat.cat) run from Lleida to Bellpuig, Anglesola, Tàrrega and Cervera, and RL4 continues to Barcelona via Terrassa and Sabadell.

The main **bus** operators in this region are Alsa (✆ 910 20 70 07; w alsa.es), which runs services between Cervera, Lleida, Agramunt and Torà, and Teisa (✆ 972 20 48 68; w teisa-bus.com), which links Lleida and Cervera with Girona. Alsa has an express bus service between Barcelona and Lleida via Cervera.

TOURIST INFORMATION There are tourist offices in all the main towns and villages, including Bellpuig (Pl Sant Roc 23; ✆ 973 32 05 36; w bellpuig.cat/el-municipi/turisme) and Cervera (Avda Francesc Macià 78; ✆ 973 53 44 42; w turismecervera.cat). In Tàrrega, there's a regional tourist office which provides info on the whole *comarca*, as well as on the city itself (C/ Agoders 16; ✆ 973 50 08 83; w turismeurgell.cat).

⌂ WHERE TO STAY

Hotel Pintor Marsà Avda de Catalunya 112, Tàrrega; ✆ 973 50 15 16; w hotelpintormarsa.com. A friendly, family-run mid-sized hotel with comfortable, traditionally decorated rooms, many with balconies, & a café-bar (€€) which serves up delicious Catalan cooking. **€**

Hotel Restaurant Hostal del Carme Ctra N-II, km 504, Villagrassa; ✆ 973 31 10 00; w hostaldelcarme.com. Run by the same family

as the Pintor Marsà (see left), this roadside inn is much the same – mid-sized, traditional, welcoming & comfortable – but has a slightly more upmarket restaurant (€€). **€**

Hostal Jaumet Ctra Barcelona-Andorra, Torà; ✆ 973 47 30 77; w hostaljaumet.com. A modern building (the old one burned down), but the same family has been running the place since 1890. The restaurant is an institution known far & wide. If

you want some real Catalan soul food, ask for the ofegat de la Segarra, with parts of the pig you don't want to know about. €
La Savina C/ Horts 2, Cervera; ☏ 973 53 13 93 . It doesn't look like much from the outside, but this is

a rather charming *hostal* with 8 inviting, if rather old-fashioned, rooms in open country just below the medieval centre. It has a swimming pool out in the leafy gardens, too. €

✖ WHERE TO EAT AND DRINK

L'Antic Forn Pl Major 18, Cervera; ☏ 973 53 31 52; w lanticforncervera.com; ⊕ 13.30–15.15 Tue–Thu, 13.30–15.15 & 21.00–22.00 Fri–Sat. Perhaps the last thing you'd expect in this rural corner of Catalunya is an outstanding Japanese restaurant, & yet that's what you'll find in the 'old bakery'. Part of the 'Slow Food' movement, the award-winning cuisine is prepared with organic Km0 produce, combining Catalan produce & Japanese techniques in dishes like prawn *suquet* (a fish stew) with seaweed tempura beef *doteyaki*, all artfully presented. €€€€
El Celler de l'Artista C/ Joan Maragall 7, Tàrrega; ☏ 973 31 00 14; w elcellerdelartista.cat; ⊕ 08.00–17.00 Mon–Tue & Thu, 08.00–17.00 & 20.00–midnight Fri–Sat. Delicious Catalan seasonal cuisine, including meat & fish cooked on a wood-fired grill, prepared with a modern twist.

They offer an outstanding set lunch (€18.90) on w/ days, which might include grilled cuttlefish with tomato chutney or slow-cooked lamb with sweet potato mash. €€
La Fontana C/ La Font, 21, Bellpuig; ☏ 973 32 05 41; ◙ restaurantlafontanadebellpuig; ⊕ 18.00–midnight Wed–Fri, noon–midnight Sat–Sun. Lively café-bar, with retro-chic décor & a menu of freshly prepared Mediterranean & Catalan favourites, from grilled cuttlefish with *escalivada* to Iberian pork fillet with mustard sauce. €€
Montfalcó C/ Rodo 6, Montfalcó; ☏ 973 53 17 55; ◙ montfalco_restaurant; ⊕ 13.00–17.00 Tue–Sun. In the tiny village square, within the old walls, this is a small, charming restaurant that specialises in grills & classic local dishes, which change depending on what's in season. €€

BELLPUIG Heading towards Barcelona on the A2, the great high road of Spain, there won't be much to detain you. Do stop at Bellpuig, though, for an apple (like fine wines they have a *denominació de qualitat*) and for an amazing small dose of the Renaissance in a very unlikely place. Barely fitting within this village's humble church of **Sant Nicolau** (Pl De l'Església s/n; ☏ 973 32 03 68; w bellpuig.cat/el-municipi/turisme/recursos/esglesia-de-sant-nicolau; ⊕ 10.00–13.00 & 15.00–17.00 Mon–Sat, 10.00–14.30 Sun; free) is the **Tomb of Ramon Folch de Cardona**, admiral of Spain and viceroy of Naples.

Everyone in the day believed that Folch was a natural son of King Fernando El Católico. Whether or not he was a literal bastard, he certainly fitted the term in every other respect. Fernando gave him Naples to rule in 1505, and Folch made himself one of the most hated men in Italy. After introducing the Inquisition to Naples, he went on a long series of campaigns across the peninsula, distinguishing himself mostly by the grisly sack of Prato in Tuscany (1512), in which thousands were massacred.

His tomb was designed and sculpted by Giovanni Merliano da Nola, a student of Benedetto da Maiano and the most renowned sculptor of his time in Naples, where most of his works are. This tomb, a few tonnes' worth of the finest Carrera marble, was originally installed in a Neapolitan church; it wasn't exactly welcome there, and was finally shipped over to Bellpuig, where Folch was born.

Merliano gave the bastard his money's worth: marble angels and mythological graces compete to shower his effigy with crowns and laurel. Note Folch's crossed legs, a convention in art that shows that the deceased was a crusader. Folch did lead a campaign in North Africa, capturing towns in Algeria, which also explains the stirring relief scenes of sea battles with galleys and the freeing of Christian captives.

8

Almost every inch of the tomb is covered in finely sculpted, intricate detail, with lots of surprises hidden among the decoration. Children can see if they can spot the crocodiles.

TÀRREGA The second city of Lleida province, Tàrrega is a cheerful (by Catalan standards) and forward-looking place, although there's not much to see beyond the **Museu Comarcal de l'Urgell** (C/ Major 11; \973 31 29 60; w museutarrega. cat; ⊕ 10.00–14.00 Mon–Wed, 10.00–14.00 & 17.00–20.00 Thu–Fri, 11.00–14.00 & 17.00–20.00 Sat, 11.00–14.00 Sun; adult/reduced/under 10 €5/3/free), with an archaeological collection and works of local artists. The city is internationally renowned for the **FiraTàrrega**, one of Spain's biggest festivals of the performing arts, and it has a vibrant year-round cultural scene.

VERDÚ South of Tàrrega, this little village is built around an unusual **castle** (Pl Bisbe Comelles; \973 34 72 16; ⊕ by guided visit only which must be booked in advance at the tourist office; w verdu.cat; €6), converted first into a palace and then into a mill, still with its medieval tower sticking out of the top. Verdú is also a ceramics town, known for its black-glazed pottery, and there are lots of shops around town. Just beyond Verdú lies Vallbona de les Monges, one of the three magnificent Cistercian monasteries of Catalunya (page 252).

CERVERA There is nothing in Cervera's early history to suggest that it would end up one of the loveliest and most distinctive towns in Catalunya. It followed the usual trajectory: hilltop Iberian settlement, followed by Romans, Visigoths, Moors and Aragonese. Its only mention in the history books would have been the conference where Aragonese and Castilian diplomats ironed out the terms of Fernando and Isabel's marriage.

But Cervera got one lucky break. In the War of the Spanish Succession it was one of the very few towns in Catalunya that picked the winning side. Its loyalty to the Bourbons was rewarded when Philip V shut down the universities of Lleida and Barcelona and combined them in a new, state-controlled university here. It may have been a disaster for Catalan culture, but it helped keep Cervera prosperous for another century and a half in which most of the other towns of Catalunya were going to pot.

It's still prosperous and happy, but being cute does mean it's increasingly popular among the 'second home' set. Modern Cervera is a sizeable new town with some industry, and the old medieval centre hangs from it like a pendant towards the south, giving it the air of a village surrounded by open country.

Universitat Old and new towns meet at this handsome building that covers an entire block. Completed in 1740, in a style that is Neoclassical with a touch of Rococo and an outlandish giant iron crown on top, its plan is something of a throwback, a great rectangle with courtyards and a chapel (called the Paranimf) at the centre, rather like the royal palace of El Escorial. The lower floor, around the stone arcades of the courtyards, housed the lecture halls and offices, while students lived in dormitories upstairs.

Showing his accustomed reverence for culture, Franco bombed the Universitat in the Civil War, and then turned it into a prison for dissidents. Parts of it are now once again being used for students, and the rest houses archives, a library and offices. Around the back, along **Passeig Jaume Balmes** there is a belvedere with views over the countryside.

Casa Museu Duran i Sanpere (C/ Major 115; ☎973 53 39 17; w museudecervera. cat; ☉ exhibition spaces 11.00–14.00 Thu–Fri & Sun, 11.00–14.00 & 17.00–19.00 Sat; Casa Museu Duran i Sanpere guided visit only 16.00–17.00 Sat; exhibitions or Casa Museu Duran i Sanpere adult/reduced/under 15 €3/2.5/free, combined €5/4/free) Continuing south into the medieval centre, Cervera's monuments line up along the Carrer Major, beginning with this museum in the former home of the wealthy Duran i Sampere family. On the ground floor is the tourist office, and behind is an exhibition called 'I'm 93' dedicated to beloved local heroes, Marc and Àlex Márquez, brothers and Moto GP world champions, as well as a collection of art from local churches, including a fine retable by Pere Girard. There are also some quaint and interesting relics from the old university, including silly lampshade hats that the professors had to wear, and an 18th-century voting machine used by the faculty to vote among themselves for positions. Upstairs, the rooms of the Duran i Sampere family have been restored to show how such a household lived in the 19th century.

Along the Carrer Major After the museum comes the 12th-century **Hospital de Sant Joan de Jerusalem**, with the Maltese cross on the façade giving it away as the property of the Knights Hospitallers. Have a look down some of Cervera's ancient narrow side streets, really nothing more than alleys with vaulting grown over them. Some, like the **Carrer de les Bruixes** (Witches' Street), have buildings that go back to the 1200s. There's a whole world underneath Cervera too; you may have noticed the little windows of thick glass placed on the pavement of the Carrer Major, to let some light into the network of cellars and storehouses that lie beneath the buildings.

The street ends with the peaceful and lovely **Plaça Major**, surrounded by arcades. The centrepiece here is the town hall, like Lleida's called the **Paeria**. This elegant building, completed in 1688, incorporates earlier structures, including a 13th-century Gothic chapel, but the best part is outside: the whimsical oversized figures on the corbels holding up the balconies. From the left, the first group are allegories of the senses; next come caricatures of the town merchants; and, finally, prisoners in the town jail.

Parròquia de Santa Maria (Pl Palau 1; ☎973 48 06 19; w bisbatsolsona.cat/ parroquies/cervera; ☉ services only; free) Directly behind the Paeria stands the Parròquia de Santa Maria, a jewel of a Gothic church begun in the 14th century and squeezed artfully into an oddly shaped site. Many of the architectural elements, including the octagonal belltower, show the influence of the Seu in Lleida; inside, it's wonderfully light and airy, with a wide nave and delicate rib vaulting. Over the main altar is a stately Baroque baldachin, covering the medieval image of the *Madonna del Coll de les Savines*, patroness of Cervera. The Anarchists wrecked most everything else inside during the Civil War, but in this case they spared the Madonna. Also surviving is some original stained glass and a pair of 14th-century tombs.

Around the castle At the tip of medieval Cervera stands its ruined, perfectly square castle, and the Gothic church and monastery of **Sant Domènec**. From here you can take a little walk into the countryside to see a little curiosity, the plain, round church of **Sant Pere le Gros** (1079), thought to have served as a funerary chapel or a pilgrim initiatory temple. But round chapels are always a bit of a mystery. This is one of only a handful in all Catalunya.

The area around the castle is a good place to have a look at Cervera's medieval **walls**, which survive almost intact in parts. Once they ran around the university, and

8

285

down the length of what is now the modern main street. Now the most picturesque bits are this stretch, and the eastern side along Carrer Pere el Cerimoniós. From the latter, you can see across the ravine to the rock called **Les Forques**, marked with a cross, where executions would take place.

In the newer neighbourhood of Cervera, near the rail station, stands a tower that looks like it might have been dropped down from Mars. Not Mars, in fact, but César Martinell. Although 1919 was a busy year for the architect, he found time to design this fantastical tower for the town's agricultural co-operative. Some Cerverans call it **La Farinera** and some call it El Sindicat.

AROUND CERVERA: THE SEGARRA Cervera is the capital of the *comarca* of the Segarra. It's hard-scrabble country, dotted with seldom-visited medieval hamlets, each one with a miniature castle that has been falling down since the 11th century. Before that, this was frontier country between the Christians and Moors, and that era left the Segarra with more castles than any part of Catalunya. Count Ermengol IV of Urgell took over the territory once and for all in the 1060s. Since then, outside of skirmishes in the War of the Spanish Succession or the Carlist Wars, the castles have had nothing to do.

One place that really does deserve a visit is **Montfalcó Murallat**, northeast of Cervera near Oluges. It's nothing more than a simple church and a handful of houses that have grown up inside a rough and ready castle, but no place evokes the old frontier days better. In the 11th century, a lot of people lived just like this. Montfalcó is packed so tightly that it seems like a single building with a little maze of passages running through it and a tiny plaça or two. Lately people have been moving in and fixing it up, and there is a restaurant and a couple of bars in summer.

TORÀ If you really mean to go chasing down curiosities in the Segarra, by all means take yourself off to Torà, on the furthest extremes of the comarca, for a look at the **Tower of Vallferosa**. In a pretty green setting, Vallferosa is a hamlet outside Torà that was largely abandoned after the Civil War. Its conical tower, over 33m tall, is a startling sight, even more so when you consider it was begun about the year AD970.

This is the true monument of the Reconquista, conjuring up as no other relic can the age when the first uncouth Catalans came storming down from the hills. Round defensive towers were commonly built to help defend newly conquered lands from the Moors. This is the biggest, built in stages over two centuries. The entrance was on the second floor; when attacked, they would just pull up the ladder.

Torà itself is a thoroughly charming village, full of steps and arcaded alleys and fountains and lovely old houses. There's a medieval bridge and an aqueduct, and a 400-year-old communal oven that has become a tiny **Museu del Pa** (bread museum) (C/ Forn s/n; ⧹973 47 30 28; call for visits, although you can see it through the gate).

THE LLOBREGÓS The valley around Torà is an excellent spot for a walking holiday (some good walking routes are listed here: w valldelllobregos.com/en/nature/all). There's a lot to see in the surrounding countryside, including plenty of Neolithic dolmens, including Catalunya's biggest, at **Llanera**, just north of Torà. There are a few more round towers like the one at Vallferosa; the most impressive are at **Castellfollit de Riubregós** and **Ivorra**. There's a rather magical ruined castle at **Sanaüja**, north of Biosca, along with an impressive medieval bridge. Among the many rustic Romanesque churches in the area, the best are at Castellfollit de Riubregós and **Cellers**, east of Torà, with some wonderfully primitive carved decoration in the crypt. Finally, in Ivorra's Baroque church you can also see the reliquary of Sant

Dubte, the 'holy doubt'. The story goes that back in the 1030s someone said that he didn't believe the eucharist was really the body of Christ, and it conveniently started bleeding for him.

NORTH OF LLEIDA: SERRA DE MONTSEC

From the north side, at least, it's one ugly mountain, a long grey mound that looks like a gargantuan bag of cement left out in the rain. The southern silhouette's a little more comely, weathered away into a long skyline of steep cliffs. The whole thing is 47km, east to west. Throughout history, it has never been much more than a lumpish obstacle, blocking everyone's way on valley paths between the Pyrenees and the southern plains. Nowadays, though, it's become a popular destination for a whole range of outdoor activities, from the death-defying hiking path that clings to the edge of the Mont-rebei Gorge to climbing, canyoning and hang-gliding. Much of it is a designated Starlight Reserve, with some of the clearest skies in Europe, making it an exceptional location for stargazing. The rise in tourism has helped stem the population drain of recent decades, giving young people an opportunity to make a living.

GETTING THERE AND AROUND Catalunya's regional rail line, the FGC, operates the year-round RL2 commuter service on a scenic route through Montsec from Lleida to La Pobla de Segur via Balaguer, Sant Llorenç de Montgai, Àger, Cellers, Guardia de Tremp, Palau de la Noguera and Tremp. On Saturdays between April and October, it offers a tourist train called the 'Tren dels Llacs' (Train of the Lakes; ☏ 932 05 15 15; w trendelsllacs.cat) along the same line, with guides on board. You can choose either the historic trains with vintage interiors from the 1960s or a modern panoramic train with huge windows.

TOURIST INFORMATION As always, the local tourist information offices are an excellent resource, offering a wealth of useful info on activities in the area. You'll find them in Balaguer (Pl Comtes d'Urgell 5; ☏ 973 44 51 94; w balaguer.cat/turisme), Tremp (Pg del Vall 13; ☏ 973 65 34 70; w ajuntamentdetremp.cat) and La Pobla de Segur (Pl del Ferrocarril s/n; ☏ 973 68 02 57; w lapobladesegur.cat).

⌂ WHERE TO STAY

Casa Perdiu C/ del Mig 5, Guardia de Tremp; ☏ 973 65 05 25; w casaperdiu.com. A handful of rustically furnished, pristine rooms & a couple of apartments in a simple casa rural – perfect for stargazing. **€**

Hotel Santuari C/ Pla d'Almata; ☏ 973 44 96 17; w hotelsantuari.cat. Next to the sanctuary & the castle overlooking the city, this mid-sized hotel has immaculate, modern rooms & an excellent restaurant (**€€**) with wonderful views. **€**

La Canonja Pg del Vall 5, Tremp; ☏ 973 65 05 58; w hostallacanonja.com. Cosy little inn in the middle of town that's been going strong since 1939, with simple rooms & a good restaurant (**€€**) for local specialities. **€**

Monestir de les Avellanes Ctra C12, Les Avellanes; ☏ 973 43 80 06; w monestirdelesavellanes.com. This lovely medieval monastery is available for everything from spiritual retreats to business conferences. The friendly Marist fathers, who've been here since 1912, are frankly in the hospitality business; that's how they keep up the buildings. There are about 50 air-conditioned rooms which, though simple, are anything but ascetic. Full- or half board is available. **€**

Palauet de la Muralla C/ Miracle 7, Balaguer; ☏ 642 614 726; w lopalauetdelamuralla.com. Set in a 17th-century townhouse full of historic artworks & books, this has 10 lovely antique-furnished suites & rooms, a pretty terrace with trailing plants & a wine cellar. **€**

Terradets Ctra Balaguer–Tremp, C13, km 75, Cellers; ☏ 973 65 11 20; w hotelterradets.

8

cat. Right on the lake in the quiet countryside. Most rooms have balconies; ask for one

on the lake side. Pool, a good restaurant & activities. €

✕ WHERE TO EAT AND DRINK

Cal Xirricló C/ Dr Fleming 53, Balaguer; 973 44 50 11; w calxirriclo.com; ⏰ 13.30–15.30 Mon–Thu, 13.30–15.30 & 20.30–22.30 Fri– Sat. A local favourite for over 60 years & one of the best in the region: sophisticated Catalan cuisine, including a 9-course *menu degustació* (€72), plus an excellent w/day set lunch (€28). €€€€

Bocca Braseria Ctra de Balaguer 16; 687 44 98 90; bocca.balaguer; ⏰ 13.00–16.00 Mon–Wed, 13.00–16.00 & 20.00–midnight Thu–Sun. Specialising in meat & fish cooked on wood-fired grills, this old *masia* on the edge of town offers a hearty menu of classic Catalan

dishes at lunchtimes & a tapas menu in the evenings. €€

Casa Vidrieres Tremp; restaurantlesvidrieres; ⏰ 07.00–17.00 Mon–Wed, 07.00–17.00 & 19.00–23.00 Thu–Sun. A popular local favourite, this has classic Catalan country dishes like chicken with prunes & pine nuts or *callos* (tripe), along with juicy burgers & sandwiches. €

Casa Xalets C/ Font 14, Àger; 622 135 985; w restaurantcasaxalets.com; ⏰ noon–17.00 Tue–Wed & Sun, noon–17.00 & 20.00–22.00 Thu– Sat. Good, honest home cooking – lamb chops, *esqueixada*, local sausages – at this family-run restaurant-bar in the middle of the village. €

SPORTS AND ACTIVITIES The Montsec region has a huge array of outdoor sports and activities. Tremp, as the largest town in the region, is the main base, but Àger is the main centre for stargazing.

Climbing This is a very popular climbing destination, with something for everyone. The two main areas are Vilanova de Meià and Terradets, which both offer a mix of routes, although those at Vilanova de Meià are considered more challenging. There are also several via ferrata in the region, including Les Arcades, near Tremp, which is suitable for beginners, and Urquiza-Olmo, near Àger, which is for experienced climbers.

Hiking The Montsec mountain range offers some spectacular routes, including the renowned path along the Congost de Mont-Rebei (Mont-rebei Gorge; page 291), which is carved into the rock walls. The Camí de Montfalcó and the Camí de la Pertusa are two of the main routes, both stunning and not for the vertiginous. Several local companies offer guided excursions, including Montsec Activa (w montsecactiva.com).

Kayaking and canoeing You can kayak through the Mont-rebei Gorge or head to the calmer waters of the Embassament de Canelles (a reservoir). Kayaking Mont-Rebei (w kmr.es) run kayaking tours through the gorge for a range of levels, from the most challenging to easier, family-friendly tours.

Stargazing The Parc Astronòmic del Montsec (Montsec Astronomical Park; page 290) is a designated Starlight Reserve, and offers exceptional conditions for stargazing.

BALAGUER At first glance it seems strangely familiar: on one side of the river there's a neat, straight row of big modern apartment buildings, on the other a venerable old town, with a great church inside a castle looming over it. It's no mistake; Balaguer is a baby Lleida in every way. And, for a town of 17,600 that no-one outside Catalunya has ever heard of, Balaguer is a pleasant surprise.

Balaguer is mentioned in Roman records, but it didn't become a thriving town until the time of the Moors. Madinat Balagi, according to the 11th-century historian al-Himyari, was a beautiful city surrounded by orchards and gardens, made wealthy by farming, linen cloth and gold panned from the River Segre. The city fell to Count Ermengol V of Urgell in 1105, with a particularly brutal sacking and the flight of most of its Muslim population. Ermengol made it Urgell's new capital, but revival did not really come until the early 1300s, when prosperity returned and the churches and bridges were built.

Balaguer's happiness would be brief; the city shared the fortune of the last Count of Urgell, Jaume II el Dissortat (the Unlucky), who pressed his claim to the Aragonese crown in 1410. Jaume lost a string of battles to the successful claimant Fernando of Antequera, abdicated in 1413, and spent the rest of his life in prison.

Around Plaça Mercadal The place to size up Balaguer is from the foot of the **Pont Nou**, the busy main bridge over the Segre. The *pont* is *nou* because the old one got blown up in the Civil War; in the closing days Balaguer was the first big Catalan town to fall, and the gateway for Franco's final march on Barcelona. Over on the modern side, this bridge leads to the tree-lined rambla, the **Passeig de l'Estació**, with all the businesses and posh shops. Looking down at the Segre, you'll probably see some of the ducks and geese that have made the riverbank their home since the city turned it into a park. Looking up, there's what appears to be an enormous fortress on the heights above the town, particularly impressive at night when it is illuminated. This is really only part of the town walls, begun by the Moors and rebuilt by the Counts of Urgell.

Walk north a block, and you'll come to the **Plaça Mercadal**, surrounded by arcades and shaded by well-clipped plane trees. This absolutely lovely square hides a dark secret. Before 1492 this was the densely packed Jewish ghetto. After the Jews were expelled, the buildings were all levelled and the ground made into a new marketplace. On the corner house coming from the bridge, note the plaque marking the birthplace of Gaspar de Portolà, the first governor of California (page 279). From this square, you can climb up to the walkway on top of the old walls for tremendous views.

Museu Comarcal de la Noguera (Pl dels Comtes d'Urgell 5; 973 44 51 94; w museucn.com; ⏱ 10.00–14.00 & 17.00–19.00 Mon–Sat, 10.00–14.00 Sun; adult/reduced/under 16 €3/2/free) Two streets south of the Plaça, this big modern museum will give you a thorough grounding on Balaguer's history.

Santa Maria (Pl Cecilia Cominge 1; 973 44 53 42; w balaguer.cat/turisme; ⏱ 11.00–14.00 Sat–Sun; free) This church with the octagonal belltower is the one that hangs so fetchingly above the Plaça Mercadal and you'll have to climb up Balaguer's oldest streets to get there. Santa Maria is a testament to Balaguer's up-and-down medieval history; this ambitious project was begun in 1351 but took over 200 years to finish. The result is a little Gothic and a little Renaissance.

On the opposite bank of the Segre, near the Pont de Sant Miquel, is the attractive Gothic church and cloister of **Sant Domènec** (Av Comte Jaume d'Urgell 1; 973 44 66 06; w parroquiabalaguer.org/informacio/temples-parroquials/st-domenec; ⏱ mass only; free).

Santuari de Sant Crist (C/ Pla d'Almatá; 973 44 53 35; w santcristbalaguer.com; ⏱ 08.00–19.00 daily; free) Part of another set of church-and-castle on a

8

commanding height, the building goes back to the Middle Ages, but most of what you see now is from 1912. Once this was a very popular pilgrimage church, for a miraculous statue of Christ said to be the work of Nicodemus, companion of Joseph of Arimathea. The legend said that angels guided his hand, and the image represented the true face of the Saviour. Before it was destroyed in the Civil War, killjoy scholars unfortunately dated it to the 14th century. Of the reconstruction you see now, only a foot survives from the original.

Next to it you can see the very sparse remains of the old Islamic medina, **Pla d'Almatà** and the remnants of the **Castell Formós**, the palace of the Counts of Urgell which replaced the Arabic *suda* (fortress) after the town was taken.

MONESTIR DE LES AVELLANES (Ctra C-12, km 181, 25612, Os de Balaguer; ✆973 43 80 06; w monestirdelesavellanes.com; ⊕ book guided visits in advance; €6) If you approach Montsec from Balaguer on the scenic C-12, you'll pass this monastery with a Romanesque cloister and a Gothic church that once held the tombs of the Counts of Urgell. These, unfortunately, were spirited away by the minions of the Rockefellers long ago, after the monastery fell into ruin, and you'll have to go to the Cloisters Museum in New York to see them. Les Avellanes is now restored, and makes an interesting place to pass the night (page 287).

ÀGER Right at the foot of Montsec, Àger is a centre for paragliding, kayaking and stargazing. Àger was once an important place, thanks to its most famous resident, Arnau Mir de Tost. Arnau, born c1000, was one of the protagonists of the Catalan Reconquista. This knight of Urgell made Montsec his personal frontier, and by the time he died he had conquered much of it and earned himself no less than 30 castles. Historians have called him the 'Catalan El Cid'.

Arnau was responsible for completing the somewhat ruined and fascinating **Col·legiata de Sant Pere**. This Catalan backwater church has suffered like the others, with some fine frescoes moved long ago to Barcelona. Still, as an example of the earliest rugged Catalan Romanesque, it has charm. Àger's better days have further witnesses in the parish church of **Sant Vicenç**, where the baptismal font is a 3rd-century AD Roman sarcophagus decorated with marine mythological scenes, and a stretch of Roman road that survives in almost passable shape.

Àger is in the heart of a designated Starlight Reserve, boasting some of the darkest skies in Europe and wonderful conditions for stargazing. Just outside town is the **Parc Astronòmic del Montsec** (Astronomic Park of Montsec) (Camí del Coll d'Ares s/n; ✆973 05 30 22; w parcastronomic.cat; ⊕ day & night visits available: see website for times & prices), with a fabulous planetarium with a retractable dome.

PAS DE TERRADETS Montsec is divided in two by the Noguera Pallaresa River. The larger, western part, bordering on Aragon, is called Montsec d'Ares while the eastern part is Montsec de Rúbies, and this pass marks the boundary between the two. The **Noguera Pallaresa** River cuts a dramatic gorge here, which has become one of Catalunya's most popular climbing destinations. Upstream from that, a grey Franco-era dam holds back an artificial lake with a lovely mountain backdrop, the **Pantà de Terradets**, now a popular spot for boating and watersports near the village of **Cellers**.

CASTELL DE MUR Up on the slopes of Montsec to the west is a remarkable sight, a narrow, triangular castle with a tall curtain wall built around a 10th-century cylindrical defence tower, like those of the Llobregós. Altogether, it looks a little like a steamboat, and a little like a steam iron. There's a church nearby, the **Col·legiata**

de Mur (\677 701 820; w castellmur.cat/el-municipi/turisme/rutes/castell-de-mur-i-col-legiata-de-santa-maria; ⏲ guided visits Feb–Jul & Sep–Dec 11.00 Sat–Sun, Aug 11.00 & 18.00 Sat, 11.00 Sun; €6), built at the end of the 11th century, with a small cloister. The church apse once held a wonderful fresco of Christ Pantocrator with the four Evangelists. The Americans got this one too; now it's in Boston, but an accurate reproduction was put in place.

CONGOST DE MONT-REBEI The best part of Montsec is also unfortunately the hardest to see, nothing less than the most isolated spot in all of Catalunya. And it is utterly spectacular. The Congost de Mont-Rebei, the long gorge of the Noguera Ribagorciana River that divides Catalunya from Aragon, has cliffs that tower over 500m, in places where the river itself is only 20m wide. You'll have to be an experienced climber to get all the way through it.

Back in the 1920s the government created a path through, but later on this was chopped short when part of the gorge was flooded for the Canelles Dam. The **Mont-rebei path** was restored in 1984, carved high into the rock. Don't come if you suffer at all from vertigo: in some stretches this narrow path is thoroughly terrifying, hanging 180m in the air on a nearly vertical cliff, with no guard rails. The highlight is the **Passarel·les de Montfalcó** – two dizzyingly high wooden walkways and a 35m suspension bridge anchored to the cliff. If you can stand it, though, it's quite an experience, and you'll be sharing it with the bats and vultures that nest in the rock face as well as royal eagles and rare lammergeiers. Down in the river there's an abundance of otters.

TREMP AND THE CONCA DELLÀ The 5,870 souls in Tremp make it the only town of any size in this region. Outside of that there's not a lot to say about it, just a sleepy little town with a miniature medieval centre and some surviving towers from the wall that once went around it.

East of Tremp is a broad, green basin between the mountains called the **Conca Dellà**. The centre is the village of **Isona**, once the Roman town of Aeso. Isona was a little more important then, and ruins from Roman times can still be seen in and around the village – but it was really a swinging place 67 million years ago, at the end of the Cretaceous period. Dinosaur fans won't want to miss the **Museu de la Conca Dellà** (C/ Museu 4; \973 66 50 62; w parc-cretaci.com; ⏲ 11.00–14.00 & 17.00–19.00 Tue–Sat, 11.00–14.00 Sun; adult/reduced/under 7 €5/4/free). Among the many Cretaceous finds in the area is an entirely new species, an unlovely, fat-tailed brute named *Pararhabdodon isonensis* in honour of the village. One floor of the museum is devoted to dino eggs, dino footprints and dino everything else.

THE SOLSONÈS AND CARDONA

There's something otherworldly about this region, with its mysterious dolmens, legends and impossibly huge salt mountain. Largely sleepy and rural, with old stone villages and remote *masies* scattered across wooded hills, it does have two sizeable and dignified little cities – Solsona and Cardona – and even a pocket-sized ski resort at Port del Comte.

GETTING THERE AND AROUND The nearest train station for Solsona or Cardona is Manresa (page 138), so it is more convenient to arrive by bus. Alsa (\910 20 70 07; w alsa.es) and Teisa (\972 20 48 68; w teisa-bus.com), operate most services in the area, including several a day from Barcelona, Lleida and Manresa.

8

WHERE TO STAY

La Freixera C/ Sant Llorenç 46, Solsona; 973 48 42 62; w hotellafreixera.com. Right in the centre, a very charming boutique hotel in a 14th-century building with 5 varying modern & spacious rooms, delightful staff & delicious b/fasts. €€

Parador Nacional Duques de Cardona Castell de Cardona, Cardona; 938 69 12 75; w paradores.es. Set in a stunning location high over the town, in part of the castle founded in AD789 by Louis the Pious. The charming restaurant (€€) in a vaulted cellar offers well-prepared Catalan grills & roasts. The rooms are furnished with Catalan antiques; some have great views. €€

Sant Roc Pl Sant Roc, Solsona; 973 48 40 08; w hotelsantroc.com. Martorell's Modernista monument still shines in all its glory – at least from the outside. Inside, sadly, it's been remodelled to death, & the 25 rooms & 2 apartments are all quite bland. There's a couple of restaurants: 1 tapas bar (€€) & a more pretentious restaurant (€€€). €€

Can Puig Ctra de Manresa, Clariana de Cardener; 973 48 24 10. A small, family-run roadside hotel, with pristine, well-equipped rooms, an excellent restaurant (€€) serving traditional Catalan cuisine, along with a pool & playground for kids. €

Casa Angrill Montpol, Lladurs; 607 30 63 23; w angrill.cat. A restored *masia* in the countryside north of Solsona, with a handful of rustically furnished rooms (you can also rent the whole house). It's a great base for hiking & mountain biking. €

Castell de Ceuró Camí de Ceuró s/n, Castellar de la Ribera; 679 378 790; w castelldeceuro. cat. This was the rectory attached to an isolated Romanesque church, set high on a hill with great views. It's been converted into a pretty small guesthouse, with simple rooms, & offers a range of holistic wellness activities, including Qi Gong & healthy food. €

Fonts del Cardener Ctra de Tuixent, La Coma; 973 49 23 77; w hotelfontsdelcardener.com. A mid-sized hotel, 12km from the ski slopes, but good in summer too; in a lovely setting with a pool, gardens & terrace with a view; also a restaurant (€€). €

Monegal Guixers, 5km east of Sant Llorenç de Morunys; 973 49 23 69; w monegal.com. A rather sophisticated establishment for the Vall de Lord, a modern place near a lake, with 9 smart rooms & an apartment, plus an ambitious restaurant (€€€). The hotel helps with any sort of outdoor activity (including mushroom hunting in season), & it also arranges exhibitions & concerts. €

Torre del Baró Ctra de la Coma, Sant Llorenç de Morunys; 973 49 26 36; albergtorredelbaro. Modest but nice, in a restored *masia*, with about a dozen dorms, dbls & family rooms, plus a shared kitchen. They'll help organise cross-country skiing & other activities. €

WHERE TO EAT AND DRINK

Cal Borrasca C/ Escorxador, Cardona; 938 69 27 30; cal_borrasca; 13.00–15.30 Mon, Thu & Sun, 13.00–15.30 & 21.00–22.30 Fri–Sat. An historic & beloved local restaurant for refined Catalan cuisine in a charming old building in the city centre. €€

Crisami Ctra de Manresa 52, Solsona; 973 48 04 13; w hostalcrisami.top; 13.00–15.30 & 19.30–22.30 Mon–Sat, 13.00–15.30 Sun. A modest but superior establishment. The rooms are fine, but come for the restaurant. The menu may feature only simple favourites like a beef *estofat*, but someone back in the kitchen really knows how to cook. €€

La Volta del Rector C/ Flors 4, Cardona; 938 69 16 37; w lavoltadelrector.cat; 09.00–17.00 Tue–Fri, 08.00–17.20 Sat & 08.00–18.00 Sun.

Modern, Catalan cuisine in a vaulted dining room in the historic heart of town; try their own wines, El Celler del Rector. €€

Mare de la Font Ctra de Bassella, Solsona; 973 48 01 52; w maredelafont.cat; 09.00–18.00 Mon, Thu–Fri & Sun, 09.00–17.30 & 21.00–midnight Sat. An elegant restaurant just outside town in a rustic setting, a long-time local favourite that concentrates on all the things Catalans like best: snails, *bacallà*, rabbit, stews & of course a crema catalana for dessert. €€

El Punxó Pl de Sant Joan 14, Solsona; 973 65 46 56; elpunxo; 18.00–midnight Wed–Fri, noon–15.00 & 18.00–midnight Fri–Sat. Vermut & delicious tapas on one of Solsona's prettiest squares. What could be more perfect? €

SOLSONA In a part of Catalunya where the economy has been difficult for a long time, the exquisite town of Solsona is thriving. It used to be known for making gloves and lace. Now, every August it runs a chamber music festival and academy for students from all over the world. Solsona takes carnival very seriously, putting on one of the best in Spain, and it's even prouder of its *gegants*.

Solsona has always been here; archaeological finds go back beyond 3000BC. The Iberians called it Xelsa, the Romans Setelsis. After some Dark Age troubles, Wilfred the Hairy helped re-establish the city; Catalunya's founder died in a battle nearby. Solsona prospered in the Middle Ages, as its merchants made a reputation throughout Spain and beyond. One of the town's barons even seized a foreign conquest, the town of Alghero in Sardinia (until recently, some of the older folks there still spoke Catalan).

The 16th and 17th centuries were very good to Solsona. The town became a city, and the seat of a bishop. It gained a university (later consolidated with Cervera's) and contributed one of the great painters of Spain's golden age, Francisco Ribalta. The 18th century was good too. Solsona thrived by manufacturing knives, gloves and lace, while most of Catalunya was floundering.

The modern era, however, brought nothing but trouble. First Napoleon's army burned the cathedral. The First Carlist War brought even worse damages. The pope took away the episcopal see in 1851, just while the city's old manufactures were losing out to the new industrial firms in Barcelona. Solsona has come through the troubles in style. It is one of the most refined and urbane towns you'll find in Catalunya, or anywhere. The people of Solsona know it's special, but they aren't very helpful in explaining why. Ask them about it and they'll just smile.

Most likely you'll come into town on the bridge over the little Riera de Solsona. After the bridge was built, the gate called the **Portal del Pont** was constructed as the new monumental entrance to the city (1805). Just outside it, a small pavilion has been built over the **Pou de Gel**. There must be a hundred of these in the towns of Catalunya – ice wells, where ice from the Pyrenees could be packed in the winter and kept all through the summer. This one was made in the 1680s. From here, Carrer Sant Miquel leads into the heart of the city.

Cathedral (C/ Campanes 1; ☎973 48 06 19; w bisbatsolsona.cat; ⊕ 08.00–20.00 daily; free) Next to a 15th-century fountain, the cathedral is a Romanesque building, completed in 1070, but it has suffered much over the centuries; the fragments on the exterior show that it must have been quite impressive in its day. To see the best thing about it you'll have to go around the back – a gorgeous Modernista dome in dark blue and yellow tiles over the *cambril*, or Lady chapel. This was built to house Solsona's beloved icon, the *Mare de Déu del Claustre*, an exceptional 12th-century image with a faraway gaze and stylised draperies that give away its origins in southwest France; the artist's name was Gilbert of Toulouse.

Plaça de Palau and the Museu Diocesà i Comarcal (Pl Palau 1; ☎973 48 21 01; w museusolsona.cat; ⊕ mid-Mar–mid-Dec 11.00–18.30 Wed–Sat (also Tue in Jul & Aug), 11.00–14.00 Sun; mid-Dec–mid-Mar 11.00–17.00 Wed–Sat, 11.00–14.00 Sun; free) A block to the north is the lovely Plaça de Palau, with a wonderful fountain decorated with begonias and ivy. The former episcopal palace is now the Museu Diocesà i Comarcal (Diocesan and regional museum). Except in summer when the tourists are about, it's usually dead quiet inside, but this little museum has an astounding hoard of medieval art, most of it frescoes taken here for preservation from village churches.

8

Before you see these, though, there's the equally astounding **Col·lecció de Sal**, sculptures made from chunks of salt from nearby Cardona. It's an old tradition in these parts; unknown madmen have contributed fantasy Gothic temples, a salty bust of a princess, and best of all, life-like sausages and slices of cantaloupe.

The medieval collection starts with fragments: original doors, a small portal carved with a not-very-Christian dragon, and some charming cartoonish painted wood icons of the Madonna. Next come perhaps the museum's star exhibits, rare pre-Romanesque paintings from Sant Quirze de Podret (11th century): some utterly exotic subjects framed by Moorish arches, and an Angel of the Apocalypse you won't forget. After that there are some exceptional 12th-century frescoes from Sant Vicenç de Rus, and a collection of items arranged to make a complete Romanesque altar ensemble that makes it easy to imagine how early-medieval churches really looked in their day. There are several altarpieces from the 14th century, including a great *Last Supper* by Jaume Ferrer.

Around the Historic Centre

Adjacent to the Plaça de Palau is the arcaded **Plaça Major**; from here, Carrer de Castell leads up to the stately Renaissance **Ajuntament (City Hall)** and the **Torre de les Hores**, the centre of the action each year at carnival. Solsonans are sardonically called 'donkey-killers' in Catalunya. The old story goes that a farmer once dragged his hungry donkey up to the top of the steeple to eat the grass that was growing out of the cornice. They used to re-enact it every year, but now, for sanity's sake, they use an effigy.

It's a delight to wander around the serene, immaculate back streets of old Solsona. A block south of the Ajuntament is the **Plaça Sant Joan**, and you'll come across other squares, **Plaça Sant Roc** and **Plaça de Sant Pere**, landscaped into attractive gardens. The other surviving town gates, **Portal de Llobera** and **Portal de Castell**, lie at the northern edge of town. Just beyond this is the Solsona's Modernista monument, the **Hotel Sant Roc** (1929), designed by Ignasi Oms and Bernardí Martorell in a fairytale sort of Modernisme that seems to fit the mood of Solsona perfectly. Just outside the city, the tiny hilltop hamlet of **Castellvell** is a favourite with photographers for its beautiful dawn and sunset views, has the remnants of a 10th-century fortress and a small Gothic church.

AROUND SOLSONA: THE SOLSONÈS

On a road map, the area around Solsona looks thoroughly empty, as if it were some rugged mountainous wasteland. It's not quite true. The Solsonès lies just inside the boundaries of 'old Catalunya', the part never conquered by the Moors. Like the Llobregós just to the south, this was a part of the country where medieval feudalism never took root very strongly. So more farmers owned their own land and, instead of living in villages, they had their own homes, or *masies*, scattered around the country.

From almost anywhere in Solsona, you can see **Castellvell**, perched jauntily on a steep hill to the west like a cap that's just a little too small. Once it was bigger. This castle was a stronghold of the Counts of Cardona, long the big shots in this part of Catalunya. Later owners took away most of the stone to build Solsona's walls, but today it serves as a private residence. Further west, the area around **Castellar de la Ribera** was a busy spot in Neolithic times. There are collections of dolmens and a menhir or two south of the village at the **Necròpolis de Clot** and the **Necròpolis de Llor**. There are more dolmens south of Solsona around Llobera, along with a **marker for the geographical centre of Catalunya**, near Pinós, and the rural **Santuari del Miracle**, built in the early 16th century after an apparition of the Virgin Mary.

Just outside Solsona to the east, **Olius** has an interesting Romanesque church, **Sant Esteve**, with a crypt, as well as a real oddity, the only entirely **Modernista cemetery**, designed in 1916 by Bernardí Martorell. Built simply, mostly from rough stone, the construction still shows Gaudíesque steeples and parabolic arches. Further east, there are a number of plain Romanesque churches around **Navès** and further north along the **Riu d'Ora**. They have some rustic charm; the best perhaps is **Sant Pere de Graudescales**, at the northern end of the river in the **Vall de Lord**.

This is a long east–west transverse valley, and, if you're coming from the south, it's about here that you really feel you're in the Pyrenees (and the highest peaks are always on the horizon to remind you). The valley won't trouble you with sightseeing, but the scenery is grand. Just west, is the small, family-friendly ski station of **Port del Comte** (℡ 973 49 23 01; w portdelcomte.net).

CARDONA They won't soon be running out of salt in Cardona. They've been mining the stuff since before the Romans came, for at least 3,500 years in fact, and there's still well over a cubic kilometre left, neatly piled up in a place just outside town called, straightforwardly enough, the **Muntanya de Sal**. In the 8th century AD, the owner of the land was Louis of Aquitaine, and he began Cardona's famous castle to protect his lucrative property.

As for the town itself, Cardona is one of the few in this country to have a birthday, celebrated each year on 23 April. On that date, in AD986, Count Borrell II issued its Carta de Poblament, one of the first such charters given. Throughout the Middle Ages, Cardona was the headquarters of one of the wealthiest noble families of Spain. The Osonas were Counts of Cardona (later Viscounts, later Dukes) and owners of 21 other castles, literally hundreds of villages and a score of towns. It is estimated that they owned 6% of everything in medieval Catalunya. You can go a long way on salt. The town that grew up around their castle became wealthy too, as capital from salt went to build thriving mercantile houses and businesses.

Nothing lasts forever, and despite its inexhaustible resource Cardona was already declining in the 1650s when the Osonas packed up and moved to a more modern lifestyle in Barcelona. Their castle stayed behind to distinguish itself in the War of the Spanish Succession, when it was the last redoubt in Catalunya to fall to the Bourbons. It kept Napoleon's men out in 1806, too. You wouldn't guess Cardona was a town of salt miners. Like Solsona, it is a lovely place, with a dignified air to it. And like Solsona it has a lovely square at its centre, **Plaça de la Fira**. Underneath the arches on the edge is the **Centre Cardona Medieval** (C/ de la Fira 1; ℡ 938 68 49 12; w cardonaturisme.cat; ⊕ 10.00–14.00 Sat & 11.00–15.00 Sun; free). Here you can see exhibits and an audiovisual show on the town's historic centre. Also on the plaça is the church of Cardona's medieval merchants, the **Sant Miquel** (C/ Flors 2; ℡ 938 69 10 45; w bisbatsolsona.cat/parroquies/cardona; ⊕ mass only; free).

Castell de Cardona (Castell de Cardona; ℡ 938 68 41 69; w patrimoni.gencat.cat/en/monuments/monuments/cardona-castle; ⊕ Jun–Sep 10.00–19.30 daily & Oct–May 10.00–17.30 daily; adult/reduced/under 16 €5/3/free) Cardona's real landmark is its castle, which stands out like a beacon above the surrounding hills, visible for miles around. Part of the castle is a parador (page 292); the rest is open for visits. In form, it's everything that Hollywood would expect of a castle, and more than a few films have been shot here (notably Orson Welles' great but seldom-seen *Chimes at Midnight*). If it seems gloomy from a distance, it's only the colour of the local stone.

There was already some kind of a fortress here in AD798, when Louis the Pious, son of Charlemagne, occupied it. Much of what you see now was begun c986,

8

possibly by Wilfred the Hairy himself. One feature gives away its early date, the Torre de la Minyona, a round defence tower like those in the frontier settlements of the Llobregós. The real surprise is that this castle contains not just a simple chapel but a nearly cathedral-sized church, one of the important works of the early Catalan Romanesque.

The **Col·legiata de Sant Vicenç** (part of the castle visit), consecrated in 1040, says a lot about the ethos of the frontier. It was built to impress, in its size and muscular strength but also in its militant austerity. Outside of the Lombard arcading on the exterior and the eight-sided cupola (one of the first of this Catalan tradition) there is hardly a bit of decoration inside or out. The majestic nave once had frescoes, but the surviving fragments of these are now in Barcelona's MNAC museum. An unusual feature is the raised altar, with steps down to the crypt underneath, a plan often seen in central Italian churches.

A World of Salt Over the centuries Cardona did everything with its salt but make it into a tourist attraction, and now it's managed that, too. The village centre has a couple of shops where you can take home a salt sculpture curio. The **Museu de la Sal Josep Arnau** (Pl de Santa Eulàlia 11–13; \938 69 08 58; w museodelasal. com; ⏰ 11.00–13.30 & 17.00–19.45 Tue–Wed & Fri–Sat, 11.00–13.30 Sun; adult/reduced/under 16 €4/3/free) is a family-run tribute to one of the most devoted mad artists; if you've never seen a perfectly lifelike plate of eggs and sausages carved in salt before, this is the place to find them.

For something a little more didactic, come to the **Parc Cultural de la Muntanya de Sal** (Ctra de la Mina s/n; \938 69 24 75; w cardonaturisme.cat/en/activitats/guided-tour-to-the-salt-mountain; ⏰ 10.00–14.00 Tue–Sun; adult/reduced/children 5–11/children 2–4/under 2 €12.50/10/6/3/free), right in the working mine area, and you'll learn everything about the history of salt and salt mining, and then they'll take you down into the underground part of the mines, through salt galleries hung with salt stalactites and stalagmites – as impressive as a good limestone cave.

THE HIGH PYRENEES

When the Bourbon Philip V ascended to the Spanish throne, his grandfather Louis XIV haughtily declared (according to Voltaire): 'Il n'y a plus de Pyrénées!' History, of course, proved him sadly deluded, although these great mountains have, of late, suffered a good deal of mental erosion as Spain takes its place as an equal partner in Europe. Yet the difference between the French and Spanish Pyrenees is striking. The former are rugged, and often forbidding, and even at the beginning of March there can be a blinding whiteout of snow, while, to the south, green valleys bask in the sun; the mountains are gentler, their aspect more benign.

In the Alt Pirineu, as these mountains are called in Catalan, think in terms of valleys. That is the natural unit of geography here. As they get closer to the mountains, the two big river valleys, the Noguera and the Segre, split off like the branches on a tree. The easternmost, the Vall del Segre, takes you to La Seu d'Urgell with its famous cathedral, and then to the odd little mountaintop hypermarket called Andorra. The Noguera Pallaresa branch splits off into many smaller ones, each with a personality of its own: the Vall de Cardós, well known to Nordic skiiers, and the Vall d'Àneu and Vall d'Asil, charming and remote, where the old traditional life of the Pyrenees still hangs on.

Further west there's the Vall d'Aran, a little bit of Gascon France that got away, and the Vall de Boí, with its world-famous Romanesque churches. In fact there are lovely medieval churches everywhere in these valleys, a testament to their greatest period of prosperity. Not much has happened here since; lately, almost all of these valleys have seen dramatic drops in population, as young people scarper off for opportunities they can't get at home. That leaves the place pretty much to the hikers and skiers, the eagles and the lizards.

Like so many other corners of Europe's mountains, this one is trying to make a future for itself in nature tourism. It has a lot to offer. Outside of Andorra, prices can be delightfully inexpensive, and the scenery is wonderful in and around the two big parks, the Parc Natural d'Alt Pirineu (comprising the tops of the Pyrenees along the French border), and the Parc Nacional d'Aigüestortes i Estany de Sant Maurici, a gorgeous region of forests and mountain lakes.

GETTING THERE AND AROUND With flights to Madrid and Palma de Mallorca, **Andorra-La Seu d'Urgell Airport** (w aeroportandorralaseu.cat) is located 7km southwest of La Seu d'Urgell and 17km from Andorra (linked by a free shuttle).

There is no train service up here, and you shouldn't expect even the buses to be much help in the mountains. The main roads will usually have only one or two a day, as from Lleida up the Noguera Ribagorça Valley to Pont de Sort and Vielha, or Lleida up the C26 to Solsona and Seu d'Urgell, or from Barcelona up through Solsona to La Seu and Andorra. And where there are buses to the villages, they'll usually be timed to get kids to school and back. The main operator in these parts is Alsa (📞 910 20 70 07; w alsa.es), which also runs express services from La Seu d'Urgell to Barcelona. Hife (📞 977 44 03 00; w hife.es) operates buses between La Seu d'Urgell and Andorra.

TOURIST INFORMATION The excellent tourist information office in La Seu d'Urgell is right in the centre of the old town (C/ Major 8; 📞 973 35 15 11; w turismeseu.com). For information on the many outdoor activities in the region – hiking, climbing, mountain biking and more – see their useful website, w pirineuoutdoor.com.

🏠 WHERE TO STAY

El Castell Ctra Puigcerdà, Castellciutat; 📞 973 35 00 00; w hotelelcastell.com. Just outside La Seu d'Urgell, an elegant modern building of wood & stone, underneath the ruins of the old castle at the entrance to the town. There's a pool with a spectacular view, sumptuously decorated rooms, & a beauty & wellness spa where they whisper of exotic pamperings involving fruits & chocolate. 2 resolutely trendy restaurants (€€ & €€€) share one of Catalunya's best wine cellars. You can try such delights as black ravioli flavoured with cuttlefish ink & stuffed with lobster. **€€€**

Andria Pg Brudieu 24, La Seu d'Urgell; 📞 973 35 03 00; w hotelandria.com. Small & central, with a pretty courtyard; 15 comfortable & prettily decorated rooms. The restaurant (€€€) is excellent, with bits of truffle & foie gras & wild mushrooms

everywhere (but note it must be reserved in advance). They raise their own chickens. **€€**

✳ **Cal Serni** Barri Poble Sec, Calbinyà; 📞 973 35 28 09; w calserni.com. In a tiny village just north of La Seu, this beautiful rural hotel has 4 lovely rooms & 6 apartments, plus a garden with pool. You can enjoy their wonderful home cooking (they use their own produce as much as possible). **€€**

Hotelet Estamariu Cal Teixidor C/ Soldevila 33, Estamariu; 📞 973 35 45 11; w hoteletestamariu.com. Utterly charming little country hotel, with a handful of beautifully designed, simple rooms in a miniature village. The restaurant, Llobarca (€€€), is excellent & it's the perfect base for hiking. **€€**

Parador Nacional de la Seu d'Urgell C/ Sant Domènec 6, La Seu d'Urgell; 📞 973 35 20 00;

8

w paradores.es/en/parador-de-la-seu-durgell. Situated in what's left of the old quarter: built around a Renaissance cloister filled with plants, this has a heated pool, modern & comfortable rooms, & a restaurant (€€€) that puts a refined twist on traditional mountain dishes. €€

✕ WHERE TO EAT AND DRINK

Lo Paller del Coc Lo Paller del Coc s/n, Surp; 690 80 52 96; w lopallerdelcoc.com. A gorgeous country house in a tiny village makes a handsome setting for this outstanding restaurant. There's no menu here: everyone is served the same extraordinary contemporary Catalan dishes, prepared with whatever is in season & all exquisitely presented. Expect to pay around €60–80 pp for cuisine that you won't forget in a hurry. It also has 3 lovely little apartments (€€) for 2–4 people. €€€€€

Cal Pacho C/ de la Font 11; 649 85 65 81; ⓕ restaurantecalpacho. A long-time local favourite in the old city centre for classic roasts & grills. €€

El Menjador C/ Major 4, La Seu d'Urgell; 612 43 28 60; ⏲ 13.00–15.00 Thu & Sun, 13.00–15.00 & 20.30–22.00 Fri–Sat. This pretty, welcoming restaurant serves up delicious Catalan & Mediterranean specialities, including *canelones de rostit* & excellent *patates braves*. €€

El Rastell Pl Jacint Verdaguer, 2, La Seu d'Urgell; 873 45 13 03; w elrastell.restaurant; ⏲ 13.30–15.30 Mon–Tue, Thu & Sun, 13.30–15.30 & 20.00–22.30 Fri–Sat. A wonderful, family-run 'slow food' restaurant where you'll find all the Catalan favourites – roast lamb, *canelones* with *botifarra negra* (black sausage), prepared with locally sourced produce. €€

SPORTS AND ACTIVITIES

Skiing Some 20km west of La Seu d'Urgell, **Sant Joan de l'Erm** (Montferrer Castellbo; 973 29 80 15; w santjoandelerm.com) is Catalunya's largest resort for cross-country (Nordic) skiing, with 40km of very pretty courses.

Watersports and rafting At the Parc Olímpic del Segre – the 1992 Olympic facilities on the Segre Canal – you can follow the Olympic canoe and kayak course, or try other watersports including rafting, hydrospeed, open-kayak and paddle surf. More info at w parcolimpicdelsegre.cat.

LA SEU D'URGELL La Seu, the 'See' of the mighty bishops of Urgell, once played as big a role in Catalan history as Barcelona itself. Those days are long gone, but La Seu is still the biggest town in the Catalan Pyrenees (population 12,200) and an urbane and agreeable base for seeing the Cerdanya (page 222), the Serra del Cadí (page 221) and the rest of this stretch of the mountains.

La Seu existed in Roman times, and seems to have been doing well even while the rest of the Roman world was falling apart. The first cathedral here was begun in the early 6th century AD. In 793 Arab armies destroyed the town, but thanks to the intervention of Charlemagne it was soon on the up again. From here, the bishops' wealth and power increased steadily, alongside that of the Counts of Urgell. They got along fine; in fact through much of the Middle Ages the two positions were usually held by the same family.

La Seu d'Urgell became the power centre from which Christian armies set off to chip away at the boundaries of al-Andalus. Its success, however, was to be its bad luck. The conquest of 'New Catalunya' had tripled the size of the county, and in 1105 the Counts moved their capital down to the plains, to Lleida. La Seu has been the back of beyond ever since – though its bishops still get to be co-princes of Andorra.

Cathedral (Pl del Deganat 16; 973 35 32 42; w museucatedralseudurgell.org; ⏲ Jun–Sep 10.00–13.30 & 16.00–19.00 Tue–Sat, Oct–May 10.00–13.30 & 16.00–18.00 Tue–Sat; adult/reduced/under 18 €4/3/free) La Seu d'Urgell's glory days have left it a tremendous Romanesque cathedral, one of the greatest in Spain. Old as it is, it is at least the third church to occupy the site. The first was from Carolingian times; next, St Ermengol, one of the great medieval bishops, began a reconstruction in 1010. Finally, came the work you see today, begun in 1184 in the Lombard Romanesque style. On the façade, the sculptural decoration is concentrated on a narrow band at the centre; lacking a square to show it off, the designers had to create an imposing view down a narrow street, much as it appears today. The decoration is fanciful enough, with pairs of lions, a pentagle, a mermaid and much more. The builders put more effort into the back than the front, a peculiarity the cathedral shares with many others that were going up at the time, such as Toulouse, Tours or Santiago de Compostela. Like these, the highlight is a beautiful colonnade of twinned columns running around the apse.

The first sight of the **interior** will be a surprise, heightened by the incense and piped-in music. The peculiar little façade gives no idea how big and imposing the cathedral really is. Dark and strong and tall, it has the air of a real national shrine, built before Catalunya was even really a nation. The **cloister**, rough and strange even by mountain Romanesque standards, has some vigorous sculpture on its dark granite capitals, including some beasts that look a lot like the winged monkeys from Oz.

From the cloister there is an entrance to the Museu Diocesà d'Urgell, one of the great hoards of medieval Catalan art. The prize exhibit is a brilliantly coloured, outlandishly stylised copy of one of Spain's greatest illuminated books, Beatus de Liébana's 10th-century *Apocalypse*. There's a fine altarpiece by Pere Serra and an entire set of 12th-century frescoes from Baltarga where everyone looks terribly sad. There are plenty of retables and other wood carvings from the Middle Ages through the Renaissance and Baroque, including a whole room of *Mares de Déu* from village churches. It's a little depressing to see all these once-beloved icons taken away from the villages where they were worshipped for centuries and lined up here in a museum; one wonders what they all talk about when the lights are out and the tourists have gone home. St Ermengol, the bishop who built the cathedral, gets a completely over-the-top gold and silver sarcophagus from 1735.

Around La Seu There isn't much else in La Seu, although a walk around the old arcaded streets of the centre is fun. Just around the corner from the cathedral on Carrer Major, you can see the old 16th-century *mesures de la bladeria* (grain measures) built into the walls. The medieval centre meets the newer side of town at **Passeig Joan Brudieu**, a rather gorgeous rambla lined with a superb avenue of plane trees – they look like the ones Van Gogh painted in Arles.

At the western edge of town, there's the pretty **Parc de la Valira** along a stream. Walk over here to see the little **cloister**, a copy of the cathedral cloister designed by Catalan writer Lluís Racionero, a La Seu native; the capitals on the cloister's columns, instead of saints and angels, have the faces of 20th-century celebrities, from Stalin and Hitler to Picasso, Groucho Marx and Marilyn Monroe.

On the other side of town, along the Segre, the **Parc Olímpic del Segre** was the venue of the Olympic canoeing and kayaking events in 1992. If you ever wanted to try out something non-fatal and non-embarrassing on a real Olympic course, here's your chance.

Just south, the ruined 18th-century fort at **Castellciutat** stands on a height, built over the original Iberian and Roman settlements of La Seu. More fine scenery waits further south, through the **Congost de Tresponts** (also called 'de Organyà') a narrow, 600m walled gorge formed by the River Segre, now dammed into a long lake. An

8

excursion into the hills west of **Organyà** is especially popular with cyclists: ask the tourist office for a map of the '**Ruta de las Dolmenes**'. It takes in seven dolmens, along with a couple of early-medieval churches and a medieval aqueduct, all strung along the road to **Cabó**. Up at the end there's a pretty mountain plain called the **Prat Muntaner**, and woods full of mushroom hunters.

Further south, **Coll de Nargó** on the Segre has one of the most interesting, and oldest, Romanesque parish churches in the area. The builders of the 10th-century Sant Climent apparently weren't too convinced of their ability to make a belltower; it's so much thicker at the bottom, it looks like it's melting. There's more noteworthy Romanesque in the villages north of La Seu. Just outside town at **Anserall**, the imposing remains of **Sant Serni de Tavernoles** mark what was an important monastic church begun in Saint Ermengol's day. Further north, at **Ars** near the Andorra border, the 11th-century **Sant Martí** has a charming circular campanile.

WEST OF LA SEU D'URGELL: THE VALL DE NOGUERA PALLARESA

The Vall de Noguera Pallaresa is a long, winding valley carved out by the most powerful of the region's rivers. It stretches from the lower slopes of the high mountains down toward Lleida, slicing through deep gorges and meadows, past glacial cirques and Romanesque churches. It's the Alt Pirineu at its most dramatic.

In spring and summer, the river swells with meltwater, surging through a string of reservoirs and hydro-electric weirs that release torrents into the valley. From the Pantà de la Torrassa above Esterri d'Àneu down to the vast Pantà de Sant Antoni near Tremp, the Noguera Pallaresa is a playground for wild watersports, drawing thrill-seekers from all over the world.

Above the river, medieval villages dotted with tiny Romanesque churches cling to cliffs. Roads twist and climb into side valleys – the Vall de Cardós and the Vall d'Àneu among them – which fill with Nordic skiers every winter, while the higher peaks offer skiing and snowshoeing.

Historically isolated, this region was long neglected and underdeveloped – one of the last places in Spain to get TV, and among the first to lose its railway line. Now it has reinvented itself as a hub for adventure and nature-based tourism, anchored by hospitable little towns like Sort, Rialp and Esterri d'Àneu.

TOURIST INFORMATION There are tourist information offices in all the larger towns and villages, including Sort, which doubles as the Pallars Sobirà regional information office, (Camí de la Cabanera s/n; 973 62 10 02; w turisme.pallarssobira.cat), Rialp (Pl del Tornal 1; 973 62 10 02; w turisrialp.cat) and Esterri d'Àneu (C/ Major 40; 973 62 63 45; w esterrianeu.cat).

WHERE TO STAY
Casa Leonardo Hotel Eco Boutique C/ La Bedoga 2, Senterada; 973 66 17 87; w casaleonardo.net. An enchanting little *casa rural*, with 8 individually decorated rooms, & delicious home cooking prepared according to time-honoured local recipes. They run all kinds of wonderful activities, from mushroom hunting to hikes with stops at local cheese producers. €€

Casa Palmira C/ Peguera 3, Espot; 973 08 30 20; w hostalpalmira.com. A less expensive choice, with just 7 immaculate rooms, a cosy restaurant (€€), & delightful staff who are full of great tips on local activities. €€

Castellarnau Avda Burgal 1, Escaló; 973 62 20 63; w hotelcastellarnau.com. A large, comfortable modern hotel in this pretty village, with a shady garden & terrace by the river. Amenities include pool, mini-golf, gym & sauna, & a good restaurant (€€) too. **€€**

Els Avets Port de la Bonaigua, Sorpe; 973 62 63 55; w elsavets.com. A large hotel in splendid isolation up near the Port de la Bonaigua, the pass into the Vall d'Aran. Simple but comfortable rooms, a restaurant (€€), garden with small pool, & a free shuttle to the ski station at Baqueira-Beret. **€€**

✳ **Hotel Roca Blanca** C/ Església s/n, Espot; 973 62 41 56; w hotelrocablanca.com. A modern hotel, built of traditional stone & wood in classic mountain style, this is an excellent choice. The interior is elegant & stylish, with 16 spacious & well-equipped rooms, & it offers all kinds of amenities including a Japanese-style area with outdoor Jacuzzi, plus a small sauna & gym. A host of activities is available, from skiing in winter to hiking or white-water rafting in summer. The staff are utterly delightful. **€€**

Hostal Vall d'Aneu C/ Major 46, Esterri d'Aneu; 973 62 60 97; w hostalvalldaneu.com. Set in a characterful stone building, this mid-sized hotel has spacious, well-equipped rooms & a restaurant (€€) that serves grilled trout or pheasant or boar stew. They'll be happy to set you up for riding, rafting & other activities. **€€**

Pessets C/ Diputació 3, Sort; 973 62 00 00; w hotelpessets.com. Modern & comfortable mid-sized hotel, with a pool, garden & small spa (including a Jacuzzi for relaxing after a day on the pistes). The restaurant (€€) serves delicious local cuisine. **€€**

Les Brases Avda Generalitat 27, Sort; 973 62 10 71; w hotellesbrases.com/en . A solid hotel overlooking the river, with 27 comfortable rooms, & a restaurant (€€) serving grilled meats & fish, as well as a few pizzas. **€**

Or Blanc Ctra Barrader, Espot; 973 62 40 13; w hotelorblanc.com. The bizarre modern architecture may make you laugh, cry, or both, but this still offers quite a good bargain in a lovely setting. Basically a large ski hotel at the foot of the Espot lifts, but staff will point you towards rafting, riding & just about every other activity imaginable. There's a pool & gardens, & a decent restaurant (€€). **€**

Roya C/ Sant Maurici 1, Espot; 973 62 40 40; w hotelroya.net. A small, comfortable modern hotel in a scenic location on the edge of town with a good, reasonable restaurant (€€). Friendly & family run. **€**

Saurat C/ Sant Martí, Espot; 973 62 41 62; w hotelsaurat.com. A very comfortable, mid-sized hotel built in traditional stone, with attractively decorated rooms, a lovely garden & a popular restaurant (€€). **€**

✕ **WHERE TO EAT AND DRINK** Most of the restaurants in this area are located in hotels (see opposite), which are almost always very good.

Fogony Avda Generalitat 45, Sort; 973 62 12 25; w fogony.com; ⏱ 13.30–15.00 Wed–Thu & Sun, 13.30–15.00 & 20.30–22.00 Fri–Sat. One of the most interesting restaurants in this part of the mountains, with a Michelin star among its many accolades; choose from the 'Km0' menu (€55) which showcases the excellent local produce at its finest or the 9-course Confiança tasting menu (€99). **€€€€€**

Els Puis C/ Dr Morelló 13, Esterri d'Aneu; 973 62 61 60; w hotelelspuis.com. A fine restaurant where you'll find classic mountain dishes, such as *palpís*, a slow-cooked lamb stew from the Pallars. It also has a handful of attractive rooms (€). **€€**

SPORTS AND ACTIVITIES This region is outstanding for pretty much any outdoor activity that you can imagine, with a host of local tour providers. **White-water rafting** is one of the biggest sports in the region, with Sort and Llavorsí the main bases for renting equipment. It's also a top destination for **canyoning** and most tour providers will offer both.

RocRoi C/ Hort de Rei s/n, C13 km 140, Llavorsí; 973 62 20 35; w rocroi.com. This company offers a host of outdoor activities including rafting, canyoning, kayaking, climbing & hiking trips, with options for all levels.

8

La Rafting Company Pl Caterina Albert, Sort; ☎973 62 14 62; w laraftingcompany.com. Rafting (from family-friendly trips to full-day guided excursions for the experienced), canyoning, kayaking, climbing & via ferratas, horseriding & mountain biking.

Skiing

Although most popular for winter sports, the ski resorts also open in summer for activities such as hiking, nature tours, riding, mountain biking and more. Check their websites for details.

Port-Ainé ☎973 62 03 25; w portaine. cat. Up in the hills above Rialp, with 8 lifts & 33km of downhill pistes plus 15km of Nordic trails.
Tavascan ☎973 62 30 79; w tavascan.net. Up at the northern end of the Vall de Cardós, this is a Nordic ski area with a small snowpark for younger kids, 5 runs & 1 lift.
Espot Esquí ☎973 62 40 48; w espotesqui.cat. Near Aigüestortes National Park, offering 25km of pistes, 14 lifts, & modest lodgings in the town of Espot.

SORT AND AROUND

From La Seu, the only way to get over to the next valley west, the Vall de Noguera Pallaresa, is over the twisty but beautiful N260, which will leave you in **Sort**. The capital of Catalunya's biggest and emptiest comarca, the Pallars Sobirà, Sort means 'luck' in Catalan, and the town is famous as a place to buy lottery tickets, although fortune hasn't left it a lot to offer visitors outside of a ruined **castle**. You can discover more about the perilous journeys that as many as 80,000 refugees fleeing the Nazis took across the mountains at the little museum of the **Camí de la Llibertat** (Freedom Trail) (Pl de Sant Eloi; ☎679 795 616; w camidelallibertat.sort. cat; ⊕ late-Jun–mid-Sep 18.00–20.00 Tue–Fri, noon–14.00 & 18.00–20.00 Sat–Sun, rest of the year noon–14.00 & 18.00–20.00 Sat, noon–14.00 Sun; adult/reduced/under 8 €3/2/free), set in the old prison where many of them would be handed over to Franco's troops.

South of Sort, the very picturesque village of **Gerri de la Sal** has the Romanesque monastery church of Santa Maria and something you've never seen before: salt pans that aren't on the seashore. A salty source fills them up, just as it has done for at least 1,200 years, and the enormous Reial Alfolí, or Royal Salt Storehouse, still stands on the Plaça Major and has been converted into a **Museu del Sal** (Pl Àngel Esteve 10; ☎630 05 61 38; w museudegerri.cat; ⊕ changes monthly, see website for details; adult/reduced/under 7 €4/3/free), which also organises tours of the salt pans. North of Sort is **Rialp**, a lively tourist centre for mountain activities.

VALL DE LLESSUI

From here a road to the left leads up to a cluster of villages in the Vall de Llessui. At the top of the valley, **Llessui** has become something of a legend for its ski station, abandoned since 1987 along with its shops, lifts and hotel-restaurant. It's an eerie place to visit but, even so, it still draws plenty of cross-country skiers. Llessui now seeks to draw on its traditional life with the **Ecomuseu dels Pastors de la Vall d'Àssua** (C/ Llessui Poble 141; ☎973 62 17 98 w turisme.sort. cat/fitxes/ecomuseu-pastors; ⊕ 09.00–14.00 & 15.30–17.45 Mon–Sat, 09.00–14.00 Sun; adult/reduced/under 8 €5/3/free), where you can learn everything about shepherding, ancient and modern, witches and local legends. The next village up the valley, **Llavorsí** where the Noguera Pallaresa Valley and the Vall de Cardós split off, attracts sporty tourists.

VALL DE CORDÓS

This is a beautiful, heavily forested 20km dead end, though if you had a mule and a couple of days to spare you could make it over to France or Andorra on the old smugglers' trails. At **Esterri de Cardós** the church of **Sant**

Pau i Sant Pere has a wonderful apse painting of Christ Pantocrator (a copy, but still worth seeing). The Vall de Cardós road ends at **Tavascán**, where there's a little ski station, but this area is more popular with cross-country skiers, snowboarders and hikers. From here you can reach a number of mountain lakes, including the **Estany de Certescans**, the biggest in the Pyrenees. One of the most remarkable things about Tavascán is the **Complex Hidràulic del Alt Cardós** (C/ Unic; \973 62 30 79; w tavascan.net/apres-ski/central-hidroelectrica; ⏱ check website for times of guided visits; adult/reduced €7/4, under 5 not admitted) an enormous hydro-electric plant built in caverns under the mountains, begun in 1958.

VALL D'ÀNEU The northernmost stretch of the Noguera Pallaresa, the Vall d'Àneu is almost as well-endowed with Romanesque art as the famous Vall de Boí, a tribute to the relative wealth and sophistication of these remote mountain villages at the dawning of the Middle Ages. Many of the churches are ruined or altered, and the medieval paintings survive only in fragments, but these monuments are often in lovely settings and worth a detour.

North of Sort, beyond Llavorsí, there are two good ones above the C13 valley road. To the east, there's the church of **Santa Maria at Ribera de Cardós**; on the other side, at **Baiasca**, there's **Sant Serni** with a spectacular, if fragmentary, Christ Pantocrator painted in the apse. **Escaló**, with its old stone houses and wooden balconies, is one of the most attractive villages in this part of the Pyrenees. Above the village, a steep but lovely 25-minute walk brings you to the 11th-century Benedictine monastery of **Sant Pere de Burgal**, which enjoyed the patronage of Llúcia de la Marca, countess of the Pallars Sobirà (and possibly of Urgell), and her image appears in the exceptional murals in the apse (the originals are in Barcelona's MNAC), attributed to the Mestre de Pedret (page 219). To the north, the artificial lake at **Mollera d'Escalarre** has already become a favoured spot for cormorants and other waterfowl, as well as for kayaking and fishing.

Esterri d'Àneu is the valley's biggest village. Esterri, like many of the place names in these parts, is a Basque word, meaning 'stone wall'. Long before there was such a thing as Catalans, the Basques occupied almost all of the Pyrenees. Esterri has a 12th-century **bridge**, the Romanesque **Santa Maria** with a fascinating carved font inside, and the **Ecomuseu de les Valls d'Àneu** (C/ del Camp 22; \973 62 64 36; w ecomuseu.com (Catalan and Spanish only); ⏱ 11.00–14.00 & 17.00–20.00 Tue–Sat, noon–14.00 Sun; adult/reduced/under 9 €5/4/free), dedicated to researching and explaining facets of traditional life in the Pyrenees. Its main sight is the **Casa Gassia**, an 18th-century farmhouse restored and furnished to something like its original appearance, but the Ecomuseu tries to be a kind of open-air museum that takes in other sites, offering tours of each. These include a Romanesque **church and comunidor at Son**, the monastery at **Escaló**, as well as a hydro-electric power station and a water-powered **sawmill**.

One road from the Vall d'Àneu leads up to the pristine wilderness of the **Parc Nacional d'Aigüestortes i Estany de Sant Maurici** (page 308); the paved part ends at **Espot**. Many people visit the park from the other side, in the Vall de Boí, but Espot too has an entrance, with an information centre, the **Casa del Parc Nacional**. Up above the village there is a small, inexpensive ski station, Espot Esquí. After Esterri, you have a choice of heading into the Vall d'Aran (page 308), or straight north into the mountains, along the short but scenic Vall d'Isil.

VALL D'ISIL At the main village, **Isil**, the lovely church of **Sant Joan** has a Romanesque apse and a charming setting on the bank of a rushing stream. Although

8

FUR REAL: THE RETURN OF THE BROWN BEAR

Once common across the Pyrenees, there were fewer than five brown bears left in these mountains by the 1990s. Since then, Slovenian bears, which are genetically similar to their Pyrenean cousins, have been introduced to the Val d'Aran, the Alt Àneu and the Bosc de Bonabé near Isil and now there are about 100 wild bears across the Pyrenees, including around 50 in Catalunya. You can find out all about the conservation efforts at the wonderful **Casa de l'Ós Bru dels Pirineus** in Isil (C/ del Pont 7, Isil; ☏ 973 08 30 44; w casaosbrupirineus. cat; ⏱ check website; €5/3).

it may have only about 50 inhabitants, Isil is famous throughout Catalunya for its summer solstice festival – the feast of Sant Joan – called *Les Falles*. Solstice bonfires are still common all over Catalunya, with the holy fire being brought every 23 June from the Catalan holy mountain Canigó (Canigou in French; page 358). Here in Isil, they continue a tradition from the old days, when the boys of the town bring pine logs down from the mountains a month ahead, and are rewarded by the girls with a rose and a pitcher of wine for each.

The Vall d'Àneu and the paved road go only as far north as **Alós d'Isil**, surrounded by towering mountains up by the French border. It has another of those wonderful high-arched medieval bridges, and a church of Sant Lliser with some remarkable survivals from the original 12th-century building, a sculpted portal and three fonts inside.

THE VALL DE BOÍ

The Alta Ribagorça is one of the smallest and emptiest comarcas of Catalunya. Its main road isn't even in it; the N230 runs up the Noguera Ribagorçana Valley, the boundary between Catalunya and Aragon, and most of the time it's on the Aragonese side. Most of this comarca is the Vall de Boí. Since it made UNESCO's World Heritage list two decades ago, this valley has become a popular spot; people from all over the world come to see the remote villages whose 12th-century Romanesque churches provided so many of the masterpieces in Barcelona's Museu Nacional d'Art de Catalunya (MNAC, page 119).

The exteriors of these slate-roofed churches and their stout square campaniles with storeys of mullioned windows (a style imported from Lombardy) have been restored, with replicas of their frescoes, offering a chance to see what they were meant to look like in situ.

TOURIST INFORMATION The information centre for the Parc Nacional d'Aigüestortes i Estany de Sant Maurici is in Boí (C/ de les Graireres 2; ☏ 973 69 61 89; w parcsnaturals. gencat.cat/aiguestortes), and has maps, suggestions for hikes, and information on the wide range of activities available. It also arranges the 4x4 taxi service to the start of the main walking trails (private vehicles are not allowed within the park's limits).

The Vall de Boí tourist information office is in Barruera (Pg Sant Feliu 43; ☏ 973 69 40 00 w vallboi.cat), and offers a whole host of information on the local area, including outdoor activities, hiking routes, and more.

The Pont del Suert tourist information office (Avda de Victoriano Muñoz 22; ☏ 973 69 06 40; w visitaelpontdesuert.com) provides information on what to see and do in the town as well as outdoor activities around the region.

⌂ WHERE TO STAY

Boí-Taüll Resort Pla de l'Ermita s/n, Taüll;
☏ 973 69 60 00; w boitaullresort.es. Really an
all-inclusive complex: 4 hotels & aparthotels,
4 restaurants in a variety of styles & prices.
Plenty of sports facilities including a spa & a
pool. €€

Caldes Caldes de Boí; ☏ 973 69 62 20;
w caldesdeboi.com. Huge, 17th-century stone
hospital converted into a pleasant hotel with
spacious rooms. As part of the Caldes spa
complex, you can take the waters & try a host
of treatments. The slightly more upmarket (but
less charming) Manantial is also part of the
complex. €€

El Xalet de Taüll C/ El Como 5, Taüll; ☏ 973
69 60 95; w elxaletdetaull.com. An attractive
mid-sized hotel of wood & stone, perfectly
located in the heart of the old village. All
rooms have beautiful views, but some look out
towards the lofty belltowers of the celebrated
churches. €€

L'Aüt Erill la Vall; ☏ 973 69 60 48; w laut.cat. You'll
get a warm welcome at this charming country
hotel, which has 16 modern rooms, including family
rooms, & a stylish, contemporary restaurant (€€)
serving organic, locally sourced produce. €€

Can Mestre Pl Major 8, Pont de Suert; ☏ 973
69 03 06; w hotelmestre.es. Simple, with 28
traditionally decorated rooms, many with
balconies covered with flowers, on the main
square. €

Casa Coll C/ Major 28, Barruera; ☏ 637 73 89
96; w casacoll.info. A wonderful little B&B in a
lovely stone house with peaceful garden, this has a
handful of traditionally decorated rooms & a small
relaxation zone with Jacuzzi. €

Hotel Pey Pl Treio 4, Boí; ☏ 973 69 60 36;
w hotelpey.com. Right in the middle of the

CHURCHES OF THE VALL DE BOÍ

The **Centre del Romanic de la Vall de Boí** in Erill la Vall has an information
office (Camí del Batalló 5, Erill la Vall; ☏ 973 69 67 15; w centreromanic.com)
which provides information on guided tours (available in English, Catalan,
Spanish and French) and sells admission tickets (which are also available
directly from the churches).

A **single joint admission ticket** (purchase on the website or at the centre)
pays for entrance to either three or five of the main churches: Sant Clement
de Taüll, Santa Maria de Taüll, Sant Joan de Boí, Sant Eulàlia d'Erill, Sant Feliu
de Barruera, Nativitat de Durro, Santa Maria de Cardet, Assumpció de Cóll,
Sant Quirc de Durro.

Three churches (Sant Clement de Taüll, including the mapping) plus two
more of your choice: adult/reduced/under 10 €7/5/free.

Five churches (Sant Clement de Taüll, including the mapping) plus four
more of your choice: adult/reduced/under 10 €10/8/free.

The **mapping** (an audiovisual projected on the walls of Sant Clement de
Taüll) takes place at: ⏰ 10.15, 11.00, noon, 12.45, 13.30, 16.15, 17.00, 17.45
and 18.30 (Jul–Aug also 19.00 & 19.30).

Opening hours are as follows:

**Sant Clement de Taüll, Sant Joan
de Boí, Sant Eulàlia d'Erill**
⏰ 10.00–14.00 & 16.00–19.00 (Jul–
Aug until 20.00) daily
Santa Maria de Taüll ⏰ 10.00–
19.00 (Jul–Aug until 20.00) daily
Sant Feliu de Barruera
⏰ 10.00–14.00 daily

Nativitat de Durro
⏰ 16.00–19.00 daily
**Santa Maria de Cardet, Assumpció
de Cóll, Sant Quirc de Durro**
⏰ summer daily (ask for specific
hours at the info centre)

8

village, this is a top choice if you're on a budget; 35 cosy rooms (with or without bath) plus a popular

restaurant (€€) with tasty home cooking (HB is also available). €

✕ WHERE TO EAT AND DRINK

El Ventador Pg Sant Feliu 49, Barruera; 📞661 86 34 00; w elventador.com; ⏱ 13.00–15.30 Wed, 13.00–15.30 & 20.00–22.00 Thu–Sun. For creative cuisine based on the best local produce, come to this stylish yet relaxed modern restaurant; choose from à la carte options (main dishes €15–25) or go for the wonderful tasting menu (€60). €€€

El Fai C/ Aiguals 10, Taüll; 📞973 69 62 01; w restaurantelfai.com; ⏱ 13.30–16.30 Mon–Tue & Sun, 13.30–16.30 & 20.30–22.30 Thu–Sat.

Cheerful, colourful restaurant with delicious local dishes, including wonderful canelones with wild mushrooms, one of the house specialities along with organic, locally reared beef & *cargols a la llauna*. €€

La Granja C/ Santa Eulàlia 1, Erill la Vall; 📞973 69 63 22; w lagranjaderill.com; ⏱ 13.30–21.00 Fri–Sun. A delightfully old-fashioned country restaurant, where meat & fish cooked to perfection on a wood-fired grill is the house speciality. €€

SPORTS AND ACTIVITIES This mountain region is paradise for outdoor enthusiasts. From hiking and paragliding to fishing and skiing, there's a wealth of activities available all year round. You'll find more info on the activities available at w vallboi.cat/en/vall-de-boi.

The Aigüestortes National Park has some spectacular **hikes**, from simple family-friendly walks to mountain lakes to multi-day loops for the experienced. If you want to spend the night at one of the *refugis*, book in advance at w refusonline. com. ECEM (📞636 63 26 38; w ecemescolademuntanya.com) runs guided hikes and mountaineering trips into the park.

Pont de Suert is the main base for **watersports** like rafting and kayaking.

For **skiing**, Boí-Taüll (📞973 29 70 85; w boitaull.cat) is a small, pretty resort overlooking the Boí valley, with 43 runs, four cross-country routes and a toboggan run.

RocRoi 📞973 62 20 35; w rocroi.com. Offers rafting, canyoning, kayak trips on the Escales

reservoir, via ferrata, climbing & guided hikes into Aigüestortes.

WHAT TO SEE AND DO The gateway into the Vall de Boí, and the only place of any size in the Alta Ribagorça, is **Pont de Suert**, a laid-back, well-worn, attractive old town with houses over stone porticoes and a little park along the riverfront. The best thing about Pont de Suert is probably its parish church, the **Església de la Asunció**, built in 1955 in a kind of interplanetary Modernista style, with an egg-shaped baptistry, painted bright green, and an equally peculiar detached belltower. It's beautiful in its way. At least, the locals think so; in the shops you can buy a model of it inside a snow globe. The church was built by the electric company ENHER, which had brought so many new people to town with its dam-building that the old one was no longer big enough. This church, called the **Església Vell**, now holds a museum of art from other local churches, the **Col·lecció d'Art Sacre de la Ribagorça** (Avda Victoriano Muñoz 27; 📞973 69 06 40; w visitaelpontdesuert.com/art-sacre; ⏱ guided visits organised by the tourist office; free), including some good medieval carvings and Baroque retables.

The turning for the Vall de Boí lies just north of Pont de Suert, at **Castello del Tor**, where a pretty medieval stone bridge helps sets the mood. The churches are opened for visitors by the **Centre del Romanic de la Vall de Boí**, which has an information office in Erill la Vall (page 305). Interestingly, there is no evidence that anyone ever lived in this valley before the Dark Ages, when Christians fled here to escape the Moorish invasions and settled down.

Plenty of other Pyrenean valleys have Romanesque churches, but these are a bit special. The story goes that a Count of Erill was one of the leaders of a great raid against al-Andalus in the 11th century, and he used the booty he brought back from Córdoba to finance the churches. The isolation and obscurity of the valley in later centuries helped ensure they would survive. The valley is lovely and green. The villages, built of the same dark granite as the churches, have a solemn dignity to them. The sites are scattered across the valley; but it would be easy to see all of them in a day.

The only thing to slow you down would be herds of cattle on the road – the Vall de Boí has far more cows than people. The first two churches are minor ones: L'Assumpció, just outside the village of Cóll, has a portal with carved capitals. Santa Maria, a few kilometres further on in Cardet, is much the same.

Next, Barruera, the biggest village in the valley, has Sant Feliu, much tampered with over the centuries, with only two apses and aisles where once there were three. In all of these, you can see the basic elements of the Lombard style: the basilican form with rounded apses and a square belltower, blind arcading (those decorative arches around the cornices). The Lombard builders of northern Italy had established this style two centuries before the churches here were built, and their architects and masons spread it all over western Europe.

Up in the hills above Barruera, a short detour takes you to the first of the great Boí churches, all of which were built at about the same time, at the beginning of the 12th century. La Nativitat, in the village of Durro, has a portal with carved capitals and another Lombard trademark, a tall belltower with more blind arcading and pairs or triplets of narrow windows, often arranged so that the fenestration gets wider with each succeeding story. Unfortunately all the interior decoration was lost centuries ago. Just outside Durro is the small, plain hermitage of Sant Quirc.

Back in the valley, Santa Eulàlia in Erill la Vall has an even taller and more graceful campanile, as well as a side porch supported by arches. Inside, placed unusually on a beam under the arch above the altar, is a sculpted wood group of the *Descent from the Cross*, a copy of the original that was carted off to Barcelona. The murals of the next church, Sant Joan in Boí, are in Barcelona too, but they have been replaced with a complete set of copies, spectacularly colourful and alive – just as the originals undoubtedly were when they were new. The main subject is the 'Revelations', though the artists used it as an excuse to throw in the whole medieval bestiary, including their best guesses as to what an elephant, a panther and a camel might look like. Another scene shows the stoning of St Stephen, while the last, one the scholars can't really explain, portrays what appear to be entertainers juggling swords. By the portal, note the medieval sgraffito of a battle scene.

They've saved the best for last; the climax of this trip requires climbing up to the village of Taüll, in a beautiful setting high above the valley. Taüll is now a little resort, and it's gratifying to see how the new villas and apartments, built of the same stone, fit in with the medieval village. Not many places get these simple things right. Taüll has two churches, and the records say they were consecrated on two successive days in December 1123.

Santa Maria, the parish church, has lost all its paintings to Barcelona save only a scene of the Epiphany with Mary, Jesus and the three kings. On the edge of the village, Sant Climent is the largest and finest of the churches, with the loftiest and most elegant belltower of them all. Inside, the building is completely dominated by the *Christ in Majesty* on the apse, surrounded by the four Evangelists, a painting that has become the most famous image of Catalan medieval art. Nothing could capture

8

the essential Romanesque better than this Christ, with his courtly yet otherworldly expression and nervously perfect folded draperies. As one critic put it, the Master of Taüll 'further stylised what was already stylised...he made the Byzantine model even more Byzantine'. Underneath Jesus, next to the window, note the figure of the Virgin Mary; according to one recent book, that dish she's holding is the first artistic representation of the Holy Grail (page 141). Up above Taüll, the **Boí-Taüll ski station** is the busiest place in the valley in winter.

Back down in the valley, if you follow it to its northern end you'll be in the old thermal spa of **Caldes de Boí**, the end of the paved road and the western entrance to the Aigüestortes park.

Parc Nacional de Aigüestortes i Estany de Sant Maurici
For beautiful mountain settings without the tax-free merchandise, this stretch of the Pyrenees can offer nothing better than this breathtaking national park, created in 1955 and encompassing $230km^2$ of forests, meadows, lakes and jagged snow-capped peaks, including the pristine **Serra dels Encantats** ('the enchanted mountains') and **Comoloforno**, at 3,029m the highest mountain in the park. As the name implies (*aigüestortes* means 'crooked streams') there is water everywhere; covering one-sixth of the park's area. Few places in the Pyrenees can match the jigsaw-puzzle scenery of the **Lake of Sant Maurici**, completely encircled by trees and mountains.

The environs have several well-marked trails of varying difficulty. Especially pretty and none too difficult is the hike from **Espot** to the refuge in the **Encantats**, with views over the lake. Boí is the major gateway into the park from the western side, as Espot with its hotels is from the east; information booths at the entrances have information on trails, refuges (book well in advance) and half- and full-day excursions into the park with an experienced guide. Private vehicles aren't allowed beyond the car parks at the two entrances.

VALL D'ARAN

North of the park and the Vall de Boí, the western and eastern Pyrenean massifs join in a rugged embrace, enfolding the verdant Vall d'Aran. Once almost inaccessible, it was first linked by road with the outside world in 1932. Today, it has become one of the most popular winter playgrounds of the Pyrenees.

A little twist in the Pyrenees guaranteed this valley a destiny apart. The chain runs in a die-straight line everywhere else, but here we have the 2,883m Pic de Mauberme to the north, and the huge massif called Maladeta (3,312m) to the south. The Vall d'Aran, caught in between, is the only place in Catalunya where the waters run down to the Atlantic. By nature it is orientated towards the north, to France. Many inhabitants still speak Aranés, a dialect not of Catalan or Spanish, but of Gascon (since 1990, Aranés has been an official language on a level with Catalan and Spanish).

Over the centuries, no country in Europe was more skilled than France at nibbling away bits of its neighbours' land. So it's a wonder that this bit got away. In fact, the Aranese cut a deal with the Kingdom of Aragon as far back as 1174 to preserve their liberties and keep the greedy king of France out. Thanks to its isolation, for most of its history the valley was in practice independent, like Andorra. Napoleon annexed it to France, but after his fall it became officially part of Spain once again.

Nowadays, thanks to that N230 road, and the Vielha tunnel that connects it with Lleida, the valley is one of the main routes between France and Spain, and it has become a big winter resort. Some of the villages are nearly a mile high, and the temperature passes below 0°C almost half the days of the year.

WHERE TO STAY

Casa Irene C/ Major 3, Arties; ☎973 64 43 64; w hotelcasairene.com. This has 22 beautifully furnished rooms in a park-like setting. Extremely pleasant & especially cosy in the winter, with its fireplaces, spa & very fine restaurant (€€€), featuring exquisite dishes such as duck with truffles, local trout with apple chutney, & Pyrenean lamb with mint tabbouleh. The Spanish royals drop in here from time to time when they're skiing in Baqueira-Beret. €€€

Parador de Arties Ctra de Baqueira, Arties; ☎973 64 08 01; w paradores.es/en/parador-de-arties. Part modern, part in a restored 18th-century mansion, this large hotel is in one of the more charming corners of the Vall d'Aran & close to the skiing at Baqueira-Beret. Garden with large outdoor pool, gym & sauna. €€€

Parador de Vielha Ctra de Túnel s/n, on N230 tunnel road, Vielha; ☎973 64 01 00; w paradores.es/en/parador-de-vielha. The large building, modern & eccentric with a panoramic circular sitting room, is prettily situated on a wooded slope; it has a pool & a good restaurant with Aranese specialities. Closed May–Oct. €€€

Casa Estampa C/ Sortaus 9, Escunhau; ☎973 64 00 48; w hotelcasaestampa.com. This has 18 comfortable rooms; the surprising amenities include an indoor pool, solarium, gym & a Jacuzzi with a view. It also boasts a very good restaurant (€€€). €€

Fonfreda Pso Libertad 18, Vielha; ☎973 64 04 86; w hotelfonfreda.com. Central, family-run hotel with 26 rustically furnished, charming rooms, superb mountain views & welcoming staff. €€

Casa Vicenta C/ Reiau 7, Vielha; ☎973 64 08 19; w pensioncasavicenta.com. Charming little *pensió*, with 20 simple rooms & a cosy little café-bar where you can enjoy the Basque-style pinxos (a chunk of bread with different toppings) & some local wine. €

Garòs Ostau C/ Cal 3, Garòs; ☎680 85 50 58; w garosostau.com. An old stone house with a pretty courtyard has been converted into a charming little inn. It's located in a tiny village, just 5km from the glitzy slopes of Baqueira-Beret, & has 8 rustic, antique-furnished rooms, & a bright b/fast room offering spellbinding views. A car is essential. €

Montarto C/ Baqueira 2, Arties; ☎973 64 80 03; w pensionmontarto.es. A simple, honest budget choice with 16 wood-panelled rooms in this upscale village. €

Saueth C/ Santa Maria 7, Tredòs; ☎629 78 79 41; w hotelethsaueth.com. A wonderful little inn, just 2km from the Baqueira-Beret slopes, this is tucked away in the pretty village of Tredòs. Great value, basic rooms & good b/fasts with homemade bread & cakes. €

SNÖ Mont Rumies C/ Major 1, Salardú; ☎973 64 58 16; w snomontromies.com. This offers 11 simple but stylish rooms & 9 apartments in the village centre. They can give advice on all kinds of activities in the area & it is popular with cyclists. €

Talabart C/ Banys 1, Les; ☎973 64 80 11; w hoteltalabart.cat. Modest but amiable establishment that has been around forever, run by a lovely family. There's a small kids' pool in the gardens & a very good restaurant (€€) for Aranese trout, snails, stews & such. €

WHERE TO EAT AND DRINK

The Vall d'Aran, as you might expect, has its own unique slant on mountain cooking, with a little touch of southwest France thrown in, in the form of foie gras and duck magrets. They're very proud of the local charcuterie, and there are some favourite dishes you'll find wherever you go: grilled trout, stewed boar and rabbit, and most notably *olla aranesa*, the valley's massive traditional stew with pork, chicken, sausage, beans and vegetables.

Casa Turnay C/ Sant Sebastià 2, Escunhau; ☎973 64 02 92; w casaturnay.es; ⏰ 13.15–15.15 & 20.00–22.25 Mon–Tue & Thu–Sun. In a village just east of Vielha, a long-established local favourite for refined olla aranesa & other valley recipes. Save room for the excellent desserts. €€€

Era Coquèla Avda Gerona; ☎973 64 29 15; w eracoquela.com; ⏰ 13.00–15.00 & 20.00–22.00 Tue–Sat, 13.00–15.00 Sun. Come to enjoy sophisticated local cuisine, from roast lamb to more unusual dishes like gazpacho with watermelon & scallops. The set lunch (€38.50) is a steal for this quality. €€€

Casa Rufus Gessa, 2km west of Salardú; ☎682 61 58 33; w casarufus.com; ⏰ 11.00–22.00 Mon–Fri & 11.00–midnight Sat–Sun. A friendly place with

8

strictly Aranese cooking, often including venison & other game dishes, as well as *bacallà*. €€
Al Fogón de Valle C/ Maladeta 8; ☏ 698 36 40 08; ⏰ noon–23.00 Tue–Sun. A relaxed local

favourite, which offers a great choice of dishes, from *trinxat* (the Catalan version of bubble & squeak) to a succulent paella. Apparently, the king likes to drop in. €

SPORTS AND ACTIVITIES The Val d'Aran is Spain's top skiing destination in winter, and superb for hiking, biking, kayaking and mountaineering in summer. You'll find more info on activities and local tour operators on the official tourist information website: w visitvaldaran.com.

Adventure sports During the summer months, you can go rafting, canyoning or mountain biking with local operators like Aran Experience (☏ 973 64 00 87; w aranexperience.com), which also run via ferrata and kayaking trips. Horseriding, fishing and paragliding are also available throughout the valley.

Hiking and mountaineering There are more than 500km of marked trails in the Val d'Aran, from gentle valley walks to challenging high-altitude routes. The popular Camin Reiau links many of the valley's prettiest villages, while the Ruta dels 7 Llacs passes a chain of alpine lakes. Camins (☏ 973 64 28 78; w camins.es) run mountaineering, hiking and climbing trips.

Skiing Baqueira-Beret (☏ 973 63 90 10; w baqueira.es) is Spain's most prestigious ski resort, famously popular with the Spanish royals. It has three valleys with 165km of runs, 36 lifts and reliable snowfall.

VIELHA The little village that turned into a town thanks to tourism, Vielha has made the transition as gracefully as could be expected. If it has a little more traffic and cute shops than is good for it, at least the development and architecture has been tasteful and fits in well with the tiny old village centre, which is only a few streets of distinctive Aran-style stone houses, with their stepped gables, dormers, slate roofs and carved wooden balconies.

Vielha has been the principal village of the Mijaran ('mid-Aran'), and really of the valley as a whole, almost forever. Jaume the Conqueror stopped here on his campaigns and granted the Vall d'Aran its royal privileges. The town lies on a pretty little stream called the Garona, which eventually becomes the mighty Garonne that flows through Toulouse and Bordeaux. The centre gathers under the shadow of the impressive Romanesque-Gothic church of **Sant Miquel** and its octagonal tower. The portal has a wonderful confusion of angels, saints, musicians and warriors around its Gothic arches, and inside is a dashing 12th-century *Christ de Mijaran* that originally belonged to Vielha's other church, nearby Santa Maria, which was wrecked by retreating Republican soldiers in 1938. The **Musèu dera Val d'Aran** (C/ Major 26; ☏ 973 64 18 15; w vielha-mijaran.org; ⏰ 10.00–13.30 & 17.00–20.00 Tue–Sat, 10.00–13.30 Sun; adult/reduced/under 10 €3/2/free), in a 17th-century mansion, has a collection that ranges from archaeological finds to medieval art from the valley's churches to exhibits on rural life.

FROM VIELHA TO FRANCE North of Vielha, the N230 that leads to France runs right beside the Garona. Along the way, there are several good opportunities for jaunts up to some of the highest accessible parts of the Pyrenees, running through beautiful forests of fir and black pine. At **Arròs** a road will take you up towards **Pic de Mauberme**; the paved road runs out a few kilometres short of a pretty waterfall, the **Sauth deth Pish**.

On foot, or even in a car, you can detour for some spectacular scenery in the opposite direction; south of the N230 at either Aubert or Es Bordes, a road leads high up the slopes of Aneto, the highest peak of the Maladeta massif, where there is another glacier-fed waterfall, called **Uelhs deth Joèu**.

At **Vilamòs**, there is a branch of the Muséu dera Val d'Aran, the **Ecomusèu Çò de Joanchiquet** (C/ Major; ☎973 64 18 15; w visitmuseum.gencat.cat/en/museum/ ecomuseu-co-de-joanchiquet-de-vilamos; ⏲ 11.00–14.00 & 16.00–18.00 Tue– Sat; adult/reduced/under 10 €3/2/free), which is a rustic house with gardens and outbuildings, furnished to show what life was like for the Aranese a century ago (and it looks to have been pretty cosy). The last villages along the road before France, **Les** and **Bossòst**, both have plenty of supermarkets for the French to stock up on booze, smokes and petrol before they get home. Bossòst's church of **Santa Maria** has a wonderful portal of Christ and the Evangelists that looks as if it was carved by a local boy who had never seen another church but decided to give it a go.

EAST OF VIELHA The Vall d'Aran has a good dozen Romanesque churches. None possess anything like the painting and lofty Lombard campaniles of the Vall de Boí, but many have interesting features, usually the sort of vigorous naive art seen on the portal at Bossòst. **Betrén**'s church of **Sant Esteve** (or Sant Sernilh in Aranés) has a portal similar to that of Vielha's. In nearby **Escunhau**, **Sant Peír** has a portal as good as the one in Bossòst, with strange carved capitals.

Arties, the second tourist centre after Vielha, has two churches, **Sant Joan**, now used as a space for art exhibitions, and the plain **Nostra Senyora de Arties**. The village once belonged to the Templars, who left a ruined castle, and the village centre has some fine old buildings, one of which has become a parador.

Next comes the attractive village of **Salardú**, traditionally, the chief village of the upper Aran, and a key fortified place in the Middle Ages. The 13th-century church of **Sant Andreu** is covered with fanciful carvings on the capitals and modillions. Rare for a simple church in the mountains, the interior has almost a complete scheme of Renaissance frescoes; there is also a fine early-Romanesque painted wood crucifix called the *Majestat de Salardú*. From here, it's a short hike to another church, **Santa Eulàlia** in the village of **Unha**, the only church in the valley to retain some vestiges of its medieval painting inside.

Up above Salardú, little **Tredòs** has yet another church, with a set of Renaissance frescoes similar to those of Salardú. There are some popular spots for walking in this area: north of Salardú and Unha you can go up through the isolated village of **Bagueregue**, and from there up to the nearly abandoned village of **Montgarri** or up to the slopes of Pic de Mauberme.

Southwards, other paths lead up to **Bany Tredòs** or along the **Arriu de Ruda**; both lead to the mountain lakes in the Aigüestortes park. This is almost the end of the valley; further east there's nothing but the lovely road over the pass, the **Port de la Bonaigua** to the Vall d'Aneu. But for most of the valley's tourists this is the most important part. Up above the valley road is the swanky ski station **Baqueira-Beret**, a favourite with the Spanish royal family.

ANDORRA

It's a sleazy little paradise, Andorra. Take a slow ride down the single, eternally congested road that runs through the little principality. It's packed tight for nearly all of its length with boutiques, shopping centres, four-star hotels, nightclubs,

ANDORRA ESSENTIALS

LANGUAGE Although Catalan is the official language of Andorra, French, English and Spanish are well understood.

TELEPHONES If you're dialling an Andorran number from Spain or France, dial ☎00, wait for the tone, and then dial the prefix ☎376 and the number.

LOCAL CURRENCY Euro

HOSPITAL Hospital Nostra Senyora de Meritxell (C/ dels Escalls; ☎(376) 87 10 00).

POST OFFICES For the French La Poste, head to Carrer Pere d'Urg 1 in Andorra la Vella; there's also the Spanish Correos (Correus in Catalan) at Carrer Joan Maragall 10.

billboards for Swiss watches and perfumes, and tyre shops. Tyre shops? At last count Andorra gets almost 10 million visitors a year, and more than half of them are day trippers. Andorra is open for business, and its business is duty-free. Decades ago, the Andorrans decided that a good living from skiing and tourism and selling postage stamps wasn't good enough. They wanted more.

Like Dubai or Qatar, the Andorrans long ago started importing 'guest workers', mostly French, Italian and Portuguese, to do all the menial work for them. Today, less than half the population is Andorran-born (the rest is mainly Spanish, French and Portuguese). The Andorrans' biggest fear, besides the diseases that come with high living, is that the emigrants will take over – or at least organise themselves. Until fairly recently there were no trade unions here, and the right to strike was only formally legislated in 2019 (after a huge workers' protest the previous year). The government's own website used to brag that 'legislation is adapted to companies' needs'. Women didn't get the right to vote here until 1970.

Today, the Andorrans have found a way to exploit every single possibility open to a grasping, sweaty-palmed pipsqueak principality. Duty-free was only the beginning, quickly followed by tax havens, offshore investment and dodgy banking schemes. In 2015 a major scandal hit, when the Banca Privada d'Andorra (BPA) was accused by the US Treasury of money laundering and links to criminal networks, forcing the Andorrans to clean up their act (they were on the EU's tax haven 'grey list' until 2021). The latest angle has been a speculative boom in Andorran real estate, stoked by overbuilding. They've turned their lovely corner of the Pyrenees into a garish supermarket. It's a worthy competitor for Europe's other Ruritanian craphole, San Marino, which, if you've never been, is the first country in the world to be paved over with factory outlet car parks.

HISTORY The Principat de les Valles de Andorra, as it is officially known, is an independent historical oddity in the manner of Grand Fenwick and the Marx Brothers' Fredonia, a Catalan-speaking island of mountains measuring 468km² that has managed to steer clear of the French and Spanish since its foundation by Charlemagne. Its name is apparently a legacy of the Moors, derived from the Arabic Al-gandûra – 'the wanton woman' – although unfortunately the story behind the name has been forgotten.

Andorra has two 'co-princes', the president of France (as the heir of the Count of Foix) and the bishop of La Seu d'Urgell. According to an agreement spelled out in 1278, in odd-numbered years the French co-prince is sent 1,920 francs in tribute, while in even-numbered years the Spanish co-prince receives 900 pesetas,

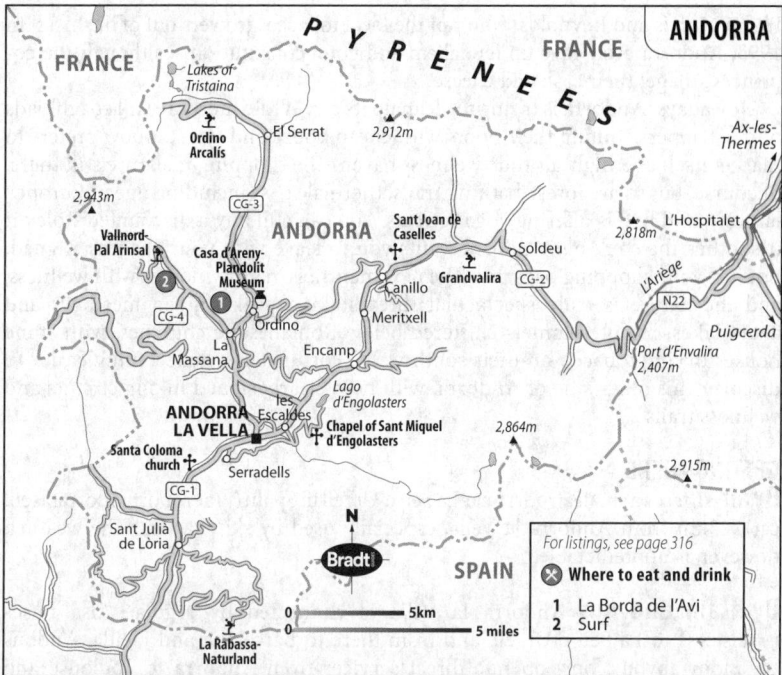

ANDORRA

FRANCE

PYRENEES

FRANCE

Lakes of Tristaina

El Serrat

2,912m

Ax-les-Thermes

Ordino Arcalís

L'Hospitalet

2,943m

CG-3

ANDORRA

Sant Joan de Caselles ✝

2,818m

L'Ariège

Vallnord-Pal Arinsal

Casa d'Areny-Plandolit Museum

Soldeu

N22

2

1

Canillo

Grandvalira

CG-2

Puigcerda

CG-4

Ordino

Meritxell

La Massana

Encamp

Lago d'Engolasters

Port d'Envalira 2,407m

ANDORRA LA VELLA

Les Escaldes

Chapel of Sant Miquel d'Engolasters ✝

2,864m

Santa Coloma church ✝

Serradells

2,915m

CG-1

Sant Julià de Lòria

N

Bradt

SPAIN

For listings, see page 316

❌ Where to eat and drink
1   La Borda de l'Avi
2   Surf

0   5km
0   5 miles

La Rabassa-Naturland

12 chickens, six hams and 12 cheeses. Napoleon thought it was quaint and left it alone, he said, as a living museum of feudalism.

The Andorrans were always most adamant about preserving their local privileges, which they maintained through the Consell de la Terra, founded in 1419, one of Europe's oldest continuous parliaments. They also claim to be the only people in the world who have avoided warfare for 800 years, though they do have an army, which enlists every able-bodied man in the country who owns a gun. They are all officers, every one, and if it pleases them, they may show up whenever the Principat needs an honour guard.

The peace was threatened twice in the last century. First came an Andorra-style civil war in 1934, when a political faction got a White Russian count to proclaim himself King Boris I. Boris soon declared war on the bishop at La Seu – a war the bishop ended after two weeks by sending four Guardia Civils, who drove King Boris to Barcelona and put him on a boat. Then, in 1939, the Andorrans realised to their horror that, since no-one had remembered to invite them to the peace conference at Versailles in 1918, they were still technically at war with Germany. A rapid treaty with Hitler soon sorted that out, and the Germans largely left them alone while they occupied France.

Until the 1940s Andorra remained isolated from the world, relying on dairy farming, tobacco-growing, printing stamps for collectors, and more than a little smuggling. Then this peaceful Ruritania began to change after the war with a popular new sport called skiing. And then came the great revelation: why bother smuggling when you can get the consumer to come to you? For many Andorrans, it was simply too much of a good thing. Their traditional society, already swamped by emigrants, all but disappeared under a wave of day trippers, passing through to purchase duty-free petrol, electronics, booze and smokes, imported tax-free by

8

Philip Morris and Reynolds, who ran the local tobacco-growers out of business. In 1993, Andorra even gave up feudalism and got a constitution – although the co-princes still get their cash and cheese.

Nowadays, Andorra is trying to clean up its act. While there are still coachloads of day trippers stuffing their boots with cheap booze and tyres, it now prefers to market itself as a high-altitude wellness haven. The shopping malls are still there, of course, but so are forest-bathing trails, thermal spas (including one of Europe's largest), and hotels offering yoga retreats. You can still buy a discounted Rolex if it soothes the soul, but Andorra wants you to leave with your chakras aligned, not just your shopping bags full. The new mantra is 'nature merges with wellness' and the nature is truly spectacular: breathtaking peaks, green meadows and azure lakes, minute hamlets clustered below Romanesque churches, with stone houses drying tobacco on their south walls. Fortunately, it's becoming easier to discover this other side of Andorra, with new, clearly signed hiking circuits and wellness trails.

GETTING THERE

By air There's a small airport near La Seu d'Urgell in Spain (w aeroportandorralaseu. cat), 23km from Andorra la Vella, especially used by ski charters. The weather, however, is unpredictable.

By train and bus Andorra la Vella is connected by regular Alsa buses (w alsa.es) to La Seu d'Urgell, and from there to Barcelona and Lleida. Andbus (w andorrabybus.com) operate direct services from Andorra to Toulouse and to Barcelona. If you're coming from France, SNCF trains on the Toulouse–Perpignan–Barcelona line (w sncf.com) get as close as L'Hospitalet, with bus connections the rest of the way. Other buses to Andorra depart from Toulouse and Ax-les-Thermes every morning. From Perpignan you can catch the Villefranche train, which links up with the narrow-gauge Le Train Jaune ('yellow train'; w letrainjaune.fr) which passes through some awesome mountain scenery on its way to Latour-de-Carol, and then catch a taxi (there's no longer a bus service) to Andorra.

By car Unless you know the old smugglers' trails, coming from Spain is straightforward – there's only one way, the N145 from La Seu d'Urgell. Driving in Andorra is unpleasant. The roads are good and kept clear, but the traffic is terrible in the built-up areas and parking is often impossible Out in the country all the beautiful narrow roads were designed for mountain goats. At the end of the shopping day, expect huge queues at the customs check to leave.

TOURIST INFORMATION

Andorra la Vella Pl de la Rotonda; \(376) 75 01 00; w visitandorra.com; ⏲ Jul–12 Sep 09.00–21.00 Mon–Sat, 09.00–19.00 Sun; 13 Sep–Jun 09.00–20.00 Mon–Fri, 09.00–21.00 Sat, 09.00–14.00 Sun

Canillo Ptge Prat del Riu; \(376) 75 36 00; w en.vdc.ad; ⏲ Jul–15 Sep 09.00–18.30 daily; 16 Sep–Jun 09.00–13.00 & 15.00–19.00 Mon–Sat, 09.00–16.00 Sun

SPORTS AND ACTIVITIES

There are a number of sports complexes and facilities all over Andorra, providing an inescapable chance for holiday fitness. Andorra la Vella's **sports complex** (Poliesportiu d'Andorra; Baixada del Molí; \81 20 20) is used for indoor sporting events and has a shiny multi-purpose court with stands for over

5,000 people. There's also a sports centre at Encamp (Pg de l'Alguer, Encamp; ✆73 27 00; w comuencamp.ad; ⊕ 07.00–22.00 Mon–Fri, 09.00–20.00 Sat, 09.00–14.00 Sun) with squash, tennis, swimming, a gym, as well as a library, exhibition hall, table tennis, billiards, martial arts and dancehall.

For more health & wellness tourism, see w healthdestination.ad.

For more **swimming**, there's the **Centre Esportiu** in Serradells (Ctra de la Comella; ✆73 00 90; w andorralavella.ad/esports/inici-esports; ⊕ 07.00–22.00 Mon–Fri, 10.00–14.00 & 16.30–20.00 Sat–Sun), with both indoor and outdoor pools, a shallow learning pool, gym, sauna, tennis courts, squash court and a snack bar.

Andorra is also home to the **Palau de Gel** (Ctra General, Canillo; ✆80 08 40; w palaudegel.ad), a giant skating rink (*patinaje*): in addition, there is a 25m swimming pool, gym, sauna, games room, and much more. Would-be skaters can book lessons for both ice hockey and normal 'artistic' skating.

If you fancy visiting a **shooting range**, there's the Club Esportiu de Tir d'Andorra (Ctra de Nagol, Sant Julià de Lòria; ✆33 70 77; w andorratir.com), with six semi-automatic posts, Olympic and universal pits, an armoured gun room and, comfortingly, a first-aid room.

Skiing
Andorra has abundant snow from December to April, combined with clear, sunny skies – a skier's heaven. The high season, when everywhere is extra busy, is from late November to mid-April, with peak periods around Christmas/New Year, Carnival and Easter. Note that Andorra's high altitude and even terrain make it especially good for ski trekking, or ski randonnée, with overnight accommodation in refuges around the rim of Andorra.

Grandvalira (2,050–2,600m); ✆89 18 18; w grandvalira.com. The oldest (1952) & largest in the country, with 138 runs that span 210km. Divided into 7 different sectors: Canillo, Soldeu, Pas de la Casa, Encamp, El Tarter, Peretol & Grau Roig. **La Rabassa-Naturland** (2,050m); near Sant Julià de Lòria; ✆74 14 44; w naturland.ad. A cross-country skiing station that features 15km of pistes through meadows & forests; separate pistes for snowmobiles; 2.6km of runs; 17 snow cannons; 13 lifts; a children's snow park complete with snow slides, sleds & the like; a sports centre with pool, gym, sauna, etc. & horseriding & guided ecology tours. There are rooms, & a café & restaurant at the refuge which is approached by a good road.

Ordino Arcalís (1,940–2,600m); 17km from town & 4km from El Serrat; ✆73 96 00; w ordinoarcalis.com. Perhaps the most dramatically beautiful & the best place to ski in Andorra. It has 29 pistes & 16 lifts, a medical centre, 8 cafés, & restaurants & hotels in Ordino itself. **Vallnord-Pal Arinsal** (1,550–2,560m); ✆87 80 00; w vallnordpalarinsal.com. The Arinsal & Pal resorts linked up in the 2000/2001 winter season for the first time. They have joint services & share lift connections, & you can get a combined pass. There's a snow park for snowboarders, 63km of runs, monoskiing, big foot, alpine, snowboarding & 78 snow cannons.

Spas and wellness
The **Caldea Spa** is Andorra's most famous spot (Parc de la Mola, Escaldes-Engordany; ✆80 09 99; w caldea.com, the largest spa centre in southern Europe and perfect for après-ski. It's a modern, mirrored, pyramidal structure with thermal water facilities (60°C), air baths, indoor and outdoor Jacuzzis, hydromassage and many, many more watery things all within luxurious, aquatic surroundings. There's also a shopping centre, restaurant and bars.

🏠 WHERE TO STAY *Map, page 316*
Andorra Park Hotel (98 rooms) 24 C/ de les Canals, Andorra la Vella; ✆87 77 77; w andorraparkhotel.com. A charming little palace set in a park with a beautiful rock-cut

8

ANDORRA LA VELLA

For listings, see from page 315

🏠 **Where to stay**

1 Andorra Park
2 Barri Antic
    Hostel & Pub
3 Exe Princep
4 Grand Plaza Hotel
    & Wellness
5 Roc Blanc
6 Suites Plaza

❌ **Where to eat and drink**

7 Celler d'en Toni

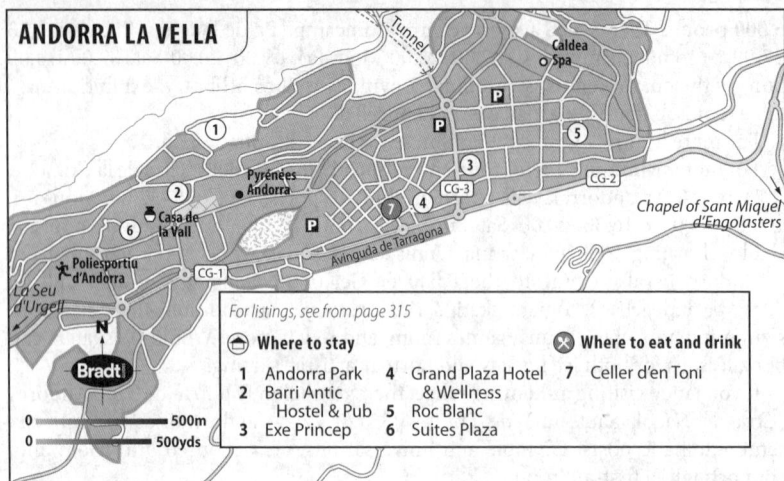

pool, croquet lawn, driving range & tennis court. Its restaurant is one of the best in Andorra, with an excellent wine cellar of the best drops from Spain & Chile. €€€€€

Grand Plaza Hotel & Wellness (90 rooms) Maria Pla 19, Andorra la Vella; ✆87 94 44; w hotelplazaandorra.com. Ultra-contemporary, elegant & classy, if right in the centre of the hubbub. The restaurant Instants (€€€€) offers fresh-from-the-market tapas, meats, seafood & more. €€€€

Suites Plaza Hotel (140 rooms) Prat de la Creu 88; ✆87 44 44; w suitesplazahotelandorra.com. Well-equipped modern hotel located next to the national stadium, with 2 restaurants & a cocktail bar. €€€

Exe Princep (50 rooms) C/ de la Unió 5, Escaldes-Engordany; ✆87 04 00; w eurostarshotels.com. A solid choice when it comes to value for money. Rooms are a bit on the small side but are colourful

& feature a thoughtful design. The location is fantastic – a short walk from everything in town. €€

Roc Blanc (157 rooms) Pl de CoPrínceps 5, Escaldes; ✆87 14 00; w rocblanc.com. In terms of glamour, this takes the cake, with a 5-storey atrium lobby & a glass elevator, sauna & a thermal spa with a number of treatment programmes offered, including 2 weeks of magnetotherapy to realign your electrons. The restaurant, El Entrecôt (€€), features an exceptionally wide selection of French, Spanish & Catalan dishes. €€

Barri Antic Hostel & Pub (11 rooms) C/ de la Vall 18, Andorra la Vella; ✆84 59 69; w hostalbarriantic.com. Basic & good accommodation in a historic building in Andorra la Vella's old town. There's also a bar downstairs with live music that's popular with locals. €

❌ WHERE TO EAT AND DRINK *Map, above, unless otherwise stated*

Borda Vella Av Príncep Benlloch 22, Encamp; ✆83 13 08; w bordavella.com; ⏰ 13.00–17.00 & 20.00–12.30 Wed–Sat (kitchen 13.00–15.00 & 20.00–22.00). Exquisite dishes using the finest ingredients on offer from the region. Highlights include the Galician veal carpaccio, the octopus with pork jowl, or beef tenderloin with white truffle oil & foie sauce. The prices are fantastic for the quality. €€€

Celler d'en Toni Verge del Pilar 4, Andorra la Vella; ✆86 27 50; w cellerdentoni.rest; ⏰ 13.00–15.30 & 20.00–22.00 Mon–Sat, 13.00–15.30 Sun. A long-established classic,

which offers modern interpretations of Catalan cuisine in rustic, delightfully old-fashioned surroundings. Try their famous *canelons*. €€€

La Borda de l'Avi [map, page 313] On the Arinsal road, outside Massana; ✆83 51 54; w restaurantlabordadelavi.com; ⏰ 13.00–15.30 & 20.00–22.30 Tue–Sun. Typical Andorran meals roasted in front of you on a wood fire, as well as fresh fish, foie gras, magrets or snails. €€€

Surf [map, page 313] Ctra General, Arinsal; ✆83 80 69; w www.surfarisnal.com;

🕐 13.00–15.00 & 19.00–23.00 daily, except Tue. A wonderful restaurant serving up delicious asado-style Argentinian beef. €€€

Topic [map, page 313] C/ Major 21, Ordino; 📞73 61 02; w hotelcoma.com/restaurants/topic; 🕐 08.00–midnight daily. Serves Belgian beer & a selection of fondues alongside pizzas. €

SHOPPING Andorra's agreement with the EU on customs allowances has considerably increased the permitted value of goods bought in Andorra and taken back to EU countries; check online for a simple table of allowances (currently under €900 per adult; minors €450). See w visahq.com/andorra/customs. Entrance formalities are a breeze, though there are checks at both French and Spanish customs and you may well be stopped twice.

In Andorra la Vella, the giant department store **Pyrénées Andorra** (Av Meritxell 11; 📞88 00 00; w pyrenees.ad; 🕐 09.30–21.00 Mon–Sat & 10.00–19.00 Sun) is a one-stop shop for everything new and shiny.

WHAT TO SEE AND DO

Andorra la Vella ('Europe's Highest Capital') and the former villages of Les Escaldes-Engordany have melded into a vast arena of conspicuous consuming. Worth a visit, however, is the old stone **Casa de la Vall** (Calle de la Valle; 📞82 91 29; 🕐 10.00–14.00 & 15.00–18.00 Tue–Fri, 10.00–14.00 & 15.00–19.00 Sat, 10.00–14.00 Sun; €5 with audio guide; €6.50 for guided tours by appt only), the seat of the Counsell de la Terra since 1580, and home of the famous Cabinet of the Seven Keys, containing Andorra's most precious documents, accessible only when representatives from each of the country's seven parishes are present. You can visit the main hall and kitchen. The latter is where the parish meetings used to take place – the councillors would walk long distances in the cold to come here, and then would warm up by the stove and eat at the table there, discussing parish business. There is also a dovecote, a fountain, ornamental gardens and a monument by Pujol. If there is a session going on you won't be allowed to visit.

Around Andorra [map, page 313] Andorra is famous for its Romanesque churches and belltowers: a 40-minute walk south of Andorra la Vella will take you to the best one, the 11th-century **Santa Coloma**, with a unique, round belltower and Visigothic arches. A winding road from Escaldes (or ride on the telecabina from Encamp to the north) ascends to the isolated 11th-century **Església de Sant Miquel d'Engolasters** (Sant Miquel d'Engolasters; 📞89 08 81; w museus.ad/en/monumentos/sant-miquel-d-engolasters; 🕐 10.00–14.00 & 15.00–18.00 Tue–Sat, 10.00–14.00 Sun; free). Its fine frescoes, now in the Museu Nacional d'Art de Catalunya in Barcelona, have been replaced by copies, and its three-storey campanile, as often in Andorra, totally dwarfs the church. Beyond the chapel lies a forest and the pretty **Llac d'Engolasters** ('lake swallow-stars') where an old tradition states that all the stars in the universe will one day fall. It's a good place for walking or fishing.

Exploring the hidden corners of old Andorra can be difficult if you're not walking or don't have a car to zigzag up the narrow mountain roads. Buses ply the two main roads through Andorra every couple of hours towards **El Serrat**, and more frequently towards **Soldeu**. **La Cortinada**, en route to Soldeu, is a good tranquil base, with only a couple of hotels, excellent scenery, and some of Andorra's oldest houses. In a 1967 restoration of its parish church, **Sant Martí**, some of the original Romanesque frescoes were uncovered. El Serrat is more touristy but worth a visit in the summer for the gorgeous panorama of snow-clad peaks from the **Abarstar de Arcalís** (via the ski resort).

8

Another branch of the road from El Serrat leads to the three stunning mountain lakes of Tristaina in Andorra's loveliest and least developed northwestern corner, and site of its finest ski resort, Ordino Arcalís (page 315). There's also a museum of note in Ordino town, the **Casa d'Areny-Plandolit Museum** (\ 83 69 08; **w** museus. ad; ⊕ 10.00–14.00 & 15.00–18.00 Tue–Sat, 10.00–14.00 Sun; adult/reduced/under 10 €7/5/free). It is the ancestral home of a long line of local nobility and has three floors; the oldest part of the building dates from 1613.

Another destination reached by bus (on the Soldeu road) is **Meritxell**, the holy shrine of Andorra – an old Romanesque church standing in ruins since a devastating fire in 1972, and next to it, a new sanctuary housing a copy of the 11th-century **Virgen de Meritxell**, designed in 1976 by Barcelona's overrated superstar architect Ricardo Bofill. The Andorrans have their doubts about this gruesome hybrid of their traditional architecture with the modern, which may explain why the principality decided a few years ago against going ahead with a Bofill-designed ski resort near Andorra la Vella. The lovely 12th-century church **Sant Joan de Caselles** is located on a hillside on the north edge of **Canillo** (the big village in these parts), its interior adorned with a Gothic retablo, painted wooden ceiling, and Romanesque paintings; the belltower has fine mullioned windows in the Lombard style.

EXPLORING SPAIN

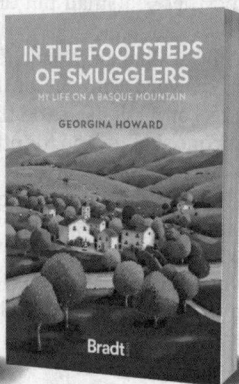

9

North Catalunya

The love of one's country is a splendid thing. But why should love stop at the border?

Pau Casals

Cross the border into France and you won't leave Catalunya behind. The accents shift a little, the names on the signs are in two languages (one of them French), and the rhythm of life tilts ever so slightly towards the Gallic, but the flag still flaps red and yellow, and stately *sardanes* are still danced on summer afternoons. This is the part of Catalunya that ended up in France after the Treaty of the Pyrenees in 1659 (page 10) – but, while the territory may have been ceded, the culture remained, even if the French state has done its best to file off the sharper edges. As a département, it's officially known as the Pyrénées-Orientales (or P-O for short), part of a super-region called Occitanie since 2016. This change caused outrage among the French Catalans, who believed their cultural identity was being erased, and there's a small but energetic campaign to rename the region 'Occitanie–Pays Catalan'.

Perpignan is the capital of North Catalunya; around it stretches the broad Roussillon plain, crowded with the dusty, introverted villages that make all that sweet wine. The real attractions are on the periphery: Collioure and the delectable Côte Vermeille on one side and, on the other, valleys that climb up into the Pyrenees and the Catalan sacred peak of Canigou.

This chapter traces a slow arc through this little-visited and beguiling region, beginning with the wooded hills and artistic enclaves of the Vallespir Valley along the border, curving east to the rugged coast of the Côte Vermeille, then inland to Perpignan (once the capital of the Kingdom of Majorca) and out across the wide Roussillon plain. From there it climbs into the Conflent Valley, rich with Romanesque heritage, before reaching the high-altitude peaks of the Cerdagne.

THE VALLESPIR

Coming from Spain, there are different ways to enter North Catalunya: the big AP7 motorway at La Jonquera (page 200), from Andorra (page 311) or from Llívia (page 224), the tiny Spanish enclave tucked just inside France. But this is perhaps the prettiest: follow the winding C38 northeast of Camprodon (page 217) and slip over the border at the Coll d'Ares, a 1,512m-high mountain pass that leads to the wooded Vallespir Valley. Known for its mineral waters since Roman times, it traditionally made its living from these and from ironworking. When the iron gave out, there was always smuggling. Now that the EU has made smugglers superfluous, the Vallespir lives by tourism, with some euros on the side from cherries and cork oak – the *primeurs*, the first cherries in the French market each year, and the *grand cru* corks that have kept the best champagne bubbly for centuries.

GETTING THERE AND AROUND The C5 bus, operated by Teisa (972 20 48 68; w teisa-bus.com), links Camprodon in Spain with Prats-de-Mollo. From Prats-de-Mollo, there are buses to Perpignan with liO (w lio.laregion.fr; 08 06 80 80 90) with stops at all the main towns of the Vallespir.

TOURIST INFORMATION

Amélie-les-Bains 22 Av du Vallespir; 04 68 39 01 98; w amelie-les-bains.com; ⊕ see website
Arles-sur-Tech Baills de la Mairie; 04 68 39 11 99; w tourisme-haut-vallespir.com; ⊕ 10.00–12.30 & 14.00–17.30 Tue–Sat
Céret 5 Rue Saint-Ferréol; 04 68 87 00 53; w ot-ceret.fr; ⊕ 09.00–12.30 & 14.00–18.00 Mon–Sat

Le Boulou 4 Rue Arago; 04 68 87 50 95; w tourisme-leboulou.fr; ⊕ 09.00–noon & 14.00–18.00 Mon–Fri, 09.00–12.30 Sat
Prats-de-Mollo Place le Foiral; 04 68 39 70 83; w pratsdemollolapreste.com; ⊕ 09.30–12.30 & 14.00–18.00 Mon–Fri, 10.30–12.30 Sat

WHERE TO STAY

Le Mas Trilles [map, page 322] (13 rooms) Pont de Reynès, Céret; 04 68 87 38 37; w le-mas-trilles.com; ⊕ closed Nov–Easter. A tastefully renovated *mas* (traditional farmhouse) with plush & comfortable rooms, most with a private terrace, & big enough to sleep 4. There's also a heated pool & a charming garden overlooking a trout stream. No restaurant, but there are 2 very nearby. €€€
Hôtel Le Cérétan (17 rooms) 7 rue de la Republique, Céret; 04 68 87 11 02; w hotel-le-ceretan.com/fr. Right in the town centre, a simple hotel with immaculate rooms, friendly owners who are happy to give tips on what to see & do & tasty b/fasts. €€
Hôtel Val du Tech [map, page 351] (18 rooms) 100m from the spa, Prats-de-Mollo-La-Preste; m 06 21 72 60 15; w hotel-valdutech.fr. Patronised by walkers & spa clients. Choose between a modern or a rustic room, & have fresh spa water brought to your room in the morning.

There's a good restaurant (€€) & they'll make a picnic if you want to go exploring. €€
Hôtel Vidal (8 rooms) 4 Pl Soutine, Céret; 04 68 87 00 85; w hotel-vidal-ceret.hotelmix.fr. In a charming, if quirky and sometimes noisy, listed building. Its colourful restaurant, Bisbe (€€), has good food & a charming terrace. €€
Mas L'Andreu [map, page 322] (4 rooms, 1 gîte) 5 mins from Corsavy village; 04 68 37 57 22; w lavieenpentedouce.com. Stay amid the lush woodlands north of Arles-sur-Tech in a choice of 4 charming gîtes (for 2–4 people) set in an 18th-century farmhouse. There's a pool, a home cinema, Wi-Fi & the choice of French or English b/fast. €€
Hôtel Le Costabonne [map, page 322] (16 rooms) Pl du Foiral, Prats-de-Mollo-La-Preste; 04 68 39 70 24; w lecostabonne.fr. Simple en-suite rooms & a bar terrace in the centre of action during the bear festival; also a restaurant (€€) serving Catalan dishes. €

WHERE TO EAT AND DRINK

Le Jardin 7 Rue de la République, Céret; 04 11 64 41 12; w lejardinceret.eatbu.com; ⊕ noon–14.00 & 19.30–21.30 Mon, noon–14.00, 14.30–18.30 & 19.30–21.30 Tue–Sat, noon–14.30 Sun. A tranquil restaurant with a very popular set menu. Try to grab a seat on the shady terrace out back. €€€
Can Bigoti 10 Pl des Neuf Jets, Céret; m 06 18 45 61 25; ⊕ 10.00–23.00 Mon–Tue & Fri–Sun.

Tiny restaurant in a pretty square, with delightful owners & good-value, simple menus. €€
Chez Françoise Rue Baptiste Pams, Corsavy; 04 68 39 12 04; ⊕ noon–15.15 daily except Wed. Part village épicerie, part excellent restaurant, serving tasty Catalan specialities for lunch. €€

SHOPPING The valley's market days are a great way to soak up the village life. Céret has its market on Saturdays, while Arles-sur-Tech has its on Wednesday. A market also happens in Prats-de-Mollo on Fridays.

9

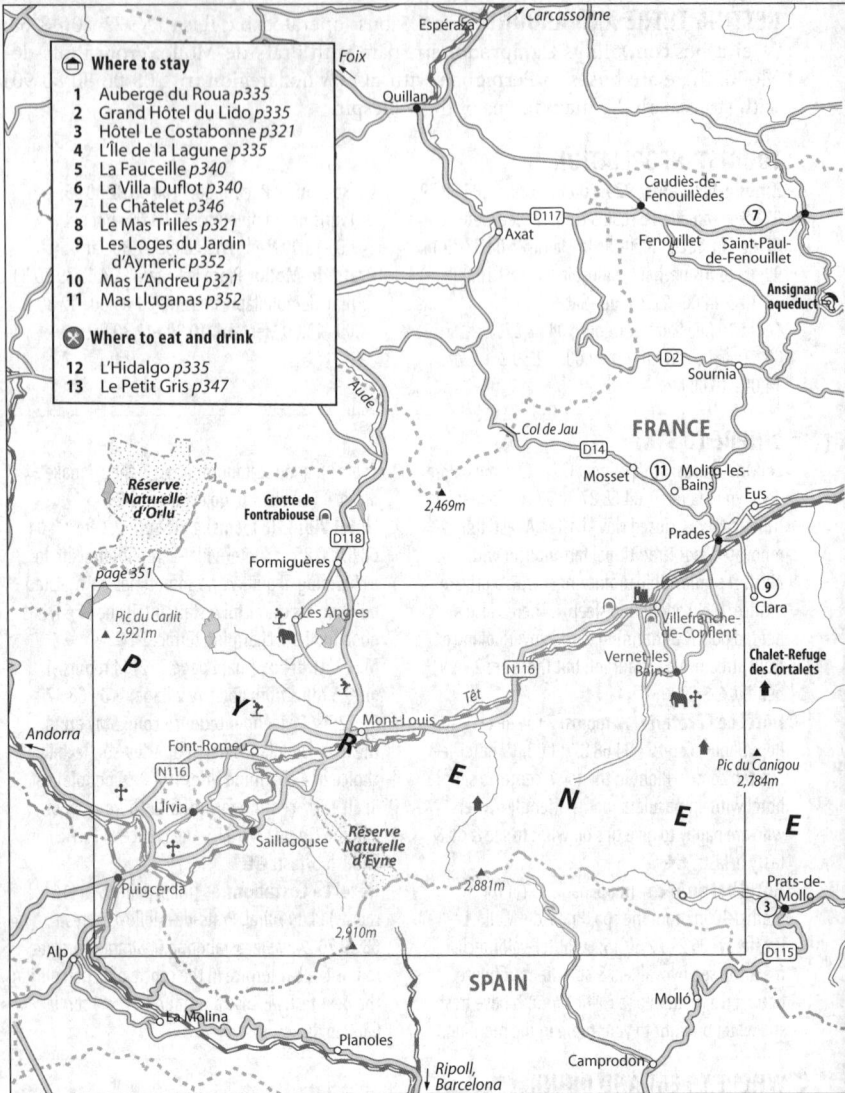

PRATS-DE-MOLLO Some towns just ask for it. As if having a name like Prats-de-Mollo wasn't enough, this tiny spa advertises itself as the 'European Capital of Urinary Infections'. Prats-de-Mollo's other claim to fame is a European record for rainfall: 33 inches in 16 hours on 15 October 1940. The **Thermes de La Preste-les-Bains** (572 Rte de la Preste; ☎04 68 87 55 00; w chainethermale.fr; ⊕ 4 Apr–19 Nov) are really at **La-Preste**, 8km up in the mountains. Prats-de-Mollo itself is an attractive old village, with remains of its walls, and **Fort Lagarde** (☎04 68 39 70 83; ⊕ Jun 14.00–17.30 Thu–Sun; 1–11 Jul 11.00–17.45 daily; 12 Jul–31 Aug 11.00–17.45 Mon, 11.00–15.45 Tue–Sun; adult/reduced/under 12 €4/3/free), a fortress refurbished by Vauban, together with other medieval buildings that recall the days when it was a textile centre, specialising in Catalan bonnets. Don't miss the whale bone stuck in the church wall.

NORTH CATALUNYA

ARLES-SUR-TECH This is the ancient capital of the Vallespir and last redoubt of the valley's medieval iron industry; the last working mine in Roussillon, up at Batère, closed down in the early 1990s. Arles is a curious old town built on a narrow maze of lanes and offers some even curiouser hagiography in its 11th- and 12th-century **Abbaye Sainte-Marie** (❀ 04 68 83 90 66; ⏱ 09.30–12.30 & 14.00–18.30 daily; adult/reduced/under 12 €4/3/free) entered by way of the tourist office. This abbey was originally founded in the late 8th century AD in Amélie-les-Bains by Sunifred, brother of Count Wilfred the Hairy, but was later relocated here for safety. Its focus of devotion was an anonymous saint – an empty 4th-century AD sarcophagus known as **Sainte Tombe** – until the day when the dreaded simiots came to town, ape-like monsters that trampled the crops and

9

323

BEAR FROLICS

There are some peculiar goings-on in winter in the upper Vallespir, starting with the Festa de l'Os (bear festival) in Prats-de-Mollo. Originally this took place on 2 February or Candlemas, a traditional Celtic cross-quarter day like Hallowe'en, although modern times have regulated it to the second Sunday of February half-term holidays.

The festival has suitably murky origins that go back to the days when there were more than a handful of bears in the Pyrenees. There may even be, deep in the Vallespir's DNA, Palaeolithic memories when humans and bears shared the same cave shelters, apparently in a friendly enough fashion, even though the now extinct cave bears were as big as grizzlies. Curious artefacts dating from c12,000BC found in French shelters suggest odd human/ursine sexual fantasies. In historic times, hunting cultures such as the Ainu in Japan would capture bear cubs to be suckled by a human mother and reared like a sibling with her children in preparation for a bear festival in which, after many apologies, the bear would be ritually strangled and eaten.

In Prats-de-Mollo, a veneer of Christianity has allowed some peculiar ancient rites to survive, notably the legend of a shepherd girl who was abducted by a lusty bear (the devil in disguise). The devil bear tried to have his evil way with her, but she prayed to Notre-Dame-du-Coral (the chapel on the hill) who saved her honour for nine days, until the bear's howls of frustration reached a band of woodcutters, who rescued her.

While basically telling the same story, each town with a bear festival (Arles-sur-Tech and Saint-Laurent-de-Cerdans are the others) celebrates it on different days with slightly different versions of atavistic weirdness. In Prats-de-Mollo, young men are divided into 'bears' (covered in sheepskins, grease and soot) with long wooden sticks, and 'hunters' who have blanks in their guns and gourds filled with wine. The action starts with a chase and high jinks to music through the streets, as the bears try to smear everyone with their soot. Once all the bears are 'shot', they are chained up and brought to the main square to be 'shaved' with axes by flour-covered 'barbers' who use a *botifarra* (Catalan black pudding) for soap. Afterwards bears, hunters and barbers do a mad dance until a gunshot rings out and the bears drop down 'dead'.

Carnival in Prats-de-Mollo also preserves odd old customs that would immediately be cancelled if Health and Safety ever got wind of them. There's the Ball de la Posta dance, in which female dancers have to choose between kissing a painted image of the Virgin or the devil, before getting a playful smack on the bottom. In the evening, masked dancers cover themselves with flour and dance the Tio-tio, each dancer bearing a rolled paper 'log' on their back and each holding a lighted candle, with the idea of setting the 'log' of the dancer in front on fire! Fortunately, a referee with a broom is in charge of putting out the flames if they actually succeed.

violated the women. In despair, the abbot of Sainte-Marie went to the pope asking for some holy relics. This was in 957, when demand for saints' bones was at its historic high, and the best the pope could offer was a pair of Persian martyrs named Abdon and Sennen. The abbot brought them back in a false-bottomed water barrel, to fool the Venetians and Germans and any other relic thieves, and they dealt with the simiots as efficiently as if they had been the bones of St Peter himself. The story is portrayed in a 17th-century retable, in the chapel where Abdon and Sennen's relics are kept; back when times were more perilous, their bones were stored in cupboards that you can see high in the square pillars in the nave. Another telling feature that betrays the church's age is the fact that it is orientated towards the west – a mistake 'corrected' with a frescoed counter-apse chapel of Saint-Michel.

The Sainte Tombe itself, once a major pilgrimage attraction, is kept in a little enclosure outside the enclosed façade. It fills continually with perfectly pure water – some 500–600 litres a year, ceremoniously pumped every 30 July. Above it, on the wall, is the early 13th-century tombstone of Guillaume de Gausselme.

Two kilometres northwest along the D44 is the world's narrowest gorge, the **Gorges de la Fou**, a giant crack in the rock with sides towering 198m, yet only a metre or so wide at its narrowest point, with waterfalls and caves along the 1.6km-long walkway. It has been closed due to dangerous rockfalls for a few years now, which is a great shame; still, legend made it the lair of witches, bogeymen and Traboucayres, an infamous band of Catalan robbers who pounced on passing diligences, whose story is told up in the hill village of **Montferrer** in the tiny **Musée de Montferrer** (ask at the Arles tourist office), which also has items dedicated to Napoleon and Charles de Gaulle. A pair of watchtowers mark **Corsavy**, even higher up; it's nicknamed 'the balcony of Canigou' and is especially proud of its beautifully restored **Chapelle Sant Martí** (1158).

A detour south of the valley, on the D3, will uncover **Saint-Laurent-de-Cerdans**, famous for making espadrilles, and Coustouges, which has a lovely early 12th-century fortified church with a slate roof and two carved portals, one inside the other. Continuing up the valley, just south of the D115, the hilltop village of **Serralongue** has a **church** dating from 1018, with a fine portal and one of the only surviving examples of a Catalan *conjurador*; this is a small, square pavilion with a slate roof and statues of the four Evangelists facing the four cardinal directions. When a storm threatened, the priest would go up to the *conjurador* and perform certain rites facing the direction of the storm to avert its wrath.

AMÉLIE-LES-BAINS

Sulphurous waters, good for your rheumatism, have been the fortune of this village since ancient times; a Roman swimming pool with a vaulted roof has been uncovered, and the **Thermes d'Amélie-les-Bains** (Pl Arago; ☎ 01 89 16 96 79; w chainethermale.fr) still does a grandstand business. Named in 1849 after the wife of King Louis Philippe, Amélie's pretty medieval ancestor, Palalda, is piled on a nearby hill, and offers a small museum on how the locals lived in the past.

CÉRET

Sitting pretty in a sea of cherry orchards, Céret is a laid-back town under enormous plane trees, with perfect little café-lined squares (especially the **Plaça dels Nou Raigs**), medieval gates, **Saint-Pierre**, modestly famous for being the biggest Baroque church in Roussillon, a war memorial by Maillol and an elegant 14th-century bridge over the Tech. Céret takes its bullfighting seriously, with ferias in July and September, and it celebrates the *sardana*, the traditional Catalan dance in a ring, with a huge three-day festival in July.

Walking around Céret is the best preparation for its **Musée d'Art Moderne** (8 Bd du Maréchal Joffre; ☎ 04 68 87 27 76; w musee-ceret.com; ⊕ Jul–Aug 10.00–19.00 daily; Sep–Jun 10.00–18.00 Tue–Sun; adult/18 & under €10/free) The Fauves may

9

have gone to Collioure, but Céret found its artistic destiny in the early 20th century as the 'Mecca of Cubism', thanks to Picasso, Braque, Gris, Manolo, Matisse, Soutine, Kisling, Masson, Tzara, Lhote, Marquet and others who came to paint here, and whose paintings line these walls. Matisse donated 14 drawings from his first stay in Collioure, but perhaps best of all are the works donated by Picasso in 1953, among them 28 little plates painted in a five-day spurt of energy, all with variations on the corrida under a blasting sun. The museum has attracted just under a dozen art galleries to Céret.

Nearby, the **Musée de la Musique** (14 Rue Pierre Rameil; ⟍04 68 87 40 40; w museemusiqueceret.com) houses traditional instruments from Catalunya and from around the world, along with items to put them in context.

LE PERTHUS Hannibal entered Gaul through Le Perthus, the last – or first – stop in France. Archaeologists have uncovered, at the Panissars mountain pass, a monumental pedestal, identified as belonging to the Trophée de Pompée. Similar to the Trophy of Augustus at La Turbie near the Italian border, this monument was erected by a victorious Pompey in 71BC on the Gallo-Hispanic frontier. Part of the stone was used to build a priory in 1011 (the ruins are nearby); the rest was quarried by Vauban in the 17th century to build the **Fort de Bellegarde** which stands guard over town. It's currently closed to visitors, but is in such good nick that it was used as an internment camp for refugees from Spain in 1939.

MAUREILLAS-LAS-ILLAS This sleepy, picturesque town is most famous for its 9th-century church of **Saint-Martin-de-Fenollar** (⟍04 68 87 73 82; ⏲ Jul–Aug 14.30–19.00 Mon–Sat; Sep–Jun 14.30–17.00 daily; adult/child €3.50/1.50) with some of the most unusual and best-preserved 12th-century frescoes in the south of France, by the so-called Master of Fenollar. Nine-tenths of all early medieval painting is lost to us, and this is a rare example of the best of what is left: brilliant colours and a confident stylisation, with an imagery untroubled by the dogma of later religious painting, as in the *Nativity*, where Mary lies not in a stable but in a comfortable bed under a chequered baldachin. The scene from the *Apocalypse*, of Christ in Majesty with the four symbols of the Evangelists and the 24 elders, was a favourite 12th-century theme on both sides of the Pyrenees. Picasso and Braque came and were suitably impressed.

LE BOULOU Le Boulou, the last town of the Vallespir Valley (and a renowned truck-stop known to every European big-rig jockey), sits just off the A9 motorway. It has been fated by geography to be an eternal transit point since Roman times, and is jammed in summer with tourists on their way to or from Spain. It also has a casino and spa, and a fine Romanesque church, **Église Sainte-Marie** with a superb white marble tympanum sculpted by the Master of Cabestany, portraying the *Resurrection of the Virgin*. The cornice shows scenes of the Nativity, the *Christ Child's first bath* (a scene banned by the Counterreformation Council of Trento), the shepherds, Magi and flight into Egypt.

COLLIOURE AND THE CÔTE VERMEILLE

The Côte Vermeille is a delicious world of crystalline rock, olive trees and uncanny sunlight, a 30km extension of Spain's Costa Brava. Forgive yourself for cynically thinking that the name 'Vermilion Coast' might have been cooked up by promoters – of course it was. The red clay soil of the ubiquitous olive groves does lend the area a vermilion tint, but as far as colours go that is only the beginning.

Every point or bend in the Mediterranean coast is a sort of meteorological vortex, given to strange behaviour: the Fata Morgana at the southern tip of Italy, the winds of the Mani in the Peloponnese or the glowing, subdued light of Venice. The Côte Vermeille gets a strong dose of the tramontane wind that can shriek like a monster in a B movie, but also has a remarkable mix of light and air, inciting the coast's naturally strong colours into an unreasonably heady and sensual Mediterranean spectrum. André Derain and Henri Matisse spent one summer here, at Collioure, and the result was a milestone in the artistic revolution known as Fauvism.

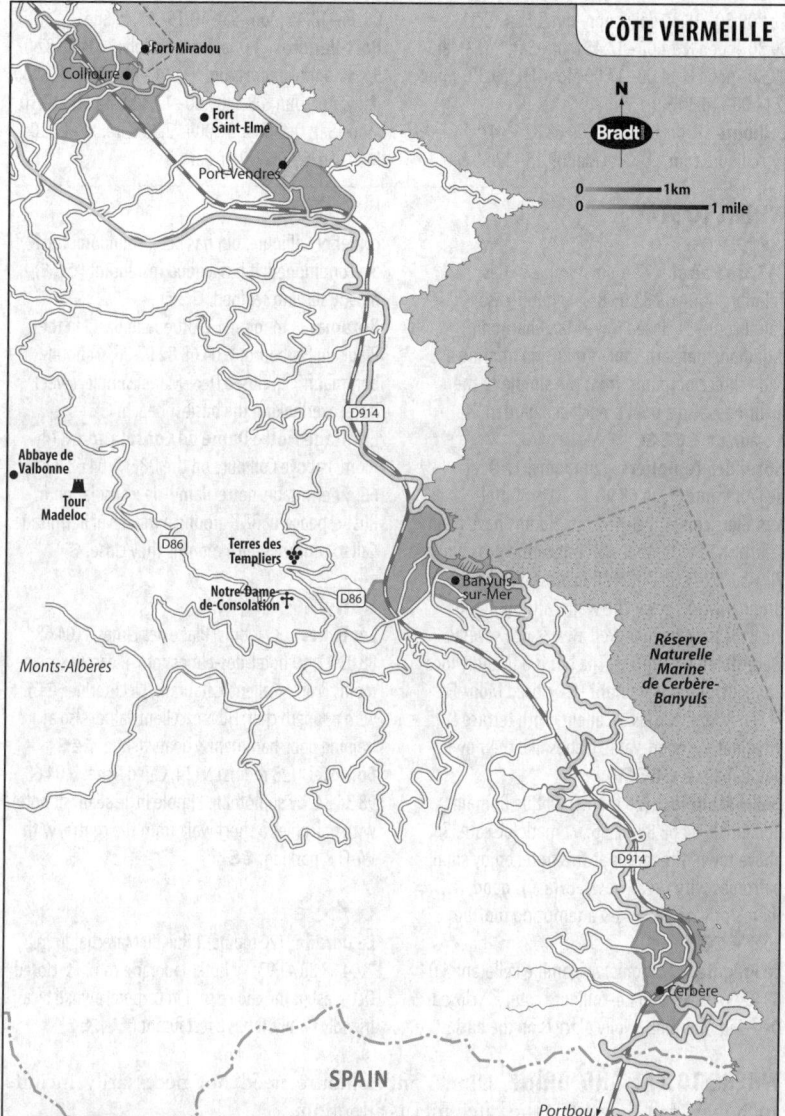

GETTING THERE AND AROUND Trains link Cerbère on the Spanish border and Perpignan every couple of hours, with stops at Banyuls-sur-Mer, Port Vendres and Collioure. Regional Occitanie **buses** make the same trip (w lio.laregion.fr).

Having your own **car** here is also recommended; the twisting roads along the coast make for a great drive, and you'll also easily be able to venture inland to visit some wineries. Make sure to arrive in town early though, as parking spaces are limited.

TOURIST INFORMATION

Banyuls-sur-Mer Av de la République; ☎04 68 88 31 58; w banyuls-sur-mer.com; ⏱ Jul–Aug 09.30–18.30 daily; Apr–Jun & Sep–Oct 09.30–noon & 14.00–17.45 Mon–Sat; Nov–Mar 09.30–noon & 14.00–17.00 Mon–Fri, 09.30–noon & 14.00–16.30 Sat

Collioure Pl du 18 Juin; ☎04 68 82 15 47; w collioure.com; ⏱ Oct–Mar 09.15–12.30 & 14.00–17.15 Mon–Sat; Apr–Jun & Sep 09.15–17.45 Mon–Fri, 10.15–17.45 Sat–Sun; Jul–Aug 09.15–18.45 Mon–Sat, 10.15–17.45 Sun

Port-Vendres 1 Quai François Joly; ☎04 68 82 07 54; w port-vendres.com; ⏱ Jul–Aug 09.00–17.30 daily; Apr–Jun & Sep 09.00–12.30 & 14.00–17.30 Mon–Sat; Oct–Mar 09.00–12.30 & 14.00–17.30 Mon–Fri, 09.00–12.30 Sat

🏠 WHERE TO STAY

Collioure

La Casa Païral (27 rooms) Impasse des Palmiers; ☎04 68 82 05 81; w hotel-casa-pairal.com; ⏱ closed Nov–Mar. Charming, dignified, mansard-roofed mansion offering a wide choice of rooms, from the simple to the luxurious; also a pool & enclosed garden. No restaurant. €€€€€

Hôtel des Templiers (20 rooms) 12 Quai de l'Amirauté; ☎04 68 98 31 10; w hotel-templiers.com; ⏱ closed Jan. Rooms have been refurbished with AC & Wi-Fi since the days when Picasso, Matisse, Dufy & Dalí all stayed here. Original works cover the walls, although the Picassos have been locked away since several were stolen by a 'guest'. The bar is a friendly local hangout, & the restaurant (⏱ closed Mon–Fri in Feb & Mar; €€) is excellent, with terrace & imaginative, good-value dishes like their own bouillabaisse. €€€€

Hôtel Madeloc (26 rooms) 24 Rue Romain Rolland; ☎04 68 82 07 56; w madeloc.com. Set above town, the rooms at this hotel enjoy small balconies with great views. B/fast is good, there's private parking & a tempting rooftop pool. €€€

La Frégate (27 rooms) Av Camille Pelletan; ☎04 68 82 06 05; w fregate-collioure.com; ⏱ closed Dec–Jan. This pink & jolly place is on the busiest corner of Collioure, but has been soundproofed & air-conditioned; it has a good restaurant (€€€), mostly serving seafood. €€€

Boramar (14 rooms) 19 Rue Jean Bart, on the Plage du Faubourg; ☎04 68 82 07 06; w hotel-boramar.fr; ⏱ closed Dec–Mar. A simple, sweet hotel overlooking the busiest beach. €€

Ermitage Notre Dame de Consolation (14 rooms) above Collioure on the D86; ☎04 68 82 17 66, w ermitage-notre-dame-de-consolation.fr. Rustic, peaceful B&B around a medieval hermitage. Call to confirm which months they close. €

Banyuls-sur-Mer

Les Elmes (33 rooms) Plage des Elmes; ☎04 68 88 03 12; w hotel-des-elmes.com. Pleasant seaside rooms & an excellent restaurant, La Littorine (€€), with a superb chef; HB is excellent value. Also a training pool, hammam & boats to hire. €€€

Solhotel (23 rooms) N114, Cap d'Osne; ☎04 68 98 34 34, w solhotel.fr. Simple little seafront hotel with balconies a short walk from the centre, with Wi-Fi & parking. €€

Cerbère

La Dorade (20 rooms) 1 Rue du Maréchal Joffre; ☎04 68 88 41 93; w hotel-ladorade.com; ⏱ closed Oct–Easter. The choice spot in Cerbère, owned by a friendly family. It has a restaurant (€€). €€

✗ WHERE TO EAT AND DRINK

Dinner in Collioure need not necessarily include anchovies, but the rest of the catch merits attention.

Le Neptune 9 Rte Port-Vendres; ☎ 04 68 82 02 27; w leneptune-collioure.com; ⊕ closed Tue. One of the best in town, with wonderful canopied sea views & the full nouvelle Catalan cuisine; menus change seasonally but you might be offered *salade chemin des Fauves*, which combines eggs, artichokes, tapenade & tomato confit in highly decorative style, or lobster ravioli with cardamom vinaigrette; desserts are delicious. €€€€

Chez Simone 7 Rue Mailly; ☎ 04 34 29 93 47; 🖂 restaurant.chezsimone ⊕ closed Mon.

Wonderful seafood & creative Catalan tapas on the seafront, with gorgeous views if you can snag a table outside looking over the church. €€€

Can Pla 7 Rue Voltaire; ☎ 04 68 82 10 00; w restaurant-can-pla-collioure.com; ⊕ closed Tue. Relaxed family restaurant with a nice terrace – one of the best for traditional Catalan dishes – & lots of seafood. €€

L'Insolite Pl de l'Eglise; ☎ 04 68 82 08 61; ⊕ all day. Suntrap by the beach, serving a mix of salads, crêpes, seafood & tapas. €€

SHOPPING Collioure's market is held on Wednesdays and on Sunday mornings. There is also a weekly market in Port-Vendres on Saturday mornings, while Banyuls's market takes place twice weekly, on Thursdays and on Sunday mornings.

Anchois Desclaux Roque 17 Rte d'Argelès; ☎ 04 68 82 04 99; w anchois-roque.com; ⊕ 08.00–18.30 Mon–Fri, 08.00–noon & 14.00–18.30

Sat–Sun. Come here to pick up a jar of Collioure's famous anchovies.

SPORTS AND ACTIVITIES There are several sea excursions available from Port-Vendres, including catamaran cruises, fishing trips and a day on a sailboat; the tourist office website has a complete list.

Since 1974, 650ha of coast between Banyuls and Cerbère has been protected as the Réserve Naturelle Marine de Cerbère-Banyuls, the oldest marine reserve in France and said to be the only one entirely underwater. You can snorkel along the Sentier Sous-Marin (Underwater Trail) – there's an information point on Banyuls's quay and at the Plage de Peyrefite – or explore it with local diving clubs: **CIP-Collioure** (15 Rue de la Tour d'Auvergne, Collioure; ☎ 04 68 82 07 16; w cip-collioure.com) and **Aqua Blue Plongée** (5 Quai Georges Petit, Banyuls-sur-Mer; ☎ 04 68 88 17 35; w aquablue-plongee.com).

CERBÈRE If you are of a certain age, you may well have already been here, but Cerbère, once the busiest rail crossing into Spain, won't bring back any pleasant memories – being herded from one train to another in the middle of the night under the gaze of soldiers with sub-machine-guns and impossible customs men who do their best to make this seem like an old Hitchcock spy film. No-one has ever seen Cerbère in daylight, but you might give it a try. The coast here is at its most spectacular and there are a few pebble beaches. With its handful of hotels, Cerbère is a minuscule resort with a World's End air about it – an impression reinforced by its solar lighthouse, '*le phare du bout du monde*' ('the lighthouse at the end of the world').

MONTS-ALBÈRES The steep and narrow D86, which links Collioure and Banyuls, is an extremely scenic route through the ancient olive groves on the lower slopes of the Monts-Albères. Several abandoned fortresses come into view, although none is especially easy to reach. There is also a ruined monastery, the **Abbaye de Valbonne**, on the heights to the west; the track to it begins at the pilgrimage chapel of **Notre-Dame-de-Consolation**. Nearby, the **Tour de Madeloc** is the climax of the trip, its lofty position affording panoramic views over the surrounding hills and coast; it was a signal tower, part of the sophisticated communications network that kept the medieval kings of Aragon in close contact with their borders.

9

MAILLOL AND HIS MUSE

Aristide Maillol had a lifelong fixation: young, nude women. This is not so uncommon, mind you, but Maillol (1861–1944) cast his idée fixe in bronze with sufficient conviction to have it lodge in museums and art history books and on the pedestals of monuments all over France.

Vicki Goldberg, *New York Times*, 1996

Maillol started off as a painter influenced by Gauguin, Puvis de Chavannes and Maurice Denis, before opening up a tapestry workshop in Banyuls, becoming one of the first to revive the art. By the early 1900s he had turned to sculpture, using his wife as a model, and introduced his first simplified, serene classical female nude, *Méditerranée*, to the world in 1905 – ironically, just as the Fauves up the road in Collioure were taking the first steps of turning representative art on its head. Rodin was impressed. Although he lived in Paris, Maillol loved Banyuls, and was proud of his Catalan heritage – he proudly wore his *barretina* (Catalan cap) and espadrilles. But by 1934 he was in the doldrums, when a friend discovered 'a living Maillol', Dina Veirny, then a 15-year-old student. Within a couple of years, posing in between her school work, she had become devoted to him, and herself offered to pose in the nude (he apparently was far too shy to ask!), inspiring a whole new period of creativity. Their relationship by mutual agreement was platonic, but it didn't stop Madame Maillol from complaining long and bitterly.

In 1939 Maillol took refuge in Banyuls. He was eventually followed by Dina, who in spite of the danger (she was Jewish) was working with the Resistance, and in particular with Varian Fry at the US Consulate in Marseille. Fry ran an organisation dedicated to smuggling Jews out of France, especially over the secret paths around Banyuls. When Dina was arrested, Maillol hired a lawyer who won her freedom, then sent her to Nice for her own safety – to Henri Matisse, where she posed for him, before Maillol, nervous of losing her, summoned her back. When Dina was arrested again, this time by the Gestapo, Maillol managed to free her after six months by appealing to Hitler's favourite sculptor. After Maillol's death in a car accident in 1944, Dina was made one of the executors of his will. She became the greatest promoter of his art, buying up all she could and opening a Musée Maillol in Paris; her foundation, run by her sons since her death in 2009, also runs the little museum in Banyuls.

BANYULS-SUR-MER (Banyuls de la Marenda in Catalan) Next town along the picturesque coastal N114, this is a resort with a beach and thalassotherapy centre, the heart of the Banyuls wine region, but also the home of the oceanographic Laboratoire Arago, affiliated to the University of Paris. Their excellent **Aquarium** (Av du Fontaulé; ⚓04 68 88 73 39; w biodiversarium.fr; ⏰ 10.00–12.30 & 14.00–18.30 Tue–Sun; closed Jan; adult/13–18/12 & under €9.50/7.50/5) was built in 1883; don't miss the grandaddy lobster and sea anemones and 250 marine species. The 650ha of coast between Banyuls and Cerbère is protected as the **Réserve Naturelle Marine de Cerbère-Banyuls**, the oldest marine reserve in France, and is well worth taking the time to explore.

To show there's nearly as much natural diversity on land in this magical niche, the Aquarium has set up the **Jardin Méditerranéen du Mas de la Serre** (⏰ Apr–Jun Tue–Thu; Jul–Aug Mon–Fri; closed Sep–Mar; adult/13–18/12 & under €6/3) located on a hill overlooking Banyuls (take Rue Jules Ferry to Route du Mas Reig to the Route des Crêtes). Admission is at 09.30 on the days it's open, but only with a pre-booked guided tour via the website.

As for art, Banyuls has a good 11th-century Romanesque church, **La Rectorie** on Rue Charles de Foucault (⊕ 10.30–noon and 14.00–18.00 Sat, 15.00–18.00 Sun; guided visits arranged by the tourist office) and takes credit for giving the world Aristide Maillol, born here in 1861 and perhaps the best-known French sculptor of the last century after Rodin. He contributed the town's War Memorial, but in general expressed everything through the medium of the stylised, voluptuous female form. His tomb and a few copies of works are displayed in his old farmhouse, La Métairie, now the **Musée Aristide Maillol**, 4km up the Col de Banyuls road (✆ 04 68 88 57 11; w museemaillol.com; ⊕ 10.00–noon & 14.00–18.00 Tue–Sun; €7).

PORT-VENDRES This is a real port, with few of the charms of Collioure, even though in ancient times it was nothing less than Portus Veneris, the Port of Venus. Louis XVI's government had big plans for developing it which were scuppered with the Revolution. A few grandiose Neoclassical buildings from this programme managed to get built around the central **Place de l'Obélisque**, along with a 30m obelisk decorated with propaganda reliefs celebrating poor Louis's glorious reign (it is one of few to survive the furious hammers of the Revolution).

Every town on the Côte Vermeille has its artist, and the one who spent the last two winters of his life (1925–26) rambling the hills and painting vibrant watercolours here was Charles Rennie Mackintosh, the great Scottish architect and designer, who loved the area so much that he had his ashes scattered in the sea off Port-Vendres. In the basement of Le Dôme Centre d'Art on Route de Collioure, a **Mackintosh Interpretation Centre** (✆ 04 68 82 60 99; w crmackintoshroussillon.com; ⊕ see website) has an exhibition and photos on his life and paintings; there's also an art walk, with 13 copies of his works.

The coast juts out east here, with a picturesque little promontory called Cap Béar, topped by another of this area's many Baroque fortresses that is now off limits to the public thanks to the area being designated as a military zone. However, you can still make your way to the very tip of the peninsula via a narrow and winding road, where you'll find a lighthouse standing guard and swoon-worthy views of the coast in either direction.

There are many isolated beaches in the vicinity, though they are hard to reach; most are south of the cape, including three at **Paulilles**, where the landmark is a dynamite factory (a mildly historic one, because it belonged to Alfred Nobel, inventor of dynamite and plywood, who used the profits to finance his prizes), which operated from 1870 to 1984; you can visit the factory, director's house and interpretation centre, the **Site de Paulilles** (✆ 04 68 95 23 40; ⊕ May–Oct 09.00–noon & 14.00–19.00 daily; Nov–Apr 09.00–noon & 14.00–17.00 daily except Tue).

COLLIOURE

Sempre endavant, mai morirem
(Always forward, we'll never die)
Collioure's motto

If the tourists would only leave it in peace, Collioure would be quite happy to make its living in the old way, filling up barrels with anchovies. As it is, the town

9

WINE: BANYULS AND COLLIOURE

Sweet and spicy and AOC since 1936, Banyuls is mainland France's southernmost wine appellation. The Romans were the first to plant vines on its steep, schisty slopes 2,000 years ago, but it was the Knights Templars who transformed the wine production process from the 13th century. Because of the climate – swept by the tramontane winds, with long sunny summers and torrential rains in winter – the Templars had to build stone terraces and construct drainage trenches and stone walls to keep the vines from being washed or blown away. They planted the dark Grenache noir grapes that were best suited for the difficult conditions.

But what made Banyuls into the Banyuls we know today was their adoption of the vinification process proposed in the 13th century by Arnau de Villanova, a Catalan alchemist and physician to the popes. While studying in Muslim Córdoba, Arnau learned the secrets of distillation and transmitted it to the West; in particular he invented the principle of wine fortification and stabilisation with a dollop of neutral eau de vie, which preserves some of the wine's natural sugar and its aroma. Afterwards the wine is aged for 3–15 years, sometimes in barrels right under the roof of a winery, or out in the full sun, to subject it to extreme variations in temperature, resulting in a distinctive rich amber wine with a raisiny taste. A fine old Banyuls is claimed to be the only wine that can accompany chocolate desserts, but be warned: a cheap young bottle may hardly do justice to a Mars bar.

Collioure, Port-Vendres, Cerbère and Banyuls are the only places allowed to wear the AOC label, and two-thirds of their wine, as well as the delightful dry red, rosé and white wines of Collioure, pass through the co-operative **Terres des**

bears their presence as gracefully as possible, though in summer parking is nigh on impossible. In a way, Collioure is unspoiled – though it has 17 hotels, it does not have mini-golf or a water slide, or all the hype projected on Saint-Tropez, that other unaffectedly beautiful port discovered at the beginning of the 20th century by the Fauves. Instead, you'll find every other requisite for a civilised Mediterranean resort: a castle, a pretty church by the sea, three small beaches, a shady market square with cafés – and warehouses full of anchovies. Its narrow streets are lined with boutiques and tall, shuttered houses painted in pink, green, blue and yellow.

It's hard to believe, looking at the map, but in the Middle Ages this was the port for Perpignan; with no good harbours on the (then) unhealthy sandy coast to the north, Perpignan's fabrics and other goods had to come to the Pyrenees to go to sea. In the 14th century, Collioure was one of the biggest trading centres of Aragon, yet nearly the whole town was demolished by the French after they took possession in 1659. They weren't angry with the Colliourencs; the town was merely in the way of modernising its fortifications. Our own century has no monopoly on twisted military logic: Collioure had to be razed so that it could be better defended.

The population moved into the part that survived, the steep hillside quarter called the Mouré, where they have made the best of it ever since. Collioure was discovered in 1905 by Matisse and Derain. 'No sky in all France is more blue than that of Collioure!' wrote Matisse. Many other artists followed, including Picasso, but these two were the most inspired, and they put a little of Collioure's vermilion tint into the deep colours of their first Fauvist experiments.

Collioure also marks the northern tip of the great Catalan 'Anchovy Coast' that extends south to the Gulf of Roses on the Costa Brava (page 157). Few of us,

Templiers (Rte du Mas Reig; ☎ 04 68 98 36 92; w terresdestempliers.fr; ⊕ see website for opening times & scheduled tours in English), a large concern happy to receive visitors for tastings and a tour of their magnificently vaulted 13th-century *grande cave*; their *cave souterraine* (⊕ Jul & Aug only) just below has enormous hundred-year-old oak barrels, and a film on the wine.

Other wineries include:

Cave l'Étoile 26 Av du Puig del Mas, Banyuls; ☎ 04 68 88 00 10; w caveletoile. com; ⊕ call ahead for visits. Co-operative where everything is done lovingly in the old-fashioned way.
Cellier des Dominicains Pl Orphila; ☎ 04 68 82 05 63; w cellierdominicain. com; ⊕ 09.00–12.30 & 13.30– 18.45 Mon–Sat, 10.00–13.00 & 15.00–18.45 Sun

Domaine de la Rectorie 65 Av du Puig del Mas, Banyuls; m 06 95 77 78 09; w rectorie.com; ⊕ call ahead for visits
Domaine du Mas Blanc 9 Av du Général de Gaulle, Banyuls; ☎ 04 68 98 74 41; w domaine-du-mas-blanc.com; ⊕ 10.00–13.00 & 15.00–19.30 daily in summer, by appt only out of season. A good selection of Collioure wine.

If you wish to try the local wines with local food in a delightful setting, book dinner (May–Sep only) at the ferme-auberge **Les Clos de Paulilles** (Domaine de Valcros, Port-Vendres; m 06 31 93 06 24; w lesclosdepaulilles.com), where different wines accompany each course.

probably, give any thought to how the little fish are apprehended in the open sea. It isn't, in fact, a terribly difficult operation. The diabolical Catalans have boats called *llampadores*, with big searchlights. They sneak out on warm summer nights, when the normally shy anchovies are making their promenade, and nab the lot. After spending a few months in barrels of brine, the unfortunate fish reappear, only to be stuffed into olives; and it must be said a proper fat brown Catalan anchovy is a very different beast from the dinky silvery salt bomb that can sneak on to your pizza.

Museums and art Fourteen sketches by Matisse are in Céret (page 325) and his best works from Collioure are in private collections, or in the Hermitage in St Petersburg. Collioure has none. To rectify the lack, the village has created the **Chemin du Fauvisme**, placing copies of Matisse and Derain's works on the spots where the two set up their easels. The Fauvism guided tours (and every other type of guided tour in town) begin in **La Maison du Fauvisme** (10 Rue de la Prud Homie; ☎ 04 68 98 07 16; w collioure.com; ⊕ 09.30–12.30 & 14.00–18.15 Tue–Fri, 09.30– 12.30 & 14.00–17.30 Sat & Mon, closed Sun); there is also the **Musée d'Art Moderne** (4 Rte de Port-Vendres; ☎ 04 30 44 05 46; ⊕ 10.00–noon & 14.00–16.00 daily, Oct– May closed on Tue; adult/26 & under €3/2) in a peaceful villa on the road to Port-Vendres with a terraced olive grove, which has works by lesser-known artists in the style of the Fauves, as well as an intriguing collection of Moorish ceramics.

Château Royal (☎ 04 68 82 06 43; w ledepartement66.fr; ⊕ see website; adult/ reduced/under 18 & EU residents 18–25 €9/7/free) Collioure (or as the locals call it, Cotllures) is a thoroughly Catalan town, and the red- and yellow-striped Catalan flag waves proudly over the Château Royal, dominating the harbour thanks to its

9

outworks that are nearly as big as the town itself. First built by the Templars in the 13th century, the castle was expanded by various Aragonese kings, and used as a summer palace by the kings in Perpignan. The outer fortifications, low walls and broad banks of earth were state-of-the-art in 1669. The great Vauban, Louis XIV's military genius, oversaw the works and the demolition of the old town. Collioure's fate could have been even worse; Vauban had wanted to level it completely and force everyone to move to Port-Vendres. The older parts of the castle have been restored and are open for visits, along with several small exhibitions on local specialities from whip-making to espadrilles.

From the castle, cross the small stream called the Douy (usually dry and used as a car park) into the Mouré, the old quarter that is now the centre of Collioure. There is an amiable shorefront, with a small beach from which a few anchovy fishermen still ply their trade; several brightly painted fishing smacks are usually pulled up to complete the effect.

Notre-Dame-des-Anges (⊕ 09.15–16.30 daily, although hours may be reduced for ongoing restoration) At the far end of the beach you'll see Collioure's landmark, painted by Matisse and many others: the church of Notre-Dame-des-Anges. The Colliourencs built it in the 1680s to replace the original church destroyed by Vauban; they chose the beach site to use the old cylindrical lighthouse as a bell tower. The best thing about the church is that you can hear the waves of the sea from inside, a profound basso continuo that makes the celebration of Mass here unique. The next best are the retables, five of them, done between 1699 and 1720 by Joseph Sunyer and others. This is Catalan Baroque at its eccentric best, drawing influence from the style of Spanish architect José Benito de Churriguera, who would often concentrate his finest efforts on these towering constructions of carved wooden figures and dioramas of scriptural scenes with intricately painted stage-backdrop backgrounds. Sunyer's inside the Notre-Dame-des-Anges are especially lifelike.

The second of Collioure's beaches lies right behind the church; really an old sand bar that has become part of dry land, it connects the town with a former islet, the Ilôt Saint-Vincent, crowned with a tiny medieval chapel.

Sentier de la Moulade A scenic footpath called the Sentier de la Moulade leads from near Notre-Dame-des-Anges along the rocky shore north of Collioure. High above, you'll see Fort Miradou, the Spanish King Philip II's addition to Collioure's defences, and still in military use. You can, however, tour the **Fort Saint-Elme** (m 06 64 61 82 42; w fortsaintelme.fr; ⊕ see website for opening times and guided tours), built by Charles V in 1552 as a key link in Spain's coastal defences; and, if that's not high enough, a road leads up to the 13th-century **Tour de Madeloc** (for more fortresses, see page 329).

Cemetery Collioure's cemetery, found back in town at 4 Jardin Navarro, has its share of celebrities: the Spanish poet Antonio Machado died here in 1939, after escaping Franco's forces in the Civil War (an annual poetry competition is held in his honour), as did translator and historical novelist Patrick O'Brian (d2000), who moved to Collioure with his wife in 1949.

UP THE COAST TO PERPIGNAN

A geographical oddity, Roussillon's coastline is almost perfectly straight and runs from Argelès in the south for 40km to Port Barcarès in the north. It isn't the most compelling landscape, but it is almost solid beach, and has been much developed since the 1960s, when de Gaulle's government decided to try to keep the French masses holidaying in France (but not on the elite Côte d'Azur) instead of spending all their hard-earned francs on the Costa Brava.

Perpignan's suburbs have sprawled out to meet the sea and the continuation of Roussillon's die-straight sands, while Elne, just inland, has one of the south's greatest Romanesque cloisters, not only surviving, but surviving in situ.

GETTING THERE AND AWAY **Trains** run by SNCF whisk visitors between Cerbère at the border to Perpignan, with stops at Banyuls, Collioure, Argelès-sur-Mer and Elne. The B40 bus links Banyuls and Perpignan, with stops at all the resorts in between. To reach Canet-Plage, directly east of Perpignan, jump on the regular number 3 **city bus** operated by Sankéo (w sankeo.com).

TOURIST INFORMATION

Argelès-sur-Mer Pl de l'Europe; ` 04 68 81 15 85; w argeles-sur-mer.com; ⏰ 09.00–12.30 & 14.00–17.30 Mon–Fri

Elne 2 bis Rue du Couvent; ` 48 98 00 08, w tourisme-pyrenees-mediterranee.com; ⏰ Jul–Aug 09.00–12.30 & 14.30–18.00 daily; May–Jun & Sep 09.00–12.30 & 14.00–17.30 Mon–Sat; Oct–Apr 09.00–12.30 & 14.00–17.30 Mon–Fri

Saint-Cyprien Quai Arthur Rimbaud; ` 04 68 21 01 33; w tourisme-saint-cyprien.com; ⏰ Jul–Aug 09.30–12.30 & 15.00–19.00 daily, Sep–Jun 09.00–noon & 14.00–18.00 Mon–Sat

🏠 WHERE TO STAY

L'Île de la Lagune [map, page 322] (30 rooms) Bd de l'Almandin, Saint-Cyprien; ` 04 68 21 01 02; w hotel-ile-lagune.com. This luxury resort enjoys a tennis court & a large central swimming pool, all set on its own little island. The restaurant, L'Almandin (⏰ noon–13.30 & 19.30–21.30 Mon–Sat, noon–13.30 Sun; €€€€), is considered one of the best on the coast, with a stylish menu of Catalan dishes, such as *blinis aux anchois de Collioure à la tapenade* and *caviar d'aubergine*. €€€€

Grand Hôtel du Lido [map, page 322] (66 rooms) 50 Bd de la Mer, Argelès-sur-Mer; ` 04 68 81 10 32; w hotel-le-lido.com. A pleasant family-friendly resort right on the beach in Argelès-sur-Mer. There's a large swimming pool &, in summer, the beachfront promenade comes to life with carnivals & things to keep the little ones entertained. €€€

Auberge du Roua [map, page 322] (20 rooms) Chem du Roua, Argelès-sur-Mer; ` 04 68 95 85 85; w aubergeduroua.com; ⏰ closed mid-Nov–Feb. Away from the hubbub, this luxurious little stone auberge has a pool & terrace restaurant (€€€). €€

Logis Hôtel Le Cara-Sol (8 rooms) 10 Bd Illiberis, Elne; ` 04 68 22 10 42; w hotelcarasol.com. A beautiful hotel set in the old ramparts of Elne. Bedrooms have views across the Roussillon plain to the mountains, & the restaurant (€€), serving Mediterranean dishes, has a lovely rooftop terrace. €€

✖ WHERE TO EAT AND DRINK

L'Hidalgo [map, page 322] 7 Quai Arthur Rimbaud, Saint-Cyprien; ` 04 68 21 15 30; w lhidalgo.business.site; ⏰ 09.00–22.30 daily. Located at the port in Saint-Cyprien, this waterfront bistro serves up Catalan tapas & seafood plucked from the Mediterranean in great portions. €€€

Le Flowers 59 Rue Victor Hugo, Argelès; ` 04 68 81 05 79; w leflowers.fr; ⏰ noon–14.00 & 19.00–21.30 Tue–Sat. World cuisine – choose between North African, Asian or Catalan – with a lunch buffet & a chance to choose your own veggies, fish or meat for the chef to whip up in the wok & serve with noodles or rice. €€

SPORTS AND ACTIVITIES For those travelling in the summer, **Aqualand Saint Cyprien** (Av Des Champs de Neptune, Saint-Cyprien; ` 04 68 21 49 49; w aqualand. fr; ⏰ 22 Jun–4 Sep 10.00–18.00 daily) is a fantastic water park that'll be popular with little ones. There are plenty of slides and pools to enjoy, making this an easy

9

family day out in the area. There are also **go-karting tracks** in Saint-Cyprien (Karting St Cyprien; Chemin du Prat d'En Veil; 📞 04 68 21 41 76; w kartingstcyprien.fr) and Argelès (Ludi Kart; 1 Imp Copernic; 📞 04 68 81 88 01; w ludikart.com), and a fabulous, 27-hole **golf course** (Golf de Saint-Cyprien; Rue Jouy d'Arnaud; 📞 04 68 37 63 01; w golf-saint-cyprien.com) that stretches from the Mediterranean along the bottom of the Étang de Canet lagoon.

ARGELÈS AND AROUND Big bland Argelès (divided into the old town, Argelès-sur-Mer, and Argelès-Plage) has 7km of sand and makes some claim as the European Capital of Camping, with over 50 campsites and a capacity for 100,000 happy campers. When you can't stand any more beach fun, head 4km inland to **Saint-André**, in the foothills of the coastal Albères mountains. It has a lofty 12th-century church with a sculpted lintel of 1030; opposite, the small **Maison Transfrontalière de l'Art Roman** (📞04 68 89 04 85; ⏰ 5 Apr–6 Jul & 29 Aug–6 Nov 14.00–18.00 Tue–Sat; 7 Jul–28 Aug 15.00–19.00 Wed–Sat) is dedicated to sculpture from this and from other Romanesque churches in Roussillon and Catalunya.

One of these is just west of Saint-André: the Benedictine monastery of **Saint-Génis-des-Fontaines** (📞04 68 89 84 33; ⏰ Jul–Aug 09.30–12.30 & 15.00–19.00 daily; Apr–Jun & Sep 09.30–noon & 14.00–18.00 daily; Oct–Mar 09.30–noon & 14.00–17.00 Mon–Sat; €2), founded around the year 800. Its church has a remarkable carved lintel dated 1020 (the earliest ever with a date) decorated with a Christ Majestat and stylised apostles shaped like bowling pins; the pretty late 13th-century cloister was dismantled and sold off in 1924, one of the final scandals of France's traditional lack of concern for its medieval heritage. In 1988 it was rebuilt as it was, using a mix of originals and copies of its capitals.

Just south of Saint-André, in **Sorède** and the **Vallée Heureuse** ('Happy Valley') filled with cork groves, rare Hermann's tortoises and 30 other species inhabit **La Vallée des Tortues** (📞 04 68 95 50 50; w lavalleedestortues.fr; ⏰ Apr–May & Sep–early Nov 11.00–16.30 daily; Jun 10.00–18.00 daily; Jul–Aug 10.00–18.30 daily; adult/12 & under €13.50/9.50, €12.50/8.50 if booked online in advance). This tortoise refuge is best visited at the cooler times of day, when the animals are more active. The adjacent Fun Valley offers plenty of activities for the small fry.

ELNE The citadel of Elne, atop a steep hill, has guarded the Roussillon plain for at least 2,700 years. Its ancient name, Illiberis, is said to be Iberian. Hannibal sojourned here on his way to Italy, waiting to negotiate an alliance with the Celts to guard his rear; the locals, apparently unimpressed even with the elephants, made him pay a toll to pass through. The name-change came in the time of Constantine, to Castrum Helenae, after the emperor's mother, St Helen, legendary discoverer of the True Cross. Throughout the Middle Ages and into the 16th century, Elne was one of the most important cities in Roussillon, the seat of the archbishops. The town is now reduced to some 6,000 souls, having lost all its honours and status to Perpignan.

But they couldn't take away its fortified **cathedral** at the top of the town. Begun in 1069, it has a wonderful stage presence, with crenelated roofline and stout, arcaded tower. Inside, the stone masons pulled some optical techniques straight out of the magic hat of antiquity to accentuate the beauty – the cornice along the nave slopes and the pillars gently lean outwards. In a chapel on the right is an Italianate 14th-century altarpiece of St Michael and there are some fine tombs, especially that of Ramon de Costa (1310).

The **cloister** (📞04 68 22 70 90; ⏰ 09.30–18.00 Tue–Sun; €4.50) is one of the best in the Midi, and also the best preserved, its capitals and pillars decorated with imaginative, exquisitely carved arabesques and floral patterns. What makes Elne's cloister particularly interesting is the fact that its four sides were completed in different periods, at roughly 50-year intervals; that closest to the cathedral is the earliest, from the 12th century, and its capitals show the influence of the sculptors of Saint-Michel-de-Cuxa (page 355).

Oddly, each generation of sculptors chose to repeat the subjects of their predecessors: all but the north gallery have central pillars carved with serpentine dragons and mermaids (who may well have been introduced in the region by the Visigoths) spreading their forked tails; other capitals repeat scenes from the Old Testament. The little **museum** tells the history of the cathedral and cloister, including its lost upper gallery, dismantled in 1827 and sold off at an auction in 1960.

Admission to the cloister includes entry to the **Musée Terrus** (3 Rue Prte Balaguer; \04 68 22 88 88; w ville-elne.fr; ⊕ May–Sep 10.00–19.00 Tue–Sun; Oct–Apr 10.00–noon & 14.00–18.00 Tue–Sun) a short walk away; painter Étienne Terrus (1857–1922) was a friend of Matisse and Derain and the museum contains mainly his landscapes. Interestingly, in 2018, a visiting art historian discovered that over half the works in the museum were fakes, created by professional art forgers and sold to the museum over a number of years. The collection today is a lot smaller than it once was, but you can now rest assured that what they do have are original pieces completed by Terrus.

SAINT-CYPRIEN-PLAGE

SAINT-CYPRIEN-PLAGE This looks just like Canet-Plage only more so, with fancier restaurants and a summer chamber music festival. Set back in Saint-Cyprien proper, 3km from the beach on Place de la République, the **Musée François Desnoyer** (Rue Émile Zola; \04 68 21 32 07; w collectionsdesaintcyprien.com; ⊕ 1 Sep–30 Jun 14.00–18.00 daily; €4) has works by Catalan artists such as Maillol, Delfau and Bone, and a small collection of paintings by Picasso, Dufy, Chagall and Miró once owned by François Desnoyer (1894–1972), along with several of Desnoyer's own colourful, figurative works.

CANET-PLAGE

CANET-PLAGE This has long been the favourite resort of the Perpignanais. After taking a beating in the last war, it has been rebuilt without much distinction. To add to the joys of the beach and endless water-based sports there's an **Aquarium** (2 Bd de la Jetée; \04 68 80 49 64; w oniria.fr; ⊕ Sep–Jun 10.00–19.00 daily; Jul–Aug 09.30–21.00 daily; adult/child €14.50/11) by the port, where the star attraction is that impossibly unlovely living fossil from the depths of the Indian Ocean, the coelacanth. The tourist office organises tours of Canet's medieval castle in summer.

South of Canet the distinctive profile of the Pic du Canigou looms as prominently as Fiji over the flamingo-filled **Étang de Canet**, while the road and bike path runs down a lido of wild beaches and dunes, complete with a reconstructed reed hut fishermen's village.

PERPIGNAN

There's a little craziness in every Catalan soul – they even have a name for it, 'rauxa' (page 12). In Perpinyà (as its residents call it), former capital of the kings of Majorca and the counts of Roussillon, this natural exuberance was until recently suppressed by French centralisation; of late, however, it's been feeling its oats, with high-speed train links with Paris and Barcelona and a busy calendar of festivals.

9

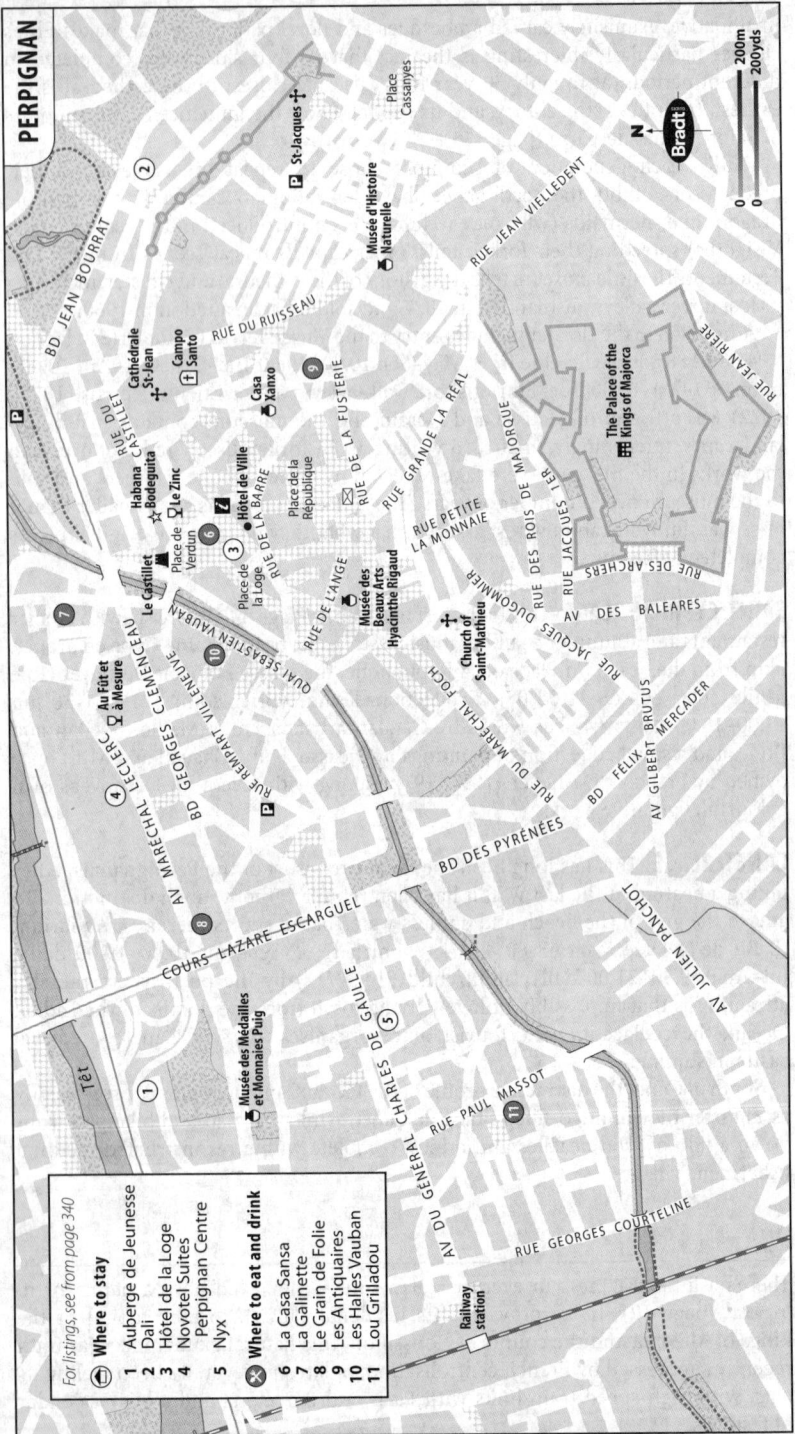

PERPIGNAN

Place Cassanyes

St-Jacques

Musée d'Histoire
Naturelle

Cathédrale
St-Jean

Campo
Santo

Casa
Xanxo

Habana
Bodeguita
Le Zinc

Hôtel de Ville

Place de la
République

Place de
Verdun

Le Castillet

Place de
la Loge

Musée des
Beaux Arts
Hyacinthe Rigaud

Church of
Saint-Mathieu

The Palace of the
Kings of Majorca

Au Fût et
à Mesure

Musée des Médailles
et Monnaies Puig

Railway
station

Tét

The king of kookiness himself, Salvador Dalí, set off the first sparks in 1963, when he passed Perpignan's train station in a taxi (he would frequently visit to ship his paintings abroad, not trusting the train station in his native Figueres) and suddenly realised it was the great hinge of existence: 'a true mental ejaculation… suddenly I saw it with the brightness of lightning: in front of me I saw the centre of the Universe.'

He painted a picture of it, one of his last masterpieces, called *Mystique de la Gare de Perpignan* (1965), which shows, among other things, Dalí himself being sucked into a vortex of light; a later revelation showed in 1983 that the entire Iberian Peninsula did really rotate precisely at Perpignan station 132 million years ago – and might some day break off, a theory which he illustrated in one of his final drawings, *Topological Abduction of Europe – Homage to René Thom*. Perpignan's otherwise ordinary Gare SNCF (with its terminal for the TGV, which puts Figueres and the Dalí Museum only 20 minutes away) has been a hot destination for Surrealist pilgrims ever since.

HISTORY Perpignan is named after Perperna, a lieutenant of the great 1st-century BC populist general Quintus Sertorius. While Rome was suffering under the dictatorship of Pompey, Sertorius governed most of Spain in accordance with his astonishing principle that one should treat Rome's provinces decently. The enraged Senate sent out five legions to destroy him, but his army, who all swore to die if he was killed, defeated each one until the villainous Perperna invited his boss to a banquet in the Pyrenees and murdered him.

In 1197, Perpignan became the first Catalan city granted a municipal charter, and governed itself by a council elected by the three estates or 'arms'. Its merchants traded as far abroad as Constantinople, and the city enjoyed its most brilliant period in the 13th century when Jaume I, King of Aragon and conqueror of Majorca, created the Kingdom of Majorca and County of Roussillon for his younger son, Jaume II. This little kingdom was absorbed by the Catalan kings of Aragon in the 14th century, but continued to prosper until 1463, when Louis XI's army came to claim Perpignan and Roussillon as payment for mercenaries sent to Aragon. Besieged, the Perpignanais ate rats rather than become French, until the king of Aragon himself ordered them to surrender. In 1493, Charles VIII, more interested in Italian conquests, gave Perpignan back to Spain. But in the 1640s Richelieu pounced on the first available chance to grab back this corner of the mystic Hexagon, and French possession of Roussillon and the Haute-Cerdagne was cemented in the 1659 Treaty of the Pyrenees.

Perpignan made little noise after that. Recent troubles over immigration and rivalries between the city's communities of North Africans and Catalan Roma seem to have dwindled, leaving a sunny, attractive town, popular with visitors.

GETTING THERE AND AWAY
By air Perpignan airport (✆ 04 68 52 60 70; w aeroport-perpignan.com) is 5km northwest of the city and linked by shuttles (navettes) from the bus station an hour before each flight, with schedules published on the airport website. **Ryanair** run regular flights between the airport and London Stansted, as well as a couple of flights every week from Birmingham between March and October. Daily flights from Paris Orly are offered by **Transavia**.

By train The famous station, decorated with Dalí style murals, is at the end of Avenue du Général de Gaulle and has frequent slow services down to the Spanish border at Port Bou and high-speed links to Paris, Figueres and Barcelona.

9

By bus Perpignan's city bus service is operated by the company **Sankéo** (w sankeo. com) with links across the urban area and to most of the beaches in summer. Bus lines across the département (☎806 80 80 90; w lio.laregion.fr) also leave from the bus station, which you'll find attached to the train station. Buses also leave for Barcelona across the border.

Car hire

Avis Gare Perpignan; ☎04 68 35 61 48; w avis.fr; ⏰ 10.00–13.00 & 15.00–17.30 Mon–Sat

Enterprise Aéroport de Perpignan & Gare de Perpignan; ☎04 68 51 09 09; w enterprise.fr;

⏰ 09.00–noon & 14.00–18.00 Mon–Sat at the train station, daily at the airport

Sixt Aéroport de Perpignan; ☎820 00 74 98; w sixt.fr; ⏰ 08.30–22.00 Sun–Fri, 08.30–19.30 Sat

TOURIST INFORMATION

Tourist Office of Perpignan Pl de la Loge; ☎04 68 66 30 30; w perpignantourisme.com; ⏰ Apr–Oct 09.30–19.00 Mon–Sat, 10.00–17.00 Sun; Nov–Mar 10.00–18.00 Mon–Sat, 10.00–13.00 Sun. Perpignan's large tourist office is located inside the beautiful & historic

Gothic Loge de Mer building (page 342). The friendly staff are immensely helpful & more than happy to share their local knowledge of the region, making this a great first port of call when arriving in the city.

⌂ WHERE TO STAY   *Map, page 338, unless otherwise stated*

La Villa Duflot [map, page 322] (52 rooms) Rond Point Albert Donnezan; ☎04 68 56 67 67; w villa-duflot.com. Near the Perpignan-Sud-Argelès motorway exit, in the middle of an industrial zone! However, you can pretend to be elsewhere in the comfortable AC rooms & garden, or in the popular restaurant (€€€) overlooking the pool. €€€€

La Fauceille [map, page 322] (35 rooms) 860 Chemin de la Fosella; ☎04 68 21 09 10; w lafauceille.com. 5km south of the centre towards Argelès, colourful contemporary rooms with a pool, spa & fine restaurant (€€€). €€€

Novotel Suites Perpignan Centre (50 rooms) Espace Mediterranee, 34 Av du Maréchal Leclerc; ☎04 68 92 72 72; w all.accor.com. Your standard chain hotel that offers all the comforts & service you'd expect. Great location makes it easy to whisk yourself into Perpignan's old town for a meal. €€€

Nyx Hôtel (17 rooms) 62 bis Av du Général de Gaulle; ☎04 68 34 87 48; w nyxhotel.ellohaweb.

com. A pleasant stroll from Perpignan's old town, this stylish hotel offers beautiful rooms, friendly service & a peaceful lobby bar to enjoy a drink before dinner. €€€

Dalí Hôtel (115 rooms) 18 Bd Jean Bourrat; ☎04 68 35 14 14, w dalihotel.fr. Plush, traditional, soundproofed rooms with tropical wallpapers. Common areas feature plenty of fun details inspired by Dalí, & the hotel restaurant (€€€) serves upscale Catalan fare. €€

Hôtel de la Loge (22 rooms) 1 Rue des Fabriques-d'en Nabot; ☎04 68 34 41 02; w hoteldelaloge.com. A small & friendly hotel in the city centre, located in a 16th-century building. Rooms are spacious & pretty, with TVs, AC & some with small terraces overlooking the plaza below. €€

Auberge de Jeunesse (49 beds) Parc de la Pépinière, Av de Grande Bretagne; ☎04 68 34 63 32; w perpignan-hostel.com; ⏰ closed mid-Nov–mid-Mar. A small youth hostel, with b/fast available. Book in summer. €

✕ WHERE TO EAT AND DRINK   *Map, page 338*

La Galinette 23 Rue Jean Payra; ☎04 68 35 00 90; w restaurant-galinette.com; ⏰ noon–14.00 & 19.30–21.30 Tue–Sat. Christophe Comes' gastronomic restaurant delights palates with fresh & seasonal produce including vegetables

from the chef's own garden. Choose between either the 6- or 8-dish tasting menu, both of which are excellent value for money considering the high quality & Michelin star billing. Bookings essential. €€€€

La Casa Sansa 3 Rue Fabriques Couvertes; ☎04 68 34 21 84; ⏰ noon–13.45 & 19.00–22.45 Tue–Fri, noon–14.00 & 19.00–23.00 Sat. The restaurant locals point you towards here when asking for a recommendation. Lively, with excellent food served in a 14th-century cellar – with dishes from Catalan escargots to rabbit with aioli, occasional live music & more than its share of Catalan flair. €€€
Les Antiquaires Pl Joseph Desprès; ☎04 68 34 06 58; ⏰ noon–13.30 & 19.30–21.00 Wed–Fri, noon–13.45 & 19.30–21.00 Sat, noon–13.30 Sun. A local favourite for reliable, excellent French specialities. Fabulous service, a friendly environment & a passionate chef make this restaurant an all-around fantastic choice. €€€
Le Grain de Folie 71 Av Maréchal Leclerc; ☎04 68 51 00 50; ⏰ 09.00–15.00 Sun & Tue–Wed,

09.00–23.00 Thu–Sat. Excellent value for money seasonal dishes, with a menu that changes every month. €€
Les Halles Vauban 37–39 Quai Sébastien Vauban; ⏰ 08.00–21.00 Tue–Wed, 08.00–23.00 Thu–Sat, 08.00–13.00 Sun. A covered food hall with fresh fruit & veg, delis & street food vendors with a wide variety of options from fresh seafood cooked on the spot to Catalan tapas bars. A lively spot to sample a range of different foods or get together some goodies for a picnic. €€
Lou Grilladou 7 Pl de Belgique; ☎04 68 34 86 81; w lou-grilladou-restaurant-perpignan. fr; ⏰ noon–14.00 & 19.00–22.00 Tue–Sat. Affordable creative cuisine (scallops & chorizo on a spit, etc) halfway between the historic centre & the train station. €€

ENTERTAINMENT AND NIGHTLIFE The lively bars around Place de la Loge and the surrounding streets are where much of the city's nightlife unfolds. There are also some great bars around Avenue Maréchal Leclerc, just across the river.

Au Fût et à Mesure 23 Av Maréchal Leclerc; m 06 81 62 80 64; w aufutetamesure.fr; ⏰ 17.00–01.00 Mon–Wed & Sat, 17.00–01.30 Thu–Fri, 17.00–midnight Sun. A convivial beer hall with a wide range of craft beers on tap.
Habana Bodeguita 5 Rue Grande des Fabriques; ☎04 68 34 11 00; 🖸 habanabodeguita;

⏰ 18.00–02.00 Tue–Sat. Music, dancing & food with a Latin touch.
Le Zinc 8 Rue Grande des Fabriques; ☎04 68 35 08 80; ⏰ 19.00–02.00 Tue–Sat. Jazz & cocktails; especially animated during Jazzèbre, Perpignan's jazz festival held in Oct.

SHOPPING Perpignan's market is held every morning on Place Cassanyes, and there is a Saturday morning market on Place de la République, selling regional produce.

OTHER PRACTICALITIES The closest **post office** to the city centre is just south of Place de la République (2 Rue Louis Caulas; w laposte.fr; ⏰ 09.00–noon & 13.30–17.00 Mon–Wed & Fri, 10.30–noon & 13.30–17.00 Thu); there's a second location across the river (19 Bd Georges Clemenceau; ⏰ same as above). The **Hospital Centre of Perpignan** (20 Av du Languedoc; ☎04 68 61 66 33; w ch-perpignan.fr; ⏰ 24hrs) is on the northern outskirts of the city towards the airport.

WHAT TO SEE AND DO
Le Castillet (Pl de Verdun; ☎ 04 68 35 42 05; w mairie-perpignan.fr/culture-patrimoine/culture/musees/casa-pairal; ⏰ 10.30–18.00 Tue–Sun) When most of Perpignan's walls were destroyed in 1904, its easy-going river-cum-moat, La Basse, was planted with lawns, flowerbeds, mimosas and Art Nouveau cafés. The fat brick towers and crenelated gate of Le Castillet in Place de Verdun were left upright for memories' sake; built in 1368 by Aragon to keep out the French, it became a prison once the French got in, especially during the Revolution. In 1946 a mason broke through a sealed wall in Le Castillet and found the body of a child, which on contact with the air dissolved into dust; from the surviving clothing fragments the corpse was dated to the end of the 18th century. And for over 50 years, people wondered: could

9

it have been Marie-Antoinette's son, the dauphin Louis Charles and briefly, before he died in 1795 at age 10, Louis XVII? After all, the child buried in the Temple prison in Paris, where the dauphin was said to have died of TB, was thought to be a substitute, and there were rumours that Revolutionaries had instead used the young dauphin as a secret bargaining chip in dealing with his Bourbon relatives in Spain.

All the many dauphin rumours and pretenders' claims were put to rest in 2000, when DNA testing of a desiccated heart stolen by the doctor who performed the autopsy on the child who died in Temple – which had resurfaced in 1975 after many adventures, and been deposited in a crystal vase in the royal Basilica of St-Denis – proved that it had indeed belonged to the son of Marie-Antoinette.

Along with this mysterious ghost, Le Castillet houses the **Casa Pairal Museum** (\04 68 35 42 05; ⊕ Jun–Sep 10.30–18.00 daily; Oct–May 11.00–17.30 Tue–Sun; €2) with items ranging from casts of Pau (Pablo) Casals' hands to a kitchen from a Catalan *mas* (farmhouse), complete with a hole in the door for the Catalan cat. The religious section includes religious poems carved on wood known as *goigs*, which people would commission to mark important events, plus a 'Cross of Insults', and a folksy 17th-century carving of the Last Supper.

Place de Verdun, nearby, is one of Perpignan's liveliest squares, while just outside the gate the **Promenade des Platanes** is lined with rows of magnificent, never pruned plane trees.

Place de la Loge

From Le Castillet, Rue Louis Blanc leads back to Place de la Loge, the medieval centre, where the cafés provide a grandstand for contemplating Aristide Maillol's voluptuous bronze *Venus* and the beautiful Gothic **Loge de Mer** or **Llotja**, built in 1397 by the king of Aragon to house the exchange and the Consolat de Mar, a branch of the Barcelona council founded by Jaume I to resolve trade and maritime disputes. This proud and noble building, with its Venetian arches, loggia and ship-shaped weathercock, fell on hard times and was until recently used as a fast-food outlet, although now it's home to Perpignan's wonderful tourist information centre.

The neighbouring 13th-century **Hôtel de Ville** has been spared the Llotja's humiliation, probably because it still serves its original purpose: on Saturday mornings, its courtyard fills with blushing brides posing for photos by Maillol's allegory of the *Mediterranean* (as a naked woman, of course). It is built of rounded river pebbles and bricks in the curious layer-cake style of medieval Perpignan; the three bronze arms sticking out of the façade symbolise old Perpignan's three estates. To the right, **the Palais de la Députation Provinciale** (1447) is a masterpiece of Catalan Renaissance, built for Roussillon's parliament but now housing dismal municipal offices. Rue des Fabriques-d'en Nabot, opposite the palace, was once the street of drapers.

Musée des Beaux Arts Hyacinthe Rigaud

(21 Rue Mailly; \04 68 66 19 83; w musee-rigaud.fr; ⊕ Jun–Sep 10.30–19.00 daily; Oct–May 11.00–17.30 Tue–Sun; adult/reduced/under 18 €8/7/free) South of the Députation, this fantastic art museum is named after the hometown boy who became portrait-painter to Louis XIV. Hyacinthe (1659–1743), master of raising the mediocre and unworthy to virtuoso heights of rosy-cheeked, debonair charm and sophistication, is well represented, most famously in his portrait of the Cardinal de Bouillon, who beams with self-satisfaction with his overflowing chest of loot (he was Grand Almoner of France) and the golden hammer he used to open the Holy Door at St Peter's in 1700. Note that he has a slight squint; because Rigaud painted it, the Cardinal refused to

pay him for the picture, so Rigaud kept the hammer instead. Another masterpiece is the *Retable de la Trinité* (1489) by the Master of Canapost, painted for the 100th anniversary of the Consolat de Mar and showing, underneath, a fanciful scene of the sea lapping at the base of the Llotja. You'll find 20th-century works by Picasso, Dufy, Maillol, Miró and Catalan-American artist Pierre Daura depicting Spanish Civil War exiles.

Cathédrale Saint-Jean (1 Rue de l'Horloge; ☎ 04 68 51 33 72; w cathedraleperpignan.fr; ⊕ 08.00–18.00 daily)

Just east of Place de la Loge unfolds Place Gambetta, site of Perpignan's pebble and brick cathedral, topped by a lacy 19th-century wrought-iron campanile with a four-octave carillon. Begun in 1324 but not ready for use until 1509, the interior is a success because the builders stuck to the design provided in the 15th century by Guillem Sagrera, architect of the great cathedral of Palma de Mallorca. Typical of Catalan Gothic, it has a single nave, 48m long, striking for its width rather than its soaring height.

The cathedral is proudest of its exquisite altarpieces or retables: on the high altar, the marble *Retable de Saint-Jean*, carved in a late Renaissance style in 1621 by Claude Perret; at the end of the left crossing, the *Retable des Stes Eulalie et Julie* (1670s); in the apsidal chapels, the painted wood *Retable de Saint-Pierre* (mid 16th century), and, to the right, the lovely *Notre-Dame de la Mangrana* (1500) – its name, 'of the pomegranate', comes from an earlier statue of the Virgin, which held a pomegranate, a symbol of fertility.

The chapels, wedged between the huge piers, hold some unique treasures along with their ornate retables, the oldest of which is a mysterious marble **baptismal font** (first chapel on the left), with a Latin inscription '*The wave of sacred fountain smothers the hill of the guilty serpent*'. Pre-Romanesque, perhaps even Visigothic, and carved from the drum of a Roman column to look like a tub bound with a cable, it bears a primitive face of Christ over an open book. Further up the left aisle, the massive **organ** of 5,075 pipes was decorated in 1504 with painted shutters (now displayed in a side chapel) and sumptuous carvings. On the pendentive under the organ, note the Moor's head – a common Catalan conceit symbolising wisdom, taken from the Templars, who exerted a powerful influence over the kings of Aragon. The jaw was articulated, to vomit sweetmeats or stick out its tongue at the children on holidays; now it's stuck, gaping open.

Beyond the Moor's head is the entrance into the **chapel of Notre-Dame-dels-Correchs**, a survivor of the original cathedral of Saint-Jean-le-Vieux (consecrated in 1025), filled with reliquaries and the effigy of the cathedral's founder, Jaume's son Sancho, his feet resting on a Chinese lion. The rest of the church was converted into an electrical generating station in 1890; it is closed to visitors, but you can see the portal with its image of Christ in Majesty just outside the present cathedral.

Repair work on the cathedral revealed that it still has a rare '**Pentecostal hole**' in the roof; on Pentecost Sunday a priest would climb on the roof and, at the appropriate moment in the Mass, light branches of dry broom and drop them through the hole on the congregation to symbolise the tongues of flame that appeared over the apostles' heads when they were filled with the Holy Spirit. So far there has been no talk of reviving the old custom.

A door in the right aisle leads out to a 16th-century chapel constructed especially to house an extraordinary wooden sculpture known as the *Dévôt Christ*. Carved in the Cologne region in 1307, this wasted Christ, whose contorted bones, sinews and torn flesh are carved with a rare anatomical realism, is stretched to the limits of agony on the Cross. Almost too painful to behold, it comes straight from the gloomy

9

age when Christendom believed that pain, contemplated or self-inflicted, brought one closer to God. It is an object of great veneration, and the Perpignanais claim that when the Christ's bowed head sags another half a centimetre or so to touch his chest, the world will end. A door from the cloister leads into the striking 15th-century **Salle Capitulaire**, its complex ogival vaulting attributed to Guillem Sagrera.

Nearby on Rue Amiral Ribeil is the cathedral's **Campo Santo** of 1300–30 (⊕ 11.00–17.30 Tue–Sun), the only cloister-cemetery of its kind in France, the Gothic tomb niches (*enfeux*) decorated with bas-reliefs; until the late 1980s it was occupied by the local gendarmerie. Today it forms the perfect setting for the city's summer concerts.

Casa Xanxo
(8 Rue de la Main de Fer; ☏ 04 68 62 37 98; ⊕ May–Sep noon–19.00 Tue–Sun; Jan–Apr 11.00–17.30 Tue–Sun) This Gothic house was built in 1507 by draper Bernat Xanxo, keen to show off his new wealth, although he made sure to decorate his proud new house with a relief of the Seven Deadly Sins. Portraits of Bernat and his wife decorate one of the doors, and there's an impressive fireplace but otherwise little else has survived, although there is a model of Perpignan in 1686, with the fortifications planned for the city by Vauban. It frequently hosts special exhibitions.

Quartier Saint-Jacques
The piquant neighbourhood south of the cathedral, built on the slopes of Puig des Lépreux (Lepers' Hill), was once the *aljama*, or Jewish quarter, of Perpignan. In its happiest days, in the 13th century, it produced a remarkable body of literature – especially from the pen of the mathematician and Talmudic scholar Gerson ben Salomon (author of the philosophical *Gate of Heaven*) – as well as rare manuscripts and calligraphy, all now in Paris. After the Jews were exiled, the quarter was renamed Saint-Jacques, and inhabited by working men's families, Romani and most recently by North Africans.

Saint-Jacques (Carrer de la Miranda; ☏ 04 68 66 30 30; ⊕ 11.00–18.00 daily) The neighbourhood landmark, this 12th- to 14th-century church is opulent and rich inside: there's a 'Cross of Insults' covered with the symbols of Christ's Passion, a statue of St James in Compostela pilgrimage gear (1450), and more fine retables, especially the 15th-century *Notre-Dame de l'Espérance*, featuring a rare view of the pregnant Virgin. Even today it's a hotbed of stalwart Catholic tradition, performing Masses in Latin since the pope gave the nod in 2007.

Musée d'Histoire Naturelle (12 Rue Fontaine Neuve; ☏ 04 68 66 33 68; w mairie-perpignan.fr; ⊕ Jun–Sep 09.30–17.30 daily; Oct–May 11.00–17.30 Tue–Sun; free) This was created for Perpignan's university in 1770 and displays creatures now rare or extinct in the eastern Pyrenees, including a plaster mould of a giant prehistoric tortoise, 'Perpiniana du Pliocene', discovered just outside the city at Serrat d'en Vaquer. The mummy was a gift from Ibrahim Pasha, sent over in 1847 after he took the cure at Vernet-les-Bains.

The Palace of the Kings of Majorca (Rue des Archers; ☏ 04 68 34 48 29; w tourism-mediterraneanpyrenees.com/palace-kings-majorca; ⊕ Nov–Mar 10.00–17.00 daily; Apr–Jun & Sep–Oct 10.00–18.00; Jul & Aug 09.30–18.30 daily; adult/reduced/under 25 €9/7/free) Enclosed in a vast extent of walls, originally medieval and later enlarged by Vauban, the Palais des Rois de Majorque is the oldest royal palace in France, begun in the 1270s by Jaume the Conqueror and occupied by his son Jaume II after 1283. Yet for all its grandeur, only three kings of Majorca were

LA SANCHE

In the early 15th century, while the fire-eating Dominican preacher St Vincent Ferrer was in Perpignan to advise in the dispute between Antipope Benedict XIII and Rome, he founded in the church of Saint-Jacques the confraternity of the Holy Blood (de la Sanch) to bring religious comfort to prisoners condemned to death. As in Seville, the confraternity reaches a wider audience on Good Friday afternoons, when it dons spooky black and red Ku Klux Klan-like robes and hoods called caparutxe (en route to an execution, the prisoner, judges and executioner were all dressed in caparutxe, to prevent anyone with enemies from being lynched along the way). Penitents in the procession carry the misteri, life-size statues representing scenes of the Passion (each one weighs up to 50kg, so carrying them really is an act of penitence); others crawl on their knees. A tambourine, and the occasional bell break the solemn silence, along with the chanting of traditional Easter goigs, or verses. Similar processions take place in the evening at Arles-sur-Tech and Collioure.

to reign here before Roussillon, Montpellier, the Cerdagne and the Balearic Islands were reabsorbed by Aragon in 1349. The scale of magnificence that they intended to become accustomed to survives, but not much else.

The throne room, with its three vast fireplaces, and the double-decker chapels in the donjon, with the queen's chapel on the bottom and the king's on top, both offer hints of the exotic splendour of the Majorcan court. The sacristy was the entrance to a network of underground passageways that connected the palace to its enormous 45m-deep wells, which also afforded Jaume II the chance to escape should his fierce and unwelcome older brother, Pere III of Aragon, come to call. The palace once stood in the midst of what the archives call 'Paradise' – partly enclosed terraced gardens, inspired by Moorish gardens on Majorca. A few traces remain to the right of the mightiest tower, the **Tour de l'Hommage**. The narrow grid of streets below the palace, around the church of **Saint-Mathieu**, were designed by the Templar tutors of Jaume the Conqueror, although most of the buildings are 18th century.

Musée des Monnaies et Médailles Joseph Puig (42 Av de Grande Bretagne; 04 68 62 37 64; ⊕ 13.00–18.00 Tue–Sat; free) This offbeat museum has an excellent collection of coins and medals from antiquity to modern times, with a section on Catalan money.

AROUND PERPIGNAN Of all the villages ingested by Greater Perpignan, none has as much star power, at least among medievalists, as **Cabestany** (Cabestanh), 4km to the southeast, which lent its name to the highly original Romanesque sculptor known as the Master of Cabestany. The Michelangelo of his day, he was in demand as far afield as Tuscany. In Cabestany's church **Notre-Dame-des-Anges** he left a remarkable tympanum of the *Dormition and Assumption of the Virgin*, and a scene of the Virgin in heaven, handing her girdle down to St Thomas, rediscovered during renovations in 1930 (now removed and displayed inside the transept). The anonymous master's itinerant life is explored in the **Centre de Sculpture Romane Maître de Cabestany** (Parc Guilhem; 04 68 08 15 31; w maitredecabestany.fr; ⊕ Jul–Aug 10.00–12.30 & 13.30–18.00 daily; Sep–Jun 10.00–12.30 & 13.30–18.00 Tue–Sun; adult/reduced/under 12 €4/2/free) which has over 60 casts of his finest works.

Cabestany was also the home of the troubadour Guilhem de Cabestanh, who wrote some of the most popular love poems of the Middle Ages. He is most famous for the legend of his demise, that Boccaccio inserted in *The Decameron* (Day 4: 9). Guilhem loved and was loved by the wife of a knight, one Raymond of Castel-Rossello. When Raymond learned of their affair, he ambushed Guilhem, murdered him and cut out his heart, which he gave to his cook to prepare with plenty of pepper. His wife ate it and praised the dish. 'I am not surprised,' said her husband, 'as you loved it so well when it was alive.' And he told her what she had eaten. 'Sir,' the lady replied, 'you have given me such an excellent thing to eat that God forbid any other food should again pass my lips.' And she leapt out of the window to her death.

NORTHERN ROUSSILLON

To venture into northern Roussillon is to discover a sparsely populated area of France. While the coast may still be filled with busy seaside resorts, inland you might drive for miles without seeing another car. There's the desolate Plateau d'Opoul, where the French army still comes to practise, and the southern edge of the barren Corbières, where digs turned up the Tautavel Man, who was one of the oldest Europeans discovered at the time. After that, the landscape becomes more interesting as it delves into the Fenouillèdes area, with ravines, forests, rushing streams and foothills.

GETTING THERE AND AWAY Local **trains** from Perpignan call at Rivesaltes and Salses-le-Château; at the former you can pick up the **Train Touristique du Pays Cathare et du Fenouillèdes** (\ 04 68 20 04 00; w letrainrouge.fr; reservations essential), which offers rides in open-air carriages through some lovely scenery as far as Axat in the Aude. Buses run by **Sankéo** (w sankeo.com) provide services to the main towns across the north.

TOURIST INFORMATION

Fenouillèdes 21 Av Georges Pezières; \ 04 68 59 07 57; w cc-aglyfenouilledes.fr; ⊕ 10.00–noon & 14.00–18.00 Tue–Sat

Le Barcarès Pl de la République; \ 04 68 86 15 56; w portbarcares.com; ⊕ 09.00–12.30 & 14.00–17.30 daily

Rivesaltes 9 Av Ledru Rollin; \ 04 68 64 73 23; w tourisme-rivesaltes.fr; ⊕ 10.00–noon & 14.00–17.00 Mon–Fri

🏠 WHERE TO STAY

Casa Montes (3 rooms) 1 Le Clos des Abricotiers, Salses-le-Château; m 06 11 10 90 28; w casa-montes.com. A charming B&B in the peaceful village of Salses-le-Château. There's a pool in the spacious garden, & it's a short 10min drive to the beach. €€

Le Châtelet [map, page 322] (15 rooms) Rte de Caudiès, Saint-Paul-de-Fenouillet; \ 04 68 59

01 20; w hotel-lechatelet.com. A Logis de France hotel, with a pool & restaurant (€€) open in the evenings for dinner. €€

Le Relais des Corbières (9 rooms) 10 Av Jean Moulin, Saint-Paul-de-Fenouillet; \ 04 68 59 23 89; w lerelaisdescorbieres.com. Smaller, more centrally located near Saint-Paul-de-Fenouillet with a restaurant (€€). Great value for money. €

✕ WHERE TO EAT AND DRINK

La Maison du Terroir 2 Av Jean Jaurès, Maury; \ 04 68 68 92 54; f maurylamaisonduterroir;

⊕ 10.00–15.00 Tue, 10.00–14.30 Wed & Sun, 10.00–22.15 Thu–Sat. Simple décor & a terrace amid the vines; contemporary Mediterranean cuisine from a chef trained at Paris's L'Arpège & a wide selection of wines from the surrounding region. €€€

Le Petit Gris [map, page 322] Rte d'Estagel, Tautavel; \04 68 29 42 42; w lepetitgris.eatbu.

com; ◷ noon–14.00 Sun & Tue–Thu, noon–14.00 & 19.00–21.00 Fri–Sat. A very popular family restaurant with great views of the plain from big windows; they serve traditional Catalan fare, including petit gris (snails), gambas & more. €€€

RIVESALTES Famous for its sweet wines (page 348), Rivesaltes was the home of Marshal Joffre, and now houses the small **Musée du Maréchal Joffre** (11 Rue Maréchal Joffre; \04 68 64 04 04; w museejoffre.fr; ◷ mid-Jun–mid-Sep 09.30–12.30 & 15.00–19.00 Tue–Sat; €2) dedicated to the Battle of the Marne.

In the nearby village of **Espira-de-l'Agly** to the west of Rivesaltes stands the impressive fortified Romanesque **church of Sainte-Marie**, built in 1136 as part of a monastery by the bishops of Urgell in Spain (powerful Catalan clerics whose successors, along with the presidents of France, are still the joint tributary lords of Andorra). The businesslike exterior has one fine carved portal, but the lavish interior (unfortunately usually locked) still comes as a surprise, with polychromed marbles and elaborate altarpieces from the 16th century.

FORTERESSE DE SALSES (Le Portichol, Salses-le-Château; \04 68 38 60 13; w forteresse-salses.fr/en; ◷ Apr–Sep 10.00–18.00 daily; Oct–Mar 10.00–12.45 & 14.00–17.15 daily; €9) Here the divorce of land and sea is startlingly complete. Set on the back end of the lagoon, the Étang de Leucate (or de Salses), on the route tramped by Hannibal and his elephants, is the last, lowest and least spectacular of all this area's many castles – but the Forteresse de Salses was the most important of them all.

Built in 1497 by Ferdinand the Catholic, first king of united Spain, Salses was the last word in castles for its time, the budget-busting masterpiece of a great military architect named Ramiro Lopez. Set squarely on the then French–Spanish border, Salses was meant to house 1,500 men to guard Perpignan and the vital coastal road. It finally had a chance to do so in 1639 – and failed. The Spaniards, caught by surprise, had only a small garrison at Salses; nevertheless, it required 18,000 Frenchmen and a month's siege to take it. The same year, a Spanish army spent three months winning it back. Both sieges were serious operations; until recently, the locals would go out cannonball-hunting for fun in the surrounding hills. When France acquired Roussillon in 1659, Salses no longer had a role to play. The famous Vauban, perhaps jealous, wanted to knock it down, but it was too expensive and survived to become a national monument in 1886.

At first glance, Salses looks strikingly streamlined and modern. It is a product of a transitional age, when defenders were coming to terms with the powerful new artillery that had made medieval castles obsolete. Salses is all curves and slopes, designed to deflect the cannonballs; its walls are not only incredibly thick (8.5m on average, 15m thick at the base), but also covered with heavy stone barrel vaulting to protect the walkway at the top.

PORT-BARCARÈS Until the 1960s (and DDT), this malarial coast was utterly deserted and no-one in the region gave it a second thought. Today in Roussillon's northernmost resort, the landmark is the *Paquebot Lydia*, a 1930s steamship brought over in 1967 by an entrepreneur and converted into a casino; in 2011 it was purchased by the town and now acts as an event space with a very popular Christmas market. Further south, the beaches are less cluttered but harder to reach; back roads lead off the D81 to **Torreilles-Plage** and **Sainte-Marie-Plage**.

9

RIVESALTES AND CÔTES DU ROUSSILLON

Catalans have a notoriously sweet tooth, and some 90% of France's dessert wine (*vin doux naturel*) comes from this département, spilling over into the Corbières to the north. Using mostly Grenache, Muscat or Macabeu grapes, these wines are made simply by stopping the fermentation at the right moment, leaving more sugar in the wine; usually a small amount of pure alcohol is added as well. Since the 13th century, Rivesaltes has been known for its fruity muscat, a wine to be drunk young, with sorbets or lemon tarts. Its AOC status, awarded in 1972 along with other Rivesaltes red and white apéritif wines, covers 99 communes in the eastern Pyrenees. Try some in Rivesaltes itself at the **Domaine Cazes** (4 Rue Francisco Ferrer; 04 68 64 08 26; w cazes-rivesaltes.com; 16 Sep–31 May 09.00–noon & 14.00–18.30 Mon–Sat; 1 Jun–15 Sep 09.00–19.00 daily), where the two talented Cazes brothers, Bernard and André, also produce AOC Côtes du Roussillon and Côtes du Roussillon Villages, plus some excellent white, rosé and red IGPs. In the past, few wine writers ever had anything good to say about this former *vin de pays* but, as in Languedoc, a number of producers like the Cazes brothers have been creating notable, individualistic wines from fine blends of Syrah, Carignan, Grenache and Mourvèdre.

Côtes du Roussillon is made all over the département, often in village co-operatives that also produce Rivesaltes or sweet muscat. Some recommended wineries include:

Château de Jau D59, Cases-de-Pène; 04 68 38 90 10; w chateaudejau.com; 08.30–12.30 & 14.00–17.00 Mon–Thu. This winery produces Côtes du Roussillon of surprisingly high quality. In summer they also host art exhibitions & have a restaurant (5 Jun–3 Oct; €€€€) that offers a fantastic lunch menu featuring local specialities & a wide range of wines.
Domaine Gauby Calce; 04 68 64 35 19; w domainegauby.fr; 08.00–noon Mon–Fri. Some of the area's finest red & white wines, full of local character.
Domaine Treloar 16 Traverse de Thuir, Trouillas; m 06 20 29 71 39; w domainetreloar.com; appointment via phone or email. Puts out a fantastic range of critically acclaimed reds & whites & a rosé.
Les Vignerons des Albères 9 Av des Écoles, St-Genis-des-Fontaines; 04 68 89 81 12; w vignerons-des-alberes.com; 09.30–noon & 15.00–18.00 Mon–Fri, 09.30–noon Sat. Produces a honey-sweet, fresh, lively rosé.

PLATEAU D'OPOUL Just above Salses, the long rocky wall of the southern Corbières spreads into a plateau that happens to be one of the most barren and isolated places in France; it is hard to believe any sea could be within a hundred miles. Don't be surprised to find tanks and suchlike growling across your path. The western half of the Plateau d'Opoul is one of the French army's zones for manoeuvres, the closest France can get to desert conditions. Most of the time, however, you won't see anyone, save old farmers half-heartedly trying to keep their ancient Citroëns on the road, on their weekly trip to the village to get a haircut or a goose.

The village is **Opoul-Périllos**, a cosy place that shuts itself off from the surrounding void. It is a relatively new settlement; its predecessor, **Périllos**, is an eerie ruined village higher up on the plateau, now inhabited by praying mantises, with another castle nearby. Both castle and village have enormous stone cisterns. Water was always a problem here – indeed, everything was a problem, and the 13th-century Aragonese kings who built both village and castle had to bribe people with special privileges so that they would agree to live on the plateau. Today there are vineyards, but until recently the only real occupation was smuggling.

Near the castle, a rocky side road leads west into the most desolate part of the plateau; at a spot called **La Vall Oriole** stands a massive, lonely limestone outcrop with a locked door at the bottom. It seems that in the early Middle Ages this rock was hollowed out by a community of cave-dwelling monks, like the famous Cappadocia ones in Turkey. There are plenty of other strange things up on this plateau, and in its history: connections with Bérenger Saunière and André Malraux, dragon legends, ley lines, an odd ruin called the 'Seat of Death', a lord of Périllos who became grand master of the Knights of Malta, a mysterious plane crash, UFO sightings and rumours of secret government installations. Enough material, in fact, for Périllos to have become a little vortex of mystery.

TAUTAVEL Descending from Opoul to the southwest, the D9 passes through some romantically empty scenery towards Tautavel, a pretty village under a rocky escarpment. Throughout Europe, prehistoric man picked the unlikeliest places to park his carcass. Around Tautavel, human bones have been found from as far back as 550,000–450,000BC, making 'Tautavel Man' a contender for the honour of First European when discovered in 1969 (although his grandad status has since been usurped by the discovery in 2008 of a 1.2-million-year-old humanoid jaw at Atapuerca in northern Spain). Back then, the climate was quite different, and Tautavel Man had elephants, bison and even rhinos to keep him company. Palaeolithic bones have become a cottage industry – over 430,000 have been found, especially in a cave called the Caune de l'Arago north of the village – the best being displayed in the **Musée de Préhistoire de Tautavel** (Av Léon Jean Grégory; \04 68 29 07 76; w 450000ans.com; ⊕ 10.00–12.30 & 14.00–18.00 daily; Jan–Mar & Sep–Dec closed on Tue; adult/reduced/under 7 €8/4/free). From April to September, during the excavation season, there's a camera link to the cave so you can watch the palaeontologists at work.

THE FENOUILLÈDES From Tautavel, the D611 continues south into the valley of the Agly. This and surrounding mountains make up the Fenouillèdes – the northernmost region of medieval Catalunya. The scenery makes a remarkable contrast to the dry and windswept Corbières. Here, limestone gradually gives way to granite, the true beginning of the Pyrenees. Some of it is covered by ancient virgin forest, broken by quick-flowing streams and ravines. The first likely stop along the D117 is **Maury**, famous for its dessert wines (page 350) and its pottery of deep blues and greens; next is **Saint-Paul-de-Fenouillet**, known for its almond biscuits.

Further along the D117, **Caudiès-de-Fenouillèdes**, has become something of an art centre, especially in summer. Three kilometres to the south, **Fenouillet** is guarded by three more ruined castles, all within a few hundred metres of each other (for the crow, anyhow). Beneath them, the simple medieval chapel of **Notre-Dame-de-Laval** has a wonderful polychrome wooden altarpiece, dated 1428.

The D619 south from Saint-Paul-de-Fenouillet is the only good road through the Fenouillèdes, passing through **Sournia** on the River Désix, the only real town. Along the way, be sure to stop at **Ansignan** to see its **Roman aqueduct**, a rustic,

9

seldom-visited version of the famous Pont du Gard. An 168m arcade with 29 arches, it is still in use today, carrying water over the Agly to the vineyards, and you can walk over it, or follow the channel towards the village. The question is why the Romans built it, with no nearby towns. It is unlikely that agriculture on the coastal plains was ever so intensive as to merit such a work. One possibility is a patrician villa – such things were often cities in themselves – but no traces of one have been discovered. Signs in Ansignan point the way up to a dolmen and to the small village of **Feilluns**; there are wide-ranging views over the mountains just beyond, on the D7 south to Sournia.

UP THE CONFLENT VALLEY

Canigou is an immense magnolia that blooms in an offshoot of the Pyrenees; its bees are the fairies that surround it, and its butterflies the swans and the eagles…

from Jacint Verdaguer's poem *Canigó*

Two major valleys, the Conflent (the valley of the River Têt) and the Vallespir (of the River Tech), slope in parallel lines towards the Spanish border. Don't think that this butt end of the Pyrenees consists of mere foothills; in between these two valleys stands the Pic du Canigou (2,785m) jauntily wearing a Phrygian cap of snow until late spring, a mountain so steeply flanked and imposing that until the 18th century it was believed to be the highest peak in the range.

The small villages in the more northerly Conflent Valley are often adorned with exceptional Romanesque churches. Upriver towards the town of Prades (the most popular spot for expeditions up Canigou), you'll pass rock formations and twisting gorges, before the mountains close in after Villefranche-de-Conflent on the small villages that cling precariously to cliffs, a handful of which make for excellent bases for trekking into the hills. The valley slopes all the way up to Cerdagne (page 359), one of the most popular skiing destinations in the Pyrenees.

GETTING THERE AND AWAY The **train** from Perpignan goes as far as Villefranche-de-Conflent, with regular departures from Perpignan's central train station. From

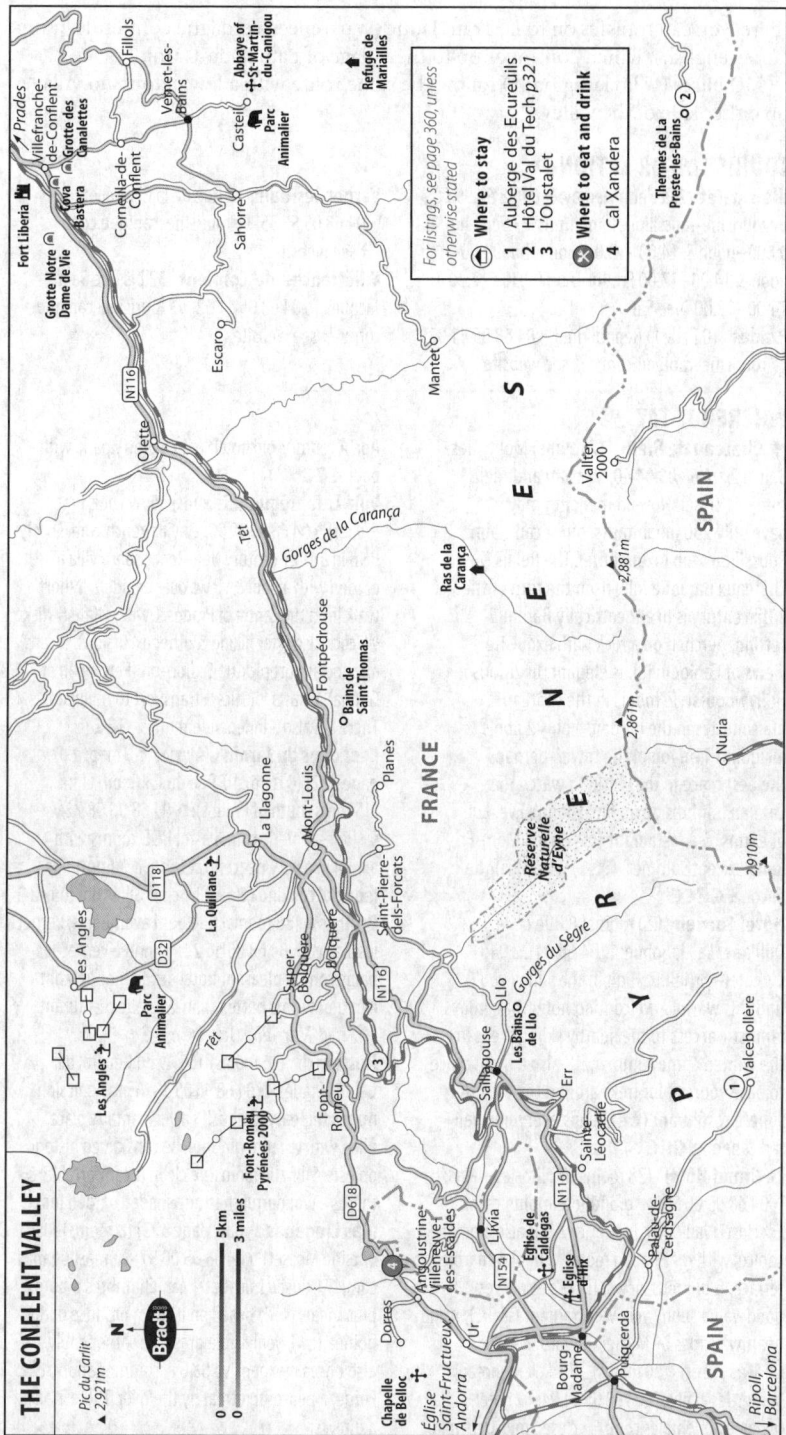

THE CONFLENT VALLEY

Bradt

N

Pic du Carlit
▲ 2,921m

0 — 5km
0 — 3 miles

For listings, see page 360, unless otherwise stated

Where to stay
1 Auberge des Ecureuils
2 Hôtel Val du Tech p321
3 L'Oustalet

Where to eat and drink
4 Cal Xandera

Prades
Villefranche-de-Conflent
Fort Liberia
Grotte Notre Dame de Vie
Cova Bastera
Grotte des Canalettes
Fillols
Vernet-les-Bains
Corneilla-de-Conflent
Castell
Parc Animalier
Abbaye de St-Martin-du-Canigou
Refuge de Marialles

Sahorre

Escaro

N116

Olette

Mantet

Thermes de La Preste-les-Bains

SPAIN

Vallter 2000

Tét

Gorges de la Carança

2,881m

Ras de la Carança

Fontpédrouse

Bains de Saint Thomas

Planès

FRANCE

La Llagonne
Mont-Louis

Saint-Pierre-dels-Forcats

2,861m

Nuria

Réserve Naturelle d'Eyne

2,910m

D118

Les Angles
La Quillane

D32

Parc Animalier
Les Angles

Super-Bolquère
Bolquère

N116

Llo
Gorges du Sègre

Saillagouse
Les Bains de Llo

Err

Valcebollère

Font-Romeu
Pyrénées 2000

Font-Romeu

Sainte-Léocadie

D618

Angoustrine-Villeneuve-des-Escaldes

Livia

É004glise de Caldégas

N154

N116

Dorres

Chapelle de Belloc

Église Saint-Fructueux
Andorra

Ur

Bourg-Madame

Église d'Hix

Palau-de-Cerdagne

Puigcerdà

SPAIN

Ripoll, Barcelona

9

351

there, you can transfer on to Le Train Jaune (w pyrenees-cerdagne.com/en/le-train-jaune-english), which continues up to the village of Latour-de-Carol.

LiO buses (w lio.laregion.fr) follow the same route with a few detours to villages on either side of the valley.

TOURIST INFORMATION

Ille-sur-Têt 2 Pl Henri Demay; \04 68 57 99 00; w tourisme-roussillon-conflent.fr; ⏰ Sep–Jun 09.00–noon & 14.00–18.00 Mon–Thu, 09.00–noon & 14.00–17.00 Fri; Jul–Aug 09.30–12.30 & 14.00–18.00 Tue–Sat
Prades 10 Pl de la République; \04 68 05 41 02; w tourisme-canigou.com; ⏰ see website

Vernet-les-Bains 2 Rue de la Chapelle; \04 68 05 55 35; w tourisme-canigou.com; ⏰ see website
Villefranche-de-Conflent 32 bis Rue Saint-Jacques; \04 68 05 41 02, w tourisme-canigou.com; ⏰ see website

---

🏠 WHERE TO STAY

✴ **Château de Riell** (17 rooms) Molitg-les-Bains; \04 68 05 04 40; w chateauderiell.com; ⏰ closed Nov–Mar. Molitg may have only 250 inhabitants, but it can claim Roussillon's top luxury hotel. The Relais & Châteaux Baroque folly from the turn of the 20th century is in a theatrically Baroque setting, perched on a rock with exquisite views of Canigou; it has elegant, luxurious Hollywood-style rooms in the château & maisonettes in the garden – plus 2 pools, including 1 on top of the tower, perhaps the best place in the world to watch the Catalan bonfires go up on St John's Eve. Lots of extras, & a restaurant (⏰ closed Mon–Fri lunch except summer; €€€) worthy of the décor. €€€€€

Hôtel Corrieu (20 rooms) 8 Rue de la Quillane, La Llagonne; \04 68 04 22 04; w hotel-corrieu.fr. High in the valley you'll find this warm & welcoming hotel that enjoys fantastic access to the nearby skiing areas in the winter. Come summer, it's also a great place to base yourself for treks around the area. A superb restaurant (€€) keeps everyone well fed & happy. €€€

Le Grand Hôtel (38 rooms) Molitg-les-Bains; \04 68 05 00 50; w grandhotelmolitg.com; ⏰ closed Jan–Mar. Less pricey, but also a great choice, with marble spa rooms, a pool & marble terrace, & glorious views. There's also a very good-value sunny yellow restaurant (€€€), using healthy recipes by Michel Guérard. €€€

Le Mas Fleuri (30 rooms) 25 Bd Clemenceau, Vernet-les-Bains; \04 68 05 51 94; w hotel-pyrenees-orientales.com; ⏰ closed mid-Oct–mid-

Apr. A century-old hotel set in a pretty park, with a pool. €€€

Villa Lafabrègue (5 rooms) 15 Av Louis Prat, Prades; \04 68 96 29 90; w villafrench.com. Lovely B&B in a 19th-century Neo-Renaissance villa in a garden with a pool & views over Canigou, a short walk from the centre of Prades. Owners Kate & Nick Wilcock also offer hiking & other excursions, & can arrange airport pick-up & drop-off (Perpignan or Girona), b/fasts, picnics & transport to trailheads. There are also 2 independent gîtes. €€€

Les Loges du Jardin d'Aymeric [map, page 322] (3 rooms) 7 Rue du Canigou, Clara (15 mins south of Prades); \04 68 96 08 72; w logesaymeric.com. Pastel B&B rooms with a pool in a very peaceful setting, & sumptuous regional cooking (€€€) by chef Gilles Bascou. €€

Princess (38 rooms) Rue des Lavandières, Vernet-les-Bains; \04 68 05 56 22; w hotel-vernet-les-bains.com. A pleasant hotel at the foot of Mont Canigou with a better-than-average restaurant (⏰ mid-Mar–end Oct; €€). €€

Hostalrich (16 rooms) 156 Av du Général de Gaulle, Prades; \04 68 96 05 38. A big neon sign makes this easy to find. It's a very vintage place, filled with what might soon be considered historic objects. Still, the rooms are clean & comfortable, & there's a wonderful chestnut-shaded garden too. €

Mas Lluganas [map, page 322] (8 rooms) Just outside Mosset; \04 68 05 00 37; w maslluganas.com; ⏰ closed mid-Oct–Mar. Chambres d'hôtes, plus meals (€€) based on its own produce of duck, guinea fowl, veal & foie gras. The same family also offers inexpensive B&B accommodation at La Forge, a peaceful retreat by the river. There is also a gîte. €

✕ WHERE TO EAT AND DRINK

Au Grill La Senyera 81 Rue Saint-Jean, Villefranche-de-Conflent; ☎04 68 96 17 65; ⏰ noon–14.00 & 19.30–21.00 Thu–Sat, noon–14.00 Sun. Solid, traditional cuisine, simply prepared & delicious. €€

Bistrot Le Cortal Rue du Château, Vernet-les-Bains; ☎04 68 05 55 79; w bistrot-lecortal.fr; ⏰ noon–14.00 & 19.00–21.00 Thu–Sun, 19.00–21.00 Mon. Lovely views from this renovated stable, featuring modern bistrot dishes. €€

Café de l'Union Rue de l'Église, Fillols; ☎04 68 05 63 06; ⏰ Mar–Sep 08.30–21.30 Mon–Tue, 08.30–18.00 Wed, 08.30–20.00 Thu, 08.30–22.30 Fri–Sat, 09.00–18.00 Sun. A famous stop for magret & morrels, & live music on many summer evenings. Limited opening in winter, so call ahead to check. €

SHOPPING In Ille-sur-Têt, market days are Wednesday and Friday, with a flea market on Sunday. In Prades, Tuesday is market day, with a wonderful farmer's market (produce, crafts, etc.) on Saturdays in summer.

SPORTS AND ACTIVITIES Summer and winter in the Conflent Valley offer plenty of chances for daredevil sports for the entire family. For details of climbing Canigou, see page 358.

Exploration Pyrénéen m 06 83 22 79 72; w pyrenees-exploration.com. Caving, canyoning, hiking & snowshoeing; based in Villefranche-de-Conflent.

Exterieur Nature ☎04 68 05 72 12; w exterieur-nature.com. Canyoning, rafting & unique hydrospeed tours (also known as riverboarding). They also operate a forest acrobatic course (ages 3 & up) just east of Prades in the village of Marquixanes.

Kap'oupa Kap m 06 88 48 06 45; w kapoupakap.fr. Tubing, snow tubing, karting, zip lines, jumping around like a kangaroo on giant trampolines & winter sports, in Eus.

THUIR Before passing through Perpignan, the fish-filled River Têt washes a wide plain packed full of vineyards and lovely villages. The largest of them, Thuir, 15km west of Perpignan, puts up signs all over Roussillon inviting us over to see the **World's Biggest Barrel** (2 Bd Violet; ☎04 68 53 05 42, w caves-byrrh.fr; ⏰ Jul–Aug 10.00–11.30 & 14.00–18.00 daily; Apr–Jun & Sep–Oct 09.30–11.30 & 14.30–16.45; Nov–Mar tours at 10.45, 14.30 & 16.00 Tue–Sat), in the cellars of Caves Byrrh – wine mixed with quinine and ten different spices, invented here in 1886, and once so popular that, when a new station was required for all the trains shipping it out, Gustave Eiffel was summoned to build it (the station has not been used since 1989, but is still an impressive sight). And the barrel? Dating from 1950, it can hold over a million litres, and an impressive sight it is, too.

CASTELNOU AND AROUND After an apéritif or two, head 6km west to this golden-hued, perfectly preserved medieval village on winding, pebble-paved lanes and steps under the spectacular 10th-century **château** (☎04 68 53 22 91; ⏰ 15 Apr–17 Jun 10.00–17.00 daily; 18 Jun–18 Sep 10.00–19.00 daily; closed 19 Sep–14 Apr; €5) built by the Viscounts of Vallespir. Restored after the roof caught fire in 1981, this six-storey castle, unlike most military castles in France, never graduated into a lordly residence, and the rooms are mostly empty today; the owners also make AOC Côtes du Roussillon and Rivesaltes, which you can purchase on site.

The narrow D48 wiggling west of Castelnou is unabashedly beautiful: if you have a couple of hours to spare, you can circle around to the Prieuré de Serrabone (page 354) by way of the D2 to Caixas and Fourques, then on to the D13 for Llauro and Prunet-et-Belpuig, where the ruins of the **Château de Belpuig** offer a superb view and the 11th-century **Chapelle de la Trinité**, with an extraordinary medieval door

9

and some rather unusual modillions (inside, its greatest treasure is a superb 12th-century Romanesque *Christ in Majesty* – on the cross, yet clothed in a kingly robe; there's also a very early polychrome wooden *Virgin and Child*). In **Boule-d'Amont**, just up the road, there's another charming Romanesque church, **Saint-Saturnin**, from the same century, with a Baroque retable squeezed into a Visigothic arch and another sculpted Virgin and Child.

A shorter alternative, but on even more dubious roads, is to take the D2 north from Fourques to **Saint-Michel-de-Llotes**, a village encircled by five dolmens, then turn back to Serrabone by way of Casefabre, with its tremendous views.

ILLE-SUR-TÊT This attractive old town at the gateway to the mountains was once famous for its **Hospici d'Illa**, a 13th-century hospice for the poor, currently under renovation (m 06 67 65 36 76 for possible visits). In the Rue des Enamorats ('lovers' lane') there's a statue believed to mark the site of a brothel, and at the corner of Rues Malpas and Carmes there's a pink marble *caganer d'Ille*, a figure in the act of defecating. The Catalans are merrily obsessed with bottoms and poo, seeing it as a sign of their essential earthy character; in southern Catalunya you can buy *caganer* figures (either traditional models or squatting celebrities) to decorate your home and Christmas manger scene.

Northwest of Ille, the Chemin de Régleilles leads to some surprising landscapes: 5-million-year-old 'fairy chimneys' and towers called **Les Orgues** (\04 68 84 13 13; w orgues.netinfo.pro; ⊕ 1 Apr–14 Jun & 15 Sep–14 Oct 09.30–19.00; 15 Jun–14 Sep 09.15–20.00; 1 Feb–31 Mar & 15 Oct–14 Nov 10.00–18.00; 15 Nov–31 Jan 14.00–17.30 daily; adult/reduced/under 10 €5/3.50/free), that resemble eroded, dream-like buildings out of Italo Calvino's *Invisible Cities*, with the forgotten ruin of a 12th-century tower and the Pyrenees forming a magnificent backdrop. The **fortified church of Régleilles** (from Ille, take the D2 over the river and after a kilometre turn right on to a little road) looks like a castle – a typical example of a monastic church, in an area without any castles, that grew into a fortress to protect the monks and the village. Ille in fact was located here before its population drifted to the present site.

Six kilometres north on the D21, in little **Bélesta**, the **Château Musée de Bélesta** (5 Rue du Château; \04 68 84 55 55; w musee-belesta66.fr; ⊕ 15 Jun–14 Sep 14.00–19.00 daily; 15 Sep–14 Jun 14.00–17.30 daily except Tue & Sat; adult/12–18/11 & under €5.50/4.50/free) holds the treasure found in a 6,000-year-old Neolithic tomb in 1983 (explanations in French only) in its restored 12th-century castle looming up from a rock.

PRIEURÉ DE SERRABONE (\04 68 84 09 30; w ledepartement66.fr; ⊕ Jun–Sep 09.30–18.30 daily; Apr–May & Oct 10.00–18.00 Tue–Sun; Nov–Mar 10.00–17.00 Tue–Sun; adult/reduced/26 & under €5/4/free) Seeing the finest medieval sculpture in Roussillon requires dedication: the most direct route to Serrabone, 'the good mountain', (for others, see page 353) requires 13km of hairpin bends on a road where you dread oncoming traffic, starting from the D618 at Bouleternère, just west of Ille, and ending in a lofty, remote, barren spot on the slopes of a mountain called Roque Rouge, in the commune of Boule-d'Amont.

Even once you finally arrive, the solemn, spare shape and dark schist of Serrabone's church are not promising, making the surprise inside that much the greater, concentrated in a 12th-century single gallery of a cloister and in the capitals of the tribune, a kind of mini-interior cloister in rose-coloured marble from Canigou. Perfectly preserved in its isolated setting, the sculpture includes a fantastical bestiary, centaurs, a grimacing St Michael, reliefs of the four Evangelists and a fellow blasting on a trumpet. The style, by the school of sculptors that grew up at Saint-Michel-de-Cuxa, will become familiar if you spend time in the Conflent. Note the figure of the Virgin; a narrow window allows the sun's rays to illuminate it one day each year – the Feast of the Assumption on 15 August.

PRADES Prades is known around the musical world in connection with the chamber music festival founded in 1950 by cellist Pau (Pablo) Casals, but few people could place it on a map. Casals, in exile after the Spanish Civil War, spent much of the 1940s and 50s here, in the one safe corner of his beloved Catalunya. From the beginning, his festival attracted many of the world's greatest classical soloists, and it still does today. Otherwise, Prades is a typical stolid, slightly bohemian Catalan town with a rather worrying road system.

There are a couple of things to see, besides the festival. In the heart of Prades, the **church of Saint-Pierre** has a fine Romanesque bell tower with a pyramid crown and, inside, an operatic Baroque retable in full 17th-century fig by Catalan chisel virtuoso Joseph Sunyer, along with an exhibition of church treasures. You can watch a film and see how the local garnets are made into opulent red and gold jewellery at **La Manufacture du Grenat** at the Rond-Point du Canigou towards Perpignan (\04 68 96 21 03; w manufacturedugrenat.com; ⊕ 09.00–12.30 & 14.00–19.00 Tue–Sat, guided tours leave at 10.30, 14.30, 15.30 & 16.30; €3).

ABBAYE DE SAINT-MICHEL-DE-CUXA (3km south of Prades; \04 68 96 15 35, w abbayecuxa.org; ⊕ May–Sep 09.30–11.45 & 14.00–18.00 Mon–Sat; Oct–Apr 09.30–11.45 & 14.00–17.00 Mon–Sat, 14.00–17.00 Sun; adult/13–18/12 & under €6/3.50/free) One of the most important monasteries of medieval Catalunya, the scale of Saint-Michel even in its reduced, semi-ruined state, is impressive: this was one of the great monastic centres from which medieval Europe was planned and built. Visigothic Catalunya had something of an artistic head start in the 9th century AD, along with the iron mines in the Pyrenees to provide the cash.

Saint-Michel-de-Cuxa was founded in AD878 under the protection of the Counts of Cerdagne, after an earlier monastery, built in AD840 on the banks of the Têt, flooded. The church, consecrated in AD974, is a landmark on the road to the Romanesque style. One of its features is the more-than-semicircular 'Visigothic' arches in the nave, a style which never became too popular in Christian Europe, although the Muslims of Spain adopted it to create the architectural fantasies of Seville and Granada.

Saint-Michel's reputation spread across Europe; in 978, Doge Pietro Orseolo slipped out of Venice and retreated here incognito, living out his life piously like a hermit (he was canonised in 1731 – his relics are now in Saint-Pierre in Prades). Another who spent time here was Gerbert d'Aurillac (cAD946–1003), the future Pope Sylvester II, who as a young man showed so much promise that the Count of Barcelona sent him to learn mathematics in Spain, where he became fascinated with astronomy, Arabic numerals and the whole sophisticated culture of Al-Andalus; he would later re-introduce the abacus and armillary sphere to Europe.

In 1008, the famous scholar Oliba was made abbot and embarked on a major building plan, adding the abbey's massive yet elegant 40m **bell tower** (originally there were two) and the unusual circular crypt, known as the **Chapelle de la Vierge de la Crèche**. This was originally located underneath a long-gone rotunda that held a prize relic: baby Jesus's swaddling clothes. The crypt, plain and rugged, is covered by toroid barrel vaulting, with a mushroom-like central column 7m in circumference that is almost unique in medieval architecture. Antonio Gaudí

9

used similar columns in Barcelona – a fascinating example of subliminal Catalan cultural continuity, especially as the crypt was only rediscovered in 1936, after Gaudí's death. (Curiously, by another great Modernista architect, Puig i Cadafalch, page 22.)

The French Revolution found Saint-Michel already in a state of serious decay. Looted and abandoned in the 19th century, one of the two bell towers collapsed, and much of the best sculptural work went 'into exile', as the Catalans put it, carted off to the Cloisters Museum in New York. When restoration began, the rest of the cloister was found in a public bathhouse in Prades. The altar was found holding up a balcony in Vinça.

After years away from the public, Pau Casals performed his first public concert in exile in 1950 in the church – which had become so run-down that it didn't even have a roof. His interest was key in initiating its restoration, and today it remains a major venue for concerts during the Prades festival.

In the rebuilt **cloister** (at 47.5m by 39m, it was one of the biggest in region) are capitals sculpted out of the rose-tinted marble of Canigou: monsters from the medieval bestiary in the corners, intertwined with men on the four faces. There is an obsession with lions, almost Chinese in their stylisation, biting and licking each other. One is said to represent the Sumerian hero Gilgamesh.

A small community of Benedictine monks from Montserrat (page 140), the centre of Catalan spiritualism, have occupied Saint-Michel since 1965 and make their own cheese, which you can buy in the abbey's shop. They also tend a beautiful **iris garden**, where every colour of iris imaginable bursts into bloom in May and early June.

EUS This beautiful, pyramid-shaped village spills down a granite hill northeast of Prades, in what it claims is the sunniest spot in France. On top, the 18th-century (but rarely open) church of **Saint-Vincent** stands amid the 11th-century ruins of a castle and a cactus garden and is rumoured to house elaborate 17th-century polychrome retables.

UP THE CASTELLARE VALLEY Northwest of Prades on the D14, **Molitg-les-Bains**, on a hill in the forest, has been a spa (specialising in skin disorders) since the Belle Époque, with a suitably grand hotel with a lake, river and lovely gardens open to the public. The 12th-century village church **Saint-Marie** with its silo of a tower is another Casals festival venue.

Beyond Molitg, the road climbs to the **Col de Jau**, a pass with stunning views, once the border between France and Spain. On the way, pause in the fortified village of **Mosset**, a little haven of artists and potters, where the landmark is the bell tower of the church of **Saint-Julien-et-Sainte-Basilisse**, with a dwarf 200-year-old pine tree growing out of the top. It also has a beautifully restored Romanesque chapel, the *capelletta*. It once boasted 'the smallest ski station in the world', with two runs and one chairlift, which survives, although the station closed in the early 2000s.

VERNET-LES-BAINS AND AROUND The D27, the narrow road that snakes around the lower slopes of Canigou to the south of Prades, is a pretty drive through the mountain forests. After Saint-Michel-de-Cuxa, it passes lively little **Fillols** before meeting Vernet-les-Bains, a bustling spa with most of the accommodation in the area and hot sulphuric waters that are good for your rheumatism and respiratory problems. Rudyard Kipling made his first of three visits in 1910, as did so many fellow Brits that they built an Anglican church and erected the only monument in France to the 1904 Entente Cordiale between the UK and France; even Vernet's waterfall (a 90-minute trek) is known as the Cascade des Anglais, perhaps because les Anglais were the first to go trekking out to look at it for fun. Kipling even wrote a story called *Why Snow Falls at Vernet*, poking fun at his compatriots' habit of talking about the weather. The weather in fact was so fine that British residents started planting exotic trees, a practice Vernet has since adopted: today it's proud to be France's first official Village-Arboretum with over 320 varieties scattered throughout town.

CASTEIL This little wooded resort 3km from Vernet has a family-run 20ha **Parc Animalier** (04 68 05 67 54; w parcanimaliercasteil.com; mid-Apr–Oct 09.30–19.00 daily; Feb–Mar & Nov–Dec 13.00–18.00 w/ends & school hols; adult/11–17/3–10/under 3 €17/16/14/free) on the mountain slopes, with deer, lions, bears, goats and more in a natural setting, visible along two discovery paths.

A taxing though lovely 40-minute walk up from Casteil or by way of jeep taxi (m 06 14 35 70 64) leads to **Abbaye Saint-Martin-du-Canigou** (04 68 05 50 03; w stmartinducanigou.org; Jun–Sep daily; Oct–Dec & Feb–May Tue–Sun; guided tours only, reserve on their website; adult/12–18/11 & under €8/6/free). A monkish architect named Sclua designed this complex in 1009 for Oliba's brother, Guifré II, the Count of the Cerdagne and the Conflent. Sclua was a designer ahead of his time; his Saint-Martin is a rustic acropolis, spectacularly sited with views around Canigou and surrounding peaks, and arranged as a series of courtyards and terraces on different levels. The church, with its immense, fortress-like bell tower, has two levels: an upper church dedicated to St Martin and a lower crypt for a certain obscure subterranean Virgin Mary, **Notre-Dame-sous-Terre**. Some good white marble capitals can be seen in the cloister, heavily restored in the early 20th century, and medieval tombs, including Count Guifré's, survive in the upper church. But on the whole Saint-Martin, damaged by an earthquake in 1428, abandoned after the Revolution and restored between 1952 and 1971, retains relatively few of its former architectural glories. Since 1988, it has been reinhabited by women and men belonging to the community of the Béatitudes, who devote their lives to prayer.

CORNEILLA-DE-CONFLENT To complete the tour of Romanesque Canigou, this village was once the summer capital of the counts of Cerdagne, and has another 11th–12th-century church founded by Guifré II along the road to Vernet-les-Bains: **Chapelle Notre-Dame de Vie**. Once part of a Benedictine priory, the chapel is full of fascinating sculpture, including a red marble tympanum of the Virgin and Child, in a mandala. An extraordinary window in the apse is decorated with five carved receding arches, and there's a capital sculpted with winged dragons; inside (rarely) are gaunt figures from a 15th-century polychrome *Deposition* and other statues, and a 14th-century Mozarabe walnut wardrobe. Above the chapel is a small **Grotte Notre-Dame de Vie**, which is worth the extra climb because of the astounding views (be careful – it can be slippery). The path begins by a small stone cross-topped pillar; allow 2½ hours there and back.

Side roads to the west, in the Rotja Valley, lead to several more churches, including rare 10th-century ones in the tiny villages of **Fuilla** and **Sahorre**. Canigou's iron, mined since 150BC, is recalled in tiny Escaro's **Musée de la Mine** (04 68 97 15 34 ; w musee-mine-escaro.fr; 1 May–14 Jun & 16 Sep–31 Oct 15.00–18.00 Sat–Sun; 15 Jun–15 Sep 15.00–18.00 Mon–Wed and Fri–Sun; adult/15 & under €4/3) with trains, tools, old equipment and photos of the days when the mines employed 420 people and the village had three schools.

9

THE PIC DU CANIGOU

I came here in search of nothing more than a little sunshine. But I found Canigou, whom I discovered to be a magician among mountains…nothing he could do or give birth to would now surprise me, whether I met Don Quixote himself riding in from the Spanish side…or saw (which each twilight seems quite possible) gnomes and kobolds swarming out of the mines and tunnels of his flanks.

Rudyard Kipling

The *muntanya sagrada* ('sacred mountain') of the Catalans is one of the most potent symbols of the nation (north and south), and the subject of national poet Jacint Verdaguer's best-loved Catalan poems. Legends and apparitions abound. Fairies and 'ladies of the waters' are said to frequent its forested slopes, and King Peter III of Aragon climbed it in 1285 and met a dragon near the top. Some say it even shelters the Holy Grail.

On 23 June, on the eve of the Festa Major or St John's Day (*nit de Sant Joan*), a bonfire is lit on the summit, and Catalans from both sides of the frontier run down the mountain in a torch relay, bringing down the flame that will ignite some 30,000 bonfires across the region. In August, there's a massive marathon run up and down the summit.

If Canigou's magnetism is working its juju, don't resist the call – but do make sure of the weather before setting out, to avoid getting caught in a late afternoon thunderstorm. The climbing season generally runs from May through September, when the mountain's 2,785m are free of snow. To do it entirely by foot takes 11 hours and means an overnight stay in one of the refuges, or you can drive up the forest road from Casteil as far as the **Refuge de Mariailles** (1,700m; 📞 04 68 05 57 99; w refugedemariailles.fr; 🕐 closed Jan) and make the 7–8hr climb there and back, by way of a 100m scramble over the stone 'chimneys'.

The easiest way, however, is to go by jeep as far as the **Chalet-Refuge des Cortalets** (2,150m; 📞 04 68 96 36 19; w refugedescortalets.ffcam.fr; 🕐 last w/end of May–mid-Oct), the base for a fairly easy 3–4-hour walk to and from the summit, requiring only a decent pair of walking shoes and a windcheater. Check the Vernet-les-Bains tourist website for other options, maps, jeep taxi services and contact numbers for Canigou's other refuges (to stay or eat at any, it's essential to book ahead).

VILLEFRANCHE-DE-CONFLENT Some villages have their own ideas for welcoming visitors. This one casually points cannons down at you, by way of an invitation to drop in. Located where the Têt valley abruptly narrows, Villefranche has had a castle ever since the Counts of Cerdagne founded Villa Franca in 1092 – the 'franca' referring to tax and duty privileges meant to attract traders and workers. After the Treaty of the Pyrenees in 1654, Louis XIV hired his crack military engineer Sébastien Le Prestre de Vauban to refortify it to guard his new frontier. Vauban gave him a model Baroque fortress-town. Almost nothing has changed since, leaving a fascinating historical record, a sort of stage set of that era, although one filled with Roussillon's greatest concentration of tourist shops.

The town's 11th-century church of **Saint-Jacques** (🕐 14.00–18.00 Mon–Sat, 14.30–18.30 Sun) is its greatest medieval relic, with a rosy pink portal and capitals sculpted by the Saint-Michel-de-Cuxa school. Inside there's another retable by

Sunyer and, by the door, note the measures engraved in the stone, used by drapers who had market stalls in the square. Vauban incorporated the church and tower into his wall.

From 2 Rue Saint-Jean steps lead up Vauban's **ramparts** (⊕ Jul–Aug 10.00–20.00 daily; Jun & Sep 10.00–19.00 daily; Apr–May & Oct 11.00–18.00 daily; Feb–Mar & Nov–Dec 13.00–17.00 daily; closed Jan; adult/10 & under €5/2.50) with their roofed walkway built through the walls – necessary because of the surrounding mountains. For those with sufficient puff and military curiosity, there's a steep climb up the remarkable 739 subterranean rock-hewn steps at the end of Rue Saint-Pierre to **Fort Liberia** (☏04 68 96 34 01; w fort-liberia.com; ⊕ Jul–Aug 09.00–20.00 daily; May–Jun & Sep 10.00–19.00 daily; Feb–Apr & Oct 10.00–18.00 daily; adult/reduced/5–10/under 5 €8/7/4.50/free, with shuttle €14/10/6/free) added by Vauban in 1681, on the one spot where an enemy could bring cannons to fire down on Villefranche. It was further fortified by Napoleon III and used as a prison, where you are invited to 'meet the villainous female poisoners' (don't be alarmed – they're made of wax). There were eight women sent here from Versailles accused of poisoning and witchcraft; one poor soul survived for 44 years chained to the wall.

Besides offering trips into the Pyrenees on the **Train Jaune** (page 314), Villefranche has two caves all in easy walking distance, awaiting your inspection. Just across the N116 is the **Cova Bastera**, which was inhabited in prehistoric times, and later served as the headquarters of Catalan rebels in 1674; French troops made short work of them, but, to make sure it didn't happen again, Vauban fortified the entrance to the cave as well. The current owners have turned it into the **Dinopedia Expérience** (☏04 68 05 20 20; w le-monde-de-dinopedia.fr; ⊕ Apr–Sep 10.00–17.30 daily, Oct–Mar 10.30–12.30 & 14.00–16.30 w/ends & school holidays only; closed Jan–Feb except school holidays; adult/child/under 1m high €15/12/free) with dioramas and animatronic dinosaurs which are always a hit with kids. Some of the Pyrenees' most peculiar stalactites await further up the road at the intimate **Grotte des Canalettes** (☏04 68 05 20 20; w grottescanalettes.com; ⊕ Apr–Jun 10.00–17.00 daily; Jul–Aug 10.00–17.30 daily; Oct 11.00–16.00 daily; closed all other periods; adult/5–12 €12/6).

THE CERDAGNE

Long ago this spectacular, sun-drenched basin at 1200m was a lake rimmed by lofty peaks; today it's filled with mountain rhododendrons and blue gentians, hordes of skiers, herds of horses, and snow on top until May or June. The Cerdagne (Cerdanya in Catalan) was an isolated and effectively independent county in the Middle Ages; from the 10th century its counts gradually extended their power, eventually becoming counts of Barcelona and kings of Aragon. In spite of this heritage, the Cerdagne was split between Spain and France in the 1659 Treaty of the Pyrenees. The completion of the Train Jaune, or Yellow Train, in 1911 brought the French Cerdagne into the modern world; skiing has made it rather opulent today. And besides skiing, you can see some good Romanesque churches, warm up at the world's largest solar furnace, visit the highest railway station in France – and circumnavigate Spain in less than an hour.

GETTING THERE AND AROUND Le Train Jaune (☏04 68 96 63 62; w letrainjaune.fr) begins at Villefranche Vernet-les-Bains (reached by regular rail connections from Perpignan) and travels 62.5km up a tremendously scenic narrow-gauge track into the Cerdagne. Begun in 1910, it's one of the most unlikely railways in France – a

9

political project, meant to bring new life into the impoverished mountain valleys, and so difficult to build through the Pyrenees, along France's highest railway bridges, that it was only completed in 1927. Restored for its centenary, it runs year-round, taking skiers up in winter and visitors to see the scenery in summer in open carriages. The last station, 3 hours away, is Latour-de-Carol (page 363), the only place in France (and one of very few in the world) where three rail gauges meet: you can catch a train to Toulouse, and even a night train to Paris (French gauge) or Barcelona (Spanish gauge).

TOURIST INFORMATION

Font-Romeu 82 Av Emmanuel Brousse; \04 68 30 68 30; w font-romeu.fr; ⊕ 09.00–noon & 14.00–18.00 daily

Les Angles 2 Av de l'Aude; \04 68 04 32 76; w lesangles.com; ⊕ 09.00–12.30 & 14.00–18.00 daily

Mont-Louis 1 Rue Émile Zola; \04 68 04 21 97; w mont-louis.net; ⊕ Apr–Jun 09.30–noon

& 13.30–17.30 Mon–Sat; Jul–Aug 09.30–17.30 Mon–Sat, 09.30–12.30 & 13.30–17.30 Sun; Sep–Mar 09.30–12.30 & 13.30–17.30 Mon–Fri

Saillagouse 1 Pl du Roser; \04 68 04 15 47; w pyrenees-cerdagne.com; ⊕ 09.00–12.30 & 14.00–17.00 Mon–Sat

WHERE TO STAY

Le Clos Cerdan (60 rooms) Mont-Louis; \04 68 04 23 29; w lecloscerdan.com. Get a room with a view at this grey stone hotel on a cliff overlooking the valley; modern but very comfortable, with a restaurant (€€). There are also apts & a spa with gym. €€€

Auberge des Ecureuils [map, page 351] (19 rooms) Valcebollère (east of Bourg-Madame); \04 68 04 52 03; w aubergeecureuils.com; ⊕ closed Nov–early Dec. Friendly mountain auberge, offering charming rooms & local produce (€€€). There's a heated indoor pool, Moorish bath, sauna & fitness room. Lots of interesting packages – go snowshoeing, horseriding or walking along smugglers' paths, or hunt for & cook wild mushrooms. €€

Hôtel Planes (19 rooms) 6 Pl de Cerdagne, Saillagouse; \04 68 04 72 08; w chezplanes. com; ⊕ closed early Nov–mid-Dec. Planes has been hosting guests since 1895; the dining room (€€€€), with its huge fireplace, is a great place to eat Catalan anchovies & red peppers. Guests can use the facilities at the Planotel. €€

L'Atalaya (2 gîtes) 37 Carrer del Senyalò, Llo; \04 68 96 59 41; w atalaya-cerdagne.com; ⊕ closed mid-Jan–mid-Apr & mid-Nov–mid-Dec. A rare example of a country inn unconcerned with the skiing business; tranquillity is assured in this setting, close to the wildflowers of the Vallée d'Eyne & infinitely far from anything else, with a pool & excellent restaurant in summer (€€€). €€

La Fontaine (5 rooms) 3 Rue de la Fusterie, Olette; \04 68 97 03 67; w olette66.com. A nice B&B on the village square in a large house run since 2006 by an English couple. Guest lounge available & terraces for eating b/fast or simply relaxing. €€

Le Planotel (18 rooms) 18 Rue de la Poste, Saillagouse; \04 68 04 72 08; w chezplanes.com; ⊕ closed Oct–May except school hols. Modern, with a heated pool & restaurant & run by the same family that runs Planes (see left). €€

L'Oustalet [map, page 351] (26 rooms) Av du Maréchal Leclerc, Font-Romeu; \04 68 30 11 32; w hotelloustalet.com; ⊕ closed Apr–mid-May. Chalet-style hotel with some family rooms & great views, a pool & a restaurant (€€€). €

WHERE TO EAT AND DRINK

La Chaumière 96 Av Emmanuel Brosusse, Font-Romeu; \04 68 30 04 40; w restaurantlachaumiere.fr; ⊕ noon–14.00 & 19.30–21.30 Wed–Sun. Ask the locals for a restaurant & this is where they'll point you. A rustic

dining room of wood & stone serving up classic, hearty Catalan dishes. €€€€

Cal Xandera [map, page 351] 49 Rte de Font-Romeu, Angoustrine; \04 68 04 61 67; w calxandera.com; ⊕ noon–14.00 Sun & Wed, noon–21.00 Thu–Sat, closed Mon–Tue. Completely different: a beautifully restored 18th-century farmhouse serving flavour-packed traditional mountain cuisine. Also 5 rustic-chic rooms (**€€**) for 2–6 people. Jazz concerts in summer. **€€€**

La Table des Saveurs 7 Av Mal Joffre, Font-Romeu; \04 68 04 88 49; w tabledessaveurs. fr; ⏰ noon–14.00 & 19.00–22.00 Mon–Sat.

Generous portions of high-end & artfully plated French cuisine. **€€€**

Moulin à Pizza 1 Pl de Cerdagne, Saillagouse; m 06 84 42 23 63; w moulin-a-pizzas.fr; ⏰ 11.30–14.30 & 18.00–21.30, closed Mon & Tue lunch. For those craving a taste of Italy in the mountains, this pizzeria on the main square serves pizza, focaccia & pasta. **€**

SHOPPING The best market in the area is over the border in Puigcerdà (page 224) and takes place every Sunday morning.

SPORTS AND ACTIVITIES The Cerdagne is great for hiking. The best parts lie to the west, up the very narrow and winding D60 from Mont-Louis, on the slopes of the 2,921m **Pic du Carlit**, with the sources of both the Têt and the Aude in the Forêt de Barrès and the idyllic Lac des Bouillouses. From mid-June to late September, a shuttle takes visitors from the Pla de Barrès car park up to the dam and the trailhead. For other sports, **Ozone3** (38 Av Emmanuel Brousse, Font-Romeu; \04 68 30 36 09; w ozone3.fr) organises cross-country skiing, dog-sledding, hot-air balloon rides, hot water canyoning, diving under ice and much more, while **Transpyr66** (6 Imp des Prés, Saillagouse; m 06 11 87 85 12; w transpyr66.com) can arrange snowshoeing, botanical and other walks around Font-Romeu and Latour-de-Carol.

Thousands come here to ski. **Les Angles** (w lesangles.com) has 55km of slopes serviced by 23 lifts. There are also smaller ski areas in **Formiguères** (w formigueres. fr) and **La Quillane** (w laquillane.fr). Serious powder hounds will want to base themselves in Super-Bolquère to experience one of France's biggest ski resorts, **Font-Romeu Pyrénées 2000** (w altiservice.com).

APPROACH TO MONT-LOUIS After Villefranche-de-Conflent, the main N116 climbs dramatically into the mountains. There are a few possible stop-offs on the way, most of which have stations along the Train Jaune as well: at **Olette**, you can turn off to explore nearly abandoned old mountain villages like **Nyer** and **Evol**. A bit further up, at **Thuès-Entre-Valls**, you can stretch your legs in the beautiful, vertiginous **Gorges de la Carança**, with its sheer cliff fitted out with gantries (allow 4 hours there and back, although you can also make this a 2-day circular trek, returning on the Cami Ramader, with an overnight at the very basic refuge of **Ras de la Carança** (\09 88 66 73 81; w refugedelacaranca.com; ⏰ year-round). Afterwards, soak your weary bones in the delightful natural hot springs of **Bains de Saint Thomas** (\04 68 97 03 13; w bains-saint-thomas.fr; ⏰ Jul–Aug 10.00–20.40 daily; Sep–Jun 10.00–19.40 daily) at **Saint-Thomas-les-Bains**, where even in a raging blizzard you can take a dip outside or in the jacuzzi, visit the hammam or have a massage.

Climb, climb, climb and at last you'll reach the gateway to the Cerdagne, **Mont-Louis**, named after Louis XIV, another work by Vauban and the highest fortress in France (1,600m). Unlike Villefranche, which it resembles, tourist shops are few and far between; the army still resides here, to train commandos and look after the world's first solar furnace built in 1949 by Félix Trombe and used, not for generating power, but for melting substances for scientific experiments; the huge mirror generates temperatures up to 3,400°C. It shares the small space inside the walls with some 200 residents. The tourist office offers guided tours of the village and of the Citadel to visit the commandos and the **Puits des Forçats**, the 17th-century wheel which lifted water from the wells dug into the rock.

9

A 7km detour up into the mountains will take you to tiny **Planès** and its equally tiny and unique triangular 11th-century church which has occasioned much speculation; some have claimed it as the centre of a network of ley lines.

Le Capcir

The road to Planès is a dead end, but there are better choices from the big crossroads at Mont-Louis. To the north, the D118 leads to the isolated plateau of **Le Capcir**. It's a perfect place to get away from it all – after a road was built into the Capcir in the 19th century, almost the entire population left, tired of scratching a living from land that would only support a few cows. They left behind beautiful pine forests and a score of little lakes. Skiing has brought the Capcir back to life since the 1960s.

On your way into Le Capcir, don't miss the church of **Saint-Vincent** in **La Llagonne**, 3km from Mont-Louis. Founded in AD866 and remodelled several times since, the centuries have left it in peace, with a remarkable collection of medieval art, including an altarpiece and painted baldachin (12th and 13th centuries), and an excellent polychrome *Majestat*, or robed Christ on the Cross.

Les Angles was formerly Vallsera, which in the 14th century vanished when the Black Death wiped out the entire population. Along with its winter sports it has a **Parc Animalier** (✆04 68 04 17 20; w faune-pyreneenne.fr; ⊕ 10 Jul–31 Aug 09.00–18.00 daily; 1 Sep–9 Jul 09.00–17.00 daily; adult/5–17/under 5 €17/15/free), a partly free-range zoo with native fauna of the Pyrenees, and both current and past residents, including bears, reindeer, wolves, bison and frisky mountain goats. A télécabine also runs in summer, affording some great views.

Formiguères (not the ski station but the village, 4km away) is one of the prettiest and best-preserved villages in the region, hardly changed since the days when the kings of Majorca sojourned here to relieve their asthma. Further north, in the village of the same name, the **Grotte de Fontrabiouse** (✆04 68 30 95 55; w grotte-de-fontrabiouse.com; see website for guided tour schedule) was discovered in 1958 while digging for alabaster; the hour-long tours take in the subterranean river and stalactites.

Font-Romeu

The western road (D618) will take you through more pine forests to Font-Romeu, which, along with Super-Bolquère and Pyrénées 2000, has been integrated into a single ski domain called Font-Romeu Pyrénées 2000. Font-Romeu grew up after 1910, around a now-closed grand hôtel. It prospers today partly from its excellent sports facilities, often used for training France's Olympic teams, and also has a golf course and casino. Stamped from the same mould as every other ski resort, it has plenty of fake Alpine chalets, innumerable pizzerias and snow machines to help out if the weather isn't co-operating.

But no other resort has the world's largest **solar furnace**, 'stronger than 10,000 suns!', the successor to the one in Mont-Louis. With its curved mirror, covering an entire side of the nine-storey laboratory building, it reflects the Pyrenees beautifully while helping scientists work out all sorts of high-temperature puzzles. It's currently closed to visitors, but still worth stopping for a look at the bizarre building. Above the town, the pilgrimage chapel of **Notre-Dame de Font-Romeu** has an exuberant altarpiece by Joseph Sunyer and a 12th-century statue of the Virgin.

Another solar experiment can be seen at **Targassonne**, west of Font-Romeu on the D618; this big mirror was built to generate electricity, but hasn't quite worked as well as intended. The glaciers that reshaped the Capcir were busy here too, leaving a strange expanse of granite boulders called the Chaos. The Cerdagne is famous for its Romanesque churches and chapels, testimony to the mountain Catalans' prosperity and level of culture even in the very early Middle Ages. One of the best is **Saint-André**, at **Angoustrine**, west of Targassonne, with fragments of 13th-century frescoes representing the months of the year.

To the west, **Dorres** is a lofty granite *village perché* with another church, this one from the 12th century, with a strikingly primitive and much venerated 'black' Virgin inside, and a chance to soak in a granite hot tub at the **Bains Romains de Dorres** (✆ 04 68 04 66 87; w dorres66.com; ⏰ 09.00–19.30 daily; €6). The local granite has been exploited since the cows came home – there's even a rather fetching granite dolmen in the next hamlet, **Brangolí**. For stupendous views from Canigou into Andorra, take the 45-minute walk up to the medieval **Chapelle de Belloc**.

The next village, **Ur**, apparently has nothing to do with its ancient Sumerian namesake; instead of a ziggurat it has another richly decorated Romanesque church, although it's usually locked.

Vallée du Carol

From Ur you can make a northern detour into the Vallée du Carol, the western edge of Roussillon. **Latour-de-Carol** (La Tor de Querol in Catalan) is a romantic name for another great border rail crossing many of us have blinked at in the dark, even if it is famous among trainspotters as the only place on earth where three different rail gauges come together at a single station. The name does not come from Charlemagne, as most people think, but the River Carol. Latour's church has more work by Joseph Sunyer. The best church in the area, however, is the **Église Saint-Fructueux** in the minuscule holiday club village of **Yravals**, above Latour-de-Carol. It has a wealth of medieval art inside, and a magnificent mid-14th-century altarpiece of St Martha by a Catalan named Ramón Destorrents, although again it's rarely open.

Further up this scenic valley, you'll pass the tower of the ruined 14th-century castle that gives Latour its name. The trees give out as the tortuous road climbs to the **Puymorens Pass**. From here, if you have a sudden hankering for some tax-free Havanas, it's only 40km to the principality of Andorra (page 311).

Bourg-Madame

Originally known as La Guingueta d'Hix and renamed in 1815 to honour the wife of the Duke of Angoulême, Bourg-Madame doesn't have a lot going on, although its outer hamlets offer more traditional Catalan Romanesque churches. The **Église d'Hix**, an impressive 12th-century edifice with finely sculpted capitals, was built when the kings of Aragon were frequent visitors and contains a majestic Romanesque Virgin with a little kingly Christ child on her lap; and the **Église Saint-Romain de Caldégas** contains six Baroque retables and 13th-century frescoes, including a hunting scene with falcons (to visit the churches, ring the town hall in Bourg-Madame; ✆ 04 68 30 11 60). Bourg-Madame is also the crossing point for Spain; just across the border lies **Puigcerdà**, with a 14th-century church and a crack ice hockey squad.

Alternatively, the N116 leads northeast from here to Mont-Louis, completing your circumnavigation of Spain – or at least the tiny Spanish enclave of Llívia (page 224).

Sainte-Léocadie

Further east along the N116, this is home to the highest vineyard in Europe, as well as the **Musée de Cerdagne** (✆ 04 68 04 08 05; w museedecerdagne. com; ⏰ Jul–Aug 10.00–13.30 & 14.30–18.30 daily; Apr–Jun & Sep 10.00–12.30 & 14.00–17.30 Mon–Sat; Oct–Mar 14.00–17.00 Mon–Fri), which occupies a restored 17th-century farm and is dedicated to oral histories and photos of rural life, and the pre-ski trades of the great plateau – shepherding and farming.

9

Eyne and Llo A by-road leads up to Eyne and the beautiful **Réserve Naturelle d'Eyne** (✆04 68 04 77 07), which offers guided tours in summer. Come in May, when it's late enough to avoid the skiers from the resort called Eyne 2600 but just in time for a spectacular display of wildflowers and medicinal herbs in the Vallée d'Eyne. Here too is **Llo**, a name that linguists say is Basque, evidence that the Basques lived here in remote times. It has another Romanesque church with a lovely sculptured portal, while climbers will love tackling the course at **Via Ferrata Llo** (m 06 85 02 23 84; ⊕ 09.00–18.00 daily). If you're not into climbing, then instead you can follow the narrow hiking trail leading you to **Gorges du Sègre**, with even more hot springs to enjoy afterwards at the indoor and outdoor pools of **Les Bains de Llo** (✆04 68 04 74 55; w bains-de-llo.com; ⊕ 10.00–19.30 daily, until 20.00 15 Jul–31 Aug; closed 2 Nov–4 Dec).

Saillagouse This market town back towards Mont-Louis on the N116, completes the circuit of the Cerdagne. It has playful statues in its square and the famous **Charcuterie Bonzom** (✆ 04 68 30 14 27; w charcuterie-catalane-bonzom.com; ⊕ 08.00–12.30 & 15.00–19.30 Tue & Thu–Sat, 08.00–noon Sun), purveyors of the Cerdagne's best confits, charcuterie and other goodies, including 1,500 hams drying in the barn.

Appendix 1

LANGUAGE

The official languages of Catalonia are Catalan and Spanish (in the Vall d'Aran, Aranes also enjoys official status). Although virtually everyone speaks both Spanish and Catalan, most people prefer to express themselves in Catalan. This is also the language used in schools, universities, and by local government. Even a simple *bon dia* or *adéu* – will be enormously appreciated by locals.

Catalan pronunciation is distinct but shares some traits with both Spanish and French. Vowels more or less follow their English equivalents, but consonants are trickier. The letter 'x' is pronounced 'sh' at the beginning of a word, as in *xocolata* (pronounced sho-ko-LA-tuh, meaning chocolate) or after 'ei', as in the Barcelona neighbourhood, Eixample, pronounced uh-SHAM-pluh. In general, the stress falls on the second-to-last syllable, but accents are used to change the stress, for example in *número*, pronounced NOO-mer-roh. There is no English equivalent for the double 'l' in Catalan, which sounds somewhat similar to the 'igl' in the Italian word 'famiglia'.

CATALAN WORDS AND PHRASES
Essentials

Good morning	*Bon dia*	bon DEE-uh
Good afternoon	*Bona tarda*	BO-nuh TAR-duh
Good evening	*Bona nit*	BO-nuh NEET
Hello	*Hola*	OH-lah
Goodbye	*Adéu*	ah-DEH-oo
My name is…	*Em dic…*	em DEEK…
What is your name?	*Com et dius?*	kohm et DEE-oos?
I am from…England/ America/Australia	*Soc de…Anglaterra/ Amèrica/Austràlia*	sok duh…ANG-luh-teh -ruh/ah-MEH-ree-kuh/ows -TRAH-lee-uh
How are you?	*Com estàs?*	kohm es-TAHS?
Pleased to meet you	*Encantat/Encantada*	en-kahn-TAT / en-kahn- TAH-duh
Thank you	*Gràcies*	GRAH-syuhs
Don't mention it	*De res*	duh RES
Cheers!	*Salut!*	sah-LOOT!
Yes	*Sí*	SEE
No	*No*	NO
I don't understand	*No ho entenc*	noh oo en-TENK
Please would you speak more slowly	*Parli més a poc a poc, si us plau*	PAR-lee mess uh POK uh POK, see oos PLOW
Do you understand?	*Ho entén?*	oo en-TEN?

Questions

How?	*Com?*	kohm?
What?	*Què?*	keh?
Where?	*On?*	on?
What is it?	*Què és?*	keh es?
Which?	*Quin/a?*	keen/kee-nuh?
When?	*Quan?*	kwan?
Why?	*Per què?*	pehr keh?
Who?	*Qui?*	kee?
How much?	*Quant?*	kwant?

Numbers

1	*un/una*	oon/oon-ah
2	*dos*	doss
3	*tres*	tres
4	*quatre*	KWA-treh
5	*cinc*	sink
6	*sis*	sees
7	*set*	set
8	*vuit*	vweet
9	*nou*	now
10	*deu*	deh-oo
11	*onze*	ON-zuh
12	*dotze*	DOT-zuh
13	*tretze*	TRAYT-zuh
14	*catorze*	kah-TOR-zuh
15	*quinze*	KEEN-zuh
16	*setze*	SET-zuh
17	*disset*	dee-SET
18	*divuit*	dee-VWEET
19	*dinou*	dee-NOW
20	*vint*	vinh
21	*vint-i-u*	veent-ee-oo
30	*trenta*	TREN-tuh
40	*quaranta*	kwuh-RAN-tuh
50	*cinquanta*	seen-KWAN-tuh
60	*seixanta*	say-SHAN-tuh
70	*setanta*	seh-TAN-tuh
80	*vuitanta*	vweet-AN-tuh
90	*noranta*	no-RAN-tuh
100, 1000	*cent, mil*	sent, MEEL

Time

What time is it?	*Quina hora és?*	KEE-nuh OR-uh es?
It's…am/pm	*Són les…*	sohn les…
today	*avui*	ah-VWEE
tonight	*aquesta nit*	uh-KES-tuh neet
tomorrow	*demà*	deh-MAH
yesterday	*ahir*	ah-EER
morning	*matí*	mah-TEE
evening	*vespre*	VES-pruh

Days of the week

Monday	*Dilluns*	dee-YOONS
Tuesday	*Dimarts*	dee-MARTS
Wednesday	*Dimecres*	dee-MEK-res
Thursday	*Dijous*	dee-ZHOOS
Friday	*Divendres*	dee-VEN-dres
Saturday	*Dissabte*	dee-SAHB-tuh
Sunday	*Diumenge*	dee-oo-MEN-juh

Months of the year

January	*Gener*	zhuh-NEHR
February	*Febrer*	fuh-BREHR
March	*Març*	mahrs
April	*Abril*	uh-BREEL
May	*Maig*	mahtch
June	*Juny*	zhoon
July	*Juliol*	zhoo-lee-OL
August	*Agost*	uh-GOHST
September	*Setembre*	suh-TEM-bruh
October	*Octubre*	ook-TOO-bruh
November	*Novembre*	no-VEM-bruh
December	*Desembre*	duh-ZEM-bruh

Getting around
Public transport

I'd like…	*Voldria…*	vol-DREE-uh…
a one-way ticket	*un bitllet senzill*	oon beet-LYET sen-ZEEY
a return ticket	*un bitllet d'anada i tornada*	oon beet-LYET duh-NAH-duh ee tor-NAH-duh
I want to go to…	*Vull anar a…*	VOOLY uh-NAHR uh…
How much is it?	*Quant costa?*	kwant KOSS-tuh?
What time does it leave?	*A quina hora surt?*	uh KEE-nuh OR-uh SOORT?
What time is it now?	*Quina hora és ara?*	KEE-nuh OR-uh es AH-ruh?
The train has been…	*El tren ha estat…*	el tren ah es-TAHT…
delayed	*retardat*	ruh-tar-DAHT
cancelled	*cancel·lat*	kan-sel-LAHT
first class	*primera classe*	pree-MEH-ruh KLAH-suh
second class	*segona classe*	suh-GOH-nuh KLAH-suh
sleeper	*llitera*	yee-TEH-ruh
platform	*andana*	uhn-DAH-nuh
ticket office	*taquilla*	tah-KEE-yuh
timetable	*horari*	oh-RAH-ree
from	*des de*	dess duh
to	*fins a*	feens uh
bus station	*estació d'autobusos*	es-TAH-see-oh dow-too-BOOS-oos
railway station	*estació de tren*	es-TAH-see-oh duh tren
airport	*aeroport*	ah-eh-roh-PORT
port	*port*	port
bus	*autobús*	ow-too-BOOS
train	*tren*	tren

A1

plane	*avió*	ah-VYOH
boat	*vaixell*	vah-SHAY
ferry	*ferri*	FEH-ree
car	*cotxe*	KOT-sheh
4x4	*tot terreny*	TOT tuh-REHNY
taxi	*taxi*	TAK-see
minibus	*minibús*	mee-nee-BOOS
motorbike/moped	*moto*	MOH-too
bicycle	*bicicleta*	bee-see-KLEH-tuh
arrival	*arribada*	ah-ree-BAH-duh
departure	*sortida*	sor-TEE-duh
here	*aquí*	ah-KEE
there	*allà*	uh-LYAH
bon voyage!	*bon viatge!*	bon VYAH-tzhuh!

Private transport

Is this the road to…?	*És aquesta la carretera cap a…?*	es uh-KES-tuh lah kah-ruh-TEH-ruh kahp uh…?
Where is the service station?	*On és la benzinera?*	on es lah ben-zee-NEH-ruh?
Please fill it up	*Ompli, si us plau*	OM-plee, see oos PLOW
I'd like…litres	*Voldria…litres*	vol-DREE-uh…LEE-tres
diesel	*dièsel*	dee-EH-sel
leaded petrol	*benzina amb plom*	ben-ZEE-nuh ahmb plom
unleaded petrol	*benzina sense plom*	ben-ZEE-nuh SEN-suh plom
I have broken down	*He tingut una avaria*	eh teen-GOOT oo-nuh ah-vah-REE-uh

Road signs

give way	*cediu el pas*	seh-DEE-oo el pahs
danger	*perill*	peh-REEL
entry	*entrada*	en-TRAH-duh
detour	*desviament*	des-vee-uh-MENT
one way	*direcció única*	dee-rek-SYOH OO-nee-kuh
toll	*peatge*	peh-AHT-zhe
no entry	*prohibit el pas*	pro-EE-beet el pahs
exit	*sortida*	sor-TEE-duh
keep clear	*deixeu pas lliure*	day-SHEH-oo pahs LEE-oo-ruh

Directions

Where is it?	*On és?*	on es?
Go straight ahead	*Vagi recte*	VAH-zhee REK-tuh
turn left	*giri a l'esquerra*	ZHEE-ree ah luhs-KEHR-ruh
turn right	*giri a la dreta*	ZHEE-ree ah lah DREH-tuh
…at the traffic lights…	*al semàfor*	ahl seh-MAH-foor
…at the roundabout…	*a la rotonda*	ah lah roh-TON-duh
north	*nord*	nort
south	*sud*	soot
east	*est*	est
west	*oest*	o-EST
behind	*darrere*	dah-RREH-ruh
in front of	*davant de*	duh-VAHNT duh

| near | a prop de | uh PROP duh |
| opposite | al davant de | ahl duh-VAHNT duh |

Street signs

entrance	entrada	en-TRAH-duh
exit	sortida	sor-TEE-duh
open	obert	oo-BEHRt
closed	tancat	tahn-KAHT
toilets – men/women	lavabos – homes/dones	lah-VAH-boos – OH-mes/ DOH-nes
information	informació	een-for-mah-SYOH

Accommodation

Where is a cheap/ good hotel?	On hi ha un hotel barat/bo?	on ee ah oon oh-TEL bah-RAHT/boh?
Could you please write the address?	Em pot escriure l'adreça, si us plau?	em pot es-KREE-roo luh-dreh-SAH, see oos plow?
Do you have any rooms available?	Teniu habitacions disponibles?	tuh-NEE-oo ah-bee-tah-SYONS dees-po-NEE-bluhs?
I'd like…	Voldria…	vol-DREE-uh…
a single room	una habitació individual	oo-nuh ah-bee-tah-SYOH een-dee-voo-AHL
a double room	una habitació doble	oo-nuh ah-bee-tah-SYOH DOH-bluh
a room with two beds	una habitació amb dos llits	oo-nuh ah-bee-tah-SYOH ahmb dos YEETS
a room with a bathroom	una habitació amb bany	oo-nuh ah-bee-tah-SYOH ahmb bany
to share a dorm	compartir un dormitory	kohm-par-TEER oon dor-mee-TOH-ree
How much it is per night/person?	Quant costa per nit/ persona?	kwant KOSS-tuh per neet/pehr-SOH-nuh?
Where is the toilet?	On és el lavabo?	on es el lah-VAH-boo?
Where is the bathroom?	On és el bany?	on es el bahn?
Is there hot water?	Hi ha aigua calenta?	ee ah EYE-gwah kah-LEN-tuh?
Is there electricity?	Hi ha electricitat?	ee ah eh-lek-tree-see-TAHT?
Is breakfast included?	L'esmorzar està inclòs?	les-moor-ZAHR es-TAH een-KLOHS?
I am leaving today	Marxo avui	MAR-shoo ah-VWEE

Food

Do you have a table for…people?	Teniu una taula per a…persones?	tuh-NEE-oo OO-nuh TOW-luh per uh…pair-SOH-ness?
…a children's menu?	…un menú infantil?	…oon meh-NOO in-fan-TEEL?
I am a vegetarian	Sóc vegetarià/ vegetariana	sok veh-zhe-tah-REE-ah / veh-zhe-tah-REE-ah-nuh
Do you have any vegetarian dishes?	Teniu plats vegetarians?	tuh-NEE-oo PLAHTS veh-zhe-tah-ree-AHNS?
Please bring me…	Porteu-me si us plau…	por-TEH-oo-muh see oos plow…
a fork/knife/spoon	una forquilla/ ganivet/cullera	oo-nuh for-KEE-yuh/gah-nee-VET / koo-YEHR-uh

A1

369

Please may I have the bill?	*Em podeu portar el compte, si us plau?*	em poh-DEH-oo por-TAR el KOM-tuh, see oos plow?

Basics

bread	*pa*	pah
butter	*mantega*	mahn-TEH-guh
cheese	*formatge*	for-MAHT-zhuh
oil	*oli*	OH-lee
pepper	*pebre*	PEH-bruh
salt	*sal*	sahl
sugar	*sucre*	SOO-kruh

Fruit

apples	*pomes*	POH-muhs
bananas	*plàtans*	PLAH-tahns
grapes	*raïm*	rah-EEM
mango	*mango*	MAN-goh
oranges	*taronges*	tah-ROHN-juhs
pears	*peres*	PEH-res

Vegetables

broccoli	*bròquil*	BROH-keel
carrots	*pastanagues*	pahs-tah-NAH-guhs
garlic	*all*	ahly
onion	*ceba*	SEH-buh
peppers	*pebrots*	puh-BROTS
potato	*patata*	pah-TAH-tuh

Fish

mackerel	*verat*	vuh-RAHT
mussels	*musclos*	MOOS-klohs
salmon	*salmó*	sahl-MOH
tuna	*tonyina*	toon-YEE-nuh

Meat

beef	*vedella*	vuh-DEH-lyuh
chicken	*pollastre*	poo-YAHS-truh
goat	*cabra*	KAH-bruh
pork	*porc*	pork
lamb	*xai*	shy
sausage	*botifarra*	boo-tee-FAH-ruh

Drinks

beer	*cervesa*	ser-VEH-zuh
coffee	*cafè*	kah-FEH
fruit juice	*suc de fruita*	sook duh FROO-ee-tuh
milk	*llet*	lyet
tea	*te*	teh
water	*aigua*	EYE-gwah
wine	*vi*	vee

Shopping

I'd like to buy…	*Voldria comprar…*	vol-DREE-uh koom-PRAR…
How much is it?	*Quant costa?*	kwant KOSS-tuh?
I don't like it	*No m'agrada*	noh muh-GRAH-duh
I'm just looking	*Només estic mirant*	noh-MESS es-TEEK mee-RAHNT
It's too expensive	*És massa car*	es MAH-suh KAR
I'll take it	*Me'l quedo*	mel KEH-doo
Please may I have…	*Em pot donar… si us plau?*	em pot doh-NAR…see oos PLOW?
Do you accept…?	*Accepteu…?*	ahk-sep-TEH-oo…?
credit cards	*targetes de crèdit*	tar-ZHEH-tuhs duh KREH-deet
travellers' cheques	*xecs de viatge*	sheks duh vee-AH-tzhuh
more	*més*	mess
less	*menys*	MEN-yss
smaller	*més petit*	mess puh-TEET
bigger	*més gran*	mess GRAHN

Communications

I am looking for…	*Busco…*	BOOS-koo…
bank	*banc*	bahnk
post office	*oficina de correus*	oh-fee-SEE-nuh duh koo-REH-oos
church	*església*	uhs-GLEH-syuh
embassy	*ambaixada*	ahm-bai-SHAH-duh
exchange office	*oficina de canvi*	oh-fee-SEE-nuh duh KAHM-vee
telephone centre	*centre de telèfons*	SEN-truh duh tuh-LEH-foons
tourist office	*oficina de turisme*	oh-fee-SEE-nuh duh too-REES-muh

Emergency

Help!	*Ajuda!*	ah-ZHOO-duh!
Call a doctor!	*Truqui a un metge!*	TROO-kee ah oon MET-zhe!
There's been an accident	*Hi ha hagut un accident*	ee ah ah-GOOT oon ahk-see-DENT
I'm lost	*M'he perdut*	meh pehr-DOOT
Go away!	*Vés-te'n!*	ves-ten!
police	*policia*	poo-lee-SEE-uh
fire	*bombers*	bom-BEHRs
ambulance	*ambulància*	ahm-boo-LAN-syuh
thief	*lladre*	LYAH-druh
hospital	*hospital*	oos-pee-TAHL
I am ill	*Estic malalt/malalta*	es-TEEK muh-LALT / muh-LAHL-tuh

Health

diarrhoea	*diarrea*	dee-ah-REH-uh
nausea	*nàusees*	NAW-sehs
doctor	*metge*	MET-zhe
prescription	*recepta*	ruh-SEP-tuh
pharmacy	*farmàcia*	fahr-MAH-syuh
paracetamol	*paracetamol*	pah-rah-seh-tah-MOL
antibiotics	*antibiòtics*	ahn-tee-byoh-TEEKS

antiseptic	*antisèptic*	ahn-tee-SEHP-teek
tampons	*tampons*	tahm-POHNS
condoms	*condons*	kohn-DOHNS
contraceptive	*anticonceptiu*	ahn-tee-kohn-seep-TEEW
sun block	*crema solar*	KREH-muh soh-LAHR
I am…	*Sóc…*	sok…
asthmatic	*asmàtic/asmàtica*	ahs-MAH-teek / ahs-MAH-tee-kuh
epileptic	*epilèptic/epilèptica*	eh-pee-LEP-teek / eh-pee-LEP-tee-kuh
diabetic	*diabètic/diabètica*	dee-ah-BEH-teek / dee-ah-BEH-tee-kuh
I'm allergic to…	*Sóc al·lèrgic a…*	sok ahl-LEHR-zheek ah…
penicillin	*penicil·lina*	peh-nee-seel-LEE-nuh
nuts	*fruits secs*	froots seks
bees	*abelles*	ah-BEH-yuhs

Gestures

OK	thumbs up
Hello	wave hand, palm out, from side to side

Travel with children

Is there a…?	*Hi ha un…?*	ee ah oon…?
baby changing room	*canviador de nadons*	kahn-vee-uh-DOR duh nuh-DONS
children's menu?	*menú infantil?*	meh-NOO in-fan-TEEL?
Do you have…?	*Teniu…?*	tuh-NEE-oo…?
infant milk formula…	*let de fórmula per a nadons*	lyet duh FOR-moo-luh per uh nuh-DONS
nappies	*bolquers*	uhn bol-KEHRs
a potty	*un orinal*	uhn oh-ree-NAHL
a babysitter	*un cangur*	uhn kahn-GOOR
a highchair	*una trona*	uh-nah TROH-nuh
Are children allowed?	*Es permeten nens?*	es pehr-MEH-ten nens?

Other

my/mine/ours/yours	*meu/meva/nostre/vostre*	meh-oo/MEH-vuh/NOS-truh/VOS-truh
and/some/but	*i/alguns/però*	ee/al-GOONS/puh-ROH
this/that	*això/allò*	uh-SHOH/uh-LYOH
expensive/cheap	*car/barat*	kar/bah-RAHT
beautiful/ugly	*bell/lleig*	behl /LYAYCH
old/new	*vell/nou*	vey/noh
good/bad	*bo/dolent*	boh/doo-LENT
early/late	*d'hora/tard*	DOR-uh/tart
hot/cold	*calent/fred*	kah-LENT/fred
difficult/easy	*difícil/fàcil*	dee-FEE-seel/FAH-seel
boring/interesting	*avorrit/interessant*	ah-voo-REET/een-teh-reh-SANT

Appendix 2

GLOSSARY

Ajuntament	city hall
Azulejos	(Spanish) painted glazed tiles used in Moorish and mudéjar work and later architecture. Note: the Catalan word rajoles is also used, but is a more general term for tiles.
banys	baths
barri	quarter, neighbourhood
cala	cove
caldes	hot springs
call	the Jewish quarter of a town
camí	path
ca	can house, like the French chez
cangost	a canyon
carrer	street
cartoixa	'charterhouse', a monastery of the Carthusian order
casino	a social club for a town's wealthy elite
castrum	Roman military camp, or a new town founded on the same grid plan
claustre	cloister; the covered walk surrounding a monastery or cathedral courtyard
cobla	sardana band
col·legiata	a 'collegiate' church; an important church that is not a cathedral, ruled by a college of canons
comarca	one of the counties into which modern Catalonia is divided
communidor	a small shrine of pagan origins to ward off storms, with a roof over four columns open to the four winds
conca	a broad basin surrounded by mountains, as the Conca de Barbéra
Corts	the Catalan parliament
cova	cave
cremallera	rack-and-pinion railroad
església	church
esgrafiat	sgraffito work, designs etched in stucco on a building façade
espai	space
estany	lake
eixample	extension, or the modern district of a town
far	lighthouse
Generalitat	autonomous government of Catalonia
jardí	garden
mas/masia	a substantial farmhouse, usually of stone
Modernisme	the Catalan manner of Art Nouveau, not to be confused with the 'Modernism' of 20th-century international architecture

A2

mudéjar	(Spanish) Moorish-influenced architecture in Chistian Spain between the 12th and 16th centuries
nou	new
oppidum	a (usually) hilltop settlement or trading base of the Iberians or Celts
paeria	in Lleida and other towns, the city government and the building it occupies
palau	a palace
pantà	reservoir
parróquia	a parish church
pla	plain, flat area
plaça	town square
platja	beach
pou de glaç	an ice well, a feature of many old Catalan towns
pujada	slope, hill
Renaixença	the 19th-century Catalan cultural reawakening
rambla	a boulevard with a broad central pedestrian strip, Catalonia's great contribution to urban design
rauxa	exuberance, madness (the opposite of seny, see page 12)
retaule	retable, carved or painted altarpiece
riu	river
seny	reason, prudence a special Catalan virtue, according to the Catalans
seu	('see' or 'seat' of a bishop) cathedral
suda or zuda	the Moorish palace that was the seat of government, usually on a height above a town
trencadís	pieces of broken tile used for decoration on Modernista buildings
vell	old
xemeneia	a factory chimney, smokestack

ADDRESSES IN CATALUNYA

Street names in Catalunya are in Catalan and are usually abbreviated when written down (see list below). Sometimes you will see 's/n', particularly in rural addresses, which means 'sense número', or 'no number' and just means that there is no number attributed to that address. Outside the big cities, addresses might include the roads by their name or number, followed by a kilometre marker (km) to indicate a location. For example, 'Ctra de Vic, km 3.2' means that the location is 3.2km along the Vic road from its starting point.

Abbreviation	Catalan	English
C/	Carrer	Street
Av	Avinguda	Avenue
Pg	Passeig	Promenade/Boulevard
Pl	Plaça	Square
Rda	Ronda	Ring road
Ctra	Carretera	Road/Highway
Trv	Travessera	Cross street
Ptge	Passatge	Passage/Alleyway
Rbla	Rambla	Promenade/Walkway
Bda	Baixada	Descent/Sloping street
C.	Camí	Path/Trail

Appendix 3

BOOKS
Non-fiction

Bisson, Thomas N *The Medieval Crown of Aragon: A Short History* Oxford University Press, 1986. An accessible academic overview of the Crown of Aragon, which once united much of medieval Catalunya with Mediterranean powers.

Guibernau, Montserrat *Catalan Nationalism: Francoism, Transition and Democracy* Routledge, 2004. This concise political history explains how Catalunya identity survived Francoist repression and re-emerged in democratic Spain.

Hooper, John *The New Spaniards* Penguin, 2006 (2nd ed). An engaging and enjoyable modern classic explaining Spain's transition after Franco: although the focus is mainly on Spain, it does offer some valuable insights into what sets Catalunya apart.

Hughes, Robert *Barcelona* Harvill Press, 1992. A fantastic, sweeping cultural and political history of the Catalan capital and beyond, written with wicked wit and an artistic eye.

Minder, Raphael *The Struggle for Catalonia* Hurst & Company, 2017. A series of interviews with locals all over the region paints a fascinating picture of the context of the ill-fated 2017 referendum on independence.

Orwell, George *Homage to Catalonia* 1938. Orwell's firsthand account of fighting alongside anti-fascist militias in the Spanish Civil War – a vivid, personal and politically complex portrait of Catalonia in wartime.

Preston, Paul *A People Betrayed* William Collins, 2020. A shocking story of the corruption and incompetence that have scarred Spanish politics in the post-Franco period. His history of the Spanish Civil War (*The Spanish Civil War: Reaction, Revolution, and Revenge* William Collins, 2016) is also recommended.

Tóibín, Colm *Homage to Barcelona* Picador, 1990. This elegant literary essay by one of the finest authors writing today combines history, memoir and cultural observation.

Tree, Matthew *Barcelona, Catalonia* Catalonia Press, 2011. An illuminating collection of essays, lectures and anecdotes from a long-time Catalunya resident, media personality and writer.

Fiction

Cabré, Jaume *Confessions* Arcadia Books, 2014 (trans. Peter Bush). A global bestseller, this sweeping novel spans centuries of Catalan history, politics and art, told through the life of a gifted violinist.

Falcones, Ildefonso *Cathedral of the Sea* Transworld Publishers, 2008. An epic historical novel follows a serf's rise in a city transformed by the building of the Santa Maria del Mar church.

Ruiz Zafón, Carlos *The Shadow of the Wind* Weidenfeld & Nicolson, 2004. A haunting literary adventure set in post–Civil War Barcelona.

A3

Rodoreda, Mercè *In Diamond Square* Virago Modern Classics, 2013 (trans. Peter Bush). Another classic, this is a beautiful, intimate portrayal of a young woman's life in Barcelona before, during, and after the Civil War.

Sales, Joan *Uncertain Glory* MacLehose Press, 2014 (trans. Peter Bush). A Catalan classic of the Spanish Civil War, originally published in 1956, focusing on young Republican idealists in Barcelona and the frontlines.

Thubron, Rupert *Barcelona Dreaming* Abacus, 2021. A trio of linked novellas set in contemporary Barcelona, this explores love, loss and cultural dislocation through the lives of an ex-pat shop-owner, a young translator and a washed-up jazz musician.

Vázquez Montalbán, Manue *Tattoo* Serpent's Tail, 2008 (original Spanish published in 1974). The first novel in the iconic Pepe Carvalho detective series, set in gritty 1970s Barcelona. Carvalho, an ex-communist and gourmet sleuth, investigates a drowned man with a cryptic tattoo. A stylish noir that doubles as a social critique of post-Franco Spain.

WEBSITES

Catalan News w catalannews.com. An English-language news site, which also has a podcast, 'Filling the Sink'. As well as news, it provides information on upcoming events, festivals and traditions, and sports.

Centre Excursionista de Catalunya w cec.cat. The official website for Spain's oldest hiking club, which offers courses, hosts events and runs seven mountain refuges. The site also provides details of the best hikes and climbs, as well as blogs and articles (in Catalan and Spanish only).

El Pais in English w english.elpais.com. One of Spain's biggest newspapers produces an edition in English, which is useful for catching up with the current events in the country in English.

Museus Catalunya w museus.cultura.gencat.cat. A searchable directory of all the museums in Catalunya (in Catalan and Spanish only).

Parcs Naturals de Catalunya w parcsnaturals.gencat.cat. This website provides extensive information on Catalunya's nature reserves and national park (in Catalan and Spanish only).

Turisme de Catalunya w catalunya.com. The official Catalan-government tourism portal is a comprehensive resource with info on all aspects of travel to the region, from what to do to where to stay, with lots of information on local gastronomy, traditions and culture.

Turisme de Barcelona w barcelonaturisme.com. The Catalan capital's indefatigable tourist board operates this excellent website, where you can find a wide range of information on visiting the city, from transport to accommodation, as well as purchase entrance tickets and guided visits (usually with a discount for buying online).

Index

Page numbers in **bold** indicate major entries; those in *italic* indicate maps.

INDEX OF ADVERTISERS